THE FIRST EPISTLE GENERAL OF JOHN.

INTRODUCTION.

§ 1. CONTENTS OF THE EPISTLE.

I. THE EXORDIUM (i. 1–4) states the object of the Apostolic annunciation (i. 2) and its purpose (v. 3); the design of the Epistle being superadded (v. 4).

II. PRINCIPAL PART THE FIRST (i. 5—ii. 18):

IF YE WALK IN THE LIGHT (i. 5—ii. 2), IN OBEDIENCE TO HIS LAW IN GENERAL (ii. 3–6), AND KEEPING THE COMMANDMENT OF BROTHERLY LOVE IN PARTICULAR (ii. 7–14), NOT BEING MISLED BY THE LUSTS (ii. 15–17), AND THE LIES OF THE WORLD (ii. 18–23), YE SHALL HEREAFTER ABIDE BEFORE CHRIST.

1. The leading thought: "*God is light*" (i. 5).
2. The first inference: *true fellowship* (i. 6. 7).
3. The second inference: *perception and confession of sins* (i. 8–10).
5. The third inference: *reconciliation and redemption* (ii. 1. 2).
6. Mark of the walk in the light; *obedience to His commandments, especially brotherly love* (ii. 3–11).
6. Consolatory warning against love of the world (ii. 12–17).
7. Warning and consolation against antichrist (ii. 18–28). Description of his forerunners, whose appearing points to the last time (ii. 18–23); Exhortation of the faithful to stedfastness in their assurance of having the truth and eternal life (ii. 24–28).

III. PRINCIPAL PART THE SECOND (ii. 29—v. 12):

HE THAT IS BORN AGAIN (OUT) OF (THE BEING OF) GOD THE RIGHTEOUS (ii. 29), IS A MIRACLE OF HIS LOVE NOW AND HEREAFTER (iii. 1–3), IS BOUND BY HIS WILL (iii. 4–10a), ESPECIALLY TO PRACTISE BROTHERLY LOVE (iii. 10b–18), IS BLESSED BEFORE HIM AND IN HIM (iii. 19–24), TRYING, LIKE GOD, THE FALSE SPIRITS (iv. 1–6), HE ENJOYS THE LOVE OF GOD AND EXHIBITS BROTHERLY LOVE (iv. 7–21), HE TRIUMPHS OVER THE WORLD AND IS SURE OF ETERNAL LIFE (v. 1–12)

1. The leading thought: *He that is born again of God the Righteous doeth righteousness* (ii. 29).
2. The glory of the Sonship (iii. 1–3).
3. The way of God's children passes through God's law (iii. 4–10a).
4. Brotherly love is the sum-total of the Divine law (iii. 10b–18).
5. The blessed consequences of our adoption by God (iii. 19–24).
6. Warning and exhortation with reference to false teachers (iv. 1–6).

7. Brotherly love and Divine love as related to each other on the ground of Christ's advent (iv. 7–21).

8. The power of faith (v. 1–5), its testimony (v. 6–10) and substance (v. 11. 12).

IV. THE CONCLUSION (v. 12–21) REMINDS US OF THE GIFT OF ETERNAL LIFE (v. 13), OF THE CONFIDENCE THAT OUR PRAYERS ARE HEARD (vv. 14. 15), EXHORTS US TO INTERCEDE FOR ERRING BRETHREN (vv. 16. 17), AND REMINDING US OF THE CERTAINTY OF OUR REDEMPTION FROM SIN (v. 18), DEHORTS US IN VIEW OF THE WORLD (v. 19) AND THE REDEEMER (v. 20) FROM IDOLATRY (v. 21).

This attempted analysis will have to be justified by the exposition, but the situation of the question has to be noted here in brief. Formerly nobody thought of seeking and finding in this Epistle a well-ordered train of thoughts, or even definite and connected groups of thought. Augustine (*Expos. in Ep. Joh.*) contented himself with the remark: "*locuturus est multa et prope omnia de caritate.*" Thus Luther in his two expositions says: "The main substance of this first Epistle relates to love." "The Apostle's object in this Epistle is to teach faith against heretics, and true love against the vicious."—Calvin (in his Commentary on the New Testament) says: "*doctrinam exhortationibus mistam continet. Disserit enim de eterna Christi deitate, simul de incomparabili, quam mundo patefactus secum attulit, gratia; tum de omnibus in genere beneficiis, ac præsertim inæstimabilem divinæ adoptionis gratiam commendat atque extollit. Inde sumit exhortandi materiam; et nunc qnidem in genere pie sancte vivendum admonet, nunc de caritate præcipit. Verum* nihil horum continua serie facit; nam sparsim docendo et exhortando varius est: præsertim vero multos est in urgenda fraterna intellectione. Alia quoque breviter attingit." Lutheran expositors, *e. g.*, Valentine Löscher and Rappolt thought that the Epistle was written without method; the latter described John's method as aphoristic. Not until the 18th century, more definitely since the middle of that century, the programme of Joachim Oporin of Göttingen led to progress in the recognition of a plan and order in this Epistle. Bengel recognized the exordium (i. 1–4), the *tractatio* (namely the special one i. 5–iv. 21, and the more general v. 1–12), and the conclusion (v. 13–21).—Lücke with his ten sections approached again the aphoristic plan (i. 1–4; i. 5–ii. 2; ii. 3–17; ii. 18–28; ii. 29–iii. 10; iii. 10–24; iv. 1–6; iv. 7–v. 5; v. 6–12; v. 13–21).—After v. Hoffmann's lead (in *Schriftbeweis* 2, 2. p. 335–337), who, independently of the exordium (i. 1–4), and the conclusion (v. 18–21), divides the Epistle into four parts (i. 1–ii. 11; ii. 12–28; ii. 29–iii. 22; iii. 23–iv. 21; v. 1–17), Luthardt in his programme of 1860 adopted the following division after the exordium: i. 5–ii. 11; ii. 12–ii. 27; ii. 27–iii. 24a; iii. 24b–iv. 21; v. 1–21.—Ebrard has six divisions; i. 1–4; i. 5–ii. 6; ii. 7–ii. 29; iii. 1–24; iv. 1–v. 3a; v. 3b–21.—Ewald has only three divisions: i. 1–ii. 17; ii. 18–iv. 6; iv. 7–v. 21.—Huther, who, at the suggestion of de Wette, in the first edition of his commentary had grouped his divisions according to the three leading thoughts:—God is light (i. 5), righteous (ii. 29), love (iv. 8), has abandoned this arrangement as untenable, and adopted the following division in the second edition of his work: i. 5–ii. 11; ii. 12–ii. 28; ii. 29–iii. 22; iii. 23–v. 17, leaving it optional to combine the first and second into one. Düsterdieck has, after the exordium, i. 1–4, two main parts (i. 5–ii. 28; ii. 29–v. 5), and a double conclusion (v. 6–13 and 14–21).

Cf. Lücke, ch. v. Düsterdieck, 1, p. XI.–XXVII.; Huther, p. 3–12.

§ 2. CHARACTER OF THE EPISTLE.

1. The Epistle treats of the following subjects: God is light, love, righteous; being of God, being God's child, born of God, being and abiding in God; His Son, who is from the beginning, sent by the Father, come in the flesh to destroy the works of the devil, who gave His life for us, who is the propitiation for all, for the sins of the whole world, our Paraclete, in whom is eternal life, in whom we are and abide, whom we shall see as He is: His Spirit, the Spirit of truth, of whom we have: His word, which is eternal; fellowship with the Apostles, with the Father and the Son, prayer, intercession, confidence even in the judgment, the faith which overcomes the world, love of the brethren even to the point of laying down our lives for them, hope that purifies itself;—the devil, the spirit of fraud, lying, darkness, antichrist, the world, the lust of the eyes, the lust of the flesh, the sin which is formally lawlessness, inwardly unrighteousness, the sin

THE

EPISTLES GENERAL OF JOHN.

BY

KARL BRAUNE, D.D.,

GENERAL SUPERINTENDENT, ETC., AT ALTENBURG.

TRANSLATED FROM THE GERMAN, WITH ADDITIONS ORIGINAL AND SELECTED.

BY

J. ISIDOR MOMBERT, D.D.,

RECTOR OF ST. JAMES'S CHURCH, LANCASTER, PA.

Wipf & Stock
PUBLISHERS
Eugene, Oregon

Wipf and Stock Publishers
199 W 8th Ave, Suite 3
Eugene, OR 97401

The Epistles General of John
an Exegetical and Doctrinal Commentary
By Braune, Karl F. C.
ISBN 13: 978-1-55635-401-4
ISBN 10: 1-55635-401-0
Publication date 4/4/2007
Previously published by Charles Scribner, 1869

unto death, being of the devil, the child of the devil, hatred, death, idols.—They are almost exclusively ethical ideas, very few dogmatical, and these are immediately delivered of the ethical references they contain, and thus linked into this chain of ethical ideas; *e. g.*, the death of Christ (ch. ii. 2; iii. 16). The author hastens in this Epistle through the whole sphere of life, although his power to do so is derived from a very small circle of ethical ideas. The advent of the Son of God in the flesh, His walk and aim as well as His intercession make up the christology he sets in operation, and the life of the Christian, snatched away from the power of the devil by regeneration and united in church-fellowship with the Father and the Son in his way through the world with its seductive power in particular things and in groups to the bliss of eternal life after death,—this is the sphere of life, the extent of ethical contemplations in this Epistle. We have therefore to deal here as much with faith in the divinity of Christ transposed into life, then with the life in Christ, as with the life in Christ theologically thought-out and leading to faith in the divinity of Christ. While the Gospel seeks to strengthen and enlarge faith in Jesus (says v. Hoffmann, *Schriftbeweis*, 2, 2, p. 337), the Epistle shows forth the moral conduct which is necessary to faith and only possible to faith.

2. But our Epistle does not treat these ideas as abstractions of the mind, but as contemplations of life, experiences of life, as facts and concrete manifestations of life. "One cannot tell whether the artless ingenuousness of a childlike disposition strikes us more in this Epistle than the grave high-tonedness of a thoughtful man, because, in fact, both are intimately blended together." (Düsterdieck). The author takes hold of the most weighty thoughts and ideas with a sure, light and dexterous hand; he is perfectly master of them, he has experienced them, they are his own, he is familiar with them. His object is to bring them home to the consciousness of his readers and to make them know them. Hence οἴδατε, οἴδαμεν, δοκιμάζετε, γινώσκετε, ἵνα γινώσκωμεν, ἵνα εἰδῆτε. Peculiar is the constant repetition of antithetical sentences, not by way of simple antithesis, but so that the predicate of a sentence becomes the subject of the antithesis or *vice versa;* the antithesis only brings out a new feature and thus carries on the thought, cf. *e. g.*, i. 6 sq., 8 sq.; ii. 4—vi. 9 sqq. 22, sq.; iii. 3–6. On the use of καί instead of δέ, of ὅτι, ἵνα, etc., see Ebrard, p. 9. [He says: *Style* and *construction* remind us strongly of the didactic passages of the Gospel, *e. g.*, Jno. i. 1–18; iii. 27–36, etc. For we recognize in the Epistle the same mode of thinking in paratactic periods and the same preference for καί in connecting together the different members of a train of thought (cf. *e. g.*, 1 Jno. ii. 1–3, where Paul would doubtless have used ἐὰν δὲ for καὶ ἐάν, and surely have put αὐτὸς γὰρ ἱλασμός ἐστι for καὶ αὐτὸς ἱλασμός ἐστι); cf. his taking up again the immediately preceding ὅτι in 1 Jno. iii. 20 with the anaphoras in Jno. i. 33; iv. 6, etc., and in general his preference for the particle ὅτι which is used in so many different senses (cf. Jno. xvi. 3. 4. 6. 17; also 1 Jno. ii. 12 sqq. with Jno. xvi. 9–11), and the use of the particles περί, ἵνα, ἀλλά. It is clear that the author of the Epistle, like the Evangelist, is in the habit of thinking in Hebrew, *i. e.*, Aramaic, and moving within the narrow range of the particles ו, כי or די, למען. To this must be added certain other modes of construction peculiar to a Hebrew cast of thought, *e. g.*, the circumlocution of the Genitive by ἐκ, 1 Jno. iv. 13, cf. Jno. i. 35; vi. 8, 70 and many other passages, the solution of a relative sentence into a conditional sentence, (ἐάν τις .... οὐκ ἔστιν ἐν αὐτῷ for ὅστις κ. τ. λ.) 1 Jno. ii. 15; iii. 17; cf. Jno. vi. 43, etc. The solution of a simple antithesis into a final or causal sentence depending on a word to be supplied (οὐκ ἦσαν ἐξ ἡμῶν ἀλλ᾽ ἵνα .....) 1 Jno. ii. 19; cf. Jno. i. 8; iii. 28, etc. The circumlocution of the Dative of the instrument by ἐν, 1 Jno. ii. 3, etc., compared with Jno. i. 26. 33; xvi. 30; and lastly the frequent use of θεωρεῖν and θεᾶσθαι, while ὁρᾶν is only used in the Perfect, and certain phrases such as τὴν ψυχὴν τιθέναι, θεὸς ὁ ἀληθινὸς, ὁ σωτὴρ τοῦ κόσμου ὁ Χριστός, κόσμος λαμβάνει, the use of φαίνειν, τεκνία, παιδία, etc.—M.].—John's method is neither dialectical like that of Paul, nor rhetorical like that of the Epistle to the Hebrews, but speculative, contemplative, noting the substance of thought without marking the mutual relation of the thoughts themselves. Huther strikingly illustrates the Apostle's peculiarity by comparing his leading thought to a key-note that he strikes and causes to sound through the derivative thoughts until a new key-note is struck that leads to a new key. It is the dialectics of contemplation, of experience. "His simplicity and unadornedness of statement are characteristic: whether he refers to the Divine truths

themselves, or addresses his readers by way of admonition or warning, his language preserves throughout the same calmness and decision; he never discloses a passionately excited frame of mind, but we see every where the reflection of the calmness of a heart resting in blissful peace, which makes him sure that the simple statement of the truth is sufficient to commend his words to the hearts of his readers. At the same time a firm, manly tone pervades the Epistle, contrary to all effeminate sentimentality of which the Apostle is so thoroughly free, that while enforcing spirituality of life, he uniformly insists upon the necessity of the exhibition of its truth in *deeds* [*i. e.*, in the life and practice of men.—M.].—It is also noteworthy that while, on the one hand, he addresses his readers as a father speaks to his children, he does not forget, on the other, that they are no longer minors and do not require to be taught new things, but that they are his equals and joint-possessors with him of all the truth he enunciates and of the life which he wants not to create, but to preserve in them." (Huther). This Epistle, "a deed of sacred love," "is to the most simple reader whose heart has made experience of Christian saving truth, immediately intelligible, but also unfathomable to the profoundest Christian thinker, although equally dear and refreshing to both. The very method pursued by the author of our Epistle in taking hold of Christian living, believing and loving from their profoundest depth, and in their inexhaustible wealth, shows with peculiar clearness how the foolishness of God confounds all the wisdom of the world; for that which our Epistle declares with almost playful ease, or at least with the perfectly artless simplicity of a heart which in its real vital fellowship with the Lord possesses all the riches of Divine wisdom and communicates them in holy anxiety of love—that which it declares with the triumphant assurance and joyful confidence of indisputable truth concerning the source and nature of the Christian life, *i. e.*, of eternal life, is infinitely more than all the wisdom of the world together can ever reach, and also more than even Christian wisdom can ever think out or fathom." (Düsterdieck). One cannot fail to see how unexcelled gentleness, tenderness and thoroughness of love are wonderfully blended with the most decided sternness and deep-cutting keenness of judgment. "It does not seem as if only a father were addressing his beloved children, but as if a glorified saint were speaking to men from a higher world. The doctrine of heavenly love, calmly active, with indefatigable zeal essaying everything and never exhausting itself, has in no writing been so perfectly demonstrated as in this." (Ewald). With such testimonies, triumphantly corroborated by the exposition, we may take comfort under the charges that the confusion of the Epistle betrays the senility of its author, who, either with planless abruptness, wanders from a thought he had suggested, or falls into the eternal sameness of an old man (S. G. Lange, Eichhorn, Ziegler). And the reproach of the master of the Tübingen school, of v. Baur, that the Epistle lacks the freshness of direct life, and that the tenderness and profound thoroughness of the Johannean mode of contemplation and statement had too much resolved themselves into a tone childishly effeminate, dissolving in indefiniteness, marked by constant repetitions and a lack of logical energy, may be met by Hilgenfeld's declaration that this Epistle is one of the *most beautiful* writings of the New Testament, that it is peculiarly rich and original with reference to the subjective, intensive life of Christianity, and that the fresh, living and attractive character of the Epistle consists just in the marked preference with which it introduces us into the inward experience of the true Christian life.

[After all this, we may well say with Ebrard to the commentator and his readers: "Put off thy shoes from off thy feet, for the place whereon thou standest is holy ground."—M.]

§ 3. THE AUTHOR OF THE EPISTLE.

If we glance at the testimony of the ancient Church and pay close attention to the statements of the witnesses respecting the author of this Epistle, all doubt must vanish that the Apostle St. John was, without contradiction, considered to have been its author. The Apostolic Fathers contain several allusions and references to our Epistle. Ebrard gives them along with similar matter in the Introduction to his Commentary, pp. 14–16. [The paragraphs in question, besides the quotation from Polycarp, as given below, are these: Papias knew and used this Epistle: Κέχρηται δ' ὁ αὐτὸς [Papias] *μαρτυρίαις ἀπὸ τῆς προτέοας 'Ιωάννου ἐπιστολῆς.* v. Euseb. H.

E., III., 39.—The anonymous Epistle to Diognetus, written about the time of Justin Martyr, contains many passages, which imply an unquestionable dependence on this Epistle. Cf. Cap., X., with 1 Jno. iv. 9–11; XII. with 1 Jno. ii. 18–25; iv. 4–6; v. 6–12; also Cap., V.–VII.; XI The Epistle of Vienna and Lyons [*Euseb.*, V., 1] contains an unmistakable allusion to 1 Jno. ii. 16: ὁ διὰ τοῦ πληρώματος τῆς ἀγάπης ἐνεδείξατο, εὐδοχήσας ὑπὲρ τῆς τῶν ἀδελφῶν ἀπολογίας καὶ τὴν ἑατοῦ θεῖναι ψυχήν.—Carpocrates, a Gnostic, who flourished about the beginning of the second century at Alexandria, sought to use for his purpose, 1 Jno. v. 19. "*Mundus in maligno positus est*," see Origen *in Genes.*, cap. I., Opp., I. p. 23,—M.].—The most important testimony is that of Polycarp, the disciple of John, who suffered martyrdom, A. D. 168, as found in his Epistle to the Philippians c. vii.: πᾶς γὰρ ὃς ἂν μὴ ὁμολογῇ Ἰησοῦν Χριστὸν ἐν σαρκὶ ἐληλυθέναι ἀντίχριστός ἐστι; which Ebrard calls "an unmistakably clear reminiscence", and Düsterdieck "a free use of Jno. iv. 2. 3."—Very important is the testimony of the Canon of the New Testament, which was edited by Muratori about a hundred years ago and is known as the Muratorian Canon. According to Wieseler's careful investigation (see *Studien und Kritiken*, 1847, pp. 815–857) it was written A. D. 170 by a Church-teacher for the purpose of instructing catechumens in the documents of the Christian faith which were received in his Church. We read, thereafter, notices of the fourth Gospel and its origin: "*Quid ergo mirum, ei Johannes tam constanter singula etiam in epistolis suis proferat, dicens in semet ipso* (1 Jno. i. 1): *quæ vidimus oculis nostris et auribus audivimus et manus nostræ palpaverunt, haec scripsimus; sic enim non solum visorem, sed et auditorem, sed et scriptorem omnium mirabilium domine per ordinem profitetur.*" And again after an enumeration of the Pauline Epistles: "*Epistolæ sane Judæ et superscripti Johannes duæ in Catholica habentur.*" This reference to the two Epistles of St. John must not be construed as denoting either the second and third, as if the citation from the first Epistle rendered further reference to it unnecessary (Schleiermacher, Lindner and Ebrard in *Herzog's R. E.*, p. 98), or the first and the third, the second being regarded as an appendix to the first (Hug), but the first and the second, as Catholic Epistles proper, the second Epistle, addressed to the κυρία, being considered to have been written not for a single person, but for a congregation; it is consequently the third Epistle which is not mentioned, not because its Johannean authorship was called in question, but because it was regarded as less instructive and as a private letter addressed to an individual.

The *Peschito*, belonging to the same age as the Muratorian fragment, also bears witness to the authenticity of this Epistle.—Quotations from this Epistle grow more frequent after the beginning of the third century in the writings of Irenæus, Tertullian, Clement of Alexandria, Origen and Cyprian.—It is very probable, but without much importance, that the Alogi, who, on the authority of Epiphanius, rejected the Gospel and Revelation of St. John, rejected also the first Epistle. Nor can it be of any moment that Marcion and his followers did not enumerate the writings of John in their Canon. Eusebius, whose defects in statement, pompous style, and disjointed treatment are considerably excelled and counterbalanced by his comprehensive and laborious historical researches, includes the Epistle among the *Homologoumena* (*H. E.*, III., 24. 25), and Jerome (*de viris illust. c.* 9) says: "*ab universis ecclesiasticis viris probatur.*"—Most excellent is also on this point Tischendorf's short but weighty essay: "*Wann wurden unsere Evangelien verfasst?*" Leipzig, 1865. [See also my article on the *Sources of the Gospels* in the *Bibliotheca Sacra*, July and October numbers, 1866.—M.]

2. This chain of *external* evidence is confirmed by the *internal* evidence arising from the comparison of the Epistle with the Gospel of St. John. Both the range of thoughts and their mode of expression, as well as the diction, are the same in the first Epistle and in the Gospel, and the remarks on the former in § 2., 1. 2, may and must be applied to the latter with slight modifications. Cf. Grimm: *On the Gospel and first Epistle of St. John as Works of the same Author* in *Studien und Kritiken*, 1847, p. 171–181, and *On the first Epistle and its relation to the fourth Gospel*, *ibid.*, 1849, p. 269–303.—"As in the Gospel we see here the author retire to the background, unwilling to speak of himself and still less to support any thing by the weight of his name and reputation, although the reader meets him here not as the calm narrator, but as an epistolary writer, as exhorter and teacher, as an Apostle, and moreover as the only surviving Apostle. It is the same delicacy and diffidence, the same lofty calmness and composure, and especially the same truly Christian modesty that cause him to retire to the background as an

Apostle and to say altogether so little of himself: he only desires to counsel and warn, and to remind his readers of the sublime truth they have once acquired; and the higher he stands the less he is disposed to humble '*the brethren*' by his great authority and directions. But he knew who he was, and every word tells plainly that he only could thus speak, counsel and warn. The unique consciousness, which an Apostle, as he grew older, could carry within himself, and which he, once the favourite disciple, had in a peculiar measure, the calm superiority, clearness and decision in thinking on Christian subjects, the rich experience of a long life, steeled in the victorious struggle with every unchristian element, and a glowing language lying concealed under this calmness, which makes us feel intuitively that it does not in vain commend to us love as the highest attainment of Christianity—all this coincides so remarkably in this Epistle, that every reader of that period, probably without any further intimation, might readily determine who he was. But where the connection required it, the author intimates with manifest plainness that he once stood in the nearest possible relations to Jesus (i. 1–3; v. 3–6; iv. 16), precisely as he is wont to express himself in similar circumstances in the Gospel; and all this is so artless and simple, so entirely without the faintest trace of imitation in either case, that nobody can fail to perceive that the selfsame author and Apostle must have composed both writings." (Ewald, *Die Johann. Schriften*, I., p. 431 sq.). Add to this the bold self-testimony with the impress of truth, ch. iv. 6.—Surprising is the number of parallel passages in the two writings:

FIRST EPISTLE OF JOHN.	GOSPEL OF JOHN.
Ch. i. 1. 2.	Ch. i. 1. 2. 14.
4.	xv. 11.
	xvi. 24.
10.	v. 38.
ii. 1. 2.	xiv. 16.
	xi. 51. 52.
	xiii. 15. 34. 35.
4–6.	xiv. 21–24.
	xv. 10.
8.	xiii. 34.
11.	xii. 35.
23.	xv. 23. 24.
	v. 24.
27.	xiv. 26.
iii. 1.	xvii. 25.
8.	viii. 44.
10.	viii. 47.
13–15.	v. 24. 38.
	xv. 18. 19.
16.	xv. 12. 13.
22.	ix. 31.
	xvi. 23.
iv. 5. 6.	iii. 31.
	xv. 19.
	viii. 47.
9.	iii. 16.
16.	vi. 69.
v. 3. 4.	xiv. 15.
	xvi. 33.
9.	v. 36.
12.	iii. 36.
	xiv. 6.
13.	xx. 31.
14.	xiv. 13. 14.
	xvi. 23.

Considerably more than half of the thirty-five passages taken from the Gospel form part of the last sayings of Christ in ch. xii.–xvii. There the receptivity of the witness was preëminently necessary, and there it showed its strength; where he made the most vital surrender of himself, there he received the most permanent impressions. This is thoroughly Johannean. Compare on this subject especially Lange, *The Gospel of John*, §§ 1–3, Vol. IV., p. 1 sqq. German edition.

3. The genuineness of this Epistle as that of an Apostle was maintained by the Church without all contradiction until Joseph Scaliger boldly enunciated the notion: "*tres epistolæ Johannis non sunt Apostoli Johannis.*" Then there arose at the time of the atomic criticism of Rationalism S. G. Lange (*Die Schriften des Johannes übersetzt und erklärt*, Vol. III., p. 4 sqq.), who although not venturing to assault the external evidence, made the subject matter of the Epistle the starting-point of his criticisms, and raised the doubt whether the Epistle was worthy of an Apostle; his strictures were as follows: that the Epistle lacked individual and local character, that its agreement with the Gospel gave rise to the suspicion of timid imitation and slavish copying; that John, before the destruction of Jerusalem, was not old enough to produce such a work of senility; that he may not have mentioned the destruction of Jerusalem, because it was a ticklish point, etc.—Bretschneider (*Probabilia*) is a more important opponent; but he lived to become convinced of the groundlessness of his doubts of the authenticity of John's writings. Claudius (*Uransichten des Christenthums*), who maintained that the Epistle was the fabrication of a Jewish Christian, and Horst (in *Henke's Museum für Religionswissenschaft von* 1803) are only mentioned on account of their boldness, and Paulus (*Die drei Lehrbriefe des Johannes wortgetreu mit erläuternden Zwischensätzen übersetzt und nach philologisch-notiologischer Methode erklärt. Mit exegetisch-Kirchenhistorischen Nachweisungen über eine sittenverderbliche* magisch-persische *Gnosis, gegen welche diese Briefe warnen.* 1829. [The three doctrinal Epistles of John literally translated with explanatory parentheses, and expounded after the philologico-notiological method. With exegetico-Church-historical references to an immoral *magico-Persian* Gnosis, of which these Epistles give warning. 1829.—This title is enough to awe even confirmed book-worms.—M.]), who like Bretschneider believed the Presbyter Johannes to have been the author of this Epistle, is referred to simply because of the manner in which he maltreated it.

4. More important are the assaults of the Tübingen school on the authenticity of our Epistle. It starts with the Hegelian idea of God, which makes man truly the other part of God; we may say that the followers of that school have already applied Darwin's theory to their conception of history: Christianity did not come down from heaven in a finished form, involves no miracle or privilege of certain persons, but originated in the inmost being of the Spirit, in the natural consciousness of man by a genuine historical development, without revelation or inspiration by a process in agreement with the general laws of historical development. The real original Christianity was a Judaism only slightly modified by Christ, quite Ebionite as exhibited by Peter and John in the Apocalypse, or Gentile-Christian as exhibited by Paul (Epistles to the Romans, Corinthians and Galatians), who, to be sure, went further in the dogma of the law. Hence there arose a contention between him and the other Apostles, in which men, well qualified to effect an understanding and reconciliation among the contending parties, advanced to Christian views and composed the other writings of the New Testament, which simply amount to unhistorical party-writings [German: *Tendenzschrift, i. e.*, a writing of a certain tendency favouring the distinctive views of a party.—M.], not without legends, and were written about the middle of the second century. This applies also to our Epistle. At first Köstlin (*Lehrbegriff des Ev.*, etc., 1843) and Georgii (*Theol. Jahrbücher*, 1845) pronounced for the identity of the author of the Epistles and that of the Gospel; then Zeller, who as late as 1842 had presupposed the identity of the author of both writings, was the first to declare, in a review of Köstlin's work, that it was conceivable that the Epistles and the Gospel were written by different authors. This view was raised by Baur, the leader of that school (in *Theologische Jahrbücher*, 1848), to apodictical certainty, and according to him the Epistle is *a weak imitation* of the Gospel, whereas Hilgenfeld (*Das Evangelium und die Briefe Johannis*, 1849, and *Theol. Jahrbücher*, 1855) identified and proved the Epistle to be *a splendid type* of the Gospel.—Baur starts on the unfounded supposition that the author manifests the intentional and most studious anxiety (1 John i. 1–3) to be regarded as identical with the author of the Gospel; in ch. v. 6–9, he sees, owing to

an exegetical misunderstanding, a wanton attempt of drawing a distinction between Divine and human testimony, and shows by this the unskilful imitation of the author. From a comparison of the eschatological statements of the Epistle (ch. ii. 18–23; iii. 2) with those of the Gospel (ch. xiv. 3. 18 sq. 23; xvi. 16. 22), and of 1 John v. 6, with John xix. 34, he infers that the mode of contemplation in the Epistle is more material and outward than that of the Gospel, which he considers to be more ideal and spiritual. The idea of the atonement, ἱλασμός (ch. i. 7; ii. 2; iv 10), and that of the interceding High Priest, παράκλητος, he thinks more suited to the range of ideas peculiar to the Epistle to the Hebrews, and foreign to that of the Gospel. Baur, lastly, considers the Epistle to be wholly *Montanistic*, because it describes the fellowship of Christians as holy and sinless, makes mention of the χρίσμα, and draws an unevangelical distinction between venial and mortal sins. But our Epistle does not distinguish a higher class of spiritual Christians from the lower classes of other Christians, the *Psychici*, but believing Christians from an unholy world; the Epistle *does* not, nor *may we* refer the χρίσμα to the baptismal anointing which is mentioned for the first time by Tertullian; and with respect to the mortal sins enumerated by Tertullian (*homicidium, idolatria, fraus, necatio, blasphemia, mœchia et fornicatio et si qua alia violatio templi dei*), Baur ought not to have made a most arbitrary selection of three, viz., idolatry (ch. v. 21; iii. 4), murder (iii. 15), adultery or fornication (from the inscription *ad Parthos*, corrupted from πρὸς παρθένους), and still less to have remarked that the author does not refer to the outward acts, but to the inward, moral disposition; for that is not Montanistic. If Hilgenfeld considers (1 John i. 5. 7) the statement that God is φῶς, ἐν τῷ φωτί, too material and local [*räumlich*, literally, relating to space.—M.], turns 1 John iii. 4, where sin is called ἀνομία, and 1 John ii. 7. 8, where love is referred to as an old commandment, into an argument for a friendly relation to the Mosaic law, and maintains that the idea of a personal Logos, clearly expressed in the Gospel, is unknown to the Epistle, although ὁ υἱὸς τοῦ θεοῦ is considered as identical with the Logos, and ἡ ζωή in Christ as hypostatical,—that the Holy Ghost is not described as a Person because He is called χρίσμα, and not παράκλητος, although He is called τὸ μαρτυροῦν (1 John v. 6), that the exhortation, addressed to the readers of the Epistle, to a conduct enabling them to look for and pass through the ordeal of the judgment without being ashamed, militates against the idea of the Gospel, which does not speak of the judgment of believers,—all this is as untenable on exegetical grounds as the recognition of *Gnostical* elements belonging to the post-Apostolical age in the idea of the σπέρμα (iii. 9), the conception of the χρίσμα, and the thought that God ought not to be feared, but only to be loved (ch. iv. 18. 19). Anointing as an Old Testament type suggested χρίσμα in the antithesis of the *Christian* and ἀντίχριστος, the representation of being born of God suggested the σπέρμα, and in that representation the fundamental view of an atonement for all the sins of all mankind prohibits any reference to a dualistic separation and to a metaphysical reason without ethical life-process, and the love of God is not a Gnostical discovery, but a purely Christian and Divine command. Of what avail is all the praise which Hilgenfeld awards to the first Epistle of John (for he solely refers to it without adverting to the second and third Epistles, although the title of his book refers to *Epistles*) and its author, in calling him a great independent thinker, if he nevertheless regards him as blindly echoing the Gnostic system of his time, and having only given a clear, practical impress to its speculative features, and considers the Epistle as less spiritual, and on that account older than the Gospel; and how can he accuse those who reject a pseudo-epigraphical literature of the New Testament, of overlooking the important circumstance that the modern idea of literary property was wanting in primitive Christian times; it has not been overlooked that the modern idea was then wanting, but even more than that, there was wanting all license of any forger. The pretensions of the Tübingen school are by no means borne out by what it gives us. Cf. Dietlein (*Urchristenthum*). Düsterdieck, Vol. I., p. XXXV—CI. Huther, p. 19–28; Brückner in de Wette's *Handbuch*, p. 316 sqq.

§ 4. THE READERS OF THE EPISTLE.

1. Augustine has a literal quotation of 1 Jno. iii. 2, which he introduces thus: *Quod dictum est ab Joanne in epistola ad Parthos* (*Quaest. Evang.* ii. 39). Possidius in his *indiculus operum S. Augustini* cites the tractates on our Epistles as "*de ep. ad Parthos sermones decem.*"

Thus has this designation found its way at least into the Benedictine edition of the works of Augustine, and even into some Latin codices and several other writings (Vigilius Tapsensis, Cassiodorus, Beda). Grotius already knew how to explain and apply it: "*Vocata olim fuit epistola ad Parthos*, i. e., *ad Judæas Christum professos, qui non sub Romanorum, sed Parthorum vivebant imperio in locis trans Euphratem, ubi ingens erat Judæorum multitudo, ut Neardæ, Nisibi et aliis in locis. Et hanc causam puto, cur hæc epistola neque in fronte nomen titulumque Apostoli, neque in fine salutationes apostolici moris contineat, quia nimirum in terras hostiles Romanis haec epistola per mercatores Ephesios mittebatur multumque nocere Christianis poterat, si deprehensum fuisset hoc quanquam innocens litterarum commercium.*"

Clement of Alexandria (*opera* ed. Potter *fragm.* 1011) observes that the second Epistle was addressed *ad virgines* (see Introduction to the second Epistle). It is easy to see how πρὸς παρθένους may have been wrongly transcribed πρὸς πάρθους, and thus originated the corrupted subscription of the second Epistle, which, being used as its superscription, may have been mistaken for the subscription of the first Epistle and connected with it, as Hug conjectures. Or, as in a codex of the Apocalypse, the subscription of the first and second Epistles may have read Ἰωάννου after παρθένοιν, and thus have given rise to the above mutilation and designation (so Gieseler, *Eccl. Hist.*, I., p. 139). There is evidently a mistake somewhere, and since Hug's supposition is even more simple than Gieseler's, it seems to commend itself as giving the solution of the riddle. The matter is not furthered if we suppose with Paulus of Heidelberg, that this subscription originated in πρὸς πάντας, or conjecture a corrupted reading in Augustine of *ad Pathmios* (Serrarius), *ad sparsos* (Wegscheider), *adpertius* (Semler). In this way, it is clear, we shall never find the readers for whom our Epistle was intended.

2. Equally inadmissible is the inference of Benson that ἀπ' ἀρχῆς (ch. ii. 7. 13. 14) points to a circle of readers in Judæa, and that of Lightfoot who, connecting the Gaius, mentioned 3 Jno. 1, with the Gaius 1 Cor. i. 14, thinks of Corinth as the Church to which the Epistle was sent. The Epistle is not addressed to any one Church in particular; and this accounts for the absence of detailed notices of a concrete or personal character. The circumstance, that while the Epistle contains only slight and incidental references to representations peculiar to the Old Testament, it expressly denounces idolatry, gives countenance to Düsterdieck's shrewd conjecture (§ 7), that it was addressed to Gentile Christian Churches; moreover, the author's contrasting the knowledge of the true God in Jesus Christ, which includes eternal life, with the dazzling form of paganism and an antichristian Gnosis, is in perfect agreement with the historical notice that John selected Asia Minor as the sphere of his labours, if we have to look to that province for the Churches to whom this encyclical Epistle was sent. But we must not think of a single Church, least of all of the Church at Ephesus (Hug), but of several Churches "of John's Ephesian circle of Churches" (Lücke), [*i. e.*, Churches within the diocese of Ephesus, as we should say, Churches under the especial jurisdiction of John.—M.], perhaps of all Churches to whom the personal labours of John extended (Huther).

§ 5. THE FORM OF THE EPISTLE.

1. Given an encyclical or circular Epistle, and it is manifest that it may and does lack features which generally belong to other Epistles: *i. e.*, the special address and particular salutations. Thus the common epistolary address is wanting in the Epistle to the Hebrews, while the Epistle of James is without the customary final salutations. Barring this circumstance all the requirements of the epistolary form are complied with: γράφω occurs seven times, γράφομεν once, ἔγραψα six times; ὑμῖν, ἐν ὑμῖν, ὑμεῖς and ὑμᾶς occur thirty-six times, the address τεκνία and παιδία ten times, ἀγαπητοί six times, πατέρες and νεανίσκοι twice each, ἀδελφοί once. The exordium (ch. i. 1–4) may be regarded with Calov (*Biblia N. T. illustrata*, Tom., II., p. 1582. Francof. 1676), who follows Estius, as founded on the usual form of an epistolary address. Lücke regards it as the amplification of such an address. The view of Baronius (*Annal. Eccl. an.* 99, II., p. 964) that the address, like a modern envelope, may have been lost, is as unnecessary as unfounded. The *spirit* of the Epistle corresponds with its form, the former being thus capitally described by Bacon: "*Epistola habent plus* nativi sensus *quam orationes; plus etiam* maturitatis *quam* colloquia

subita." Hence Düsterdieck very correctly remarks (I., p. X.) : "The whole writing rests so thoroughly on a living, personal relation between the author and his readers, the pertinence of the written exhortation is so absolutely personal, that this ground is sufficient to make us consider the writing as a genuine Epistle. This epistolary character belongs moreover to the whole keeping and structure of the short writing. With all logical order, there reigns in it that free and easy naturalness and unconstraint of statement, which suits the immediate interest and hortatory tendency of an Epistle, while the strict, progressive dialectical development, peculiar to a treatise or homily, is held back."

2. Receiving this writing with the ancient Church as an *Epistle* of John, is therefore every way commendable. Heidegger (*Enchiridion Bibl.*, p. 986) advanced his new view as late as the end of the seventeenth century: "*Accedit, quod scriptum hoc, licet epistola insigniatur, censeri tamen possit brevis quædam Christianæ doctrinæ epitome et evangelii a Johanne scripti succinctum quoddam enchiridion, cui adhortationes quædam pro communi totius ecclesiæ conditione adjectæ sunt. Non enim, ut reliquæ epistolæ, inscriptione ac salutatione inchoatur, neque etiam salutatione et voto clauditur.*" Although Bengel calls the writing *epistola*, he rather regards it as a *libellus*. Michaelis (*Introd.*, p. 1520) calls it a *treatise*. Storr (*Ueber den Zweck der evangelischen Geschichte und Briefe Johannis*, pp. 384. 401 sq.) calls it the *polemical*, and Berger (*Versuch einer moralischen Einleitung ins N. T.*, II., p, 179 sq.) *the practical part* of the Gospel; while Reuss (*Die Geschichte der Heiligen Schriften, N. T.*, p. 217) describes it as "a *homiletical essay*, at the most a pastoral Epistle, the readers being present." Augusti calls the Epistle an *anacephalæosis* of the Gospel, and Hug, Fromman (*Studien und Krit.*, 1840, p. 853), Thiersch (*Versuch zur Herstellung des historischen Standpunkts*, p. 78, *und die Kirche im apostolischen Zeitalter*, p. 266) and especially Ebrard (*Kritik der Evangelischen Geschichte*, p. 148, and *Comment.*, pp. 29–39) designate it as a companion-writing of the Gospel, or regard it in the light of a preface as an *epistola dedicatoria* without an independent designation *per se*, but we ought to have some notice or reference to that effect. This view certainly does not explain the want of an address, salutation and benediction, and we shall show in § 8, 3 that such a view is impossible.

§ 6. RELATIONS AND CIRCUMSTANCES OF THE CHURCHES.

1. The external relations cannot have been peculiarly difficult; there is no reference whatsoever to persecutions, like those to which the Christians were exposed either by the Jews as in the time of Paul, or by Nero at Rome (A.D. 54–68), or at the end of Domitian's reign (A.D. 81–96), and under that of Trajan (A.D. 98–117), and his proconsul Pliny in Bithynia. The Epistle speaks of the hatred of the world (ὁ κόσμος μισεῖ ὑμᾶς, ch. iii. 13). The notices of the victory of young men (ch. ii. 13. 14, νενικήκατε τὸν πονηρόν) and the victory over the world (v. 4, ἡ νίκη ἡ νικήσασα τὸν κόσμον, ἡ πίστις ἡμῶν), point rather to spiritual struggles, in the Church and in the individuals themselves; but they afforded opportunity for a reference to and description of external conflicts. The external relations must have been, on the whole, favourable; at least external fears cannot have been of sufficient moment to be taken into account (cf. Ewald, p. 437 sq.).

2. The disquiet and motion reigning within, which characterize this Epistle, point to rest without. The Churches were not necessitated to cling together and to remain closed by themselves. The writing is deficient in words of consolation, but not in exhortations to brotherly love, to stedfastness in the fellowship of faith and life with the Father and the Son, in cautions against the seductions of worldly lusts and false brethren. The time of their first enthusiasm has passed; their zeal and love lack the vibration produced by the weighty pendulum of obstacles and enmity. The reaction of evil from without is followed by the more pernicious reaction from within; falling away has begun without a violent crisis; the energy of evil, as well as of good, has abated. The first generation which had torn loose from idolatry and the world, and earnestly laid hold of God in Christ, has died; a showy and nominal Christianity has crept into the Churches Believers, like Gaius, exhibit all the Christian virtues (3 John 5. 6), old men full of Christian wisdom, young men full of vigorous aims (1 John ii. 13. 14), are pleasing evidences of the Christian life. But ambition spreads itself, as in Diotrephes (3 John 9. 10), the lusts of the world assert their claims (1 John ii. 15–17), false brethren arise, and not only tear themselves, but also

others from the true fellowship (ch. ii. 18 sq.; iii. 7; iv. 1 sqq.). And the influences from the world are rather those of pagan frivolity, than those of Judaistic narrowness.

3. The *heresy*, against which the Epistle is directed, is a pagan Docetism. Jesus is the Christ, the Son of God! Jesus is the incarnate Son of God! The Epistle, from the beginning to the end, raises high and holds fast confession as the banner under which we must fight and are sure of victory, thus pointing to Docetism, which had not yet developed into a system, but had appeared as a tendency, as is certified by Cerinthus, the contemporary of John. For Cerinthus held that Jesus was the son of Joseph, with whom the Logos united at His baptism, but left Him again after His crucifixion. Cf. Dorner, *Entwickelungsgeschichte*, I., 314 sqq. Pressensé, *Hist. of the First Three Centuries*, II., p. 233 sqq. The Epistle insists upon knowing and knowledge in opposition to the false spiritualistic *Gnosis* which had already begun with Docetism and opposed to the ergism of Judaism a syncretistic philosophy, and set in motion an ingenious theory operating intellectually, in the place of the work of redemption operating ethically.

In opposition to the pagan Dualism, which is the basis of Docetism in fixing metaphysically the antinomy of spirit and matter, the Epistle points to the opposites of light and darkness, of truth and falsehood, of the world with the evil one, and God with His Son and His children, opposites which are altogether ethical and in the fusion of an ethical life-process, so that the opposing element is overcome, dissolved and rejected, or may and shall be saved.—We do not yet find the full-blown Gnosticism, nor yet the rigid Docetism (as maintained by Lücke, Sander and Thiersch), nor any longer the antinomism combated by Paul, nor yet the later antinomism of the Gnostics (as Hilgenfeld assumes). Nor do we find the least trace of opposition to the disciples of John the Baptist, whom Paul met at Ephesus (Acts xix. 1 sqq.), whom John may have had regard to ~~in his Gospel (John iii. 22–36), and a reference to whom was suggested by the very lan~~guage of this Epistle (1 John v. 6. 8).

4. The Epistle knows no other division of the Church than that by age, fathers and young men (1 John ii. 12–14). But John gives distinct prominence to the circumstance that every one receives the unction of the Holy Ghost (1 John ii. 20. 27); he joins his readers in the confession of sins (1 John i. 8. 9), does not set himself above his brethren, and acknowledges the inalienable rights of Christians to try the spirits (1 John iv. 1), as well as their own responsibility to the Lord (1 John ii. 28).

[The heresy of Cerinthus and other heretics is thus described by Irenæus in his great work against heresy:

"*Et Cerinthus autem quidam in Asia* non a primo Deo factum esse mundum *docuit, sed* a virtute quadam valde separata et distanto *ab ea principalitate, quæ est super universa, et ignorante eum, qui est super omnia, Deum.* Jesum autem, *subjecit,* non ex virgine natum, (*impossibile enim hoc ei visum est*) *fuisse autem eum* Joseph et Mariæ filium similiter ut reliqui omnes homines, *et plus potuisse justitia et prudentia et sapientia ab hominibus. Et post baptismum* descendisse in eum *ab ea principalitate, quæ est super omnia,* Christum *figura columbæ: et tunc annuntiasse incognitum patrem et virtutes perfecisse; in fine autem* revolasse iterum Christum de Jesu, et Jesum *passum esse et resurrexisse; Christum autem impassibilem perseverasse, existentem spiritualem.*" (*Adv. Hær.* 1, 26).

"*Hanc fidem annuntians Joannes Domini discipulus, volens per evangelio annuntiationem auferre eum qui à* Cerintho *inseminatus erat hominibus errorem, ut confunderet eos et suaderet quoniam* unus Deus qui omnia fecit per Verbum suum; *et non, quemadmodum illi dicunt,* alterum, quidem fabricatorem, *alium autem* Patrem Domini; *et alium quidem fabricatoris filium, alterum vero de superioribus Christum, quem et impassibilem perseverasse, descendentem in Jesum filium fabricatoris, et iterum revolasse in suum Pleroma; et initium quidem esse Monogenem, Logon autem verum filium Unigeniti; et eam conditionem, quæ est secundùm nos, non à primo Deo factam, sed à virtute aliquâ valdè deorsum subjecta, et abscissa ab eorum communicatione, quae sunt invisibilia et innominabilia. Abstulit autem à nobis dissensiones omnes ipse* Joannes *dicens,* In hoc mundo erat et mundus per ipsum factus est, et mundus eum non cognovit. In sua propria venit, et sui eum non receperunt. *Secundùm autem Marcionem et eos, qui similes sunt ei, neque mundus per eum factus est; neque in sua venit, sed in aliena; secundùm autem quosdam Gnosticorum ab angelis factùs est iste mundus, et non per Verbum Dei. Secundùm autem eos, qui sunt à Valentino, iterum non per eum factus est, sed per Demiurgum. Hic enim operabatur similitudines tales fieri, ad imitationem eorum quæ sunt sursum; quemadmodum dicunt. Demiurgus autem perficiebat fabricationem conditionis. Emissum enim dicunt eum à matre Dominum et Demiurgum ejus dispositionis, quæ est secundùm conditionem, per quem hoc mundum factum volunt quùm Evangelium manifestè dicat, quoniam per Verbum, quod in principio erat apud Deum, omnia sunt facta: quod* Verbum, *inquit,* caro factum est, et inhabitavit in nobis.

Secundùm autem illos, neque Verbum caro factum est, neque Christus, neque qui ex omnibus factus est, Salvator. Etenim Verbum et Christum nec advenisse in hunc mundum volunt; Salvatorem verò non incarnatum neque passum; descendissè autem quasi columbam in eum Jesum qui factus est ex dispositione, et cum adnunciasset incognitum Patrem, iterum ascendisse in Pleroma. Incarnatum autem est passum quidam quidem eum, qui ex dispositione sit, dicunt Jesum, quem per Mariam dicunt pertransisse, quasi aquam per tubum: alii verò Demiurgi filium, in quem descendisse eum Jesum qui ex dispositione sit: alii rursum Jesum quidem ex Joseph et Mariâ natum dicunt, et in hunc descendissè Christum, qui de superioribus sit sine carne et impassibilem existentem. Secundùm autem nullam sententiam hæreticorum, Verbum Dei caro factum est. Si enim quis regulas ipsorum omnium perscrutetur, inveniet quoniam sine carne et impassibile ab omnibus illis inducitur Dei Verbum, et qui est in superioribus Christus, alii enim putant manifestatum eum, quemadmodum hominem transfiguratum; neque autem natum neque incarnatum dicunt illum: alii verò neque figuram eum assumpsisse hominis: sed quemadmodum columbam descendisse in eum Jesum, qui natus est ex Mariâ. Omnes igitur illos falsos testes ostendens discipulus Domini, ait: "Et Verbum caro factum est et habitavit in nobis." (Iren. iii. xi. p. 462). The English reader is also referred to the valuable notices of those early heresies in Bp. Bull's *Defence of the Nicene Creed,* iii. 1; Dr. Burton's *Bampton Lectures,* 1829, Lecture VI. pp. 158–160; Dr. Waterland *on the Trinity,* v. 139; and Pearson's *Vind. Ignat.* II. c. I. p. 351, ed. Churton.—M.]

§ 7. SCOPE OF THE EPISTLE.

The Apostle distinctly specifies in two passages the scope of this Epistle, viz.: ch. i. 4: ἵνα ἡ χαρὰ ὑμῶν ᾖ πεπληρωμένη, and ch. v. 13: ἵνα εἰδῆτε ὅτι ζωὴν ἔχετε αἰώνιον. The Church therefore has already the joy of faith, the joy of the possession of eternal life; but it must increase and grow until it is perfected; the Church has eternal life, but she must know and be conscious of it. Further particulars relating to the scope of the Epistle may be gleaned from the preceding paragraph. They must abide with Christ, without whom they have neither joy nor eternal life, the object of joy, without whom also they have no undimmed and clear consciousness of what they are and have, of what they may acquire or preserve; John desires to keep his Church with Christ, who is from the beginning, and will come again as Judge, but in the form of a Servant, became our Redeemer and Saviour (ch. i. 1 3. 5–10; ii. 1–3. 22–28; iii. 1–6; iv. 1–6; v. 1–2; 18–20). By obedience to the law and commandments of God and by a faithful following of Christ, he desires to establish his people more and more in the communion of God and in the participation of the Divine nature as the children of God (ii. 3–11; iii. 4–18). In Christian humility before the Father and the Son, and in Church-fellowship he desires to fill them with courage in confronting all proud spirits and the anti-Christian powers of the world; he wants them to be timid lest in any way they should injure the truth, the word of God, or themselves, but courageous and fearless in reliance on God and in the conflict with the world and its lusts and threatenings (ch. ii. 12–21; iv. 7–27). On that account they must not think lightly of the faith, as if the wisdom of the world were superior to it, but cling to it as the means by which they lay hold of Christ and eternal life and of the Father Himself, and make them so thoroughly their own, that thereby they may be glorified in and with Christ (ch. iii. 1–3; iii. 23. 24; v. 1–5). "Thus John, like Paul at the very close of the apostolic age, plants with a firm hand the cross before the Church, as the lighthouse destined to shed its friendly light in all the storms through which she has to pass. The foolishness of the Crucified shall always be her wisdom, and all the efforts of false doctrine shall split on it." (Pressensé, *History of the First Three Centuries,* II. p. 234 sqq.).

[Huther specifies three chief points as essential to the understanding of the construction of the Epistle:

1. The manifest purpose of the Apostle to preserve his readers in the fellowship with God, that their joy may become perfect.

2. For the accomplishment of his purpose he develops the thoughts that fellowship with God is possible only in a holy life of love, rooted in faith in Jesus Christ, and answering to the Being of God, and that the Christian is not only obliged to lead such a life, but that he necessarily does lead it in virtue of his being born of God (whereby he is absolutely opposed to the world, which is ἐκ τοῦ πονηροῦ).

3. The Apostle develops these thoughts both with reference to the anti-Christian lie that had already appeared, and the nearness of the advent of Christ.

Huther then states his reasons for his division of the Epistle into six parts, viz.: The exordium, ch. i. 1–4; i. 5–ii. 11; ii. 12–28; ii. 29–iii. 22; iii. 23–v. 17; v. 18–21, the conclusion, and leaving aside the exordium and conclusion, he says that of the remaining four parts,

The *first* (i. 5–ii. 11) warns against the danger of moral indifferentism, the *second* (ii. 12–28) warns against the love of the world and antichrist, the *third* (ii. 29–iii. 22) shows that nothing short of a righteous life in brotherly love is compatible with the nature of Christians, and the *fourth* (iii. 23–v. 17) indicates faith in Jesus Christ, the Son of God, as the Divinely authenticated foundation of the Christian life.—M.].

§ 8. DATE OF THE EPISTLE.

The material already produced in the foregoing paragraphs furnishes us with three points of view from which we may determine the date of this Epistle; *first*, the Epistle itself; *secondly*, the author, the Apostle John; *thirdly*, the writing related to the Epistle, viz.: the Gospel.

1. From the Epistle itself we glean these particulars:

a. It contains no reference to seasons of persecutions when it was written (§ 6, 1.); consequently it must have been written before the time of Trajan (A. D. 98—117), even before the end of the reign of Domitian, who reigned until A. D. 96, and also after the reign of Nero and the destruction of Jerusalem, consequently between A. D. 70 and 96, and rather about 90 than soon after 70, since the greatness and importance of that catastrophe would render some reference to it most natural, unless a sufficient period of time had elapsed to account for the want of such reference. Ch. ii. 18 cannot be made to supply a chronological date; ἐσχάτη ὥρα is too indefinite an expression for that purpose; besides, the context in which it occurs must not be explained of external events, but relates to internal disturbances occasioned by antichristian heresies. Hence we cannot see with Düsterdieck (I. p. ciii.) a prophetical reference to the judgment impending on Jerusalem, but join him in decidedly rejecting the reference of this passage to the end of the Jewish state, as maintained by Grotius, Benson, *al.*

b. The more so, because cognizance is taken not of Jewish opposition, but of Gentile corruption, the strength of the former having been broken with the destruction of Jerusalem.

c. The Church-life, well-ordered in its course and of many years' standing, points likewise to the time after A.D. 70 (§ 6, 2).

d. The heresies also point to the time after the destruction of Jerusalem to the end of the century (§ 6, 3).

2. The Apostle John cannot have entered upon his labours among the Churches of Asia Minor until after the death of Paul, A.D. 64 (§ 4, 1. 2); he lived at Jerusalem until about A.D. 60; after that time no trace of him is found there. Moreover, the whole tenor of the Epistle forbids the hypothesis that it marks the beginning of his ministry in that sphere, as a kind of pastoral Epistle. Huther, who had advanced this view in the first edition of his Commentary, has retracted it in the second edition: this view is too modern to suit the ancient Church. The Apostle was banished to Patmos during the reign of Domitian, consequently before A.D. 96, and died after A.D. 100, in a good old age. Cf. Lange on the Gospel of John in the *Bibelwerk*, IV., p. 8. 9. (German edition).

3. The *Gospel* at all events was written before the Epistle. If we read in the Gospel, ch. **xx** 31: ταῦτα γέγοαπται ἵνα, π ι σ τ ε ύ σ η τ ε ὅτι ὁ Ἰησοῦς ἐστιν ὁ Χριστὸς ὁ υἱὸς τοῦ θεοῦ, καὶ ἵνα πιστ

εὐοντες ζωὴν ἔχητε *ἐν τῷ ὀνόματι αὐτοῦ, believing* in Jesus the Christ and *life* in His Name are the end contemplated; but if we read in the Epistle, 1 John v. 13: *ταῦτα ἔγραψα ὑμῖν, ἵνα* εἰδῆτε, *ὅτι ζωὴν ἔχετε αἰώνιον, τοῖς πιστεύουσιν εἰς τὸ ὄνομα τοῦ υἱοῦ τοῦ θεοῦ*, the reference is simply to the *knowledge* of believers who already possess faith and eternal life. This would indicate that the Gospel was written prior to the Epistle, that both could not have been written at the same time, and that the Epistle was not a companion-writing of the Gospel. John could not have thus written *simultaneously to the same readers:* the Epistle realizes what is only aimed at in the Gospel.—Düsterdieck (I., p. LIX.) thinks it only possible, while we think it inevitably certain, that the Epistle was written after the Gospel, and believe that this opinion may also be proved by many passages of the Epistle in which thoughts developed in the Gospel are expressed in a briefer and more pregnant form. Compare

1 John ii. 2. with	John xi. 52.
ii. 4.	xv. 10.
27.	xiv. 26.
iii. 8.	viii. 44.
13.	xv. 18. 19.
14.	v. 24.
22.	ix. 31; xvi. 23. 29.
iv. 6.	viii. 47.
16.	iii. 16.
v. 12.	iii. 36; xiv. 6.
14.	xiv. 13. 14.
	xvi. 33.

As a rule, the briefer form is the later and riper form of thought; a splendid illustration of the truth of this position may be found on a larger scale in Luther's Lesser Catechism, which, being the more difficult of the two, followed his Larger Catechism. But we must not disregard the circumstances under which the Epistle was written, and the relations to which the author had respect. Hence the comparison of the exordium of the Epistle with the beginning of the prologue is at any rate irrelevant, because the Apostle begins there in a monologue, whereas he begins here moved by the double impulse of vivid joy in the Lord and tender care for the Church. And the comparison of *ὁ λόγος σάρξ ἐγένετο*, John i. 14, and *Ἰησοῦς Χριστὸς ἐν σαρκὶ ἐληλυθώς*, does not show that the former expression is more definite, and therefore of a later date than the latter, because that was chosen and held fast with particular reference to the heresy intended to be opposed (against Huther)

[As Dr. Braune's view may fail to carry conviction to the mind of the reader, we add that of Huther (in Meyer's *Comment.*, p. 33): "The greater number of critics assume that the Epistle was written after the Gospel, and that the date of the latter is subsequent to the destruction of Jerusalem. As to the first point, the chief argument is that derived from occasional references in the Epistle to the Gospel; but this is not the case; there is not a *single* passage in the whole Epistle, which presupposes the *known* existence of the *written* Gospel." (Reuss: "We need the Gospel as a commentary on the Epistle; but as the Epistle had a commentary in the oral instructions of the author, this circumstance does not prove the later date of the Epistle"). It seems more probable *per se* that John, moved by the pernicious influence of the false teachers, wrote first the Epistle for the admonition and warning of the Churches confided to his care, and afterwards the Gospel for the benefit of all Christendom, as "a hallowed document of the historical basis of salvation," than that he wrote first the Gospel, and then the Epistle. (The general observation of Thiersch, "that, as a rule, the proposition: *writings of a momentary destination, among which most of the Epistles have to be classed, are of an earlier origin than the writings of a permanent destination, which include the Gospels,* may be proved historically true," may also be applied to the relation of the Gospel to the Epistle of John.)—And this seems to be confirmed by some of the very passages adduced to show the dependence of the Epistle on the Gospel. The passage, 1 John i. 1–4, compared with John i. 1 sqq., appears to be not the later, but the earlier, because the Apostle in the former struggles to give a proper expression to his idea, whereas in the latter he has already found it, and the expression: ὁ λόγος σὰρξ ἐγένετο, compared with Ἰησοῦς Χριστὸς ἐν σαρκὶ ἐληλυθώς, shows the latter to be less definite, and on that account perhaps earlier than the former. Moreover, the affinity of the two writings warrants the supposition, that in point of time they are not far distant from each other; and this affinity appears not only in the character peculiar to both, but also in their form, seeing that both not only commence with an exordium embodying the same ideas, but that also the concluding thoughts of both writings exhibit a singular correspondency, cf. John xx. 31, with 1 John v. 13.—As to the second point: while no conclusive proof can be drawn from the Gospel itself that the Epistle was written after the destruction of Jerusalem, it contains on the other hand nothing to contradict the ancient tradition that John wrote the Gospel towards the close of his life. Nor is it improbable that it was not published during the life of the Apostle; at least it is more natural to assume that the twenty-first chapter was added at the time of its publication, than at a later period when it had already become the possession of the Christian Churches. In *that* case John wrote his Gospel as a legacy for the time subsequent to his death; but this would require the Epistle also to have been written at the close of the Apostle's life, but before the Gospel. The Apostle indeed states nowhere that his readers had heard the Gospel *of him*, notwithstanding his reiterated reference to their acquaintance with the Gospel, nor is there a single passage to prove his personal labours among them, although we must not infer from this that he wrote this Epistle when he settled in Asia Minor, after the decease of Paul, as a pastoral introductory of his work there (first edition of Huther's Commentary); for on the one hand, we lack all indications of such a tendency of the Epistle, and on the other, said circumstance may be accounted for by the consideration that the Apostle intended this Epistle not exclusively for the use of those Churches among whom he exercised his ministry, but also for that of others not included in the round of his visitations.—An unbiassed consideration of all the circumstances renders it probable that John wrote this Epistle during the last quarter of the Apostolical age."—M.].

4. Putting all things together, the year A.D. 90 seems to mark the date of this Epistle; so Ewald (*Die Johann. Schriften*, I., p. 471). It is impossible to fix the date of the Epistle with Hilgenfeld, who gives A.D. 150 for the date of the Gospel, at A.D. 125–150, unless it be classed with the Tübingen school among the pseudo-epigraphical literature of the New Testament.

§ 9. PLACE WHERE THE EPISTLE WAS WRITTEN.

It is not known and cannot be determined. Some mention Ephesus, after an old supposition found in several subscriptions by Mill, Wetstein, Griesbach and Matthæi, but hardly entitled to the name of tradition. This is also the view of Bengel, who observes: "*non videtur peregre misisse, sed coram impertiise auditoribus.*"—Hug, Grotius and Ebrard name Patmos as the place where the Epistle and the Gospel were written, the former with reference to 2 John 12, and 3 John 13, as if the want of writing-material pointed to the Apostle's exile. But ancient tradition names Ephesus also as the place where the Gospel was written. See Lange, *Bibelwerk*, IV., p. 26. (German edition).

§ 10. LITERATURE.

Compare, (and it is worth comparing) LUECKE's section on the principal features of the history of the first Epistle of John.

Of the Commentaries of the *Greek Fathers* some have been lost entirely (DIODORUS of Tarsus, CHRYSOSTOM), others with the exception of small fragments (CLEMENT of Alexandria), and others with the exception of fragments not wholly unimportant (DIDYMUS of Alexandria).—The *Catenæ* of OECUMENIUS, THEOPHYLACT and two Scholiasts have been preserved.

Of the *Latin* fathers we have the *Expositio* of AUGUSTINE and that of BEDE. From the time of the Reformation we may notice, besides the *Annotationes in Novum Testamentum* by ERASMUS, two expositions of LUTHER (*Werke* ed. Walch IX., 909–1079; and 1080–1252), the Commentaries of CALVIN and BEZA, the lectures of ZWINGLI taken down and edited as an *expositio* by MEGANDER, and BULLINGER's *Brevis et Catholica Expositio.*

Along with the Lutheran A. CALOVIUS, the Arminian HUGO GROTIUS should be named. BENGEL, in his Gnomon, is here, as always, very noteworthy.

Among the moderns we specify in particular LUECKE, whose Commentary passed through a third edition in 1856, and DE WETTE, whose hand-book has in several respects been happily improved by BRUECKNER. EBRARD has contributed the Epistles of John to OLSHAUSEN'S Commentary. Excellent is DUESTERDIECK'S: *Die Drei Johanneischen Briefe*, 2 Bände; Göttingen, 1852–1854. HUTHER'S Commentary in Meyer's Critico-exegetical Hand-book is very well done; 2d ed., 1861.

For practical exegetical purposes we name after SPENER'S *Exposition*, 1699, ZELLER'S (Archdeacon at St. Nicolai, Leipzig) *Explication of the First Epistle of John in* 206 *sermons*, 1709.—STEINHOFER, *The First Epistle of John*, 1762; Hamburg, 1848.—RICKLI, *Johannis* 1 *Brief Erklärt und Angewendet in Predigten;* Luzern, 1828.—JOHANNSEN, *Sermons on the First Epistle of John;* Altona, 1838.—K. BRAUNE, *the Epistles of John;* Grimma, 1847.—A. NEANDER, *the First Epistle of John, practically explained;* Berlin, 1851. [A good translation of this work by Mrs. H. C. CONANT, New York, 1853.—M.].—WOLF, *Practical Comment. on the first Epistle of John in Church Catechizings;* Leipzig, 1851.—HEUBNER, *Practical Exposition of the N. T.*, Vol. IV., pp. 378–440.—BESSER, *Bibelstunden*, Vol. V. *The Epistles of John*, 3d ed., 1862.

On the doctrine see SCHMID, *Bibl. Theology of the N. T.*, 1853, Vol. 2, p. 359 sqq. Cf. LANGE in *Bibelwerk*, Vol. IV., p. 27. (German edition).

[We may add, besides the General Commentaries, the following works:

PRICÆUS, J., in *Crit. Sacr.*

WHISTON, W., *Comm. on the Three Catholic Epistles of John, in agreement with the ancientest records of Christianity now extant.* London, 1719.

HAWKINS, T., a *Comment. on the First, Second and Third Epistles of John.* Halifax, 1808.

BICKERSTETH, E., *Family Exposition*, etc. London, 1846.

SHEPHERD, *Notes on the Gospel and Epistles of John.* London, 1840.

MAURICE, F. D., *The Epistles of John. A Series of Lectures on Christian Ethics.* Cambridge, 1857.

MESTREZAT, JEAN, *Exposition de la Première Epistre de l'Apostre St. Jean.* 2 Vols. Geneva, 1651.

PATERSON, S., *a Commentary on the first Epistle of John.* London, 1842.

PIERCE, *An Exposition of the First Epistle General of John, in 93 Sermons.* Lond., 1835. M.].

COMMENTARY.

THE FIRST EPISTLE (GENERAL) OF JOHN THE APOSTLE.

Ιωαννου α in A. B. *Ιωαννου επιστολη α* Cod. Sin. al. [other Codd. read *επιστολη Ιωαννου πρωτη*; l. r. *Ιωαννου του αποστολου επιστολη χαθολιχη πρωτη*.—M.].

I. THE EXORDIUM.

Chapter I. 1–4.

OBJECT AND PURPOSE OF THE APOSTOLIC ANNUNCIATION (1–3). DESIGN OF THE EPISTLE. (Ver. 4).

1 That which [1] was from the beginning, which we have heard, which we have seen with
our eyes, which we have looked upon, and our hands have handled, of the Word of
2 life; (For [2] the life was manifested, and we have seen *it*, [3] and bear witness, and show
unto you that eternal life, which [4] was with the Father, and was manifested unto us;)
3 That which we have seen and heard declare [5] we unto you, that ye also may have fel-
lowship with us: and truly our fellowship [6] *is* with the Father, and with his Son Jesus
4 Christ. And these things write [7] we unto you that your joy [8] may be full.

Verse 1. [1] German [" What was from the beginning, what we have heard, what we have seen with our eyes, what we gazed upon and our hands handled, of the Word of the Life."—M.]

Verse 2. [2] German ["And the Life was manifested, and we have seen and testified and declare unto you the eternal Life, as which it was with the Father and was manifested unto us."—M.]

[3] [*It*, supplied by E. V., not necessary; it is better to construe ἑωράκαμεν, μαρτυροῦμεν and ἀπαγγέλλομεν with ζωὴν τὴν αἰώνιον. So Lachm., Hahn, Theile, Tischend. and Lillie.—M.]

[4] [On the whole, the rendering of E. V., " that eternal Life which was with the Father," is preferable to the German, and the meaning is clear without the adoption of the Greek idiom, " Life Eternal," by Wordsworth.—M.]

Verse 3. [5] [German: " What we have seen and heard, declare we also to you, that ye . . . . us; and our fellowship indeed is with . . . . Christ." καὶ—δὲ; the καὶ adds something, and δὲ is slightly adversative, cf. 2 Peter i. 5, also Matt. xvi. 18; Mark iv. 36; Luke ii. 35; Acts iii. 24; xxii. 29; Heb. ix. 21; John vi. 51; viii. 16. 17; xv. 27.—*Indeed* or *truly* seem to bring out this slightly adversative sense better than *again* (Lillie).—M.]

Cod. Sin. has καὶ ἀπαγγέλλομεν καὶ ὑμῖν. The first καὶ occurs also in Theoph. and Vulg. (*Cod. Amiatinus;* it may have crept in from v. 2). The second καὶ is found in A. B. C. Cod. Sin. has before this second καὶ an erased ι, as if ἵνα καὶ ὑμεῖς was to have followed forthwith; καὶ ὑμῖν seems therefore to be copied.

[6] Cod. Sin. has ὑμῶν after ἡμετέρα, but a disapproval in the margin.

Verse 4. [7] B. ἡμεῖς for ὑμῶν, [Cod. Sin. ἡμεῖς and ἡμῶν.—M.]

[8] B. G. al. ἡμῶν; so Vulgate with the variation, "*ut gaudeatis et gaudium nostrum sit plenum.*" Both ἡμεῖς and ἡμῶν have probably arisen from the μεθ' ἡμῶν and ἡμετέρα of v. 3, [ἡ χαρὰ ὑμῶν. A. C. K. al. Copt.; Tischend.—M.]

[German: "And these things we write unto you that your joy may be fulfilled." Wordsworth: "filled up to the full;" but *fulfilled* is better.—M.]

EXEGETICAL AND CRITICAL.

The exordium (v. 1–4) describes in vivid and definite language the object and purpose of the Apostolical annunciation and of this Epistle.—The *affinity* of this exordium with the prologue of the Gospel of St. John is unmistakable.

THE GOSPEL.	THE FIRST EPISTLE.
VER. 1. In the beginning (ἐν ἀρχῇ) was the Word.	VER. 1. What was from the beginning (ἀπ ἀρχῆς.)
1. 2. And it was with God (ποὸς τὸν Θεόν.)	2. Which (Life) was with God [with the Father] (πρὸς τὸν ϑεὸν.)
1–4. The Word (λόγος) in Him was Life (ζωή.)	1. The word of the Life (τοῦ λόγου τῆς ζωῆς.)
4. 5. The Life was the Light of men, and the Light shineth (φαίνει)—	2. The Life was manifested, appeared (ἐφανερώθη.)
9. He was the true Light, who lighteneth every man, come into the world.	
14. We gazed upon His glory (ἐθεασάμεθα.)	2. What we have seen with our eyes, what we gazed upon (ἐθεασάμεθα.)

Equally unmistakable is the *difference* between the two exordia; the prologue of the Gospel is a monologue, a testimony and confession, where the Apostle, soaring aloft like an eagle, is raised in calm contemplation above all the tumults of life; the exordium of the Epistle, however, is written in profound emotion under the impressions of a blessed experience in the past, and of the present in hearty sympathy with and tender anxiety for the readers of the Epistle; its address is eloquent, pathetic and lively.

In point of *form* this exordium differs from that of almost all the Epistles of the New Testament, and resembles only the exordium of the Epistle to the Hebrews; it is alike devoid of the name of the writer, of a description of the readers, and of the salutation. But even in the second and third Epistles, although addressed to individuals, and specifying their name or description, the name of the author is not given, his office only being mentioned (ὁ πρεσβύτερος).—As in the Gospel, so in the Epistles, John loves to suppress his name (John i. 35. 40; xiii. 23; xviii. 15; xix. 26; xx. 3; xxi. 20, and cf. J. P. Lange, the *Ev. Jo.*, p. 63. 2). But although he does not name himself, the Apostolical office and vocation of the author are accurately marked; and although the readers are not even designated, his relation to them is made sufficiently prominent, so that we must say that the Epistle is written not only *for* them, but *to* them. But the salutation (χαίρειν) may be alluded to in ἵνα ἡ χαρὰ ὑμῶν ᾖ πεπληρωμένη.

The *structure*, v. 1–3, owing to its liveliness, is not quite simple; it is repeatedly interrupted and has been variously given. The fundamental or leading word (the *verbum finitum*), is doubtless ἀπαγγέλλομεν, v. 3, which for the sake of clearness is appropriately placed between the object of the annunciation and its purpose. The *purpose* is simply and definitely indicated: ἵνα καὶ ὑμεῖς κοινωνίαν ἔχητε μεϑ' ἡμῖν. In defining *the object*, the Apostle seems to struggle for the right expressions, and renders it prominent in a double series of clauses, first, v. 1: ὃ ἦν ἀπ' ἀρχῆς—ἐψηλάφησαν; then v. 1: περὶ τοῦ λόγου τῆς ζωῆς—ἐφανερώθη ἡμῖν. He marks it first according to its import and being, v. 1. ὃ ἦν ἀπ' ἀρχῆς, in the second part of v. 1; περὶ τοῦ λόγου τῆς ζωῆς, and v. 2, ἡ ζωὴ ἡ αἰώνιος ἥτις ἦν πρὸς τὸν πατέρα, and then according to its manifestation, v. 1: ὃ ἑωράκαμεν—ἐψηλάφησαν, v. 2: ἐφανερώθη—ἡμῖν, or first according to its mysterious sublimity and fulness, and then according to the manifold internal relations in which it stood and stands to John and his associates. The Apostle, while strongly marking the object of the Apostolical annunciation after the first series of relative clauses by περὶ τοῦ λόγου τῆς ζωῆς, takes occasion to introduce with the Genitive ζωῆς a parenthesis, v. 2, which concludes with ἐφανερώθη ἡμῖν, and cannot be resolved or broken up. This constrains him to connect the sentence, thus interrupted by the parenthesis, with what goes before by ὃ ἑωράκαμεν καὶ ἀκηκόαμεν, and so that, as the sentence begins with a relative, now that the object has been distinctly defined by περὶ τοῦ λόγου τῆς ζωῆς, it also concludes with a relative. We have therefore here no period with protasis and apodosis, but a simple sentence, much enlarged indeed and interrupted by long parentheses, the structure of which however is plain enough and does not allow any other construing.

THE OBJECT OF THE APOSTOLICAL ANNUNCIATION. VER. 1–3*a*

a. The First Series of Clauses.—VER. 1.

VER. 1. **What was from the beginning.**—The opening words remind us of John i. 1: "In the beginning was the Word," and of Gen. i. 1: "In the beginning God created." Not the moment of creation, but the purely eternal existence until the beginning of the world and its history. The word ἀρχή must always be defined by the context, *e. g.*, in 1 John ii. 7: "Ye had *from the beginning*," the beginning denotes the time when they became Christians, in ch. iii. 8, "the devil sinneth *from the beginning*," *i. e.*, from the time when he became the devil, which happened immediately after the creation of the world; in ch. ii. 13, 14: "Ye have known him that is *from the beginning*," *i. e.*, from eternity, Jesus Christ.—The beginning of the devil dates from the creation of the world (ch. iii. 8), the beginning of faith lies in the life of the readers themselves (ch. ii. 7), and the beginning here and at ch. ii. 13, denotes eternity *before* the creation of the world. The sense is clear from the parallel sentence, v. 2, "ἦν πρὸς τὸν πατέρα," and corresponds with πρὸ πάντων Col. i. 17, πρὸ καταβολῆς κόσμου Eph. i. 4, πρὸ τοῦ τὸν κόσμον εἶναι John xvii. 5, or with ἀπὸ τῶν αἰώνων Eph. iii. 9; Col. i. 26. But ἀπό does not equal πρὸ, nor is ἀπ' ἀρχῆς equal to ἐν ἀρχῇ, John i. 1.—In the Gospel the Apostle describes and considers the Existence of the Logos with the Father before the Creation, and then proceeds to denote His agency in the creation; but here the Apostle passes from the Existence of the Logos to His manifestations in history. He *was* therefore *before* the world was, and He *was*, before He appeared in history [*i. e.*, before His incarnation.—M.]. The Apostle looks back from his personal experience to the eternity *from* whence He came; His eye travels over thousands of years from the beginning to the time of His personal experience. As He became not the Logos when He became man, so He became not [began to exist—M.] when the world was made, began to exist. The reference is consequently not to the *μυστήριον Θεοῦ* (Theophylact, Oecumen.), or to the Gospel of Jesus Christ (Socinus), or to the *res a Deo destinatæ* (Grotius).—The simplest explanation of the designation of the personal Logos by the Neuter ὅ, is the supposition that the Apostle, moved by the mysterious sublimity and the fulness of essential [belonging to the Being or Essence of Christ—M.] glory (which will not be fully recognized and known before His ultimate revelation in His second advent, ch. iii. 2: *καθώς ἐστι*), writes with a soaring sense of indefiniteness, and views the Person to whom he refers at the same time as the principle of the world and its history, although this does not pass into a reflecting consciousness [*sic* in German.—M.]. Similarly *τὸ κατέχον* precedes *ὁ κατέχων* in 2 Thess. ii. 6; similar terms may also be seen in Luke i. 35; John iii. 6; vi. 37; Heb. vii. 7; 1 Cor. i. 27 sq.; Col. i. 26; 1 John v. 4. The reference is consequently not to abstraction, the Word of Life, the Life (Huther), or to the connection of the Person of Jesus with His history and doctrine (Lücke, Ebrard), or the taking together of His preëxistence and historical appearance (Düsterdieck), or to the mere designation of the Apostolical annunciation (Hofmann). [Braune's explanation lacks perspicuity, and really seeks to combine the views of Huther and Düsterdieck, with the addition of a reference to the second coming of Christ; we doubt whether it will convince many readers, while Huther's explanation, which we give in full, supplies a clear and natural reason for the use of the Neuter ὅ. "The Apostle points to the Apostolical annunciation, namely, the personal Christ, by the Neuter because he thinks of Him as 'the Word of Life,' or 'the Life.' The reference then being to an abstract (*per se*) or general idea, *ζωή*, the Neuter ὅ seems to be in place. The Apostle might indeed have used ὅς for ὅ, because this *ζωή* is to him the personal Christ; but considering that the characteristic import of Christ consists in His being *the Life* (not only a living individual) and that John, full of this idea, begins this Epistle, it was more natural that he should use ὅ than ὅς."—M.]

What we have heard—seen—gazed upon—handled is a rising gradation; *hearing* is the lowest degree of the climax, it strikes the ear from a certain distance, perhaps unsought for; **with our eyes** intensifies the word *seen;* seeing indeed may be involuntary, but the beginning of self-activity is already marked; *gazing upon* gives prominence to this self-activity [voluntary exercise of the sense of sight—M.], with the secondary idea of continuance; **handled with our hands** denotes the nearest and most direct intercourse. By "*what we have heard*" the Apostle naturally passes from the eternal existence of the Logos to His historical appearing; the *λόγος ἄσαρκος* becomes the *λόγος ἔνσαρκος*. He makes Himself known first and most naturally in the Word. Not what he had heard of Him in the Word of the Old Testament, in the prophecies until John the Baptist, but that he had heard *Himself.* "O cannot be another object than in the first clause; the same word, ὅ, is used in all the clauses, and designates the same object, the Logos; the perceptions and modes of revelation only differ. The Apostle had not only heard words of the mouth, words from human lips, but in such human words, and through them the speaker Himself, the Logos; not the Apostle's ear, but he himself has heard, his soul of course through the instrumentality of the material organ of hearing.—He had seen, as he says, in order to lay peculiar emphasis on the testimony of his ears and eyes, *with his own eyes*, the form of a servant, the Son of man, but of course what lived therein shown forth therefrom in look and mien, in manner and motion; the soul of John, therefore, looked with bodily eyes into the Nature of the manifested, incarnate Logos. Hence again the same object. Indeed He says Himself: "He that hath seen me, hath seen the Father," Jno. xiv. 9 compared with ch. xii. 45.

What we gazed upon—handled are Aorists, not Perfects, as just before. This change of tense is neither arbitrary nor inaccurate, but designed and wise. The Apostle had *heard* and *seen* in single moments; these are finished acts, facts with their effects; but now he intends by the use of these Aorists to point to the past as an expiring present, how he had ever and anon had continuous intercourse with Him in the most direct nearness and lively self-activity.—The verbs "*heard*" and "*seen*" rather denote involuntary perception, while the others, "*gazed upon*" and "*handled*," signify voluntary, intentional perception for the purpose of making sure of the reality and nature of the Logos. (Huther).—The man Jesus only was gazed upon, His body only was handled, but through all that sensuousness the Son of God was recognized and felt, and His Divine glory perceived and experienced. We have, therefore, to deal with the same object throughout. The verb "*gazed upon*" reminds us of the language of John in his Gospel (ch. i. 14): "The Word became flesh and dwelt among us, and we gazed upon (*ἐθεασάμεθα*) His glory;" the verb "*handled*" is connected with the words of the risen Saviour, Lke. xxiv. 39: "Behold my hands and my feet that it is I myself; handle me (*ψηλαφήσατέ με*), and see; for a spirit hath not flesh and bones as ye see me have," cf. Jno. xx. 27. John, who leaned on His bosom, Jno. xiii. 23: *ἐν τῷ κόλπῳ*, Jno. xiii. 25; xxi. 20: *ἐπὶ τὸ στῆθος*, denotes thereby the most intimate relation, rendering shaking of hands and kissing proper, and thus places the real humanity and bodily existence of Christ beyond the possibility of doubt. "He patiently allowed murderers to handle Him, why should He not have suffered those who love Him to do the same." (Pfenninger) Thus the Apostle marks here two things, first, the fulness of his perceptions, and, secondly, their authentication. Luther says correctly: "He multiplies words, and thus makes the matter great and important. We have, says he, looked and gazed upon with the utmost care and diligence; we have not been deceived, but are sure that it was not an illusion. He says this in order to make his hearers perfectly sure of the matter." Thus both the glory of the incarnate Word, so difficult to understand, and the authentication of the testimony, so important in its bearing, are portrayed in such lively colours on account of the object.

b. The Second Series of Clauses.—VER. 1–3*a*.

Of the word of the Life is neither an independent appositive addition to the preceding definitions of the object (Huther), nor governed by the last verb, ἐψηλάφησαν (Erasmus, al.), nor, indeed, by ἦν ἀπ' ἀρχῆς (S. G. Lange, "What happened to the Word of Life from the beginning!"). It is the beginning of a new clause, parallel with the series of relative clauses as to matter (Düsterdieck), which terminates with them in ἀπαγγέλλομεν. That which before had been taken indefinitely as a Neuter, is here described for the first time as a Person. The Word of Life, *per se*, may stand both for the *Gospel of Life* and the *Personal Logos of Life*, and taken as the *Apostolical Word*, or the *hypostatical Word.* If it be taken in the former sense as *verbum simpliciter* (Bengel), the Genitive τῆς ζωῆς may designate the quality (Socinus, Grotius), like ὁ ἄρτος τῆς ζωῆς, Jno. vi. 35, τὸ φῶς τῆς ζωῆς, or the object (Luther: "we *speak* of the life," Düsterdieck), as in 1 Cor. i. 18: ὁ λόγος τοῦ σταυροῦ. But this construction of περὶ τοῦ λόγου τῆς ζωῆς is impossible, because it must be connected with ἀπαγγέλλομεν (1 Thess. i. 9: περὶ ἡμῶν ἀπαγγέλλουσιν); the construction with περὶ instead of the Accusative is designed to guard against the possible misunderstanding of making the Word designate the Gospel and not Christ. To speak the Gospel *concerning, respecting* the Word, although in the manner of a declaration, pertains rather to the province of science, is more the work of the theologian than of the Apostle. But grammatically it is inadmissible to infer from the parenthesis after ζωῆς, namely from the words ἀπαγγέλλομεν τὴν ζωὴν τὴν αἰώνιον, that λόγος τῆς ζωῆς is equal to said words, *i. e.*, the declaration or annunciation of life. The *Word*, ὁ λόγος, the object of the Apostolic annunciation, must be, as in Jno. i. 1, sqq., the original, eternal, personal Word, the eternal Son of the eternal Father, and fully accords with ὃ ἦν ἀπ' ἀρχῆς, with the sole difference that the *neutrum* becomes a *masculinum*, in order to bring out the personal character of the Logos according to His historical manifestation. On ὁ λόγος see J. P. Lange, *The Gospel According to John*, p. 38, sq., Germ. edition.—The Genitive τῆς ζωῆς is explained by Jno. i. 4: ἐν αὐτῷ ζωὴ ἦν. The Word has Life in itself, is Life Itself, and imparts Life to others. It is the true, eternal, primal Life, and this Life is the Nature of the Logos, but the object of the annunciation is the Logos Himself. (Düsterdieck).

VER. 2. **And the Life was manifested.**—καὶ adds in a vivid manner an explanation by introducing a parenthesis and interrupting the sentence; ἐφανερώθη recalls Jno. i. 4. 5, "And the Life was the Light, and the Light shineth (φαίνει) in the darkness." The Life of the Logos appeared, was manifested, so that we may infer His Being and Nature from His Life, and thus acquire a knowledge of the Son. This epiphany is the immediate consequence of the Incarnation, of the ἐνσάρκωσις. Jno. i. 14: ὁ λόγος σάρξ ἐγένετο.

And we have seen—testify—declare.—Antithesis of Jno. i. 5, "And the darkness has (Luther: had) not comprehended it." The climax is: ἑωράκαμεν connected with ἐφανερώθη, he had been a *spectator*, but did not see in vain; for he became a *witness* through intercourse with the manifested One, and in his capacity of witness he fixes his eye on what had become visible, the acts and events which he had experienced: what he thus sees and utters is purely objective without reference to his hearers and their wants or relations, but in the interest in and for the matter itself. But he does not stop there; he now *declares* also what he has seen; he explains and applies at the same time; he unfolds in their fulness, and with a special interest in his readers, the thoughts and facts comprised in his personal experience. The objective is brought near through the subjective. Thus he joyfully recalls to himself that blessed manifestation, and is constrained to testify for himself, and to declare to others, that they also may have such an experience. 'Απαγγέλλειν = καταγγέλλειν, Acts xvii. 27; and=κηρύσσειν, Rom. x. 14, sq., cf. Matt. xxviii. 8. 11; Acts xxvi. 20. In John's writings, ὁρᾶν and μαρτυρεῖν are frequently joined together, Jno. i. 34; iii. 32; xix. 35; but the last of these passages, like Jno. xv. 27, is without an object, which, however, may be readily supplied from the context. The object of the *three* verbs is **the Eternal Life** (Oecumenius, Lücke, Huther), and not only of ἀπαγγέλλειν (Fritsche, de Wette, Düsterdieck). The life is called *eternal*, ἡ αἰώνιος, because it did not take its beginning in the world, but rather gave a beginning to the world and the life in the world. It is Absolute Life, the source and root of all life in the world, physical and ethical (Lücke on Jno. i. 4). It *was* before it appeared, became visible; it did not *become* [come into being] perchance, when it appeared. On that account the Apostle adds ἥτις ἦν πρὸς τὸν πατέρα.—The relative ἥτις is not=ἥ, but=*ut quæ*, hence, eternal life as which it was, that is to say, which *was* (ἦν) as such before its revelation in the *direction towards the Father*, not with, alongside of Him; it denotes not a mere juxtaposition, but a being together, having mutual intercourse; it is directed towards Him, turned to Him, longing for and leading to Him, according to its nature. It is not *in the Father*, but from Him, and hence directed towards Him. Here is asserted of the ζωή what Jno. i. 1 predicates of the λόγος; in Him truly is such life, in Him also it has become manifest. Because John had just had such a lively conception of the Life of the Logos, he was able to begin in the Neuter, ὃ ἦν ἀπ' ἀρχῆς; for it *is* without the world, before the world, with and for God in the Logos.

And was manifested unto us.—*Eternal* Life has appeared, and just now become manifest to us the Apostles. Thus closes the parenthesis with a return to the thought at the beginning, and it is because of this conclusion (ἐφανερώθη) that John resumes the interrupted sentence, the words "**what we have seen and heard**" being placed before, and, in consequence of the prolonged interruption, breaks off and drops the series of clauses beginning with περὶ τοῦ λόγου, and resumes the first series of clauses, in a brief and concise form. The object is the same as in v. 1.

The Subject of the Annunciation, VER. 3.

On ἀπαγγέλλομεν see the notes on v. 2.

VER. 3*a*. **Declare we also to you.**—Καὶ ὑμῖν places the readers of this Epistle alongside of other Churches who had heard the Apostolical annunciation; hence John, in using the Plural in the verbs from v. 1 onward and ἡμῖν in v. 2, probably did not only refer to himself after the manner of authors, but to himself and his brethren, more particularly to the disciples of Jesus and the Apostles; the opposition of ἡμῖν and ὑμῖν is only the opposition of the first Christians and the immediate disciples of the Lord, or the Apostles and the Churches formed by the instrumentality of the former, or founded by the agency of the latter. John is fond of including himself among the whole of Christendom, ch. i. 6–8; ii. 1. 28; iii. 1. But the comparison of Jno. xv. 27 seems to render it probable that John in this place speaks of himself as connected with the Apostles, the reference being to the founding and conservation of Christian Churches. He does not stand alone, but like him all the **Apostles** have heard, seen and handled, and bear witness with him.

Purpose of the Annunciation, VER. 3*b*.

VER. 3*b*. **That ye also may have fellowship with us.**—The word *also*, καὶ before ὑμεῖς after the preceding καὶ ὑμῖν, renders it very prominent that the purpose of the Apostolical annunciation is always and every where the same with all the Apostles in all Churches, namely: unity and fellowship. *Fellowship with us* is not the same as *fellowship such as we have it*, like us, with the Father and the Son (Socinus, Episcopius, Bengel). The position of the words forbids such a construction. It is rather the fellowship *with us*, the Church-fellowship of Christians among themselves.—Μετά (from μέσος, *between*, *among*) τινος denotes the circle into which one enters, consequently cöexistence, whereas σύν τινι signifies connection with, coherence (so Krüger). The Church of the first disciples, of the Apostles, is the primitive Church into which they must enter in order to partake [of its fellowship—M.]; mere connection with it is not sufficient. The Apostles are and remain the foundation on which we must take our stand (Eph. ii. 20); the mediators who must take us by the hand (Eph. iv. 11. 12); they are the stem out of which the Churches break forth and grow like branches. All (καὶ) the Churches are to be in Church-fellowship with the Apostles.—ἔχητε is not: *acquire* (Fritzsche), nor does it denote *progress* (à Lapide [who says: "*pergere et in ea*, κοινωνίᾳ, *proficere et confirmari*"—M.]), but indicates simply permanent possession, constancy.

And our fellowship indeed is with the Father, etc.—καὶ does not connect with the preceding clause, so that also that which follows depends on ἵνα (Luther: and our fellowship *be*; so Augustine, Calvin, Grotius, Ebrard); for there is also a δὲ after κοινωνία [see Appar. Crit., v. 3. 5.—M.]. The reference, therefore, is to a κοινωνία here as well as in the preceding clause, hence καὶ ἡ κοινωνία ἡ ἡμετέρα; but this fellowship is yet another μετὰ τοῦ πατρὸς, etc. The other stands in some sort of antithesis to this; it must go beyond the former, and in it come to the latter, hence δὲ. Similar is the construction, Jno. vi. 51; viii. 17; Matt. xvi. 18; Mk. iv. 36; Lke. ii. 35. Winer, p. 393. We have here a separate clause, in which ἐστί must be supplied, which adds a new and somewhat different particular as if we did read: καὶ ἡμεῖς ἔχομεν κοινωνίαν μετὰ τοῦ πατρὸς κ. τ. λ., so that they have not only fellowship with the Apostles, but also with the Father and the Son. The thought itself forbids a close connection with ἵνα. The purpose of the Apostolical annunciation is not to effect a union with the Father and the Son, for that is the office of Jesus Christ, the Mediator. The Apostle insists upon Church-fellowship, and that is sufficient, because in it is the fellowship with the Father and the Son; a fellowship with God in Christ is not to be created from Church-fellowship; the Church-fellowship is not without the former, and the former is in the latter; otherwise the Church-fellowship would be no Church-fellowship, the Apostolical fellowship, no fellowship with the Apostles. Κοινωνία is a fellowship with the Father and the Son, so that we form part of Them and are personally united with Them; They are in us and we in Them (Jno. xiv. 23); Their Life is our Life (v. 6). Besides the Father, **His Son Jesus Christ** is particularly named, and thus the full designation of Him ὃ ἦν ἀπ' ἀρχῆς, of the λόγος τῆς ζωῆς serves to show His identity with the Incarnate Saviour; and thus the conclusion is found. Cf. Jno. xvii. 22–26. [This κοινωνία is one of *essence* and *being*, founded on the circumstance that its subjects are *begotten* of the same σπέρμα θεοῦ (1 Jno. iii. 9), and that the same power of a heavenly and glorified life animates them; so Sander. The definition of Zuinglius deserves transcribing: "*De qua loquatur societate, quodque intelligat consortium, exponit; non qua homines hominibus solum pace, concordia et amicitia fraterna juguntur, sed qua homines Deo animo, mente atque adeo fide hic uniuntur indissolubiter et posthanc cum eo aeternum viventes. Hoc est quod Christus orat Patrem*, Jo. xvii."—M.].

The Epistle and its Design, VER. 4.

VER. 4. **And these things we write unto you.**—*And* not only connects, but continues, leads us further, and marks the next progress; the fellowship just described promotes joy, operates in the depth of the heart. Ταῦτα is neither what precedes (Sander), nor what follows immediately (Socinus), but the whole contents of the Epistle (Lücke, de Wette, Düsterdieck, Huther, Ebrard). John considers the Epistle with its contents as documentary evidence connected with the oral annunciation.

We write.—Although the personal relation of the Apostle to the readers is here more prominent than in the Plurals of the preceding clauses, the Plural is not used, after the manner of authors, for the Singular. John continues impressed with the convictions of the common Apostolical annunciation; he knows that he is in perfect agreement with all the Apostles, that he speaks as they speak, and that their speech is like his; nor does he stand alone, but has his associates and assistants, like Paul (1 Cor. i. 1, Παῦλος και Σωσθένης ὁ ἀδελφός; 2 Cor. i. 1; Col. i. 1; Philem. 1, Παῦλος καὶ Τιμόθεος; Phil. i. 1, Παῦλος καὶ Τιμόθεος δοῦλοι Ι. Χρ.; 1 Thess. i. 1;

2 Thess. i. 1: Παῦλος καὶ Σιλουανὸς καὶ Τιμόθεος). *Writing* is indeed another species of μαρτυρία, coördinate with oral communication. Bengel:—*Testimonium genus; species duæ: annuntiatio et scriptio; annuntiatio ponit fundamentum, scriptio superædificat.*" The Epistle seems only to build up and perfect the life already existing in the readers. Düsterdieck.

That your joy may be fulfilled.—The reading ἡμῶν would make the joy of the Apostles over the Churches [*i. e.*, joy, because their word yields fruit among their hearers. Theophylact: "ἡμῶν γὰρ ὑμῖν κοινωνούντων πλείστην ἔχομεν τὴν χαρὰν ἡμῶν, ἥν ταῖς θεριστaῖς ὁ χαίρων σπορεὺς ἐν τῇ τοῦ μισθοῦ ἀπολήψει βραβεύσει, χαιρόντων καὶ τούτων· ὅτι τῶν πόνων αὐτῶν ἀπολαύουσι."—M.]. So does Bede with reference to Phil. ii. 2: "*gaudium doctorum sit plenum, cum multos prædicando ad sanctæ ecclesiæ societatem perducant.*" Jno. xvii. 13; xv. 11 cannot be adduced in support of this reading; said passages, besides the reason already stated above in Appar. Crit. [v. 4. 8—M.], may have suggested this reading. The identical language occurs at Jno. xvi. 24: ἵνα ἡ χαρὰ ὑμῶν ᾖ πεπληρωμένη. To be sure, according to Jno. xv. 11: ἵνα ἡ χαρὰ ἡ ἐμὴ ἐν ὑμῖν ᾖ καὶ ἡ χαρὰ ὑμῶν πληρωθῇ, the joy of Christians is the joy of Christ, of which they had become partakers. For Christ has in Himself the Life, Life eternal, true, full, unobstructed Life, which is happiness and peace. Whoso derives Life from Christ becomes a convalescent, recovers health, the health of the soul, and that is peace and joy. Surely, he who is holy, must be happy, and none but the holy and sanctified are happy. If Christ's high-priestly intercession (Jno. xvii. 13) still continues the object and ground of great joy, it contemplates also the growth of joy in individuals going on to eternity, even as John remarks in a private Epistle addressed to a friend (2 Jno. 12).—Hence Christ speaks of His joy, which shall become our joy, even as Christ's Life shall become our Life through faith; hence χαρὰ πίστεως, Phil. i. 25.—*Given* is the joy by Him, but only like a grain of wheat, which must grow in order to become perfect and to yield fruit. But that which is to be perfected must *exist.* The perfection, however, is not instantaneous, magical or miraculous, but has its stages and maladies of development,—struggles—dangers; hence: ἡ πεπληρωμένη. Now this takes place in the fellowship, both in that of the Church and in that with the Father and the Son; there, joy is not only a transient emotion, but an habitual state becoming ever more perfect. Luther (*Schol.* ed. Bruns.):—"*Principium hujus gaudii est, quum incipimus credere; postea quum fides augescit meditando, docendo, studendo, tum fit plenum gaudium.*" The reason why the Apostle dwells on joy (χαρὰ) rather than on peace, may be that at the beginning of the Epistle he thinks with reference to the readers of the greeting, χαίρειν, which, apart from the Epistle of Claudius Lysias to Felix (Acts xxiii. 26–30), occurs only in the circular of the Apostles at the Council of Jerusalem (Acts xv. 23) and at James i. 1. [Wordsworth contrasts the πλήρωμα χαρᾶς with the πλήρωμα of the Gnostics. —M.]

[Düsterdieck:—"The peace of reconciliation, the blessed consciousness of sonship, the happy growth in holiness, the bright prospect of future completion and glory,—all these are but simple details of that which in all its length and breadth is embraced by one word, Eternal Life, the real possession of which is the immediate source of our joy. We have joy, Christ's joy, because we are blessed, because we have Life itself in Christ." Compare the beautiful extract from Augustine, below in *Doctrinal and Ethical*, No. 7 —M.]

DOCTRINAL AND ETHICAL.

1. On the word λόγος cf. J. P. Lange on Jno. i. 1, Vol. IV., p. 41, sq., of the *Bibelwerk*, German edition.—It is characteristic of John, and perfectly analogous to the Gospel, to start from the historical stand-point, vv. 1. 2. 3., cf. Jno. i. 14, and draw the *à posteriori* conclusion of the Eternal Being and Nature, and then taking there, as it were, a firm position, to trace the epiphanies and operations of the Logos in the world, in time and among men. On this account the Apostle begins here, as in the Gospel, with the Prëexistence of the Logos (ὃ ἦν ἀπ' ἀρχῆς ἡ ζωὴ ἡ αἰώνιος, ἥτις ἦν πρὸς τὸν πατέρα). He does not lose himself in the genesis of the Logos, like the Gnostics with their theogonies, but only dwells upon His *Being*, as ζωὴ αἰώνιος, in relation to the Father (πρὸς τὸν πατέρα). Hence we must not connect the λόγος and the ζωὴ as a (third) syzygy with Valentinus (†160 on the island of Cyprus), "that most profound, spiritual, thoughtful, intelligent and imaginative" Gnostic (see Gieseler, *K. G.*, I., p. 155; particularly Kurtz, *K. G.*, I., 136, sqq.). Eternal, true, full life is only the Being of the Logos, as it is the Being of the Father. But this Life He has not only in Himself as a possession, as Jno. i. 4: ἐν αὐτῷ ζωὴ ἦν, but He Himself was truly and altogether Life, eternal Life in His Being (v. 2), of the same Life-substance with God the Father, indissolubly united with Him, although different from Him in Person, there is nothing in Him which is not likewise in the Father, but He is self-dependent, turned to and belonging to the Father (πρὸς τὸν πατέρα).

2. Threefold is the *mode of existence* of the Logos: *a. anterior to the world* of time; *b. earthly-human; c. glorified.* The first is made prominent in the beginning of this Epistle: ὃ ἦν ἀπ' ἀρχῆς, ὁ λόγος τῆς ζωῆς, the second is intimated in ἐφανερώθη, and in conjunction with the third in υἱὸς αὐτοῦ Ἰησοῦ Χριστοῦ. For λόγος and υἱός are to be distinguished, so that the historical Christ is called *Son,* cf. vv. 1. 3 with Jno. i. 1. 14. But in reality it is the same Person. The incarnate Logos does not *become* the *Son of God,* and this designation is not so much of ethical as of metaphysical import. He is called and is the Son of God only because of the relation essential to His Person, and of His eternal and ante-temporal relation to God.

3. The *humanity* of the Logos is referred to with marked emphasis, in the terms ἀκούειν, ὁρᾶν, θεᾶσθαι, ψηλαφᾶν, vv. 1. 2. 3. The Son of Man has become audible, visible, sensible to the children of men. His being ἐφανερώθη to the disciples was only brought about by His human nature, but so that He really σὰρξ ἐγένετο and

ἐσκήνωσεν ἐν ἡμῖν (Jno. i. 14). He is perfect man. But His becoming man is not brought out as much by John as by the other Apostles with reference to His humiliation, because John recognized the Divine glory in the form of the Servant, the Divine attributes in the form of His human appearing, sought their traces with peculiar love, and found them with a jubilant soul. John was more concerned with what the Son of God brought with Him, His eternal Life which He had in Himself, than with what He did assume, human flesh and blood. The Apostle sees in all the epiphanies and exhibitions of the Incarnate One, in all the humiliations of His earthly-human Being and Life, the Love, the Wisdom and the Power of Christ; he follows their traces with ardent attachment, and he follows them not in vain. He bears more testimony to the κρύψις than the κένωσις, but also more to the Lutheran intermixture [German: Into-one-another—M.] of the Divine and the Human in Christ.—Traces of the transcendency and immanency of God may also be found and proved here, and how both have to be held fast together.

4. Christ is the eternal principle of the life of men and of the world in general; He is the Mediator of all the activity of the Father exerted with reference to the world. The thought expressed in the Epistle to the Hebrews by φέρων τὰ πάντα τῷ ῥήματι τῆς δυνάμεως αὐτοῦ is the fundamental pre-supposition of ὃ ἦν ἀπ' ἀρχῆς, ζωὴ αἰώνιος, ἥτις ἦν πρὸς τὸν πατέρα, κοινωνία μετὰ τοῦ πατρὸς καὶ μετὰ τοῦ υἱοῦ αὐτοῦ Ἰησοῦ Χριστοῦ, as well as of ἵνα—πεπληρωμένη. John, by the use of ἀπ' ἀρχῆς—, which, as opposed to ἐν ἀρχῇ, Jno. i. 1, within the beginning, points as a definite sphere, and as opposed to κατ' ἀρχὰς (Heb. i. 10) along the beginnings, following the beginnings, —points, although fastened to a longer line, more than ἐξ ἀρχῆς, Jno. vi. 64, out of the beginning as out of a fountain, to a source of history after the beginning—intends to mark the power existing in eternity as present and real in time and the course of history. [The peculiarly involved and occasionally obscure style of Dr. Braune will tax the patience of the reader, as it does that of the translator, who tries his best to express B's meaning in idiomatic English. The last sentence was peculiarly difficult, but the use of dashes and other marks of punctuation will, it is hoped, enable the reader to catch the author's meaning.—M.]. But it must be remembered that the Apostle is more concerned with the life of individuals, of the Apostles and of Churches, than with that of the whole world. Still what holds good in the case of individual man, the microcosm, must also apply to the whole world, the macrocosm. Christ could not be the principle of salvation to individuals, unless He were potent and destined for the whole world. Because in the creation He is the Mediator of the beginning of the world's life (Jno. i. 3) so also in the redemption He is of course the Mediator of the consummation of the world's life. The earth requires no new suns, and mankind no other Saviour. The truth of Christ is the only and eternal truth for all nations and times. Christ is not a world-historical personage, like Alexander the Great, but the Living One that has the keys of hell and of death (Rev. i. 18).

4. Ver. 3 indicates the relation of *Churchliness* and *Christianness*, of *Church-dom* and *Christianity*, [I am not altogether satisfied with these terms, but they express as nearly as possible the German words, *Kirchlichkeit*, the quality of being Church-like, *Christlichkeit*, the quality of being Christ-like, or Christian, *Kirchenthum*, the state, existence or establishment of the Church, and *Christenthum*, the religion taught by Christ.—M.] For ἡ κοινωνία μεθ' ἡμῶν, the fellowship of the Churches with the Apostles and among themselves is *Church*, while κοινωνία μετὰ τοῦ πατρὸς καὶ τοῦ υἱοῦ αὐτοῦ Ἰησοῦ Χριστοῦ denotes the nature of Christianity. John insists only on Church-fellowship for the promotion of Christianness. It is Apostolical that the Churches should keep to the Apostles and their annunciation, and be united among each other without independentism, but it is equally and only Apostolical that the Christ-like or the Christian-like should be the basis and aim of the Churchly. The Churchly must ever be measured and adjusted by the Christ-like.

5. The *Church* is a whole, an organization embracing heaven and earth in the Church militant and triumphant, and in the Church militant all the different local Churches (καὶ ὑμῖν, καὶ ὑμεῖς, v. 3), and all the Churches of all centuries (ἀπαγγέλλομεν) gathered by the Apostolical ministry in general, with its continuous activity (Lücke). What Paul says (1 Cor. iii. 9–11. 16; Eph. ii. 20 sq.; cf. 1 Peter ii. 5) of the Church, that it is a building of the temple of God founded on Christ the corner-stone, or a body of which Christ is the head (Eph. i. 22 sq.; v. 23; Col. i. 18), is here also present to the mind of John, who, with a leaning to John xv. 1, seems to think of a growth, in which the Church is the stem founded by Christ, out of which believers come forth on all sides like branches (John xvii. 20).

6. *The Apostolical annunciation*, ἀπαγγελία, presupposes an eventful experience from personal intercourse with the Redeemer, and is accompanied by the Apostolical writings (γράφόμεν). All information derived from oral communication must be strengthened, guided, cleared and completed by the written communication. He only is able to work for the Lord and the brethren that has lived with Him in intimate converse, to whom He did yield Himself and whom he did draw to Himself, so that he "cannot but speak the things which he has seen and heard," (Acts iv. 19. 20).

7. *Joy* is the essence of Christianity. Augustine, *Conf.*, 10, 22, says: "*Est enim gaudium, quod non datur impiis, sed iis tantum, qui te gratis colunt, quorum gaudium tu ipse es. Et ipsa est beata vita gaudere ad te, de te, propter te, ipsa est et non altera.*"—The Christian faith does not move in a circle of different objects, thoughts, words and works, some of which must be done and others shunned; but it moves in that which it does gladly, and shuns that which it scorns to do. The Word and Life of Christ are as much the Christian's element as air is the element of birds, and water that of fishes. The exercises of godliness are to him not charms against an evil, or the worship of God a slave-work, or prayer a burden. The godliness, which is kindled by the loving-kindness of God is true happiness and

felicity. The fear of God does not bring to the Christian gloomy self-denial and renouncing of the world, as if the Christian's life consisted solely in the suppression of ardent desires and want, but in joys which he experiences, according to the exhortation of the Apostle Paul in the Epistle for the fourth Sunday in Advent (Phil. iv. 4): "*Rejoice in the Lord alway; and again I say rejoice.*" Or according to the Lord's promise in the Gospel for the third Sunday after Easter (John xvi. 22): "*Your heart shall rejoice, and your joy no man taketh from you.*" Hence the reiterated monition: "Be not afraid," and the promise of the Comforter and of peace. In the praise and love of God we have a token and a standard of true Christianity. Delight in the Lord (Ps. xxxvii. 4) with His creating, preserving, overruling, pardoning, atoning and glorifying (John iii. 2) love, is the Christian's duty and life. Only that he ABIDE, AND THE JOY OF CHRIST ABIDE IN HIM, AND THAT HIS JOY MAY BE FULL (John xv. 1–11).

HOMILETICAL AND PRACTICAL.

Seek Jesus and His light; all without that is unprofitable.—Seek in all your experience in time for that which is from all eternity.—Seek in all sensuous manifestations for the supersensuous kernel with its life, which continues to all eternity, even as it is from all eternity.—Nothing is more sure than that which is of Christ: He is from all eternity, and brings His own into the Kingdom of the Father.—Learn more and more that God is not only above thee, but in the world, not far from thee, but very nigh thee.—Speak of Christ only as His witness. Speak of Him, because thou hast known and felt Him within thee, not because thou art a preacher or a theologian, or because thou art baptized.—Do not despise Church-fellowship; it contains a blessing, even an eternal blessing.—Be not satisfied with thy churchliness (churchmanship) unless it make thee more happy in, and more sure of the Father and the Son.—Christian knowledge, like all science, is possible only in fellowship with the whole, especially in going back to the fountain-head in the writings and the testimony of the Apostles.—Holiness and joy are indissolubly united in the Christian, but impiety and lust in the worldly-minded.—Be ashamed, if for want of faith or courage, or even because of a desponding mind, thou dost not rejoice in thy Lord.—Be afraid lest thy joy in Christ and the Kingdom of heaven decrease.—Strive that thy joy in Christ grow fuller and fuller. Delight in the Lord is thy duty, in order that thy duty become thy joy and honour, not thy task and burden.—A Christian must be joyful, for his is the truth which maketh free, the righteousness that availeth with God, the liberty of the children of God, the peace that passeth all understanding, the joy that no man may take away, the Divine sonship and inheritance, the life which death cannot kill, and the happiness which endureth and groweth forever.

STARKE:—Christ is Absolute Life, and our life depends upon Him, not only this earthly life, but also blessed, eternal life through faith in Him.—He that despises the word of the Gospel, despises also the Absolute Word of God, for Christ is the star and kernel of the whole Bible.—Christ liveth, and the believers shall live too. Glorious consolation! Mighty strengthening of our faith, in adversity and temptation and in the hour of death! Because Life and Light have appeared unto us in Christ Jesus, we should most diligently use them, for sure he will be without excuse that notwithstanding remaineth in darkness and blindness.—What shall it profit an unconverted teacher, to testify of Christ the Life, and to urge the people to receive Him, if he himself remains in death and in his life and by his works denies Him?—In order to be saved, it is not enough that a man know and believe Christ to have come into the world, but he must know and believe Him to have also risen and shone as the Morning-star in his heart.—The design of the Gospel is to lead men to fulness of joy, for God has not called us to sadness, but to joy.—If our joy turns sometimes into sorrow when affliction without and temptation within, as it were, threaten to take it by storm, we know, for our edification and comfort, that Christ will come again and turn our sorrow into joy. [Cf. Dr. Muhlenberg's hymn, "*I would not live alway.*"—M.]

SPENER:—Our life in Christ is eternal life, and out of (*extra*) Him there is no life; although hidden now, it shall be revealed hereafter.—The Divine word of the Gospel is given unto us for the purpose of restoring us to the fellowship with God, and it is therefore an inestimable benefit that it gives us not only the knowledge of certain truths, but actually bestows upon us the blessings which it announces.—The written Word of God is not less potent to produce faith than the preached word, and this Word the Apostles have left us as a legacy which may be heard and read at all times, and therefore we ought to consider the written Word as more sure and trusty than the declarations of men.

LANGE:—In spiritual matters every man should for himself examine and understand the truths of God, and not blindly believe the report of others, lest like a blind man he be led astray and miserably cheated.—All human fellowship should be so arranged and constituted that it do not oppose the fellowship with God. We should regard the Epistles of the Apostles as Epistles of God addressed to ourselves, and know that they are most surely addressed to us in order that we may become, as it were, living Epistles of God, known and read of all men.

BESSER:—There is no fellowship with the Head of the Church apart from the instrumentality of the joints of the Apostles. Those who are inserted in the edifice of the Church, rest upon the foundation of the Apostles and prophets, with Jesus Christ Himself as the chief corner-stone.—Out of infinite Love the Son of God became what we are, in order that He might give us power to become what He is; He became partaker of our nature, that we should become partakers of the Divine nature. (Irenæus.)

HEUBNER:—Christianity demands a solemn and deep contemplation wholly absorbed in Christ [or entering into Christ.—M.]; hasty and superficial looking and hurrying away is unprofitable; Christianity wants profound natures.—Christianity rests mainly on facts, as external revela tions of God, in order that thus the Godhead may become visible to the sensuous man [to our senses.—M.], without any injury being done to its dignity.—The Apostles as such eye-and-ear-witnesses are also most sure and reliable, and it is impossible that their account of so many facts, their harmonious and many-sided account, could have been fabricated or be spurious.—These Apostolical writings compensate us for that which we can no longer see with our own eyes. We have, moreover, the testimony of the Church for those facts, for without them it [the Church.—M.] could not have come into existence.—The vocation of the Apostles was most philanthropic and beneficent: the design of their testimony and of the preached Gospel in general, is to lead all men to the fellowship of the same life which was enjoyed by the Apostles. The Apostles did not wish to keep their life to themselves, but loved to communicate it. The true nature of life is its impulse, wherever it is, to pour itself into others. The Apostles were to the first Christians, and are still to all Christians, channels and conductors to the Life Eternal; without the Apostles we should have neither Christ nor Christianity. The Apostles conduct us to it. Those who reject the Apostles and their testimony, cannot reasonably continue to discourse of Christianity; they have only left to them a Christianity of their own making.—Holy Scripture is a standing monument of history that may not be interpolated; it remains a pure and ever-accessible fountain; oral delivery would have grown more and more unreliable, the memory would have lost much, and our delight in the enjoyment of the Gospel would have lessened.—The evangelical history the most sublime history: 1. We will convince ourselves of it, *it comes from God, continues in God, and leads us to God;* and, 2. Lay to heart the conclusions we draw: behold the poverty of those who despise and neglect it! Give more attention and diligence to it!

Christian joy is from its very nature the highest joy. For,

I. *a. Whence is it?* Of God, of heavenly origin. *b. What does it aim at?* The eternal salvation of our souls. *c. For whom does it exist?* For all in the same manner (without exception).

II. (Conditions on our part). *a. Acquire a thorough understanding* of the truth that sin is our common misery, and that none can save us therefrom but Jesus Christ alone. *b. Believe in Jesus,* the Son of God. *c. Animate this faith* by habits of devotion.

The Apostolical testimony of the Word of Life.—1. How it is attested (as to its verification); 2. How joyful it is (as to its *object:* the Life was *manifested,* and as to its *effects:* Fellowship of Christians among themselves and with God).

The firm foundation of our faith.—It rests, 1, *upon the Apostolical annunciation of the witnesses* of Him who is the Beginner, Fulfiller and Object of our faith (v. 1); 2, *on its joyful object* (contents, *German*) v. 2, which could not have spontaneously entered into any man's heart; 3, *on the testimony of the Holy Ghost* in those who receive the word of faith from the lips of the aforesaid witnesses.

SPURGEON:—It is indeed written (Prov. xiv. 10): "A stranger doth not intermeddle with his joy." The secret is with them that fear Him, and their joy no man taketh from them. But we would remind you of the proverb, "Still waters run deep." The brook rushing over the stones dries up in summer, but the deep river flows uniformly along in freshets, or in heat and drought, and yet glides calmly through the fields. We do not speak or boast so loudly of our joys, as you do of your pleasures, because it is unnecessary; ours are as well known in silence as in lively company. We do not want your company to indulge our joy, still less the manifold condiments with which you try to flavour your joy. We require no cups, no banquets, no fiddles, no dance in order to be joyful.—Our joy does not depend on transitory things, but rests in the eternal, unchangeable Creator of all things. I know very well, notwithstanding all we shall say, the slander will continue that the children of God are a wretched people.—We *have* joy, we *have* delights, so precious that we would not exchange an ounce of ours with a ship-load of yours; not drops of our delight for rivers of your pleasures. Our delight is not tinsel, painted joy, but solid reality; our joys are such as we take along with us to our quiet resting place beneath the dust; joys which sleep with us in the grave and will wake with us in eternity, joys on which we may courageously look back, and which, therefore, we enjoy a second time in memory; joys also which we enjoy beforehand, and know already here below as the antepast of eternal joy and delight. Our joys are no soap-bubbles which only glitter and sparkle in divers colours in order to burst, they are no apples of Sodom which crumble in your hand into ashes; true joys are real, true, solid, lasting, enduring, eternal! What more shall I say? Joy and true piety are eternally joined together like root and blossoms, as inseparably as truth and assurance; they are indeed two precious jewels, set side by side in the same gold setting."

[*Sermons and Sermon-Themes:*

CH. I. II. BINNING, HUGH: Fellowship with God, or twenty-eight sermons on the first and second chapters of the first Epistle of St. John Works, II., 177.

Vv. 1-3. MILL, W. H.: The Word Incarnate, the essential basis of individual and social Christianity. Sermons, (Advent, 1846), I.

VER. 3. *The same author:* The Word Incarnate in the totality of His exhibition in the Church, the true centre of Christianity. Sermons, (Ad vent, 1846), XXVIII.

BRADLEY, C.: Fellowship with God. Sacramental, 216.—M.]

II. PRINCIPAL PART THE FIRST.

CHAPTER I. 5–II. 28.

IF YE WALK IN THE LIGHT (I. 5–II. 2)—OBEDIENT TO HIS LAW IN GENERAL (II. 2–6). AND TO THE COMMANDMENT OF BROTHERLY LOVE IN PARTICULAR (II. 7–14), NOT MISLED BY THE LUSTS (II. 15–17) AND THE LIES OF THE WORLD (II. 18–23) YE SHALL ABIDE BEFORE CHRIST.

1. *Leading thought: God is Light.*

5 This then is[1] the message which we have heard of him, and declare unto you,[2] that God is light, and in him is no darkness at all.

[German:—And this is the message, which we have heard from Him, and announce you again, that God is Light and darkness in Him is none whatsoever.—M.]

Verse 5. [1] ἔστιν αὕτη, B. C. G. K., Cod. Sin., al. [Syr., Theoph., Oecumen., Tischend., Buttmann, Wordsw. καὶ αὕτη ἐστὶ, A., Vulg., Lachm., Rec.; this is altered from the original reading.—M.]

[2] Instead of ἀγγελία, A. B. G., al. [Griesb., Scholz., Lachm., Tischend., Wordsw.—M.] we find ἐπαγγελία in C., and in Cod. Sin., over ἀπαγγελία, the following correction, probably emanating from the transcriber himself: ἀγάπη τῆς ἐπαγγελίας; but a later hand has added ἀγγελία as the right reading.

[[3] ἀναγγέλλομεν, RE*nuntiamus*, announce again, RE*port* (Lillie). *Declare*, E. V., is too weak, it denotes a repetition of an announcement already made and known, brought out by the preposition ἀνα. See the notes of Bengel and Erasmus in *Exegetical and Critical*.—M.]

EXEGETICAL AND CRITICAL.

VER. 5. **And** is not like οὖν (*igitur*, Beza) or δὲ (Episcopius); for it is neither an inference, nor even a delicate antithesis; it simply connects with the preceding, as does καὶ—γράφομεν, v. 4, with ἀπαγγέλλομεν, and while ταῦτα points to the contents of the now opening Epistle, καὶ connects with the exordium, in which preparation is made for what follows, and αὕτη ἡ ἀγγελία points to the subsequent words [ὅτι ὁ θεὸς κ. τ. λ.—M.].

This is the message.—Contrary to the usual position of the words (αὕτη ἐστίν, ch. ii. 25; iii. 11. 23; iv. 3; v. 11. 14, cf. Jno. xvii. 3), ἔστιν is emphatically placed first to denote the existence and reality of the message. The poorly authenticated reading ἐπαγγελία is very awkward, the word denoting not *annunciation* (Oecumen., Beza, de Wette contrary to the grammatical usage of the N. T.), either here or elsewhere (ch. ii. 24; iii. 11; cf. var. 2 Tim. i. 1; Acts xxiii. 31), and if taken in the sense of *promise* would have required here an enlargement of the thought. Calov: *non jubemur tantum in luce ambulare ac mundari sanguine Christi, sed utriusque etiam gratia nobis promittitur, illius per Spiritus Sancti illuminationem, hujus per expiationis Christi applicationem; quia utraque fruimur per beatam cum Deo et Christo communionem.* [Huther thinks that the reading ἐπαγγελία in the sense of *promise* might be justified on the ground that every announcement of the New Testament is fraught with promise, and cites Spener, who says: "*Promise*, as the sequel indeed conceals a promise. God is not only a light in Himself, but He is also the light of believers. And that is the promise."—M.].—ἀπαγγελία, which occurs no where in the New Testament, as Socinus and Episcopius read, is an arbitrary correction. The outwardly best authenticated reading is strongly supported by the context, for it seems to rëecho in the following ἀναγγέλλομεν: the message of Christ is announced *again* by His Apostles. Erasmus: "*Quod filius annunciavit a patre, hoc Apostolus acceptum a filio* RE*nunciat nobis.*"

Which we have heard from Him.—The Apostle alludes to v. 1. He thinks of the first disciples, and more particularly of the Apostles. Hence both the ἀγγελία, the ἀκηκόαμεν, and the contents of the message: ὁ θεός κ. τ. λ., suggest the reference to Jesus, the Christ; this is also rendered necessary by the preposition ἀπό, which indicates the Prophet-speaker, the Person of the Master, on whose lips the Apostles hang as hearers and disciples. John uses ἀκούειν παρά, ch. viii. 26. 40; xv. 15, but there it is the Father who speaks and the Son who hears; this (παρὰ) presupposes the nearness, the being together, and had to be used when the Son was hearing the Father, the other (ἀπό) denotes distance, and could hardly have been used in the aforecited passages; παρὰ points also to familiarity, ἀπό only to derivation in general. αὐτοῦ denotes, with reference to v. 3: τοῦ υἱοῦ αὐτοῦ, Christ; the assertion that αὐτοῦ, as distinguished from ἐκεῖνος, which always relates to Christ, invariably refers to the Father (Paulus, Baumgarten-Crusius) is incorrect. The sense then is: From Him, the Incarnate Son of God, whom we have heard, etc., v. 1, we have received the message concerning God the Father (Düsterdieck, Huther). Socinus, who takes the relation of God and Christ not as *conjunctio essentiæ*, but only as *conjunctio voluntatis et rerum aliarum omnium*, understands *a Deo et Christo, i. e., a Deo per Christum*, thus representing Christ as the mere mediator and not as the author of the message.

And announce to you again.—Next to the note of Erasmus, as quoted above, we cite the admirable exposition of Bengel: "*Quæ in cre Christi fuit* ἀγγελία *eam apostoli* ἀγγέλλουσι; *nam* ἀγγέλιαν *ab Ipso acceptam reddunt et propagant.*" ἀναγγέλλειν is not exactly=ἀπαγγέλλειν, the latter denotes *to continue announcing* [rather to bear tidings from one person (ἀπὸ) to another—M.]

the former to announce *anew*, *back*, *again*, as in Jno. iv. 25; xvi. 25, where, however, ἀπαγγελῶ is the more authentic reading. As our Lord conversed with the Syrophœnician woman as the Messenger of God REporting what the Father had told Him before, so the Apostles *re*port what the Lord had told them before (Jno. xx. 21).

God is light.—This is the substance of the ἀγγελία. But Christ did not say so, although He called Himself *the Light*, Jno. xii. 12; xv. 46; and speaks of *the children of the Light* (Jno. viii. 36), even as James refers to the *Father of the Lights*, τῶν φώτων, Jas. i. 17, see the note above *ad loc.* But Christ, as the Son of God, is ἀπαύγασμα τῆς δόξης καὶ χαρακτὴρ τῆς ὑποστάσεως αὐτοῦ (Heb. i. 2), and this it is which John and his fellow Apostles (v. 1) had heard, seen and gazed upon, so that the sum-total and centre of the message of Christ, as well as His personal manifestation and revelation in the flesh, may truly be expressed in the words "*God is Light.*" Christ reveals this, but no philosopher is able to find it; without Christ the wise men of the world pass it by. It is not *a* light, as Luther translates, as if there were other lights beside and out of Him. The Being of God is Light. Neither is it *in the light*, as if it were only surrounding Him, nor *as the Light.* It is not *secundum similitudinem* (Bullinger), but *secundum substantiam.* Light is His garment (Ps. civ. 2); Ezekiel (ch. i.) and Habakkuk (iii. 3, sqq.) beheld the glory of the Lord as fire, pure and bright as lightning. He is not only the *Author* of light, to whom belongs His first creative *fiat* (Gen. i. 3), but the *Father of all light* (Jas. i. 17), a mighty sphere of light surrounds Him (1 Tim. vi. 16); and the marvellous light wherein Christians walk is God's (1 Pet. ii. 9). This sentence is parallel to the sentence: "*God is Love*" (ch. iv. 8. 16), with the same fundamental thought, although in the one instance the expression is figurative, and in the other literal, and the figurative expression lays peculiar emphasis on one side of the Divine Being, and this, on account of the antithesis in the following verses (vv. 6–10), is also *holiness*, perfect pureness, but not omniscience, as Calov maintains, although in Dan. ii. 22 light is the symbol of the omniscience of God; it may include, however, the *wisdom* of God. [Alford:—"Of all material objects, light is that which most easily passes into an ethical predicative without even the process, in our thought, of interpretation. It unites in itself purity, and clearness, and beauty, and glory, as no other material object does; it is the condition of all material life and growth and joy. And the application to God of such a predicative requires no transference. He is Light, and the fountain of light material and ethical. In the one world, darkness is the absence of light; in the other, darkness, untruthfulness, deceit, falsehood, is the absence of God. They who are in communion with God, and walk with God, are the light, and walk in the light."—M.]

And darkness in Him is none whatsoever.—This second negative member, stated with marked emphasis (οὐκ ἔστιν οὐδεμία, similar to John xv. 5, see Winer, p. 521. ["The two negations produce *one* negation, which is the more frequent case, and serve, originally, to make the principal negation more distinct and forcible, and exhibit the sentence as negative in all its parts."—M.]), rejects any and every darkness, *i. e.*, impureness [or absence of all admixture.—M.]. Oecumenius: ἤτοι τὴν ἄγνοιαν, ἢ τὴν ἁμαρτίαν Rather both: neither an untruth or a lie, nor any sin is in Him. The fulness of the reference contained in this expression is brought out by Lorinus in the following passage cited by Huther: "*Deus lux est, quia clarissime se ipsum percipit, omniaque in se ipse, utpote prima et ipsissima veritas, quia summe bonus, ac summa et ipsissima bonitas, fidelis absque ulla iniquitate, justus et rectus, quia fons omnis lucis in aliis, i. e., veritatis atque virtutis, non solum illustrans mentem, docensque quid agendum sit, verum etiam operans in nobis, ut agemus et sic radiis suis liberans mentem ab ignorantiæ tenebris, purgans a pravitate voluntatem.*"—John's speculation or mysticism is so thoroughly ethical, that he is solely concerned with the practical working out of the truth: "God is Light." As he connects this sentiment with the preceding by καί, namely, the fellowship with the Father and the Son, so he develops the nature of this fellowship-life in the sequel (v. 6–ii. 28). Now, since the nature of this fellowship and of the life in it depend upon the nature of the Father, he begins with the leading thought (v. 5) and with reference to errors in a sentence of two members, the one positive, the other negative. [Huther: "John properly makes the truth that God is Light, as the chief substance of the ἀγγελία of Christ, the starting-point of his development; for it is the essential basis of Christianity, both as to its objective and subjective substance, and it involves both the consummation of sin and the redemption from sin by the incarnation and death of Christ; both the necessity of repentance and faith and the moral problem of the Christian life."—M.]

DOCTRINAL AND ETHICAL.

1. *Monotheism and the absolute-personal existence of God* are with John two chief points, which may be also identified here, although one side only is made prominent. Of the two sentences, "*God is Spirit*" (John iv. 24), and "*God is Love*" (1 John iv. 8. 16),—the former denoting the Being of God *physically*, the latter *ethically*; the former describing the nature and substance, the latter the character of God,—the second only will have to be connected with the sentence, "*God is Light*," and thus be further defined by a metaphorical expression. *Spirit* and *Love* are indeed correlative fundamental ideas, since *Spirit* denotes "free self-glory in self-consciousness and spontaneity over a substantial fulness of real vital powers," and *Love* "free self-surrender with conscious and intentional conservation of the essential original determinateness both of oneself and of others" (Plitt). But the phrase "*God is Light*," declares "the superiority of God to all sensuous wants" (Köstlin), the holiness of God, and thus defines further the character of God, His *Love*, and this as a *holy* Love, while it enables us to take the *Love of God* as contemplating also the communication of His Holiness. We may add, "God is—eternal Life" (v. 20) as a correlative, so that His Love as well as His Holiness are live. *There is* NO MANNER *of darkness in Him.* He is not a God

in process of being coming to Himself in the history of creation, the world or in the spirit of man, as Plato maintains: He is operative prior to all the ὕλη of Plato, or the *dark Urgrund* of Schelling, as a self-conscious, holy, loving and living God. Nor has sin, evil, its original beginning in Him, as was taught by the Gnostics in their doctrine of emanations. [Wordsworth: "A sentence opposed to the error of most of the Gnostics, who asserted the existence of *two hostile Deities*, one a God of *Light*, the other of *Darkness*. Irenæus I., 25. 28, ed Grabe. Theodoret, *Hæret., fab. prœm.* Epiphan., *Hæres*, XXVI., cf. Ittig. *Hæres*, p. 34; note in his Comment. on John i. 5; and Bp. Andrewes, III., pp. 371–376. Almost all the Gnostics adopted the theory of *dualism*, derived from the Magians, and afterwards developed by the Marcionites and Manichæans."—M.]

2. *God is Light*—must not be taken as a notice, a truth without reality, a reality without efficiency. As the sentence "*God is Spirit*" (John iv. 24) is immediately followed by "and those who worship Him, must worship Him in Spirit and in truth," so this sentence must be taken as a principle, the application of which is contained in the sequel. The sentence is through and through ethical and practical. John wants no science without practice. He does not allow an enlightenment of the mind without a corresponding bias and purifying of the will.

3. The question "*Whence comes sin, evil* into the world?" the Apostle here decides very distinctly in a negative form: *in no event from God.* Evil though *connate*, is not *co-created.*

4. Nothing must be taught or announced that does not rest upon or does not agree with the testimony of Christ. Those who pretend to know eternal truth which maketh free, different from Him, do not know it better, and are not servants, but adversaries and rebels.—It is at once *Apostolical* and *Protestant* to go back to the beginning of the Gospel in Christ. We are much more the Apostolical Church than the Church of Rome with its claims to Apostolicity.

HOMILETICAL AND PRACTICAL.

God is Light. 1. Whence do you know it? 2. What does it mean? 3. Whither does it point?—Whatever right and true views you may have of God the Father, you have them from Christ, no matter whether a messenger of salvation, a servant of the Church have announced them to you, whether they were told you by your mother or commended by the counsel of a friend, whether Christian hands brought them to you in the Bible, or the Holy Ghost excited them in your heart.—Nothing gladdens the hearts of men more than light; but how have they abused the Word and deprived it of its best part, and try to make it chime in with unholiness in thought, in word and in deed!—The world's light dazzles without illumining, shines without producing a spring with blossoms or an autumn with fruit.—The world's light may be useful, build you in this life bridges of honour, bring wreaths to artists and fame to the wise, make account of order in the land and in the streets, rejoice the heart in the social circle and refresh the mind, but also undermine and destroy the salvation of your soul. But it cannot carry a shine of consolation into the night of life, still less into the night of death; it cannot help the soul to find love and the life which death cannot destroy.—The world's light sets like the sun in the sky; but the Light which is God the Lord, shines through all the night of sin, of life, of death.—Try every light, whether God be in it.—If He, the Holy One, is absent, that light is no light worthy of the name, but a false light, a will-o'-the-wisp.—Do not look for salvation in any light of science or civilization, if it denies the holy light. Fear only the darkness in which God the Father is not found.

STARKE:—Teachers should not pronounce any thing in things Divine but that which they have heard from the Lord in His Word; for if the Apostles themselves were firmly tied by it, how much more are they bound to cleave to it? The thoughts of man, being fallible, are not sufficient for the foundation of the faith.—Because God is Light, and in Him is no darkness whatsoever, it is wholly impossible that He can be the Cause of sin, which is the greatest darkness.—God is all Light, Wisdom, Holiness, Consolation and Joy; who would not desire to be united with Him?

LANGE:—Because God is Light we have often to sigh in our fellowship with Him: "Lord, cause Thy face to shine upon us, and be gracious unto us."

SPENER:—God is Light. 1. Holiness and Righteousness, showing that He not only has no evil within Himself, but also cannot suffer sin or evil in His creatures. 2. All wisdom and All-wisdom. 3. Glory and salvation.

HEUBNER:—Christianity has showed to all men the light-nature of God in Christ in the clearest brightness; that He is through and through perfect Knowledge, Omniscience, Wisdom, Love, Grace, Holiness and Happiness, and delights in the happiness of His creatures. Why does John specify this as the chief announcement? 1. Because it is of the first importance and indispensably necessary for sinful man to know that it is not by the hostile and malicious purpose of an omnipotent Being that he has been cast into this misery, that God did not plan his ruin, and that it does not come from Him, because He is pure and good. 2. Because salvation, a restoration of happiness may be expected from this God who desires all men to be happy. This belief is man's first support [holding-point] of salvation. And this His Will God has proved most strongly in fact—through Christ.

BESSER:—John convicts of falsehood three classes of spirits by declaring the vanity of the boast of fellowship with God on the part of such as walk in darkness instead of walking in the Light, of such as comfort themselves with the assurance of being perfectly pure instead of relying upon the continual cleansing of the blood of Christ, and lastly, of such as, instead of confessing their sins, deny their sinfulness. Worldly-mindedness, boast of sanctity and self-righteousness are exposed by John to the condemnatory light of the truth, and accompanied by an exhortation to a sincere, humble and penitent walking in the Light.

[BP. HALL:—*Divine Light and reflections.* Sermons, Works, 5, 419.—M].

2. *First Inference: The True Fellowship.*

CHAPTER I. 6–7.

6 If we say that we have fellowship with him, and walk in darkness,[1] we lie, and do not
7 the truth: But if we walk in the light, as he[2] is in the light, we have fellowship one
with another,[3] and the blood of Jesus[4] Christ his Son cleanseth[5] us from all sin.[6] [7]

Verse 6. [[1] ἐν τῷ σκότει, in the darkness; so German, Lillie, al., Dutch, Ital., French verss.—M.]
Verse 7. [[2] ὡς αὐτὸς ἐστιν, as He Himself is, etc.; so Meyer, Lillie, Wordsworth, al. Winer: "Among the Greeks, as is well known, αὐτός in the *casus rectus* does not stand for the mere unemphatic *he*, nor could any decisive examples of this be found in the N. T."—M.]
[3] μετ' ἀλλήλων. The best Codd., also Sinait., have this reading; μετ' αὐτοῦ is substituted chiefly by Latin Codd., but the less authentic reading, and clearly a correction designed to conform v. 7 to v. 6.
[4] After Ἰησοῦ A. G. K., al. read Χριστοῦ, probably on account of v. 3. [It is omitted by B. C., Sin., al., Lachm., Tischend., Buttm. M.]
[5] καθαρίσει or καθαριεῖ lacks sufficient authority.
[[6] Sin. reads ἁμαρτίας ἡμῶν.—M.]
[[7] German of the last clause:—"and the blood of Jesus, His Son, cleanseth us from all sin."—M.]

EXEGETICAL AND CRITICAL.

The sequence is clear: the Apostle concludes from the Being of God the nature of their life who are and live in fellowship with God. He postulates that spiritual fellowship necessitates an affinity among persons in fellowship with one another, and that this internal fellowship must manifest itself externally in their life, so that fellowship with God is impossible without a corresponding godlike life as exhibited in the walk and conversation of men.

VER. 6. The *negative* part of the inference stands first, connecting with the last clause of the preceding verse ("and darkness in Him is none whatsoever").

If we say.—John is very fond of this phrase, vv. 7. 8. 9. 10; ii. 1; iv. 12; it is similar to ἐάν τις, ch. ii. 1. 15; iv. 20, or ὃς ἄν, ch. iii. 17; iv. 15. As to the sense, the following phrases present parallels: πᾶς ὁ ἔχων, ch. iii. 3; πᾶς ὁ ποιῶν, ch. iii. 4; πᾶς ὁ μένων, ch. iii. 6; πᾶς ὁ ἀρνούμενος, ch. ii. 23; without πᾶς, ch. ii. 4. 6. 9. 10. The Apostle is thus wont to describe an *objective* possibility (Winer, p. 308), *i. e.*, he assumes that it may be so, and that the event would show whether it will be so. The Apostle renders this hypothesis general by the use of the communicative Plural, and thus makes his speech more lively; if we,—not excluding myself and the Apostles, beginning with myself down to the most humble reader of this Epistle, or to any individual Church-member,—should say. Thus John combines in the communicative and hypothetical form generality of application and considerate delicacy (Lücke). *Saying* does not denote here the inaudible language of the heart, that is *thinking*, but articulate utterance and assertion induced by the force of conviction. But it is not on that account *nos gerere* (Episcopius), as if the reference were to a testimony of our walk and practical conduct, although this saying and alleging must be taken as equivalent to an act, a fact or an action. [Wordsworth suggests that ἐὰν εἴπωμεν contains a reference to the *saying* of the Gnostics, who alleged that by reason of the *spiritual seed* in them, and of their superior *spiritual knowledge*, and communion with the light, they were free to act as they chose, and were not polluted thereby, and were not guilty of sin (Irenæus, I., 6, 20). Some of them even ventured to extol the workers of the most audacious acts of darkness, such as Cain, Korah and Judas, as persons gifted with superior freedom of thought and intrepidity of action, and to affirm that, since the soul could not attain unto perfection except by *knowledge*, it was even requisite for men to make themselves familiar with all manner of evil, in order that by a universal empiricism of evil they might arrive the sooner at their ultimate consummation. See Irenæus, I., 25, 4, ed. Stieren; p. 103, ed. Grabe; II., 32, ed. Stieren; p. 187, ed. Grabe, and cf. Blunt on the Heresies of the Apostolic Age, *Lectures*, ch. IX., p. 179.—M.]

That we have fellowship with Him.—See the notes on v. 3. Here the Father only is mentioned, of whom it was said above that He is Light, in order to draw therefrom a conclusion bearing on the nature of the Christian life. [Fellowship with God is the centre and foundation of the Christian life.—M.]

And walk in the darkness.—*And* combined with *say* makes one sentence.—*Walk*, περιπατεῖν, ch. ii. 6; 2 Jno. 6, occurs also Rom. vi. 4; viii. 4; its synonymes are πολίτευμα, Phil. iii. 20, ἀναστροφή and ἀναστρέφειν, Eph. iv. 17, sq., ii. 2, sq.—Bengel: "*actione interna et externa, quoquo nos vertimus.*" It embraces all our actions, not only those perceptible to men (Ebrard), but also that on which these depend, whereby they are caused, the inward actions of our life.

In the darkness indicates the sphere and element in which that walking takes place, cf. Jno. viii. 12. Darkness, which is not at all in God, does not in any way belong to Him, is the undivine, the unholy, that which is separate from Him—sin, evil. It is therefore not: to have still adhering to one sin or evil, or failure and falling through haste or weakness in temptation, in the struggle; but as the *walk* does not denote gross and common sin only, so *walking in the darkness* does not imply the presence of satisfaction with sin, or the entire passing through the whole territory of sin in all directions; the reference must be to one particular phase of life; some want to be Christians and make good their profession in every thing except honour; others are not severe with themselves or unfaithful to God and His Word in matters of worldly possession or in some master-passions, although in other respects they are strict and faithful. Such men walk, nevertheless, in the darkness, and the words "**we lie**" apply also to them. It is a contradiction and opposition, cf. 2 Cor. vi. 14, sqq. Not exactly intentional lying and conscious hypocrisy, but actual contradiction between Christian principle and the Christian sphere of life, and the real exhibition of life, certainly not without personal guilt; it is our guilt and our sin, *our own lie, we ourselves* are liars. Whenever, under those circumstances, we say that we have fellowship with Him, we lie; we lie to ourselves, if we say it only within ourselves, in our heart, think or imagine it, or we lie to others, if we say it to them in our words or our works. Such lying consists, therefore, in thoughts, words and deeds.

And do not the truth.—This is not the same as ψεύδεσθαι, as if ποιεῖν τὴν ἀλήθειαν were identical with ἀληθεύειν, Eph. iv. 15. It is neither the same as *agere recte* (Socinus), nor *sincere* (Beza, Grotius, Carpzovius), nor *veraciter* (Calvin). The truth consists not only in words, but also in thoughts and deeds; its sphere embraces the whole life, the whole man. The truth, according to John's view, must be *done;* saying with him implies acting; not to do the truth is here parallel with walking in the darkness, while to do the truth corresponds to walking in the Light. "It is one and the same truth, which is apprehended in faith and confessed with the mouth, which, as a holy, Divine power, recreates the life of the new man and manifests itself in internal and external deeds." (Düsterdieck), cf. Jno iii. 19–21 [where ποιεῖν τὴν ἀλήθειαν is opposed to φαῦλα πράσσειν, and where special reference is made to the ἔργα.—M.]—Thus the Apostle raises his powerful protest against every form of show-, word- or lip-Christianity, but his reference is to Christians, and therefore he passes on to VER. 7, to the *positive* part of the inference. **But if we walk in the Light.**—δὲ marks an antithesis. *In the Light* is explained by the antithesis ἐν σκότει, and by the additional clause, **as He is in the Light**, with reference to v. 5. [But this, it seems, is not the only antithesis, for it is also antithetical to ἐὰν εἴπωμεν, ὅτι κοινωνίαν ἔχομεν μετ' αὐτοῦ, v. 6, viz.: if we not only *say* that we have fellowship with God and not walk in the darkness, but if we *really* walk in the Light; so Huther, Ebrard.—M.].—Our walk in the light embraces, therefore, the holiness of our inner and outer life, a holiness which in its consequences operates a communion among the brethren, and fully corresponding to the Light-Being of God, which is also Love, exhibits its essential strength in the formation and preservation of fellowship. *As He is in the Light* is only formally different from *God is Light;* the latter phrase denotes Light as the Being of God, the former designates the element in which He is and lives.—ὡς indicates the oneness of element [in which Christians walk and God lives and moves—M.] and ground in God and ourselves; His holiness must be traceable in us if we have fellowship with Him. He indeed *is* in the Light, while we *walk* in the light, it matters not how poor and defective our efforts may be. The sense is very similar to 1 Pet. i. 14–16; 2 Pet. i. 4. [Cf. ἐστι and περιπατῶμεν. God is infinite—man finite.—M.]

We have fellowship one with another—The reading μετ' αὐτοῦ cannot be right; for to walk in the Light and to have fellowship with Him coincide. But we naturally expect an advance in the argument. It is, therefore, not right to take μετ' ἀλλήλων as ἡμῶν τε καὶ τοῦ φωτός (Theophrast., Oecumen.), especially because God and men, the Creator and His creatures, are not of sufficient equality to be comprised in μετ' ἀλλήλων. Equally inadmissible is the construction of Beza (*cum illo mutuam communionem*), and that of de Wette, who renders *our fellowship with God.* It is the fellowship of Christians one with another, as v. 3, μετ' ἡμῶν, cf. iii. 11; iv. 7. 11. 12. To *have* (see note on v. 3) and to *keep* this fellowship is not a light matter; it is the fruit of the walking in the Light, of the fellowship with God, of a holy life and of holy aspirations. For sin separates, impedes and constantly destroys that fellowship. [This passage shows that the fellowship of Christians, or the "communion of Saints," as it is expressed in the Apostles' Creed, rests on a truly *Catholic basis*, and that its restriction to the narrow limits of a sect is at once un-evangelical, un-Apostolic and un-Christian.—M.] Hence the Apostle continues:

And the blood of Jesus His Son cleanseth us.—The copula καὶ establishes a parallel with the preceding words, and points consequently not to fellowship with God and the brethren to be established, but to a fellowship already existing, and so well established that the first, viz.: fellowship with God, has already yielded the fruit of the second, viz.: fellowship with the brethren. It is impossible to take and interpret καὶ=γὰρ, as alleged by Oecumen., Bede, Calov, Semler, al. The question is not to supply *proof* of the fellowship with the brethren, but to state a *consequence* of walking in the Light. The only question is whether the cleansing through the blood of Christ takes place *alongside* or *inside* the fellowship of the brethren with one another. The work of redemption is a *whole*, and not mechanical, but organic and moral, so that this cleansing takes place *inside* the fellowship of the Church, of the fellowship essential to and established for redemption. Exegetically important is, moreover, the *meaning* and the *Present form* of καθαρίζει. This word cannot be the same as ἀφιέναι τὰς ἁμαρτίας, because it recurs, v. 9, by the side of and after that phrase. The reference is, therefore, not to the remission of sins, to exemption from punishment or the pardon of guilt, but to the cancelling of sin and redemption from it. The Apostle does not advert here to justification, regeneration, conversion, the *actus judicialis* or *forensis* concerning the sinner, but to *sanctification*. The Present may suggest the idea of daily repentance and forgiveness of sins, but the meaning of the verb forbids also this reference. But wherein that *cleansing* consists is defined by the cleansing subject: **the blood of Jesus His Son**. It is said αἷμα, consequently not: God's new covenant with us established by the blood of Christ (Socinus), not: our faith in the sufferings of Christ (Grotius), not: Jesus Christ who shed His blood for us, not: the contemplation of the death of Jesus (Paulus), not: the reasonable belief of the moral end of the crucifixion of Jesus (Oertel); τὸ αἷμα Ἰησοῦ is the blood shed upon the cross, the bloody death of Jesus on the cross, as in ch. v. 6, sqq. [The blood which Jesus, so-called because of His incarnation, shed as a sacrifice at His Crucifixion, or the bloody sacrificial death of Jesus, so Huther, Düsterdieck, Ebrard.—M.]. This indicates the historical fact when the man Jesus died upon the cross at Golgotha, the sufferings of the Lord when He made experience of the sins of men, suffered for them, carried them also, assumed them (ἀμνὸς τοῦ θεοῦ ὁ αἴρων, etc., Jno. i. 29), and took them away as Reconciler, but takes them away also as our Saviour, having died *for* us, but now lives and works *in* us, cf. ch. iii. 5. [Wordsworth: "No less a sacrifice than the death of the *Son of God* was required to *propitiate* the offended justice of God for sin; and no less a price than His *blood*, to ransom us from the bondage of Satan, to which we were reduced by sin."—M.]. The addition of τοῦ υἱοῦ αὐτοῦ points to His relation to God the Father, consequently to His Divinity, where two things are to be considered, first, the exaltation and glory, secondly, the humiliation and servant-form of the Crucified One; the blood of the God-Man is the subject which cleanses. Now the death of Jesus is a sacrificial death, His blood sacrificial blood, shed for the atonement of committed guilt, for reconciling the offended majesty of God and the inimically disinclined sinner, a ransom for mankind doomed to death and condemnation. See ch. ii. 2; iii. 5; iv. 9; v. 6, sqq. He creates to believers justification before God, but the power that creates preserves also that which it creates. The redeemed congregate at the cross of Jesus; sin is forgiven, the debt remitted, sin must now be cancelled and fresh guilt avoided; in believers *peccatum manet* but *non regnat*. Thus in the Church congregated at the cross and preserved in unity, sanctification continues in operation, after having begun its operativeness in justification. It is not our walking in the Light, not our own efforts in sanctification, but the blood of Jesus which cleanses us. (See *Doctrinal and Ethical*, No. 3).

[The whole doctrine of this verse is very fully and admirably set forth in Düsterdieck. The sum of what he says we give in the language of Alford: "St. John, in accord with the other Apostles, sets forth the Death and Blood of Christ in two different aspects:

1. As the one sin-offering for the world, in which sense we are justified by the application of the blood of Christ by faith, His satisfaction being imputed to us.

2. As a victory over sin itself, His blood being the purifying medium, whereby we gradually, being already justified, become pure and clean from all sin. And this application of Christ's blood is made by the Spirit which dwelleth in us.

The former of these asserts the imputed righteousness of Christ put on us in justification: the latter, the inherent righteousness of Christ wrought in us gradually in sanctification. And it is of this latter that he is here treating."—M.]

From all sin—whether sins of thought, word or deed, sins of rashness or sins of ignorance, sins of malice, sins of omission or sins of commission, sins in *affectu* or sins in *defectu*, sins of pleasure or sins of pain, sins committed at our work or during our recreation, sins against the first or the second table of the decalogue. Bengel: *originale, actuale*.

[Wordsworth notices the completeness of this doctrinal statement, which declares that *Jesus* is the *Christ*, against the Cerinthians (but this rests on the doubtful reading χριστοῦ, see App. Crit., v. 7, 4), that He is the *Son of God*, against the Ebionites, that He shed His *blood* on the cross, against the Simonians and Docetæ, that it *cleanseth from all sin*, against those who deny pardon on earth to deadly sin after baptism, and that it cleanseth us if *we walk in the Light*, against the Antinomian Gnostics, who changed the *grace* of God into *lasciviousness* (Jude 4), and alleged that a man might *walk in darkness* and yet be clean from all guilt of sin.—M.]

DOCTRINAL AND ETHICAL.

1. *As He is in the Light*, v. 7—is not a Gnostic dogma simply required to be known and understood, but an ethical principle for the governance of our walk. Light, as it is the Being of God (v. 5), so it is also the element of God, and because it is the Being of God, therefore it is also His element, wherein He dwells and lives. Light must become our element in order that it may also become our Being; we must live in Him that He may more fully live in us, for we are destined to *become* θείας κοινωνοὶ φύσεως, 2 Pet. i. 4. To *strive* after resemblance of God (Lücke) is saying too little. Nor is Bengel altogether right in saying: "*imitatio Dei criterium communionis cum Illo.*" For if the Lord says (Matt. v. 48): "Be ye therefore perfect, even as your Father which is in heaven is perfect" (cf. Lke. vi. 36), perfection or compassion is not set down as a foreign and distant goal, or held up as an ideal rule, but the experience and enjoyment of the perfect compassion of God is to become an impulse for receiving and appropriating it, in order that we, in our turn, may exhibit it. 1 Pet. i. 15. 16 is similar. Even Paul says (Eph. v. 1): γίνεσθαι οὖν μιμηταὶ τοῦ θεοῦ ὡς τέκνα ἀγαπητά. As children they are in their converse with the Father to inhale and receive what they experience at His hands, in order that they may have within themselves a living fountain, causing in its turn the streaming forth of Divine life, and to do as the Father doeth. The reference is not to an artificial imitation, but to a filial following the Father in ardent attachment to Him. The child is not so much literally to imitate as to cleave to the Father, to receive Him, and as the Lord so often requires it, to *follow* Him. Such a life in converse with God, in the life-sphere of God, John emphatically demands as the chief requirement of individual Christians, as well as of the whole Church.

2. *The Person of Jesus* is again taken as uniting the Godhead and Manhood, when His blood is spoken of as αἷμα τοῦ υἱοῦ αὐτοῦ (of God). The word αἷμα testifies against Docetism, because it is operative as a real power, and against Ebionism the words "His Son," whose the blood is, the

Godhead, in brief, is a factor in the work of redemption. This combined expression opposes as much Nestorianism, which separates the two natures, as Eutychianism, which confounds them, and testifies for the Lutheran doctrine with its *communicatio idiomatum*, and against the Reformed principle: *finitum non capax infiniti.* Luther, in his Confession of Faith, A. D. 1528–29 (Guerike: *Symbolik*, p. 666), says: "Again I believe and know that the Scripture teaches, that - - God the Son - - did assume a whole, full humanity, and was the true seed or child promised to Abraham and David, and was born as the natural son of Mary, every way and in every form a true man, as I am myself and all others; but that He came without sin, of the Virgin alone, by the Holy Ghost. And that this man is truly God, and became (other reading: was born) one inseparable Person of God and man, so that Mary the holy Virgin is a very and true mother not only of the man Christ, as the Nestorians do teach, but of the *Son of God.*" But if Luther in a Trinity Sermon (Erlangen edit., 9, p. 25), on the ground of Acts xx. 28, calls the blood of Christ straightway *the blood of God*, it is to be borne in mind that in that passage κυρίου and not θεοῦ is the best authenticated reading, and that such an *oxymoron* must not be pressed beyond seeing in it the doctrine of the inseparable God-Man. Calov's following Luther cannot be regarded as a precedent of great moment, since the Scripture, with its wisdom in the choice of terms, does not require us so to do.—Cf. *Doctrinal and Ethical*, on v. 3, No. 3. [Also the last note on v. 7, in *Exegetical and Critical.*—M.]

[Article II. of the 39 Articles of the Church of England and the Prot. Episc. Church in the U. S. states thus briefly the doctrine of the Person of Christ: "The Son, which is the Word of the Father, begotten from everlasting of the Father, the very and eternal God, and of one substance with the Father, took man's nature in the womb of the blessed Virgin, of her substance: so that two whole and perfect natures, that is to say, the Godhead and Manhood, were joined together in one Person, never to be divided, whereof is one Christ, very God and very Man; who truly suffered, was crucified, dead and buried, to reconcile His Father to us, and to be a sacrifice, not only for original guilt, but also for all actual sins of men." And the *Athanasian Creed*, vv. 28–35, thus defines:

28. *Est ergo Fides recta, ut credamur et confiteamur, quia Dominus noster Jesus Christus, Dei Filius, Deus pariter et Homo est.*

29. *Deus ex substantia Patris ante sæcula genitus: Homo, ex substantia Matris in sæcula natus.*

30. *Perfectus Deus, perfectus Homo ex anima rationali et humana carne subsistens.*

31. *Æqualis Patri secundum Divinitatem: minor Patre secundum Humanitatem.*

32. *Qui licet Deus sit et Homo, non duo tamen, sed unus est Christus.*

33. *Unus autem, non conversione Divinitatis in carnem, sed assumptione Humanitatis in Deum.*

34. *Unus omnino, non confusione Substantiæ, sed unitate Personæ.*

35. *Nam sicut anima rationalis et caro unus est Homo; ita Deus et Homo unus est Christus.*"—M.]

3. The work of Jesus is strongly characterized in one direction: "*His blood cleanseth from all sin.*" This statement involves the following particulars:

1. We can nevermore cleanse ourselves, our cleansing remains the work of Christ.

2. It is just the death of Christ that effects and accomplishes our cleansing; dying for sin, He conquers it; the victory of sin is its defeat, and the defeat of Christ is His victory; fighting unto death, He acquires the life of His own, and sin in its triumph over Him on the cross is discomfited. For His sake God turns to the world His reconciled countenance, and through faith in the Crucified One the world abandons sin, which is enmity against God. The cross, the death upon the cross, possesses an overwhelming power of attraction, and the life of the Son of God shut up in the life of the body breaks through in the life of the Spirit, in the working of the Spirit sent by Him and the Father, who now becomes operative in believers (Jno. vii. 39; Col. xvi. 7; Acts ii. 33).

3. Sin still cleaves to the justified; justification does not miraculously or magically cancel sin by a judicial decree, it only absolves us from punishment, guilt and condemnation, but requires the carrying on of the work of redemption (of which it is the beginning), and of its consummation in sanctification; justification does not end, but it does begin redemption.

4. Justification does not even effect the independence of the believer, but merely introduces him into the walk in Light, to the fellowship of the brethren one with another, as into the sphere within which redemption may be carried on and consummated, and also in the individual; redemption, like the knowledge of infinite Love, is a common experience (Eph. iii. 18, sq., σὺν πᾶσιν τοῖς ἁγίοις).

5. Sanctification is the continuation of justification, it must ever return to it and recur to its power and might.

6. Sanctification is a work gradual in its growth.

7. It has respect to *all* sin, not only to its manifestation, but to its seat and origin.

8. Justification and sanctification, the power of the death upon the cross and the fellowship with the brethren, the walk in the Light and the cleansing from all sin, all these reciprocally operate on and promote each other; this holds more particularly good of brotherly, of Church-fellowship, and of the hallowing power of the Saviour's death upon the cross, so that we are reminded of the words of Cicero: "*Nisi in bonis amicitia esse non potest.*" Or, we must distinguish, but not separate Christ *for* us, *before* us, and *in* us.

HOMILETICAL AND PRACTICAL.

Every thing depends on the reply you give to the question whether sin rules you or as yet only adheres to you. If sin reigns over you, you belong as yet to the darkness, but if the reign of sin is broken in you, though there be still sin in you, you belong to the children of light.—It is not with pride, but with gratitude to God, that the Christian contemplates his being in the light.

—Love of God and of the brethren is the power of sanctification, and this is the life of love.—It is just the sanctified who see even the smallest sins with painfulness and perceive that they stand in need of cleansing through Jesus Christ. —If thy sin troubles thee in its deep motions, know that in the cross thou hast a well, whence thou mayest and must draw consolation. It is not sufficient that thou art a Christian who is *shone upon*, thou must become an enlightened Christian.

Starke:—The ungodly are children of darkness without admitting it, they walk in the darkness without perceiving it, they commit the works of darkness without believing it. O, terrible blindness! Lord, open thou their eyes that they may see, tremble and return from their evil way.—How busy are people during the natural day! O, that they would not suffer the acceptable time and the day of salvation to pass by idly and without profit! Walk in the Light!—The virtue of the blood of Jesus Christ effects not only our first cleansing from dead works, but also our daily cleansing.

Spener:—We may say it and glory that we have fellowship with God; nor is it spiritual pride to acknowledge the grace of God which we have received, provided we do not ascribe it to ourselves.—Light is impatient of darkness, and God of sin. By this test thyself, whether thou art God's. Moses shone beautifully through long converse with this light; why should not the soul wherein He dwelleth do likewise? Let thy light shine, and do not deceive thyself by false conceits.

Neander:—To those who sincerely strive to walk in the Light, yet make daily experience of the still remaining influence of sin, and are disquieted in their conscience on hearing that fellowship with God, who is Light, can only be had by those who walk in the light,—to such is offered the comfortable assurance of entire cleansing from the sin as yet adhering to them. But the self-deception of those is also met, who trust to cleansing through the blood of Christ, without a corresponding course of life. The close connection between Christ *in* us and Christ *for* us is here indicated.

Heubner:—Only among the pure is fellowship, *i. e.*, true concord, love, confluence of the hearts. Evil separates, and is the source of discord.—The kingdom of God is the kingdom of love and peace; that of Satan the kingdom of discord.

Ahlfeld:—Which are the seals and evidences of true fellowship with God? 1. That we walk in the light; 2. that we have fellowship one with another; 3. the humble confession that we owe the cleansing from our sins solely to the blood of Jesus Christ.—Providence moves *pari passu* from the first creative fiat to the last judgment.—Thou knowest that every transgression enshrouds thy heart in night.—True fellowship does not flow from our natural life, not from leagues for the commission of common sin, not from common pleasure or common profit, but only from the walk in Light.—First *His* passion, then *thy* passion; first *His* dying, then *thy* dying.—As long as *Christ is our Righteousness, you also must go with Him into the walk in Light. As long as He is truly your Surety and Sacrifice,* you also must with Him present to God your heart and will as a sacrifice of sweet savour. *But he that learns to sacrifice himself, remains also in the fellowship with the brethren.*

Besser:—But how many, who, perchance, do not know the school-name of the modern Nicolaitanes, the Pantheists, yet do their works, while from the fear of a separateness from sin, grievous to the flesh, they change the frontier-line between good and evil, put light for darkness and darkness for light, and then spread a figment of their own thoughts, which they call God, as a pillow for their worldly-mindedness.—Our fellowship with *God*, whom we do not see, is evidenced by our fellowship *with one another*, where one sees the other.—There are also will-o'-the-wisp-fellowships, and the mere *saying* of any Church-fellowship that it has fellowship with God is not sufficient.—Anna, the electress of Brandenburg, ordained in her will: "Our text shall be 1 Jno. i. 7: The blood of Jesus Christ His Son cleanseth us from all sin."

Steinhofer:—"A soul washed in the blood of Jesus Christ has very delicate perceptions. The light which has risen in her shows her the smallest dust-particle of sin and the most subtle motions of the flesh, and makes her perceive whatever accords with her happy frame in gladsome converse with God and the Saviour, and whatever disturbs it."

[Rieger:—The Bible-verse of the blood of Jesus Christ and its cleansing virtue is a verse for the children of God, for the children of the Light, and says to them: your love of the light, your hatred of darkness with its unfruitful works were insufficient to warrant your access to God, your joyous appeal to His Love; with these only your approach of the Light would have caused you to melt away as wax exposed to the heat of fire; but it is *the blood of Jesus Christ the Son of God*, that is, God's sending His Son into the world to make atonement for your sins, whatever He did and suffered, especially His sacrificial blood-shedding in the voluntary surrender of Himself, and His present priestly appearance before the face of God with His blood and the treasure of all His merits contained therein, it is this which must be of avail to you. The design of this blood-shedding was *the cleansing of your sins;* and thus we find it declared in the Gospel, for our use in penitence and faith; thus it was sprinkled over us in Holy Baptism; and thus the Holy Ghost applies it in our daily renovation, bestowing upon us the double benefit of the forgiveness of our sins and the cleansing from all unrighteousness. At every motion of sin in our conscience or in our members, we may, under the influence of the Spirit, apply to this blood and its cleansing virtue, and thus prevent the calling into question or the sundering of our fellowship with God, and that in the power of the power of the high-priesthood of Christ we may ever become and remain nearer to God."—M.]

[Bp. Hall:—As He is Light, so every aberration from Him is darkness; if we then say that we have fellowship with this pure and holy God, and yet walk in the darkness of any sin whatsoever, we belie ourselves, and do not according to that truth which we profess.—M.]

[*Sermons:*—

GRIFFITH, M.:—The spiritual antidote to cure our sinful souls.

CHARNOCK, STEPHEN:—The virtues of the blood of Christ.

EARLE:—The Popish doctrine of purgatory repugnant to the Scripture account of remission through the blood of Christ.—M.]

---

3. *Second Inference.—Perception and Confession of Sins.*

CHAPTER I. 8–10.

8 If we say that we have no[1] sin, we deceive ourselves, and the truth is not in us.[2]
9 If we confess our sins, he is faithful and just[3] to forgive us *our* sins,[4] and to cleanse[5]
10 us from all unrighteousness. If we say that we have not sinned, we make him a liar,
and his word is not in us.

Verse 8. [[1] German: "If we say that we have *not* sin," but the rendering of E. V. is better and idiomatically more correct, for ἁμαρτίαν ἔχειν is to have sin, and ἁμαρτίαν οὐκ ἔχειν denotes to have *no* sin, to be absolutely free from it.—M.]

[2] ἐν ἡμῖν οὐκ ἔστιν A. C. K. al. [Lachm., Tischend., Wordsw.—M.] is a more authentic reading than οὐκ ἔστιν ἐν ἡμῖν B. G. al. Sin. Vulg.; which is probably a correction according to v. 10.

Verse 9. [[3] German: "He is faithful and *righteous* to forgive us *the* sins." δίκαιος "ocurs other five times in this Epistle, and is always in E. V. so rendered. The opposition, moreover, between God as δίκαιος and the ἀδικία from which the Church is cleansed, is lost in E. V." Lillie.—The omission of *our*, supplied in E. V., is idiomatic German, but hardly English.—M.]

[4] ἡμῶν, *Cod. Sin.*, but otherwise feebly sustained, is probably added from the first clause of the verse.

[5] καθαρίσει A. al. [perhaps also in C**] cannot be received as the original reading. καθαρίσῃ has the the weightier authority of Sin. B.

EXEGETICAL AND CRITICAL.

Connection.—The structure of these verses is unmistakably the same as that of those immediately preceding them: negative (v. 8) and positive (v. 9), while the negation (v. 8) is continued (v. 10) with reference to the positive (v. 9), and the parallel is even indicated in the form: *ἐὰν εἴπωμεν.* vv. 8. 10. The connection of v. 8 with the presuppositions at the end of v. 7 (*καθαρίσει ἀπὸ πάσης ἁμαρτίας*) that sin is still inhering in us, is equally unmistakable. But it is just as unmistakable that the *perception and confession of sins* are here emphatically dwelt upon as following and accompanying the true fellowship with its walk in the Light. The continuance of the Plural form (*we, us, our*) denotes also the general character both of what is said here and in the preceding verses. After all, we have here a second inference drawn from the leading thought that "*God is Light,*" (v. 5).

VER. 8. *Perception of Sin.*—**If we say**, cf. v. 6, above in *Exegetical and Critical.*

That we have no sin.—'*Αμαρτία* in the Singular denotes sin in general; the absence of the Article points out that the reference is neither to a particular sin, nor to the whole, full sin [but to *any* sin.—M.]. Hence the application of the term to original sin as contrasted with actual sins (*peccata actualia*), as maintained by Augustine, Bede, Luther, Calvin, Beza, Calov, Baumgarten-Crusius, Neander, Sander and Düsterdieck, is as inadmissible as that which refers it to a particular sin or a particular kind of sins, as in ch. v. 16; *ἁμαρτία πρὸς θάνατον*, or *μὴ πρὸς θάνατον*, sins of infirmity, light offences, against which so early a writer as Augustine remarks: "*Multa levia (peccata) faciunt unum grande.*" Nor can *ἁμαρτία* designate the *guilt* of sin, as held by Socinus, Episcopius, Löffler and Grotius, the latter saying: "*Habere peccatum non est: nunc in peccato esse, sed: ob peccata reum posse fieri,*" nor describe sins committed or inhering anterior to entrance into fellowship with God the Light, where the Greeks Oecumenius, Theophylact and the Scholiasts have the precedence. '*Αμαρτία* is simply *sin*, nothing more or less, but it is certainly sin. Nor does *ἔχομεν* make any change in the matter, so as to designate the *state* "in which sin has not yet wholly disappeared" (Lücke). But it is less the state which is the result of continued sinning, than the state from which results such sinning, *i. e.*, the state which is not the product of former sin, but the producer of new sin. John says: *We have sin*, and that denotes, both that original sin gives us still trouble, and that we still do sin in thought, in word and in deed; if not as servants, under the dominion of sin, who looking for reward are in the service of sin, yet by hastiness, infirmity or ignorance, now only suffering it by the force of habit or because of its congenital strength, or again by offering it too little resistance; sin insinuates itself into our good and our good works, even into prayer, partly *in affectu* (self-love, hardness in firmness, etc.), partly *in defectu* (gentleness even to parting with virtue, the love of our neighbour, as well as the love of self with fear, etc.). '*Αμαρτία* is a sinful demeanour of any kind, falling away from true godliness, from that which is well-pleasing to God; here we may name particular inclinations, tendencies, principles, and especially the forms of the life of the imagination [German: *Artung* *des Phantasielebens*, an expression of Ebrard, who alludes to the impure representations of a depraved imagination preceding the overt acts of vice and sin.—M.]. This we must not deny. The sentence with its substance and bearing becomes clearer if we take it in connection with περιπατεῖν ἐν σκότει. *The darkness* is the territory of the undivine, well marked off in every direction and containing the whole system of sin,—the sphere of the *walk*, the life and doings of men. A Christian cannot and may not be said to walk thus in the darkness, but he still has sin. There is still within him a territory which is constantly receiving some kind of admixture from the territory of darkness. He is no longer in sin, but sin is in him; the degrees, indeed, are infinitely different and adjusted to the degree of the cleansing and growth of the inner man. But even John is constrained to say: "We have sin."

We deceive ourselves.—Here we have the Active, not the Middle Voice; ἑαυτὸν πλανᾶν. This form brings out the self-activity which sinks more into the background by the use of the Middle with its Passive form. This brings out a difference like that in the German, "*ich selbst ärgere mich—ich ärgere mich selbst.*" In the latter case the cause is excluded in others, while in the former it is definitely laid within myself, and thus gives prominence to my own guiltiness, whereas the second case describes only a suffering without any one else's guilt. The pronoun of the third person ἑαυτοῦ in the Plural is used frequently both for the first (Rom. viii. 23) and the second person (John xii. 8). See Winer, p. 163, No. 5. The context removes all doubt that the reference is here to deception, to lying and error, as in 1 John iii. 7; Matt. xxiv. 4. 11, and elsewhere. This is also the proper meaning of this verb. It is parallel with ψευδόμεθα of v. 6, but gives greater prominence to self-guilt; there he lies before others in word or deed, here he lies to himself and this sin works into himself greater perdition. There an unregenerate man wants others to believe that he is a Christian, here a regenerate man deceives himself through pride. [Augustine: *Si te confessus fueris peccatorem, est in te veritas: nam ipsa veritas lux est. Nondum perfecte splenduit vita tua, quia insunt peccata: sed tamen jam illuminari cœpisti, quia inest confessio peccatorum.*"—M.]

And the truth is not in us.—Since deceiving oneself runs parallel with the lying of v. 6, so this sentence concludes parallel with *not doing the truth*, (v. 6). The truth, ἡ ἀλήθεια is to be taken objectively (Düsterdieck, Ebrard, Huther); the subjective lies in ἐν ἡμῖν (Bengel: *non in corde, neque adeo in ore*"). It is the Divine truth in Christ; the absolute principle of life from God, received into our heart. Hence it is neither *studium veri* (as maintained by Grotius and Episcopius), nor a truthful disposition (Lücke), nor the truthfulness of self-knowledge and self-examination, of purity (de Wette), nor that which is true in general (S. G. Lange, Paulus), nor better moral perception, *melior rerum moralium cognitio*, as Semler interprets. Moreover, the being, the existence of the Divine truth as the principle of life in us is also denied (οὐκ ἔστιν). Hence this is even stronger than the former οὐ ποιεῖν τὴν ἀλήθειαν, v. 6; the latter is without the deed of the truth, the former without its existence; here the truth being in us is denied, in v. 6, only its manifestation and expression in our life.

VER. 9. *Confession of Sins.*—**If we confess our sins.**—The connection of this sentence with the preceding is not like that of v. 7 with v. 6, by δὲ, as Luther renders; the negatives of the preceding verse are strongly and abruptly antithetical to the positive of this verse; [Ebrard: "Now follows the second thought-member in a conditional sentence which introduces the opposite case. Ἐὰν ὁμολογῶμεν τὰς ἁμαρτίας ἡμῶν. Here also John scorns a merely tautological repetition; he does not say: ἐὰν ὁμολογῶμεν ὅτι ἁμαρτίαν ἔχομεν, but where he opposes to the negative the positive, Confession, he does not speak of sin in general (as a state), but of definite, concrete, specific sins. For this is the form which the confession of sins must assume, in order to be inwardly true and efficacious. The mere confession *in abstracto* that we have sin, would be without truth and value and shrink into a hollow phrase, unless it be attended by the perception and acknowledgment of concrete particular sins. It is much easier to make pious speeches concerning repentance and the greatness of the misery engendered by sin, than in a specific case of sin to see one's wrong, admit and repent it, and to be sorry for it. John requires the latter." —M.].—The Apostle is not satisfied with εἴπωμεν as before, but uses ὁμολογῶμεν, which is much more comprehensive than the former, and of course involves it as well as the inward opining, thinking, saying and feeling convinced, which finally develops into audible utterance and declaration before men; nor is this all, for it involves the additional particular of confessing one's guilt before God, and this confession of guilt must be so lively and profound as to become public and ecclesiastically ordained, and stands in nothing behind the former εἰπεῖν. It is therefore not enough to see here only a *perception* or *recognition* (Socinus: "*Confiteri significat interiorem ac profundam suorum peccatorum agnitionem.*" Baumgarten-Crusius: "ὁμολογεῖν is to perceive, to be sensible, and to become conscious of, as contrasted with εἰπεῖν μὴ ἔχειν ἁμαρτίαν"), or "an *inward* act grounded in the whole inward bias of the mind" (Neander), all which is taken for granted. Nor is it only the real utterance of sin inwardly identified and confessed to oneself (Huther, Düsterdieck), for this also is implied as a consequence. Nor must we exclude the acknowledgment before God, and "*the confession*" ordained for the comfort of a disquieted conscience, from which no truly penitent man will withdraw himself, and which is gladly sought and made by such as are of a contrite heart. [The reference here is to the Lutheran "confession," which must not be confounded with the R. C. auricular Confession. Luther himself distinguishes three kinds of confession: the first, before God (Ps. xxxii. 6), which is so essential that it ought to be the sum-total of a Christian man's life; the second, *towards our neighbour*, and is the confession of love as the former is that of faith (Jas. v. 16. This confession, like the former, is necessary and ordained. The third is that ordered by the Pope to be made secretly into the ears of a priest with an enumeration of sins. Luther condemned compulsory private confession, and left it optional with individuals to determine if, and what they should confess. Still he commends *private confession*, saying, "it is advisable and good." The *Augsburg Confession*, II., IV., says: "Confession has not been abolished in our Churches, and the usage is not to give the Lord's Body to those who have not been previously examined and absolved," and Luther in his Larger Catechism supplies a form of confession which is very full of private matters (*Catech. Minor.*, IV., 16–29). The present practice varies in different Lutheran establishments, some retaining private confession, others substituting general confession. The latter custom prevails, I believe, among Lutherans in the United States. —M.].—The proud εἰπεῖν stands in antithesis with the humble ὁμολογεῖν, which includes all the aforesaid particulars. The original ὁμολογεῖν signifies *to speak together* [hence *to hold the same language.*—M.], then *to accord, assent to*, and points to a *dialogue* between God accusing and reproaching us in our consciences by His Word and His Spirit, and man assenting thereto in humility, faith and prayer, even unto pouring out his heart before loved fellow-men, from his nearest friend to the spiritual guardian of his soul, the servant of the Word, the Minister of the gifts and Steward of the mysteries of God. Hence the object is designated by τὰς ἁμαρτίας. *The sins* are "the particular manifestations of ἁμαρτίαν ἔχειν" (Huther), "definite, concrete, specific sins" (Ebrard), of whichever kind they may be, lesser and even the least sins, even as repentance goes ever deeper and deeper and attains more clear and distinct perceptions of sin in its endless turns, in its hideousness and wrong. See below on v. 10, and on ch. iii. 4.

He is faithful and righteous.—That is only God the Father (so Lücke, de Wette and the majority of commentators), who is the ruling subject in the work of redemption, since for Christ's sake, and through Christ the Mediator, He forgives and makes us happy, although Christ is referred to in v. 7, and below in ch. ii. 1. The reference to the Father and the Son is inadmissible (J. Lange, Sander, S. Schmid). The subject is not defined, because the reference is to God the Father, who is the principal subject throughout [vv. 5–10]. God *is* faithful, He does not *become* so through forgiveness consequent upon our repentance. God is *faithful* because His Essence accords with His workings, and these in all particular manifestations accord with one another and all of them together. The primary reference is to God's faithfulness towards *us*, to the truth-and-light-essence which reigns in us, if we confess our sins, and is related to and in accordance with His Own Essence (Ebrard); but to this must be added a secondary reference to His Word with its promises of help, blessings, redemption and remission of sins (Düsterdieck, Huther, al.), and this secondary reference follows from the context v. 10, which re-adverts to the Word of God, although it had already been mentioned in vv. 1. 3. 5, and is in perfect harmony with the grammatical usage of both Testaments and the views they express (cf. Ps. xxxii. 3 sqq.; Ezek. xviii. 31 sq.; 1 Cor. i. 9; x. 13; 2 Cor. i. 18–21; 1 Thess. v. 24; Heb. x. 23; xi. 11). And more than this, the term πιστός, held thus absolute and undefined, has surely a wider bearing. It concerns something which He has produced as Creator and suggested as Regent in dispensations, to which the Father and the Lord have given consciousness in the Word, and which is in perfect harmony with the Light-nature of God. He is faithful to His Own Being, to His doings for, and in man as Creator, Preserver, Governor, Redeemer and Revealer. He is "stiff and firm" (Luther) in cleaving to His holy purpose of grace, that is, His faithfulness; πιστός therefore is not only *misericors* (S. Schmid). Besides this we have the epithet δίκαιος, RIGHTEOUS, JUST, which applies to one who acts in accordance with the duties arising from his position; it denotes the disposition and righteousness which gives to every man his due. God is righteous or just, when He *punishes* those who walk ἐν σκότει, 2 Thess. i. 5. 7, where the reference is to δικαία κρίσις, then He κατακρίνει but *blesses* those who walk ἐν φωτί, forgiving, cleansing and ultimately glorifying them. It is only the juxtaposition of πιστός and the context which render the limitation of δίκαιος to the judicial character of God with reference to the penitent admissible in this passage. Faithful towards the penitent, agreeably to His Love, His eternal purpose of grace, His Word of promise and His work of redemption, He is also righteous, just, to them as promising them forgiveness and cancelling what is still unrighteous in them in conformity to His appointed laws. Hence δίκαιος is not=*bonus*, *lenis* (Grotius, Schöttgen, Rosenmüller), nor=*æquus*, *benignus* (Semler, G. S. Lange, Carpzov, Bretschneider), nor again=πιστός (Hornejus, "*in promissis servandis integer*"), nor=δικαιῶν (Ebrard). Nor does the righteousness of God appear here as *justitia vindicativa*, which was revealed in the death of Christ, so that the forgiveness of sins is *Christo justa non nobis* (Calov), or in that the sinner, appealing to the ransom paid in the blood of Christ, has his sin cancelled, because it would be unjust to insist upon a twofold payment (Sander). Luther's explanation is excellent; he says, "God is righteous who gives to every man his due and accords to those who confess their sins and believe, the righteousness acquired through the death of Christ, and thus makes thee righteous." This righteousness of God is closely connected with His faithfulness. But we must guard against the distinction that πιστός relates to PECCATA MORTALIA, δίκαιος to PECCATA VENALIA, "*quia sc. justi per opera pœnitentiæ, caritatis etc. merentur de condigno hanc condonationem*" (Suarez). *Faithfulness* is rather the soil and foundation from which *righteousness* springs up. [The blessings conferred upon Christians conformably to the δικαιοσύνη of God, are in fulfilment of the Divine *promises*.—M.]. In Holy Scripture goodness and righteousness, truth and righteousness are syzygies (Nitzsch, *System*, 6th ed., p. 176). Cf. Ps. cxliii. 1, and notes on ch. ii. 29.

To forgive us our sins.—Ἵνα is not=ὥστε, *so that*, or ὅτι with which it alternates, v. 5, ch. iii. 11. The difference is, whether we have here simply the contents of the message (v. 5), or its purpose (ch. iii. 11). The meaning here seems to be: "He is faithful and righteous *for the purpose* of forgiving. It is His Law and Will to forgive (de Wette), but of course the Will manifests its energy in action (contrary to Huther). [I should prefer putting this with Winer thus: "He is faithful and righteous *in order to* forgive us," *i. e.*, the Divine attributes of faithfulness and righteousness are exercised *in order to* our pardon, as Wordsworth puts it.—M.]. The *sins* which have been confessed He remits. Pardon, forgiveness of sins, *i. e.*, the cancelling of the debt of sin and its culpability as well as of the consciousness of guilt or of an evil conscience; justification and reconciliation are therefore the *first* consequence of the confession of sin; the *second* consequence is:

And cleanse us from all unrighteousness.—Neither an epexegetical addition (Semler) nor an allegorical repetition of the preceding (Lange). It is a coördinated clause describing sanctification as the continuation of justification, or redemption as the consequent of reconciliation. On καθαρίζειν see notes on v. 7. Unrighteousness, ἀδικία, is synonymous with ἁμαρτία, and consequently not=*pœna peccati* (Socinus); the latter denotes the *formal*, the former the *material* side of sin; the latter indicates the genesis of sin (or its course of development) which does not coincide with the law, the former the fact of the effect of sin as violating, transgressing and offending against the Law, and on that account liable to punishment and conducing to ruin and perdition.

VER. 10. *Conclusion.*—**If we say.**—Cf. v. 8, of which this verse is not merely the repetition, but the intensification and continuation.

That we have not sinned goes back to ἁμαρτίαν οὐκ ἔχομεν, but οὐχ ἡμαρτήκαμεν is a much stronger expression; the former denotes a state or condition of which the latter is the actual expression [v. 10 describes the concrete act, v. 8 the abstract state—M.]; we have here the conduct (v. 10) in a certain relation (v. 8) in connection with ἀδικία, v. 9. The use of the Perfect does not warrant an exclusive reference to sins *anterior* to entrance into the Church (Socinus, Paulus), but denotes active sinfulness reaching down to the present and sins just committed; τὰς ἁμαρτίας, v. 9, show that the separate acts, the actuosity [*actuositas*—M.] of the ἁμαρτία (v. 8) are here dwelt upon. [Huther: "The Perfect does not prove that ἡμαρτήκαμεν denotes sinning prior to conversion (Soc., Russmeyer, Paulus, etc.); the reference here, as well as in all the preceding verses, is rather to the sinning of Christians; for no Christian would think of denying his *former* sins. The Perfect is in part accounted for by John's *usus loquendi*, according to which an activity reaching down to the present is often expressed by the Perfect tense, and in part by the fact that confession always has respect to sins committed before.—M.]

We make Him a liar.—This clause answers to ψευδόμεθα and ἑαυτοὺς πλανῶμεν, but is a much stronger expression; we not only lie for ourselves, we not only deceive ourselves, but we make God (αὐτὸν) a liar, and this takes place not without pride, stubbornness or bitterness even unto blasphemy (cf. Jno. v. 18; viii. 53; x. 33; xix. 7. 12). He who is πιστός is blasphemed as ψεύστης, of course only by such men.

And His word is not in us, *i. e.*, His word of promise containing the ἀλήθεια, v. 8; not only the truth and its knowledge are wanting to such persons, but they are also without the Word, the frame and vessel of the truth. As the reference is to Christians, His word probably designates the Gospel of, or concerning Jesus (Socinus, Calov, Neander, Luther, Huther, Düsterdieck), and not the Old Testament in particular (Oecumenius, Grotius, de Wette, al.), or only the New Testament (Lachmann, Rosenmüller), nor in general the revelation of God absolutely, His entire self-disclosure, including the λόγος, Jno. i. 1 (Ebrard).—It is not stamped into the heart in living characters (Spener), it has remained or become again "outwardly or inwardly strange to us" (Huther); for the regenerate may fall from grace. A man that is not conscious of sin still adhering to him, not conscious, therefore, of the true nature of the holiness for which he was born and born again, cannot be or have been wont to contemplate and examine himself in the mirror of the Divine Law, in the Light of the Divine Word, by the pattern held up to us in the revelation of Jesus Christ. Such a one does actually, carelessly or maliciously accuse of falsehood the Word of God and the God of the Word, who looks upon us sinners and calls us to the consciousness of sin. Such men may remember the Word of God, know it by heart, but it is not to them an animating life-principle and impelling power; it is not extant in their inward life and consciousness.

DOCTRINAL AND ETHICAL.

1. *The want of redemption* which is *universal* is also *permanent*, which even in the Church of the redeemed *has not disappeared* (v. 8), although it is *disappearing* more and more (v. 9). The certainty of the difference between walking in the darkness (περιπατεῖν ἐν τῷ σκότει) and walking in the light (περιπατεῖν ἐν τῷ φωτί) is not greater than the certainty that those who are walking in the light have sin adhering to them (ἁμαρτίαν ἔχομεν). Vast as is the difference between these two modes and spheres of life, yet the import of the difference among Christians still affected with sin, but experiencing a daily growing redemption from sin, vanishes before the purity of God the Father, no matter how marked and important the difference may be between a John and individual Church members. The perception and cognition of sin, especially of one's own sin, and the clear consciousness of it in all humility, are indispensable requisites for the walk in the Light. Though your sin, as compared with that of the unregenerate, be light, take care lest you esteem it light. The smallest stain soils a clean garment. If you despise it when you weigh it, be afraid when you count it up. Many little sins make one great sin; many drops make a river.

2. *Self-deception* is so fearful because it will progress to the denial of the truth and the truthfulness of God and His Word, even to open and formal blasphemy (we lie, v. 6; we deceive ourselves, v. 8; we make God a liar, v. 10). Christians are *saints*, but only *in process of being*, and not already complete and perfect. [German:—*becoming*, not yet *become*.—M.]. This contradicts the Donatist error.

3. *Justification* is before *sanctification*, its antecedent; τὰς ἁμαρτίας ἀφιέναι precedes the καθαρίζειν ἀπο πάσης ἀδικίας (v. 9); this is the fixed order in the kingdom of God.—Both are acts of God; the first an act occurring once only, the second involving the continuous doing of God [the first is a solitary act, the latter a continuing process—M.]. Although the former is only a solitary, momentary act, and not a process like the latter, the former repeats itself whenever there occurs an interruption in the walk in light, or a loosening or sundering of the fellowship with God (v. 9).

4. *The forgiveness of sins*, as the principal part of justification, consists of different elements: 1. cancelling or diminishing of the punishments of sin; 2. cancelling of the debt of sin and the culpability connected therewith (*culpæ et debiti*); 3. removal of the consciousness of guilt or of an evil conscience; 4. the inclination of Divine grace to the sinner as actually evidenced in the communication of positive, and especially of spiritual and eternal riches; 5. abrogation of the strength and power of sin, wherewith the blotting out of sin did begin, redemption, loosening from the power of evil, the purification of the reconciled sinner from sin. While the two last elements (Nos. 4. 5) mark the transition from the realm of justification to that of sanctification (καθαρίζειν, v. 7) that named first and relating to the punishment of sins is so externally related to the subject needing the forgiveness of sins, that its centre may be sought and found only in the other two, viz., the cancelling of the guilt and the removal of the consciousness of guilt, in perfect analogy with the confession of a justified man, as supplied by St. Paul in Rom. v. 1–5, a passage which may be called classical in this matter: εἰρήνην ἔχομεν. The centre of the forgiveness of sins is the *non-imputatio peccati*. Temporal ills appointed as punishments of sin cease to be punishments to one who has received the forgiveness of sins, they are to him only δοκιμασία or παιδεία; they are not always or altogether cancelled and removed, and are not the worst, particularly as they do not terminate in damnation, ἀπώλεια, whereas guilt and an evil conscience disquiet and cause pain. The forgiveness of sins simply changes the sinner's *relation* to and before God, but afterwards there springs up a different *conduct of God towards the sinner and of the sinner towards God* in sanctification, wherein sins are forgiven and forgotten, the sinner is no longer regarded by God as a sinner, but as another man, and God appears to, and is felt by the sinner no longer as Judge, but as a merciful Father. But such a relationship springing from the forgiveness of sins may indeed be disturbed and impaired and needs therefore repeated renewing and quickening.

5. *The factor of the forgiveness of sins* is God the Faithful and Righteous with His purpose of grace and its revelation (v. 9). No man can forgive his sins to himself; self-redemption is a lie. Very beautifully says Luther in execrable Latin: "*Amor Dei non invenit, sed creat suum diligibile; amor hominis fit a suo diligibili.*"

6. The *condition* of the forgiveness of sins is the *confession of sins* (ὁμολογεῖν τὰς ἁμαρτίας) resting upon and conditioned by *perception of sins* and *self-knowledge*. After the death of Christ with its sufferings as well as with the proof of His perfect obedience (v. 7) has operated on the sinner's conscience and caused him by that light to perceive his own sinfulness, and to feel at the same time the mercy of God, as having special regard to, and influence upon him, he ceases in the love of faith in Christ to love himself and sin within himself, is afraid of himself in his ugliness, afraid of sin and its perdition reaching to the bottom of his heart and to eternal damnation, afraid of the wrath of God in the holy energy of holy love, and confesses his sin, which he has discovered, before himself, before God and before men. Thus penitent he not only confesses his sins, but he is also another man, he is regarded as such by God, who now remits to him the debt of sin. This is the initial phase of sanctification, which begins with the forgiveness. The reconciliation of sinners is effected through the reconciliation in the bloody sacrificial death of Jesus, so that as the sons of God by grace, through the Son of God by nature, they make experience of the further communication of His grace, and in virtue thereof grow up into heirs of His glory. This was very correctly perceived by Luther: "Here John meets the objection: 'What must I do then? my conscience reproaches me with my many sins, and John says, Confess thy sins. Thereby he confounds all such objections as if conscience says: What must I do to be saved? How shall I set about to grow better? Nothing else, says he, but this: Confess thy sins to Him, and pray Him to pardon thy grievous guilt.'" "This must be the form of confession," says Ebrard, "in order to be inwardly true and efficacious." The mere confessing *in abstracto* that we have sin, etc. [See above in *Exegetical and Critical* on v. 9.—M.] The child after the deed and with his deed, which is evil, is a very different child, if he goes and sorrowfully and truthfully confesses his sins to his father. ["I will arise and go to my Father and will say unto Him, Father, I have sinned against heaven and before thee, and am no more worthy to be called Thy son," etc. Luke xv. 18, 19, compared with vv. 21–24.—M.] It is wholly unwarranted that the *Concil. Trident.* XIV. c. 5, p. 37, cites this passage along with Luke v. 14; xvii. 14; Jas. v. 14, in proof of auricular confession, that *auricularis carnificina* and alleges "*Dominus noster Jesus Christus, e terris ascensurus ad cœlos, sacerdotes sui ipsius vicarios reliquit tamquam praesides et judices, ad quos omnia mortalia crimina deferantur.*" Likewise à Lapide says: "*Quam confessionem exigit Johannes? Hæretici solam, quæ fit deo, admittunt; catholici etiam specialem requirunt. Respondeo, Johannem utramque exigere. Generalem pro peccatis levibus, specialem pro gravibus.*" Equally unwarranted is the inference drawn in favour of purgatory from καθαρίσῃ as if *the forgiveness* (ἀφιέναι τὰς ἁμαρτίας) took place here and the *cleansing from all unrighteousness* (καθαρίζειν ἀπὸ τῆς πάσης ἀδικίας) not until hereafter in another state of existence; even the reading καθαρίσει would not warrant such a construction. It is Paul's particular aim to guard his readers against all such false satisfactions and hopes as those in which auricular confession and purgatory entangle men, and pas-

ters and friends also should bear this in mind in private confessions. [See above note on v. 9.—M.]

HOMILETICAL AND PRACTICAL.

The truth that we are altogether sinners is very bitter, universal in its application and reaches deep. But those who flatter themselves, and think higher and better of themselves than they really are, lose the truth. If you think any thing of yourself, you ruin yourself. God only knows and is able to make something of man. Without the perception of sin no confession of sin, without confession of sin no forgiveness of sin, without forgiveness of sin no cancelling of sin, *ergo* without grace no salvation. The denial of our sin and sinfulness will hardly avail with a human judge, but it will ruin us with the Judge Eternal. Without truthfulness and the love of truth you will have no room for God and His word in your heart and lose all susceptibility for them. Be afraid of desiring to know any thing, and especially thy heart, better than God, the Lord.

STARKE :—We must not look for perfect holiness in this world; those who entertain the fancy that they may be or are perfect are like those who walk on stilts or over precipitous cliffs: before they are aware of it they will fall and come to naught. Whoso seeks righteousness in absolute deliverance from sin, will lose it if he has it already, and never get it if he has it not. Confession of sins before God is necessary to the forgiveness of sins; but we cannot merit forgiveness by confession of sins. The confession of sins is here simply adduced as a sign of hearty, contrite repentance; it comprises all these parts and is founded on a thorough knowledge accompanied by a perfect hatred and detestation of sin; but it must take place without all cloaking and concealment, sincerely and from the heart. Moreover it must take place with the heart and with the mouth, first and foremost before God whom we have offended therewith and who, we hope, may forgive it us; but also before men, whom we have either offended or vexed thereby. It is a congenital fault of men to love making themselves innocent by their own efforts [literally "to burn themselves white"—M.]; but let none act the hypocrite to himself; for God has concluded all under sin, and no man living is righteous before him.

SPENER :—Those also who walk in the light, stand in fellowship with God and are cleansed by the blood of Christ, have sins adhering to and remaining in them, from which they still require to be cleansed. If God has forgiven your sins, He will also cleanse you from all unrighteousness: now if you desire the one benefit without striving for or refusing to receive the other, you seek to overturn the righteousness of God and therefore cannot get it; for God has ordered that they must remain together. If the word of God is to be profitable to us, it must be kept and planted within us in order that it may be powerful and efficacious in us.

[*Collect for second Sunday in Advent:* "Blessed God, who hast caused all holy Scriptures to be written for our learning: grant that we may in such wise hear them, read, mark, learn and *inwardly digest them*, that, by patience and comfort of thy holy Word, we may embrace and ever hold fast the blessed hope of everlasting life, which Thou hast given us in our Lord Jesus Christ. *Amen.*"—M.]

J. LANGE :—If God daily forgives penitents their sins, how much more ought we to forgive one another's sins; if we have been offended by men and we do not willingly and truly forgive them, neither will God forgive us.

If one thinks himself perfectly holy and pure he comes short of,

1. Daily renovation;
2. The sense of godly poverty of spirit;
3. The daily prayer for the forgiveness of the sins and transgressions he has committed;
4. Spiritual watchfulness and carefulness;
5. Avoiding what may excite his inward desires and appetites;
6. The right use of the means of grace which are appointed for the furtherance of virtue;
7. The proper regard and daily appropriation of the blood of Christ for cleansing from all unrighteousness;
8. Bounden sympathy with, and compassion on his faulty and erring brethren. Thus he will at last fall from the grace of God into abominable selfishness and spiritual pride; and, unless he turn from the error of his ways, into eternal perdition.

WHISTON :—Although we should like David and Peter fall from fellowship with God, He will, if we humbly and penitently confess those repeated sins and beg for mercy for Christ's sake, forgive them also and cleanse us from all unrighteousness. We must not however boldly go on sinning; but rather shun sin the more.

HEUBNER :—The beginning of all wisdom is to know one's sin. There is a difference between *having* and *doing sin.* The first is partly former guilt, partly the remaining bias to sin which misleads us to the commission of many sins of infirmity; the second is living in some master sin, to be wholly the servant of sin. The matter stands thus: God says on every page of His Book: All men, consequently you and I also, are sinners; but man says, I am not a sinner. One or the other therefore must lie. If man denies his sin, he affirms that God has lied in His Word; yea, the whole Christian religion, Christ's coming into the world would become a lie; for He came for the salvation of sinners—and there would be no sinners! Hence pride, self-righteousness is so dangerous, hateful and loathsome to God, because the proud accuse God of lying.

NITZSCH :—I. *The warning against the false method of getting acquitted of the burden of our guilt before God.* The Apostle warns,

1. Against the *false interpretation* and depreciation of the law; the precepts, which I have not violated, cannot preserve my righteousness and innocence in the one which I have broken; nor is ignorance of any avail to me, how often I have unconsciously or half-consciously transgressed; more malice may lie concealed in a word than in a deed, and more still in a thought. *Knowledge of sin is the only gain we can derive from the law.*

2. *Against excuses of sin* from external or in-

ternal circumstances (*the world, fate, human nature*); we lose more by taking from God what is His, than if we give up all self-praise. Why did you not threaten or entice with God when men threatened or enticed you with the world, and seek to lead those to virtue who wanted to mislead you to vice? and have you always done the good you knew and were able to do? *That* ignorant sinner remains to be found who has not knowingly transgressed the Divine precepts.

3. *Of false satisfactions;* for they contain one and all an untrue and unhappy release from the state of guilt.

II. *The true way of getting acquitted of our guilt before God:*

1. *Ask what the confession of our sins is;* and,

2. *Consider how on the right confession of sin God the True and Righteous will forgive us our sins and cleanse us from all unrighteousness.*

The man who confesses his sins in Ps. xxxii., does not make a show of his wickedness, nor regard his transgressions with the fear or carelessness of the natural man, nor say *yea* to the general situation and complaint, and yet feel his guilt as he feels the regular pulsation of his heart, satisfied with his condition. No, his whole being, thinking, moving and life fully participate in his confession, which insists upon the full act and truth of our separation from sin and the accomplishing of all that to which grace in Christ will lead us. It is full knowledge of sin and of *our* sin in us; we feel truly the guilt and misery of sin and that sin imperils our life, we confess in despair unto salvation, yet not without faith, but in faith in holy Love. This is the way with the beginning and progress of being cleansed from all unrighteousness.

T. A. Wolf:—*Of the true constitution of those who live without the knowledge of sin.*

1. *Its marks:* rude security, tender selfishness, self-contented pride.

2. *Its consequences:* without the light of the truth, without the consolation of forgiveness, without strength for real amendment.

3. *Its end: either dying without the knowledge of sin,* partly with fearful presumptuousness, partly with a firm courage that might make us doubt our belief, *or attaining to a penitent and sincere knowledge of our sin.*

Krummacher:—*The throne of grace*—1. Is *concealed* from *ignorant* or *bad* self-righteous men; 2. *Unveiled*—to believers; 3. *Left too soon* by levity, idleness, or culpable opinionativeness.

Friedrich:—Either *God* is a *liar*, or *we* are *altogether sinners*. 1. A *call to decision* as to whether we will believe God's Word in general or not. 2. A *call from sleep* whether we will continue to yield ourselves to the dream of self-deception or not. 3. A call of the *judgment*, whether we will seek the grace of the forgiveness of our sins, or be lost forever.

Clauss:—*The Confession:* 1. What it is? 2. What are its effects?

Besser:—God grant that the truth be written not only in our confessions, but in our hearts!—No sanctification unless its root be forgiveness; and no forgiveness unless its fruit be sanctification.

[Stanhope:—On v. 9, "That the true purport of this condition be not mistaken, it is fit we remember that nothing is more usual in Scripture than to express a man's duty by some very considerable branch of it. Thus the whole of religion is often implied in the love or the fear of God; and thus confession here, no doubt, denotes not only an acknowledgment of our faults, but all that deep humility and shame, all that afflicting sorrow and self-condemnation, all that resolution against them, all that effectual forsaking them for the future, all that diligence to grow and abound in the contrary virtues and graces, all that entire dependence on the merits and sacrifice of our crucified Redeemer, all that application of His Word and sacraments ordained to convey this cleansing blood to us, which accompany such acknowledgments, when serious and to the purpose, and which are elsewhere represented as constituent parts of repentance and necessary predispositions to forgiveness. In the mean while, as the mention of this singly was sufficient, so was no part of repentance as proper to be mentioned as this; for it was directed to persons vain and absurd enough to suppose themselves void of sin, and thereby evacuating, so far as in them lie, the whole Gospel of Christ; for the Gospel propounds a salvation to all men, to be obtained only by His death,—a death undergone on purpose that it might propitiate for sin, and consequently a death needless to them who had no sin; a death of none effect to any who do not allow the necessity and trust to the virtue of it, for the remission of their own sins; but to all who do, so beneficial that God can as soon renounce His Word, as disappoint their reasonable expectations. His promise is passed, and He is faithful; the Judge of all the earth cannot but do right; His Son has paid the debt, and He is just; He will not therefore require from the principal what the Surety has already discharged. So sure are we to be happy, if we be but sensible how miserable we have made ourselves; so sure to be miserable, if puffed up with vain confidence in our own real impotence, and insensible that to Jesus Christ alone we owe the very possibility of our being happy."]

[Barrow:—"When from ignorance or mistake, from inadvertency, negligence or rashness, from weakness, from wantonness, from presumption we have transgressed our duty and incurred sinful guilt; then, for avoiding the consequent danger and vengeance, for unloading our consciences of the burden and discomfort thereof, with humble confession in our mouths, and serious contrition in our hearts, we should apply ourselves to the God of mercy, deprecating His wrath and imploring pardon from Him, remembering the promise of John: "If we confess our sins, He is faithful and just to forgive us our sins, and to cleanse us from all unrighteousness."—M.].

[*Sermons:*

Vv. 8. 9. Augustine: If we say that we have no sin, etc. Libr. of the Fathers, 20. 947.

Trench: Sin forgiven by a faithful and just God.

Ver. 9. Burnet, Gilbert: God's readiness to receive returning sinners. Pract. Serm., 2. 321.

Hook, W. T.: Auricular Confession. Controversies of the Day, 187.—M.].

The Third Inference.—Reconciliation and Redemption.

Chapter II. 1–2.

1. My little children, these things write I unto you, that ye sin not. And if any man
2 sin, we have an advocate with the Father, Jesus Christ the righteous: And he[1] is the
propitiation for our sins: and not for ours only, but also for *the sins*[2] *of* the whole world.

Verse 2. [[1] καὶ αὐτὸς—ἐστι. "And He is Himself." Lillie: "Here the emphatic or exclusive force of αὐτὸς is important. He is the only propitiation for sin. The penitent may trust the Advocate who, righteous Himself, died for him. Such an Advocate God will hear." The emphatic force is retained by Tyndale, Cranmer, Geneva (he it is that); Syr. Latin versions except Castal. (*ipse*), German (the same); French vss. (*c'est lui qui*) Bengel (*ipse. Hoc facit epitasin.* PARACLETUS *valentissimus, quia ipse* PROPITIATIO).—Lachmann following A. B. Vulg. places ἐστι before ἱλασμός.—M.]

[[2] German: "But also for the whole world." Winer, p. 599, specifies this clause as an instance of *oratio variata*, pointing out that in περὶ τῶν ἁμαρτιῶν ἡμῶν, οὐ περὶ τῶν ἡμετέρων δὲ μόνον ἀλλὰ καὶ περὶ ὅλου τοῦ κόσμου, instead of the last words περὶ τῶν ὅλου τοῦ κόσμου, or instead of the first περὶ ἡμῶν might have been used.—M.]

EXEGETICAL AND CRITICAL.

Connection.—Luther is prepared to call him a theologian who is able to show the consistency and agreement of this passage. He agrees however with Augustine, who says: "*Et ne forte impunitatem videretur dedisse peccatis, quia dixit: fidelis est et justus, qui mundet nos ab omni iniquitate, et dicerent jam sibi homines: peccemus, securi faciamus, quod volumus, purgat nos Christus,—tollit tibi* malam securitatem *et inserit* utilem timorem. *Male vis esse securus, solicitus esto; fidelis enim est et justus, ut dimittat nobis delicta nostra, si semper tibi displiceas et muteris, donec perficiaris. Ideo quod sequitur? filioli.—Sed forte surrepit de vita humana peccatum. Quid ergo fiet? Jam desperatio erit? Audi: Si quis, inquit, peccaverit, etc.*" So Bede, Calvin, Calov, Düsterdieck. [Alford thinks that there is more in the connection than this: "It is not corrective only of a possible mistake, but it is progressive—a further step taken in the direction of unfolding the great theme of this part of the Epistle, enounced in ch. i. 5. The first step for those walking in the light of God was, that they should confess their sins: the next and consequent one, that they should forsake them, and agreeably to their new nature, keep His commandments. This verse introduces that further unfolding of our subject, which is continued, and especially pressed as regards the one great commandment of love, in our vv. 3–11."—M.]. The difficulty lies not so much in the sequence of ideas as in the ethical relation and agreement of the points under consideration, viz.: the grace of God and reconciliation through Christ, the universality and power of sin and man's wrestling with it. On the one hand, the aid of God and Christ must neither make us disheartened in the struggle with sin, nor render us confident that we are sure to have it, and, on the other, the power of sin must not terrify us as if all were in vain.

Ver. 1*a*. *Call to the contest.* **My little children.**—Thus "*tum propter ætatem suam, tum propter paternam curam et affectum*" (Hornejus), and because he was their spiritual father (Gal. iv. 9), and as John called out to the lapsed youth (Euseb. *H. E.* III, 23); τί με φεύγεις, τέκνον, τὸν σαυτοῦ πατέρα; Lorinus ("*Diminutiva nomina teneri ac blandientis sunt amoris signa*"). So Ch. ii. 12, 28; iii. 18; iv. 4; v. 21, only μου is certain, but in ch. iii. 18, it is uncertain. Here, just in view of the danger, the most tender and heartfelt love is awake.

These things write I.—The Plural ταῦτα (not τοῦτο), has respect, not to a particular point, but to the whole in its vital harmony. We should be eager for the contest with sin, because God is light; because walking in the light is the preservative of our fellowship with God, and the means of deriving the benefits of the blood of Christ; because we must not deny having sin, and because God will gladly rid us of it.

That ye sin not.—This is the design of his writing. *Sinning* applies to particular sins, not to small faults and inadvertencies only which would properly be no sins; they might gradually fall even into mortal sin (ch. v. 16). It is neither = *peccatis manere* (Socinus, Episcopius), still less = to continue unbaptized (Löffler).

Ver. 1*b*. *The aid.* **And if any man sin** [better: and if **any one** sin.—M.].—Not an antithesis (*Vulg.* δὲ), but simple copulation (καὶ); since even in zeal against sin there ever recurs the indubitable case of sinning (ἐάν τις cf. the note on ch. i. 6). [ἐὰν simply admits the *possibility* of sinning.—M.]. Both fighting against sin and sinning, go always together. The reference is general, and hence the apostle continues in the Plural. But the apostle does not affirm an inward necessity, that it *must* be so, as Calvin supposes: *nam fieri non potest, quin peccemus;* it may be so in fact, but the conditional particle must not be turned into a causal. Socinus also disfigures the thought; "*si quis peccat, i. e., post Christum agnitum, et professionem nominis ipsius adhuc in peccatis manet, necdum resipuit.*" The note of time and the intensification of the thought, are purely arbitrary; "for, on the one hand, a true Christian *may* sin, but he cannot *remain* in sins, and on the other, to one remaining in sins Christ is not the παράκλητος" (Huther). "If any one sin—not with the wilfulness of sin, but in spite of the will of his mind, which says *no* when sin is present." (Besser).

We have an advocate with the Father.—On παράκλητος see Lange on John xiv. 16, Vol. IV. p. 311 sq. [German edition.—M.]. The word has here undoubtedly a Passive sense, viz.: *advocatus* *orator, causæ patronus* (Luther, *Vormund*), *intercessor.* Its application to Christ, although its application in the Gospel, is limited to the Holy Spirit (Jno. xiv. 16, 26; xv. 26; xvi. 7), is anticipated in the first of these passages by the words ἄλλος παράκλητος; Christ is also Paraclete, the Holy Ghost only another Paraclete; this is clear from the context. ["Christ is the real παράκλητος, the Holy Ghost His substitute" Huther.—M.]. Here Christ is παράκλητος πρὸς τὸν πατέρα (cf. on ch. i. 2), there the Holy Ghost is μεθ' ὑμῶν εἰς τὸν αἰῶνα. The Holy Ghost carries on the work of Christ in His followers, the world with its threatenings notwithstanding, but Christ pleads the cause of His followers before God the Father, interceding for them with Him, even as Heb. iv. 14–16; vii. 25–28; 8, 1sqq.; Col. ix. 24, relate to a transaction between the Father and the Son. The ὑπερεντυγχάνειν of the Holy Ghost, Rom. viii. 26, is a different matter, and does not affect the difference marked by John. The apostle says *Father*, not *God*, because the new relation into which those who are reconciled through Christ have been translated, is assumed as already existing; hence not only because the *Son* intercedes with Him, but because He intercedes for believers who, through Him, have become τέκνα τοῦ θεοῦ (ch. iii. 1, 2). The activity of the Paraclete is ἐντυγχάνειν ὑπὲρ ἡμῶν (Rom. viii. 34; Heb. vii. 25).—Ἔχομεν indicates two things. 1. The Plural, as in ch. 1, 6 sqq., denotes the general character of the intercession and the universal want of Christians of such an intercessor. Augustine's note is capital: "*Non dixit:* habetis, *nec:* me habetis *dixit, sed et Christum posuit; non se, et* habemus *dixit, non habetis. Maluit se ponere in numero peccatorum, ut haberet advocatum Christum, quam ponere se pro Christo, advocatum et inveniri inter damnandos superbos.*" [The same Father says in the same connection after the words cited at the head of this section under *Connection:* "*Ille est ergo advocatus: da operam tu ne pecces: si de infirmitate vitæ subrepserit peccatum, continuo vide, continuo displiceat, continuo damna; et cum damnaveris, securus ad judicem venies. Ibi habes Advocatum: noli timere ne perdas causam confessionis tuæ. Si enim aliquando in hac vita committet se homo disertæ linguæ et non perit: committis te verbo et periturus est?*"—M.]. 2. The Present indicates that the intercession is continued and permanent in its operation.

Jesus Christ the Righteous.—Δίκαιος is evidently put in antithesis to the still sinning children of God, and is not=ἅγιος, *innocens et sanctus* (a Lapide), but His sinlessness and holiness as manifested in His life, "righteous, unblemished and sinless" (Luther). While the sense of *bonus, lenis* suggested by Grotius is too weak here, as also in ch. i. 9, that given by Ebrard=δικαιῶν, says too much, and is incorrect, because it is not the province of the intercessor to δικαιοῦν, and that of Bede, who says, "*justus advocatus, injustas causas non suscipit,*" is equally inadmissible, because δίκαιος is not the adjective belonging to παράκλητον. Nor can it be taken in the sense of "*fidelis et verax*" (Socinus), like πίστος ch. i. 9. It corresponds exactly with the description of the interceding High-priest, Heb. vii. 26; cf. 1 Pet. iii. 18. Moreover here, where we have neither χριστὸν alone, nor υἱοῦ αὐτοῦ, but χριστὸν, preceded by Ἰησοῦν, with emphatic force, the reference is not to the λόγος ἄσαρκος, but to the λόγος ἔνσαρκος, who has shed His blood (ch. i. 7). For both in Heb. vii. 25 sqq.; iv. 14 sqq., and Rom. viii. 34, the intercession of Christ is connected with His suffering on the Cross, as part of His high-priestly work and office. If Grotius supplies, and on the strength of ch. v. 16; Gal. vi. 1; 2 Cor. ii. 6, puts after ἐάν τις ἁμάρτῃ "*Et se ecclesiæ regendæ sanandæque tradiderit*" remarking, "*non dicit: habet ille advocatum, sed ecclesia habet, quæ pro lapso precatur,*" and "*preces ecclesiæ Christus more advocati deo patri commendat,*" (Jno. xvi. 26,) it is not *a Spiritu Sancto, sed a Grotiana audacia*, as Calov expresses himself. The Plural ἔχομεν does not involve the idea of the Church, but designates rather every individual, even the most advanced Christian, for every one is the object of our holy Saviour's intercession. And this very thing is the comfortable help vouchsafed to those who fight against sin.—All this shows that Christ, who died for us and is now at the right hand of the Father, is our Advocate pleading the cause of every Christian with the Father, provided that, clearly and profoundly conscious of his guilt, he appear before God as a penitent, and fight manfully against the sin in his heart. Christ, as the Sinless and Righteous One, lays before the Father the supplication of the penitent sinner, supported by His intercession, and as He has died for him on the cross, as He has wooed and drawn him to Himself to walk in light, so He desires to preserve him therein, and to aid him towards the attainment of sanctification, in the continued activity of an advocate in glory, even as He did intercede for His followers in the days of His humiliation (Jno. xvii. 9; Luke xxii. 32; xxiii. 34).

VER. 2. *The assurance.* **And He is the Propitiation for our sins.**—Καὶ is here the simple *copula*, which adds a further particular, and, therefore, neither=*quia* (a Lapide), nor=*nam* (Beza). This particular relates to the Person of the Intercessor (καὶ αὐτος=*et ipse, idemque*) and is of perpetual validity and operation (ἐστὶ); like and parallel to the preceding ἔχομεν παράκλητον. The word ἱλασμὸς occurs only here and in ch. iv. 10, and there also connected with περὶ ἁμαρτιῶν ἡμῶν. The verb ἱλάσκεσθαι is also found in a *Passive* sense, Luke xviii. 13: ἱλάσθητί μοι τῷ ἁμαρτωλῷ, where the reflexive sense is not wholly quiescent; be (become thou) mercifully disposed, suffer thyself to be mercifully disposed, it is consequently ἵλεων γενέσθαι, *propitium fieri.* Or with the obliteration of the reflexive force peculiar to the Middle, it has an *Active* sense, *e. g.*, Heb. ii. 17: ἱλάσκεσθαι τὰς ἁμαρτίας τοῦ λαοῦ, to atone, expiate for the sins of the people, *expiare.* In classical Greek ἱλάσκεσθαι denotes only *propitium facere aliquem*, indicating the attempt of the pagan sacrifices to reconcile *God.* In Holy Scripture, and especially in the New Testament, God *is* not reconciled by us, but *reconciles*, as we learn from the instructive passage, 2 Cor. v. 18, 19, cf. Col. i. 20; Eph. ii. 16. Man is καταλλαγείς, God only καταλλάξας, ἀποκαταλλάξας ἑαυτῷ, εἰς αὐτόν. In *Clement Rom.* we find already ἐξιλάσκεσθαι τὸν θεόν, but it does not occur in a canonical writing. The Socinians have not overlooked this. Schlichting says: "*Non est ergo cur quispiam ex hac* *placandi voce concludat, deum a Christo nobis fuisse placatum*" (see Delitzsch, Note on Heb., p. 97). The same view is very distinctly contained in our parallel passage, ch. iv. 10: *αὐτὸς ἠγάπησεν ἡμᾶς καὶ ἀπέστειλεν τὸν υἱὸν αὐτοῦ ἱλασμὸν περὶ ἁμαρτιῶν ἡμῶν*, God the Father has constituted the propitiation by sending therefor His Son. *He* Himself **is the propitiation**, which comprises the High-priest and the sacrifice. For according to Kühner 1, § 378, p. 418, *ἱλασμὸς* denotes "the intransitive relation of the stem verb." It is, therefore, neither=*ἱλαστήρ* (Grotius, al.), for He is also the propitiatory sacrifice, nor=*ἱλαστήριον* (Bengel, Lücke, de Wette al.), for He is the Agent accomplishing the propitiation (or expiation). As He *is* the Light of the world, the Truth, the Life, the Way in Himself, and not only has, shows or brings it, so He is Himself the Propitiation; it is "really existing in His Person" (Düsterdieck); He is "not the Reconciler or Propitiator through something external to Him, but through Himself" (Lücke). Thus He is called our *ἁγιασμός*, 1 Cor. i. 30; cf. 2 Cor. v. 21.—Nor is He *ἱλασμὸς* Θεοῦ, but *περὶ τῶν ἁμαρτιῶν ἡμῶν*. The sins are the points with which the propitiation is concerned, to which it has reference (*περί*); neither substitution is mentioned here, nor the manner and means how this propitiation is accomplished and brought about. John evidently designates church-members by *ἡμῶν* (*fidelium*, as Bengel explains the word); he writes to Christians, not to Jews. The sequel also simply contrasts Christians and non-Christians. Bengel justly observes with reference to ch. v. 19: "*quam late patet peccatum, tam late propitiatio.*" On that account the apostle adds:

Yet not for ours only, but also for the whole world.—Here is simply *oratio variata.* He might have said: *ἀλλὰ καὶ περὶ τῶν ὅλου τοῦ κόσμου*, joining what precedes with *ἁμαρτιῶν*, or connecting before with *ἱλασμός, οὐ περὶ ἡμῶν δὲ μόνον*, which would answer to the conclusion as it stands. See Winer p. 599; [also Appar. Crit. v. 2, 2.—M.]. A similar variation is found Heb. ix. 7. The point is, therefore, not breviloquence (Ebrard), nor the supplying of *τῶν* (Grotius, de Wette, Düsterdieck). Nor was it because of the evil inhering in the *κόσμος*, since it is equally applicable to Christians (contrary to Huther). The Apostle's design was manifestly to show the universality of the propitiation, in the most emphatic manner, and without any exception. This renders any and every limitation inadmissible. We must not except with Calvin the *reprobos*, because of predestination; it is rather the double *decretum absolutum* which is here excluded. Neither is it admissible to take *κόσμος* as *ecclesia electorum per totum mundum dispersa* (as Bede does), nor to explain it of the heathen only (Oecumenius, Cyrillus, Hornejus, Semler, Rickli). In like manner we must not think only of the apostle's age, but rather of the totality of unbelieving mankind in general (Spener, Paulus, de Wette, Lücke, Sander, Neander, Düsterdieck, Huther). As in ch. i. 7, the work of Christ extends to *all the sins* of His people, so it extends here to the sin of the *whole world*, without distinguishing between contemporaneous and successive generations (Baumgarten-Crusius), or finding here any reference to the difference between *sufficientia* and *efficacia*. This renders it also perfectly clear that while Christ is the Paraclete of believing penitent Christians only, His propitiation has respect to, and is sufficient for all men in general. The idea of *παράκλητος* is, therefore, not wider than and including *ἱλασμὸς*, as Bede supposes ["*advocatum habemus apud patrem qui interpellat pro nobis et propitium eum ac placatum peccatis nostris reddit.*"—M.]; or, *vice versa*, *ἱλασμὸς* 'is not the wider idea including *παράκλητος* (de Wette, Rickli, Frommann); the two ideas are rather coördinate, yet so that *παράκλητος* pre-supposes *ἱλασμὸς*; Christ has made a propitiation sufficient for all men. He *is* Himself the propitiation, and would fain appear before the Father as the Paraclete of all men. There are two different parts of the Redeemer's work, each having its real mode of action and effect, but of course in an ethical life-sphere.

DOCTRINAL AND ETHICAL.

1. *The frontiers of Christianity.*

Systems which, like Pelagianism, do not acknowledge the *necessity* (*ἐάν τις ἁμάρτῃ*) or like Manichaeism with its fundamental dualism, deny the *possibility* (*ἵνα μὴ ἁμάρτητε*) *of redemption*, if the question bears on the objects of redemption, and systems which, like Ebionism, deny the *Divinity* (*δίκαιον*), or in the opposite case, like Docetism, the *humanity* (Ἰησοῦν) of the Redeemer, if the question bears on the *subject* of redemption; such systems are wholly foreign to Christianity.

2. *Of Christ.*

a. Sinlessness and holiness is the fundamental trait of His Being. He requires neither an expiation nor the help of an advocate, but He makes the one and accords the other.

b. His work on earth is indicated by His being *ἱλασμὸς περὶ τῶν ἁμαρτιῶν ἡμῶν—καὶ ὅλου τοῦ κόσμου.* This implies,

α. As He is *δίκαιος*, and according to 1 Cor. i. 30: *σοφία—δικαιοσύνη τε καὶ ἁγιασμὸς καὶ ἀπολύτρωσις*, so He is Himself, so there is existing in Him, also *ἱλασμός*; and beside Him and without Him there is no propitiation for our sins.

β. As He only is *δίκαιος*, and all men *ἄδικοι*, so it is He only who has made and does make a propitiation for all men; this affirms the universality of the only *ἱλασμὸς*.

γ. The atonement extant relates to the sins which violate the majesty of God, disturb the holiness of the order of His Kingdom, and are the products of an enmity to the Glorious One, so that they arouse the reaction of the *ὀργή*; and therefore, as distinguished from *καταλλαγή*, reconciliation which bears on sinners and creates a disposition, *reconciliatio*, *ἱλασμὸς* is to be taken in the sense of atonement, propitiation [or expiation] *expiatio*, and as regulating a disturbed relationship. *Expiation* renders quiescent the *ὀργὴ τοῦ θεοῦ*, whereas reconciliation allays the enmity of man in his *ἁμαρτία*, cf. Nitzsch, *System* § 135.

δ. The effect of the *ἱλασμὸς* is that he, whose sins are expiated, ceases to belong to the *κόσμος*, but not irresistibly, nor by a physical process, but only as a real beginning and supporting foundation, on which we must take our stand, and progress, in order that the *καταλλαγή* may ensue.

and that we may become partakers thereof; in our *ethical* demeanor we must do our part whenever occasion and aid are afforded us, otherwise we shall lose the ground of salvation, the beginning of blessedness, and the receptivity for the same. But our passage is silent as to the manner how it is done; even the αἷμα (ch. i. 7) is tacitly pre-supposed. Nor may an inference respecting *substitution* be drawn from this passage, as Nitzsch (*System*, p. 284) has done.

η. Christ is and remains the ἱλασμός—both for *all* sins and the sins of *all*, and for all ages and generations; His atonement is permanent in its operativeness. Not only in a general way, but the individual, every individual, is the object of expiation and reconciliation. This passage teaches the predestination of the salvation of all men.

c. *His work in heaven* is indicated by παράκλητος πρὸς τὸν πατέρα; which imports,

α. That it concerns a work after His entrance into His original glory, consequently that which the glorified Redeemer does for us in heaven; He is not only a *historical* person and power, whose influence is felt for centuries, like Luther and his reformation, and the Greeks with their civilization, but He is an *ever living person* above, and at the same time in the world's history.

β. Jesus, the Christ, is consequently the Paraclete, not only as to His Divine, or as to His human nature, but in His Divine-human person in its glory with the Father.

γ. This work concerns our need of help remaining after our expiation and reconciliation effected by Him on earth, which need of help consists in our repeated sinning anew, and the consequent peril threatening anew our filial relation to God the Father effected by him; He desires "to cancel again the effects of our sins on our relation to God," (Hofmann, *Schriftbeweis* 11, 1, p. 545), on the object of this work, are "believers still sinning in their walk in the light" (Huther), and that without any exception.

δ. This work of the exalted Redeemer is an *intercession* for Christians belonging to Him in faith; it is a real work of the Lord, since He not only silently waits for the effects of His reconciliation, but is actively engaged in pressing His merit with the Father, and that, as a *vocalis et oralis intercessio*. Our passage excludes all the intercessions of Romanism, those of the Virgin Mary, and of all the saints, who, as well as St. John, stand in need of intercession. See *Conf. Aug.* XXI., *Apol.* XXI. 10, sqq. For the saints are not *deprecatores*, still less *propitiatores, ut orent, non tamen invocandi*. It also dismisses the "grossly sensuous view" combated by Calvin when he says: "*nimis crasse errare eos, qui patris genibus Christum advolvunt, ut pro nobis oret;*" the *intercessio* is not *humilis*. But it is equally false to regard it as only symbolical, as *nuda interpretiva* (*per ostensa merita*), as *Bede* does, or only as the continuing effect of the work of redemption consummated by Christ in His death (Baumgarten-Crusius). Unfounded is the view of Köstlin (*Lehrbegriff*, pp. 31, 192), who understands παράκλητος to denote the eternal High-priest, who does not pray, but, as the Father for His sake loves also those who believe in Him, directly excludes intercession, because Jno. xvi. 26 expressly deprecates ἐρωτᾶν πρὸς τὸν πατέρα περὶ ὑμῶν. The intercession of the Paraclete, which contemplates the perfection of believers and their preservation in the Sonship, must be well distinguished from the asking intercession of the High-priest, which contemplates the acceptance of the Sonship, cf., Lange on John xvi. 26, Vol. 4, p. 343, n. 16. [German edition, M].

3. *Of Christians.*

a. Sinfulness continues even in the most advanced Christians, and manifests itself in the constant recurrence of particular sins.

b. *The warfare against sin*, however, is earnestly insisted upon. John does not say whether it is possible to a believer *not* to sin; nor does he say that he *must* sin (Calvin: "*nam fieri non potest, quin peccemus*"), but demands that Christians should strive not to commit sin. The Apostle's love of the Church (τεκνία μου) constrains him to charge them not to sin, because those who sin not, keep themselves, (τηρεῖ ἑαυτὸν, ch. 5, 18) preserve their sonship with God and their regeneration (ch. iii, 6. 9). He views sin as man's ruin and ungodliness.

c. The Christian requires no other *human* mediator, or priest; he has become spiritual himself, and no longer secular, himself a priest and not a layman. These antitheses vanish to those who live in faith in Christ the Redeemer, do every thing through Him and for His sake, and refer every thing to Him.

HOMILETICAL AND PRACTICAL.

Sin should not be denied, but fought and conquered. Seek with Jesus the Sinless One for true humility in the knowledge of thy sin, and thou wilt find with Him the right courage to overcome thy sin. As thy perception of sin grows more keen, thy sensibility even of the most secret and most trifling sin more acute and delicate, thy sorrow for sin more profound, thy struggle with it more desperate, so thy perception of the Saviour's life and work will also grow more keen, thy hearing of God's still small voice more acute, thy joy over the cleansing power of His word and work more profound, the Lord's victory over thee and thy triumph with Him more certain. Although a man sanctify himself, he still sins. It is Jesus Christ, the Righteous, in His glory, who prays for the fallen, for an unrighteous world, that cannot forgive and forget any thing that judges and condemns. The *demand* not to sin is not devoid of *consolation*, if we do sin; but he only that strives to satisfy the demand will be satisfied with the consolation. Never forget that Christ has expiated sin, and that *He* had to expiate it, and thou wilt take a serious view of sin.

AUGUSTINE:—"*Ibi habes advocatum, noli timere, ne perdas causam confessionis tuæ. Si enim aliquando in hac vita committit se homo disertæ linguæ et non perit, committis te verbo et periturus es?*"

LUTHER:—The righteousness of Jesus Christ is on our side; for the righteousness of God is ours in Jesus Christ.—It is a certain fact, that thou art a part of the world: lest perchance thy heart might deceive thee and say: "The Lord died for *Peter* and *Paul*—*not for me!*"

STARKE:—Teachers should deal with their hearers as a father deals with his children; but then the hearers should so demean themselves that such a course is possible.—Whoso serves the Church of Christ with his writings, should examine himself as to the motive which prompts him; if he does unite with the motive of ambition or covetousness, it is sin to him; but if his motive is really and truly the glory of God, and he desires to make his gifts useful to men, it is well-pleasing to God.—Blessed consolation! Christ is our advocate and spokesman, who has taken our cause in hand! Rejoice, ye tempted ones! there is no danger. Our Saviour claims His right.—

HEUBNER:—The Christian promises of grace are holy and not designed to abet idleness; they are not given to careless and hardened sinners, but to sorrow-stricken, contrite and penitent sinners.—Here is expressly taught Christ's intercession for His people. It is of infinite value before God, because it is the intercession of the Righteous, of the perfectly Holy One, who may dare to intercede with God.

[CRANMER, ABP.:—"Christ was such an High Bishop, that He, once offering Himself, was sufficient by one effusion of His blood to abolish sin unto the world's end. He was so perfect a Priest, that by one oblation He purged an infinite heap of sins, leaving an easy and ready remedy for all sinners, that His one sacrifice should suffice unto all men that would not show themselves unworthy, and He took unto Himself not only their sins, that many years before were dead and put their trust in Him, but also the sins of those, that until His coming again, should truly believe His gospel. So that now we may look for none other Priest or sacrifice to take away our sins, but only Him and His sacrifice. And as He dying once was offered for all, so, as much as pertained to Him, He took all men's sins unto Himself."—M.].

[CHURCH HOMILIES:—"All men are God's creation and image, and are redeemed by Christ."—M.]

[BEVERIDGE:—"If any man's sins be not pardoned—it is not for want of sufficiency in Christ's sufferings, but by reason of his own obstinacy or negligence in not performing the conditions required for applying the sufferings of the human nature in Christ unto his own particular person. For seeing that that death, which was threatened to all mankind in the first Adam, was undergone by the whole nature of man in the second; hence all particular persons comprehended under that general nature, are capable of receiving the benefit of those sufferings, if they will but apply them rightly to themselves."—M.].

[BARROW:—"*The whole world* is here mentioned in contradistinction from all Christians to whom St. John speaketh in this place; that *the whole world* of which he says below, that it 'lieth in wickedness.' Ch. 5, 19. In this and in various other places, where Jesus is called the Saviour of the world, that the world, according to its ordinary acceptation, and as every man would take it at first hearing, doth signify the whole community of mankind, comprehending men of all sorts and qualities, good and bad, believers and infidels; not, in a new unusual sense, any special restrained world of some persons, particularly regarded or qualified, will, I suppose, easily appear to him, who shall, without prejudice or partiality, attend to the common use thereof in Scripture, especially in St. John, who most frequently applieth it as to this, so to other cases or matters."—M.].

[NEANDER:—"What now is the practical significance of this truth, that Christ, the Holy, is our ever-abiding Advocate with the Father? To this perpetual mediation through the living Christ, to His ever-abiding priesthood for those who are reconciled to God through Him, corresponds the ever-remaining need of mediation in believers, their constant dependence upon the priesthood of Christ, in union with whom they are a generation consecrated to God. Under every feeling of sin and infirmity, in all their temptations and conflicts, they may securely trust in their indissoluble union with this Divine human Personage, who Himself has felt all their necessities, and is near to them in the intimate sympathy of perfect love. Moreover, their whole inward and outward Christian life, flowing as it does from this sense of continual need of redemption, will take its character from this ever-continuing mediation of Christ, and their own conscious connection therewith."—M.].

[VER. 1. BUNYAN, JOHN: The work of Jesus Christ as an Advocate, clearly explained and largely improved, for the benefit of all believers. Many editions.

CHARNOCK, STEPHEN: The Intercession of Christ. Works, 8, p. 1.

FULLER, A.: Christianity the Antidote to presumption and despair. Sermons, 326.

HOOK, W. F.: Jesus Christ the Righteous. Sermons, 307.

Vv. 1. 2. CRISP, T.: Sermons, 2, pp. 251–386.
Revelation of grace no encouragement to sin.
The faithful Friend at the bar of justice.
Christ's advocateship for all the elect.
Christ's righteousness only dischargeth the sinner.
The act of believing is not our righteousness.
Faith the fruit of union.
Christ alone our Mercy-seat.

BEVERIDGE, BP.: The satisfaction of Christ explained. Works. 4. 162.

SEABURY, BP.: The atonement of Christ. Disc. 2. 113. M.].

5. *Mark of the walk in the light. Obedience to the commandments of God, especially brotherly love.*

CHAPTER II. 3—11.

3 And hereby we[1] do know that we know[2] him, if we keep[3] his commandments.
4 He that saith,[4] I know[5] him, and keepeth not his commandments, is a liar, and the

5 truth is not in him. But whoso keepeth his word, in him verily is the love of God
6 perfected[6]: hereby know we that we are in him. He that saith he abideth in him
7 ought himself also so[7] to walk, even as he walked. Brethren,[8] I write no new commandment unto you, but an old commandment which ye had from the beginning
The old commandment is the word which ye have heard from the beginning.[9]
8 Again, a new commandment I write unto you, which thing is true in him and in
9 you;[10] because the darkness is past,[11] and the true light now shineth. He that saith
10 he is in the light, and hateth his brother, is in[12] darkness even until now. He that
loveth his brother abideth in the light, and there is none occasion of stumbling in
11 him.[13] But he that hateth his brother is in darkness, and walketh in darkness, and
knoweth not whither he goeth, because that[14] darkness hath blinded his eyes.

Verse 3. [[1] German: "And hereby we know;" the emphatic *do* know in E. V. suggests an idea foreign from the text. —M.].

[[2] German: "That we *have* known him." Lillie: "Have attained to this knowledge." Where knowledge is spoken of *merely* as present, γνώσκω. or οἶδα is used, not ἔγνωκα. See John's epistles *passim*.—E.V. vv. 13, 14; ch. iii. 6; iv. 16; 2 John i., and generally elsewhere."—M.].

[3] Cod. Sin. has φυλάξωμεν for τηρῶμεν; which is, however, given as well. The future by no means suits the Apostle's thought.

Verse 4. [4] A. B. Cod. Sin. al. insert ὅτι before ἔγνωκα. John usually employs the *oratio indirecta* with the *infin.*, as in vv. 6. 9; ch. i. 6, or *temp. fin.* with ὅτι, as in ch. i. 8, 10. The *oratio directa* with ὅτι occurs only in one other place, ch. iv. 20. It is difficult to understand why ὅτι should have been introduced here from there. [Rather: ὅτι was possibly omitted by later transcribers, on account of the difficulty it presented.—M.].

[[5] German: "I *have* known Him," ἔγνωκα see above on v. 3, note 2—M.].

Verse 5. [[6] German: "In such an one the love of God is truly perfected." Lillie: "Truly in this man hath the love of God been perfected."—M.].

Verse 6. [7] C. Cod. Sin. insert οὕτως before περιπατεῖν. There is no reason why it should be inserted, although it might have seemed superfluous to some. [It is wanting in A. B. Vulg.—M.] It renders the thought very emphatic.

Verse 7. [[8] German: "*Beloved*" M.] ἀδελφοί, Oecum, Mill, Wetstein, is weakly supported; ἀγαπητοί is manifestly the correct reading [A. B. C. Cod. Sin. Syr. Vulg. Griesb. Bengel, al. sustain it.—M.].

[[9] German omits the words "from the beginning," at the close of the verse. The corresponding ἀπ' ἀρχῆς, omitted by A. B. C. Sin. al., are cancelled by Lachm., Tischend., Buttm., Theile.—M.].

Verse 8. [10] ὑμῖν, B. C. Cod. Sin., although the more difficult reading, is better authenticated than ἡμῖν (A.)

[11] σκιά instead of σκοτία lacks the weight of authority, and is clear as to its tendency or origin from the contrast between the economy of the Old and New Testaments.

[German: "Passeth away," παράγεται. The Present should by all means be retained. German: already, ἤδη, better than *now*.—M.].

Verse 9. [[12] German: "*The* darkness," ἡ σκοτία, both here and below in v. 11. The omission of the Article in E. V. obscures the sense.—M.].

Verse 10. [[13] German: "An offence" or "stumbling-block is not in him."—M.].

Verse 11. [[14] German: "The darkness;" "because that darkness" (E. V.) is perplexing and ambiguous, better retain the more correct rendering, "because *the* darkness," ὅτι ἡ σκοτία. German: "where he goeth to." —M.].

EXEGETICAL AND CRITICAL.

The Connection. The call to the contest with sin on the ground of the Saviour's antecedent propitiation and lasting intercession is connected with this section of the mark of the true knowledge of and fellowship with God, as that of vital Christianity: see whether thou really art the object of the intercession of the Sinless One with Him who is Light! The *mala securitas* and the *utilis timor* move the Apostle to set this section with the given marks of a true Christian into close connection with the immediately preceding section of the atonement for the sins of the *whole* world, and namely, as a link in the chain of thoughts depending on v. 5.: "That God is Light." His object is to excite a salutary, moral seriousness of purpose in his readers; their obedience to the commandments of God, and especially their practice of brotherly love are given to them as tokens by which they may determine whether they are really in God's kingdom of grace. He warns, therefore, "against the false security of a show-Christianity," and guards his churches "against false confidence and carnal security" (Neander); similar are the views of the greater number of commentators, from Episcopius and Calov down to Düsterdieck, who, however, confines himself to pointing out the dependence of this section also on the leading thought in ch. i. 5, 6, while the former take too narrow views of the connection with ch. ii. 1, 2. The copula καὶ denotes the close connection and appurtenance of the sequel to the preceding section. Hence it is not correct to make here the beginning of a new section, (Sander: "Having thus far spoken of the proofs of salvation, he now proceeds to exhort his readers to its preservation"), or to connect with ch. i. 5, 6 (Huther).

Obedience to the commandments of God is the general characteristic of true Christianity. (v.v. 3–6).

Ver. 3. **And hereby we know.**—John uses ἐν τούτῳ in order to refer to the sequel, as here, ch. iii. 16, 19, 24; iv. 9, 10, 13, 17; v. 2, or to the preceding, as in v. 5: iii. 10; the reference is generally plain from the context. In the former case the Apostle is wont to indicate the mark *whereby* we know, by the addition of the preposition ἐκ (iv. 13), or by ὅτι (ch. iii. 16, 19; iv. 9, 10), or ἵνα (ch. iv. 17), or ἐὰν (vv. 3, 5), or ὅταν (ch. v. 2), according as he wants to supply either "a really existing, historically given and objectively sure token" (Düsterdieck), or one only ideally existing and described as possible or conditional. The Apostle, who lays a strong emphasis on *knowing*, understands to express in writing the different shades of thought with the same nicety and correctness. ["John uses the formula ἐν τούτῳ γινώσκομεν first as referring the demonstrative pronoun back to what has gone before, as *e. g* in our v. 5, and in ch. iii. 10. If, however, the demonstrative pronoun in this or a like formula, looks onward, and the token itself, with the circumstance of which it is a token, follows, he expresses this token variously and significantly, according to the various shades of meaning to be conveyed. Sometimes the token implied in the demonstrative, follows in a separate sentence, as in ch. iv. 2; sometimes the construction is slightly changed, and the sentence begun with ἐν τούτῳ is not regularly brought to a close, but continued in a new and correlative form; *e. g.* ch. iii. 24, where ἐν τούτῳ γινώσκομεν is taken up by ἐκ τοῦ πν. And this way of expression is closely parallel to that where ὅτι completes the construction begun with ἐν τούτῳ. So ch. iii. 16, 19; iv. 9, 10, 13. In these cases the full objective reality of the token, as a fact, is set forth. It is an undoubted fact that He has given us of His Spirit, that He has sent His Son: and from these facts our inference is secure to the other facts in question, that He abideth in us, etc. But in other passages we find instead of this ὅτι an ἵνα, ch. iv. 17, or an ἐὰν, as here, John xiii. 35, or ὅταν, ch. v. 2. This ἐάν, ὅταν, mark the token implied in ἐν τούτῳ as one not actually existent, an historical or objectively certain fact; but as a possible contingency, something hypothetically and conditionally assumed: in other words as ideal." Düsterdieck, pp. 172, sq.—M.]. He is concerned with the fact,

That we have known Him.—The context must determine who is meant by αὐτὸν, God the Father or Christ; the reason must be sought in the section itself, where in vv. 3–6 we have first the repeated forms αὐτοῦ, αὐτῷ and αὐτὸν and once ἐκεῖνος, v. 6. As the latter evidently denotes Christ, so the former applies with equal certainty to God the Father. Hence it was not the immediately preceding verse in which Christ is spoken of, which induced the Apostle to use αὐτὸν and to understand thereby the Father, but rather the all-controlling thought, "God is Light," ch. i. 5. —So Bede, Oecumenius, Erasmus, Lücke, Jachmann, Baumgarten-Crusius, de Wette, Brückner, Düsterdieck, Huther, Ebrard. It is referred to Christ by Augustine, Episcopius, Grotius, Luther, Calov, Wolf, Lange, Sander, Neander. Socinus and Calvin are undecided. The word γινώσκειν, occurring twice in juxtaposition, bears each time substantially the same meaning: *to know.* But to know God is not a matter of the understanding only, a knowledge, a knowing, but matter of the whole man; it is an inward life, both matter of the will and of the mind; an entering into, a perceiving in order to be penetrated thereby, in order to receive it in receptivity. The object of this knowing becomes the substance of him that knows; the nature of the object of our knowing determines His coming near us and entering into relationship with us. God cannot be known without Himself; it is only by converse with Him that He allows Himself to be known (Oecumenius; συνεκράθημεν αὐτῷ, Clarius "*societatem habemus cum eo.*"); the knowledge of God presupposes and promotes life-fellowship with Him. This last particular is also intimated by the perfect ἐγνώκαμεν; the real fact of having known Him is described as finished, attended by an after-effect and still further development in continued and ever-growing knowledge; it is parallel to κοινωνίαν ἔχειν μετ' αὐτοῦ, ch. i. 6. Col. 3. "Inward affinity of life, real appurtenance is the unconditional pre-supposition both of knowing and loving; for only those in affinity with each other know and love each other" (Düsterdieck). *We,* the Christians, renewed in Christ, created to His image, are those who know. Hence it is false to take γινώσκειν like the Hebrew יָדַע in the sense of to *love* (Carpzov, S. G. Lange), or only as a theoretical understanding of Divine truth (Socinus, Episcopius); nor may we intermingle knowledge and love, and regard the latter as essential to the former (Bede, Oecumenius, Lücke), although knowledge is conditioned by love (de Wette).—[It is not mere theoretical knowledge, but vital, experimental knowledge flowing from God, being received into the heart, and His influencing our thoughts, our will and our actions. —M.].

If we keep His Commandments.—The verb τηρεῖν, probably connected with τέρας, [more probably with τήρος, a watch, M.], a sign, denotes properly to pay attention, to observe, ἄνεμον (Eccl. xi. 4), τὴν φυλακὴν (Acts xii. 6), the beloved disciples (Jno. xvii. 11, sqq.), τὴν ἑνότητα τοῦ πνεύματος (Eph. iv. 3), ἑαυτόν (1 Jno. v. 18). Hence to preserve [keep in safety] (*observare, servare*) from loss, danger, injury. Fear, selfishness, hatred or love may be the motives of such preserving; the object of τηρεῖν enables us to infer the motive. *His* commandments=the commandments of *God the Father;* for the reference to Christ here is valid not so much because He gave commandments as because He kept them (cf. v. 6). *To keep the commandments* is not the same as ἐν φωτὶ περιπατεῖν (ch. i. 7), but an indispensable part of it, and moreover a distinct, cognizable part of the greater, wide and profound whole, and as a sign or token peculiarly fitted to mark a conclusion. The commandments of God are clear, simple, well-defined; the expression of His will, given as much for His glory as for our salvation, evidences of His holy love, of His sanctifying compassion, and of His salutary righteousness; they answer to His Being, and in like manner to the nature of His Law, and particularly to the nature of His creatures. If they originate in the love of God, the motive of obedience to them must also be the love of God, who gave them, and the love of themselves as the gifts of His love. But the words themselves do not warrant the opinion of Augustine and Bede, that John insists here upon love. He only demands the unexceptional keeping of the commandments of God, and by the use of the Article and the Plural (τὰς ἐντολὰς), excludes any and every arbitrary selection. He lays down a sure and infallible token; and the erroneous view just stated proves it to be such. But he does not lay down this keeping as a fact by the use of ὅτι, but as a supposition by ἐὰν; with this agrees also the choice of the word τηρεῖν instead of ποιεῖν (which is likewise conditioned by the words of our Lord in Matth. xxviii. 20: τηρεῖν πάντα ὅσα ἐνετειλάμην ὑμῖν). We cannot *do,* but only *keep* the commandments of God. And even this is very limited, unsatisfactory, liable to frequent and manifold interruptions. Least of all can it be John's meaning (according to ch. i. 8–10) to suppose Christians capable of fully keeping and practising the commandments of God. But notwithstanding all the shortcomings of obedience to the commandments of God, and despite all the imperfections and sins of Christians and their life, there still remains a sharp contrast between those who remember the commandments of God to do them (Ps. ciii. 18), and those who do not mind them at all, or only know them. However great may be the difference of believers among themselves, their knowledge of God and their obedience to the commandments of God will be reciprocally related, and the latter will always remain a sure token of the former, which cannot be a fact in the life of Christians without the latter. On that account the Apostle, as is his wont, (as in ch. i. 8, 9), gives prominence to the opposite with a progression in the thought and by way of explanation. [Huther thinks it note-worthy that John never designates the Christian commandments by νόμος, a term used by him *only* with reference to the Mosaic code of laws, but mostly by ἐντολαί (only occasionally λόγος θεοῦ, or χριστοῦ); nor by the verb ποιεῖν (except in Rev. xxii. 14), but τηρεῖν. Paul uses the term τηρεῖν ἐντολήν only at 1 Tim. vi. 11; it occurs besides in the N. T. at Matth. xix. 17 (cf. ch. xxviii. 20). M.].

Ver. 4. **He that saith I have known Him, and keepeth not His commandments, is a liar.**—The progression in the development and unfolding of the thought lies in the Singular, which sets it forth not as indefinitely general, but as general and true in its application to each individual. It lies moreover in the negative form, so that we may and must not only infer the knowledge of God from the keeping of God's commandments, and from other facts as well, but that the keeping of the Divine commandments, obedience, cannot and must not be wanting where there is a knowledge of God, which deserves that name. The words "*he is a liar*," moreover, are intensive and stronger than "he lies" (ch. i. 6), or "he deceives himself" (ch. i. 8). Not a single act, but his whole nature and being, is thus designated; the *lie* reigns in him. There may first of all be wanting self-examination in the light of divine truth, or it may be self-deception and unconscious hypocrisy, but the conscious lie will follow; one *desires* to appear more than one is. The further particular,

And the truth is not in him, gives emphatic prominence to the status, the emptiness of such a person, cf. ad. ch. i. 8, in *Exegetical and Critical.*

Ver. 5, similar to ch. i, 8—10, in antithesis with v. 4, refers back to v. 3, by δὲ, but progressing both in the subject-clause and in the predicate-clause.

But whoso keepeth His word; literally: "*but whoso keepeth of Him the word.*"—Τηρῇ, keepeth, stands emphatically first, so αὐτοῦ precedes τὸν λόγον, and λόγον instead of the manifold ἐντολαί, in order to mark the unity. "*Præcepta multa, verbum unum,*" observes Bengel, and a Lapide correctly says: "*Dicit verbum ejus in singulari, quia præcipue respicit legem caritatis: enim ceteras omnes in se comprehendit.*" Hence ὁ λόγος is not the synonym of αἱ ἐντολαί (Huther), nor the comforting message of the gospel, nor the requirement of faith, but the revelation of the will of God as a unit, or the revelation of His commandments in their relation as a unit to His purpose of grace (Ebrard). As this sentence corresponds with "if we keep His commandments" (v. 3), and is more definite by the *pron. rel* than is the other sentence by ἐάν, so the ἐγνώκαμεν αὐτὸν is parallel with ἐν τούτῳ ἡ ἀγάπη τοῦ θεοῦ τετελείωται. It matters not how much we distinguish *knowledge* and *love*, and warn against their being confounded, they are nevertheless intrinsically connected and correlatives: "*Amor præsupponit cognitionem*" [says Grotius, which Huther admits, and adds M.]: "*Cognitio præsupponit amorem.*" Both are true. From this it is evident both that we must apply αὐτὸν, v. 3, to God the Father, and that ἡ ἀγάπη τοῦ θεοῦ must denote *our love of God* (as ch. ii. 15; iii. 17; iv. 12; v. 3.) *The knowledge of God* and *the love to God* must correspond with each other. This is the view of the majority of commentators, viz.: Bede, Oecumenius, Luther, Beza, Lorinus, Socinus, Grotius, S. G. Lange, Lücke, Jachmann, Baumgarten-Crusius, de Wette, Brückner, Neander, Huther, Düsterdieck, and others. Others (Flacius, S. Schmid, Calov, J. Lange, Bengel, Sander), understand the *love of God to us* (as in ch. iv, 9, 10), first in opposition to the Romish exposition of the meritorious *perfectio caritatis. nostræ aut operum nostrorum*, and secondly on account of τετελείωται, which, they say, cannot be predicated of our love. But neither is it "the love commanded by God" (Episcopius) in which we have to exercise ourselves, nor the relation of reciprocal love between God and man, the *communio, societas* and *conjunctio, mutua amicitia et conjunctio* (Ebrard following several commentators, chiefly [German] Reformed), nor "*the love of God in us*, comprising both *God's love to us, through* which, and *our* love *to God*, in which we live." (Besser.) The explanation of τετελείωται, *is perfected, perfect*, is difficult. We have no right to dilute the word with *Beza*, as if John were speaking not of a *perfecta caritas*, but of an *adimpleta caritas*, without all show and hypocrisy, so that the reference were only to *sincere* love and τελειοῦν were only *mettre en exécution* [to put into execution.—M.]. Nor can it be right to hold with Socinus and his successors, the rationalists, that the reference is to a relative perfection adapted to the powers of man, because ἀληθῶς prohibits such an interpretation. It signifies, as in ch. iv. 12, 17, 18, *perfected, has become perfect.* "John supposes the case that somebody really keeps the word of God, and from this ideal stand-point says with the fullest right that such a keeping of the Divine commandments evidences a perfected love to God in practice (cf. Lücke). The more the ideal keeping of the sentence becomes apparent to us, so much the more do we perceive in it a paracletical power, an incentive to the realization of that ideal, a holding up of Christian duty, ὀφείλει, v. 6." (Düsterdieck). Calvin says: "*Si quis objiciat, neminem unquam fuisse repertum, qui deum ita perfecte diligeret, respondeo, sufficere, modo quisque pro gratiæ sibi datæ mensura ad hanc perfectionem adspiret. Interim constat definitio, quod perfectus dei amor sit legitima sermonis ejus observatio. In ea nos progredi sicut in notitia proficere decet.*" But Huther is perfectly right in his strictures of Calvin's view which approaches that of Socinus, who says: "*Est autem perfectio ista caritatis in Deum et obedientia præceptorum ejus ita intelligenda, ut non* omnino requiratur, ne ei quicquam deesse possit, sed tantum ut ejusmodi sit, qua Deus pro sua ingenti erga nos bonitate contentus esse voluit."—M.]. "Where the word of God is perfectly fulfilled, there the love to God is perfect; perfect love shows itself in perfect obedience. It is certainly true that the Christian at no moment of his life has reached this perfection, but is always only growing in that direction. John, however, does not refer to that here." The Apostle now quickly subjoins the concluding thought: **Hereby** (not "by the perfection of love" (Socinus), but "by obedience to the commandments of God," Huther, Ebrard; for this thought concerning obedience as the token of the knowledge of God and of life-fellowship with Him governs this whole thought-complex) **we know that we are in Him.** Ἐν αὐτῷ ἐσμέν is the final and summary expression of ἐγνώκαμεν αὐτόν, v. 3, and of κοινωνίαν ἔχομεν μετ' αὐτοῦ, ch. i. 6, of the inward life-fellowship of *Christians* with God. It is more than *man's* dependence on God in virtue of his inward relation to Him (as in Acts xvii. 28). As having known Him is not without *being in Him*, obedience of His commandments must stand as the mark of the knowledge of God, while the love of God [i. e., our love to God, M.] must supervene. What is said here amounts therefore to more than the explanation given by Grotius: "*Christi ingenii discipuli sumus.*"

VER. 6 is the final and full conclusion of this section.

He that saith he abideth in Him, ought himself also so to walk.—First: "*Synonyma, cum gradatione:* ILLUM NOSSE, IN ILLO ESSE IN ILLO MANERE, *cognitio, communio, constantia,*" (Bengel); then ἐντολὰς τηρεῖν, τὸν λόγον, περιπατεῖν καθὼς ἐκεῖνος. Ἐν αὐτῷ, particularly by the side of ἐκεῖνος (Jesus), and different from it, evidently denotes God the Father, and not Christ, as maintained by Augustine, Wolf, Neander, al., although the recollection of μένειν, the favourite expression of Jesus, which occurs ten times in John xv. 4–11, may have influenced the language of the Apostle in this passage; at all events, the *abiding* spoken of in the Gospel is also connected with a reference to the commandments. "*Being* and *abiding* in God denote one and the same fellowship with God. The latter term merely superadds the description of its *permanence* and *continuance*, which is not contained in the former." (Frommann.)

Ought (ὀφείλει) does not designate a mark or sign, but only the *obligation.*

So to walk even as He walked.—(*i. e.* Christ). This walking is not a mark or sign, which exists or might exist, or given as a touchstone to determine the Christianity of individuals, but simply designates the duty and obligation of Christians, as the disciples of Christ. Nor is it consequently a moment of *abiding* or *being* in God, a part thereof, but a goal to be reached, and a problem to be solved by every Christian, with the obligation of which none may dispense. So (οὕτως) to walk as Christ walked—is a requirement, compliance with which involves constant learning and ceaseless labour. The reference to Christ by καθὼς ἐκεῖνος occurs several times in this Epistle, ch. iii. 3, 7; iv. 17.

As He walked points neither to particular traits in the life of Christ, *e. g.* prayer for His enemies (Augustine), contempt of the world and its pleasures, and patience in sufferings (Bede), nor, as in 1 Pet. ii. 21, sqq., to His self-humiliation and suffering, nor only to His perfect obedience of the commandments of God, nor to His doing only; but it is the concrete representation of walking in the Light (ch. i. 7), of the Divine life in Christ, whose essence and kernel is love. So that Paul may even exhort us to *imitate, copy, follow God* (Eph. v. 1,) and *to walk in love* (v. 2). But this must not be confined to the inward disposition, but must have an adequate expression in all our doings, in our whole conduct, at every step of our life; hence περιπατεῖν. John and his mysticism are certainly not afflicted with sentimentalism. The emphatic οὕτως can hardly be dispensed with here [See Appar. Crit. v. 6, note 7.—M.].

Brotherly love in particular is now specified as a mark of true Christianity (vv. 7–11).

VER. 7. **Beloved,** so in ch. iii. 2, 21; iv. 1, 7, 11; in the last two passages it is particularly connected with the commandment of brotherly love. *Beloved* of God the Father in Christ, whom they ought to follow in that they walk in love to the brethren, as He did. [Huther: "Such an address does not necessarily indicate a new paragraph, but it bursts forth also in cases when the matter in question is to be brought home to the hearts of readers or hearers; which is the case here."—M.].

I write not a new commandment to you.—The whole context, both what immediately precedes and what follows, requires us to regard this ἐντολή as a *commandment*, even as the commandment of *brotherly love.* The consideration of v. 6 teaches first that ὀφείλει constrains us to hold fast to the meaning of ἐντολή, *commandment*, and secondly exhorts us to walking after Christ; while v. 9 treats of love to the brethren. The latter is the definite and explicit declaration of what is implied in the former. It is improper to say that the reference here is to the different commandments; the commandment, to walk after Christ, and the commandment, to love the brethren; the two commandments are not *alongside* one another, but *inside* one another, and so that the latter is included in the former, not *vice versa*, that consequently the former is more general and less definite than the latter, whereas the latter is particular and clearly defined [*i. e.* Walking after Christ is the general, loving the brethren the particular.—M.]. A separation is impossible here; nor must vv. 7–11 be subdivided as if vv. 7, 8 treated of something different from vv. 9–11. That which is stated in such explicit and definite terms in the second half, with reference to the first half of the whole section, must be already contained and intimated in the first half. The argument proceeds from the *formal*, as given in the walk of Christ, to the *material* which is contained therein. The connection is supported by the Apostle's mode of treatment. For in ch. iii. 11, 23; iv. 7, 21, he uniformly passes from general precepts to the commandment of love. Jno. xv. 13, 17, and particularly ch. xiii. 34, present an analogy, and supply the basis for this part of the Epistle. 2 Jno. 4–6 is the perfect parallel passage which specifies walking in truth, walking after His commandments, walking in the new commandments, which we had from the beginning, and which they had heard. The corresponding points here are walking in the light, walking as He walked, after the commandments of God, in love of the brethren. But the reference cannot by any means be to walking after Christ *per se* in v. 6, because just there the ἐντολή is described as ὁ λόγος ὃν ἠκούσατε. The commandment given is therefore, not Christ's *walk* which is *seen*, but His *Word*, which is *heard;* the commandment was not only given in acts, but *spoken* in the word. Of course we must not understand ὁ λόγος as designating the Gospel which is preached, and make it the ἐντολή. Lastly, the general grammatical usage forces us to take ἐντολή [in its usual sense—M.] as *commandment*, and not in the sense of doctrine or truth, as Flacius, Calov, J. Lange, Rickli, Ebrard understand it. We ought therefore to agree with Augustine, Bede, Oecumenius, Theophylact, Luther, Calvin, Baumgarten-Crusius, de Wette, Neander, Sander, Huther and Düsterdieck, who understand the commandment of brotherly love, and not with expositors like Beza, Socinus, Episcopius, Lücke, Frommann and others, who hold that the commandment applies only to walking after Christ. [It is doubtful whether Braune's view of the relation between *walking after Christ* and *loving the brethren* is correct. It strikes me that the case is stated with greater lucidity and correctness by Huther, who says with reference to the two views of the commentators: "These two views seem to be opposed to each other, but they *are* opposed only when it is assumed that John's design was to specify a particular commandment in contradistinction from other commandments. But that assumption is erroneous: the commandment to keep the commandments (or the word) of God after the pattern of Christ, or to walk in the Light, is none other than that of loving one's brother. From ch. i. 5, onwards John does not refer to different commandments, but to a general commandment of the Christian life, which flows from the truth that God is Light. The reference is to this commandment when John, in order to bring the matter right home to the hearts of his readers, says: οὐκ ἐντολὴν καινὴν γράφω ὑμῖν, so that ἐντολή does not refer to a commandment he is about to specify, but to the commandment he had already specified before (however, not in v. 6 *only*), and which he is about to define more clearly in the sequel as its *concrete* substance." This view Huther pronounces in agreement with that of Düsterdieck: "The solution of the riddle is . . . . that the holy commandment to walk as Christ did walk, is fully and essentially contained in the commandment of brotherly love." "We encounter here the view that as the whole exemplary life of Christ is contained in His love of us, so our whole walk in the Light is substantially nothing else than following after Christ in this full brotherly love."—M.].

The words "*not a new commandment*" are explained by what follows:

But an old commandment, which ye had from the beginning; this old commandment is the word which ye heard.—The commandment, therefore, is not *new*, but *old*, because the readers do not only now learn to know it by his writing, (γράφω), but because they have it already, and had it *from the beginning*. It is also said how they did receive it; they had *heard* it, that is, it had been announced to them. This renders it necessary to refer ἀπ' ἀρχῆς to the beginning of Christianity, and the Christian standing of the readers; for the beginning, as far it concerns their life, cannot be anterior to their time, but must coincide with their life and the time when it was announced to them. So, also, v. 24; ch. iii. 11; 2 Jno. 5, 6. *Ye* can never mean *majores vestri* (Grotius), but designates the readers themselves, the Church, to whom the Epistle is addressed. Nor is there room for a distinction between Jewish Christians who had it already formerly, and Gentile Christians who had only heard it by the preaching of the Gospel, as Wolf draws it, and for saying that the beginning in the case of the former denotes what is written in the Old Testament by Moses (Flacius, Clarius), and that in the case of the latter the beginning dates even from the creation, written in their heart and conscience (the Greeks, fully corresponding with what Luthardt, *on free-will*, p. 12, sq., 22, observes as a characteristic of the Greek Church which is fond of connecting Christianity with the sphere of the universally *human* as contradistinguished from the Latin Church, which prefers to give prominence to the specific newness of the *Christian*, Baumgarten-Crusius, Credner). But we must not say that ἀπ' ἀρχῆς bears precisely the same meaning as in ch. i. 1; ii. 13, 14; iii. 8, since the meaning is determined by the context, which points here to the beginning of the Christian life. This is the view of most commentators, viz.: Calvin, Beza, Socinus, Episcopius, Lange, Rickli, Lücke, de Wette, Sander, Neander, Besser, Düsterdieck, Huther and al.—The Article in the addition (ἡ ἐντολὴ ἡ παλαιά) marks once more the age of the commandment which had already been indicated by the antithesis (οὐκ-καινὴν, ἀλλὰ παλαιάν). It is called straightforth ὁ λόγος, ὃν ἠκουσάτε, because, as all ἐντολαὶ run together in the one ἐντολή, as this one ἐντολή runs through and fills the whole λόγος, the evangelical ἀγγελία: "We should love one another as Christ has loved us;" wherefore ὁ λόγος is not the chief substance of the word, but the word itself. As εἰχετε meant that they had, knew and used the commandment, so ἠκούσατε adds how they came to possess it: by the preaching of the Apostles. The addition is, therefore, not a correction of γράφω, as if John wanted to say: it is not I that give it to you now while I am writing, but you have heard it long ago of Christ (Baumgarten-Crusius), [for ἠκουσάτε has no immediate relation to γράφω, but to εἰχετε.—M.].

VER. 8. **Again I write unto you.**—Πάλιν indicates a close connection with the preceding verse, rendered unmistakable by the repetition of the same word in the same form: γράφω, v. 7,—πάλιν belongs to the verb (Lücke, de Wette), although ἐντολὴν καινὴν stands before γράφω, and signifies *again*, once more, a second time, and Erasmus, with whom most commentators agree here, is not wrong in saying (against Huther): "*et contrarietatem declarat et iterationem*," because πάλιν is used by Homer and Hesiod in the sense of *back*, *backward*, and *against*, πάλιν ἐρεῖν to *gainsay* [*i. e.*, say *against*—M.], but in Herodotus and Attic, and later writers generally, it bears almost the exclusive signification of *again, once more, anew*; but Erasmus errs when he adds: "*hic non repetitionis sed contrarietatis est declaratio*;" it is here corrective and epanorthotic (Beza, Episcopius, Calov, Wolf, Lücke, al.).—Γράφω, both here and in v. 7, denotes the present act of the Apostle, and has its ordinary, literal sense, not=I *prescribe* (Baumgarten-Crusius), nor does the Accusative following γράφω admit the construction =I write *of, concerning* the commandment.

[As] a new commandment, which thing is true in Him and in you.—[Knapp's paraphrase πάλιν (ὡς) ἐντολὴν καινὴν γράφω ὑμῖν (τοῦτο) ὅ ἐστιν ἀληθές is the basis of *as* bracketed in the text.—M.].—This is a further proof of the close connection of this verse with v. 7; John adheres to what he had just said, writes still on the same point, and it is, therefore, simply impossible to make v. 8 begin a *new* paragraph, as does Ebrard. The clause ὅ ἐστιν ἀληθὲς relates to the preceding matter, as is evident from the relative pronoun, and cannot be connected with the following clause introduced by ὅτι, as Ebrard thinks. The Neuter forbids our regarding it as a relative clause belonging to καινὴ ἐντολή, as maintained by Düsterdieck, who assumes a *constructio ad sensum*, and says that "the real substance of ἐντολή is declared to be true, both in Christ and in the readers," but this would require ἡ—ἀληθής (Lücke), and "the thing required by ἐντολή is nothing else but the ἐντολή itself" (Ebrard). We must take it rather as coördinated with ἐντολὴν καινήν, and construe it like ἐντολὴν καινήν, as the object of γράφω. The abovementioned paraphrase of Knapp is the most simple construction, although we must not attach to the inserted ὡς the meaning of "*tanquam si nova esset*," as Knapp does, for then it could not be called a new commandment; yet both the Apostle and our Lord Himself describe it by the epithet *new* (Jno. xiii. 34); ὡς, moreover, denotes the reality (Rom. xv. 15, and elsewhere), and is well adapted to being supplied, in order to point out the right explanation.—But we have to begin with the explanation of ὅ ἐστιν, which stands emphatically first; the reference is consequently to **that**, *which is—in Him and in you.* Αὐτός by the side of ὑμῖν denotes a person, so that ἐν αὐτῷ is not—*per se ac simpliciter* (Socinus), and the context requires its being explained of Christ and not of God (Jachmann, who is then compelled to understand ἀληθὲς in connection with ἐν αὐτῷ, in a different sense from the same word in connection with ἐν ὑμῖν: *in God* it has its reason, *in you* it has its evidence). There is no reason why the preposition should be rendered *respectu*, in respect of, or *by* (which something may be known, identified as true, de Wette); it simply means: *in* or *with* Christ and you. At the same time ἀληθὲς bears of course the sense of *real*, as in Acts xii. 9 [*i. e.*, it denotes *actual reality* (Huther, Meyer)—M.]. The sentence, moreover, must not be torn to pieces after the manner of Erasmus, Episcopius and Grotius: "*quod verum est in illo, id etiam in vobis verum est, esse debet.*" But brotherly love evidenced in the walk is true in Christ the Head and in the readers of the Epistle, as the members of His Body. No matter how great the difference of that reality may be, it is still there [is actually, really extant.—M.]. This stands as a *new* commandment, and, therefore, John writes it thus. He considers the ἐντολή as the main point, places it first, and then predicates of it that it is *new* after having previously called it *old*.—He called it *old* from the stand-point of the present with regard to the former entrance into Christianity, which took place long ago; he describes as new that which is true in Christ and His people, and sees first in Him what is now also in His people, what Christ required of His followers as a new commandment (Jno. xiii. 34), and from this stand-point, from their entrance into Christianity and their fellowship with Christ, he, like the Lord Himself, calls this a commandment which is *new*. The Apostle consequently does not refer here to the permanent duration of the commandment of brotherly love, which requires to be constantly inculcated anew (Calvin: "*perpetuo vigere*," Socinus, Knapp, al.), nor to man's new birth (Augustine, Bede, al.). It is new by the very words added by Christ Himself in Jno. xiii. 34: "καθὼς ἠγάπησα ὑμᾶς," as He has proved it in fact, and as he does effect and operate it in His people. [Huther: "The sense is: that which is already true, *i. e.*, a reality, in Christ and in you, to wit: the τηρεῖν τὰς ἐντολὰς τοῦ θεοῦ (cf. Jno. xv. 10, where Christ says of Himself: ἐγὼ τὰς ἐντολὰς τοῦ πατρός μου τετήρηκα), I write to you as a new commandment," and then he adds in a foot-note, "It is manifestly not more surprising that John sets up before his readers anew as a commandment that which has already become a reality in them, than that he announces to them truths, of which he says himself that they know them already."—M.].

Because the darkness passeth away and the true light shineth already.—This sentence answers the question: Why does the Apostle write as a commandment which is new that which is true in Him and the readers of the Epistle? Hence ὅτι is simply causal, *because;* and this whole sentence corresponds exactly with the preceding (Düsterdieck, Huther). Ὅτι, consequently, is not merely dependent on ἀληθές or ἐντολή (Socinus, Bengel, Ebrard), so that it has declarative force=*that;* the point is not to prove that the light shineth and that the darkness passeth away, nor could that be the substance of a commandment. Nor can we divide (with Lücke and Brückner) the sentence that the commandment of walking in the light manifests itself as *new* in Christ (in whom the true light has appeared), and in the readers (in whom this light diffuses itself and shines already, scattering the darkness), and refer the former to ἐν αὐτῷ, which is not said at all, or to τὸ φῶς φαίνει, and the latter to ἐν ἡμῖν or ἡ σκοτία παράγεται. We have no occasion or warrant for doing so. The antitheses ἡ σκοτία and τὸ φῶς ἀληθινόν must be taken in an ethical sense, and denote the sinful and the holy, as the elements in which one lives and walks; and this construction is rendered necessary by the subsequent verses and the whole context. Both are opposed to each other, but they exist alongside each other, increasing or decreasing (παράγεται—ἤδη φαίνει). The former consequently does not denote the economy of the Old Testament or paganism, which indeed were never without light, nor the latter only the person of Christ, as in John i. 9 (Oecumenius, Bengel), nor "*Christus una cum doctrina ejus et effectus fide et caritate*" (Lange); for the expression has a wider reach. The σκοτία denotes the whole power and sphere of the ethical life, separate from communion with God (the Light in Whom there is no darkness), still fighting against the Light, but evermore condemned (Jno. iii. 19), constantly overcome and consuming itself; but the Light, which is God (ch. i. 5), embraces whatever belongs to His Kingdom, and keeps believers in communion with Himself (Düsterdieck). The Light is called τὸ ἀληθινόν, which is not only real (ἀληθὲς), but the true light answering to the real truth, embracing and effecting the real truth. (Ibid.) [Eternal, essential Light, of which earthly light is only a transitory image.—Huther, Neander.—M.]. So Luke xvi. 11; 1 Thess. i. 9. It is just the life of the Lord, wherein *is* that which shines, bursts and shines forth with ever increasing strength; this real Being is the Light, the true Light (John i. 4). In παράγεται we have first of all to preserve the Present form. The Vulgate renders falsely "*tenebræ transierunt;*" so do Luther, "is past," Calvin [and E. V. "is past"—M.]. It is unnecessary to construe it passively with Besser, Sander, Bengel, (*traducitur, commutatur, ita ut tandem absorbeatur*); it is Middle, like παράγει, 1 Cor. vii. 31 (so Oecumenius, Wolf, Lücke, de Wette, Düsterdieck, Huther): it is passing away, vanishing, disappearing. With this corresponds ἤδη φαίνει, said of the Light, it shineth, *shineth already*, not *now* (Luther, E. V.); the darkness makes room for the light, the light begins already to break through. [Huther, who adds, "so that neither the darkness is entirely past, nor the light entirely established."—M.]. The transition from the reign of darkness to that of the Light is thus indicated and referred to the future, when the conflict thus begun will end in the full victory of the Light. Hence in the words ὅ ἐστιν ἐν ὑμῖν John expresses not so much an encomium on his church, as a declaration of his joy in the continued working and the commencing and progressing victory of the Lord and His Kingdom. From this point of view the reading ὑμῖν only can be received as authentic, as bringing out the true sense of the passage in an undiluted form, which would certainly be awakened by the reading ἡμῖν, and lessen the Apostle's pure rejoicing over his church, as the work of Jesus Christ. [Rickli: "John says this in relation to the *time* in which they live, and during which the great work of the Lord took a wondrously rapid course of development. The true Light, the Lord in His perfect revelation of Divine truth, *shines already;*—already the great morning dawns for mankind. When the Lord returns, then will be the full day of God. This revelation . . . believers go to meet.—M.].

VER. 9. **He that saith he is in the light and hateth his brother.**

For the form cf. v. 4, for the thought see ch. i. 6, 7. Φῶς here denotes neither Christ (Spener), nor the Church (Ebrard: "The Church of those in whom the fact ὅτι τὸ φῶς ἤδη φαίνει has become an ἀληθές"); for since τὸ φῶς, v. 8, denotes the holy, the sphere of the Divine life, no other sense can be admitted here. The Apostle regards as his *brother* particularly the believer in Christ, as γεγεννημένος ἐκ τοῦ θεοῦ (ch. v. 1); the love of the brethren, as the children of a loved Father, rests on the love of God, who has regenerated them (ch. v. 1; iii. 10.). Likewise in the Gospel (Jno. iii. 16; xv. 12, sq.; xiii. 34; xx. 17: xxi. 13); St. Peter also gives φιλαδελφία in the same sense (1 Pet. i. 22, sq.), and actually distinguishes it from ἀγαπή which he takes in the sense of φιλανθρωπία (2 Pet. i. 7), (Luther, common love). "*Ipsa appellatio amoris causam continet* (Bengel). Whether ἀδελφὸς denotes elsewhere an actual brother or a cousin, Jno. vii. 3, 5 [see my article "*Are James the son of Alphæus and James the brother of the Lord identical,*" in Princeton Review, January, 1865—M.], or members of the same nationality, Acts xxiii. 1, or=ὁ πλησίον, ὁ ἕτερος, (Matth. xviii. 35; vii. 3; Luke vi. 41; Jas. iv. 11), the context must always determine the sense, and the context here refers decidedly to Christian fellowship. Hence Grotius is wrong: "*sive Judæum, sive alienigenam; fratres omnes in Adamo sumus*"), as well as Calov and Lange [who give a similar exposition.—M.]. It is improper to take μισεῖν as "*post habere, minus diligere, non colere*" (Bretschneider); it means *to hate;* but it is not specified here to which degree of hatred he has come to whom reference is made; it is left undecided whether his hatred be germinating and initial, or mature and fully developed. Not even the faintest degree or colouring of hatred can be compatible with this ἐν τῷ φωτὶ εἶναι. That saying and this hating are so little in agreement, and this hating imports so much more than that saying, that John continues, saying,

Is in the darkness until now—in sin, in the atmosphere of the sinful, *until now, yet*, at this hour, this very moment. But along with all this severity and profound earnestness which insists upon one thing or the other, runs the intimation of a hope of return. [Huther: "Like φῶς and σκοτία, μισεῖν τὸν ἀδελφόν and ἀγαπᾶν τὸν ἀδελφόν mutually exclude each other. They are two diametrically opposed biasses of life; a man's doings belong *either* to the one *or* to the other; that which does not belong to the sphere of the one, appertains to that of the other. Each denial of love is hatred, each conquest of hatred is love." Düsterdieck:—"Nothing can be more shallow and weak as compared with the ethics of the whole Scripture. All the truth, depth, and power of Christian ethics rest on the '*aut . . . aut*,' so distinctly insisted on by St. John. On the one side is God, on the other the world: here is life, there is death; here love, there hate, *i. e.* murder; there is no medium. In the space between, is nothing. Life may as yet be merely elementary and fragmentary. Love may as yet be weak and poor, but still, life in God and its necessary demonstration in love, is present really and truly, and the word of our Lord is true: "He that is not against me is with me," Luke ix. 50; and on the other side, the life according to the flesh, the attachment to the world, and the necessary action of this selfishness by means of hatred, may be much hidden, may be craftily covered, and with splendid outer surface; but in the secret depth of the man, there where spring the real fountains of his moral life, is not God but the world; the man is yet in death, and can consequently love nothing but himself, and must hate his brother; and then the other word of the Lord is true, "He that is not for me is against me," Luke ix. 23. For a man can only be either for or against Christ, and consequently can only have either love or hate towards his brother."—M.].

VER. 10. **He that loveth his brother, abideth in the light, and a stumbling-block is not in him.**—Not only an antithesis to v. 9, but also a progression in the argument: *μένει*, for every thing depends on the *abiding* which must be the result of *being* cf. v. 6. The sentiment is prepared in *ἕως ἄρτι* v. 9 by the fine allusion that hatred of the brother and being in the darkness, must be overcome, and that being in the light and in love must be maintained. Hence we cannot say with Ebrard: "The exercise of brotherly love is of itself a means of strengthening and confirming the new life; from brotherly fellowship there flow for the new man refreshing and quickening streams of his faith." But the love of the brother acts and moves within the sphere of light, not without growth which strengthens itself there; the impelling power is that which evinces itself in brotherly love, faith in the Father, faith in the Only Begotten of the Father, who gives us the power to become the children of God. He that loves his brother ever grows more firmly rooted in holiness, the kingdom of light; growth takes place *in* brotherly love, but brotherly love does not produce it; He only produces it who produces fellowship with Himself and the love of the brother. John knows only *aut—aut*, hating or loving: "*ubi non amor est, odium est, cor non est vacuum*" (Bengel). The sentence, *σκάνδαλον ἐν αὐτῷ οὐκ ἔστιν* fully corresponds with v. 4; *ἐν τούτῳ ἡ ἀλήθεια οὐκ ἔστιν*. The comparison of these two verses facilitates the understanding of our passage. *τὸ σκάνδαλον*, or *ὁ σκάνδαλος* (Hesychius) is [the rendering of the LXX, M.] for מִכְשׁוֹל or מוֹקֵשׁ properly *ἐμπόδισμος*, *σκανδάληθρον* (*τὸ ἐν ταῖς μυάγραις*), *πρόσκόμμα*; hence *βάλλειν*, *τιθέναι σκάνδαλον*. So *λίθον προσκόμματος*, *πέτρα σκανδάλου* Rom. ix. 33; 1 Pet. ii. 7; cf. Is. viii. 14; xxviii. 16; Rom. xiv. 13. It is always a stumbling against, an offence given, but it is left undefined whether it is given with or without guilt. Christ Himself, the Crucified One, is 1 Cor. i. 23: *Ἰουδαίοις σκάνδαλον*. The guilt of the *σκάνδαλον* may reside in him to whom it is given, who takes it, who is offended at it and falls. Here it is said: *ἐν αὐτῷ οὐκ ἔστιν*. In him, who loves his brother and abides in the Light, in the holy, is not *σκάνδαλον*, is not that which offends, gives offence, causes himself or others to stumble and fall, such as envy, suspicion, want of sympathy, harshness of judgment, pride—all *σκάνδαλα* to himself and also to others. "*Qui fratrem odit, ipse sibi offendiculum est et incurrit in se ipsum et in omnia intus et foris; qui amat expeditum iter habet.* Bengel. This seems also to be the exposition of Düsterdieck, who says: "Occasion of stumbling and falling, the lust of the flesh is still extant in believers, but they are always sure of the virtue of the blood of Christ which hallows and increasingly removes every *σκάνδαλον* (ch. i. 7, sqq.). It is inadmissible to explain *ἐν αὐτῷ*=*αὐτῳ*, as Grotius does (*est metonymia et ἐν abundat; sensus: ille non impingit.* Ps. cxix. 165), or de Wette (*with him* [for him] there is no offence), or Neander (there is no offence with him, he himself does not stumble) or to explain *αὐτῷ* with Lücke and Sander of the external sphere of life, because in the case of Christians *σκάνδαλα* lie in the world, not in himself. What Vatablus says is only half true; *nemini offendiculo est;* the same applies to Johannsen: "he gives no offence; Ebrard: "there is nothing in them whereby they give offence to the brethren; and Huther, "there is nothing in him which becomes an offence to himself:" the reference to others has also been given by Calov, Jachmann, that to himself by Bede, Luther and Calvin.

VER. 11 concludes this section in antithesis to v. 10, taking from that antithesis that which helps the further development of the thought.

But he that hateth his brother is in the darkness and walketh in the darkness.—Here we find *περιπατεῖν ἐν τῇ σκοτίᾳ*, superadded to *εἶναι ἐν τῇ σκοτίᾳ* v. 10. The latter denotes the *status* or *habitus* (Sander), or *affectus* (Grotius) the disposition, state, the former the *actus*, operation; so also de Wette and others. "Both the being (the assumption) and the doing (the consequence) of the unloving belong to the darkness; cf. Gal. v. 25" (Huther). "He that hateth his brother, both as to his *person* and as to his *walk*, belongs to the darkness, the sphere of the sinful" (Ebrard). Closely connected with this is:

And he knoweth not where he goeth to—answering to the *σκάνδαλον ἐν αὐτῷ οὐκ ἔστιν*, v. 10. The particle *ποῦ*, *where*, not *whither*, denotes rest; *ὑπάγειν* however is not *to go*, but to *go away to, to go to;* the word describes a calm walking, not a mere moving to and fro, but a progressive moving towards an end or goal. So Jno. iii. 8; viii. 14; xii. 35; also Jno. vii. 35; *ποῦ—πορεύεσθαι*; ch. xx. 2, 13; *ποῦ ἔθηκαν*. The unloving man sees and knows not which way he is going; he walks with darkened eyes on a dark way. Luther ("they fancy that they are going to rest and glory, and yet go to hell"); and Cyprian ("*it nescius in gehennam, ignarus et cæcus præcipitatur in pœnam*") look at the extreme goal, but we should not lose sight of the immediate consequences of a selfish and unloving being and walking. The matter is so very important, that the Apostle substantiates his statement, saying:

Because the darkness hath blinded his eyes.—*Τυφλοῦν*, to blind, to make blind must not be changed into "surrounding with darkness," or diluted by a *tanquam* (Lücke and others). The unloving man himself is dark, and the darkness is in him, in his eyes, not only round about him. Jno. xii. 40; cf. Is. vi. 9, sq.; Matth. xiii. 14, sq.; and N. pp. Acts xxviii. 26, sq.; also 2 Cor. iv. 4.

DOCTRINAL AND ETHICAL.

1. Here we see quite plainly the different sides of the Christian life; *γιγνώσκειν θεόν*, *τὰς ἐντολὰς αὐτοῦ τηρεῖν*, *τὸν λόγον αὐτοῦ τηρεῖν*, *ἀλήθεια*, *ἀγάπη τοῦ θεοῦ*, *ἐν αὐτῷ εἶναι*, *μένειν*, appear as *correlates*. The *dogmatical* and the *ethical* are in one another. The ethos is contained in the dogma, waiting to be delivered in the life; the ethos rests on the dogma as on a root; both are inwardly related to each other, refer to each other, belong together, may be distinguished, but not

separated; the one without the other falls to ruin or runs to waste. Christian knowledge loses experience, clearness, sharpness of outline, assurance, and breadth, without a life of Christian morality; Christian morality loses unity, depth, endurance, joyfulness, grace and beauty, if not founded on Christian knowledge. If it is affirmed concerning him who, while disobeying the commandments of God, still makes his boast of the knowledge of God, that the *truth* is not in him, and concerning him who loving his brother, abides in the light that *offence* is not in him (vv. iv. 10), it is evident that the ἀλήθεια and the σκάνδαλον cannot be made to agree, and that the former is also an immoral thing.

2. Since John makes τὰς ἐντολὰς and τὸν λόγον τηρεῖν perfectly parallel, and regards the Law with its particular commandments, and the revelation of God in His word as a unit, and contemplates the love of God as growing and maturing toward perfection by the obedient observance of the same, the presumption is that *the same loving Will of God* has revealed itself both in *the Law* and *in the Gospel*, and that man's love of God lives on, ought and has to live on the wholesome food of both. But this decidedly excludes any and every *meritoriousness of obedience* and of good works; just as in the Gospel faith in the love of God does not constitute a merit, so in the Law obedience to the loving Will of God is not a merit. Obedience is simply a sign and mark of the Christian life begun on the foundation and in the efficiency of the reconciliation accomplished by Christ. Our only merit before God is Christ, and beside Him no man can have any merit before God.

3. John does not in any way countenance the doctrine of the Council of Trent (Sess. VI., chap. 16) that "the justified are able fully to satisfy (*plene satisfacere*) the divine law by means of works wrought in God" [*Nihil ipsis justificatis amplius deesse credendum est, quo minus plene illis quidem operibus quæ in Deo sunt facta, divinæ legi pro hujus vitæ statu satisfecisse.*—M.], because he does not speak of that which *has an historical existence*, but of that which is to *become a reality;* he refers not to *actual* reality, but to *ideal* reality. On this account the words of John rather sustain Luther's paradox: "The righteous sins in every good work *mortaliter*, at least *venialiter*"—or Schleiermacher's translation of it: "even in our good works there is something in consequence of which we stand in need of forgiveness for them." Though [Roman] Catholicism debase the Law and blunt its requirements in order to exalt man, we are bound to exalt the Law, though man be debased and humbled, since the case as put by John is and remains only ideal truth, Christ alone being the exception, whom alone all are bound to follow.

4. The *unity* and *difference* of the characteristics of the *Old* and *New Testaments* appears in one point, namely, the commandment of brotherly love. This commandment is valid in either sphere; it derives in both spheres its origin from God; it has the same meaning in both, and is one in both, the old [commandment] which remains. But in virtue of Christ's example in His love of the brethren, it is more lucid, attractive, powerful, comprehensive and pure in the New than in the Old. It is new only in that which the Person of Christ has added thereto in His personal love; He is the new, which has been superadded to the old commandment.

5. The Perfect τετελείωται, v. 5, evidently denotes no historical truth, since the historical is marked by ἡ σκοτία παράγεται, τὸ φῶς ἤδη φαίνει. But these Presents indicate the assurance of victory and the joyfulness of hope with which that Perfect is anticipated. It signifies: "the whole power and sphere of the ethical life, separate from communion with God, (the Light in whom there is no darkness), still fighting against the Light, but evermore condemned, constantly overcome and consuming itself" (Düsterdieck), both in respect of the great totality of the world, and in respect of individual persons.

6. The progress in evil to perdition, and in good to the salvation of eternal life, is inward. The hidden life of the children of God has been commenced by the Forerunner; walking after Him, it grows in them, daily increasing in completeness, so that salvation, pursuant to divine appointment, is the consequence of a holy life on earth. But disobedience and unlovingness exert a reaction on the unloving, which forms their inward being and operates their perdition, which, in its turn, is also the result of their conduct here on earth.

7. As Christ is the principle of ethical life (v. 6), and love the principle in Him, as in the λόγος and the Law, so the love of Him, of God and of the brethren, must be the principle of obedience and of ethical life. Ultimately every thing concurs in brotherly love, which is the mark, while the love of God is the principle, the love of the loving God the fountain of all inward, Christian and godly life.

HOMILETICAL AND PRACTICAL.

Examine thyself.

1. *What* is to be investigated? Whether you know God; and the *knowledge* of God is not without *fellowship* with God. The question is not knowledge concerning and about God, not having heard and learned certain truths relating to Him, but the *being* and *abiding in Him* (vv. 3, 5, 6). You are intimate only with those between whom and yourself there is habitual intercourse. Otherwise you have only a more distant and superficial acquaintance, but never an intimate knowledge.

2. *Why* it should be investigated? Without God you are in darkness, without Him you walk in darkness, you become more and more darkness yourself, you run to ruin, and perish at last in the darkness of condemnation; you reach the point that you hate, and are hated, hateful and abominable (vv. 9, 11). But with and in God you are in the light, you walk in the light, and light and truth and love are in you, you become more and more light, love in truth grows more perfect, and all offence will be put away from you (vv. 4, 5, 11).

3. *How* it should be investigated? Look after your *obedience* to the commandments of God (vv. 3, 4), more especially after the old and yet new commandment of the love of the brethren (vv. 7–11), and see whether you *walk after the Lord Jesus* (v. 6). He that keeps the commandments of God in thought, in word and in deed, keeps

himself; he that observes the commandments of God, preserves himself.

AUGUSTINE:—Christ says not, learn of me to create the world, to work miracles, to raise the dead, but that I am meek and lowly in heart.

LUTHER:—The commandment of love is a short commandment and a long commandment, one commandment and many commandments, it is no commandment and all the commandments. Short and one it is of itself, and soon mastered as to its meaning; but long and manifold in point of practice, for it is the sum and chief of all commandments. And it is no commandment at all in respect of the works, for it has no special work of its own by name; but it is all the commandments, because the works of all the commandments are and should be its works. The commandment of love therefore abrogates all the commandments and yet establishes all the commandments; and all this in order that we may know and learn thus much: *no commandment and no work is to be kept and binding, but in as far as it is the demand of love.*

SPENER:—There is a vast difference between living and dead knowledge; the one flows from the revelation of Jesus Christ (Jno. xiv. 21), from the Holy Ghost, and is therefore the operation of God; the other flows from reason, and consists in man's imagination; the latter knows only what people are wont to say of God, the former ascertains the mind of God; the one is a knowledge like that which I have of a man, concerning whom I have heard something, the other like that of one with whom I have had converse; the one is a feeble light, letting in only a beam into the understanding, the other is a heavenly light which fills and irradiates the whole soul, and in which we should walk.—It is a great consolation that God gives us a sure test, whereby we may be assured of our faith and consequently of our participation in the reconciliation of Christ, a test moreover which we may use also in a state of temptation, when the sense of faith is wanting.—Saying that we know God, amounts to nothing. Simon the sorcerer gave out that himself was some great one, but was not (Acts viii. 9); some say that they are Jews, and are not (Rev. iii. 9); but confession demands first of all a believing heart.—The imitation of Christ is not something that is left to our option, or only incumbent upon certain people desirous of attaining unto a peculiar perfection, but it is the universal obligation of all those who are in Christ Jesus, and is therefore binding on the high and on the low, on the clergy and on the laity, on men and women, in every manner and walk of life.—Teachers should treat their hearers as brethren, and use the paternal power within such limits, as never to forget their brotherly equality (Philem. x. 16). No condition of life gives to a man the liberty to hate his brother; but in whatsoever condition a man may be, he is never and in no wise permitted to hate his neighbour; and although he have occasionally to hurt him, as e. g., the authority of the land, which has to punish the wicked, yet must such condign punishment flow from love, as in the case of others so in his case, and be administered with a compassion that would, if it were able, rather withhold the severe remedy, just as a physician, moved by love, yet because of urgent necessity, will amputate the arm or leg of a patient.—There is no lack of offences in the world; let every one take care not to give offence, nor condemn others, but judge every thing in love. He that hateth his brother knows not the injury he inflicts upon himself, and into what misery he precipitates himself; for whereas he thinks that he loves himself and for his own interest, honour or pleasure, hates his neighbour, even as selfishness is the cause of all hatred, he hates himself most of all, when he fancies that he is loving himself. (John xiii. 9).

LANGE:—The true followers of Christ have not a transient faith, but they are firm and steadfast like a branch in the vine, a bough in the tree, a house on its foundation. The duties of *common love* towards *every man* are these: 1. Intercession for the promotion of his conversion; 2. friendly admonition and correction at convenient seasons; 3. the careful avoidance of whatever may deter him from the practice of good; 4. the diligent warding-off of his loss under all circumstances; 5. kindly demeanour in words, manner and works. The duties of *particular love* towards *believers* are partly the same, partly those which are necessary to the maintenance of intimate brotherly converse and spiritual affinity.

STARKE:—A piece of coin stands the test; lead betrays itself that it is not silver, and brass that it is not gold. Perhaps by sound? No, by the streak; and this is to keep the commandments of Christ. Have a care, my soul. The loss of the fraud is thine own.—Faith worketh by love (Gal. v. 6); wherefore the faith, whence no good works do proceed, is only dead faith (Jas. ii. 17, 26).—The perfection of believers' love of God consists in that it is honest, sincere, pure, undivided, upright, faithful and without hypocrisy, lacking neither a truly divine impulse nor holy ardour, neither true reverence of God, nor ardent zeal for and towards God, although as yet unable to take and hallow all the thoughts of the mind, or to present all its powers as an offering of love to God.—As we know that a branch which bears good fruit is truly in the vine (for were it otherwise how could it bear fruit?) so we may surely say of a man that does truly good works, that he is truly planted in Christ.—Come hither, ye that refuse to believe that it is necessary to be pious. Christ is your Forerunner! Do as He did! Look upon His example. Arbitrary choice and presumptuous conceit pave the road to hell.—It is a great comfort that our Christian doctrine is sure and established, not liable to change and to be presented now in one way, now in another, but remains always the same, because God, who has wisdom and truth, is its Author, and needs not at any time to change that which He has given us once for all. Examine thyself, O man! who art thou? The child of God, or of the devil? Consider only whether thou lovest or hatest thy neighbour? If thou lovest him in deed and in truth, thou art in the light and in God's; but if thou hatest Him and showest thy hatred either outwardly in works, or concealest it inwardly in thy heart, and withdrawest thyself from Him, then thou hast a sign that thou art in darkness and the devil's. Tremble at thyself, and amend thy ways!

HEUBNER:—To know Christ is to know, experience and delight in Him as our Friend and Saviour, and to enjoy His grace and fellowship. The mark of it is the keeping of His commandments, vital, active Christianity. Works are not the ground of justification, but a mark to ourselves, whether justifying faith is in us, and whether we *are* justified; because Christ when He gives Himself to us, never gives Himself half but entire; to whom He becomes justification, to them He also becomes sanctification. We may therefore conclude backwards, to whom He has not yet become sanctification, to them also He has not yet become justification —The assertion of justifying faith and want of holiness, fidelity and conscientiousness, constitutes a contradiction and makes the assertor a liar.—In those who keep the words of Christ, we may plainly see that they have really tasted the forgiving love of God, that it has carried captive their hearts and filled them with love to God.—Hatred, selfishness, is a state of darkness because the lightsome knowledge of God, of the love of Christ is still wanting, because it has not yet penetrated and illuminated the heart, because therefore the soul also is still in a dark, rent state, at discord with itself, without seeing the gracious countenance of God which renders us light, and, as it were, resplendent of countenance.—He knows not 1, how far this evil, unloving mind may carry him, and 2, what will be his end, what his reward,—exclusion from the kingdom of light.

NEANDER:—Believing aright in John's sense, is a matter of life.—His commandments are only separate traits in which His life-forming word develops itself.—As genuine love can evidence itself only in the observance of Christ's word, so there are different degrees of the manner how this love has more or less interpenetrated the life of men.—He Himself is in His commandments, and they also are only separate parts of His self-revelation.—The life of every believer should be only a peculiar representation of the image of Christ, the original of the new and glorified humanity.—Either love or hatred of the brethren; love which is ready for any sacrifice, or selfishness that may also pass into hatred; even as Christ indicates only the two fundamental biasses: to serve God or the world.

BESSER:—Would I know whether I know God, I must not examine my knowledge but my walk; and would I know whether thou knowest God, I do not ask that which thy mouth may have to say of Him, but that which thy life does testify of Him.—Just in the sense of John we read in the Epistle to Diognetus: There is neither life without knowledge, nor right knowledge without the true life.—It is characteristic of love that it would do nothing to grieve but every thing to please the Beloved, surrendering its will and weal, its honour and life to the Beloved; His pleasure is its pleasure; what displeases Him, it hates.—The motto of St. Francis was: "*Tantum quisque scit, quantum operatur.*"—Cursed be all science that cannot stand the test of the commandments of Jesus Christ!—This indisputable *ought* (*v.* 6), is at the same time a blessed *may* to John and to all who have John's mind [That is, the *duty* is to them a blessed *privilege*, which they receive with grateful hearts.—M.].—When the pagans looked with amazement on the love of the early Christians, and exclaimed: "See how these Christians love one another, and are ready to die for one another," when the mark of Christians was described in the words: "They love each other even before they know each other," then there shone the resplendent light before which darkness recedes. Would that this day, when it comprises *already* a much longer period of light, there could be found no Christian Church, in whose new walk that is not truth and reality which John writes to the Christians as an old commandment.

[SECKER:—*If we keep His commandments*, v. 3. Whosoever doth so, though imperfectly, yet sincerely and humbly, hath nothing to fear. Whosoever doth not, hath nothing to hope. Strong feelings of joyful assurance may be given to the pious from above as a present reward; and strong feelings of vain presumption may lead on the wicked, secure and triumphant, to their final destruction. Very reasonable terrors from consciousness of their guilt, may torment the bad beforehand; and very unreasonable ones, from constitution or the suggestions of Satan, may assault the good. Therefore we are to judge of our condition by none of these things; but by the Scripture rule, fairly interpreted: "Little children, let no man deceive you: he that doeth righteousness is righteous; he that committeth sin is of the devil" 1 Jno. iii. 7, 8.—M.].

[BARROW:—(v. 5). If a man perform any good work not out of the love to God, but from any other principle or any other design (to please himself or others, to get honour or gain thereby) how can it be acceptable to God, to whom it hath not any due regard? And what action hath it for its principle, or its ingredient, becomes sanctified thereby, in great measure pleasing and acceptable to God; such is the work and value thereof. It is also the great commandment for efficacy and influence, being naturally productive of obedience to all other commandments; especially of the most genuine and sincere obedience; no other principle being in force and activity comparable thereto; fear may drive to a compliance with some, and hope may draw to an observance of others; but it is love, that with a kind of willing constraint and kindly violence carries on cheerfully, vigorously and swiftly, to the performance of all God's commandments.

(v. 6): "To *abide in Christ*, to *be in Christ*, to *put on Christ* and reciprocally Christ's *being in us, living, dwelling, being formed in us*, and the like expressions, occurring in Holy Scripture, do not denote any physical inherence, or essential conjunction between Christ and us, such as those who affect unintelligible mysteries, rather than plain sense, would conceit; but only that mutual relation accruing from our profession of being Christ's disciples, our being inserted into His body, the Church, being governed by His laws, partaking of His grace, with all the privileges of the Gospel, relying upon His promises, and hoping for eternal salvation from Him. By virtue of which relation we may be said, in a mystical or moral manner, to be united to Him, deriving strength and sustenance from Him, as the members from the head, the branches from the tree, the other parts of the building from the foundation, by which similitudes this mysterious union is usually expressed in Scripture; in effect, briefly, *to be in Christ*, or *to abide in Christ* implieth no more, but our being truly in faith and practice Christians; so that the meaning of St. John's words seemeth plainly and simply to be this. Whosoever pretends to be a Christian, that is, to believe the doctrine and embrace the discipline of Christ, *ought to walk*, that is, is obliged to order the whole course of his life and actions, *as Christ walked*, that is, as Christ lived and conversed in the world; or, it is the duty of every one professing Christianity to conform his life to the pattern of Christ's life, to follow His example, to imitate His practice.—M.].

[HORNE:—(v. 6). No one can fail to see that the life of Christ was designed as a pattern for His followers, who considers how admirably it is calculated for that purpose. We meet not here with legendary tales of romantic austerities, ecstasies and abstractions, tending only to amaze and embarrass the consciences of men with unprofitable and unnecessary scruples, but we behold a life, which though holy and without spot or blemish from beginning to end, was conducted after the manner of men, and so as to be imitable by them; being passed into the midst of civil society, and in the exercise of all those lovely graces, by which that is preserved and improved, sweetened and sanctified. And we should find it the best compendium of morality, the most perfect and unerring rule whereby to direct ourselves in all cases, if we would only ask our own hearts, before we enter upon an action, how the blessed Jesus would behave in our circumstances. A conscience, but moderately informed from the Gospel, would seldom perhaps give a wrong determination.—M.].

[BURKITT:—(v. 7). The commandment of love might be called an *old commandment*, as being a branch of the law of nature, and a known precept of the Jewish religion: although in other respects it might be called *a new commandment*, because urged from a new motive, and enforced by a new example.—M.].

[CLARKE:—There is a saying in *Synopsis, Sohar*, p. 94, n. 51, that may cast some light on this passage: "That way in which the just have walked, although it be *old*, yet may be said to be *new* in the love of the righteous."

(v. 11). Love prevents him from giving any offence to his neigbour, and love prevents him from receiving any from his neighbor, because it leads him to put the best construction on every thing. Besides, as he walks in the light, he sees the stumbling-blocks that are in the way, and avoids them; every part of his path being illuminated. Many fall into sin because they do not see the snares that are in their way; and they do not see the snares because they either have not received, or do not abide in the light. M.].

[PYLE:—Wherefore it is an effect of the most malicious prejudice and stupid ignorance of plain truth, for any man to profess himself a true disciple of Christ, while he harbours revengeful thoughts and uncharitable principles towards other men. On the contrary, a kind behaviour and tender disposition towards all our brethren is one of the best instances of Christian perfection, and secures us from all the scandal and mischievous effects of a censorious and persecuting temper.—M.].

[NEANDER:—(v. 8). Thus, too, John contemplates Christ as Himself the true light, holding the same relation to the spiritual as the sun to the natural life. What he here says then is this: With those who have been so long attached to Christianity, the darkness proceeding from their former heathen state is passing away, and the true light is now breaking. *Now*, he says,—meaning their present in contrast with their former state of heathenism, or while still affected by its remaining influence. The light derived from Christ, the true Light, was already banishing the former darkness—they were becoming constantly more and more enlightened. So Paul says to his readers, Rom. xiii. 11 sqq., that now their salvation is nearer than when they believed, that the end of the night approaches, the day of the Lord draws near. It is, therefore, *true*, both with reference to Christ, the true Light which has dawned upon their souls, and with reference to believers who have received this light and been illuminated thereby, that this fundamental law of Christianity now verifies its character as the new command. To those who live in the light of Christ, who have become at home in the new world of Christianity, the old commandment now, in contrast with the former state of darkness, presents itself in new glory as the new command. In new power must it be revealed to their hearts, that BROTHERLY LOVE constitutes the essence of the Christian life, is the essential mark of fellowship with Christ.—M.].

[WORDSWORTH:—Christian *Praxis* is the test of Christian *Gnosis*.—True Christians are the genuine *Gnostics*.—The Gnostics pretended to have *light*, to have special *illumination;* but their light is a false light, it is the light of wandering stars, to whom is reserved the blackness of darkness" (on v. 8).—M.].

Sermons:

[VER. 4. SMALRIDGE, BP.: Disobedience to the commandments of God, a mark of unbelief. Sermons, 199.

VER. 5. DWIGHT, T.: His example. Theology, II. 359.

VER. 6. FLAVEL, JOHN: Imitation of Christ in holiness. 2 Serm. Works II. 299.

BARROW, IS.: Abiding in Christ to be demonstrated by walking in Christ. Serm. Works II. 362.

VER. 8. ALFORD, H.: The shining light. Hulsean Lecture, 1842. 1.—M.].

---

6. *Consolatory warning against the love of the world.*

CHAPTER 2, 12—17.

12 I write unto you, little children, because your sins are[1] forgiven you for his name's
13 sake. I write unto you, fathers, because ye have known him *that is* from the begin-

ning. I write unto you, young men, because ye have overcome the wicked one.[2] I
14 write[3] unto you, little children, because ye have known the Father. I have written
unto you, fathers, because ye have known him[4] *that is* from the beginning. I have
written unto you, young men, because ye are strong, and the word of God abideth in
15 you, and ye have overcome the wicked one. Love not the world, neither the things
that are in the world.[5] If any man love the world, the love of the Father[6] is not in
16 him. For[7] all that *is* in the world, the lust of the flesh, and the lust of the eyes, and
17 the pride of life, is not of the Father, but is of the world. And the world passeth
away, and the lust thereof:[8] but he that doeth the will of God abideth forever.

Verse 12. [[1] ἀφέωνται, Perf. Pass. formed after the Perfect Active ἀφέωκα, here and Matth ix. 2. 5; Mark ii. 5; Luke v. 20, 23; vii. 47; Syriac=*remissa sunt*, "HAVE BEEN FORGIVEN YOU" more correct than E. V. "are forgiven you."—M.]

[[2] Cod. Sin. reads τὸ πονηρόν.—M.]

Verse 13. [3] ἔγραψα, A. B. C., Cod. Sin. The reading γράφω is without critical authority, and opposed to the ructure of this series of sentences.

Verse 14. [4] τὸ ἀπ' ἀρχῆς in B., which might allude to ch. i. 1, is evidently a slip of the pen, since the same Codex reads τὸν in v. 13.

Verse 15. [[5] μηδὲ τὰ ἐν τῷ κόσμῳ=*nor the things in the world*, more correct than "the things that are in the world" E. V.—M.]

[6] τοῦ πατρὸς, B. [G. K.] Cod. Sin.; the best verss. Fathers [Oec. Theophyl.—M.]. The reading Θεοῦ A. C. must yield the place to the former authorities, and to the context v. 16.

Verse 16. [[7] ὅτι=because, so German.—M.]

Verse 17. [[8] αὐτοῦ after ἐπιθυμία, although wanting in A, and cancelled by Griesbach, is the true reading. The difficulty readily accounts for the omission.—M].

EXEGETICAL AND CRITICAL.

The structure of vv. 12–14.—The six members are evidently divided into two triads: the thrice repeated Present γράφω, and the thrice-repeated Aorist ἔγραψα, as well as the address τεκνία, πατέρες, νεανίσκοι joined to the Present, and παιδία, πατέρες, νεανίσκοι joined to the Aorist, clearly intimate as much. The sentences subjoined by ὅτι exhibit the same correspondency, and confirm this arrangement. This has to be proved by the exegesis.

The addresses, vv. 12–14. Τεκνία must be taken here in the same sense as in the other passages of the Epistle where it occurs, ch. ii. 1, 28; iii. 18; iv. 4; v. 21. It applies to all readers, the whole Church, and should not be made to designate a particular age (as has been done by Erasmus, Socinus, J. Lange), or a peculiarly near relation to the author. The diminutive form is chosen for the sake of intimacy and cordiality, and is indicative of the paternal relation and advanced age of the Apostle. The addition μου, ch. ii. 1, may have a still more intimate sound, but there is no want of intimacy here or in ch. iii. 18; iv. 4; v. 21, although μου is wanting. It is altogether parallel to ἀγαπητοί, ch. ii. 7; iii. 2, 21; iv. 1, 7, 11, or to παιδία, ch. ii. 18; iii. 7, (*var lect.*). Although παιδία is thus rarely used, nevertheless it is used, and, if we take it here= τεκνία, it is used thrice. Hence there is no reason whatsoever why παιδία, v. 13, should not be applied to the whole Church, but, like πατέρες and νεανίσκοι, be understood to designate a particular age (with Calvin, Luther, Calov, Sander, Neander, Besser, Ebrard, al.), and to disturb the harmony of the structure of this group of sentences. Particularly as the comprehensive παιδία, little children, offered a more natural sequence to πατέρες and νεανίσκοι than τεκνία, little *sons*. The order in which τεκνία and παιδία occur, forbids their being referred to a particular age, for either νεανίσκοι, πατέρες would have to follow, or πατέρες, νεανίσκοι to go before. Hence τεκνία and παιδία must be construed as denoting the general address, and πατέρες and νεανίσκοι the specialization of church-members, πατέρες describing those of maturer years (πρεσβύτεροι, γέροντες, heads o families, the more experienced), and νεανίσκο those younger in years. This is the view of most commentators. Augustine's view, according to which the Apostle refers throughout to the *same* persons, only designating them by different names from different points of view, is consequently untenabl : he says: "filioli, *quia baptismo neonati sunt*, patres, *quia Christum, patrem et antiquum dierum agnoscunt*, adolescentes, *qui, fortes sunt et validi;*" nor must we refer, with a Lapide, the different addresses to a "*triplicem Christianorum in virtute gradum;* pueri *enim repræsentanti incipientes et neophytos;* juvenes *proficientes*, senes *perfectos*." Similar explanations are given by Clement, Oecumen., Grotius (with reference to 1 Cor. xiii. 11, 12; Heb. v. 13; Eph. iv. 13, 14) and others.

The *tenses* of the otherwise clear verb, γράφω and ἔγραψα, vv. 12–14, present great difficulties. It is clear that ὅτι does not denote the *substance* of his present or former writing. John writes not *that* their sins are forgiven, and *that* they have known the Father, *that* they have known Him that is from the beginning, *that* they have overcome the wicked one, *that* they are strong, *that* the word of God abideth in them, all this he does not write, and has not written to his church, but other things. Hence ὅτι can only be taken as a *causative* particle; it denotes *the reason* and *cause* of his writing, and must be rendered "*because.*" It is self-evident that ὅτι, if translated "*because*" once, must be translated thus throughout, in all the six consecutive places where it occurs, and not be rendered with Luther the first, fifth and sixth time "*that,*" and the second, third and fourth time "*for*" (=*because*).—Socinus, Schott, Sander, Neander translate "*that;*" Calvin, Beza, Lücke, de Wette, Huther, Düsterdieck, al. "*because;*" while Erdmann gives to ὅτι a declarative meaning in the first three sentences, without determining whether it should be construed objectively and causatively in the last three sentences. *I write*—simply defines the act of writing: *I write just now* what I write, *because*—. The object is the *Epistle*, even this Epistle. Now, if John, after this thrice-repeated γράφω signifying this Epistle, says again three times ἔγραψα, the reference cannot be to the Epistle; neither to the preceding exhortations (Grotius), nor to the first chapter (Calov), neither in respect of the thrice-repeated ἔγραψα to ch. i. 5–7; i. 8–ii. 2, 3–11 and γράφω to ch. ii. 15–17; 18–27; ii. 28—iii. 22 (Rickli and Lücke), nor so that the reference is general, the *Aorist* denoting that part of the Epistle which is already written, the *Present* the part as yet unwritten, but in process of development [the very act of writing, *i. e.*, the Epistle itself.—M.] (so de Wette, Brückner, Huther) nor can the reference be to vv. 12, 13, as if the apostle had said "I write, and I have written, it is a settled thing" (J. Lange, Neander, Sander, Ewald, Heubner, Bengel ["*innuit commonitionem firmissimam*"]), nor are Beza and Düsterdieck any more satisfactory, who suppose the *Present* to indicate the present stand-point of the Apostle, his present act of writing, and the *Aorist* to describe the stand-point of the readers after they had received the Epistle, when, of course, it was written;—all these explanations are so many attempts whose very forced and artificial character shows them to be mere make-shifts, which, even in their more simple forms, do not remove the appearance of *trifling*, and explain as little the position of the *Present* relating to what follows before the *Aorist* relating to what goes before, as that the author by this change of tense tears asunder that which he has written from that which he is about to write, both of which belong together as one. If we are thus constrained to think of another writing, we must not think of a previous Epistle (Michaelis), but of the *Gospel* (Socinus, Lange, Schott, Baumgarten-Crusius, Ebrard, Hoffmann), to which this Epistle is not only nearly related in the exordium, but also in its very kernel and essence. Cf. *Introduction*, § 8, 3. The consciousness of the importance of the Gospel he had written, fully justifies in the Epistle the threefold repetition of ἔγραψα in consideration of the reasons relating to different groups of persons in the Church, and warranting such repetition; nor can it be thought singular that he had no other reasons (ὅτι) for having written the Gospel than those for writing the Epistle. Nor may an objection be raised to the Apostle's not specifying the object either of ἔγραψα or γράφω, and his not describing the writing to which he refers, because both the Gospel and the Epistle were in the hands of the readers, and enabled them both to find the necessary explanation, and to prevent possible misunderstanding. [The peculiarly involved statement of Braune renders it desirable to supply the English reader with a more lucid account of the views he advocates. Γράφω, denotes the present act of writing, not only the particular sentence in which that word occurs, but the present Epistle; ἔγραψα, a writing already written, finished and complete in the hands of the readers of the Epistle, to which they might refer; and that writing was the Gospel, which would clear up every doubt, remove every difficulty, and furnish a commentary on the statements and exhortations contained in the Epistle It must be confessed that this is, on the whole, the most simple and satisfactory solution of a very knotty question, although that advocated by de Wette, Brückner and Huther is not so *trifling* as Braune, echoing the words of Ebrard, asserts. Said authors explain ἔγραψα of that part of the Epistle which the Apostle had already written, and γράφω of the immediate act of writing, that is, to the Epistle in general; in their view it is proper that John should begin with γράφω while his reference to the part already written by ἔγραψα may be explained by the fact that that part (especially ch. i. 5—ii, 11) contains the fundamental principles of the subsequent exhortations and developments. Personally we prefer the view of Braune, but many readers will, doubtless, incline to that set forth by Huther and others.—Ebrard gives the following synopsis of the two triads:

TRIAD THE FIRST. γράφω.	TRIAD THE SECOND. ἔγραψα.
1. τεκνία=all readers.	1. Children (in point of age).
2. Fathers.	2. Fathers.
3. Young men.	3. Young men.

and Wordsworth (who, however, does not discuss the details of his arrangement, and carries the series down to v. 28) makes a series of *seven*, closed by an *eighth*, the octave of the first, with a *symbolical* reference to the number *seven* and *eight*. His arrangement is this:

γράφω ὑμῖν, τεκνία, v. 12.

γράφω ὑμῖν, πατέρες, v. 13.	ἔγραψα ὑμῖν, πατέρες, v. 14.
γράφω ὑμῖν, νεανίσκοι, v. 13.	ἔγραψα ὑμῖν, νεανίσκοι, v. 15.
ἔγραψα ὑμῖν, παιδία, v. 13.	παιδία, ἐσχάτη ὥρα ἐστί, v. 18.

καὶ νῦν, τεκνία, μένετε ἐν αὐτῷ, v. 28.

This arrangement is more curious than valuable or logical, and merely added to complete the catalogue of representative views begun above. M.].

The *reasons* of the Apostle's writing vv. 12–14.

First series, vv. 12, 13*b*.

Ver. 12. **I write unto you, little children, because your sins have been forgiven you.**—The Perfect ἀφέωνται (See Winer, Grammar, § 14, 3, p. 93, on the form of this word) points to the forgiveness of sins, mentioned ch. i. 8, sqq.; ii. 1, 2, as a completed fact, which, as a ground whereon they stand, as a sphere wherein they move, as a benefit they have received, has and is to have on them and the rest of their life a lasting effect and an efficient power. [The forgiveness of sins is the *ground* of the Christian life.—M.]. Vulg., Augustine and Calvin render falsely "*remittuntur*," so Luther, "are forgiven you," [and E. V.—M.] **For His name's sake.** The reference is not to Him who forgives sins, God the Father, but to Him, for whose sake the Father forgives; that is

Christ; for *διὰ* with the *Accusative* is not *per*, through (*instrumental*), but *propter*, on account of, for the sake of, indicating the *ground* of the forgiveness of sins, and here, where the cordiality of the address (*little children*), and the direct application to the persons addressed (I write unto *you*, *your* sins have been forgiven *you*), are to be brought out, it denotes the objective ground, rendered *subjective:* since His name is with you, in you and among you; His name is He Himself and what He is, but revealed and known, believed and confessed; hence=since ye have believed on Him, confess and invoke Him, individually and collectively, and since He has manifested Himself and may yet further manifest Himself as *ἱλασμὸς, παράκλητος*; consequently *for Christ's sake in you.* Thus we might combine with Neander the explanation of Düsterdieck, who insists with the majority of commentators on the objective ground of the forgiveness of sins, and that of Luther, who understands the subjective ground. [Neander says: "He comforts them with the assurance of sins forgiven through the mediation of Christ. For the name of Christ are their sins forgiven; that is, for the sake of what Christ is as the Son of God and the Son of Man, the divine-human Redeemer—it being as such that they invoke Him as their Mediator."—M.].

VER. 13*a*. **I write unto you, fathers, because ye have known him that is from the beginning.**—Ὁ ἀπ' ἀρχῆς, according to ch. i. 1 and the context, can only signify Christ, with reference to His eternal, Divine Nature; for the *ἀρχή* reaches beyond the beginning of time and of the world, into God's eternal life, and must not be weakened into "*initium novi fœderis et evangelii patefacti*" (Socinus). Grotius and a Lapide, without all contextual sanction, explain "*novistis Deum, qui Senex dierum,*" Dan. vii. 9; xiii. 22. Ἐγνώκατε consequently denotes only the more profound understanding of the nature and eternal glory of Christ, spiritual knowledge, and not personal acquaintance, not even on the part of *some* (Bengel: "*vivebant patres eo tempore, quo Christus in terris fuerat conspiciendus, et eorum nonnulli eum et facie et fide, omnes fide cognorant*") so the *ἐγνώκατε τὸν πατέρα*, v. 13*c* must on no account be explained of personal acquaintance. Nor does this exhortation warrant the idea that the Fathers, the aged, love to hear and talk of old things, and that to them, in particular, knowledge ought to belong. (The Greek Fathers, Augustine, Erasmus, Luther, Calvin, Neander). But more profound knowledge in general, and knowledge of Jesus Christ, His Person and work in particular, is peculiarly suited to the calmness and experience of old age.

VER. 13*b*. **I write unto you, young men, because ye have overcome the wicked one.**—While young men are exposed to the power of temptation in respect of the world, both within and without, they have also fresh vigor and courage to fight against and overcome the wicked one, *τὸν πονηρόν*, the devil, who is thus designated in the N. T. in general (Matth. xiii. 19, cf. xxviii, 38, sq.; Eph. vi. 16); and in this Epistle in particular (ch. iii. 12; v. 18 sq.) Carpzov: "*Viris fortibus et robustis tribuitur supra fortissimum et robustissimum victoria.*" But we must not narrow the idea with Bengel, who says "*Insigne quoddam specimen virtutis a juvenibus, quibus scribit, exhibitum, cujusmodi erat constantia confessionis in persecutione Domitiani, itemque reditus juvenis illius, quem apostolus summa mansuetudine a lactrocinio ad pœnitentiam reduxit, suavissime descriptus a* Clemente Al. *lib. quis dives salv. c.* 42, *ab.* Eusebio H. E., *lib.* 3, *cap.* 20 *et a* Chrysostomo, *Paræn.* 1 *ad Theodorum lapsum, cap.* 11. We may think of it, but take it in the widest reach That which John says to all, the *τεκνίοις*, that their sins have been forgiven, applies indeed to all, and it does not apply exclusively to the fathers, that they have known the Lord, or exclusively to the young men, that they have overcome the wicked one; for it may be that there are fathers who have just gained the victory, and young men who have acquired profound knowledge; but besides the general truth of the forgiveness of sins, those particular affirmations are admirably distributed among the different classes, and only possible and real on the condition of that general declaration. "Christian life-truth is essentially one; in whichever direction its riches may be developed, or to whichever relations it may be applied, all these different exhortations and instructions are always of *one* casting, resting on one foundation, and animated by one spirit" Düsterdieck). But John has a particular word, a word of peculiar application for the whole Church, as well as for the separate groups and individuals.

Second series, v. 13*c*—v. 14.

VER. 13*c*.—**I have written unto you, little sons, because ye have known the Father.** To know the Father, that is, to know God as our Father, to cast deeper looks into the peace-thoughts of His heart concerning us, into the holy Love which is His Being, is possible only in the more intimate converse with Him which He opens in the forgiveness of our sins and our reconciliation. The child, with its child-like ways and mind, with its humility, attachment, diligence, teachableness and receptivity, is nearer to God than an adult. Here also apply the words, "*Become as little children*" Matth. xviii. 3. It is easy to see that we have here the parallel of the clause, "Because your sins have been forgiven you;" adoption and forgiveness of sins interpenetrate each other, and more than mere correlates. He now writes to the fathers precisely the same thing as before:

VER. 14. **I have written unto you, fathers, because ye have known Him that is from the beginning.**—His object is not to write something else; for he has rightly divided the word.

I have written unto you, young men, because ye are strong, and the word of God abideth in you, and ye have overcome the wicked one.—"*Alii juvenes corpore, vos fide.*" (Bengel). Matth. xii. 29; Luke xi. 21, sq.; Heb. xi. 34. It is the strength of the Spirit for the combat and victory, the strength of their own spirit, and derived from the Spirit of God, given from above, through and with the adoption and the forgiveness of sins. The *ἀγγελία* (ch. i. 5). with the *ἀλήθεια* ch. i. 6. 8; ii. 4), in the word of God, (ch. i. 10; ii. 2. 5. 7), creates and moves this vital strength and vital courage for the combat. Hence ἰσχυροί ἐστε is immediately followed by καὶ ὁ λόγος τοῦ θεοῦ ἐν ὑμῖν μένει. Ὁ λόγος τοῦ θεοῦ, therefore, does not denote Christ, although He is the centre and star of that word. The word of God, with its eternal power, must not only be brought to them, but it must have entered into them and remain in them; then it happens: καὶ νενικήκατε τὸν πονηρόν. The strength is grounded on the word of God, which abides in them (μένει), and in virtue of this strength they have overcome the devil [the thought belongs to Huther—M.]; the decisive battle, of course, has been fought by Jesus Christ, but His people ought to follow up His victory by continuous warfare, and gain further triumphs in their heart and sphere of life, cf. Jno. xvi. 33. A retrospective view of the preceding verses, assigning the reasons for the Apostle's writing and having written, characterizes the readers as possessing not a small degree of Christian knowledge and ability, and the writings in question as taking for granted such a degree of Christian culture. While we may therefore think of the Epistle and the Gospel, we cannot say with Ebrard that the Gospel is wholesome and pleasant food for the *little ones* (παιδία), but that the Epistle can be understood by adults only. Now has been laid down an important and sure foundation for the subsequent warnings and exhortations (Luther, S. Schmid, Episcopius, Bengel, Lücke, de Wette, Düsterdieck, al.): You have received and acquired so much, and succeeded so well, that you ought to progress, and not to retrograde! You stand in life-fellowship with God—do not dissolve it!

The warning. VER. 15*a*. **Love not the world, neither the things in the world.** The correct exposition of the whole depends on the meaning of ὁ κόσμος, which signifies according to Suidas: εὐπρέπειαν, τὸ πᾶν, τάξιν, τὸ πλῆθος, or according to Hesychius: κάλλος and then the beautiful fabric of the material universe. "*Quem* κόσμον *Græci nomine ornamenti appellaverunt, eum nos a perfecta absolutaque elegantia mundum*" (Plinius. *H. N.* 2, 3). The LXX *do not apply the word* κόσμος, *strictly taken*, to the universe. In the New Testament we find it used in all these senses, 1 Pet. i. 3=εὐπρέπεια, τάξις; Acts xvii. 24; Jno. xxi. 25; xvii. 5; Matth. xxiv. 21; Rev. xii. 8; xvii. 8=τὸ πᾶν, and especially by John in the Gospel ch. i. 9; xi. 9; xii. 19; xviii. 36; 1 Jno. ii. 2; iv. 1. 3. 9. 14.=the creation of the earth, especially of the world of man (Düsterdieck)=τὸ πλῆθος. Now the difference between οὗτος ὁ κόσμος=τὰ κάτω and τὰ ἄνω (Jno. viii. 23), which is at the same time the opposite of both, makes κόσμος to denote the whole kingdom of sin and death, inimical to God, under Satan its prince, and more particularly the world of man as fallen away and estranged from God (Jno. xii. 31; xiv. 30; xvi. 11; 1 Jno. iv. 4; v. 19; 2 Cor. iv. 4; Eph. vi. 11, sq.). But all this without the faintest trace of dualism. For the κόσμος, as originally created by God, was very good (cf. Gen. i. 31, with Jno. i. 3, 10), but became evil and is the object of redeeming love (Jno. iii. 16; 1 Jno. ii. 2; iv. 14), so that the children of the world become the children of God in their faith in Christ and His Word (Jno. i. 12; xii. 45–50); there is no man who is not first born flesh of the flesh, and yet born spirit of the spirit may not and should not become the child of God (Jno. iii. 6; 1 Jno. iii. 9, 14),—Now the sum-total of this earthly kingdom of evil is alternately applied in a *real* sense to the earthly sphere in general, and in a *personal* sense to the world of man, sinful, and abiding in sin; and these two conceptions frequently and easily play the one into the other. The present passage must be interpreted by the *usus loquendi* current in the N. T., and we must "lay down the rule that κόσμος bears the same meaning in all the three verses, so intimately connected together" (Düsterdieck). We cannot say with a Lapide "*omnibus hisce modis*" (*i. e.* three different meanings: "1. *homines mundani, in his proprie est concupiscentia*; 2. *orbis sublunaris, in hoc mundo proprie et formaliter non est concupiscentia; sed in eo est concupiscentia materialis, i. e. objectum concupiscibile*: 3. *ipsa mundana vita vel concupiscentia in genere*) : *omnibus hisce modis* mundus *hic accipi potest et Johannes nunc ad unum, nunc ad alterum respicit*; ludit *enim in voce mundus*." Points of support necessary to the right explanation of our passage are these: κόσμος is the opposite of God, it is a whole consisting of various parts and members, it is easily the object of love: it has a life, but lacks permanence and endurance. Hence it is evidently the earthly sphere of life, especially as filled with the world of man and opposing God, whose *real* side often alternates or concurs with its *personal* side; as applied to things, we have to think not so much of trees, flowers, mountains and stars as of whatever forms part of and constitutes the world-of-man, such as rank or dignity, possessions and gifts of the mind and of the body and such like. Consequently the κόσμος must not be taken as the sum-total of transient creatures as far as they are natural things as Lücke (sum-total of all sensuous manifestations, exciting sensuous pleasure), with whom we must rank, de Wette, Brückner, or J. Lange (*systema totius mundi*), Neander (the world and worldly things), and others construe the word. But equally objectionable is the interpretation which makes κόσμος=the evil inhering in the world, as given by Greek authors (ἡ κοσμικὴ φιληδονία καὶ διάχυσις), Luther (=the world, *i. e.* ungodliness itself, human passions according to which man does not rightly use the creature), Calvin (*omne genus corruptionis et malorum omnium abyssum*), Morus (*malum morale*) Semler (*vulgata consuetudo hominum, res corporeas unice appetentium*), Erdmann (*totus complexus et ambitus mali*), Ebrard (τὰ ἐν τῷ κόσμῳ=kinds of sinful living, thinking and demeanor [*e. g.* covetousness, ambition, sensuality.—M.]). Lastly, we must not limit the application of κόσμος to "*the heathen world*" (Lange), "the mass of ordinary men" (Oecumenius: ὁ συρφετὸς not συνφυτός, as Braune corrects M.] ὄχλος, ὃς οὐ τὴν τοῦ πατρὸς ἔχει ἀγάπην ἐν ἑαυτῷ; Calov.: *homines dediti rebus hujus mundi*), "the major part of men" (Grotius: *humanum genus, secundum* partem majorem, *quæ in malis actionibus versatur*), "to that part of the world which constituted the anti-christians" (Storr, Socinus). Cf. Düsterdieck and Huther *ad loc* [the latter giving all the passages cited by Braune.—M.].—Now while John, according to the Lord, urges love, notwithstanding Jno. iii. 16: οὕτως ἠγάπησεν ὁ θεὸς τὸν κόσμον he says here μὴ ἀγαπᾶτε τὸν κόσμον. There is a difference, if the Lord our Saviour and Redeemer, who is above the world, loves, or if we love that are of the world, needing salvation, although salvable. To love is to surrender oneself; God surrenders Himself in order to save, overcome and glorify; the creature can only surrender itself to the world to be ruined, swept along and carried off. The creature is forbidden to enter into intimate and vital communion, or entire life-fellowship with that sphere of humanity which has fallen away from God. The Saviour does it in order to save from it those who suffer themselves to be seized by Him.—Μηδέ=*but not even*, or *no, not even*. The Apostle consequently draws a sharp distinction between τὸν κόσμον and τὰ ἐν τῷ κόσμῳ, the whole or the general, and the particular or the specific. You are not even to love a particular, a specific part of the κόσμος; one may be fascinated by this thing, another by that, it all amounts to the same; the love of the world is there where we find the love of the particular or of one particular in the world, be it the gold of the earth, which is highly valued among men, or human wisdom, or honour with men, or power and dominion, or only influence of a less degree and in a limited sphere.—This warning is obviously addressed to all, the πατέρες and νεανίσκοι. "*Omnibus hæc generaliter ecclesiæ filiis scribit*" (Bede). It is not said to *the children* only (Oecumenius); for παιδία and τεκνία denote the whole church (see above); nor to the *young men* only (Bengel, Sander, Besser), although it follows the last address. The next verse, which is purely general, as well as the import of this warning, require us to understand it as being universal in its application.

The reasons. vv. 15*b*–17.

First reason. vv. 15*b*, 16. **If any one love the world, the love of the Father is not in him.**—"*Unum cor duos tam sibi adversarios amores non capit.*" (Bede) "*Contraria non sunt simul*" (Bengel). Since ὁ κόσμος is the object of love, since the Apostle is concerned with the love of the world and the heart of man which loves, ἡ ἀγάπη τοῦ πατρὸς is of course our love of the Father; for the love of the Father is not incompatible with the love of the world (Jno. iii. 16). Hence ἀγάπη τοῦ πατρὸς denotes neither "*amor Patris erga suos et filialis erga Patrem*" (Bengel), nor "the love of God toward us" (Luther II., Calov.), nor the "*caritas quam Pater præscribit*" (Socinus). We have here the same antithesis which is noted in Matth. vi. 24: θεῷ καὶ μαμωνᾷ δουλεύειν, Rom. viii. 5 (σάρξ and πνεῦμα), v. 7 (φρόνημα τῆς σαρκός ἔχθρα εἰς θεόν); 2 Cor. vi. 15 (Χριστός and Βελίαρ); Jas. iv. 4 (ἡ φιλία τοῦ κόσμου ἔχθρα τοῦ θεοῦ and in this Epistle ch. i. 5 (φῶς and σκοτία). This is the reason of the warning against the love of the world; the love of the world is incompatible with the love of God, as our Father; the love of the world cannot consist with the sonship of God. [Christians are the *children* of God, God is their *Father;* their vocation is to love their *Father*, not to love the world. —M.]. This is explicitly brought out in

VER. 16. **Because all that is in the world, the lust of the flesh and the lust of the eyes and the pride of life, is not of the Father, but is of the world.** The connection of this verse with the one preceding by ὅτι=*because*, compels us to emphasize π ᾶ ν; for, because there is *nothing* in the world, the κόσμος, which is of the Father, the love of the world is utterly incompatible with the love of the Father.—Πᾶν τὸ ἐν τῷ κόσμῳ is evidently not identical with τὰ ἐν τῷ κόσμῳ (v. 15); the Singular denotes the transition from the particular to the unit: what is in the world is conceived as a whole, a totality comprehending the particular; hence the reference is not *to objects only*, as all those maintain who make it identical with τά ἐν τῷ κόσμῳ (although Ebrard's exposition correctly adverts to particular forms of demeanour, and Düsterdieck speaks of a "transformation of the conception of the objects of the love of the world into the conception of subjective love itself and its essential modes of representation"); still less to *persons* ("*omnes mundi dilectores non habent nisi concupiscentiam*" Bede); but as Huther excellently puts it: "All that which constitutes the substance, *i. e.* the essence of the κόσμος, its inward life, which animates it." The apposition indicates the nature of πᾶν τὸ ἐν τῷ κόσμῳ, and shows how we are to take, and what is the true import of these words. The apposition has obviously respect to life-manifestations in the world of man: the whole, the sum and substance, the totality of those life-manifestations in the God-forsaken world of man, is not of God, but without, and opposed to God. In dealing with the difficulty connected with the exposition of the apposition: ἡ ἐπιθυμία τῆς σαρκὸς καὶ ἡ ἐπιθυμία τῶν ὀφθαλμῶν καὶ ἡ ἀλαζονεία τοῦ βίου, we have to remember that all the three clauses must be taken as coördinated, and that the Genitive must be construed alike in all three cases. The three ideas are placed in juxtaposition by καί. Hence Düsterdieck errs in making ἡ ἐπιθυμία τῆς σαρκὸς the principal idea governing ἐπιθυμία τῶν ὀφθαλμῶν and ἀλαζονεία τοῦ βίου. This is confirmed by the explanation of the separate ideas. In ἐπιθυμία τῶν ὀφθαλμῶν we have evidently the Genitive of the subject; it cannot mean: lust after the eyes. We have therefore three times the Genitive of the subject. In ἐπιθυμία τῆς σαρκός the Genitive of the subject is analogous to the idea: ἡ σὰρξ ἐπιθυμεῖ (Gal. v. 17), and to the grammatical usage of the N. T., where, with the exception of 2 Pet. ii. 10, the Genitive connected with ἐπιθυμία always denotes the subject; but σάρξ denotes here what it signifies elsewhere, *e. g.* in Eph. ii. 3 (ἐπιθυμίαι τῆς σαρκὸς) 1 Pet. ii. 11 (αἱ σαρκικαὶ ἐπιθυμίαι), the desire, the lust of the flesh, as suggested by the antithesis of πνεύματι ἄγεσθαι, ἐν πνεύματι περιπατεῖν. Limitations like those of Augustine ("*desiderium earum rerum quæ pertinent ad carnem, sicut cibus et concubitus et cætera hujusmodi*"), Grotius, Baumgarten-Crusius, Sander and Besser, who agree with him, or those of Brückner, who suggests "carnal lust in the strict sense," Bengel ("*ea quibus pascuntur sensus qui appellantur fruitivi: gustus et tactus,*) Gerlach ("every kind of the lust of enjoyment") and Ebrard ("sexual enjoyments")—are not in agreement with the context and more or less arbitrary. Only the limitation required by the coördinated ἐπιθυμία τῶν ὀφθαλμῶν is justifiable; but even this is an ἐπιθυμία, and as such equal to the former, yet not τῆς σαρκὸς, but τῶν ὀφθαλμῶν. This ἐπιθυμία must not be subordinated to the former (as is done by Lücke, de Wette and Düsterdieck), but it is coördinated with it. Nor must the Genitive be taken at once subjectively and objectively: "the lust of the eyes, and at the same time that, wherein as the sensuous-worldly, the eyes delight themselves" (Brückner). The lust of the eyes has respect to seeing, consequently the lust to see, and to see that which is the object of such lust. Hence Spener explains correctly: "all sinful lust which seeks for enjoyment in the very seeing," and so does Huther: "the desire of seeing that which is unseemly, and the sinful gratification afforded by seeing it." Hence it must not be restricted to "*omnis curiositas in spectaculis, in theatris*" (Augustine, Neander); nor is it sufficient to say with Calvin: "*tam libidinosos aspectus comprehendit, quam vanitatem, quæ in pompis et inani splendore vagatur.*" Nor may it be referred with Bengel to "*ea, quibus tenentur sensus investigativi, oculus sive visus, auditus et olfactus.*" Nor must extraneous ideas be added thereto, so as to make it denote a desire of possession excited by sight (Rickli), or straightforth *πλεονεξία* (Luther, Socinus, Grotius, Lorinus, Wolf, Baumgarten-Crusius, Gerlach, al.), or even "the whole sphere of the desires of selfishness, envy, covetousness, hatred and revenge" (Ebrard). Thus the lust of the flesh and the lust of the eyes are arbitrarily distinguished from each other or rather confounded, since the former is taken as sensuality and the latter as covetousness, or *vice versa.* The eyes, instruments of the senses, are preëminently the ministering members of the life of the soul and the spirit: here is flesh, become transparent, whereby surrounding objects and manifestations produce impressions on the life of the soul, and the soul requires insight of them. As the Scripture draws a distinction between grass and the flower of grass, and understands thereby the flesh and the glory of the flesh (1 Pet. i. 24: *σὰρξ ὡς χόρτος* and *πᾶσα δόξα αὐτῆς ὡς ἄνθος χόρτου*), and thus points beyond the nearest sphere of carnal life to the life-sphere of the soul, so we may distinguish the *ἐπιθυμία τῆς σαρκός* from the *ἐπιθυμία τῶν ὀφθαλμῶν* in such manner that the former denotes absolute, purely sensuous lust, and the latter lust which through the instrumentality of the soul, points to the spiritual sphere of life. It is noteworthy that as Peter subjoins the words (v. 25) "*τὸ δὲ ῥῆμα τοῦ θεοῦ μένει εἰς τὸν αἰῶνα,*" so John has almost the identical addition: "*ὁ δὲ ποιῶν τὸ θέλημα τοῦ θεοῦ μένει εἰς αἰῶνα.*" Hence the former includes all the desires of possession and enjoyment, of covetousness and sensuality, of vulgar or refined form, while the latter embraces the desire which longs for, seeks and finds gratification in social intercourse and the manifestations of social joys, in works of art down to the rude outbreaks of festal joy.—To this is now added as a third *καὶ ἡ ἀλαζονεία τοῦ βίου.* While *ἐπιθυμία* refers twice to *acquisition*, *ἀλαζονεία* has respect to *spending.* The noun occurs, besides this place, in the N. T. only at Jas. iv. 16: *ἐν ταῖς ἀλαζονείαις ὑμῶν*, the adjective in Rom. i. 30, after, and in 2 Tim. iii. 2, before *ὑπερήφανος.* In classical Greek it signifies arrogance and vaunting, with the secondary idea of untruthfulness and boasting about one's rank or wealth. In James it evidently denotes the outbreaks of that arrogance which overlooks the vanity and nothingness of earthly happiness, and boastingly confides in it. The *ἀλαζών* is the vain braggart at whom and with whom one may perhaps smile; the *ὑπερήφανος* is the haughty man, who is irritable and injurious; the one recognizable in the national character of the French, the other in that of the English. The Genitive *τοῦ βίου*, of the life, with reference to sustenance and necessaries, as is evident from ch. iii. 17; Mark xii. 44; Luke viii. 14, 43; xv. 12, 30; xxi. 4; 2 Tim. ii. 4, designating occasionally personal property (living), indicates the side on which this braggart arrogance does and is wont to appear, as well where there is little or great abundance as where it is merely coveted and want is concealed; braggart arrogance is wont to appear in connection with bodily sustenance and necessaries. Augustine: "*Jactare se vult in honoribus, magnus sibi videtur, sive de divitiis, sive de aliqua potentia.*" Bengel: "*Ut velit quam plurimus esse in victu, cultu, apparatu, supellectili, ædificiis, prædiis, famulitio, clientibus, jumentis, muneribus,* etc., Rev. xviii. 12. *Chrysostomus appellat τὸν τῦφον τὸν βιωτικὸν* et *τὴν φαντασίαν τοῦ βίου.*" Examples occur in Gen. xi. 2–4; 1 Chron. xxii. 1, sqq.; Eccles. ii. 1, sqq.; Ezek. xxviii. 12–19; Dan. iv. 27; Rev. xvii. 4–6; xviii, 4–7. So Lücke, Sander, Besser and Huther; Neander, Gerlach and Düsterdieck may be included in this category. Hence it is not correct to restrict the meaning to ambition, *superbia, ambitio* (Cyrillus, Socinus, al.).—We should hold with Bengel that: "*Non coincidunt cum his tribus tria vitia cardinalia, voluptas, avaritia, superbia: sed tamen in his continentur.*" The hypothesis that this trinity contains a complete indication of all the forms in which evil is apt to manifest itself, has become traditional, and goes so far that Bede following Augustine said: "*Per hæc tria tantum cupiditas humana tentatur; per hæc tria Adam tentatus est et victus; per hæc tentatus est Christus et vicit.*" A Lapide actually discovered in them the correlatives of the three Persons of the Holy Trinity answering to the three *primariæ virtutes, continentia, caritas, humilitas* [which according to Huther are closely connected with the three monastic vows of chastity, poverty and obedience.—M.]. The majority of practical expositors have followed this track with various modifications, even Pascal (*Pensées*, 28, 55) says: "*libido sentiendi, sciendi, dominandi.*" Lücke very rightly opposed this interpretation and maintained that the point in question did not relate to cardinal *vices*, but to the chief forms (Brückner; "leading biasses") of worldly-mindedness. These, as Bengel observes, sustain an intimate relation to one another: "*Etiam ii, qui* arrogantiam vitæ *non amant, tamen* concupiscentiam oculorum *sectari possunt, et qui hanc superarunt, tamen* concupiscentiam carnis *persæpe retinent: hæc enim profundissima et communissima, apud minores, medioximos et potentes: apud eos etiam, qui abnegationem sui colere videntur; et rursum, nisi vincatur, ab ea facile progreditur homo ad* concupiscentiam oculorum, *ubi materiam habet; et ab hac ad* superbiam vitæ, *ubi facultatem habet; tertioque includitur secundum, secundo primum.*" Thus ambition is *ἐπιθυμία τῆς σαρκός* only in so far as it wants to cast others in the shade, it is *ἐπιθυμία τῶν ὀφθα-*

ιῶν as far as it aims at recognition and marks of recognition, and it is ἀλαζονεία τοῦ βίου as far as it is indulged in the consciousness of position and wealth, and in every form there are degrees of intensiveness and coarseness. The same holds good of avarice, voluptuousness and the love of pleasure. We have here by no means a complete catalogue of the biasses and forms of manifestation of evil. *Unlovingness* specified above (vv. 2–11) and *mendacity* mentioned below (vv. 18–20) although connected with this [trichotomy M.], are not contained in or denoted by it. Hence Luther, followed by Sander, rightly observes: "These three particulars are not of the Father: 1. Hatred of the brethren. 2. The three idols of the world. 3. False and corrupt doctrine.—The terms ἐκ τοῦ πατρός, ἐκ τοῦ κόσμου εἶναι denote origin and indicate similarity, congruity and connection. This is the profound truth that nothing is esteemed with God except His own Image; whatever is to have respect to Him, to belong to Him, to be, and able to be united with Him, must come from Him; ch. ii. 29; iii. 7 sqq.; iv. 2 sqq.; 7 sqq.; v. 1 sqq.; Jno. viii. 44. So Düsterdieck, Huther, and Ebrard in opposition to de Wette [Paulus and Baumgarten-Crusius—M.], who deny the reference to origin and restrict the application of the terms to congruity and similarity. The antithesis, intensified by the repetition of ἐστί "*is not of the Father, but is of the world*" marks with peculiar pointedness the *world* as the source of ungodliness. The world will not tolerate any thing that does not derive its being from it or belongs to it. We see therefore how God and the world are just here opposed to each other, irreconciled and irreconcilable; both are inflexible and neither can yield the place to the other. [Düsterdieck: "Through our whole Epistle runs the view which is also manifest in the Gospel of St. John, that only the mind which springs from God is directed to God. He who is born of God, loves God, knows God, does God's will. God Himself, who first loved us, viz. in Christ His incarnate Son, begot in us that love which of moral necessity returns again to the Father, and of like necessity embraces our brethren also. This love is hated by the world, because it springs not from the world. It depends not on the world, any more than that perverted love which springs from the world and is directed towards the world, the lust of the flesh, etc., can be directed to the Father or to God's children. So that John grasps in reality down to the very foundations of the moral life, when he reminds his readers of the essentially distinct origin of the love of the world, and the love of God. The inmost kernel of the matter is hereby laid bare, and with it a glimpse is given of the whole process of the love of the world and the love of God, even to the end; and this end is now set forth expressly with extraordinary power."—M.]. But

The second reason: v. 17.

And the world passeth away and the lust thereof; but he that doeth the will of God abideth for ever.—The world can only be taken here in the same sense as in the preceding verses, viz.: the world of man fallen away from and opposing God, which is a power, and as a power awes many, but does and has great things. But what is true of the σκοτία, v. 8, applies also to it: παράγεται, it passeth away, it is passing away and disappearing; the sense must not be limited to the transitory world, to be destroyed in the judgment (Bede: "*mundus transibit, quum in die judicii per ignem in meliorem mutabitur figuram, ut sit cœlum novum et terra nova*"), nor must the term be so construed as to express the consciousness of the approaching advent of Christ and the judgment of the κόσμος connected with it (Luther, with reference to vv. 8. 18: ἐσχάτη ὥρα). It is, in effect, the uninterruptedly peculiar nature and destiny of the world (Oecumenius: "τὰ κοσμικὰ ἐπιθυμήματα οὐκ ἔχει τὸ μένον τε καὶ ἑστώς, τὰ δὲ κατὰ τὸ θέλημα τοῦ θεοῦ διακρῇ καὶ διαιωνίζοντα (Düsterdieck: "because of its alienation from God, doomed to *passing away*, to death"). The antithesis μένει requires and confirms this view. Although Düsterdieck distinguishes his view, according to which he finds here more permanently valid axiomatic truths concerning the course of the love of God or the love of the world, from that of Oecumenius, who gives prominence to the properties of the love of the world and of the obedience to the commandments of God, the two views ought really to be combined thus: it fares with the world according to its nature, and the nature of the world agrees with its passing away. And as it passes away, so also passes away its lust, the lust which inheres in it, emanates from it, and governs it. Hence αὐτοῦ is the Genitive of the subject, as maintained by most commentators; it cannot mean lust after it or in it, as if αὐτοῦ were the Genitive of the object (Lücke, Neander, Sander, Besser, al.). Of course, the lust of the world refers also to the world and the things and manifestations in it, and not to God and the riches of His Kingdom. If the whole, the world, belonging to death, passes away, then also its parts, the life that is in it, its separate manifestations and exhibitions of life in individuals, must pass away. This makes one thoroughly loathe the love of the world—the ἀγαπᾶν τὸν κόσμον. Who wants to seize and hold as the object of his love that which is perishable, doomed to death and perpetual defeat? The clause ὁ δὲ ποιῶν τὸ θέλημα τοῦ θεοῦ supplies not only an antithesis, but affirms that the ἐπιθυμία τοῦ κόσμου does not the will of God, that the ἀγάπη τοῦ πατρός shows and verifies itself in the ποιεῖν τὸ θέλημα τοῦ θεοῦ, even as unfolded in vv. 3, sqq., that the child does not trifle with the will of the Father, for the Father is God. To such applies the μένει εἰς τὸν αἰῶνα, the antithesis of παράγεται, he abides therefore unto, into eternity, sharing and assured of the imperishable and beatific life; redeemed from θάνατος, from the σκοτία, he gains φῶς, ζωὴ αἰώνιος. [Huther: "The destiny of the κόσμος is θάνατος, that of the children of God ζωὴ αἰώνιος."—M.]. This antithesis points to the fact that the παράγεται of the world will sooner or later have run its course, and that the world will have ceased to exist Most singular and arbitrary is the opinion of Ebrard, who says that "αἰών is the æon which will gloriously begin with the visible establishment of Christ's Kingdom on earth," and that consequently ὁ ποιῶν—εἰς τὸν αἰῶνα signifies that "he that does the will of God will abide until then, until the Kingdom of Christ is established.

and be suffered to witness the victory of Christ's Kingdom." The addition, "*quomodo et deus manet in æternum,*" found in several Latin translations, but not in Jerome's, is rather remarkable.

DOCTRINAL AND ETHICAL.

1. The gift of the forgiveness of sins (v. 12), which is, at the same time, the gift of adoption, [of being made the child of God—M.], v. 13*c*, establishes a relationship which must verify itself in corresponding conduct, in the way of sanctification. God *has* taken the initiative, but man must seize it and hold fast, keep and verify it in striving after more profound knowledge, and in struggling for the peace of victory. On the gift of the forgiveness of our sins, and on that of our adoption with the Father, rest the more intimate knowledge of Christ, the victorious fight against Satan, and the enjoyment of the fruits of victory. In the fellowship with the Father and the Son are given us life, light, forgiveness, truth, wisdom, and understanding, and victory over the world and the devil. The victory of Christ (John xvi. 33) is the presupposition of all true victories, and His victory must continue in ours. John grounds the duties of Church members on the high privileges and immunities of the Christian state, and makes *gratitude* the principle of morality.

2. The peace-work of profound meditation and mature knowledge in men can only take place and prove successful if preceded by the struggles and triumphs of young men [i. e., the *man* must have passed through the discipline of the *young man*.—M.]. Great purity and integrity are indispensable to the clear perception and more thorough knowledge of the glory of Christ, of His Person, His Word, and His work. True knowledge presupposes life in fellowship with the Person known; it is a living reality and not a mere dogmatical formula (concerning the Person of Christ). Nothing but fighting against Satan will facilitate our knowledge of the eternal glory of Christ.

3. The κόσμος is diametrically opposed to God, and the heart of man cannot combine the love of the world and the love of the Father; the latter cannot thrive because of the former, or the former must be overcome, and disappearing, yield the place to the latter in the course of its growth and development. Where the life of [emanating from —M.] God is extant there may still be the world, but its power must be broken, it must wane more and more, and its still surviving remainder must recede before increasing and waxing knowledge and joy. Worldly life and godly life are not only two different biasses, but two opposite inclinations, incompatible and destroying each other.

4. It is not in point of space that we must flee from the world, but it is with reference to ethical principles that we must shun it, without loving it, turned away from it, to prevent our dying and perishing in and with it; some one thing may so effectually lay hold of one or another as to sweep him along with the fearful destruction of the whole κόσμος.

5. The definite superiority of the divine to the worldly may be gathered from the transitoriness of the world. Here is "afforded a vista through the whole process of the world's history, as well as of the love of God, right on to the end" (Düsterdieck), and at the same time an insight into the biography of individuals.

6. He that has separated himself from God, has estranged himself from Him, falls into the power of death; the world contains death in the love of itself. None but those who love the Father have the life; yet none love the Father but those who have and with true fidelity keep His word. But there exists no eternal kingdom of evil, the principially dualistic predisposition to evil, but only a condition which has become so, from which any and every man may and shall be redeemed, who does not offer any resistance.

HOMILETICAL AND PRACTICAL.

The gift of the forgiveness of sins sets us the task of fighting against the destroyer, and acquiring the knowledge of the Saviour. The gift of the forgiveness of sins is sonship with God and the knowledge of the Father. Holy Scripture directs us first to the knowledge of sin, then to fight against and overcome the wicked one, and lastly to acquire the knowledge of the God-man. Holy Scripture addresses first children—that is to say, the children of God; the word of God is the word of the Father to His children; the word of God calls all, whom it addresses, children, because He is the Father of all. Young men and fathers cannot go beyond this *child*-ship [I retain this Germanism in this place in order to render the thought more perspicuous; neither the word sonship nor adoption conveys the precise shade of thought.—M.]. No age of life can or may desire to surpass the stage of childhood before God. The life-truth of the Gospel is only one, emanating from one Spirit, resting on one foundation, consisting in one Spirit, but like the sun, shedding its illuminating and vitalizing beams in all directions: away with all false individualizing and all dry moralizing! He that loves not the world in God as the object of redemption to its salvation, loves it only without God to his own perdition. The world, which thou lovest, reacts more on thee than thou art able to influence it; thou wilt sooner become worldly through it, than it will become Christian through thee. Shun not the world, but love it not; be not afraid of it, but be afraid of thy love of it.

BODMER:—John the Apostle survived twelve Roman emperors: Augustus, Tiberius, Caligula, Claudius, Nero, Galba, Otho, Vitellius, Vespasianus, Titus, Domitianus and Nerva; great expectations and hopes were entertained of each one of those lords of the world, but all failed in the case of the best of them: instead of healing, they inflicted wounds, and many came to a miserable end.

GERSON:—*Amor habet vim uniendi, si terram amas, terrenus es; si deum, divinus.*

SPENER:—Every age should diligently cultivate the virtue becoming it before others, which is especially done by each particular age applying its natural gifts to the growth of life (understanding in the case of the old, strength in the case of young men, simplicity in the case of children).—Those who have overcome Satan as young men, may afterwards truly and fully know Christ as fathers, while those who have served him do not easily attain such knowledge, which is a kind of reward of grace.—The word of God does not only *come to us*, but *abides* also *in us*, and consequently is not a dead or passing sound.—That which does not abide forever is not worthy of our love; for God has created, appointed and called us unto eternal things.

STARKE:—Preachers should particularly urge obedience to the commandments of God, and renunciation of the love of the world on the plea of the grace of God in the forgiveness of sins, as a more powerful incentive than considerations founded on the Law.—Although you have conquered the devil once, he will return and assault you with sevenfold strength to rob you of your crown. Therefore, ye warriors of Jesus, grow not secure, but think that your task is not done with one well-fought battle.—O the deluded souls that fancy that it is the privilege of their rank to use the world at their pleasure, to lead a worldly and carnal life, and to be good Christians for all! They will terribly deceive themselves, for the mere name is not sufficient.—Christians, would you love the Father, you must content yourselves with the necessaries of the body, bridle your eyes, and lead a life of simplicity.—The world and its lusts pass swiftly away; like an arrow cuts through the air, like smoke blows away, like a river flows along, like a bird flies past, like a sound dies away. What folly to set one's hope and pleasure on such changeable and transitory things!—It is well, but not enough to know the will of God, we must do it in the strength of God, with all diligence, at all times, in all things, if we would abide forever.—It is a great mercy of God that He accepts our poor, imperfect doing, provided it be done with a childlike heart, as the doing of His will.—None can do the will of God without denying his own will; for the will of God and corruptible self-will are utterly opposed to each other.

HEUBNER:—*Fathers* are spiritual adults, matured Christians; they have known Christ, the Son of God, from personal experience, made proof of His power, or He has been fully formed in them (Eph. iv. 13; 1 Thess. ii. 7, 11; Heb. v. 14). The image of Christ has a feeble and tender beginning in childhood; it continues growing in youth, but does not attain perfect clearness with open face until manhood. No warrior can go beyond this: Christ and His knowledge excel all perfection. We have here the case of souls that long since have acquired forgiveness and cleansing from their sins, overcome the wicked one, stood severe trials and hard conflicts, in victory have been planted in the likeness of Christ's death, and made experience of the power of His resurrection. As *fathers* they possess *spiritual generative powers*. They are the mellow old wine. They are called τέλειοι, they are the nearest friends of the Lord, His intimates, that have a better understanding of His counsel: but, although thus highly raised by God, they never divest themselves of their childlike disposition. The sense of redemption in Christ, true poverty of spirit, voluntary and constant self-denial and strong love are their characteristics. But they still stand in need of instruction and caution (an *old* Christian had been victorious in the fight for thirty-nine years, but was overcome in the fortieth year.) They must fight *senectute contra senectutem*. They have more works than words. They are engaged in ceaseless intercessions for all the people of God, and gather riches for the children (2 Cor. xii. 14). But they must be very careful not to usurp an authority and power, in virtue of which they require others blindly and unconditionally to follow and agree with them; the moment they fall into this snare they cease to be fathers, and become the destroyers of the Christlike spirit in the children.—*Young men* are those who are still engaged in active warfare, and have to fear most the assaults of the flesh, the world and the devil; they ought to have begun to taste the better delights [of religion] and should overcome Satan. Hence they are always prepared for the battle. He that has become a true child of God must not care for the age of youth. Can any one, by anxious care, add one cubit unto his stature [age]? He that preserves that which he has, to him shall be given more; the process of growth is imperceptible (Mark iv. 28). They ought to have the spirit of power and vigilance; as valiant soldiers they must always be at their post, warring against the enemy. Their dangers are rashness, undue ardor, temerity and negligence. They must have work to do, they must destroy Babylon, but abstain from all things, and fight faithfully unto death. They must not be discouraged in the first ardor of their zeal, for that first ardor may lose its intensity. Their strength will be in proportion to their allowing their strength quietly to strike root; even Christ walked in silence and retirement during His youth, and John was in the wilderness. They must learn to enter into the mystery of godliness, abstain from *their* doing in order that *God may work in them*, that thus they may resist the πονηρός, the spoiler, who comes from without and forces his way into them, and would fain seize the youthful warriors. Hence they need circumspection and weapons (Eph. vi).—*Children* are beginners in Christianity who have already tasted the paternal love of God, who receive from the Father more tokens of love, as it were, more caressing. But they must be truly born of God, have a new mind, the Spirit of adoption whereby they cry Abba, Father. Their general characteristics are these: a childlike disposition, lowliness, obedience, sincerity, joyfulness. Their childlike failings are: credulity, carelessness, rashness, inconstancy, or even wandering from the simplicity in Christ. They are strongly attached to the sweet taste of grace. They require oversight, guidance, nursing, care, keeping; they require milk until they are able to take stronger food and grow. (Here we may refer to the choral divisions among the *unitas fratrum:* children, older boys, single brethren, single sisters, the chorus of married people, widowers and widows, to the *incipientes*, *proficientes* and *profecti* of the Moravians, and to the analogies of paganism, Plato *de legg.* II., where the chorus of boys, of young men to the age of thirty, of men to the age of sixty, used fascinatingly to implant the true and the good into the minds of the people in songs, and Plutarch *lacon. instit.* according to which, among the Spartans, *old men* used to sing: "Once we were vigorous youths;" *men*, "We are so; if thou desirest it, try;" and the *boys*, "Some day we shall even be better").—*Love* is the noblest power in man, which he ought not to waste on unworthy objects, but he ought to love God only.—The world is set before men to try them, whether they will lay hold of it or of heavenly things.—The objects of our desires, as far as they are creatures, are not evil in themselves (1 Tim. iv. 4; 1 Cor. x. 26), but the passionate desire of them is evil, and of the evil spirit. The *excusatio* of worldlings is: "it is natural, it is innocent." That is to lay the responsibility of sin on God.—Worldly-mindedness and religion are incompatible. There are, indeed, many degrees of this worldly-mindedness and fondness of worldly pleasures, but this much is certain: 1. Those in whom this fondness is strong and supreme, to whom non-gratification causes anger and a blank, are without the divine life. 2. Every worldly pleasure, though indifferent of itself, becomes sin if it leads astray from God, and has to be enjoyed without God. 3. In proportion to the growth of religion is the decrease of a mind and taste for worldly lusts, and *vice versa*.—It is disgraceful in clergymen [Germ. *Geistliche*, a technical term for clergymen, of which the English *divines* is the nearest approximation, or we may also say "*spiritual* and *secular*," but, of course, without any reference to the Roman Catholic use of these terms—M.], who ought to be the opposite of the worldly, to exhibit worldliness in the bias of their mind and conversation.—What comes of the transitoriness of the world and of the things which lust desires? What harm does it do to the worldly? 1. Even in respect of this earthly life it is painful and humiliating to take pleasure in enjoyments which are wholly idle and transient, and leave behind them nothing that is refreshing or ennobling, but, perhaps, something that will fill the mind with gloom, paralyze and deject the spirit—a melancholy blank. 2. This holds good still more in respect of the life to come. The objects will cease, but not the desire, which will then lack the instruments and means of its gratification. Painful condition. Such a soul will then behold itself in its miserable emptiness and vileness. Therefore consider the transitoriness and consequences of every sinful lust. (Oriental saying: The treasures of the world are so constituted that they will deprive thee of life, if thou gatherest them).—

NEANDER:—It is not part of the nature of the love of God that we must retire from the world and worldly things, but rather that we should use them according to the purpose which God has assigned to all men, to His glory.

DESSER.—The forgiveness of sins is the bread on which the great and the small, Apostles and malefactors, the wise and the illiterate, kings and beggars (kings as beggars, and beggars as kings), live in the kingdom of God, even as the fourth and fifth petitions of the Lord's Prayer are significantly joined together by *and*.

JOHANN BUGENHAGEN's motto was: "*Si Christum bene scis, satis est, si cetera nescis: si Christum nescis, nil est, si cetera discis.*"

LEO THE GREAT:—There are two kinds of love from which proceeds every lust according to its kind: man, who cannot exist without love, loves either God or the world.

SPENER.—This *either—or* is an established thing which will never yield the place to an *as well—as*. To contribute one cent to ungodliness is as much as to give up to it the whole. St Bernard calls pride the arch-artificer of fraud and the true fountain of vice, the tinder of sin the rust of virtues, the moth of holiness, the beguiler of hearts, that turns medicine into poison and cordials into stupefying draughts. A soul has nothing in eternity but what it has gathered in time.

NITZSCH:—The principal question of the divine word addressed to fathers: Do you know Him that is from the beginning? Let us consider: 1. Why this question is peculiarly suited to the *aged?* The excellency and glory of old age is experience, its natural avocation to gather and to have gathered it, its supreme requirement to have wisdom by and in experience. How much more important is it to have *seen* and *felt* a thing, to have *shared* its suffering, than merely to have *heard of it!* 2. Which *knowledge* does it speak of? The First and the Last has been revealed in the centre of history, He by whom and for whom all things consist; time has become conscious of eternity. Humanity has been raised from profound misery to high glory. This knowledge compensates the eye for every unavoidable want of light, supplies the solution of many riddles, finds the kernel of many experiences, marks the holy line of human effort, cherishes the sweet hope of beholding [God], and thinks well done that which God doeth. 3. The great *monition* and the glorious *consolation* contained therein. Many things improve by age, but not the fundamental error, erring from God. Self-will and unbelief do not break spontaneously by mere events; the secret will of the natural man grows to a fearful height and resoluteness; rather die in sins than present oneself blind and naked, miserable and poor before the only Mediator, the Conqueror on the cross. Do you *still* know Him, do you know Him *again?* Be overcome and ye shall conquer; His knowledge rejuvenates you like eagles, makes you wise, and crowns all knowledge and experience with faith in the eternal words. *The monition of the divine word to young men that they have overcome the wicked one.* Regard it—1, as a *congratulation on their participation in the victory of Christ*, but also as *a threefold test-inquiry of the reality of their Christianity.* After the victory of Christ, the time of the mere doubtful struggle between the death and life of mankind, the time of invincible sin, of the immeasurable progress of corruption, belongs to the remote past. If you fear *already*, or are *still* afraid in this world, be of good courage and know that you enter into a reconciled world, and stand in eternal peace, and partake of a happiness and liberty that have not to be fought for and devised, but may be seized and enjoyed in true faith. But here you have to *inquire after faith in this word*,—since the tendency prevails not to believe that which was believed by the fathers; many, all believe to indemnify themselves for childlike faith with the conceits of the unvanished beauty of the world, of the power of the mind of man and of the innocence and goodness of the heart of man,—to inquire after the *knowledge* of this truth, after the *decision and conversion of the heart*, whether that will reigns supreme which says, How should I do this great evil and sin against my God? whether you are consciously or unconsciously under the jurisdiction of the prince of this world, and unfitted for the true work of your calling. . . . 2. As *a call to resistance*, and at the same time as a *promise of assistance*. This bears on your bravery, your honour, your independence, ye that are in such hurry to be men. There are many adversaries from without that reappear again and again; fight the invisible battles in your souls. It is good for a man to have worn the yoke in his youth, but how much better this yoke; thus you will gain a clear and pure view of your future, thus you spend the time of your transitory youth for the purpose of securing eternal youth, thus you care to-day for to-morrow and ever, even unto the judgment; all things are yours.

Hast thou broken with the world? 1. Art thou perhaps still wholly entangled in its lust? 2. Art thou convinced that it is impossible to love God and the world at the same time? 3. Dost thou daily fight victoriously against the lust of the world tempting thee?

What is the Christian's relation to the world? 1. He knows that its lust, without any exception, is sin (v. 16), and such sin as is incompatible with the Christian profession (v. 15), and on this very account 2. He shuns and flies it (v. 15).

Consider how little the love of the world comports with sincere conversion towards God. 1. The latter imposes renunciation of the world and its lust as a necessary condition. 2. It affords strength for overcoming the world. 3. And is itself a continued combat with the temptations of the world.

The infamy of a Christian being the slave of worldly lust. 1. He thereby enters the service of worldly vanity, 2. becomes the enemy of God, and 3. will perish with the world (L. in "*Gesetz und Zeugniss*" for 1860).—

[Ezekiel Hopkins:—v. 15. "For these things (Pleasures, Riches, Honours), though they make a fair and gaudy show, yet it is all but show and appearance. As bubbles, blown into the air, will represent great variety of orient and glittering colours, not, as some suppose, that there are any such really there, but only they appear so to us, through a false reflection of light cast upon them: so truly this world, this earth on which we live, is nothing else but a great bubble blown up by the breath of God in the midst of the air, where it now hangs. It sparkles with ten thousand glories: not that they are so in themselves, but only they seem so to us through the false light by which we look upon them. If we come to grasp it, it breaks and leaves nothing but wind and disappointment in our hands: as histories report of the fruits that grow near the Dead sea, where once Sodom and Gomorrah stood, they appear very fair and beautiful to the eye, but if they be crushed, turn straight to smoke and ashes."

There is nothing in the world vain in respect of its natural being or of God the Creator—but all the vanity that is in worldly things, is only in respect of the sin and folly of man. [Augustine: "*Utendum est hoc mundo, non fruendum; ut invisibilia Dei, per ea quæ facta sunt, intelligantur; hoc est, ut de temporalibus æterna capiantur.*"—M.]

The vanity of the world appears in:

1. That all its glory and splendour depend merely on opinion and fancy.

2. In its deceitfulness and treachery. It is not only vanity, but a lying vanity.

3. As all things in the world are lying vanities, so are they all vexatious. "Uncertain comforts but most certain crosses."

4. A little cross will embitter great comforts—another mark of the vanity of the world.

5. The longer we enjoy any worldly thing, the more flat and insipid doth it grow.

6. All the pleasure of the world is nothing else but a tedious repetition of the same things.

7. The world can stand us in no stead, when we have the greatest need of support and comfort.

8. All things in the world are vain, because they are unsuitable.

The soul is spiritual and immortal, worldly things are material and perishable.

Its wants are spiritual—but the world supplies only material wants.

9. The vanity of the world appears in its inconstancy and fickleness and—

10. In that it is altogether unsatisfactory.—M.].

[Barrow:—The *world* is an enemy, an irreconcilable enemy to our salvation. The world, that is, the wicked principles, the bad customs, the naughty conversation and example which commonly prevail here among men; alluring to evil and deterring from good; the cares also, the riches, the pleasures, the glories of the world, which possess or distract the minds, satiate and cloy the desires, employ all the affections and endeavours, take up the time of men; all in the world which fasteneth our hearts to earth, and to those low transitory things; or which sink them down toward hell and which detain them from soaring toward heaven.

The world passeth away and the desire (ἐπιθυμία) *thereof;* whatever seemeth most lovely and desirable in the world is very flitting; however, our desire and our enjoyment thereof must suddenly cease. Imagine a man, therefore, possessed of all worldly goods, armed with power, flourishing in credit, flowing with plenty, swimming in all delight (such as were sometime Priamus, Polycrates, Crœsus, Pompey) yet since he is withal supposed a man, and mortal, subject both to fortune and death, none of those things can he reasonably confide or much satisfy himself in; they may be violently divorced from him by fortune, they must naturally be loosed from him by death; the closest union here cannot last longer than till death us depart; wherefore no man upon such account can truly call, or, if he consider well, heartily esteem himself happy; a man cannot hence receive profit or content from any labour he taketh under the sun. (Eccles. i. 3 sqq.)—M.].

[On ἀλαζονεία τοῦ βίου v. 16. "It was a pertinent discourse of Cineas, dissuading Pyrrhus from undertaking a war against the Romans. Sir, saith he, when you have conquered them, what will you do next? Then Sicily is near at hand, and easy to master.—And what when you have subdued Sicily? Then we will pass over to Africa and take Carthage, which cannot long withstand us.—When these are conquered, what will be your next attempt?—Then we will fall in upon Greece and Macedon and recover what we have lost there.—Well, when all are subdued, what fruit do you expect from all your victories? Then we will sit down and enjoy ourselves. Sir, replied Cineas, may we not do it now? Have you not already a kingdom of your own? and he that cannot enjoy himself with a kingdom, cannot with the world." Plutarch *in Vita Pyrrhi.*—M.].

[PYLE (v. 12–14):—The cautions I here give you ought to be equally regarded by all degrees of Christian professors. The new converts and younger Christians are to consider themselves as newly put into a state of salvation, the pardon of sin, and the favour of God, through Jesus Christ; and to endeavour to confirm themselves in it by the careful practice of true Christian virtue. Such as are come to more maturity in their profession and are in the strength and vigour of their age, have a great advantage, and ought to employ the utmost of that vigour in resisting the strongest temptations of the devil, and perfecting their conquest over him and all his wicked instruments. And the aged Christians cannot but have so dear a knowledge of God, and the revelation of His will by Jesus Christ, during the long season from their first conversion, that it would be utterly inexcusable for them to be wanting in their essential duties or be drawn from them by the false teachers.—M.].

[VER. 12. SIMEON, C., The different growth and privileges of God's children. Works xx. 393

VV. 13. 14. MARSHALL, N., Peculiar temptations attending every stage of life, with the special advantages and counter-motives that are found in each, considered particularly with regard to old age.

The temptations that most endanger our first stage of life, with the duties most incumbent upon us in that early period, and the motives to discharge them.

Peculiar temptations treated in reference to such as are in the bloom and vigour of life. Sermons, iv. 433, 459, 485.

VER. 15. FULLER, THOS., An ill match well broken off. Joseph's party-coloured coat.

VV. 15–17. BOSSUET, Traité de la Concupiscence. Œuvres, xiv. 26.—M.].

---

7. *Warning and consolation against Anti-Christ.*

DESCRIPTION OF HIS FORERUNNERS, WHOSE APPEARANCE POINTS TO THE LAST TIME (VV. 18–23). EXHORTATION OF THE FAITHFUL TO STEADFASTNESS IN THEIR ASSURANCE OF POSSESSING THE TRUTH AND ETERNAL LIFE (V. 24–28).

CHAPTER ii, 18–28.

18 Little children, it is the last time[1], and as ye have heard that[2] antichrist[3] shall come,
even now are[4] there many antichrists; whereby[5] we know that it is the last time[6].
19 They went out from us[7], but they were not of us; for if they had been of us, they
would *no doubt*[8] have continued[9] with us: but *they went out*[10], that they might be
20 made manifest that they were[11] not all of us. But[12] ye have an[13] unction from the
21 Holy One, and ye[14] know all things[15]. I have not written unto you because ye know
22 not the truth, but because ye know it, and that no lie is of the truth[16]. Who is
a[17] liar but he that denieth that Jesus is the Christ? He[18] is antichrist, that
23 denieth the Father and the Son. Whosoever[19] denieth the Son, the same hath not
24 the Father[20]: [*but*] *he that acknowledgeth the Son hath the Father also*[21]. Let that
therefore abide in you, which ye have heard from the beginning[22]. If that which ye
have heard from the beginning shall remain in you, ye also shall continue in the Son,
25 and in the Father[23]. And this is the promise that he[24] hath promised us[25], *even* eternal
26 life[26]. These things have I written unto you concerning them that seduce you[27].
27 But the anointing which ye have received of him abideth in you[28], and ye need not
that any man teach you: but as the same[29] anointing teacheth you of all things, and
28 is truth[30], and is no lie, and even as it hath taught you, ye shall abide in him[31]. And
now, little children, abide in him; that when[32] he shall appear[33], we may have[34] confi-
dence, and not be ashamed before him[35] at his coming.

Verse 18. [1 ἐσχάτη ὥρα=the last *hour*.—M.].
2 B. C. Sin. read ὅτι after ἠκούσατε. *Est lectio difficilior.*
3 B. C. Sin. omit the Article before ἀντίχριστος. In Sin. it is clearly a later addition. It would hardly have been omitted, had it been originally there. [Lachm. Tisch. Buttm. reject it.—M.]
[4 German: "Even now have there come into existence" Lillie: "even now are there many *become* "—M.]
[5 ὅθεν=whence.—M.]
[6 German: "that there is a last hour." Lillie: "that it is the last hour."—M.]

Verse 19. [7 Better to retain the Greek order with German: "From us they went out."—ἐξῆλθαν, A. B. C Lach Tisch. Buttm. Huther, is more authentic than ἐξῆλθον G. K., but less common.—M.]

[[8] *No doubt* supplied by E. V. is arbitrary and unnecessary.—M.]

[[9] No reason why μεμενήκεισαν should be rendered "*continued*," since "abode" makes as good sense here as other forms of the same verb in other places. Better to render μένειν uniformly *abide*.—M.]

[[10] German: "but—that they might be made manifest," *i. e.* nothing is supplied, although the context requires something to be supplied. E. V. supplies "they went out," Beza, following the Syriac "*egressi sunt ex nobis*," Wakefield: "this was done," Newcome, "this hath come to pass," Lillie "it was," etc. See below in Exeget. and Critical.—M.]

[[11] German: "that not all are from us" better than the more inferential rendering advocated by Lillie "that none of them are of us," and the less correct translation of E. V. "that they *were* not all of us."

Verse 20. [[12] German: "And." There seems to be no necessity for "but," although καί may here have slightly adversative force.—M.]

[[13] German omits the Article before unction and renders "and ye have unction."—M.]

[[14] German omits "ye;" B. omits καί before οἴδατε.—M.]

[15] B. Sin read πάντες instead of πάντα, August. "*Ut ipsi vobis manifesti sint.*"

Verse 21. [[16] German: "and that every thing which is lie is not out of the truth," but the rendering of E. V. is a happy inferential translation of the Greek idiom.—M.]

Verse 22. [[17] German: "who is *the* liar." The Article is emphatic here and must be retained.—M.]

[[18] German: "This is the antichrist, who." οὗτος has demonstrative force.—M.]

Verse 23. [[19] German: "Every one that denieth;" *omnis qui*, Vulg. Aug. Calv. Bengel, and "every one that" Greenfield, Allioli, de Wette, Lillie.—M.]

[[20] German: "Hath also not the Father." Better render with *Rhemish* and most foreign versions "neither hath he the Father."—M.]

[21] A. B. C. Sin. [Griesb., Scholz, Lachm., Tisch. Buttm. Wordsw. Lillie.—M.] have the final clause: "ὁ ὁμολογῶν τὸν υἱὸν καὶ τὸν πατέρα ἔχει," and it is required by the parallel passage 2 Jno. 9 as well as by John's fondness of antithesis. [ὁμολογῶν however should be rendered "confesseth" and not "acknowledgeth" as in E. V.—M.]

Verse 24. [[22] German: "You, that which ye have heard from the beginning, let that abide in you." In this rendering οὖν is left out; but the emphatic *you*, in the sense of *as for you*, is decidedly in favour of the German rendering; translate, "you, let that which ye have heard from the beginning, *abide* in you."—A. B. C. Sin. Vulg. al. omit οὖν. M.]

[[23] German: "If that *abide* in you which ye have heard from the beginning, ye also shall *abide* in the Son and in the Father." The three-fold rendering of μένω in one verse: "*abide, remain, continue*," adopted in E. V. should by all means be avoided. Lillie calls this sacrificing of the simple beauty and force of the original to "a great number of good English" words an "unprofitable exuberance."—M.]

Verse 25. [[24] German: "And this is the promise which He *Himself*;" αὐτός. The reference seems to be to an *oral* promise.—M.]

[25] A. C. Sin. read ἡμῖν. The context warrants the transition to the Plural.

[[26] German: "*The* eternal life." The supplement in E. V. is hardly necessary, the Article is indispensable and the order "life eternal" seems preferable; see on the last point E. V. Matth. xxv. 46; Jno. iv. 36; xvii. 3; Rhemish version, Wakef. Macknight, Berleburg Bible, and Lillie.—M.]

Verse 26. [[27] πλανώντων ὑμᾶς, "who would deceive you." "The context (vv. 20. 21. 27) shows that this is a case of the Present '*de conatu, i. e.* an *endeavour* or *purpose*' (Buttm. § 137. n. 10), and so it is generally understood." Lillie.—M.]

Verse 27. [[28] German: "And you—the ointment which ye received from Him, abideth in you."—M.]

[29] τὸ αὐτοῦ χρῖσμα is the reading of C. Sin., many versions (Syr. *unctio quæ est a Deo*) and fathers instead of τὸ αὐτὸ χρῖσμα A. B. G. K. and the Greek fathers.—Cod. Sin. reads really πνεῦμα afterwards corrected into χρῖσμα [or χάρισμα]; B reads χάρισμα. [But both in point of authority and in point of sense τὸ αὐτὸ χρῖσμα seems to be the right reading. German, following the less authentic reading, renders "but as the ointment of Him;" E. V. follows τὸ αὐτὸ χρῖσμα.—M.]

[[30] καὶ ἀληθές ἐστι=and is true, better than "and is truth" of E. V.—M.]

[31] The reading μένετε A. B. C. Sin. is on external and internal grounds preferable to μενεῖτε [G. K. al. Tisch.—M.]

Verse 28. [32] A. B. C. Sin. read ἵνα ἐὰν instead of ἵνα ὅταν [G. K. Theoph. Oecum. Tisch.—M.]

[[33] German: "shall be manifested" decidedly preferable both for the sake of uniformity and on doctrinal grounds ("the agency and love of the Father in the second as well as the first coming of the Saviour" Lillie) to "when He shall appear" E. V.—M.]

[34] σχῶμεν.—B and Cod. Sin. give it as a correction of ἔχωμεν.

[[35] German: "and not be put to shame away from Him in His coming." Calvin: *Pudefiamus ab ejus præsentiâ;* Steph. *ab eo discedamus pudefacti;* Hammond: "Turned with shame from Him;" Green and Bloomfield: "shrink from Him with shame;" Peile: "put to confusion of face *as being* cast away from Him." Wordsworth: "Driven to shame from Him;" Lillie: "Shamed away from Him at His coming."—M.]

EXEGETICAL AND CRITICAL.

The connection. The groundwork on which this portion of the Epistle rests is contained in the individualized addresses (v. 12–14), introducing both warning and consolation against the love of the world (v. 15–17), as well as in the subsequent warning and consolation against antichrist (v. 18–28). As the former particularly connected with the final clause νενικήκατε τὸν πονηρόν whose kingdom is ὁ κόσμος, so this connects with ἐγνώκατε τὸν ἀπ' ἀρχῆς, τὸν πατέρα, ὁ λόγος τοῦ θεοῦ ἐν ὑμῖν μένει. The opening words ἐσχάτη ὥρα ἐστίν in the sequel (v. 18) connect also with ὁ κόσμος παράγεται (v. 17). This portion which began (ch. i. 5 sq.) with the Light–Being of God and the Light–walk of believers, concludes with a warning against the lie which is directed against the fundamental pillar of eternal truth, the glory of Christ, and an exposure of its attempt to annihilate the promise of eternal life. The *address* παιδία, v. 18, applies to all the readers of the Epistle, and requires us to consider the sequel addressed to the whole Church (contrary to Bengel). It is incomprehensible that Ebrard on account of the peculiarly childlike character of this section should hold the opinion that the reference is only to the little ones, to children.

The last hour, v. 18. This important and difficult idea, which is liable to many interpretations and has been variously understood, can only be understood and explained with reference to the whole *usus loquendi* current and the sum-total of clear views on the subject contained in the New Testament. It is not sufficient to refer the reader to Lange on Matth. xxiv., Moll on Heb. i. 1, and Fronmüller on 1 Pet. i. 5. 20. Compare particularly Riehm, *Lehrbegriff des Hebräerbriefs*, pp. 72 sqq.; 204 sqq., and Düsterdieck *ad loc.*—The representation of two ages of the world is rooted in the Old Testament idea

באחרית הימים which constantly recurs in prophetical passages, beginning with the blessing of Jacob (Gen. xlix. 1), especially in Jeremiah, denotes "the most distant future, beyond which the eye cannot penetrate" (Hitzig on Mich. iv. 1), and is therefore well rendered by "in the end of the days." The prophets use it almost exclusively to denote the Messianic times. The LXX. translate it ἐν ἐσχάταις ἡμέραις (Is. ii. 2), ἐπ' ἐσχάτων τῶν ἡμερῶν (Gen. xlix. 1), ἐπ' ἐσχάτου τῶν ἡμερῶν (Numb. xxiv. 14), ἐπ' ἐσχάτῳ τῶν ἡμερῶν (Deut. iv. 30), ἔσχατον τῶν ἡμερῶν (Deut. xxxi. 29). Hence comes primarily the *talmudical* and *rabbinical* idea of the עולם הזה and the עולם הבא; inside these two ages of the world are the ימות המשיח, the days of the Messiah, *the Messianic age proper*, which is alternately counted with either age of the world, and consequently may be either *after* or *before* the end of the days, or *the end* of the days itself. The Lord Himself distinguishes ἐν τούτῳ τῷ αἰῶνι from ἐν τῷ μέλλοντι (Matth. xii. 30), ἐν τῷ καιρῷ τούτῳ from ἐν τῷ αἰῶνι τῷ ἐρχομένῳ (Mark x. 30; Luke xviii. 30); and this distinction, as well as Luke xx. 34, sq. (*οἱ υἱοὶ τοῦ αἰῶνος τούτου γαμοῦσιν —οἱ δὲ καταξιωθέντες τοῦ αἰῶνος ἐκείνου τυχεῖν καὶ τῆς ἀναστάσεως τῆς ἐκ νεκρῶν*) show most plainly that the earthly development-period of the kingdom of God preceding the second coming of Christ in glory, and beginning with the first coming of Christ in the flesh, belongs to the first age of the world, and that the future time is the time of the completed kingdom of God. According to this ἡ ἐσχάτη ἡμέρα (Jno. vi. 39, 40, 44, 54; xi. 24; xii. 48) is the day of the resurrection of the dead and the judgment, the last day of the first age of the world and the transition to the second. The turning-point between both ages of the world is *the time of Christ's return to judgment* (Matth. xiii. 39 sq.; 49; xxiv. 3; xxviii. 20). Thus Paul also contrasts ἐν τῷ αἰῶνι τούτῳ with ἐν τῷ μέλλοντι, and the sufferings τοῦ νῦν καιροῦ with the μέλλουσα δόξα (Rom. viii. 18), and describes Christians as living ἐν τῷ νῦν αἰῶνι looking for the blessed' hope and the glorious appearing of the great God and our Saviour Jesus Christ (Tit. ii. 12. 13). The ἔσχαται ἡμέραι in which there shall come καιροὶ χαλεποὶ (2 Tim. iii. 1), and the ὕστεροι καιροί (1 Tim. iv. 1), like the αἰῶνες οἱ ἐπερχόμενοι (Eph. ii. 7), denote the period immediately preceding the second coming of Christ. While, according to Paul, Christians still live outwardly *in* the first age of the world, yet are they *ethically* beyond it and the character of this present age of the world is described by him as tainted with immorality and alienation from God, Rom. xii. 2; 1 Cor. ii. 6. 8; iii. 18; 2 Cor. iv. 4; Gal. i. 4; Eph. ii. 2; 2 Tim. iv. 10. He regarded also the present age of the world as running on towards its end since the first coming of Christ; hence he speaks of τὰ τέλη τῶν αἰώνων (1 Cor. x. 11) having set in. We have not to inquire here whether he regarded the second coming of Christ to be near at hand.—Peter considers his time as the ἔσχαται ἡμέραι (Acts ii. 17) and laid the first coming of Christ ἐπ' ἐσχάτου τῶν χρόνων (1 Pet. i. 20 cf. v. 5: ἐν καιρῷ ἐσχάτῳ or τῶν ἡμερῶν, 2 Pet. iii. 3 cf. Jude 18).—So also James: (v. 13: ἐν ἐσχάταις ἡμέραις).—In the Epistle to the Hebrews also the close of the first age of the world is described as beginning with the first coming of Christ (ch. i. 1), but the συντέλεια τῶν αἰώνων denotes the turning-point of the two ages of the world, ch. ix. 26, and this turning-point is more particularly described as found in the sacrificial death of Christ on account of its important consequences (ch. x. 14; xi. 39. 40), since that which is eternal, is now extant (Χριστὸς—ἀρχιερεὺς τῶν μελλόντων ἀγαθῶν ch. ix. 11; cf. v. 14; x. 1. 18; vi. 5; xii. 22). The beginning of the new time has set in, but only the ideal and objective beginning; since the αἰὼν μέλλων as to the δύναμις is already extant in the redeemed, but will not enter into ἐνέργεια until the second coming of Christ (ch. xiii. 14), so that the first age of the world still continues outwardly and that consequently our time is only a transition-period; with respect to the ethical sense of these ideas we have here the point of contact between the Epistle to the Hebrews and the views of Paul.—John's ἐσχάτη ὥρα ἐστίν must be understood as lying within the limits of these views. The use of ὥρα instead of ἡμέρα, the day which with God is equal to a thousand years (Ps. xc. 4; 2 Pet. iii. 8), indicates a peculiar feature, and the absence of the Article leaves it undefined. We have to think of a period of time belonging to the last days or last times which exhibits their character in a concentrated form, and since the ἐσχάτη ἡμέρα in the Gospel adverts particularly to the κρίσις, the reference seems to be to peculiarly *critical* manifestations. If now we have to translate: "*it is the last hour*," the reference to the antichrist and the antichrists is in admirable keeping with the announcements of the coming of false prophets and teachers for the purpose of temptation and trial, so that in them there already takes place a separation of true believers from false believers. Cf. Matth. xxiv. 24 sqq.; 1 Tim. iv. 1 sqq.; 2 Tim. iii. 1 sqq.—Hence ὥρα is neither=the season of the year, the wintry season of the world (Scholiast II), nor ἐσχάτη=χειρίστη (Oecumen., Schöttgen: *tempora periculosa, pessima et abjectissima*, Carpzov and others), which is also forbidden by 2 Tim. iii. 1. Bengel's explanation that it denotes the last hour of John's old age (*ultima, non respectu omnium mundi temporum, sed in antitheto puerulorum, ad patres et juvenes*), is a singular make-shift in order to guard John from the error that his prediction of the last hour had not been fulfilled. Nor can ἐσχάτη ὥρα designate the time immediately preceding *the destruction of Jerusalem* (Socinus, Grotius), for the last time is not to be taken with such chronological precision. Nor is there any warrant for the assertion of Huther, that John wrote with a *presentiment* of the second coming of Christ (an assertion based on what is said v. 8 of the σκοτία and v. 17 of the κόσμος, that they παράγεται which simply marks the transitory character inhering in the σκοτία and the κόσμος), since he writes only under the impression and with a sense of the transitoriness of the powers of this first age of the world, and that he indicates thereby the nearness of Christ's second coming (Lücke, Neander, Baumgarten-Crusius, Gerlach, Ebrard, Huther). Hence we may say with Düsterdieck that "John did not wish to supply a *chronological* but only a *real* definition" [that is, one relating simply to the object—M.], which is clearly indicated by ἐὰν φανερωθῇ (v. 28), since ὅταν is hardly the true reading there. "The prophetical substance of the Apostolical declaration is true," "the extension of the time from the *real* beginning (the destruction of Jerusalem, which does not disconcert John, and of the import of which, with reference to the history and the judgment of the world, his mind is fully made up), to the actual end of beings" denotes rather no measure at all than one that is too short. The first Messianic transition-period inaugurated by the Saviour in the form of a servant, governed by Him and terminating the first age of the world is the ἐσχάτη, during which men pass through peculiar troubles, perils and conflicts on to the promised advent of the second world-age of glory. In this transition-period there are however peculiar hours of development, one of which had come when John wrote his Epistle. The term ἐσχάτη ὥρα has therefore to be taken in a prophetical and eschatological sense; it has moreover an important bearing on *the history of Christ's kingdom* and constitutes a *historical* reference to the *second coming* of Christ as the commencement of the second world-age, but not a *chronological* reference to the *time when* the second coming is to take place.—Noteworthy is Calvin's explanation: *ultimum tempus, in quo sic complentur omnia, ut nihil supersit præter ultimam Christi revelationem*, and with reference to the absence of the Article also that of Besser: the time before a special revelation of the judicatory glory of Christ prefiguring *the* last hour before the universal final judgment.—

The Antichrist and the Antichrists. v. 18.

1. The word ἀντίχριστος occurs only here, v. 22; iv. 3 and 2 Jno. 7. and its meaning has to be ascertained first philologically and then exegetically.

2. ἀντὶ may mean both hostility and substitution. In the former case it denotes the antagonist of Christ, the *anti*christ, in the latter the *pretender*-Christ or *pseudo*-Christ. Thus ἀντίτυπος is a τύπος set in opposition to another τύπος, and ἀντίλυτρον a λύτρον, paid or given for something; so ἀντίθεος in Homer, denotes *godlike*, but other authors use it in the sense of *adverse to the gods; one and the same* word may then be used in *both* senses; but no word can have both meanings in one and the same place; hence we must not endeavour to combine the ideas of *anti*-Christ and *pretender*-Christ as Huther maintains ("the enemy of Christ, who, under the lying appearance of being the true Christ, endeavours to destroy the work of Christ"), although it must be conceded that the enemy of Christ appears at the same time with the pretension of being able to supply His place, of becoming His substitute, and that the pretender-Christ does occupy His place in hostility to Him. But the ἀντίχριστοι manifestly cannot be taken in this double sense. And still less allowable is it with Sander first to attach to the word in the Singular the sense of pseudo-Christ and mimic of Christ, and then immediately afterwards to make the Plural designate the enemies of Christ. We cannot get on purely philological considerations beyond the possibility of taking the word in one or the other of said senses.

3. We have to hold fast the fact that the word denotes *persons*. This is required of the Plural ἀντίχριστοι in v. 19: ἐξ ἡμῶν ἐξῆλθαν, οὐκ ἦσαν ἐξ ἡμῶν, μεμενήκεισαν μεθ' ἡμῶν. But if the ἀντίχριστοι are persons, then ἀντίχριστος must also be a person, for this is required by ἔρχεται. Hence *Bengel's* exposition is incorrect: "*Sive id vocabulum phrasis apostolica, sive sermo fidelium introduxit, Johannes errores, qui oriri possent, prævisurus, non modo* antichristum, *sed etiam* antichristos *vult dici; et ubi* antichristum vel spiritum antichristi vel deceptorem et antichristum *dicit, sub singulari numero omnes* mendaces *et veritatis inimicos innuit. Quemadmodumque* Christus *interdum pro* christianismo (where?), *sic* antichristus *pro* antichristianismo *sive doctrina et multitudine hominum Christo contraria dicitur. Antichristum jam tum venire, ita assentitur Johannes, ut non unum, sed multos, id quod amplius quiddam et tristius esse censet, antichristos factos esse doceat. Sæpe totum genus eorum, qui bonam aliquam aut malem indolem habent, singulari numero cum articulo exprimitur* (Matth. xii. 35; xviii. 17. 29.). *Igitur* antichristus SIVE antichristianismus *ab extrema Johannis ætate* (see above: the last hour=old age!) *per omnem sæculorum tractum se propagavit et permanet, donec magnus ille adversarius exoritur.* This view is adopted by Lange, Baumgarten-Crusius, Besser and others.

4. We have here before us a law of historical development, a fixed ordinance of the history of the kingdom. The point in question is the ἐσχάτη ὥρα and the marks by which it may be known; the reference is to ἀντίχριστος ἔρχεται and to ἀντίχριστοι γεγόνασιν, to that which has happened νῦν, to that which is still to be looked for and has been announced (ἠκούσατε):

And as ye have heard (through the announcement of the Apostles) **that an antichrist cometh, even now have there come into existence many antichrists** (καὶ νῦν—γεγόνασι).—It is by no means allowable to insert *ita est* before καθὼς ἠκούσατε (Bengel): nor must the Present ἔρχεται be put on a line with γεγόνασι, so that the antichrist now cometh and is present even as the others also have appeared; nor must ἔρχεται and γεγόνασι, made equal in point of time, be only so distinguished from each other that the former comes *aliunde*, while these have come *ex nobis*. Γεγόνασι, they are become, they have come into existence, denotes the antichrists as a historical product, on whom the surrounding powers operating in time have operated. Hence it is not equal to *coeperunt esse* (Erasmus) but to "they are become, they are existing."—Ebrard incorrectly renders ἔρχεται=*is future*, although he correctly explains it by=*will some day appear*. The Future is implied in the idea of coming and the Present indicates the certainty of the event. [Huther: The Present ἔρχεται instead of the Future; it denotes the future as an event which is sure to occur.—M.]. Accordingly the ἀντίχριστοι exist before the ἀντίχριστος, who however is sure to follow them, and that which appears in the former, the προδρόμοις, only in an isolated, undeveloped and feeble form, is gathered together by the latter in his individual person, and developed in a powerful form. In the course of time malice will so surely become intensified and opposition to God and Christ will reach such a degree of development that the existence of many antichrists warrants the certain result of a future concentration and formation of this spirit in one person.

5. The *ἀντίχριστοι* come out of the Christian Church, they have themselves been Christians before (*ἐξ ἡμῶν ἐξῆλθαν* v. 19); the antichrist, in like manner, will of course come forth from the ranks of the Christians, he will also be a man. Hence *ἀντίχριστος* is not Satan himself (Pseudohippolytos, Theodoret); the idea of Satan becoming man is inexecutable, since the Eternal Word only, the Image of the Father, in which man has been created, can become man.

6. The antichrists deny that Jesus is the Christ (v. 22; iv. 3; 2 Jno. 7); that He did not come in the flesh, that He is not the Son of God, that He is not of God (ch. iv. 14 sqq.; v. 5 sqq.; v. 20 sq.). The doctrine is the denial of the truth, the *lie*, they themselves are LIARS, and according to John viii. 44, the children of the devil, of the father of the lie (ch. iii. 3–10). The Greeks strikingly observe: *ὁ ψεύστης, ἐναντίος ὢν τῇ ἀληθείᾳ, ἤτοι τῷ Χριστῷ, ἀντίχριστός ἐστιν* (Theophylact) and *ὁ ψεύστης τὸ τοῦ διαβόλου ὄνομα* (Scholiast II.). The antichrist and the antichrists are to be taken "as expressly connected with Satan" (Düsterdieck), and the two words here denote not substitution, but hostility to Christ exhibited in the form of eminent strength; the antichrist is pre-eminently the instrument and tool of Satan. Hence we have to exclude the exposition of Irenæus, Hippolytus, Cyrillus and others, that the antichrist was *tentans semet ipsum Christum ostendere*, and mimicking Christ.

7. The comparison of this passage with 2 Thess. ii. 1 sq. (Hofmann, *Heilige Schrift* I., p. 307 sqq.) requires this explanation. The name *ἀντίχριστος* used by John corresponds with the description given by Paul, *ἀντικείμενος καὶ ὑπεραιρόμενος ἐπὶ πάντα λεγόμενον θεὸν ἢ σέβασμα*, to denote his hostility with reference to his pretended ability to supply the place of God (*ὥστε αὐτὸν εἰς τὸν ναὸν του θεου καθισαι, ἀποδεικνύντα ἑαυτὸν ὅτι ἐστὶν θεός*). John contrasts the *πνεῦμα τοῦ ἀντιχρίστου* with the *πνεῦμα τοῦ θεοῦ*, while Paul calls him *ὁ ἄνθρωπος τῆς ἁμαρτίας, ὁ ἄνομος, ὁ υἱὸς τῆς ἀπωλείας*. His appearing also is preceded by an *ἀποστασία*, and he himself is the precursor of the *παρουσία τοῦ κυρίου ἡμῶν*, just as in John. But we must not overlook a difference belonging to this agreement. John speaks in a more general way, and uses less definite terms than Paul, who gives more distinct prominence to the person and approach of the dreaded and dreadful one; but he also refers to *τὸ κατέχον* and *ὁ κατέχων* as a power wielded by a living person, and specifies that for the benefit of the Church his progress will be arrested and his appearing delayed, thus pointing, like John, to a historical development. —Remembering all these particulars, we have, *first* of all, to reject those expositions which limit the application of the subject to a solitary historical fact or a single personage, and regard this statement of the Apostle in the light of a prophecy of a church-historical fact. Thus the Greek expositors, and many others (Augustine, Luther, Calvin, al.) after them apply it to heretics or heresiarchs, e. g., to Simon Magus, Cerinthus, Ebion, the Gnostics, to Basilides, Valentinus, and others, the Nicolaitanes (Rev. ii. 6) to Diotrephes (3 John 9.), Hymeneus and Philetus (2 Tim. ii. 17), and Grotius actually applies it to Barcochba, Calov to Mohammed, Luther (*Art. Schm. tract. de pot. et prim. papæ*, § 39; cf. Melanchthon, *Apol. Art.* VII. VIII., § 23; XV. § 18) to the pope, and Roman Catholics to Luther All this is purely arbitrary and unwarranted, and not only depreciates the word of prophecy, but actually deprives it of the prophetical element, as if it had ceased to be valid. *Secondly*, we have also to reject the modern exposition (both that of rationalistic commentators and that of Lücke, de Wette and Neander) which insists upon separating the *idea*, "that simultaneously with the development of Christianity, *evil* also would gradually increase in intensity, until having reached its culmination, it would be completely conquered by the power of Christ," from the *form* as here indicated, and that the form, as the mere shell, might be dropped. On the contrary, both the *idea* and the *form* have to be held fast, for we have here the expression of a law ever recurring in historical manifestations which belongs to the development of the history of the Kingdom [of God] up to and until the end of the time of Messiah and the Church, and this expression is so clearly and distinctly asserted that John feels warranted to draw the emphatic conclusion: "**whence we know that there is a last hour.**" By the appearing of many antichrists we may know and infer thence (*ὅθεν*) as from a distinct premise, that there is an onward progress in the direction of Christ's coming, which is preceded by the concentration of the antichristian element, thriving and luxuriating of course in different persons according to its different forms of manifestation. [On the different views of the antichrist see Lünemann on 2 Thess. ii. 1–12; p. 204 sqq., and Düsterdieck *ad locum;* also Trench, *Synonyms of the N. T.*, p. 145 sqq.—M.].

Relation of the Antichrists to the Church. First there is noted the fact that,

VER. 19. **From us they went out.**—The most natural and primary meaning of *ἡμῶν* is that it designates the Apostle and his readers, consequently the Church, which is addressed by *παιδία*, and to be understood in *ἠκούσατε*. The reference is neither to the Jews (Grotius, Rickli), nor to the Apostles only (Spener, Besser), nor only to the Church with exclusion of the children (Ebrard). Apart from the *form ἐξῆλθαν*, which in this very verb is by no means uncommon in the New Testament (Winer, pp. 86, 87), the sense is various: *prodire, exire, egredi, secedere.* Two ideas play into each other: origin and separation, coming out and going away. The nature of the *ἀντίχριστοι* who are engaged in the *ἀποστασία*, not *μεμενήκεισαν μεθ' ἡμῶν*, requires us to translate *secesserunt, evaserunt* (Augustine, Bede, Erasmus, Lücke, Düsterdieck, Ebrard, Huther). *Prodierunt* (Vulgate, al.) misapprehends the origin of the antichrists, and denotes origin only. *ἐξῆλθαν* does not point to their development and origin, but only to their separation, their apostasy, which ἐξ ἡμῶν requires us to regard as their apostasy from the Church; γεγόνασιν, to be sure, shows that they are within that Church from which they have now separated. This is brought out "by the emphatic position of ἐξ ἡμῶν before the verb" (Huther), for ἐξ ἡμῶν in connection with the verb ἐξέρχεσθαι merely denotes the circle, the fellowship from which they have separated. "John does not indicate the extent to which that formal separation has been carried; still ἐξῆλθαν implies that they had not only opposed the Apostolical doctrine (Beza: "*ad mutationem non loci, sed doctrinæ pertinet*"), but also those who, by the faithful preservation of the unadulterated Gospel, had proved themselves to be children of God" (Huther).

But they were not of us.—Εἶναι ἐξ ἡμῶν indicates the internal relation. Here the idea of origin combines with that of appertaining and affinity. Ἀλλὰ (Winer, pp. 462, 472, ἀλλα) denotes the strong opposition of ἐξ ἡμῶν ἐξῆλθαν and ἐξ ἡμῶν ἦσαν. While the former simply betokens external origin and coming out from, the latter indicates internal relationship; they were the former, not the latter; the aforesaid fact expressly denies this internal relation. Both origin (coming from) and relationship (affinity, appertaining to) are contained in εἶναι ἐκ τοῦ πατρὸς, ἐκ τοῦ κόσμου (v. 16) and in ἐξελθεῖν ἐκ τοῦ θεοῦ (Jno. viii. 42; xvi. 28; while ἀπὸ θεοῦ, Jno. xiii. 3, and παρὰ τοῦ θεοῦ, xvi. 27, denote only the former.) [Augustine: *Quandoquidem adhuc curatur corpus Domini nostri Jesu Christi, et sanitas perfecta non erit nisi in resurrectione mortuorum; sic sunt in corpore Christi, quomodo humores mali. Quando evomuntur, tunc revelatur corpus: sic et mali quando exeunt, tunc revelatur ecclesia. Et dicit quando eos evomit atque projicit corpus, ex me exierunt humores isti, sed non erant ex me. Quid est, non erant ex me? Non de carne mea præcisi sunt, sed pectus mihi premebant dum inessent.*"—M.]. But John here sharply contrasts the two and excludes the one by the other, adding moreover,

For if they had been of us, they would have abode with us.—Consequently, they had been μεθ' ἡμῶν, they had belonged to the Christians, they had lived among and with the Christians, they were Christians outwardly and to be considered as such. Although they had been μεθ' ἡμῶν, they were not ἐξ ἡμῶν, for in that case they would have abode μεθ' ἡμῶν. On the very frequent omission of the augment in the Pluperfect see Winer, p. 85. On the dogmatical and ethical import of this passage, see below in *Doctrinal and Ethical*, especially sub. Nos. 4. 5.

But—that they might be made manifest, that not all are of us.—Here is an imperfect and involved construction. After ἀλλὰ we have of course to supply the thought suggested by the previous words: but they did not abide with us, that—(Huther, Winer, *Grammar* p. 333. where may be found the corresponding illustrations Jno. xiii. 18: ἐξελεξάμην, ἀλλ' (ἐξελεξάμην) ἵνα;—Jno. xv. 25: μεμισήκασιν—, ἀλλ' (μεμισήκασιν) ἵνα—). In general γέγονε τοῦτο would have to be supplied, which would however depend on the context for its meaning, as in Jno. i. 8: ἀλλ' (ἦλθεν) ἵνα—; ix. 3: ἀλλ' (but he was born blind) ἵνα—. But de Wette has very correctly pointed out that *two* sentences are here interlaced, and Huther has rightly arranged them thus: 1, ἵνα φανερωθῶσιν ὅτι οὐκ εἰσὶν ἐξ ἡμῶν, 2, ἵνα φανερωθῇ ὅτι οὐκ εἰσὶ πάντες ἐξ ἡμῶν. The secession of the antichrists has taken place and constitutes an event that does not take place without some providential design, an event in which God the Lord takes an active part both as Ruler and Judge, hence ἵνα, *to the end that, in order that.* The Apostle's design is to mark a *purpose* and not a *consequence*, as Lange and Paulus maintain without any reason for their view. The purpose is *first*, that they shall manifest themselves as those who do not sustain to us an inward and ethical relation of kinship and appertainment, and *secondly*, that it shall become manifest in general that not all those who are in the Church and outwardly belong to it (μεθ' ἡμῶν, *in ecclesia*) do also belong to it inwardly (ἐξ ἡμῶν, *de ecclesia*). We have to connect οὐ πάντες in the sense of *nonnulli;* for if we were to connect οὐκ εἰσὶν so that the negation would belong to the predicate, John would have written οὐκ εἰσὶν ἐξ ἡμῶν πάντες, and we should be obliged to explain. "*All* are not of us," or "*none* is of us." In this case there would be something predicated of the antichrists, they would be the subject in πάντες. But this is not allowable on account of the position of the words. The meaning is rather: "Not all are of us, only some, although the majority are of us." But this cannot be predicated of the antichrists; for they are not all true, living church-members, none of them belongs truly to the Church. But their seceding furnishes actual proof that not all Christians (*baptizati, vocati*) are and remain real Christians (*electi, fideles*). "While in φανερωθῶσιν the seceders only are considered as the subject, the conception is enlarged in the clause ὅτι—ἡμῶν, and the Apostle declares, in respect of the former, that in general *not all* who belong outwardly to the Christian Church, *are* really members of the same (Düsterdieck). It is not allowable to understand οὐ πάντες with Socinus in the sense of *nulli:* the connection is right, the explanation is wrong. [Wordsworth: "They *all* pretend to be of us, and the heathen confound them with us. But their secession *from* us, and opposition to us, clearly *prove* that they are not all of us. *Some* false teachers [or false brethren M.] there are still who propagate heresies *in* the Church. They are tares in the field, but as long as they are *in* the field, it is not easy to distinguish them from the wheat. They are not of us, but they are *not manifested* as such by going out from us. But the *going out* of those who *have* left us, and who resist us, is a *manifest* token to all men, that they and their associates are not *all of us*, as they profess to be, and as the heathen suppose them to be; and as even some of the brethren in the Church imagine that they are, and are therefore deceived by them. By their going out they are manifested in their true light; and by their opposition to us Truth is distinguished from Error and Error from Truth." —M.].

Testimony of the gifts of believers. vv. 20. 21.

Ver. 20. **And you have ointment from the Holy One and know all things.**—The address ὑμεῖς has regard to the readers, to the Church, from which the antichrists have seceded. They are referred to a gift: ἔχετε

This gift is *χρῖσμα*, *unguentum*, not *unctio* as explained by Vulgate, Augustine, Luther, de Wette, Sander, al. It is chrism. "*Alludit appellatio* CHRISMATIS ad ANTICHRISTI nomen" (Bengel). [They have the *chrism* from *Christ*.—M.]. Thus John came to use this word which besides this place occurs only in v. 27. In obedience to the command of God kings (1 Sam. x. 10; xvi. 13, 14; Ps. xlv. 8), priests (Ex. xxix. 7; xxx. 31) and prophets (Is. lxi. 1) were anointed, and ointment is both figuratively, and in the ordered act itself, a symbol of the Holy Spirit. Thus Christ is anointed (Acts iv. 27) and that with the Holy Spirit (Acts x. 38), and thus Christians also are anointed. The chrism or ointment will have to be understood as the Holy Spirit and ὑμεῖς ἔχετε χρῖσμα reminds the readers of the great gift which makes them priests, kings and prophets, the γένος ἐκλεκτόν, βασίλειον ἱεράτευμα, ἔθνος ἅγιον, 1 Pet. ii. 9; cf. Ex. xix. 6; Is. xliii. 20. 21. This gift of the Holy Spirit must not be made the "*divinum beneficium cognoscendi ipsas res divinas, quatenus homini est opus*" (Socinus), or the "*auditio evangelii, institutio christiana*" (Episcopius, Rosenmüller), or the "*docendi auctoritas*" (Sauler), or "the true tradition concerning Christ distinguished by its being primitive, originating with the Apostles and vitally propagated" (Köstlin, *Lehrbegriff*, p. 243), or the "*caritas quæ diffunditur in cordibus nostris per spiritum sanctum*" (Didymus). And this having is a gift ἀπὸ τοῦ ἁγίου, they have received what they have; hence v. 27: τὸ χρῖσμα—ἐλάβετε. Christ is called ἁγνός ch. iii. 3 and δίκαιος ch. ii. 2; in Jno. vi. 69 He is called: ὁ ἅγιος τοῦ θεοῦ, Acts iii. 14: ὁ ἅγιος καὶ δίκαιος, Rev. iii. 7: ὁ ἅγιος ὁ ἀληθινός. The primary reference therefore seems to be to Christ who received the Spirit without measure (Jno. iii. 34), and baptized with the Holy Ghost (Jno. i. 33) and sends Him from the Father (Jno. xv. 26; Acts ii. 33) and hence the idea is that the Χριστός makes the χριστούς.—Ἀπὸ τοῦ ἁγίου consequently denotes neither God the Father (Socinus, Episcopius, Rickli, Neander, Besser, al.) nor the Holy Ghost (Didymus, Grotius).—It must be remembered that nothing is said here of the time when they received this gift nor of the means by which it was conveyed to them, but we read simply: ἔχετε. Hence there is no warrant for finding here an allusion to baptism (Augustine, Bede, Oecumenius), and the inference of the ungenuineness of the Epistle from the supposition of an allusion to a usage connected with baptism introduced at a later period, is wholly unjustifiable (Baur). [The argument *for* an allusion to baptism, rests on the hypothesis that this whole section is addressed to παιδία, *pueruli, children*, who received the gifts of the Holy Spirit in their baptism; it is then by implication extended to adults, and the use of chrism in baptism, a practice which does not belong to the Apostolical Age, seems to have been occasioned by this passage. Bengel: "*Eam unctionem spiritualem habent τὰ παιδία, pueruli: namque cum baptismo, quem susceperunt, conjunctum erat donum Spiritus Sancti, cujus significandi causa ex hoc loco deinceps usu receptum esse videtur, ut oleo corpora baptizatorum ungerentur.*"—M.]. It is more allowable to connect with v. 24 cf. v. 18, and to refer to the *preaching of the word of God* (Düsterdieck). We read simply "*ye have—!* Thus John reminds his readers of an important and responsible gift from which they might derive comfort and enjoyment in opposition to the antichrists, but which they ought also to keep, use and show against these adversaries. Hence the thought is introduced by καὶ, as John is wont to do, without indicating an antithesis which is contained in the matter itself; his object being to develop his argument by way of comfort and exhortation. [It is doubtful whether there is even an adversative implication in the *thought*, for John surely did not want to inform his readers that because they had the χρῖσμα they were the opposite of the antichrists. I do not mean that ὑμεῖς is not antithetical, but doubt whether καὶ is intended to mark an emphatic antithesis; in which case the Apostle would most probably have used δὲ or dispensed with the particle altogether. So Huther.—M.]. There is no reason at all to discover here with Semler a "*captatio benevolentiæ*," or with a Lapide an apology for the shortness of the Epistle; and still more objectionable is the view of Lange that "a certain anxious care is unmistakable which puts forth even rhetorical efforts;" nor is Calvin right in saying: "*modeste excusat apostolus, quod eos tam sollicite admonet, ne putent oblique se perstringi, quasi rudes ignarosque eorum, quæ probe tenere debuerant.*" The further particular

And know all things denotes the immediate gain they derive from this gift. Bengel rightly explains "*et inde.*" Πάντα is evidently neuter. The Syriac translates therefore falsely "*omnes.*" Although Calvin rightly says of πάντα: "*omnia non universaliter capi, sed ad præsentis loci circumstantiam restringi debet,*" we must not restrict it with Bengel to "*ea, quæ vos scire opus est: hoc responso repellendi erant seductores.*" Still less must it be applied with Estius to the Church, as knowing all things, whereas individual Christians know only *implicite* if they hold to the Church [He says: "*Habetis episcopos et presbyteros, quorum cura ac studio vestræ ecclesiæ satis instructæ sunt in iis quæ pertinent ad doctrinæ christianæ veritatem.*"—M.]. The reference, according to v. 21. and agreeably to Jno. xvi. 13: τὸ πνεῦμα τῆς ἀληθείας ὁδηγήσει ὑμᾶς ἐν τῇ ἀληθείᾳ πάσῃ cf. ch. xiv. 26) is rather to πᾶσαν τὴν ἀλήθειαν (so Huther and most expositors). The sentence οἴδατε τὴν ἀλήθειαν, v. 21 is wholly=οἴδατε τὰ πάντα.

VER. 21. **I have not written unto you, because ye know not the truth, but because ye know it.**—Ἔγραψα refers to the words immediately preceding v. 19 [that is to what the Apostle had just said concerning the antichrists—M.], and not to the Gospel, as Ebrard arbitrarily asserts. Not ignorance or want of knowledge on the part of the Church induced the Apostle to write this Epistle, on the contrary it was their knowledge and ability to form a right judgment of what was transpiring among them which prompted him to indite this Epistle, anxious as he was to foster and stimulate the truth possessed by his Church. Lorinus: "*non ut vos hæc doceam, sed ut doctos confirmem.*"—Ἀλήθεια is "the truth as announced by the Apostles, determining the whole walk in the light of believers (ch. i. 8; ii. 4), begetting all love, giving life and founded on Christ (v. 23 sqq.).

Whatsoever falls within the compass of this truth is the object of Christian knowledge, all this is known by believers" (Düsterdieck).

And that every thing which is lie is not of the truth.—Καὶ ὅτι is not connected with ἔγραψα: *and because*—as if indicating the motive which prompted the Apostle to write this Epistle, but the sentence depended on the second οἴδατε and is an object-sentence coördinated with αὐτήν: ye know it (the truth)—*and that*—. Thus render almost all commentators. Hence springs the question (v. 22) τίς ἐστιν ὁ ψεύστης; John assumes that they know who is the liar, as well as what and whence the lie is. Here εἶναι ἐκ τῆς ἀληθείας denotes not only origin but also appurtenance conditioned and defined by the origin. Of course πᾶν—οὐκ must not be explained here as a Hebraism (Grotius and al.)=οὐδέν, since οὐκ evidently belongs to the predicate, but=*every* lie is *not* out of the truth, which, however, amounts to=*no* lie is out of the truth. The reference to the antichrists is plain and the sense manifest: every thing which is lie neither originates from the truth, nor can it remain with the truth; it is not matter of complaint or of surprise that the antichrists with their lies and denials are seceding. Ψεῦδος consequently is not only *error*, but the distinct opposite of the truth, nor is it the abstract put for the concrete, viz.: the false teachers (Lange). Our Lord Himself tells us whence the lie originates, it is from the devil (Jno. viii. 44). The truth is *from* God and full of God, and therefore incompatible with any and every lie. [Diversity of origin renders the truth and the lie incompatibles. Christ is the truth (Jno. xiv. 6). Lorinus: "*Lex vero non nisi verum sequitur et verum vero consonat.*"—M.]. All knowledge and ability to form a right judgment of moral phenomena are founded on the χρῖσμα, the Holy Spirit, consequently on a gift, even the gift which begins with sanctifying the will and renewing the heart. Sanctification leads to illumination. This points to the powerful exhortation which accompanies the consolation.

The substance of the antichristian lie. vv. 22. 23.

VER. 22. **Who is the liar but he that denieth that Jesus is the Christ?**—The interrogative form marks the vivacity with which John passes from the general abstract (πᾶν ψεῦδος) to the definite concrete (ὁ ψεύστης) as in ch. v. 4. 5. [Huther.] There is here surely no reference to *children* (Ebrard). Hence Bengel rightly explains: *ὁ vim habet ad abstractum* v. 21=*quis est* plains: *ὁ vim habet ad abstractum* 21=*quis est illius mendacii reus?*" The Article is by all means to be retained (Luther translates wrongly: who is *a* liar? [also E. V.—M.]) and to be explained as bringing out with emphatic distinctness the idea "*the* liar κατ' ἐξοχήν *i. e.* he in whom the lie appears in concrete form=ὁ ἀντίχριστος" (Huther). It must not, however, be restricted to one individual besides whom there is none like him, but rather be taken generically or collectively with reference to the genus of antichristians, like ὁ νικῶν in ch. v. 5 (Düsterdieck); πᾶν ψεῦδος of course concentrates in him, if we exclude lies in other spheres, *e. g.* those of the natural sciences, history or jurisprudence; here we have to do with the sphere of religion, with church-life. All comparative explanations dilute the conception of the Apostle; under this head we may enumerate those of Calvin ("*nisi hoc censeatur mendacium, aliud nullum haberi posse*"), Socinus ("*mendacium quo nihil possit esse majus*"), Grotius ("*Quis potest esse major impostor?*"), Episcopius ("*enormitas mendacii*"), J. Lange ("*mendax præcipuus et periculosior?*"), de Wette ("who deserves more the name of liar?").—Huther very justly says that Baumgarten-Crusius has altogether missed the Apostle's meaning in his explanation: "What is an erroneous doctrine, if not etc."—In the sentence εἰ μὴ ὁ ἀρνούμενος, the term εἰ μὴ is=*nisi*, except; εἰ οὐ, *si non* would be inapplicable (Winer, p. 499) cf. ch. v. 5; Luke xvii. 18; Rom. xi. 15, etc.. The negative οὐκ in the sentence: ὅτι Ἰησοῦς οὐκ ἔστιν ὁ Χριστὸς might have been omitted, since it is preceded by ἀρνούμενος; but the affirmation of the liar is fully indicated, although it is couched in the form of a negation; this is in perfect agreement with the genius of the Greek language. Similar terms are found Luke xx. 27; Gal. v. 17; Heb. xii. 19; cf. Kühner, II. p. 410; Winer, p. 532 β. The essential feature and the height of the lie of the antichrist is this: Jesus is not the Christ, the Saviour promised by and come from the Father, the λόγος σὰρξ γενόμενος; this is the gnostic error which does not distinguish Jesus from Christ, but tears them asunder and thus constitutes the strongest antithesis to the Gospel of Jesus Christ. The reference therefore is neither to the form of Jewish unbelief that Jesus is not *omnium hominum patronus* (Semler) nor to the two forms of heresy one of which denies that Jesus was the Eternal *Word*, and the other that the *Eternal Word* became flesh (Besser following Tertullian), [who says: *de Præscript.* c. 33: *Joh. in ep. eos maxime antichristos vocat, qui Christum negarent in carne venisse et qui non putarent Jesum esse Filium Dei; illud Marcion, hoc Ebion vindicavit.*"—Wordsworth, following Irenæus and Waterland, refers also to Cerinthus and his followers, who denied that *Jesus* was the *Christ*, dividing *Jesus* from *Christ*; and they denied *the Son*, because they did not acknowledge that *Jesus* was personally united with the *Word*, the Eternal Son of God; nor that the Word was the only begotten of the Father; and so they disowned the divine Sonship of Jesus and Christ; and thus they denied the *Father* and the *Son*."—M.]. The reference is only to *one* lie.

This is the antichrist who denieth the Father and the Son.—Ὁ ἀντίχριστος here and ὁ ψεύστης in the preceding clause, are evidently identical, and for the very reason that the liar denies Christ [or as Huther puts it: the liar, who denies the identity of Jesus and Christ, is the antichrist.—M.]. John adds "a new particular, exhibiting the wholly fatal consequence of that antichristian lie," (Düsterdieck) to this name in the following clause: ὁ ἀρνούμενος τὸν πατέρα καὶ τὸν υἱόν; here, to use the terse language of Luther, John knocks the bottom out of the barrel.—The antichrist denies also the Father. First he denies *Christ* and then proceeds to deny that He is the Son of and with the Father until he reaches the extreme position of denying the *Father* Himself. The Χρίστος belongs to history, to the economy of salvation. The idea υἱός reaches further, even down to the innermost Being of God; the denial of the Son violates the very Being of God, consequently the Father and thus far must it come with one who denies Christ. In *Jesus* appeared as *Christ*, as the Saviour of the world, the *Son* of the Father full of grace and truth, the Eternal Word which is from the beginning, and in the Son is manifested the Being of the Father, His Spirit and His Love, so that the knowledge of the Father is impossible without the knowledge of the Son. Hence he who denies Christ is led to the point that he has an ideal conception of God of his own making, an εἴδωλον, as Huther puts it, but not the true God. [Huther, to whom Braune is indebted for the thought, puts the logical sequence more lucidly than the latter; he says: He who denies the identity of Jesus and Christ, denies first the Son, for the Son is none other than Ἰησοῦς ὁ Χριστός (neither an Aeon called Christ who did not become man, nor Jesus who is not Christ, or according to Jno. i. 14, who is not the Logos); but whoso denies the Son, denies also the Father not only in as far as Father and Son are logically convertible terms, but because the Being of the Father manifests Itself only in the Son and because all true knowledge of the Father is conditioned by the knowledge of the Son, so that the God of those who deny the Son is not the true God, but a false creation of their own thoughts—an εἴδωλον.—M.].

VER. 23. **Every one that denieth the Son, hath also not the Father** [*neither hath he the Father*].—Here is the progression from *denying* (ἀρνεῖσθαι) to *having* (ἔχειν), and from the particular (ὁ ψεύστης) to the general (πᾶς).—Ἀρνούμενος evidently cannot be without an object, so that we have to connect πᾶς ὁ ἀρνούμενος τὸν υἱὸν, but not: every one that denieth hath not the Son also (hath not) the Father; neither ὁ ἀρνούμενος nor the immediately succeeding ὁ ὁμολογῶν can be independent subjects, and πατέρα joined to υἱὸν cannot be governed by ἔχειν as in 2 Jno. 9.—Ἀρνεῖσθαι τὸν υἱὸν signifies to disown the Eternal Word of the Father, the Logos (not only in Jesus who without the Logos is not and cannot be the Christ, but *absolutely*), and as such disowning implies not only mere ignorance or a limited understanding, but also infirmity and impurity of the heart and the will, it points to a separation of man from the Son of God, so that it becomes an οὐκ ἔχειν, and contains and operates an οὐκ ἔχειν 2 Jno. 9. It is therefore "*habere in agnitione et communione* (Bengel), a possession in vital fellowship (Düsterdieck); "*habere in mente et fide, in ore et confessione*" (a Lapide), "in faith and in love" (de Wette), "in knowledge, faith and confession" (Lücke). False are the expositions of Socinus ("*non habere opinionem, quod Deus sit*"), Grotius ("*non cognoscere Deum seu quæ sit ejus voluntas erga humanum genus*"), Episcopius and others.—Οὐδὲ emphatically denotes the further loss that one cannot separate oneself from the Son without giving up the Father. The Apostle now concludes affirmatively:

He that confesseth the Son hath the Father also.—On ὁμολογεῖν see above on ch. ii. 9. It is an act of the inner life and of a more intimate fellowship. Cf. Matth. x. 32; Rom. x. 10. [Düsterdieck: "In the denial of the Son is involved necessarily the denial of the Father, since the Father cannot be known without the Son, and the Father cannot be received, believed on, loved, by any man, without the Son, or otherwise than through the Son, *i. e.* the Son manifested in the flesh, the Christ, which is Jesus. So that in John's development of the argument there are three essentially connected points: denial of the Christ, of the Son, of the Father. The middle link of the chain, the denial of the Son of God, shows how the denial of the Father is of necessity involved in the denial of Christ. And the cogency of this proof is made yet more stringent by another equally unavoidable process of argument. The antichristian false doctrine consists mainly in a negation, in the denial of the fundamental truth, that Jesus is the Christ. But in this is involved the denial of the Essence of the Son as well as of the Father, and again in this denial is involved the losing, the virtual *not having* of the Son and of the Father. In the sense of John, we may say, taking the first and last steps of his argument and leaving out the intervening ones: *He who denieth that Jesus is the Christ, hath not the Father.* And this necessary connection between denying and not having is perfectly clear, the moment we understand the ethical character, the living realism of John's way of regarding the subject. As (v. 23) we cannot separate the knowledge and confession of the Christ, the Son, the Father, from the *having*, the real possession of, the practical fellowship with, the actual remaining in the Son and the Father, so conversely, together with the denial is necessarily given the *not having*: together with the loss of the truth of the knowledge, the loss of the life which consists in that knowledge (Jno. xvii. 3). In such a connection, the *confession* of the truth is as essential on the one side, as the *denial* on the other. Each is the necessary manifestation of the belief or unbelief hidden in the heart. And this ὁμολογεῖν is not to be understood of the "*confessio cordis, vocis et operis*," (Bede), but only as ch. i. 9, of the confession of the mouth (στόματι ὁμολογεῖται, Rom. x. 9, see Jno. xii. 42). It is parallel with φέρειν διδαχήν, 2 Jno. 7. 10; and indicates the definite utterance of the doctrine which was made known by the Apostolic preaching, verse 24."—M.].

Paternal exhortation founded on promises, vv. 24. 25.

VER. 24. **Ye, let that which ye have heard from the beginning, abide in you.**—The sentence is anacoluthic. It is well explained by Theophylact: ἐκεῖνοι μὲν οὖν οὕτως ὑμεῖς δὲ ἅπερ ἠκούσατε ἀπ' ἀρχῆς—φυλάττετε παρ ἑαυτοῖς.—ὑμεῖς therefore must not be connected with ἠκούσατε, as if it were a mere transposition; there would be no reason whatsoever for such a connection and no reason or necessity for such an emphasis. So in v. 27, and frequently. See Winer §. §. 28, 3; 64, 2. d. Kühner II, 160. Hence the explanations of Bengel ("*antitheton est in pronomine; ideo adhibetur trajectio*"), de Wette ("ὑμεῖς is really the subject of the relative sentence, placed before"), and others are erroneous. Neither can ὑμεῖς be the pure Vocative (Ebrard, Paulus), nor be taken as an absolute Nominative (Myrberg).—The spurious οὖν after ὑμεῖς is not improper *per se* (Düsterdieck in opposition to de Wette with whom Huther agrees), for it is not an antithesis of what goes before, which is also assumed by Theophylact, because the preceding sentence closes affirmatively thus: ὁ ὁμολογῶν τὸν υἱὸν, καὶ τὸν πατέρα ἔχει; and this is the ground of the present exhortation.—On ὃ ἠκούσατε cf. v. 7. John points to the apostolical announcement. Ἀπ' ἀρχῆς is more clearly defined by it (*ex quo institui cœpistis in primis christianæ religionis rudimentis*, Beza, so also Lücke and others). There is no necessity to think of the *prima ecclesiæ nascentis tempora* (Bede). The substance of ὅ, not ἅ, seems to be simple. But it is not enough to understand in general *evangelium Christi* (Calvin), or the truth that Jesus is the Christ (Huther, Lücke), or θεολογούμενον τὸν χριστὸν (Theophylact), but we had better understand with Bengel (*de patre et filio*) the theologoumenon of the Father and the Son besides that fundamental truth (Düsterdieck), as indicated in the preceding verses.—Ἐν ὑμῖν μενέτω describes ἔχειν as a possession that has to be kept. The preposition must preserve its proper meaning; that which has been heard must "be in dwelling within as something that determines the life" (Neander). This meaning is also urged by the parallel passage Jno. xv. 1–10, where μένειν appears as a favourite expression of our Lord. In the sentence immediately following it is indeed impossible to render ἐν, *with*. The same holds good here. Hence Theophylact's παρὰ and Luther's *with* are false. The truth and doctrine as announced by the Apostles "is really to dwell *in them*, as a living power in their hearts" (Düsterdieck), and if that takes place, ἐὰν ἐν ὑμῖν μείνῃ ὃ ἀπ' ἀρχῆς ἠκούσατε,

If in you—emphatically placed first—**abides that which ye have heard from the beginning, ye also shall abide in the Son and in the Father.**—Bengel well observes: καὶ: *vicissim*. Düsterdieck hits the mark: "John denotes by the position of καὶ before ὑμεῖς the promised consequence which will correspond with the indicated destination while at the same time he makes prominent the fine turn contained in the thoughtful change of ἐν ὑμῖν μείνῃ and ὑμεῖς ἐν τῷ υἱῷ μενεῖτε." The reciprocal effect of the Word abiding in you and of the Church abiding in Christ does not refer to the origin of the relation of the Church and of her conduct, but only to the further development of the same. But the expression and its order intimate that the word must first be brought, preached and explained, and then be heard, received and kept, and that it must have found in individual Christians an element in which it is vitally efficient, even as it is full of life, in order to enable them to have (ἔχειν) and to live in Christ as their element. ἐν τῷ υἱῷ stands naturally before καὶ τῷ πατρὶ because the Son is the Mediator of this life-fellowship. Hence Theophylact's exposition, based on Jno. xvii. 2. 21: κοινωνοὶ αὐτοῦ ἔσεσθε, goes hardly far enough. The life of believers must really and essentially be rooted in God, derive nourishment, grow and mature to completeness from Him. Faith has not only brought news and intelligence and become acquainted with God, but has entered into personal intercourse with Him and carries away from Him the separate gifts, benefits and powers. The possession of this life is not left to the distant future, although the life is an eternal life, but the object of Christian hope in respect of its perfection and at the same time something present and the object of present experience; to speak with Calvin: *deum se totum nobis in Christo fruendum* dedit, not *dabit* (Düsterdieck). Besides the principal passage Jno. xv. 1 sqq. the following places are very similar Jno. vi. 56; xvii. 23; Gal. ii. 20; 1 Cor. iii. 16; Eph. iii. 17. Hence the evaporating and diluting views of Grotius ("*conjunctissimi Patri et filio eritis, summo eorum favore et amicitia fruemini*") Semler ("*sitis certi, nobis patere omnem hanc felicitatem unice veram*") and others, as well as the scholastic, orthodox views of Schmid ("*gratiosa filii et Patris inhabitatio*") and J. Lange ("*unio cum deo mystica, communio cum eo jam inchoata, communicatio, per quam omnes regni divini dotes homini in usum sanctum et beatum contingunt*"), are insignificant to bring out the mind and the thoughts of John in their living fulness.

Ver. 25. **And this is the promise which He hath promised us, the life eternal.**—Αὕτη ἐστίν should be explained here as in ch. ii. 23. v. 11. 14 where the same words occur in the same position or as in ch. i. 5: καὶ ἔστιν αὕτη; the reference is to the words which follow—τὴν ζωὴν τὴν αἰώνιον. The substance or object of ἐπαγγελία is qualified here by a Substantive, while the substance or object of ἀγγελία or ἐντολή or μαρτυρία or παῤῥησία in the other passages is indicated by a clause connected with ὅτι or ἵνα according to the context. Instead of the Accusative (ζωήν), the Nominative (ζωή) ought to have been in apposition with ἐπαγγελία, but it was both attracted as apposition to the relative clause ἣν αὐτὸς ἐπηγγείλατο ἡμῖν annexed in the same case as ἥν. See Winer, p. 552 sq. Therefore *manere in filio et patre* is not the ἐπαγγελία and ἡ ζωὴ ἡ αἰώνιος not a pure apposition, so that the abiding itself is described as eternal life (Sander, Besser), but "the life eternal is the promise" (so Huther and most commentators). The ἐπαγγελία is *promissio*, consequently not *res promissa* (J. Lange, Estius), as if it were true contrary to the genius and usage of Greek to add ἣν—ἐπηγγείλατο. Αὐτὸς designates Him "who is the centre of this whole section" (Huther), that is Christ, and neither the Father (Hunnius), nor the Father through the Son (Socinus). But ἡ ζωὴ ἡ αἰώνιος, as the substance and object of the ἐπαγγελία of the Son, is not viewed as a gift remote from and subsequent to this promise, but as present and experienced, acquired and enjoyed wherever the pre-requisite of the promise is complied with, namely the abiding of the word in you. Where the promise applies, it is forthwith fulfilling itself. Therefore it is not said that we should acquire the life eternal, but that at which this promise is aimed is simply mentioned and connected by attraction with ἐπηγγείλατο.—Καὶ accordingly has here its ordinary force as copula, connecting this sentence with the one preceding, adding and explaining something implied, but not yet particularly mentioned in the preceding sentence; the reference is to something directly connected with abiding in God; καὶ therefore must not be taken αἰτιολογικῶς (Oecumenius) or as designating the further consequence of holding fast the Gospel (Lücke). Düsterdieck strikingly observes: "The present reality of eternal life in believers is no more annulled by the fact that it is not yet perfected in them than that inversely continued growth, a holy and fruitful development, and the final glorious perfection are excluded by its real possession."

Conclusion, with repeated warnings and exhortations vv. 26-28.

VER. 26. **These things I have written unto you concerning those who deceive you.**—Here ταῦτα connected with ἔγραψα refers back to the preceding verses, and the object περὶ τῶν πλανώντων ὑμᾶς points back as far as v. 18. The πλανῶντες ὑμᾶς are the antichrists, and denotes that they are dangerous *per se*, really and not only unsuccessfully dangerous, as is evident from v. 19. [It is doubtful whether the reference to v. 19 warrants the inference of their actual success in the case of those whom the Apostle is addressing. The deceivers themselves had seceded; that is all we can gather from v. 19, and that they were anxious to deceive others we learn from this verse, but nothing is said of their having been successful in their endeavour.—M.]. This is also intimated by the Accusative ὑμᾶς and 2 Jno. 8; Matth. xxiv. 5, 11, 24. [This is certainly a singular conclusion, for ὑμᾶς indicates that they, the readers of the Epistle, the Church, are the object of the deceiver's endeavours.—M.]. The word itself denotes an act, a continuing activity, and therefore more than a "*studium, conatus*," "*seducere conantibus*" (Bengel, Huther). [See *Apparat. Critic.* v. 26, note 27.—M.]. Hence the reiterated exhortation to fidelity.

VER. 27. **And you—the ointment which ye received from Him, abideth in you, and ye have no need that any one teach you.**—Thought, expression and construction, as in vv. 20, 21: καὶ ὑμεῖς τὸ χρῖσμα—φυλάττετε= μένει ἐν ὑμῖν. From ὑμᾶς, v. 26, the Apostle takes καὶ ὑμεῖς, and contrasting them with οἱ πλανῶντες, places said words emphatically in anteposition, for they would be too strongly emphasized if we were to connect them with the relative clause. cf. v. 24. Τὸ χρῖσμα here, as χρῖσμα, v. 20, is in the Accusative, but must not be connected with the relative clause, *per trajectionem*. The Article denotes what is known and what has already been mentioned. Ἐλάβετε distinctly marks their reception and points to a greater obligation than the previous reference to possession (ἔχετε, v. 20). The gift is not without its task and work, here, under the impulse of gratitude. Ἀπ' αὐτοῦ of course designates Him round whom the Apostle's thoughts revolve as round their centre, the same who is described in ἀπὸ τοῦ ἁγίου, Christ, v. 25. This verse proves that τοῦ ἁγίου, v. 20, relates to Christ (Huther). While the Future was used in v. 24 (μενεῖτε), we have here the Present (μένει) in order to express the Apostle's certain assurance (Huther) and to exhort at the same time to that which he does expect. Bengel ("*Habet hic indicativus perquam subtilem adhortationem* (*conferendam ad* 2. Tim. iii. 14) *qua fideles, a deceptatoribus sollicitatos, ita iis respondere facit:* unctio in nobis manet: non egemus doctore: illa nos verum docet: in ea doctrina permanebimus. Vide *quam amœna sit transitio ab hac sermocinatione ad sermonem directum versu sequenti* "Manet in vobis: manebitis in Illo" *correlata*).—Καὶ, and because the Holy Spirit is and *abideth in you* (Bengel: *et ideo*), οὐ χρείαν ἔχετε, ye have no need whatever; thus is brought out here the αὐτάρκεια θεοδιδάκτων, and we have here a new particular, which was not expressed in v. 20. The construction with ἵνα occurs also Jno. ii. 25; xvi. 30.—Τοῦ διδάσκειν, Heb. v. 12. The Infinitive only, Matth. iii. 14; xiv. 6; 1 Thess. i. 8; iv. 9. This teaching is taken here not as a simple consequence, but as the end and aim because of the condition of the persons to be taught. Love prompts thereto, for love deems it its duty and cherishes the intention to teach. Hence the meaning is: "You are not at all in the situation that somebody should or ought to teach you" (Düsterdieck after Lücke and against Huther, who takes ἵνα in a weakened sense and thinks that it is simply used to indicate the object). Hence we may think also of Apostolical instruction, fraternal encouragement and (with reference to τις v. 21) friendly teaching, perhaps that of the Apostle himself (Bengel, de Wette, Lücke, Düsterdieck). There is no occasion here to think of πλανῶν; so Semler, Spener, (τὶς=who asserts a new revelation), Sander, Gerlach, Besser. But with reference to πάντα v. 20 and περὶ πάντων we must not restrict ἵνα διδάσκῃ ὑμᾶς to instruction concerning the false teachers (as Lücke does), although that is included (Huther).—It is important to bear in mind that this passage does not hold out the least encouragement, or give support to the vagaries of fanatics, because the Holy Spirit works on the basis of the word given and received, and does not communicate any thing *new*, but only imparts to believers clearer perceptions and views of that which they already have.

But as the ointment of Him teacheth you concerning all things, and is true and is not lie, and as it hath taught you, so abide in Him.—As we read τὸ αὐτοῦ χρῖσμα and not τὸ αὐτὸ χρῖσμα, it is only necessary to observe that Bengel ("*idem semper, non aliud atque aliud, sed sibi constans, et idem apud sanctos omnes*) finds here the unchangeableness, and Düsterdieck and others the identity of the chrism, which unceasingly teaches believers and which they have received from Him, the Christ; our reading brings out this identity and also reiterates its origin: [See *Appar. Crit.* v. 27., note 29, where the other reading is advocated, according to which we render "the same ointment," i. e., the identical χρῖσμα, ὃ ἐλάβετε.—M.].—The structure of this sentence presents peculiar difficulties. Ἀλλὰ introduces the antithesis μένετε ἐν αὐτῷ. While, on the one hand, the Apostle had assured them that they have no need of being taught by any one, because they have the Spirit reminding them of the words of the Lord and leading them into all truth, he now declares, on the other, and by way of antithesis, that they have need of abiding faithful with Him. Hence the words in parenthesis belong to the first ὡς, although the vivacity [of the Apostle's diction] which never repeats without indicating some new feature, has occasioned various modifications. The exhortation: μένετε ἐν αὐτῷ requires fidelity toward and steadfastness with *Christ*, as is unmistakable from the context and v. 28. Erasmus explaining ἐν τῷ χρίσματι erroneously thinks of the Holy Spirit, and Baumgarten-Crusius of the doctrine of the Spirit, while Schottgen strikingly observes: "*in Christo, quem Johannes semper in mente habet.*" The motive for abiding with Christ is: τὸ αὐτοῦ χρῖσμα διδάσκει περὶ πάντων. Hence the context also recommends the well authenticated αὐτοῦ [the authorities on Braune's own showing are all the other way; they stand thus: αὐτοῦ C. Sin (?) against αὐτὸ A. B. (?) G. K.—M.]; it is the ointment of the Holy Ghost from Him [αὐτοῦ?], Christ, with [ἐν?] whom they are to remain; and this ointment teaches them concerning all things, as we read v. 20: οἴδατε πάντα. But not only the extent of that concerning which they are taught of the Holy Spirit is the motive for his exhortation that they should abide with Him. The chief motive is the characteristic: καὶ ἀληθές ἐστιν. The χρῖσμα is called absolutely ἀληθὲς, implying of course that that also which it teaches, is true; the Holy Spirit is the Spirit of truth (Jno. xiv. 17), therefore He leadeth you also into all truth (Jno. xvi. 13). So Düsterdieck; also Lücke, de Wette, Brückner, Ebrard. There is no ground for restricting the reference to that which the χρῖσμα teaches, as do Oecumenius, Theophylact, Luther, Neander, Besser, Huther. The importance of the true essence and substance of the χρῖσμα occasions the additional clause which denies all lie: καὶ οὐκ ἐστὶν ψεῦδος, and lie is not, is not extant. John evidently here recurred to the thought expressed in v. 21: πᾶν ψεῦδος ἐκ τῆς ἀληθείας οὐκ ἔστιν, and that there is no lie where the Spirit teaches. Now the Apostle resumes with the fuller form καθὼς that which he had begun with ἀλλ' ὡς, and moreover, by way of reminding them that the Holy Spirit had taught them for some time: καθὼς ἐδίδαξεν ὑμᾶς. This Aorist after the preceding Present ought not to occasion any difficulty; and the καὶ before καθὼς instead of the ἀλλὰ before ὡς is readily accounted for by the one immediately preceding it; the sentence, thus resumed, connects with the testimony of the truth of the Spirit and His teaching; agreeably to which He has taught and teaches believers. Hence we should not divide the second clause of this verse into two parts (with Luther, Calvin, Baumgarten-Crusius, Sander, Brückner, Besser, Huther, and others), so that ἀλλ' ὡς τὸ αὐτοῦ χρῖσμα διδάσκει ὑμᾶς is the first antecedent, and καὶ ἀληθές ἐστιν καὶ οὐκ ἐστιν ψεῦδος its consequent, and again καὶ καθὼς ἐδίδαξεν ὑμᾶς is the second antecedent, and μένετε ἐν αὐτῷ its consequent. The explanation given by us is supported by Oecumenius, Theophylact, Lücke, de Wette, Neander, Düsterdieck, Ewald and others. [This applies only to the structure of the sentence, not to the exposition of the passage. As to the former we cannot but think that the one adopted by Huther and the many authorities who agree with him, is preferable to that of Braune, and on the following grounds: 1st, it assigns to περὶ πάντων its proper position, whereas in the former view is no relation whatsoever to μενεῖτε (μένετε) of the consequent; 2d, ἀλλὰ indicates that the Apostle is about to introduce an antithesis to οὐ χρείαν ἔχετε, a sentence in which the teaching of the χρῖσμα is to be described as exempting them from the necessity of another human teacher, and 3d, because the clause καὶ οὐκ ἐστι ψεῦδος added to ἀληθές ἐστι raises this thought above the character of a mere parenthetical and secondary observation, and stamps it as the leading thought. These are the grounds on which Luther, Calvin, Baumgarten-Crusius, Sander, Brückner, Besser, Huther, and many more, deem it preferable to divide the whole into two clauses, and to take καὶ ἀληθές ἐστι καὶ οὐκ ἐστι ψεῦδος as the consequent of the first clause. "But as the anointing teaches you all things, so it is true and is no lie," etc. (Luther).—M.].

The conclusion of the whole section, v. 28.

VER. 28. **And now, little children, abide with [in, ἐν] him.**

Καὶ νῦν connects the exhortation, repeated on account of its great importance and already expressed as a hope and in confidence v. 27, with the preceding verses. Καὶ νῦν occurs very often (Jno. xvii. 5; Acts iii. 17; iv. 29; vii. 34; x. 5; xxii. 16; 2 Thess. ii. 6), or καὶ νῦν ἰδοὺ (Acts xiii. 11; xx. 22, 25), or νῦν οὖν (Acts xvi. 36; xxiii. 15), on the other hand ἀλλὰ νῦν (Luke xxii. 36), νῦν δὲ (Jno. viii. 40; ix. 41; xv. 22, 24; xviii. 36), but always so that out of the originally sentient description of the present there has sprung a certain logical significance in order to mark the consequences from a present situation, to draw an inference or conclusion, to annex the features involved in a given case or to denote an antithetical relation (Düsterdieck). Hence Paulus errs in rendering: "Even already now—as in opposition to the Parthian-magian doctrine, that union with God cannot take place except in the future kingdom of light."—The seasonable address τεκνία frees the Apostle's earnestness from all severity, and intensifies his exhortation as a paternal right, by reminding them of the fellowship of love as the consequence of his Apostolical discharge of duty. "*Repetitio est præcepti cum blanda appellatione, qua paternum erga eos amorem declaret*" (Estius). It is inconceivable how Socinus applies the ἐν αὐτῷ not to Christ, but to *Deus per Christum*, and how Semler could hit upon this doctrine. Rickli, who explains v. 27 of abiding in the confession that Jesus is the Christ, suggests here abiding in righteousness.—Now follows a reference to the judgment.

That if He shall be manifested we may have confidence and not be shamed away from Him at His coming.—Since ἐὰν and not ὅταν is the true reading, we have here not an intimation of the *time*, or the nearness of the time, but of the *reality* of the manifestation of Christ (Huther, Düsterdieck). Although the same word is applied to our Lord's appearing in flesh, in the form of a servant (ch. iii. 5. 8. ἐφανερώθη), still it may be applied with equal propriety to the future manifestation of His glory as in Col. iii. 4. That will be manifested which as yet is hidden. The Apostle now passes to the first person Plural: παῤῥησίαν σχῶμεν. He ever places himself under the laws (ch. i. 6 sqq.; ii. 2 sq.; iii. 16, 18 sqq.) and promises (ch. iii. 1 sqq.; 21; iv. 17; v. 11. 20), applicable to all without being able to exclude himself from the hope here presented (de Wette, Düsterdieck). Hence it is not from modesty (S. Schmid), nor because he would suffer loss if any members of his Church were falling away (Sander). Παῤῥησία is literally frankness, free-spokenness (Acts iv. 17. 29. 31; xxvi. 26; xxviii. 31; 1 Thess. ii. 2) then confident assurance with respect to all the threats and terrors of the judgment. The Vulgate translates *fiducia*; Luther properly *freudig* (vreidic *i. e.* free), *Freudigkeit* (*vreidicheit i. e.* freeness), which sheer ignorance has turned into joyful (*freudig*) and joyfulness (*Freudigkeit*). Compare Vilmar *Pastoral-theolog. Blätter* 1861, Nos. 1. 2; Jütting, *Biblisches Wörterbuch* (1864) s. v.—A *Strasburg* edition of 1537, indeed, has already *Freudigkeit*, but the original word is *Freydigkeit* (Nürnberg ed. 1524), *Freydigkeyt* (Wittenberg ed. 1525), *Freidigkeit* (1530), and in a sermon on Jno. iv. 16–21 he speaks of *boldness* (*Trotz*) in the last day. The Greek Scholiasts and Lexicographers explain the word by ἄδεια, ἐξουσία, ἡ ἐπὶ τοῖς κακίστοις εὔτολμος ἀπολογία. The ordinary antithesis is αἰσχύνεσθαι (Prov. xiii. 5; Phil. i. 20) to be ashamed, to shame oneself or feel ashamed, so as to depart from Him the Judge. The preposition ἀπὸ therefore is not=ὑπὸ (Socinus), nor=*coram* (Luther, Ewald), nor both together (S. Schmid, Sander), but=away from (Calvin, Beza, de Wette, Düsterdieck, Huther); but it is necessary to retain the Passive and not the Middle, because we do not retire and withdraw ourselves, but are rejected and driven away. Cf. Matth. xxv. 41. It is impossible to agree with Erasmus, who says: "*ut illum non pudeat nostri.*"—Παρουσία occurs only here in John's writings, but often elsewhere (Matth. xxiv. 3, 27, 37, 39; 1 Cor. xv. 23; 1 Thess. ii. 19 etc.), corresponds with φανερωθῇ, and as φανερωθῇ answers to παῤῥησίαν ἔχειν so παρουσία answers to αἰσχύνεσθαι. All this, connected with ἵνα, constitutes a motive for abiding with Him, walking in the light, in fellowship with Him.

DOCTRINAL AND ETHICAL.

1. The unmistakable reference here to the immanent Trinity is *theological* in the strictest sense of the word. According to the final clause of v. 22 and v. 23 we have here a reference to a *paternal relation* with respect to the Son, and to a *filial relation* with respect to the Father existing above and before the world within the Godhead. The Son is not only a power or principle before He became personal in the Christ, but He is personal in virtue of his Being, the Son of the Father who is a Person, the Son who as the Image of the Father is also a Person. But He became a historical Person, a Person belonging to the history of man in the Christ who did appear in Jesus. See EXEGETICAL AND CRITICAL.

2. The knowledge of God without the knowledge of *Christ* is impossible, because the *knowledge* of God is impossible without *fellowship* with God, which is solely the result of confession of Jesus the Christ.

3. Fellowship with God is not the act of men but the act of God through Christ. It begins in the word which is preached and heard, continues in the communication and reception of the Chrisma, the Holy Spirit, and it consists in the truth and in the constancy of faith and confession. The Word of Christ and the Spirit given of Him must first come to us and do His work and in us and then we shall be able to abide with Him in virtue of His power.

4. The question here is as to what constitutes the difference between *esse in ecclesia* and *esse de ecclesia*. As surely as these two conditions must be distinguished from each other, so certain it is that in point of fact they do coëxist alongside each other. So CONFESS. AUG. Art. 8.: "*Quid sit ecclesia?—in hac vita multi hypocritæ et mali admixti—*; APOL. IV. *de ecclesia* ¶. 11: *malos nomine tantum in ecclesia esse, non re, bonos vero re et nomine: Hieronymus enim ait: qui ergo peccator est aliqua sorde maculatus, de ecclesia Christi non potest appellari nec Christo subjectus dici.*"—"Like tares they stood in the same field alongside the wheat (Matth. xiii. 23 sqq.) and had part in the divine manifestations of grace whereby the whole field is made fertile and the genuine wheat brought to ripeness. But they shewed themselves to be tares and by their seceding did execute on themselves the divine judgment. Augustine and Bede, with whom Luther agrees in his second exposition, also compare the antichrists with the evil humours of the body. The body of Christ also, so long as it is undergoing the process of being cured, that is so long as it has not attained to perfect health through the resurrection, has such noxious humours (*quandoquidem adhuc curatur corpus ipsius et sanitas perfecta non erit nisi in resurrectione mortuorum; sic sunt in corpore Christi, quomodo humores mali*). Their expulsion liberates the body and enables it to attain unto perfect health (*quando evomuntur, tunc relevatur corpus*). But this does not happen to keep up Bede's figure, with the providential care of God" (Düsterdieck).

5. The present section cannot be pressed into the service of predestinarianism. Augustine, indeed, says with reference to this passage (*de bon. persev.* 11, 8): "*non erant ex nobis, quia non erant secundum propositum vocati, non erant in Christo electi ante constitutionem mundi—non erant prædestinati secundum propositum ejus, qui universa operatur.*" So Calvin, *Inst.* III. 24, 7. But although Calvin the theologian [German "*Dogmatiker*," not=*dogmatist*, *i. e.*, one who is certain or presumes to say he knows, whether he be mistaken or in the right, but the teacher of a theological dogma—M.] cannot be corrected by Calvin the interpreter, yet Augustine the theologian can be corrected by Augustine the interpreter in his *Tractat. ad h. l.*, where he says: "DE VOLUNTATE SUA *unusquisque aut antichristus, aut in Christo est; qui se in melius commutat, in corpore membrum est, qui autem in malitia permanet, humor malus est.*" The Apostle distinguishes inward and true Christian fellowship from that which is only outward and in appearance; those who belong to the former are so thoroughly fettered in their believing and regenerated mind, that, as Lücke thinks, they can nevermore separate from that fellowship. It is, to use the striking language of the *Oxymoron* of Didymus, a *voluntaria necessitas;* but no *contrarietas naturarum*, although in the course of moral development there should arise a *diversitas substantiæ*.—The phrases οὐκ ἐξ ἡμῶν εἶναι and ἐξ ἡμῶν εἶναι used by the Apostle to denote simply the opposite results of the ethical life-process, which in the former case leads to ἐξελθεῖν and in the latter to μένειν μεθ' ἡμῶν. But, as Augustine says, every Christian may become an antichrist, according as his will refuses to be determined to μένειν ἐν Χριστῷ, which beginning with the hearing of His word and advancing to πίστις εἰς αὐτόν, to childlike and unremitting trust and cleaving to Him, develops itself by ever determining

guiding, strengthening, purifying and confirming the will, is a veritable history of the word heard with the outward ears and inwardly in the heart filling and conquering the heart until it has become *wholly* believing, but for all that may and does offer resistance at every point, so that it often does resist for some length of time and so undoes all its previous acquirements, that it often conceals unpardoned sins which may again draw it down or at least arrest its progress and bring it to the point that, unless it submit to being cleansed anew, it will apostatize and thus a Christian may become an antichrist, which is however of rare occurrence, because the eternal powers of the word of Christ and His Spirit are very strong and mighty and the heart of man has been created for and with special adaptation to said powers. Hence the universal experience that it is difficult to get to Christ through self-denying and world-renouncing penitence, but that it is even more difficult to get away from Christ through the denial of the conscience and of faith as well as of the word of Christ quickened in the conscience by faith,—and the Apostle speaks from this experience. But in all this there is neither predestination nor necessity, especially since the Apostle's exhortation to abide leaves room for the *possibility* of their apostasy, as to the reality of which the Apostle confidently entertains no fear in the case of those who are vital Christians. Nor is it to be overlooked that John does not throw out the faintest allusion to the difference between the *electi* and *vocati* and the *donum perseverantiæ*. In the passage Heb. vi. 4–6 the lapse of the truly regenerate (as is evident from their description) is supposed to be possible, but the re-conversion of such apostates only is said to be impossible, so that we ought to be afraid. [Huther: the words εἰ ἦσαν ἐξ ἡμῶν, μεμενήκεισαν ἂν μεθ' ἡμῶν contain the idea that he who truly belongs to the Church will never leave it, but he that leaves it shows thereby that he did not truly belong to it. This confidence of the Apostle in the love of the Lord which keeps and preserves those who are His, and in the fidelity of those who have been redeemed by Him, seems to contradict the idea pre-supposed in Heb. vi. 4–6, that they also who were once enlightened and had tasted of the heavenly gift and were made partakers of the Holy Ghost, can fall away. But John speaks here, as he does throughout his Epistle, absolutely, without any reference to the state of gradual development, from whence however it does by no means follow that he did not know it. The one circumstance that he *exhorts* believers, as such to abide in Christ, is sufficient to show that he does not wish to deny the *possibility* of their apostasy, all he is sure of, and rightly so, is this that he that does *not* abide, had never truly entered into fellowship with the Lord with his *whole* heart, but although he was touched by His love and felt somewhat of its power, he had not entirely abandoned and renounced the world."—M.].

6. The Apostle here asserts a double law of historical development in its definite application to the development of the kingdom of God. "Evil by a gradual process of development culminates, then in the conflict between the kingdom of God and evil, the former develops itself, and at length, through a new coming of Christ in power, the kingdom of Christ is once more subdued." (Neander). This is the one, and of the other the same author speaks thus: "In this respect also we shall see how the workings of one uniform law ever appear in the course of the development of the kingdom of God, that in good and evil there are certain individual personages constituting as it were, the centre and appearing especially as representatives of the conflicting principles, uniting and concentrating in themselves as one great whole, the fragments scattered in many individuals." "When in the times before the Reformation the secularized Church under the secularized papacy, was especially instrumental under the cloak of Christianity to obscure and oppose true Christianity, people might believe that they saw in this the visible manifestation of antichrist, and Matthias of Janow, the Bohemian reformer before Huss, might suppose to have detected the effect of Satan's craft in the circumstance that believers instead of identifying antichrist in the present, viz., the rule of the secularized Church and the sway of a superstition even unto the idolizing of the human, were beguiled into seeking it at some distant period." The increasing revelation of the depths of evil in the world, runs therefore parallel to the development of the kingdom of God even up to its ultimate completion and both pass through personages in whom the former does concentrate. See also Düsterdieck: "The development of the Christian principle, and that of the antichristian principle are reciprocally related. Christian truth cannot be revealed without forthwith exciting the contradiction of the darkness. The wheat and the tares grow together until they are ripe. The antichristian spirit works already in many antichrists; but the one antichrist is still future, still to come, and is only announced by his precursors. Although therefore the last hour has already come, yet its full close is still to come, viz., the real, personal advent of the Lord which will take place immediately after the appearance of the personal antichrist. But John did neither tell us *when* this antichrist would come nor give us a chronological clue to the exact time of the personal advent of Christ. In both respects he confines himself to the statement *that* the events are to take place."—

7. Athough John in giving prominence to the marrow and vitalizing centre of Christianity, viz., to the belief that Jesus is the Christ and the Son of God, does not warrant us to undervalue the articulated confession of faith as a whole or as to its component parts, which are only developments of the pushing germ, he yet attaches, and for this very reason, the greatest importance to the *faithfulness of abiding*, the *fides qui creditur*, with reference to said centre.

8. His account of the χρῖσμα and its gifts, characteristically and emphatically adverts to the universal priesthood, indicating its origin and glory.

9. The "critical ability" (Düsterdieck) of Christians founded on the full knowledge of the truth, like the advancing knowledge of the truth itself, goes hand in hand with progressive holiness. The point throughout is not mere knowledge, tidings or information of a life *in* and of

(from) God, but the actual possession and enjoyment of this life, the life itself and the personal converse of the human soul with the living and revealed God; and it concerns man's inmost and most profound being, which is neither the understanding nor the reason, but the will, and the point in question is not *science* but *conscience*.

10. It is only in the way of obedience to the word and will of God that man is able to keep and intensify fellowship with Him in order that he may become a partaker of the divine Being, the divine Nature. It is *contrary* to the *will* of God that man departs *from* the *Being* of God until he is wholly rejected.

11. The decision and the separation will not take place until the last, the last judgment; consider this.—

HOMILETICAL AND PRACTICAL.

See what time it is in the kingdom of God? 1. Hearken to the *word* which is preached (vv. 18, 24); 2. be led by the *Spirit* whom thou hast received (vv. 20, 27); 3. take note of the *separations* which take place in the Church (vv. 19, 22); 4. hold fast to Jesus the Christ, who is the Son of the Father (vv. 26, 28).—In all the separations in the Church be sure not to forget to decide.—In every separation the sorrow of having been deceived before is connected with the joy of greater purity hereafter.—In the uncertainty as to who are true vital Christians take care lest thou lose the conviction that the vital Christian abides constant.—Act as Gideon did who encountering the Midianites numbering 135,000 with an army of 32,000 at the Lord's bidding reduced the same by 22,000 and made a selection of 300 from the remaining 10,000 even as directed by the Lord, and then gained a glorious victory with them (Judg. vii.).—The source of the anointing is the Holy Ghost, its pre-requisite regeneration, its power an assured conviction of the importance of the truth, its impulse an earnest desire to bring it home to the hearts of others; it was a protection from the hierarchism and episcopalianism of the 2d and 3d centuries. Is. xli. 15 applies to it. [I should rather say in more strict agreement with the text that the chrism of the Holy Ghost from Christ is a sure protection from any and every form of spiritual secessionism, separatism and individualism.—M.]. Because of a sorrowful experience in the Church do not give up the joy of the glory of the Church.—Comparison of the ointment as the figure or symbol of the Holy Spirit: 1, its value; 2, its use in the anointing of kings, priests and prophets; 3, its power of strengthening and stimulating the spirit of life; 4, its influence on a life well-pleasing to God; 5, its far-spreading fragrance.—The fundamental doctrine of salvation is: Jesus is the Christ. 1, With it and in it we find our way into the rich heart of God and bring God into our poor heart; 2, in opposition to it we bring eternal ruin into our heart and ourselves into eternal ruin. Or, 1, By it you learn the corrupting false teachers; 2, in it the true and living Christian shows himself; 3, out of it you pass to the inheritance of God.—Do not drive Christ and His word from thy heart, or Christ will drive thee from His kingdom.—v. 28. *Confirmation-address.*

GREGORY:—"*Nisi Spiritus Sanctus intus sit qui doceat, doctoris lingua extus in vanum laborat.*"

AUGUSTINE:—"*Cathedram in cœlo habet, qui intus docet.*"

LUTHER:—It is dangerous and terrible to believe something against the uniform testimony, faith and doctrine of the universal holy Church, which has now thus held it unanimously in every place from the beginning these fifteen hundred years past.—Many a man has a paternoster round his neck and a rogue in his heart.

STARKE:—As the betrayer of Christ was one of His most intimate Apostles, so antichrist did not arise among Jews or Turks, but in the very midst of Christendom.—The Church remaineth not without offences of which that is not least that within her fold there arise men who hold false doctrine and apostatize from the known truth; the tares do not grow by themselves, but in the midst of the wheat.—Constancy in good is an infallible sign of a true Christian, just as temporizing and changeableness indicate a false heart.—Christians are anointed, and their name should daily remind them of what they owe to God and their neighbour, as spiritual kings, priests and prophets.—A teacher ought not to despise his hearers, for they also, if they believe, are anointed with the Holy Spirit and the knowledge of divine truths, although there may be differences in the measure of their anointing.—He also denies Christ the Saviour, who does not prove in deed that He is *His* Saviour who has indeed delivered him from the guilt and punishment of sin.—We have need to be especially on our guard against the denial of Christ which takes place, not only in words and in doctrine, but also in our life.—The word of God must remain in the whole man, and not only enter his understanding.—A Christian, an anointed one, that is his name, but also the greatest prerogative to divine wisdom, it opens to him the school in which the most learned are seated below on the bench of humility, who follow in the simplicity of their heart, who know all things, and ever learn what they know, love and do.—As is a king without a kingdom, a ruler without subjects, a general without soldiers, so is a Christian without the anointing. Because the last coming of the Lord will be terrible, we should be diligent to be so well prepared that we may be found worthy to stand before the Son of Man.—The day of our Lord's coming may properly be called the believers' day of honour, for they shall be manifested, declared righteous, and advanced to the full enjoyment of heavenly blessing.

SPENER:—It is a great blessing that God does not allow the heavenly [?] deceivers to remain in the Church but overrules it that they are made known and we learn to be on our guard against them, that they must manifest themselves and make themselves known, whereby the danger is lessened and believers rendered more cautious and prompted to be diligent in prayer and to work out their own salvation with fear and trembling.—Even those who truly believe and have made great advances in the faith, may be deceived, and therefore let those who think that they stand, take heed lest they fall. None but those who have the Holy Spirit and the anointing can be sufficiently on their guard against the lies of antichrist. All other knowledge is too weak by far to be able to withstand temptation and spiritual conflicts.

UHLHORN:—*He only has God, who has Him as the Triune God.* Let us only begin with what the Apostle puts in the middle, *He that hath not the Son, neither hath he the Father*, add that with which he begins, *of the Son we can only know through the Holy Spirit*, and conclude the statement in virtue of what the Apostle says, that the anointing cometh from Him who is holy: *The Holy Ghost cometh from the Father and the Son.*

LAVATER:—Every one who is not an *evangelical* Christian, does not believe in Jesus Christ, is an atheist.

HEUBNER:—A hostile power, an opposition to Christianity, has stirred from the beginning. And this is a recommendation of Christianity; a proof of the mighty power of Christianity against evil, which is terrible to the wicked one. The more the good raises itself the more also does evil bestir itself. Where God builds a temple, Satan is sure to build a chapel by the side of it. —It serves also to exercise and try the soldiers of Christ. Without an opposing power, the divine drama would be without life or interest.—Unbelief which pretends that the kernel and characteristics of Christianity are irrational, is a very important epoch in this history.—Who thought Christianity imperilled by the growth of antichrist would betray great weakness of heart and understanding and want of confidence. The Christian should rejoice at every further manifestation: the end is drawing nearer: the catastrophe in the kingdom of Christ is the point to which the eyes of Christians are longingly directed.—The enemies of Christianity draw nourishment from the Church: it is in their interest not to suffer themselves to be deprived of the name "Christian;" they would then accomplish less and be less dangerous.—The manifestation of all, the good as well as the bad, is the design of the Kingdom of God. The evil cannot long conceal or disguise itself or stand back: it only waits for the time of coming out. God wills it thus. The appearance of evil tries and purifies the Church. It is a refreshing relief to Christians to see the separation of the unclean.—A Christian is insured and protected from false teachers. He has the Holy Spirit 1. Who interpenetrates every thing like precious perfume, enters into every thing, and imparts to it fragrance and the breath of life—to his thinking, judging, feeling and willing. The Christian is thereby clothed with a royal and priestly dignity in the Kingdom of God (Rev. i. 6). The anointing is the signature of the Christian. 2. The Spirit enables him to try, to identify the spirit of error, to judge; to such a Christian no false teacher can be dangerous.—The Christian has a fine sense of discrimination (*sagax odoratus*); he quickly perceives the essence and tendency of every doctrine; hence his Christian severity of judgment and his antipathy to syncretism.—Bad opinions, seductive principles among Christians, originate not in Christianity. The Church of Christ must not be charged with the evil that is in it.—He that will not know God in Jesus—where else will he know God?—There is no revelation of God which resembles the revelation in Christ; if one is not satisfied with this revelation, which revelation will satisfy him?—Whether they like or do not like it, neologians are obliged to assert that true Christianity was unknown before them; for what they now call Christianity is known to the whole antiquity.—The true Christian faith is immutable and needs no perfecting.—This faith is of the utmost importance; our eternal salvation depends upon it; it is not a useless, subtle question raised by the schools, but it concerns *the promise of eternal life*, and the virtue of this promise depends on the Person of Jesus; only if He is truly the Son of God He is able to promise and give eternal life. This must attach us strongly to the faith, and those who have felt the power of this faith, live and die for this faith.—Even anointed Christians stand in need of warning and admonition, because deceivers are never quiet and because within us there is not wanting that which meets them half-way.—Other gifts decrease in the course of time, the Holy Spirit does not decrease. Other frames of mind and tendencies of thought change, the Holy Spirit does not change. Yield to the promptings of the Spirit and be vigilant lest thou mistake thy own spirit for the Holy Spirit and be deceived. Be pure and meek.—Abiding with Christ and in Him in steadfastness of faith and faithful following Him is the more *honourable*, the more fall away from Him, and it is necessary, because our acceptance depends on it. If one becomes unfaithful to Christ, how can he appear before Him with joyfulness [confidence?]? *That* thought has an overwhelming influence on the heart of a Christian. How shall unbelievers appear before Him who to please the world leave Christ, and esteem the world's honours more highly than the grace of Christ? How well it would be if all men would only examine themselves in all their judging and doing; could you act thus in the presence of Jesus? would you dare to say such and such a thing in the presence of Jesus? would you dare to maintain such an opinion before Him? If you are honest and conscientious according to your interpretation, so that He may not even blame you, why have you twisted my words after your liking?

BESSER:—It *is* the last hour. But those who read the history of the Church wrongly, and consider the time of her highest inward beauty and manifest power over the world to belong to an earthly future, will be inclined to suspect the holy Apostle, to have been in error for assuring us to have experienced the beginning of the last hour; those, on the other hand, who consider that the Sun of the Gospel shone in his brightest splendor, when in the preaching of the Apostles he came forth as a bridegroom out of his chamber and rejoiced as a giant to run his race from one end of the heavens back to the same end again and that there sounds through the whole history of the Church the sigh of the saints "Abide with us, Lord Jesus, for it is toward evening"—aye, that even her most glorious victories, like the victory of the Reformation, are only like the reflection of the setting sun on the darkening clouds,—those who see this cease to be surprised at what the Apostles tell us of the last hour and read the merciful cause of this prolonged duration of the last hour, prolonged for more than eighteen hundred years, in the words of the Apostle "the Lord is long-suffering to us-ward" (2 Pet. iii. 9).—We must not only be on our guard against one antichrist, one great adversary and deceiver, but against a multitudinous progeny of the antichristian seed.—When somebody praised the sainted Oettinger shortly before his death, on account of his great wisdom, he replied with a smile: "Yes, I have learned many things; but the most precious knowledge I learned as a child in Luther's Lesser Catechism, which comprises every thing which I desire to keep and carry away with me to the seeing face to face." —A learner of the Catechism, that hath the Holy Spirit, is able so far to discover all errors which militate against the Gospel, that he is protected from deception and may immoveably stand on the foundation of his faith.—Neither the Jesus of the rationalists nor the Christ of the philosophers hurts the kingdom of Satan.—The antichrists showed themselves to be antitheists — Declension begins with men's loathing that which they have heard from the beginning (Rieger.)— Every true doctrine the assertion of which is assigned to the church during the time of her growth, is already contained in the treasury of Holy Scripture.

Johann Tauler had preached many a learned sermon when Nicolaus of Basle, the Waldensian, visited and told him: "You are a kind-hearted man and a great priest, but have not yet tasted in truth the sweetness of the Holy Spirit." From that time Tauler sought the true Teacher in the Scripture and the cross, who teaches us more in one hour than all earthly teachers can teach us to the last day.

[WARBURTON:—The late appearance of antichrist was a doctrine so universally received in the primitive Church, that it was like a proverbial saying among them; and thence St. John takes occasion to moralize on the doctrine, and warn his followers against that spirit, which in after times was to animate "the man of sin." "Little children," says he, "it is the last time; and as ye have heard that antichrists shall come, even now there are many antichrists: whereby ye know that it is the last time." As much as to say, we are fallen into the very dregs of time, as appears from that antichristian spirit, which now so much pollutes the Churches; for you know it is a common saying, that antichrist is to come in those wretched days. The Apostle goes on to employ the same allusion through the rest of the Epistle; v. 22. ch. iv. 3; 2 Jno. 7. Where we see the appellation "antichrist" is employed to signify an enemy of God and godliness in general, by the same figure of speech that Elias was designed in those times to signify *a prophet*, and Rachel, *a daughter of Israel;* and that in these times Judas is used for *a traitor*, and Nero for *a tyrant*. But as these convertible terms necessarily suppose that they originally belonged to persons of the like characters, who had them in proper, so does the name "antichrist" transferred by St. John to certain of his impious contemporaries, as necessarily suppose, that there was one who should arise in the latter times, to whom the title eminently belonged; as marked out in the prophecies by the proper name of antichrist.—M.].

[HURD's two sermons on 1 Jno. ii. 18, the one entitled "*Prophecies concerning Antichrist*," the other "*Prejudices against the doctrine of Antichrist*," are well worth reading, as they embody much of the literature on the subject.—M.].

[WHITBY:—To deny the Father here, is not to deny Him to be the true God, as the heathens did: but 1. to deny the truth of His testimony, see ch. v. 10; Jno. iii. 33; 2. to deny the doctrine of the Father, or that doctrine which proceedeth from Him; "for He whom God hath sent, speaketh the words of God," Jno. iii. 34. Whence it is evident, that he who denieth the Son, cannot thus retain the true knowledge of the Father; Jno. i. 18; Matth. xi. 27. By Him alone can we come acceptably to the Father, so as to have life; for "He is the Way, and the Truth and the Life," Jno. xiv. 6. And by Him alone are we taught how to "worship the Father in spirit and in truth," Jno. iv. 23, 24. Hence Christ so often tells the Jews, they therefore wanted the true knowledge of the Father, because they knew not Him, Jno. viii. 19; xiv. 7; xvi. 3.—M.].

[ABP. SHARP:—Abundance of fanaticism, enthusiasm and other mischiefs have been brought into the Church of Christ, by the misinterpreting and misapplying of those texts which speak of the gifts of the Spirit, which some men so understand as to make no distinction between the times then and the times now.—(Joel ii. 28; Acts ii. 17; Jer. xxxi. 34; 1 Jno. ii. 27.)—Hence they conclude that in these days, which are the last days, the Spirit of God is poured upon all flesh, and that every one hath a right to expect immediate impulses and revelations, as to what he is to believe and to practise: that by this assistance of the Spirit, every brother may understand the mysteries of the Holy Scriptures, without the troublesome way of studying human learning; nay and may take upon himself the pastoral office, and become a guide and teacher of others, without any warrant from human authority, merely upon the impulse of the Spirit of God. These consequences have been drawn from these and such texts of Scripture: and so far have they been promoted and improved by several amongst us, that reason and prudence and all acquired learning, are rather accounted by them hinderances to the work of God's Church, than any ways contributing to it. Nay, they are arrived to a pitch above the Scriptures themselves, which they look upon as a dead letter in comparison of the light within them, the witness, the anointing which they have received from above, which is the only measure with them of truth and falsehood, of good and evil. The colour, which these enthusiasts derive for this their notion from the letter of some passages of the Old and New Testament, would quite vanish, if they would but take care to distinguish between the effects of the Spirit, which belonged to the converting of the world, and those which were to be His constant permanent operations among such as were already Christians. There is no one will deny but the Apostles, and those in their times, had these inspirations, these revelations they speak of: and the texts, that they produce, are some of them plain proofs that those promises were made good.

They did see visions, and were endowed with extraordinary talents of wisdom and knowledge, without human methods, and might expect particular impulses of the Holy Ghost upon occasions, where they wanted either light or direction; and all this was indeed little enough for the discharge of that great work they had upon their hands, namely, the bringing of the world over from Judaism and heathenism to Christianity. But that being done once, and the Gospel of Christ, and all things pertaining to it, being plainly left in writing by the Apostles or Apostolical men, as there would be from henceforward no need of those assistances of the Spirit, so it would be a vain thing to expect them. We are not to desire those immediate revelations, nor to expect that God should vouchsafe them, if we prayed for them. God hath declared all His will, that is necessary for us to know, by our Saviour and His Apostles: and the rules which they have given us, together with our own natural light and reason, and the other outward means and helps of instruction, which are every day at hand among us, are sufficient, abundantly sufficient, to guide and direct us, both as to belief and practice, through all the cases and emergencies that can ordinarily happen to us. And in extraordinary cases God will take care, some way or other, that we shall not be at a loss. And therefore to pretend to the Spirit in these days, either for preaching, or praying, or prophesying, or denouncing God's judgments, or for any other thing, in such a way as implies immediate inspiration; or to set up a light within us, contrary to the light of reason, or different from the light of Scripture without us, is the extreme of folly, enthusiasm and madness."—M.].

[The *chrism* is 1. a *general* gift, vouchsafed to all *Christians;*
2. not transient but permanent;
3. leads them into all truth;
4. moves them to the practice of all the precepts of Christ;
5. assures them of their Christian privileges; (children of God, members of Christ and inheritors of the kingdom of heaven);
6. teaches them in all things; they are therefore disciples and learners all the days of their life;
7. preserves their fellowship with the Father and with the Son; (*abide*).
8. and makes them the Temples of God.—M.].

III. PRINCIPAL PART THE SECOND.

Chapter II. 29—V. 12.

HE THAT IS BORN AGAIN (OUT) OF (THE BEING OF) GOD THE RIGHTEOUS (II. 29) IS A MIRACLE OF HIS LOVE NOW AND HEREAFTER (III. 1–3), IS BOUND BY HIS WILL (III. 4–10*a*), ESPECIALLY TO PRACTISE BROTHERLY LOVE (III. 10*b*–18), IS BLESSED BEFORE HIM AND IN HIM (III. 19–24), TRYING LIKE GOD THE FALSE SPIRITS (IV. 1–6), HE ENJOYS THE LOVE OF GOD AND EXHIBITS BROTHERLY LOVE (IV. 7–21), HE TRIUMPHS OVER THE WORLD AND IS SURE OF ETERNAL LIFE (V. 1–12).

1. *The leading thought: He that is born again of God the Righteous doeth righteousness.* Ch. ii. 29.

29 If ye know that he is righteous, ye know[1] that[2] every one that doeth righteousness is born of him.[3]

Verse 29. [[1] German: "If ye know that He is righteous, know ye." The Imperative is found in the margin of E. V., Wicl. Tynd. Cranm. Rhemish, Syriac. Latin (except Pagn. Beza), German, Dutch. Italian and French versions, and adopted by the authorities cited below in *Exeget. and Crit.*—M.]

[2] καὶ after ὅτι and before πᾶς is the reading of A. C. Sin., many cursives and versions. "*Cujus addendi nulla causa erat; ex Johannis vero usu est.*" (Tischendorf, who omits it in his 7th edition). [If καὶ is genuine it serves "to mark the congruity of the inference and the premise," as Ebrard observes.—M.]

[[3] German: retaining καὶ: "that also every one that doeth the righteousness hath been born of Him."—M.]

EXEGETICAL AND CRITICAL.

The *subject* of δίκαιος is not specified. It has to be ascertained either from the connection with the preceding verses, or from the verse itself. On this point Sander very justly lays down the Canon: "If δίκαιος designates Christ, ἐξ αὐτοῦ refers to Him. But if the latter is impossible, that is, if ἐξ αὐτοῦ must be referred to God, δίκαιος also must designate God." There is no *formal* connection of this verse with the preceding verses containing reference to Christ; it is the beginning of a new section. Hence this verse, standing alone, must be explained by itself, and the question of the subject has to be determined from an examination of the verse itself. Hence there is no warrant for an outward occasion of a reference to Christ, especially since the oneness of the Father and the Son, of God and Christ, is everpresent to the mind of John, so that he frequently and easily passes from the one to the other without a special indication of such transition. Nor can we gather from the word δίκαιος whether the reference is to Christ or to God, for it is applied to God in ch. i. 9 and to Christ in ch. ii. 1. But ἐξ αὐτοῦ γεγέννηται decides the point. The idea of γεννᾶσθαι ἐκ Χριστοῦ or τέκνα Χριστοῦ notwithstanding Spener's reference to Is. ix. 6; liii. 10; Ps. xxii. 31, cx. 3; Matth. ix. 2; Jno. xiii. 33; Heb. ii. 17 occurs nowhere. But γεγεννημένος ἐκ τοῦ θεοῦ occurs ch. iii. 9; v. 18 cf. vv. 1. 4; ch. iv. 7; and τέκνα θεοῦ in the very next verse ch. iii. 1: consequently: he is born of (out of) *God.* "*Justus justum gignit*" (Bengel). We have therefore the valid conclusion: God is righteous, he that is born of (out of) God doeth righteousness. [*Like begets like.*—M.]. Hence Christ is neither the subject of δίκαιος and ἐξ αὐτοῦ (a Lapide, Bengel, Rickli, Frommann, al.), nor *Christ* the subject of δίκαιος and *God* the subject of ἐξ αὐτοῦ (Storr, Lücke, Heubner al.); but *God* is the subject of δίκαιος and ἐξ αὐτοῦ (Neander, Köstlin, Düsterdieck, Ebrard, Huther, al.).

VER. 29. **If ye know that He is righteous.**—Besides what has been said on δίκαιος at ch. i. 9; ii. 1, we have further to add that if God is ἅγιος as to His *Essence*, He is δίκαιος as to His *doing*, and just because He is ἀγάπη (ch. iv. 16), His energizing Will aims at the revelation of His holiness in laws at once agreeable to the holiness of His Being and adjusted to the nature and destination of His creatures, for whose benefit they are enacted, showing how His words are to be kept and His promises to be fulfilled, and how those who obey Him are to be rewarded and those who disobey him are to be punished. Legislation, denunciation and promise, punishment and reward, redemption and the forgiveness of sins are the acts and exhibitions of His δικαιοσύνη, which is the energy of His holy love directed outwardly, or the energy of His love conjoined with His holiness. Accordingly there is no righteousness whatever outside of God, or separate from God and His energizing, so that He is not only the prototype and original, but also the primordial source of all human righteousness. This is an important object of Christian knowledge, which, whilst it may indubitably be presupposed in the case of all Christians, is not always and readily found in the desired strength and purity in individual Christians. Hence ἐὰν εἰδῆτε. The Apostle appeals to the consciousness of the Church, desiring not to teach anything new but to render their knowledge vital and fruitful. [Hollaz: "*Justitia Dei est attributum divinum ἐνεργητικόν, vi cujus Deus omnia quæ æternæ suæ legi sunt conformia, vult et agit; creaturis convenientes leges præscribit, promissa facta hominibus implet, bonos remuneratur et impios punit.*" M.].

Know ye.—Since it is grammatically correct (Kühner II., p. 550) that such a supposition may be followed either by the Imperative or the Indicative of a chief tense, especially of the Future, the prominent use of the Indicative Future, which is very nearly related to the Imperative, renders it highly probable that our γινώσκετε is the Imperative. Now since we read at ch. v. 15 (referred to by de Wette and Düsterdieck) ἐὰν οἴδαμεν—οἴδαμεν, but in the verse immediately succeeding ch. iii. 1, ἴδετε (to which Huther calls attention), the latter consideration decidedly outweighs the former and constrains us to take γινώσκετε in the Imperative. To this must still be added the sense of the verb and the verse. The verb γινώσκειν denotes an activity ever deepening, quickening and enlarging, the knowing (εἰδέναι) grows thus into experimental knowing (γινώσκειν). The truth is the object of all knowing, and the Christian shall be led into *all* truth, that is, he is to know thoroughly, to pass on from one point which he knows and whereof he has cognition, to another [and a deeper knowing and insight—M.], even by the aid of the Holy Spirit. If ye know that He is righteous, ye know not yet, but are to know that—. Hence we must not construe here in the Indicative (Beza, Bengel, Düsterdieck, Ewald, Neander and al.) but in the Imperative (Vulgate, Grotius, de Wette, Lücke, Ebrard, Huther and al.).

That also every one who doeth righteousness has been born (out) **of Him.**—Καὶ indicates the relation of appurtenance and congruity of the second to the first thought. It does not belong, however, to γινώσκετε, as if only expressing a logical relation (Düsterdieck): if ye know—then ye know also (Neander); but it belongs to the subject, πᾶς ὁ ποιῶν, and sets forth the relation of the two truths: God is righteous, and every one who doeth righteousness, is born of God. We have here to do with a real relation.—Ὁ ποιῶν τὴν δικαιοσύνην is he that has the δικαιοσύνη within himself and causes it to be operative in his walk, his works, his words, his conduct and thinking, in his judgment, attitude, bearing and appearance, to come forth and become perceptible in himself. Doing is here not a merely outward and isolated act but an activity continuous and connected, having as much respect to the inward as to the outward, the energy of something possessed inwardly, of a gift received, of a communicated nature and life. Ποιῶν is emphatic; righteousness must be *done*, and not only lauded, confessed, preached, known, felt and believed. It may be done as yet imperfectly, in weakness, under repeated interruptions, but *every* Christian must and does do righteousness, πᾶς "*omnis et solus*" (Bengel). Nor is it enough to do only some parts of this righteousness, respect must be had to the whole τὴν δικαιοσύνην. As to the nature of this δικαιοσύνη we have to think of the righteousness which comes from God, passes before Him, is His and His work. It is, therefore, a righteousness, Divine as to its kind, an effluence of God's primordial righteousness, from God Himself. It manifests itself in obedience to the Divine commandments, in shunning sin, in striving after holiness, in love of the brethren, in the life and growth of faith; and although much be wanting in its full exhibition and its perfection lie far remote, still this is the righteousness here referred to. Compare ποιεῖν τὴν ἀλήθειαν ch. i. 6 and צְדָקָה עָשָׂה Gen. xviii. 19; Is. lvi. 1; Ps. xiv. 15.—This points to a powerful and specific cause and condition, without which ποιεῖν τὴν δικαιοσύνην is impossible and inconceivable: ἐξ αὐτοῦ γεγέννηται. The Present ποιῶν, and the Perfect γεγέννηται denote the sequence; the first in order of existence is: *to be born of* (out of) *God*, the second, which is the effect and result of the former, is: *to do the righteousness.* Precisely this order was necessarily implied in the exposition of the substance of ποιεῖν τὴν δικαιοσύνην.—As with regard to δίκαιος the turns δικαιοσύνη and ποιεῖν τὴν δικαιοσύνην have to be taken in a full and living sense, so likewise the phrase ἐξ αὐτοῦ γεννᾶσθαι. The reference is consequently to a beginning life, a birth, a coming into existence (becoming) of something which did not or does not yet exist; not only a change or an improvement, but something altogether new—and that *out of God.* The sense of the preposition ἐξ also, has doubtless to be held fast; out of Him, that is out of God's Self-own Holy Essence. "*Nasci ex Deo est naturam Dei acquirere*" (Luther) or "*constituitur in quadam participatione supernaturali esse divini*" (de Lyra), having received a new being or nature out of God (Spener), perfectly analogous to γένησθε θείας κοινωνοὶ φύσεως, 2 Pet. i. 4.—Cf. Jno. iii. 3, 5, 6; i. 12, 13; Tit. iii. 5; Eph. iv. 23, 24; Rom. xii. 2; 1 Pet. i. 3, 23. There is a Divine seed (ch. iii. 9) in those who are born out of God; they have not become God, deified or absorbed in God or God absorbed in them, but only partakers of the Divine nature, germ-like, like new-born babes, so that a beginning has been made, but only a beginning, although the beginning of a life, Divine, coming from and leading to God, whose perfection is not wrought magically or by enchantment at one stroke, but is subject to the law of Divinely appointed growth. This birth out of God is a translation of man from death to life (ch. iii. 14), brings him to the Light of the world and gives him eternal life (ch. v. 11, 20), and effects the blessed result that God is in us and we in Him (ch. iv. 15), as the children of God (ch. iii. 1, 2, 9, 10), out of God (ch. iii. 10). But this is brought about by means of an ethical life-process (ch. iii. 9; v. 1). We *become* the children of God. But nothing is said here on this point, or on the mediation of Christ and faith in Him. We have therefore to set aside all expositions, which weaken the thought, like those of Socinus ("*Dei similem esse*") and Rosenmüller ("*Amari a Deo*" and "*beneficiis ab eo ornari,*" or introduce a foreign element, like that of Hilgenfeld (a destiny and necessity of nature represented in gnostico-dualistic manner), and those which misapprehend or reverse the right order in making the doing of righteousness the condition of our adoption (Socinus, Episcopius, Semler, al.); the false relation also of doing righteousness to standing in the judgment (a Lapide, Emser, Estius) has to be excluded as irrelevant.—Lücke (2d ed.) says "properly one ought to have expected ὅτι πᾶς ὁ γεγεννημένος ἐξ αὐτοῦ ποιεῖ τὴν δικαιοσύνην;" this is not correct although the thought is correct *per se.* John makes the perceptible and cognizable ποιεῖν τὴν δικαιοσύνην a sure token of the hidden life of the inner man, which began with the birth out of God, of the adoption, of the life out of which death cannot destroy and which can glory against the judgment. The relation between γεγεννῆσθαι ἐκ θεοῦ and ποιεῖν τὴν δικαιοσύνην is exactly like that between κοινωνίαν ἔχειν μετὰ θεοῦ and περιπατεῖν ἐν τῷ φωτί in ch. i. 6.

Connection with the preceding, and development in the sequel.—The rich and independent thought is the *introduction* to or the *text* of the next part. Its fundamental tone is δίκαιός ἐστι, parallel to φῶς ἐστι, which is a further confirmation of the presumption that God is the subject. It is impossible to restrict the notion δίκαιος by the side of the inference which is here drawn from it, to *justitia judicialis.* Hence we must not seek or find an internal reciprocal relationship between the *judgment,* (to which v. 28 is supposed to refer, but of which nothing is said, the reference being simply to Christ's Advent), and *righteousness;* we need not think of the *judicial* function of the Divine righteousness nor of our being able to stand before the *righteous* Judge only through doing *righteousness.* But John in concluding the first part with the strong consolation which on the ground of the walk in light, adverts with hopeful promise to the blessed destination of Christians, passes from the παῤῥησία in the Advent to the thought of the Sonship, of the hope, the glory and heritage of the children of God. This is the connection with what goes before. The next main part of the Epistle is analytically divided by the development of this idea of a glorious birth out of God.

DOCTRINAL AND ETHICAL.

1. God's attribute of righteousness is not only energetically active, but also communicative.

2. The import of regeneration should be laid hold of by its indispensable consequence; viz. ποιεῖν τὴν δικαιοσύνην, and even its nature defined as a beginning of a new, Divine life.

3. The vital power and root of a truly valid righteousness in our being and walking, lie not in man as he is, but only in God, and out of God only in man as he has become a Christian.

HOMILETICAL AND PRACTICAL.

Determine [find out experimentally,—M.] what thou knowest.—Not only every gift of God is good and perfect, but both all the good, and all perfection are the gifts of Him, the Righteous one.—God gives and man—not only *has* but *becomes* [comes into existence.—M.].—God rules over thee and has His work in thee, that thou mayest become and remain His child.—Whatever is Divine prompts and impels the ethical, by which the Divine may be identified.—The *cause* of regeneration is the righteous God, and an ethical status is its *mark* and *sign.*

SPENER:—No man has by nature the power to do right or to work righteousness, but it comes only from his regeneration, from Christ, who makes us strong by regeneration and His dwelling in us.

LANGE:—The Gospel is careful with the law to connect the righteousness of faith with the righteousness of life and therein lies a true mark of a sincere evangelical preacher and a sincere evangelical hearer.

STARKE:—Believers are assured by their *doing right,* that they have become the children of God by grace, that consequently they may joyfully appear before the judgment seat of God knowing that no Father will suffer his children to be put to confusion of face, and in this faith and undoubting hope they may joyfully take leave of this world.

BESSER:—The Apostle's rejoicing over the

present power of the children of God over sin is, as it were, a ladder on which he ascends to the glory that is still reserved for them; and the hope of this future glory impels him once more to charge his little children to use with all diligence the Christian virtue already accorded to them, uninfluenced by the seducers who pretended to be able to see the Lord without holiness.

[EZEK. HOPKINS:—Those who do God's commandments, have a right of heirship and inheritance unto eternal life. For they are born of God and therefore heaven is their patrimony, their paternal estate: for the Apostle saith "Every one that doeth righteousness is born of God," and if they are born of God then according to St. Paul's argument Rom. viii. 17: "If children, then heirs; heirs of God and joint-heirs with Christ," who is the "heir of all things." The trial of thy legitimacy, whether thou art a true and genuine son of God will lie upon thy obedience to His commands, for "in this the children of God are manifest and the children of the devil; whosoever is born of God does not commit sin . . . . and whosoever doeth not righteousness is not of God." 1 Jno. iii. 9. 10. Now if by our obedience and dutifulness, it appears, that we are indeed the children of God, our Father will certainly give us a child's portion; and that is no less than a kingdom. So saith our Saviour Luke xii. 32; "Fear not, little flock: for it is your Father's good pleasure to give you the kingdom."—M.].

---

2. *The glory of the Sonship.*

CHAPTER III. 1–3.

1 Behold, what manner of love the Father hath bestowed[1] upon us[2], that we should be
called the sons[3] of God[4]: therefore the world knoweth us not, because it knew him
2 not. Beloved, now are we the sons of God[5], and it doth not yet appear[6] what we shall
be: but[7] we know that when he shall appear[8], we shall be like him; for[9] we shall see
3 him as he is. And every man that hath this hope in him[10] purifieth himself, even as
he is pure[11].

Verse 1 [1] δέδωκεν B. C. Sin; others, A. G. ἔδωκεν. [German: "hath given."—M.]

[2] ἡμῖν A. C. Sin; others read ὑμῖν; so B. K. [The latter reading probably originated in the reference to the 2 pers. Plural; ἴδετε.—M.]

[[3] Greek: τέκνα θεοῦ; German: "children of God;" the Article is superfluous and unauthorized and "*children*" is decidedly preferable to "*sons.*"—M.]

[4] καὶ ἐσμέν after κληθῶμεν is inserted by A. B. C. Sin; many cursives and versions. Vulg.: *et simus;* others: *et sumus.* Erasmus took it to be an addition; the Recept. omitted it. The false translation of the Vulgate was a stumbling-block to many, also Luther, and they omitted the words accordingly. [The German retains καὶ ἐσμέν and renders in an independent clause: "*and we are* (it *i. e.* God's children)." Oecumenius explains: ἔδωκεν ἡμῖν τέκνα αὐτοῦ γενέσθαι τε καὶ κληθῆναι and Theophylact: γενέσθαι τε καὶ λογισθῆναι. The authorities are decidedly in favour of the genuineness of the addition.—M.]

Verse 2 [[5] τέκνα θεοῦ; German: "children of God."—M.]

[[6] German "and it hath not yet become manifest." Lillie: "A Passive verb with or without an adjective, is employed by Syr.; Dutch, Italian verss.; Aug. Beza, Hammond, Pearson, Berleb. Bible, Bengel," and many others. He himself renders: "and it hath not yet been manifested;" the German seeks to retain the Aorist in preference to the Perfect, but it is difficult to do so in idiomatic English.—M.]

[7] G. K. insert δὲ after οἴδαμεν. [A. B. C. Sin. al. omit it; the insertion may be readily accounted for by the apparent contrast with the preceding. The German omits δὲ and begins a new sentence thus: "*We know* etc."—M.]

[[8] φανερωθῇ, German: "when *it* shall be manifest;" Lillie: "when it shall be manifested" and in paraphrase: "when the mystery of our future being is unveiled, this is what shall be disclosed: '*we shall be like Him,*' whatever of glory and blessedness that involves.—M.]

[[9] German "*because.*"—M.]

Verse 3 [[10] German "*on Him*" in lieu of the ambiguous and deceptive "*in him*" of E. V.—M.]

[[11] German: "halloweth himself even as He is holy."—M.]

EXEGETICAL AND CRITICAL.

Origin of the adoption.[1] v. 1*a.*

VER. 1*a.* **Behold!**—John desires to call the attention of his readers to their filial state, (Mark xiii. 1; Jno. i. 29), not without his own amazement at its glory, whereof, he himself, as a child of God, had made experience and therefore he uses in the sequel *ἡμῖν* not *ὑμῖν*. The former (noted only by Augustine, Sander and Huther) should be combined with the latter (to which Lyra and Grotius call attention), so that the right view lies not midway between these two thoughts (Düsterdieck), but in their combination.

What manner of love the Father hath given to us.—Ποταπός, of frequent occurrence in the New Testament, and (according to Buttmann, Lexicog. 125, 302) probably derived from *ποῦ*, *πόθεν*, and *ἀπὸ* (*πο-ἀπός*) with an inserted *δ* (*pro-d-ire, pro-d-esse*), and properly ought to be

[1] Would it not be well to coin the word *child-ship* after the analogy of son-ship, fellow-ship, friend-ship, etc.? The word rendered "adoption" denotes "*childship,*" and for the want of such a word in English the terms "sonship"—"adoption" have been used for the German "Kindschaft." M.]

written ποδαπός, as it used to be written formerly, denotes literally *wherefrom? whence? cujas?* The question relates to extraction and race. Descent and quality are inquired after. So Luke i. 29: ποταπὸς εἴη ὁ ἀσπασμός; Matth. viii. 27: ποταπός ἐστιν οὗτος. Descent and extraction are wholly lost sight of and there remains nothing but kind and quality. Luke vii. 39; 2 Pet. iii. 11; Mark xiii. 1. In the last passage the word slightly touches the sense of *quantus*. Hence it is wrong to translate "*qualem et quantum amorem*" (Socinus, Episcopius, Estius), what or "how great love" (Lücke, de Wette, Sander, Ewald) although we may admit that the signification of "*qualis*" plays into that of "*quantus*" (S. Schmidt, Düsterdieck, Huther).—Luther renders very well: "*what glorious, sublime love!*" The quality has, at any rate, to be retained. The fact, however, of its being undeserved is not implied in ποταπήν (Calvin), but rather in ἡμῖν, *indignis, inimicis, peccatoribus* (a Lapide), just as the ἀγάπη and its nature involves the idea of its greatness, even as the strength and greatness, the intensiveness and extensiveness of love are concentrated in Jno. iii. 16: οὕτως ἠγάπησεν ὁ θεός. Luther pertinently observes in his Scholia: "*Usus est Johannes singulari verborum pondere: non dicit, dedisse nobis deum donum aliquod, sed ipsam caritatem et fontem omnium bonorum, cor ipsum, idque non pro operibus aut studiis nostris, sed gratuito.*" Ἀγάπη does not mean *caritatis munus* (Beza), *effectus, documentum, beneficium*, token or proof of love (Socinus, Episcopius, Grotius, Spener, Neander, al.); this is occasioned by δέδωκεν. Bengel: "*non modo destinavit et contulit, sed etiam exhibuit.*" God has not only given in love, but He has given love itself, made it our own, absolutely given it to us so that His love is now ours. [a Lapide explains ἀγάπην in the R. C. interest, thus: "*i. e. charitatem tum activam (actum amoris Dei quo nos mire amat), tum passivam nobisque a Deo communicatam et infusam. Videte quantam charitatem—nobis—præstitit et exhibuit Deus, cum—charitatem creatam nobis dedit et infudit, quia filii Dei nominamur et sumus.*" Calvin's turn lies hardly in the Apostle's expression: "*Quod dicit* DATAM *esse caritatem, significat: hoc meræ esse liberalitatis, quod nos Deus pro filiis habet.*"—M.]. The Apostle, writing from a sense and consciousness of the adoption, says ὁ πατήρ and thus points to the sequel.

That we should be called children of God.—As we have not ὅτι as in Matth. viii. 27, the reference is not merely to the substance, the standing fact that we are called God's children (in opposition to S. Schmidt, Episcopius, al.); as we have not ὅπως, as in Jno. xi. 57, the reference is not purely telic, as maintained by Lange, Lücke, de Wette, Brückner, Neander, al., who are compelled to specify as the gift of love something which is not contained in the text, *e. g.* that of God sending the Son in order to indicate the purpose of our sonship. But being God's children is not a gift shortly to be communicated, not simply a present fact, but a task and problem, a fact only in process of becoming, only gradually accomplishing, not a creation of instantaneous occurrence or an immediately finished act of creation, but a work of God passing through different stages of development, and a history of man, a life wrought by God in man from a beginning to a high end, like the forgiveness of sins. Hence here, as in ch. i. 9, ἵνα signifies=that we *should* be called. Our adoption by the Father is the substance and aim of His love.—Καλεῖσθαι (Jno. ii. 23: φίλος θεοῦ ἐκλήθη does not denote a predicate without substance, a name without a meaning or an empty title, for He that calls us children is God, and the blessed and glorious spirits in heaven. Then we are called so by men, by the brethren in earnest, by the world in mockery. "Where God gives names, He always gives also the being [the thing signified by the name M.]." Besser.—We have not the name of children without the sonship, even as we do not only *call* God Father; He *is* also our Father. But the acknowledgment of this sonship given by God and exhibited in the life, is here brought out. Although Augustine is wrong ("*hic non est discrimen inter dici et esse*"), yet is Calvin right ("*inanis titulus esse non potest*"). Hence the Greek commentators explain: εἴδετε γὰρ ὅτι ἔδωκεν ἡμῖν τέκνα αὐτοῦ γενέσθαι τε καὶ κληθῆναι (Oecumenius), or καὶ λογισθῆναι (Theophyl.).—Baumgarten-Crusius and Neander after him, explains καλεῖσθαι with reference to Jno. i. 12, by ἐξουσίαν ἔχειν γενέσθαι, but this is only the presupposition of καλεῖσθαι and it is not said that *we* should have the right to call ourselves children.—The position τέκνα θεοῦ indicates the notion of the sonship, the choice of the word τέκνα instead of υἱοί the beginning, the birth, the dependence, and the Genitive θεοῦ instead of αὐτοῦ the glory and highness of this sonship. Bengel: "*Quid majus, quam Deus? quæ proprior necessitudo, quam filius?*

And we are!—This adjunction, externally testified and internally required, is neither a gloss nor governed by ἵνα (Vulgate "*et simus*") but an independent sentence designed to give special prominence and testimony to the reality of the sonship and the essence of the name; it is the gladsome expression of the certainty and of the consciousness founded on experience respecting this gift, although not exactly a triumphant exclamation over a hostile world. The assumption of Ebrard that κληθῶμεν indicates the relation of God to us and ἐσμὲν our relation to God, the former the fact of His being reconciled, the latter that of our changed nature and renovation, is unfounded. Both, indeed, are implied but not thus separated and distributed.

Antithesis of the Sonship v. 1b.

Therefore the world knoweth us not.—Διὰ τοῦτο refers back to what goes before: Because we are the children of God, the world knoweth us not. The Apostle mentions a necessary consequence of our being children of God, viz.: the world knoweth us not. He desires neither to meet an objection of believers (S. Schmidt), nor to express a ground of consolation [with respect to the persecutions to which they are exposed on the part of the world M.] (Luther, Grotius, de Wette, Lücke al.), but to adjoin an ever-recurring truth of our experience [I should prefer to say with Huther that the Apostle here describes the contrast between believers, τέκνα θεοῦ, and the world and the greatness of the love of the Father who gave them that endearing name. M.]. Ἡμᾶς denotes the relation and attitude, the nature and walk of the children of God, not external personality or relation.—On ὁ κόσμος compare notes on ch. ii. 15, and on γινώσκειν notes on ch. ii. 3.—"The essence of the notion ὁ κόσμος according to John's manner of thinking is antagonism to God; this,—and not the consideration of the numerical strength and influence of those who were opposed to the few and obscure Christians, and without being properly godless were wont to judge every thing by the standard of worldly wisdom (Episcopius),—is the basis of the Apostle's argument." (Düsterdieck). γινώσκειν signifies a knowing which moves the whole man, rests on personal experience, voluntary agreement and lively interest, and agrees with the frame of mind, and the bias of life. The world does not understand Christians, seeks no intercourse with them, takes no part with them, or stands by them, and has no liking for them: all this is involved in οὐ γινώσκειν and signifies: does not know them [thoroughly or experimentally; the world has no conception of the spiritual nature of Christians.—M.]. Cf. v. 13; Jno. xvi. 33; xv. 20, 21. Hence the explanations of Grotius "*non agnoscit pro suis*," Semler "*rejicit, reprobat*," Baumgarten-Crusius and others=μισεῖ, are wrong. This relation subsisting between an ungodly world and the children of God the Apostle further explains in the following proposition:

Because it knew Him not.—Ὅτι does not depend on διὰ τοῦτο; John's purpose is to explain how it happens that the world does not understand the Christians, because they are children of God, and he observes accordingly that the fault lies not with the children of God, but it is the fault of the world itself, because it has not known God. Γινώσκειν of course must be taken here in the same sense as in the former clause and, neither=*credere in Deum* (S. Schmidt), nor=*nôsse doctrinam, curare divinam legem, jussa Dei observare* (Episcopius), but "the whole contrast in mind and bias, also hatred and persecution" (de Wette) are embraced in the world's not knowing God, both with reference to the children of God and to God Himself. The conclusion is valid: οὐκ ἔγνω τὸν υἱοθετήσαντα (Oecumenius), therefore οὐ γινώσκει τὰ τέκνα αὐτοῦ. Hence αὐτόν must designate God and not Christ. Because we are born of God, and have been made partakers of the Divine nature, the world knoweth not us, which did not know God.—The change of tense in γινώσκει and ἔγνω must not be overlooked. The fact of the world not knowing the children of God is conditioned by the fact of its not knowing God. This is the first, on which depends the second. The knowledge of God is the ground of the knowledge of man and the knowledge of the world, which are not wanting in the children of God; self-knowledge also depends on it. All these are wanting where the knowledge of God is wanting; there is wanting the knowledge and understanding of believers and personal knowledge with respect to the whole and the general to which people belong, and with respect to the particular, even down to their own heart and nature. They know nothing, not even, what they do (Luke xxiii. 34).

The hope of the Sonship. v. 2.

VER. 2. **Beloved.**—This address, ἀγαπητοί, denotes a relation in which love is experienced, and in the present case experience of the love of God, whose children they are, and of the love of those with whom they are connected, and accordingly constitutes an antithesis to the preceding clause: We are children of God and therefore the world knoweth us not.

Now are we children of God.—The former ἐσμέν culminates in τέκνα θεοῦ and the preceding particle νῦν and is repeated after the parenthetical antithesis pointing first to the fact that the world does not know the children of God now, and secondly to the future. The context and position of νῦν require it to be taken as a particle of time (in opposition to de Wette: now, pursuant to that purpose of love). Thus it is emphatically asserted, that, notwithstanding the opposition of the world, we are already the children of God, although the glory of our sonship is still concealed and imperfect. So Lücke and Düsterdieck against Huther [who denies a reference to the preceding verse and considers νῦν used with respect to the future (οὔπω) to indicate the present glory of the children of God; adding that the Apostle before mentioning the future glory, notices the fact that it is as yet concealed.—M.].

And it hath not yet been manifested what we shall be.—Antitheses to the preceding are νῦν and οὔπω, ἐσμέν and ἐσόμεθα, τέκνα θεοῦ and τί, which is further answered by ὅμοιοι αὐτῷ, just as οὔπω ἐφανερώθη is carried further in ἐὰν φανερωθῇ and οἴδαμεν continued in ὀψόμεθα. These antitheses, however, are not *contraria*, but developments of the present τέκνα θεοῦ ἐσμέν, the development of the adoption into the inheritance. The argument therefore is properly carried on by καί (in opposition to Beza, Grotius, Spener and others, who construe καί as a Hebraism in the sense of ἀλλά), and δέ after οἴδαμεν is rightly wanting (contrary to S. Schmidt, Lücke, Sander and others).—Οὔπω ἐφανερώθη points to something actually existing but as yet concealed. For φανεροῦν means to make manifest, to bring to light, so as to be open to sight and to be known; not from the word itself, but from the context it has to be determined whether this manifestation is to take place factually, by means of historical development and events, or logically by means of instruction and teaching; here the former course is very distinctly marked (so Huther in opposition to Ebrard) so also ch. ii. 19; Jno. ii. 11; vii. 4; xvii. 6; xxi. 1. The context in like manner implies to *whom* this manifestation is to be made, if it is not explicitly stated. The primary reference is here probably to the world; the secondary to believers (Düsterdieck). The interrogative (τί ἐσόμεθα) presents no difficulty, and contains nothing to favour Ebrard's opinion, since not only after verbs of knowing, inquiring etc., and in *direct* questions, but also in cases where classical writers would certainly have used ὅ, τι, the N. T. writers use the interrogative pronoun; cf. Winer p. 181; Buttmann p. 216. On the thought itself compare Col. iii. 3 (ἡ ζωὴ ὑμῶν κέκρυπται σὺν τῷ Χριστῷ ἐν τῷ θεῷ) Rom. viii. 17 (εἰ δὲ τέκνα, καὶ κληρονόμοι—θεοῦ, συγκληρονόμοι δὲ Χριστοῦ) and v. 18 (οὐκ ἄξια τὰ παθήματα τοῦ νῦν καιροῦ πρὸς τὴν μέλλουσαν δόξαν ἀποκαλυφθῆναι εἰς ἡμᾶς), also Gal. iv. 1 (ἐφ' ὅσον χρόνον ὁ κληρονόμος νήπιός ἐστι, οὐδὲν διαφέρει δούλου κύριος πάντων ὤν.)

It is important to remember that what is said is: "it has not yet appeared what we shall be" and not, that "we shall be something which as yet we are not": οὔπω negatives not the being, but the having appeared, the being manifested. There is only *one* Divine sonship (child-ship); *non dantur gradus* υἱότητος (Calov). But it has its *status* or stages, its unfolding and development, the development of the inner being of a child of God and the unfolding of their manifold privileges and possessions. "The future already exists in the germ and is latent in the present" (Düsterdieck). Augustine: "*Quid est ergo, quod jam expectamus, si jam filii Dei sumus? quid autem erimus aliud, quam filii Dei?*" However different the future state may be from the present and although we must distinguish the one from the other, the former is not absolutely *new* [Huther—M.]. This is the force of οὔπω ἐφανερώθη, which only brings out and opens to sight that which is concealed, and this is the ἐσμέν become ἐσόμεθα. [Oecumenius: τὸ γὰρ νῦν ἄδηλον φανερὸν γενήσεται, ἐκείνου ἀποκαλυπτομένου. ὅμοιοι γὰρ αὐτῷ ἀναφανέντες τὸ τῆς υἱοθεσίας λαμπρὸν παραστήσομεν. οἱ γὰρ υἱοὶ πάντες ὅμοιοι τῷ πατρί.—M.]. But what does that consist in?

We know that when it shall be manifested, we shall be like (similar to) **Him.**—Οἴδαμεν signifies certainty of knowing, not only guess-knowledge (Jachmann), and knowing participated in not only by the Apostles (Episcopius), but by all Christians (Calvin), by all of whom it is said: τέκνα θεοῦ ἐσμέν. The object of that knowing is: ὅτι ὅμοιοι αὐτῷ ἐσόμεθα. The occurrence of this future condition is indicated by ἐὰν φανερωθῇ. As we have ἐὰν and not ὅταν the reference is not only to the time when (Socinus and al.), but to the reality of the matter, cf. notes on ch. ii. 28. Also Jno. xii. 32; xiv. 3; xvi. 7. The Vulgate gives the precise shade of thought: *cum apparuerit*, bringing out the force of the *Fut. exact.* applied in the *Subj. Aorist.* The subject of φανερωθῇ is τί ἐσόμεθα, which is clear from the unmistakable reference to ἐφανερώθη τί ἐσόμεθα. No expositor has seriously thought of *God*, but several supply *Christ* (Augustine, Bede, Calvin, Calov and others.).—Φανεροῦσθαι τί ἐσόμεθα coincides with the coming of Christ and *quoad rem*, it is very possible to think here of Christ. But φανεροῦν would then have to be explained here of His appearing in glory, whereas it is used in v. 5 of His appearing in the flesh and expressly referred to Him by the demonstrative pronoun ἐκεῖνος, and the same verb had different subjects in the two sentences immediately succeeding each other. We may admit here "the possibility of that reference, the reality of which" is stated in v. 5, but have to maintain with the greater number of expositors that the concinnity of the diction requires us to supply to φανερωθῇ the same subject which belongs to ἐφανερώθη, namely τί ἐσόμεθα, especially since the latter is explained by ὅμοιοι αὐτῷ ἐσόμεθα; the latter two as well as the two forms of φανεροῦσθαι are correlatives. Oecumenius excellently remarks: τὸ γὰρ νῦν ἄδηλον φανερὸν γενήσεται, ἐκείνου ἀποκαλυπτομένου: ὅμοιοι γὰρ αὐτῷ ἀναφανέντες τὸ τῆς υἱοθεσίας λαμπρὸν παραστήσομεν. οἱ γὰρ υἱοὶ πάντως ὅμοιοι τῷ πάτρι.—Ὅμοιος is resembling, similar to and not=equal to (Sander); it is not=ἴσος [the English "*like*" is ambiguous signifying both "*similar*" and "*equal.*" I have retained "*like*" in the text, but given "*similar*" in brackets.—M.]. Of Christ Paul says: τὸ εἶναι ἴσα θεῷ Phil. ii. 6; and His enemies: ἴσον τῷ θεῷ, Jno. v. 18. Luke calls υἱοὶ τοῦ θεοῦ—ἰσάγγελοι but not ἴσοι θεῷ.—Recollect the controversy of ὁμοούσιον and ὁμοιούσιον.—Ὅμοιος signifies similarity in external form and appearance (ὁράσει, Rev. iv. 3; cf. i. 13, 15; ix. 7, 10, 19), and then in kind and authority (Jno. viii. 55; Rev. xiii. 4; xviii. 18). It is certain that "the creature will never become Creator" (Luther I), and "*Non erimus idem, quod Deus, sed similes erimus Dei*" (Luther, Schol.). That the connection requires us to to apply αὐτῷ to God and not to Christ, is clear and almost universally acknowledged; hence Bengel says very pointedly: "*Deo, cujus sumus filii.*" Now although the notion of resemblance to God is somewhat vague, the question arises whether the context does not shed light on the subject. Huther indeed rightly observes that commentators are not warranted in *arbitrarily* restricting it, but the attempt of deriving more light from the context must not be absolutely repudiated. Much will depend on the right understanding of the adjoined sentence.

Because we shall see Him as He is.—The annexation by ὅτι points to a *casual* relation of resemblance to God and seeing God. This is almost universally acknowledged. Hence it is wrong to take ὅτι=ἀλλὰ καὶ (Oecumenius), or=ὅτε καὶ (Scholiast. II.), or=*et* (Luther, *Schol.*), for this disturbs and negatives the internal relation of the two. Nor does ὅτι describe the "*Modus hujus transformationis*" (Lyra). It is most natural to take the internal relation of resemblance to God and seeing God, so that the *cause* of resemblance to God lies in seeing God: we shall be similar to God, because we shall see Him face to face. For grammatically and dialectically this course is pointed out to us. We shall be similar to Him, because we shall see Him, says the Apostle, and not: ὀψόμεθα αὐτὸν, ὅτι ὅμοιοι αὐτῷ ἐσόμεθα (Düsterdieck). The resemblance to God is the end of the love of God, and not the seeing God which is simply the instrument of the former. Cf. Jno. xvii. 24. As γινώσκειν conduces to having (ἔχειν), so seeing God effects the being, and more particularly the being similar to Him. Hence the internal relation of the two is reversed if ὅτι is supposed to add only a "*testimonium aut signum similitudinis*" (Carpzov), not the cause of it, or if the seeing God is taken as the effect, from which is inferred the cause, resemblance of God (Calvin, Socinus, Episcopius, Rickli). Nor may we infer with Huther that because we *shall* see Him, therefore we know *now* (οἴδαμεν) that we shall be similar to Him; particularly as that knowledge rests on the sonship, which is a fact, and the word of promise given to the children of God. But this seeing must be taken in the full acceptation of the word, a real perfect seeing in the resurrection-body, and not only a real knowing The believer is in the σῶμα πνευματικόν (1 Cor. xv. 44) and sees face to face (1 Cor. xiii. 12); it is "*maxime practica visio, summi boni αἴσθησις plenissima*" (J. Lange).—The object of this seeing is God, καθώς ἐστι: "As He is not only in His Image etc., but in Himself and in His Being, His perfect majesty and glory (Spener). Such a seeing of God is a real ground of resembling God according to Rev. xxii. 4: *καὶ ὄψονται τὸ πρόσωπον αὐτοῦ καὶ τὸ ὄνομα αὐτοῦ ἐπὶ τῶν μετώπων αὐτῶν.* 2 Cor. iii. 18: *ἡμεῖς—ἀνακεκαλυμμένῳ προσώπῳ τὴν δόξαν κυρίου κατοπτριζόμενοι τὴν αὐτὴν εἰκόνα μεταμορφούμεθα ἀπὸ δόξης εἰς δόξαν, καθάπερ ἀπὸ κυρίου πνεύματος.* Hence Bengel: "*ex aspectu similitudo.*" Spener: "The seeing is the cause of the likeness." So likewise de Wette, Neander, Düsterdieck, Ebrard. The seeing God must react on him who sees by glorifying him into that which is the object of his seeing, making him similar to Him whom he sees. Thus is fulfilled the promise that we shall be *θείας κοινωνοὶ φύσεως* (2 Pet. i. 4). Hence we must not think with Ebrard of "the light-nature of God," or with de Wette of "the *δόξα* of God," and still less with S. Schmidt and Düsterdieck only of ch. ii. 29: *δικαιός ἐστιν*, but rather with the Greek expositors (*συμβασιλεύσομεν καὶ συνδοξασθήσομεν αὐτῷ*) also of our joint inheritance with Christ, since ch. ii. 28 (of. Rom. viii. 17; 2 Tim. ii. 12) suggests as much, and we may say with Luther that we have become lords of sin, of death and the devil. But although Calov clearly passes the bounds of exegesis in his dogmatical thought ("*ratione mentis sapientia, ratione voluntatis sanctitate et justitia, ratione corporis immortalitate, ratione utriusque gloria et felicitate æterna deo similes erimus*"), those who are held fast in the enlightenment of the understanding by no means do justice to the text; and of these men Oertel caps the climax in his philosophical exposition: "I believe that the reference here is simply to the higher perfection of the knowledge of the Christian religion and the sense to be as follows: Some day, after several generations and centuries, mankind, which as yet clings overmuch to the spirit of coarseness, will be more enlightened, ennobled and happy and thus by means of the more perfect light that is to rise, attain to a perfect knowledge of the plan of God and the purpose of Jesus.—Ah, John, if thou hadst had a presentiment of the bloody Nicæades, Costnitziades, Dragoonades, edicts, etc. and the times when thousands were slaughtered in honour of religion!—But—thy presentiment of the education of mankind in religion, virtue and philanthropy will yet be perfected by the Providence of the Almighty Father." [Augustine (*Tract. in Ep. Jno.* iv. 5) who however understands *αὐτῷ* and *αὐτόν* of Christ, exclaims: "*Ergo visuri sumus quandam visionem, fratres, quam nec oculus vidit, nec auris audivit, nec in cor hominis ascendit: visionem quandam, visionem præcellentem omnes pulchritudines terrenas, auri, argenti, nemorum atque camporum, pulchritudinem maris et aëris, pulchritudinem solis et lunæ, pulchritudinem angelorum, omnia superantem, quia ex ipsa pulchra sunt omnia.*"—M.].

The power of this hope. v. 3.

VER. 3. **And every one that hath this hope on Him, halloweth himself.**—With *καί* which is not=*οὖν*, John annexes the sentence expressing "the moral effect of Christian hope" (Huther), which although it contains an exhortation in point of sense, yet formally expresses it as a fact and that more emphatically, since it intimates in decided terms that he who does not hallow himself, surrenders that hope in ingratitude. For *πᾶς ὁ ἔχων* is *omnis et solus;* "Every one—and only such an one; for as this hope (v. 2) peculiarly and exclusively belongs to the children of God, they and they only enjoy the power of such a hope whether it is to exhibit itself in sanctification, as here, or to afford patienee and joyfulness (Rom. viii. 14 sqq.; 23 sqq.)" (Düsterdieck), and *ἐπ' αὐτῷ i. e. θεῷ* denotes "the fulcrum" (Huther), or still better "the real foundation of this hope" (J. Lange), the ground and soil out of which it grows up, so that S. Schmidt rightly observes: "*Deus gignit spem.*" Grotius weakens the thought: "*Sicut Deus eam spem vult concipi.*" Besides *ἐλπίζειν ἐπ' αὐτῷ* (*God*) occurs Rom. xv. 12 and *ἐπὶ πλούτου ἀδηλότητι, ἀλλ' ἐν τῷ θεῷ* 2 Tim. vi. 17, although *ἔχειν ἐλπίδα ἐπὶ cum dat.*, occurs only here and with *εἰς θεὸν* Acts xxiv. 15.—*Ὁ ἔχων τὴν ἐλπίδα* is not the same as *ὁ ἐλπίζων*, the latter denoting only the act of hope, but the former describing hope as a permanent property, as a fixed possession, so that the act of hoping is uninterrupted and lasting. Hence it is neither necessary nor correct to explain *ἔχειν*, as holding fast or preserving (Benson, Spener), or to take here *ἐλπίδα* as the object of hope, that which one is objectively entitled to hope (Ebrard). *Τὴν ἐλπίδα ταύτην* naturally leads us to think of *ὅμοιοι αὐτῷ ἐσόμεθα.* This was v. 2 the object and substance of *οἴδαμεν.* Now it is designated by *ἔχειν τὴν ἐλπίδα ταύτην ἐπ' αὐτῷ* as the object of a yearning desire in the power of God, in order to bring out the purifying reaction in our earthly life. The mere *ἐλπίζειν* would be incongruous with the *ἁγνίζειν ἑαυτὸν*, which is affected and to be effected. Primarily, however, this hope and self-sanctification only are here connected (Hofmann), but the state of having hope and participation in this hope are presupposed in the case of the acts of such sanctifying of oneself. "*Qui habet hanc spem et credit, se esse filium Dei, et expectat donec fides sua reveletur, is sine dubio ita accendetur spe illa, ut se purificet, nec involvat se sordibus carnis, sed carnem mortificabit*" (Luther). Self-sanctification necessarily combined with Christian hope (de Wette) is its *effectus* (Hunnius). Hope is the mother of sanctification, not the reverse, as Grotius maintains. Nor is sanctification the condition of the fulfilment of this hope (Lücke and several Roman Catholic commentators), nor must we find here the combination of both views (Schlichting, Episcopius). *Ἁγνίζειν* from *ἁγνός=καθαρός* (Suidas), טָהוֹר (Numb. viii. 21; vi. 2, 3; Ps. xi. 7) clean, pure; applied in the New Testament to wisdom (Jas. iii. 47), to one fulfilling a vow (Acts xxi. 24, 26; xxiv. 18), to the Christian walk (1 Pet. i. 22; Jas. iv. 8; 2 Cor. vi. 6; 1 Tim. v. 22), and to the chaste (Tit. ii 5; 2 Tim. iv. 12; v. 2; 2 Cor. xi. 2). It signifies accordingly *ἐλευθερία παντὸς μολυσμοῦ σαρκὸς καὶ πνεύματος* (Phavorinus), *ἡ τῶν ἁμαρτημάτων ἀποχή* (Clement. Alex.). Hence it is the opposite of *impure*, and *ἅγιος* the opposite of *profane*, although the latter denotes inward impurity and the former outward profanity [pollution] as a consequence and in a secondary sense. The reference to God, who is *δίκαιος* and whom we are to resemble, necessitates us not to restrict the meaning of ἁγνίζειν to *castificare* (Augustine), but to take it in a wider sense like καθαρίζειν (ch. i. 7, 9.). "*Hoc non tantum de illa turpitudine carnis intelligendum est, sed de omnibus passionibus animi vitiosis, ira, avaritia, invidia, odio, superbia, gloriæ cupididate etc.*" (Luther). The object of this hallowing is ἑαυτὸν, that is to say our own self, and not only particular details of our life or our outward life. The exhortations of Peter (2 Pet. iii. 13, 14) and Paul (2 Cor. vii. 1) are analogous in point of matter. The Present denotes uninterrupted self-purification (Beza, Spener, Grotius, al.), because the Divine life in us constantly encounters impurity and unrighteousness and because these must be done away (Düsterdieck). But this self-purification does not proceed from our own self in the same manner as it bears upon it; hence there is no αὐτὸς by the side of ἑαυτόν. Augustine pointedly says in this respect: "*Quis non castificat nisi Deus? Sed Deus te nolentem non castificat. Ergo quod adjungis voluntatem tuam Deo, castificas te ipsum. Castificas te, non* de te, *sed* de illo, *qui venit, ut habitet in te. Tamen quia agis ibi aliquid voluntate, ideo et tibi aliquid tributum est.*" The power, the impulse and initiative of self-purification do not reside in the *liberum arbitrium* of man, but in that on which rests the hope which impels self-purification. [See Huther.—M.].

Even as He is holy.—Ἐκεῖνος is Christ, according to the constant use of that word in juxtaposition with αὐτὸς, in the writings of John. Cf. ch. ii. 6. While the context required us to apply αὐτὸς to God, ἐκεῖνος may and must be applied to Christ, as the more remote subject. We cannot refer both to Christ (Aretius, Estius, Calvin), or both to God (Lyra, Socinus, al.). Christ is the pattern, and expressly shows us how we may become similar to God. If the Apostle had said only: καθὼς ἐκεῖνος, we should then have been obliged to supply ἁγνίζειν. This is impossible, and the Apostle therefore adjoins ἁγνός ἐστι; purity belongs to Him essentially, He is absolutely and originally holy and righteous, "in most perfect harmony with the original righteousness as well as the original purity of the Father" (Düsterdieck) see vv. 5, 7, ch. ii. 1. "The ἁγνότης is an attribute inhering in Christ" (Lücke), and ἐστι, not: ἦν, indicates an uninterrupted and permanent condition (Jno. i. 18). There is no reason why καθὼς should be explained by *quandoquidem* and the purity of Christ should be construed into a second motive of self-purification (as Ebrard does). Even the externally direct relation to Christ is sufficiently manifest to the specifically Christian way of thinking, in virtue of the position of Christ as our only and eternal Mediator, and indispensable to John's manner of contemplation; the immutable state of Christ is the perfect standard of Christians, and not only an outward example set before us, but a vital power. Cf. i. 1; ii. 1, 6; iii. 5, 7, 16; iv. 17; [that is: the purity of Christ is the immutable and perfect standard and pattern according to which Christians should shape and mould their whole life, not only outwardly in acts, but inwardly in the disposition of the heart and the determination of the will.—M.].

DOCTRINAL AND ETHICAL.

1. The state of our being the children of God is a gift of the preëminent love of God; this is a point to be insisted upon in opposition to Pelagius and all Pelagian errors. A chaste exegesis requires us not to go beyond this general character of this passage and neither to beat (with Calvin) with it "*the sophists*" who postulate the foreseen future dignity of those whom God adopts, nor to find here the Lutheran principle "*regeneratio præcedit fidem,*" while the (German) Reformed hold: "*fides præcedit regenerationem.*" Here is simply the assertion of the prevenient love of the Father as the cause of our adoption, as in ch. iv. 10.

2. But not only from God, but from God only, from God exclusively proceedeth all the divine life, which passes before him. Our life of faith takes us back to Him, the Father, whose Nature is love.

3. Christianity brings not new information but a new life, not a new doctrine but a new nature, which like the natural, bodily birth has however its growth and development from the hidden, germ-like beginning to the most glorious perfection.

4. The world with all its glory does neither understand the kingdom of God nor the people and history of this kingdom; here is the ground and beginning of all enmity against the Church of Jesus and Christian Church-ordinances (Luke xxiii. 34). Our Lord's prayer: ἵνα ὁ κόσμος πιστεύσῃ—Jno. xvii. 21, does not contradict the language of John. Christ adverts to the means designed to break through the mind and hardness of the world, while John here bears testimony to the mind and hardness of the world without intending to exclude that they may and should be counteracted and that not in vain.

5. But the first thing the world ought to be helped to get is that it may know God and the Divine. The knowledge of God, which however is only excited under the influence and manifestations of His love, conditions the knowledge of His people and kingdom.

6. The adoption of God has a history from its first beginning to its perfected glorification in the likeness of God, which takes place in consequence of the perfect vision of God, the seeing God effecting the transformation into the Image of God.

7. That which one day will become perfect in seeing God must begin here on earth in faith, and the glorification into the Image of God has its beginning in the sanctification wrought on earth. But this does by no means put the *sanctificatio* in the power of man. For first it does not go before the *justificatio* (as is assumed by Roman Catholics) and secondly it has respect only to those who are born of God and takes place only by means of the power conveyed and appropriated in regeneration; consequently although it takes place with our own power, yet is this power not originally our own but only bestowed by the grace of God and made our own in faith, so that Wolf is perfectly right in saying: "*aliud est* δικαιοῦν,

aliud ἁγνίζειν, prius illud in hominem non cadit,—ut vero posterius." Compare the quotation from Augustine in *Exegetical* and *Critical* on v. 3.

HOMILETICAL AND PRACTICAL.

Two wonderful things: 1. The love of God which desires to adopt us as children; 2. The perverseness of the world which does not know such a Lord.—Art thou more astonished at God's loving attitude to the world, or at the world's hateful attitude to God and His children? Dost thou think it more strange that God treats thee as a child than that the world does not and will not understand thee? Dost thou not see that it is more natural and reasonable that the world is against thee than that God is for thee?—See that thou find thy way through all the proofs of the love of God even to that of His adoption of thee and through all the enmity of the world even to the knowledge of its ignorance and want of understanding! He only that does the former is able to do the latter.—Think of thy own and thy children's adoption by God and inquire even in the case of one who is distasteful to thee, whether he is not as well as thou a child of God, and perhaps better entitled to be one than thou art thyself. This is very important and profitable for one's own discipline, the education of one's children and one's intercourse with and among men.—Hope for the future, but do not expect to reap hereafter without sowing now; wouldst thou hereafter see God and become like Him it is necessary for thee to begin here to purify thyself by strenuous application.—Thy adoption rests on the foundation of God's eternal love, reaches even into God's eternal felicity, but in this temporal present and the present transitoriness it may be lost and therefore must be preserved all the infirmity of thy own flesh and all the enmity of the world notwithstanding.—Happy is the man whose joy flows from the grateful love of God and whose troubles proceed from a hostile world, but woe to him, whose joy is from beneath and whose troubles come from above, who is the friend of the world and the enemy of God, because he will not be His child.—At peace with God and at war with the world is a wholesome foundation for the alternatives of joy and trouble in thy life.—The import of our adoption by God: 1. Its *Origin*—the love of God. 2. Its *Opposite*—an ignorant world without understanding. 3. Its *hope*—blessed likeness to God. 4. Its *power*—the zeal of self-purification.—Vital questions and answers for the guidance of life. 1. Who is for thee? God in His eternal love. 2. Who is against thee? The world in its short-sightedness. 3. Whence? From God. 4. Whither? To God's glory. 5. How? In the work of sanctification.

Clemens Romanus:—How blessed and how wonderful are the gifts of God! Life in immortality, splendour in righteousness, truth in joy, faith in confidence, chastity in holiness—all these are goods present to our mind.

Chrysostom:—Those who depise and deride us, know not who we are, citizens of heaven, belonging to an eternal fatherland, associates of the Cherubim; but they will know it in the day of judgment when they will exclaim with sighs and amazement, these are they whom we used to despise and deride.

[Cassiodorus:—Let us therefore so live, that when He shall come again, we may be able to behold Him, as He is, in all the fulness of His grace and glory.—M.]

Augustine:—The whole life of a Christian is a holy longing. What we long for, we do not yet see; but by longing thou art enlarging thyself so that when it is visible, thou mayest be filled therewith.—It is God alone who purifies us; but He does not purify thee, thyself unwilling; thou purifiest thyself, but not of thyself, but of Him [de Illo] who comes to dwell in thee.

Luther:—If God were strictly to reckon with us, He would owe us nothing but hell; but if He gives us heaven, it is of grace.

Starke:—Dost thou bear here the image of the devil and thinkest to become like Christ there? O, folly! O, deceit! Without the renovation of the divine Image none can attain to the glory of God.—Without purification hope of the future glory is impossible. The hope of the impure is daring, impudence and insolence.—Our Christianity is not so much a being pure as a continuous purifying oneself.—Believers purify not only one thing or another, but themselves, wholly, body and soul. The main work lies within and in the soul.—O, the shameful abuse of the Gospel! to be ever appealing to Christ and His merits, and yet never to follow His example!

Daniel:—Christian, whose is the best nobility? His, who is born of God. Who is the most honoured man? He whom God regards in grace.—A missionary in India (Ziegenbalg) is translating the New Testament with the assistance of a native. Coming to this verse the Hindoo youth translates: that we may be allowed to kiss his feet. The missionary asks: Why do you render thus? The Indian replies: A child! that is too much! too high!—That had never entered into a heathen's heart.

Steinhofer:—A child of God is always an enigma to the world.

Heubner:—The children of God bear the image, the glory of the Father, enjoy his whole fatherly love and are destined to own what He owns. All this God bestows upon us, apostates and former enemies. Every one is asked to become such a child.—The Christians should have *called* themselves the children of God? 'Twere pitiable indeed, if they did assume this title and as it were raise themselves to the divine nobility, and worse than if a fool would presume to call himself baron or count. We should be called thus by God and the heavenly children of God; in the Bible the name and the thing are one; the Bible does not know empty trifles.—The sonship is nothing that dazzles the eye, fascinates and attracts in a worldly point of view; it is rather something that is hidden. The world has no eye for it; why? because it knows not God, whereas we see in God the highest and most glorious good, and deem that only glorious which comes from God.—The Christian is quiet, calm, courageous under all the want of appreciation he experiences at the hands of the world; it neither surprises nor disturbs him; being misunderstood by the world cannot injure him.—Christians are the children of a prince, who are obliged to travel in lowly garb, incognito, and as it were in order to be tried, through a foreign country before they take possession of their kingdom. A secret, inward sense of his sonship accompanies the Christian on his journey through the world, through its busy noise; in his heart he walks with God—virtue is not to become a display and an ostentation, therefore the children of God have neither coat of arms nor the badge of an order. The future dignity of Christians cannot be guessed from his appearance any more than it could be determined from the appearance of Christ in His manger-cradle. — They are not condemned to eternal obscurity.—O day beyond compare when God will call His children, saying; Come forth from your obscurity, rise from your lowliness!—The promises of Christianity are transcendently glorious; Christians are not to be like the blessed, the perfected saints or the angels, but like God; what man could have laid hold of this daring hope without revelation?—The Christian should, as it were, keep himself up in a state of excitement. He is terrified at the thought: What? Shouldst thou exchange thy heavenly birthright for the world's mess of pottage? denounce thy faith and lose thy Christian rank for the lust of the flesh, mammon or worldly honour? —Sanctification, though it does not acquire salvation (for it is the gift of grace), yet preserves it. Purification continues day by day; we are often polluted.

EBRARD:—Our future glory is *not an object of curiosity*, not an object for inquisitiveness to be exercised about.—Not to purify oneself is tantamount to saying to God: "I do not want the jewel which thou holdest up before my eyes as the most precious jewel and promisest one day to give me: to be freed from sin I do not esteem a jewel."

BESSER:—Says David as a Christian before Christ: "I am as a wonder unto many," Ps. lxxi. 7; much more are Christians after Christ the real children of wonder. The world, indeed, which *will* remain in the Wicked One, sees in the name of our sonship nothing but an empty, imaginary title.—Even though rejuvenated to the state of apostolical power and consecration the Church would yet have the world—although *against* her, yet not only *outside* of her (for bad fish also are found *in* the net), and woe to her, if she were ever to forget in the time of her militant state that her holiness is not perfected in those who are sanctified but only in Him who sanctifies them, and that in the administration of discipline over her members with which she is solemnly charged, she must use the sword of the Spirit, which is the Word of God for the condemnation of sin and the salvation of sinners, and not the winnowing shovel for cleaning the threshing-floor.—John, in particular, cherishes the most profound conviction that there is only *one* life for the children of God in time and in eternity, and he knows of no future happiness but that which, like the rose in the bud, is already contained germ-like in faith. —As the eye cannot endure the presence of the smallest particle of dust but sheds tears until it is clear again, so also the Christian's eye of hope eagerly looking forward to the coming glory will not tolerate the presence of a particle of the world's dust, and if any fly into it, it contracts with the keenest sensibility and the Lord gives tears of penitence which wash away the dust.—

THOLUCK:—*How blessed is the lot of a believing disciple of the Saviour.*

1. *How blessed such a disciple is even now.* Who recognizes in mankind, as we see it, who recognizes in it a *family of God?* The heathen, when they saw how Christians were so intimately united in the bonds of so novel a life, exclaimed; "*See, how they love one another!*—Blissful joy and astonishment at one and the same time. A child-like mind cannot understand how and why it was thought worthy of so much grace and favour.

2. *How blessed he will be hereafter.* If you like, you may call it a defiance, but it is a divine defiance, as Luther says: "That faith gives man a *defiant* heart toward God and toward all creatures." But what is the centre of all the hope of these poor and miserable people? is it honour, glory, enjoyment? Certainly. Rom. ii. 7–10.

3. *Whereto that faith and this hope impel him.* It cannot be the centre of Christian longing and hope in the hour of death that we shall see again our loved ones, but its centre is rather that we shall see Him again. Does it well forth from a *weakly* sense, or from that *manly-strong sense*, that *seeing Him* and *to be like Him*, *freedom from sin and error*, are one and the same thing? Purify your faith, steel your hope in the faith and hope of the disciple whom you regard only too often as the preacher of a weakly, morbid love.—That resemblance will not fall to thy share *without thy own will*. Thou must feel within thee the *thirst* for it and ask and examine thyself with holy love, what is still unclean in me?—Compare the notes on vv. 4–10.

BIAROWSKY:—The Holy Communion a glorification of the Triune God: 1. in that the Triune God glorifies Himself in it; 2. in that we glorify thereby the Triune God.

GENZKEN (*Baptismal address*):—What a gift! what a task! what a blessed end even for this child.

[BURKITT:—*We shall be like him:* in holiness as well as in happiness; as well in purity as immortality.—M.]

[SECKER:—To be "like God" implies in few words everything desirable, that ever so many words can express.—M.]

[BP. CONYBEARE:—The state of good men in the other world will carry with it a resemblance not in degree, but in kind, to the absolutely perfect Being, in those perfections of which man is capable: and that these will be produced in us by "seeing God as He is;" that is, by a vastly more distinct and more full sight of Him, than the present condition of human nature will admit of.—M.]

[MACKNIGHT:—*And every man that hath this hope of* seeing Christ, and of being like Him "purifieth himself." The felicity, which the Gospel teacheth us to expect in the world to come, is not that of a Mohammedan paradise, in which animal pleasures are the chief enjoyments. The happiness of the children of God in the kingdom of their Father will consist in being like Christ, not only in respect of His immortality, but in respect of his transcendent virtues, especially His boundless benevolence. And the joy which will flow from the possession and exercise of virtues similar to Christ's is so great, that no one, who hopes to become like Christ in virtue and happiness, will indulge himself in the unrestrained enjoyment of sensual pleasures; but will purify himself from the immoderate desire of those pleasures, in imitation of the purity of Christ.—*Purifieth himself,* namely, from the lusts of the flesh and from every sin. The Apostle, as Beza has observed, does not say, "hath purified himself," but "purifieth himself," to show that it is a good man's constant study to purify himself, because in this life no one can attain unto perfect purity. By this text therefore, as well as by ch. i. 8, those fanatics are condemned, who imagine they are able to live without sin.—M.]

[HORSLEY:—Would God a better conformity to the example of his purity, than actually obtains, were to be found in the lives of nominal Christians! the numbers would be greater, which might entertain a reasonable hope that they shall be made like to Him when He appeareth. But thanks be to God, repentance, in this as in other cases, genuine, sincere repentance, shall stand the sinner in the stead of innocence: the sinner is allowed to wash the stains, even of these pollutions, in the Redeemer's blood.—M.]

[Compare also the thoughtful lecture of JOHN FOSTER on 1 Jno. iii. 2: "Our Ignorance of our Future Mode of Existence."—M.]

[EZ. HOPKINS:—*We shall see Him as He is:* we must not understand it as if we could ever arrive to such a capacity as to see and know God as He is in His Infinite Essence: for God's Essence being altogether indivisible, to know God essentially, were to know Him comprehensively; to know Him, as much as He is to be known in Himself; that is, to know Him as much as He knows Himself; which is impossible, for no finite understanding can comprehend an infinite object. And, yet, our sight and knowledge of God shall so far surmount those dim and glimmering discoveries which here He makes of Himself to us, that, comparatively, the Apostle might well call it, a seeing Him as He is, and a knowing Him as we are known by Him.—M.]

[On Chapter III. MANTON, T., Thirty-two Sermons. Works, 5, 577.

Ch. 3, 1. HIERONYMUS, S., The spiritual sonship. 2 Serm. Works, 349.

Vv. 1–3. STOUGHTON, JOHN. The dignitie of God's children: or an exposition of 1 Jno. iii, 1–3, plentifully shewing the comfortable, happie and most blessed state of all God's children, and also, on the contrarie, the base, fearfull, and most woful condition of all other that are not the children of God. 4to. London. 1610.

V. 2. TILLOTSON, ABP. Of the happiness of good men in a future state. 2 Sermons. Serm 10, 56.

SAURIN, J. Heaven. Sermons 3, 321.

VENN, JOHN. The effect of seeing God as He is. Serm. 1, 210.

DWIGHT, T. Adoption. Theol. 3, 167

HAMILTON, R. W. The heavenly state. Congregat. Lecture, 235.

V. 3. SOUTH, R. The hope of future glory, an excitement to purity of life. Sermons 6, 441 (Epiph. 6). Hope of resembling Christ. Pitman, 2d course, L. 206.

ALFORD, H. The pure in heart. Hulsean Lecture, 1842. 41. M.]

---

3. *The way of God's children passes through God's Law.*

CHAPTER III. 4–10*a*.

4 Whosoever committeth sin transgresseth also the law[1]: for sin[2] is the transgression of
5 the law[3]. And ye know that he was manifested to take away our[4] sins; and in him is no
6 sin[5]. Whosoever[6] abideth in him sinneth not: whosoever[7] sinneth hath not seen him,
7 neither known him. Little children[8], let no man deceive you[9]: he that doeth righteous-
8 ness is righteous, even as he is righteous. He that committeth[10] sin is of the devil; for
the devil sinneth from the beginning. For this purpose[11] the Son of God was mani-
9 fested, that he might destroy the works of the devil. Whosoever[12] is born of God
doth not commit sin; for[13] his seed remaineth in him: and he cannot sin, because he
10 is born of God. In this the children of God are manifest, and the children of the
devil.

Verse 4 [1 German: "Every one that doeth (the) sin, doeth also (the) lawlessness."—M.]
2 ἡ ἁμαρτία A. B. C. G. K. al. Sin. The Article is very strongly supported and syntactically required.
[3 German: "And (the) sin is the lawlessness."—M.]
Verse 5 4 ἡμῶν, omitted in A. B. Vulg. al., is found in C. G. K. Sin. [Also the reading of Syr. Theophyl. Œcum. Bede, Lachm. Tischend. Buttmann.—M.]
[5 German: "That He (that One) was manifested to take away our sins and sin is not in Him."
Verse 6 [6 German: "Every one that."—M.]
[7 Same as 6.—M.]
Verse 7 8 παιδία A. C. al. τεκνία B. Sin. [Undecided which is the true reading.—M.]
[9 German: "Let no one seduce you."—M.]
Verse 8 [10 German: "He that doeth sin."—M.]
[11 German: "For this" (εἰς τοῦτο). No warrant for the additional "purpose" in E. V.—M.]
Verse 9 [12 Same as note 6. German: "Every one that is born (out) of God, doeth not sin."—M.]
[13 German: "Because."—M.]

EXEGETICAL AND CRITICAL.

Connection. The Apostle having traced the glory of the sonship up to the power (which it derives from hope in God) of working out self-purification, annexes v 4 with a more general antithesis which, as usual, contains a progression of the argument. The positive: "Every one that hath this hope purifieth himself;" is contrasted with the negative: "Every one that doeth sin, doeth lawlessness." He does not negatively resume the notion of the subject ("every one that hath this hope"), but that of the predicate ("purifieth himself"). However, by this annexation of the notion of the predicate he denies also, by implication, that such an one is the child and heir of God, and adds a new point, viz. such an one not only injures himself and his portion but he violates also the law and ordinance of God, at the same time, referring back to the leading thought in ch. ii. 29, since all doing of sin is repugnant to the righteousness of God revealed in the law (v. 4) and in Christ (vv. 5–7), and delineates rather the children of the devil (vv. 8–10), than the children of God, who, abiding in Christ, do righteousness and not sin (vv. 6, 9, 10).

The nature of sin. v. 4.

VER. 4. **Every one that committeth sin, committeth also lawlessness.**—"The Apostle is anxious to show that the truth of the thought is unexceptionable." (Huther.)—The first point to be determined here is the notion ἁμαρτία. Suidas derives ἁμαρτία from μάρπτω to grasp, to seize, consequently=missing the mark (Rom. xxi. 8, 302, 311, 23,.62); then moral omission. Oecumenius: ἀποτυχεῖν σκοποῦ, ἡ τοῦ ἀγαθοῦ ἀπόπτωσις, on the other hand ἀνομία=ἡ περὶ τὸν θετὸν νόμον πλημμέλεια (πλὴν—μέλος contrary to the mélody, a false note, an error). Ἁμαρτία, of course, is as much an opposition to the Divine righteousness (ἀδικία), as a departure from the Divine law, a violation of the same (ἀνομία), and this ἡ ἀνομία is here not only a not having the law (as ἄνομος 1 Cor. ix. 21 denotes one who has not a law), but signifies the refractoriness opposed to the law. Neither ἁμαρτία nor ἀνομία are qualified by anything which would narrow this their meaning, nor may such a qualification be added from the context. Although the Article distinctly takes sin in the sense of an *offence* [old English: *missing.* M.] towards *God*, and ἀνομία as an opposition to the *law of God*, and removes all indefinite generality, yet no qualification within this ethico-religious sphere is admissible. But we must not attach too much importance to this, since the Article is wanting in v. 9: ἁμαρτίαν οὐ ποιεῖν and ποιεῖν τὴν ἁμαρτίαν and ἁμαρτάνειν (vv. 4, 6, 8, 9) are used *promiscue*, so that we must not attach too much importance to ποιεῖν. To this must be added that καὶ before τὴν ανομίαν conveys the idea that the doing of the ἁμαρτία is as such also as the doing of the ἀνομία." (Düsterdieck.) "*Quisquis committit peccatum, idem committit iniquitatem.*" (Erasmus.) Καὶ must neither be taken in a causal sense, nor changed into "yea" (Brückner); but we have to hold with Ebrard that the fuller idea, ποιεῖν τὴν ἁμαρτίαν, in the beginning helps to qualify the other terms, ποιεῖν ἁμαρτίαν, and ἁμαρτάνειν, and that the antithesis ἁγνίζειν ἑαυτὸν is also coëfficient, and that the reference, so far from being to sins of haste or infirmity, is rather to sin, though only a single act, yet a *voluntary* act. Hence the following explanations cannot be received: that ἁμαρτία denotes *peccatum mortale* (Estius and the Roman Catholics), or "grave, unrepented sins" (Luther, al.), or that ποιεῖν τὴν ἁμαρτίαν is=*peccare contumaciter* (Aretius), *contra conscientiam et impœnitenter* (Rosenmüller), or *peccato operam dare* (Beza), *peccare scientem e: volentem* (Spener), or the actual moral bias of life (Brückner). It is equally inadmissible to assume an intensification of the notion ἁμαρτία into ἀνομία (Baumgarten-Crusius, Bengel), or that ἀνομία includes crimes and vices proper, as if ἁμαρτία were the principle and source of the ἀνομία (de Wette). Paraphrases of ποιεῖν ἀνομίαν, such as *Deum offendere* (Grotius) and *religioni adversari* (Carpzov), do incorrectly weaken the idea. The two ideas, although distinguished from each other, are not convertible. We have here the general proposition: "whoever doeth sin, of whatever kind it be, doeth also lawlessness, violates the Divine rule and order;" which is not directed against Antinomians, but against all those who are loose on the subject of sin; the idea of ἀνομία imparts a peculiar severity to that of sin.

And sin is lawlessness.—We must of course take ἁμαρτία here in the same sense, as in the clause immediately preceding, and in the same generality. Hence the first ἁμαρτία is not sinful doings, and the second an offence against God (Köstlin). The Article also forbids our taking ἁμαρτία as the predicate of the subject ἀνομία, as in Jno. i. 1. Ὁ θεὸς ἦν ὁ λόγος (Köstlin). Ἀνομία also is as general here as in the preceding clause. Νόμος denotes not only the Mosaic law of the O. T. but also the law of the N. T. in Christ, and by Him explained in the word and exhibited in the life (ii. 16; ii. 7; iv. 21; v. 3. cf Matth. v. 17-19), as the law written in man's heart for his special direction; it embraces the whole complex of the divine ἐντολαί. Hence this proposition contains not so much a definition (Sander), as the nature of sin viewed from that side on which its absolute opposition to every Divine fellowship shows itself in the most decided form (Brückner); "the Apostle could not have more sharply drawn the contrast of the naturê of a believer who *is* a τέκνον θεοῦ and *will be* ὅμοιος θεῷ than by declaring ἁμαρτία to be ἀνομία." (Huther); or he that leads an ungodly life, abrogates the Divine rule of life to which he is subject as a Christian (Hofmann). Hence Hilgenfeld's exposition disfigures the thought: "not every one who deviates from the *ceremonial laws*, but the sinner only falls under the category of ἀνομία." Calvin also goes far beyond the contents of the verse in affirming the sum and substance of the thought to be that the life of those who yield themselves to sin is *hateful and unendurable to God.*—The Apostle annexes the sentence with καὶ and not with ὅτι, because he thereby gives the thought a more independent form. We cannot agree with Bengel in explaining καὶ by *imo*, as if before there had been only *conjuncta notio peccati et iniquitatis*, but now *eadem;* the identity is already expressed in the first sentence.—[The following definitions will shed additional light on this passage. Ambrose: "*Quid est peccatum nisi prævaricatio legis* *divinæ, et cœlestium inobedientia præceptorum."*—Augustine: "*Peccatum est factum vel dictum vel concupitum aliquid contra æternem legem.*"—"*Quid verum est, nisi et Dominum dare præcepta, et animas liberæ esse voluntatis, et malum naturam non esse, sed esse aversionem a Dei præceptis?*"—"*Neque negandum est hoc Deum jubere, ita nos in facienda justitia esse debere perfectos, ut nullum habeamus omnino peccatum; nam neque peccatum erit, si quid erit, si non divinitus jubeatur, ut non sit.*"—M.]

Aid against sin. vv. 5. 6.

VER. 5. **And ye know that He was manifested in order that He might take away our sin.**—Appealing to their own consciousness, as at ch. ii. 12-14, 20, 27, the Apostle now refers to the Lord and affirms of Him two things: *First:* the purpose of His manifestation is the redemption from sin. Ἐκεῖνος denotes Christ, as in v. 3. It is wholly untenable to understand here the Gospel (Socinus, Episcopius, Grotius), concerning which it surely cannot be said that it τὰς ἁμαρτίας αἴρει, or that this is its end and aim.—Ἐφανερώθη the context requires us to apply to Christ's manifestation in the flesh. Cf. 1, 2. It points to Christ's previously hidden existence in heaven (Huther). The purpose of this manifestation is, ἵνα τὰς ἁμαρτίας ἡμῶν ἄρῃ. The reading ἡμῶν is well authenticated and intensifies the appeal to personal experience, without restricting the forgiveness of sins to those only who "suffer the beneficial purpose of the incarnation of the Son of God to be carried out on them in faith" (Düsterdieck), and to set back the universality of the Divine purpose of salvation (ch. ii. 2.); we would rather say that paracletic element, which after all is the main point here (v. 3), comes out more strongly; the οἴδατε, at least, does not contain sufficient ground for finding here a specific indication of the doctrinal. Nor is there any necessity for extending ἡμῶν to all men (Spener). "The Plural, τὰς ἁμαρτίας, affords a far more lucid and forcible view than if we had here, as in v. 4, τὴν ἁμαρτίαν; John does not take sin in its general character, but he adverts to all the forms of it." (Düsterdieck). It is wrong to explain it by *peccati reatum, dominium, pœnam* (J. Lange and others); but it signifies: the sins themselves. The αἴρειν connected here as at Jno. i. 29, with ἁμαρτία signifies in John's writings (Jno. xi. 48; xv. 2; xvii. 15; xix. 31, 38) *auferre*, to carry away, to take away. The ἀμνός, Jno. i. 29, the idea of the sacrificial lamb, implies what is expressed at 1 Pet. ii. 24, with reference to Is. liii. 4 sqq., by the verb ἀνάφερειν: to take upon oneself by way of atonement, substitution, death and reconciliation, while αἴρειν indicated a taking away by sanctification; Jno. i. 29 we have a blending of both meanings, while Peter adverts to one, the first, and John to the other, the second work of Christ, the former to His atonement, the latter to His work of redemption. John, who discusses the former at ch. ii. 2, dwells here upon the latter, and hence denies neither; nor does he separate the one from the other, as if the first were without this consequence, and the latter without that cause (ch. i. 7; iv. 9, 11; v. 6). But the context with its ethical import, that sin must be avoided and shunned, suggests the reference to the fact that Christ came for the purpose of removing sin, or taking it away from us; what Christian would then oppose or frustrate the design of Christ! Hence Oecumenius correctly observes that Christ came ἐπ' ἀναιρέσει τῆς ἁμαρτίας (so also Luther, Calvin, Neander, Ebrard, Düsterdieck, Huther, and al.)—Bede's remark, "*Tollit peccata et dimittendo, quæ facta sunt, et adjuvando, ne fiant, et perducendo ad vitam, ubi fieri omnino non possunt,*" is perfectly true, but considerably transcends the measure of what is contained in this passage. The same applies to those who combine here said two references, e. g. Spener, Bengel (explains indeed "*tolleret,*" but refers to his exposition of Jno. i. 29: "*primum a mundo in se recepit, deinde a se ipso devolvit peccati sarcinam*"), Lücke (in his 1st ed.), Sander, Besser.—Lücke (in the later edition), de Wette and others take αἴρειν=carry; false!

Secondly: He is sinless.

And sin is not in Him.—Καὶ coördinates this clause with the former. Oecumenius errs in his καὶ ἀντὶ τοῦ διότι as well as in the paraphrase: καθ' ὅτι ἀμέτοχος ἦν ἁμαρτίας. So also Augustine: "*In quo non est peccatum, ipse venit auferre peccatum; nam si esset et in illo peccatum, auferendum esset illi, non ipse auferret,*" and a Lapide: "*Ideo Christus potens fuit tollere peccatum, quia carebat omni peccato, imo potestate peccandi.*" So also Sander, Neander and al. Ἐστι also must be retained and is not to be taken in the sense of ἦν Oecumenius, Grotius: "*peccatum in eo non erat, nempe, cum vitam mortalem* ageret," and al.); the reference here, as in v. 3, is "to the nature of Christ in its eternal consistence" [Huther]. Hence we may not say with Winer (p. 283) that "the sinlessness of Christ is considered as still present *in faith.*" Ἐν αὐτῷ, the reference of which has always to be determined by the context, denotes Christ understood in ἐκεῖνος, it denotes Christ Himself as to His Person and not (as Calov supposes) *totum corpus*, the Church, or as if we ought to explain ἐν αὐτῷ by ἐν κοινωνίᾳ μετ' αὐτοῦ. Thus the clause "and sin is not in Him" coördinated with that preceding it, is the foundation of the sequel, since the Sinless, Pure and Righteous One is held up not as an example or pattern, but as the vital power and element of life in which the Christian must *be* and *abide*.

The immediate consequence.

VER. 6. **Every one that abideth in Him sinneth not.**—By all means retain the full force of μένειν ἐν αὐτῷ to be and abide in Him, to derive nourishment from Him and His life (ch. i. 3. 6; ii. 5. 6; 23 sq.; 27 sq.), and do not exchange it for *credere in Christum*, or weaken it into *Christi discipulum esse* (Semler and al.); nor is ἁμαρτάνειν to be taken as—*persistere in peccato* (Luther), *sinere regnare peccatum* (Hunnius), *sceleratum esse* (Capellus), *peccata mortalia committere* (Roman Catholics), and to be thus enforced. The Apostle sets forth "abiding in Christ and sinning as irreconcilable opposites; but he does not mean to say that believing Christians entirely cease to sin or that those, who are yet sinning, are not yet in Christ (ch. i. 8-10; ii. 1, 2; iii. 3)" (Huther). "John is here dealing with realities and about to give us the signs whereby we may know whether we love the Lord or not, whether we are the children of God or of the wicked one" (Sander). Hence it is rather hazardous to refer here with de Wette and Düsterdieck to the Apostle's *ideal* mode of representation, and a misapprehension of the fact that the Christian, though he sins, is yet free from sin, has actually parted company with it, and it is his properly Christian and inmost being in decided opposition to it, so that not sin, but his opposition to it (as something alien to his being), determines the conduct of his life, exactly as St. Paul puts it (Rom. vii. 17): "νυνὶ δὲ οὐκέτι ἐγὼ κατεργάζομαι αὐτό, ἀλλ' ἡ οἰκοῦσα ἐν ἐμοὶ ἁμαρτία." Augustine: "*Etsi infirmitate labitur, peccato tamen non consentit, quia potius gemendo luctatur.*"—"*In quantum in ipso manet, in tantum non peccat.*" Besser excellently says: "A Christian *does* not sin, but *suffers* it."

Every one that sinneth hath not seen Him, neither known Him.—As usual John turns the thought and develops it by an antithesis. The verb ἁμαρτάνειν has the same sense as in the preceding clause; actual sinning in word, or work or in the thought of the heart. Of such an one he says quite generally οὐχ ἑώρακεν αὐτὸν οὐδὲ ἔγνωκεν αὐτόν. First of all we have to take οὐδὲ *disjunctively* (Winer, p. 509 sqq.); and although this does not decide the question which of the two verbs ὁρᾶν and γινώσκειν is the stronger and more important, yet it does indicate that they are different from each other. The pronoun αὐτὸν requires us to think in both verbs of the Person of Christ. Hence the sentence: ἁμαρτία ἐν αὐτῷ οὐκ ἔστιν is not the object of ὁρᾶν, nor is the sentence: ἐφανερώθη ἵνα τὰς ἁμαρτίας ἄρῃ the object of γινώσκειν, in order to indicate the purpose of the whole redemptive work of Christ (Rickli, Neander). Ὁρᾶν, to *see*, physically (ch. i. 1, 3; iv. 20; Jno. i. 18; vi. 36, 46; viii. 57; ix. 37; xv. 24), spiritually (3 Jno. 11; Jno. iii. 11, 32; vi. 46; viii. 38; xiv. 7, 9), and that directly and immediately if used of Christ in heaven, or indirectly and mediately if applied to believers in consequence of their illumination,—denotes consequently in this passage "seeing Christ," "when we become absolutely conscious of the glory of Christ so that our spiritual eye beholds Him as He is in the totality of His Essence" (Huther); γινώσκειν means to know as the result of searching contemplation of His word, His life, the history of His kingdom, or of one's own experience in the life around us, or within ourselves, and indicates here "the right understanding of Him," brought about by said instrumentality, "so that we have become fully conscious both of His Nature and of His relation to us" (Huther). This intimates already that in the case of the former, viz. spiritual intuition and contemplation, the efficient agency belongs more to the object which represents itself before the eye of the spirit, and that in the case of the latter, viz. knowledge acquired by reflection in the way of reasoning and inquiry, the efficient agency belongs more to the subject, which makes it the object of contemplation (Sander, Huther). Hence it follows that ἑώρακεν is not something less, and οὐδὲ="much less" (Sander, Lücke 1st ed. al.), nor something more than ἔγνωκεν and οὐδὲ="and not even" (Socinus, Neander and al.); there is no reference whatever to a difference in degree. Although despite all their difference the two have something in common, we cannot, because of this latter circumstance, overlook or underrate the former [the difference] and say with Düsterdieck that the two notions are essentially equal and that ἔγνωκεν is simply added in order to indicate the spiritual import of ἑώρακεν. Of course it is impossible to interpret (with Lücke) ὁρᾶν of outward knowledge in spite of which one may sin, and γινώσκειν of real, spiritual knowledge. This connection is analogous to that of πιστεύειν and γινώσκειν (ch. iv. 16; Jno. vi. 69), so that ὁρᾶν and πιστεύειν might be combined yet so as to keep up the difference of πιστεύειν=ὁρᾶν from γινώσκειν. The force of these notions is very shallow in the explanation of Grotius: "*Neque de Christo sic cogitat, ut oportet, neque facto ostendit, se scire, quanti sit habenda Christi voluntas.*"—The Perfects, ἑώρακεν, ἔγνωκεν are to be preserved; they point to the past when the beginning of seeing and knowing took place, yet so that that which had its beginning in the past still acts and continues in the present, which is especially noticed by Erasmus (*cognitum habet*), Lücke, Brückner, Düsterdieck and Huther. It is wholly unwarranted to take the Perfect in the sense of the Present (Didymus: "*non videt eum;*" Augustine: "*non credit;*" Bede, Grotius, Estius, who construes the Perfect as a Hebraism for the Present). John's idea therefore is this: Every one that sinneth, and that while he is sinning, is one in whom seeing and knowing Christ is a fact of the past, but without continuing to act and to last to the present. Hence Bengel says not amiss: "*In ipso peccati momento talis fit, ac si eum nullo viderit modo.*"—Instructive is the reference to ch. ii. 19 (J. Lange, Sander) and the comparison with Matth. vii. 23: οὐδέποτε ἔγνων ὑμᾶς (i. e. as mine). The reference is, as the ancients rightly observe, to an *efficax scientia* (Dydimus), an *affectiva et dilectiva* (Estius), although Lyra goes as much beyond the mark with his *fides formata caritate*, as Ebrard with his *loving* knowledge, or S. G. Lange with his γινώσκειν=*amare*. [Ignatius, the disciple of John, says: "No one who professeth *faith, sinneth;* and no one who hath *love, hateth*. They, who profess themselves *Christians*, will be manifested by what they *do*." (Ignatius, *ad Eph.;* also Jerome *in Jovin.* ii. 1, and *contra Pelagianos* I. 3).—M.]

The issue. vv. 7, 8, 9.

VER. 7. **Little children, let no one seduce you.**—This impressive address, (unchanged whether we read παιδία or τεκνία) introduces an admonition in respect of the clearly-perceived and ruin-fraught danger, unless they avail themselves of the aid provided in their glorious Lord and Saviour. The Apostle speaks of ἑαυτοὺς πλανῶμεν, ch. i. 8. Here, however, he adverts not to self-deception, but refers "in matters affecting the energizing and outwardly operative exhibition of the Divine life" (Düsterdieck), to deception and seductions coming from without, not springing from relations and events, but from men (μηδεὶς), who are more dangerous by far than relations or events. But there is no reason why we should think here of distinct forms of error, say e. g. those of the antinomian Gnostics (Düsterdieck, Huther). [On the other hand Ebrard and Wordsworth see here an unmistakable reference to the Gnostics. The latter observes: "that these verses cannot be understood without reference to their tenets and practices," and then mentions the followers of Simon Magus, who said that they could please God without righteousness, and that whatever might be the case with others, who had not their spiritual *gnosis*, they themselves had *no need to work righteousness*, but that they would be saved by *grace*, whatever their works might be. "Liberos agere quæ velint; secundum enim ipsius (Simonis) *gratiam* salvari homines, sed non secundum *operas justas*." Irenæus I. 20 *ed. Grabe*. Hippolytus, *Philosoph.* p. 175; Theodoret, *Haer fab.* i. 1, who testifies that on the presumption of the indefectibility of special grace within themselves, they fell into all kinds of lasciviousness."—M.].—This admonition is in point of form like 1 Tim. iv. 12; Tit. ii. 15, in point of sense like μὴ πλανᾶσθε, 1 Cor. vi. 9; 15–33; Luke xxi. 8. But that form at the same time exhibits a more lively sense of danger.

He that doeth righteousness is righteous, even as He is righteous.—On δικαιοσύνην ποιεῖν and δίκαιος, see notes on ch. ii. 29. The Apostle does not say here πᾶς ὁ ποιῶν, but only ὁ ποιῶν; the idea of unexceptional universality makes room for the importance of the fact. Instead of the predicate ἑώρακε αὐτὸν καὶ ἔγνωκεν αὐτὸν (v. 6), or μένει ἐν αὐτῷ (v. 5), or ἐξ αὐτοῦ γεγέννηται (ch. ii. 29), there follows, as usual with the addition of a new particular, the consequence thereof, viz.: δίκαιός ἐστιν, either with reference to ὅμοιοι αὐτῷ ἐσόμεθα (v. 2) or in order to denote the corresponding attitude towards the law. It is evident that the predicate is not acquired after that which is affirmed in the subject-sentence has taken place; the predicate is immanent in the subject, the nature of the righteous appears from his *doing* righteousness, it *is already in its existence* and does not only *become so*, as held by the Roman Catholics (Lyra, Emser, Estius, al.), and the Socinians, Arminians and Rationalists (Socinus, Grotius, al.) against the Protestants (Luther, Calvin). "He that *doeth* not righteousness, proves thereby that he *is* not righteous" (Huther). [Compare the words of Ignatius in the last note on v. 6. M.] The additional clause refers to the righteousness of Christ, as manifesting the righteousness of God and standing out as a bright pattern. The Apostle once more uses ἐκεῖνος, although the previous αὐτὸς designated Christ, so that he might have put αὐτὸς without giving rise to misunderstanding, and thus have absolutely removed any and every want of clearness, that αὐτὸς in ch. ii. 29 had reference to Christ. By Him the Christian should ever measure and adjust himself. Baumgarten-Crusius's explanation is altogether irrelevant; viz.: "he that is good, follows the example of Christ," or "he only that hath been righteous through Christ, doeth righteousness." [Huther justly observes, that as there is no reference whatever to justification in this passage, a Lapide's assertion, that the thought of this verse contradicts the Protestant Dogma of justification by faith, is altogether futile. The explanation of Lorinus also, that "ὁ ποιῶν τὴν δικαιοσύνην is =*qui habet in se justitiam, i. e. opus gratiæ, videlicet virtutem infusam*," is manifestly false.—M.].

VER. 8. **He that committeth sin, is of the devil.**—This is the progressive antithesis. On ὁ ποιῶν τὴν ἁμαρτίαν compare note on v. 4. It is "the more significant and precise" expression for ἁμαρτάνειν v. 6 (Düsterdieck). Of such an one John does not say: ἀδικός ἐστι but ἐκ τοῦ διαβόλου ἐστίν and thus states the final cause of the thought. The phrase ἐκ τοῦ διαβόλου εἶναι must be interpreted after the analogy of ἐκ τοῦ θεοῦ εἶναι (cf. on ch. ii. 16), and this is the more incumbent upon us because verse 10 specifies τὰ τέκνα τοῦ θεοῦ and τά τέκνα τοῦ διαβόλου, and the paternal name is actually given to Satan at Jno. viii. 44. Still there is wanting an analogy to γεγεννῆσθαι ἐκ τοῦ θεοῦ (cf. on ch. ii. 29) both for the adherents of the devil and the κόσμος, although we have ἐκ τοῦ κόσμου εἶναι at ch. ii. 16 and οἱ υἱοὶ τοῦ αἰῶνος τούτου at Luke xvi. 8. Hence, although ἐκ τοῦ διαβόλου εἶναι contains no reference to a regeneration from beneath,—as if the devil had created the sinner, into whom he has only infused evil (Russmeyer), so that the Apostle adverts simply to *corruptio* and not to *generatio* (Bengel), and that consequently the phrase must be construed ethically and not physically (so that we cannot say τέκνον τοῦ διαβόλου in the same sense and with the same right as we say τέκνον θέου, see note on v. 10*a*),—yet are we obliged to think of an origin from the devil and of a sameness in kind and an intimate union with the devil as well as of an inheritance of woe in hell to be meted out to the devil and his adherents, and to reject the volatilization of the idea by perversion into a mere belonging to (de Wette), following (Semler), resembling and spiritual affinity with the devil (Grotius, Socinus, al.). Nor does the analogy warrant the assertion that it is not at all necessary to assume John to believe the existence of the devil, that this is only a mode of representation current among heretical Jewish Christians (Semler), or a Jewish formula of teaching without all dogmatical importance, or used only for the purpose of intensifying the idea of sin as hostility to God (Baumgarten-Crusius). See no. 4 below in "*Doctrinal and Ethical.*"

Because the devil sinneth from the beginning.—The connection by ὅτι specifies the reason of the sentence, "He that doeth sin is of the devil;" hence the reference is to man's sinning and his relation to the devil. For this reason ἀπ' ἀρχῆς emphatically put first, is to be interpreted of the beginning of man's sinning, like Jno. viii. 44, and the Apostle declares that from that beginning the devil has been showing himself as the sinner [the sinning one], he is not only a sinner in himself, but he did also bring about the first sin of man as a seducer, and not the first sin only, but he does bring about every sin even until now (the Present ἁμαρτάνει); sinning is his work from the beginning. Bengel: "*Omnium peccatorum causa est; nunquam satiatur.*" Hence there is no reference here to the beginning of the devil's existence from the creation of the world (Bede; for that would contradict Jno. viii. 44, οὐκ ἔστηκεν), or to the beginning of the creation of the earth and the solar system (Estius), or to the beginning of the *res humanæ* (Semler), or to the beginning of the devil's fall (Calvin, Calov, Bengel: "*Ex quo diabolus est diabolus; minime diu tenuisse videtur statum primitivum,*" Neander,

Sander and others.). Nor may we interpret ἁμαρτάνει like Bengel: "*Peccat et ad peccandum inducit*," but rather compare Rom. vii. 17. The *influxus, suggestio, inspiratio, directio, coöperatio* of the devil (Calov) lie not in the verb ἁμαρτάνει, but in the whole context: because the devil has sinned from the beginning and goes on sinning, every one that is sinning is of the devil; for the real connection of the person sinning with the devil or of the devil with the person sinning, is here evidently presumed, yet so that the first proposition describes the state of the sinner as essentially belonging to the sphere of the devil's life and kingdom, while the second proposition, connected with the former by ὅτι, marks the continuing activity of the devil, so that the latter is the cause of the former.

For this was the Son of God manifested that He might destroy the works of the devil.—Bengel: "*Diabolus peccandi finem non facit; peccatum solvere filii dei opus est.*" Without using a conjunction the Apostle rapidly and in terse language specifies with sharpness and distinctness of outline the antithesis: διάβολος—υἱὸς τοῦ θεοῦ; ἐκεῖνος would have been too weak and inadequate here, and contrasts the hidden seduction of Satan with the manifestation (ἐφανερώθη) of the Son of God for the destruction of the works of the devil (Jno. xii. 31; xvi. 11; Matth. xii. 29; Luke x. 18). He is not only δίκαιος (v. 7) but He also destroys sins (λύσῃ). This is the end of His coming, as in v. 5: αἴρειν τὰς ἁμαρτίας is parallel to λύειν τὰ ἔργα τοῦ διαβόλου. The last expression consequently denotes sins and, with reference to διάβολος ἁμαρτάνει, as the works of the devil who committeth them. Hence the reference is here to the ἔργα τοῦ διαβόλου, sins, not to the wages of sin—affliction, death, condemnation (Calov, Spener). For these are rather the works of God who is righteous and decrees the penalty, and only by way of consequence the object of the redemptive work of Christ, but not the object of λύειν. This verb signifies the destruction of a building (Jno. ii. 19; 2 Pet. iii. 10–12), or of a ship (Acts xxvii. 41) and also the loosing of chains (Acts xxii. 30). Bengel: ("*Opera confortissima quæ solvere res digna erat filio Dei*"), Spener, Besser and others retain the sense of "*loosening, untying*,' as if sins were the cords or bands of Satan; but this is manifestly a departure from the plain sense of the words and although useful for practical purposes, a rather artificial interpretation. Since nothing is said here of the three offices of Christ concurring in this work, or how that concurrence is to take place, the text neither authorizes us to assume that the *officium sacerdotale* and the *officium regium* without the *officium propheticum* will be engaged in the destruction of the works of the devil and to think only of the passion of our Lord, nor to infer anything for or against that sentence from "*Etiamsi Adam non peccasset, Christus incarnatus esset.*" Besides, John adverts only, as he had written (ἐφανερώθη—λύσῃ,) "to what Christ did purpose and achieve by His manifestation in the flesh" (Düsterdieck), without intending to describe or even to deny the continuous victory of Christ; he refers to that ch. i. 7; ii. 1, 2, 13, 14; iv. 4, 14; v. 5, but not primarily here. [Ignatius, the disciple of John, uses λύειν in the sense of the text, viz., the destruction of evil, *ad Eph.* i. 3, 19, λύεται ὄλεθρος, ἐλύετο πᾶσα μάγεια.—M.].

VER. 9. **Every one that is born of God, doth not commit sin, because his seed abideth in him.**—This is the antithesis of v. 8*a*, and ὅτι here like there denotes the reason why; the structure of the sentences too is alike, with the sole difference that by the usual inversion the subjects and predicates have changed places. Ὁ γεγεννημένος ἐκ τοῦ θεοῦ *opp.*: ἐκ διαβόλου ἐστιν,—ἁμαρτίαν οὐ ποιεῖ *opp.*: ὁ ποιῶν τὴν ἁμαρτίαν,—ὅτι ἀπ' ἀρχῆς ὁ διάβολος ἁμαρτάνει *opp.*: ὅτι σπέρμα αὐτοῦ ἐν αὐτῷ μένει. Thus John contrasts sinning in its extreme and inmost nature with the children of God in the possession of their highest and most glorious gift and an attitude conformable thereto. Πᾶς denotes the general character of the sense. We know from ch. ii. 29; iii. 6, that being born of God, doing righteousness or not sinning belong together and that the former is incompatible with the commission of sin. Cf. ch. i. 5. Hence ἁμαρτίαν stands emphatically in ante-position; the Apostle regards sin as devilish, and righteousness as divine; and hence righteousness and sin are as absolutely and diametrically opposed to each other as are God and the devil. The clause annexed by ὅτι specifies the reason why one born of God does not commit sin, and being parallel to the similar clause in v. 8, sheds a light on the latter in confirmation of the interpretation given here. The reference of σπέρμα αὐτοῦ to θεοῦ is obvious. The seed of God necessarily denotes something that proceeds from God, is instinct with vital power and full of life, develops itself, blossoms and bears fruit, and begets the Divine. We cannot see here a reference to the word of God (with Clement of Alex., Augustine, Bede, Luther, Calov, Spener, Bengel, Besser, Socinus, Grotius and others), notwithstanding Matth. xiii. 3 sqq.; Jas. i. 18; 1 Pet. i. 23; cf. 1 Cor. iv. 15; Gal. iv. 19, because that simile from the vegetable kingdom does not answer to the reference to begetting and birth, and because the Word of God or the Gospel in other passages is mentioned only as the instrument of begetting, as a carrier and conductor of the Divine σπέρμα, but not the σπέρμα itself. [Alford, who takes the view impugned here, says: "But whether we regard the generation of plants, or animal procreation, which latter is more in question here, what words can more accurately describe the office of the seed, than these? And what is the word of God but the continually abiding and working seed of the new life in the child of God? Nay, it seems to be that exactly of which we are in search: not the Holy Spirit, the personal agent; not the power of the new life, the thing begotten; but just that which intervenes between the two, the word, the utterance of God,—dropt into the soul of man, taking it up by Divine power into itself, and developing the new life continually. This is in the most precise and satisfactory sense the σπέρμα τοῦ θεοῦ; and in this all Scripture symbolism is agreed: cf. 1 Pet. i. 23; Jas. i. 18. In fact, the very passage which is the key to this, is Jno. v. 38, τὸν λόγον αὐτοῦ οὐκ ἔχετε μένοντα ἐν ὑμῖν. Nor should any exception have been taken by Huther and Düsterdieck to the comparison with the para ble of the sower ("*wie viele ältere Ausleger mit ungeschickter Vergleichung von Matth.* xiii. 3 sqq." Düsterdieck), for though the attendant circumstances of generation are different, the analogy is the same."—M.] It follows from this that the reference is to the *Spirit of God*, even the *Holy Spirit*, who communicates Himself in and of His own. Hence σπέρμα must not be applied to His whole Person but as the πνεῦμα radiating from Him which is at once He Himself and His gift, a gift from Him and of His Nature. This construction is rendered imperative by ἐκ τοῦ θεοῦ in the final and substantiating clause of this verse which runs parallel to σπέρμα. Just as one who is born of God is not on that account God and has not like Christ the fulness of God bodily indwelling, so σπέρμα is not the full Person of the Spirit of God, of the Holy Spirit, but something that comes forth from His Being, which, while it cannot be separated from Him, must be distinguished from Him. Therefore we have to say with the Greek expositors that σπέρμα is πνεῦμα υἱοθεσίας, τὸ πνευματικὸν χάρισμα, the *Spiritus Sanctus et ejus virtus* (Calvin, Beza, Düsterdieck), *nativitas spiritualis* (Estius), *vires regenerationis* (S. Schmidt), *Divine life-powers* (de Wette, Neander), *the* πνεῦμα *begotten of the Holy Spirit* (Sander), *the germ of the new life, of the new man, Christ implanted in us* (Ebrard, Lücke, Huther). But it is not σπέρμα as analogous to זֶרַע=τέκνον (Bengel: "*semen dei i. e. qui natus est ex deo*"), or "*semen quasi divinum*" (Semler), *the formative principle of the good* (Paulus), or *religion* (Fritzsche).—It is important to recollect that while μένει is used of σπέρμα, μένει is also said of the believer (v. 6), and that he is bidden notwithstanding: μένετε= (ch. ii. 28). On this account, and because the reference is not to a full ear of grain gathered in the barn, but to σπέρμα cast into the earth destined to grow under the influence of all kinds of weather, we need not suppose, that therefore it *must abide* and could neither be lost again nor perish. Nothing is said on this point, it is neither affirmed nor denied, and therefore we are not warranted to introduce or assume it here; the subject in question is simply and solely that in the σπέρμα and its abiding in conformity with its nature, the child of God receives the power of not committing sin. Although we cannot explain ὅτι by ἐφ' ὅσον as if it were=*quantum, quamdiu, quatenus*, it is involved in the thought (The Greek, R. Catholic and Evangelical commentators).

And he cannot sin, because he is born of God. Now the Apostle adds the most important particular, viz., his inability of sinning on the ground of his having been born of God, with which St. John began, as he now concludes this section. With reference to the seed of God abiding in the child of God, he now asserts the absolute contrariety of a child of God and sinning in the words: οὐ δύναται ἁμαρτάνειν. *Non potest peccare* is at all events much stronger and more than *potest non peccare*; it declares not the possibility of not sinning, but the impossibility of sinning. A servant of sin has become a servant of righteousness (Rom. vi. 16-23); in virtue of the seed of God abiding in him he only wills and only can do the Divine, righteousness (Düsterdieck and most expositors); hence ἁμαρτάνειν must neither be intensified into "*committing mortal sins*" (the Romanists), *to sin diabolically* (Besser), *to sin deliberately and intentionally* (Ebrard), nor be limited to *hating the brethren* (Augustine, Bede), nor must οὐ δύναται be weakened into *ægre, difficulter est* (Grotius, "*res aliena est ab ejus ingenio*;" Paulus, "*his whole spiritual nature and* HABIT *resist it*"). Nor must it be changed into οὐ βούλεται (the Greek commentators) or *non debet*. Nor is this declaration of the Apostle only a goal and standard far above the reality of the Christian life on earth, only of relative importance and without reality. Bengel: "*Res se habet, ut in abstemio, qui non potest vinum bibere, et in variis antipathiæ generibus.*" On the substantiating clause Bengel strikingly observes: "*priora verba ex deo majorem habent in pronunciando accentum; quod ubi observatur, patet, non idem per idem probari, collato initio versus.*" Because he is born *of God*, he that is *born* of God cannot sin; the *child* of God cannot sin, because it is the child of God. Very pertinent also is the note of Luther: "*In summa nos Christiani nascimur, non fuco quodam aut specie, sed ipsa natura sumus Christiani, quare non est possibile ut peccemus.*" [Wordsworth: "He that hath been born of God, and liveth as a son of God *cannot be a sinner*. It is inconsistent with the essential condition of his *spiritual birth*, by which he is *dead* to sin. It is contrary to the nature which he has as a *child of God*. This is well expressed by Didymus here, who says, "St. John does not assert that the man who has been born of God *will never* commit sin; but he asserts that he does not *work sin*.—*Non scriptum est non peccabit, sed non peccatum facit, non idem est peccare et peccatum facere*; a child of two days old, by reason of his *natural* childhood, cannot sin, but a child of *God* cannot be a *sinner*." This distinction he draws from the difference between the Present Infinite and the Aorist Infinitive; see Winer § 44, p. 346, 348, 349, who quotes from Stallbaum, *Plat. Euthyd.*, p. 140: "*Aoristus* (*Infin.*) *quia nullam facit significationem perpetuitatis et continuationis, prouti vel initium vel progressus vel finis actionis verbo expressæ spectatur, ita solet usurpari, ut dicatur vel de eo, quod statim et e vestigio fit ideoque etiam certo futurum est, vel de re semel tantum eveniente, quæ diurnitatis et perpetuitatis cogitationem aut non fert aut certe non requirit, vel denique de re brevi et uno veluti temporis ictu peracta.*" Thus e. g. πιστεῦσαι is to make a *profession* of faith, or *an act* of faith, at a particular time; but πιστεύειν is to *believe*, to be a *believer*; δουλεῦσαι is to do *an act of service*, δουλεύειν, *to be a slave*; οὐδεὶς οἰκέτης δύναται δυσὶ κυρίοις δουλεύειν, no servant can be a *slave to two masters*; so ἁμαρτεῖν is to commit *a sin*, but ἁμαρτάνειν is much more than this, it is *to be a sinner*."

Ignatius, *ad. Eph.* 8 says: "Let no one *deceive* you. They who are carnal *cannot* do the things which are *spiritual*; nor can they who are *spiritual* do the things which are *carnal*. Faith *cannot* do the works of unbelief, nor can *unbelief* do the works of faith. The works which ye do in the flesh are spiritual, because ye work all your works in *Jesus Christ*."—M.].

Conclusion. v. 10*a*.

VER. 10*a*. **In this are manifest the children of God and the children of the de-**

vii.—Ἐν τούτῳ refers back to the preceding. Cf. on ch. ii. 3. The point under notice is ἐκ τοῦ θεοῦ and ἐκ τοῦ διαβόλου εἶναι. This is apparent in the doing of righteousness or in the working of sin, the sinner entangling himself in sin, as a child of the devil, while the believer, as being born of God, resists it. *Being* a child of God or a child of the devil is hidden and manifest in *doing*. Hence this clause must not be referred to the sequel (Grotius, Spener, Ebrard and others) as there is not the least occasion for it; de Wette, Sander, and others leave this point undetermined. It is not said here to whom τὰ τέκνα τοῦ θεοῦ and τὰ τέκνα τοῦ διαβόλου φανερά ἐστιν, but v. 1 (κόσμος οὐ γινώσκει ἡμᾶς) renders it certain that it is not manifest to the world but only to the Christian. That difference is only manifest in the light of the divine κρίσις, the uncritical world blends together and confounds good and evil, God and the devil (Lücke, Sander). "To the children of the devil their own moral nature remains a mystery until they accept the judgment of the Holy Spirit and through the divine seed are born of God and become the children of God." Cf. Matth. vii. 16–21; Luke vi. 43–46.—The phrase τὰ τέκνα τοῦ διαβόλου occurs only here in the New Testament although we encounter the following variations: υἱὸς διαβόλου said of Elymas Bar-Jesus, Acts xiii. 10; ὁ υἱὸς τῆς ἀπωλείας said of Judas, Jno. xvii. 12; and υἱοὶ τῆς ἀπειθείας and τέκνα φύσει ὀργῆς, Eph. ii. 3, instead of which τέκνον τοῦ διαβόλου might have been used, if that expression had not been studiously avoided in order to prevent the misunderstanding that we might as well speak of a birth (out) of the devil as of a birth (out) of God (see notes on v. 8) and in order not to give nourishment to the dualistic notion that their conversion or regeneration is impossible, to intimate, on the contrary, that it is more probable to see a child of the devil become a child of God than a child of God become a child of the devil. But it cannot be inferred from these different expressions that the terms τὰ τέκνα τοῦ θεοῦ and τὰ τέκνα τοῦ διαβόλου denote the two extremes between which other men are found. This antithesis embraces rather the totality of mankind just as ἁμαρτάνειν and οὐχ ἁμαρτάνειν comprise the whole attitude of men. Socinus is surely right: "*Ex apostoli verbis satis aperte colligi potest, quod inter filios dei et filios diaboli nulli sint homines medii.*"

DOCTRINAL AND ETHICAL.

1. *The nature of sin.* The word ἁμαρτία while indicating aberration from the right way, the right goal, the straight direction and order does not tell us wherefrom said aberration takes place. On this account the word ἀνομία is added. It is evident that sin is in direct antagonism to the νόμος, the divine ordinance. Hofmann pertinently compares 2 Thes. ii. 7 (*Schriftbeweis* I., 487). The first thing is that sin contradicts the divine ordinance. The extent of ἀνομία is also that of ἁμαρτία; whatever does not accord with the divine ordinance of life, be it little or small or as it please, is ἁμαρτία, which is always to be regarded primarily as an injury done to God who has appointed the νόμος. Hence the notion of guilt adheres at all events to the notion of sin, although the sinner be not conscious of it at the time or soon after the act; the sense of guilt is sure to come sooner or later, but invariably with the knowledge of sin, even as David expresses it: "Against *thee only*, have I sinned" (Ps. li. 4) and St. Paul ὑπόδικος τῷ θεῷ (Rom. iii. 19). The injury done to one's own soul which lies at the bottom of ἁγνίζειν ἑαυτὸν, and is declared in τηρεῖ αὐτὸν as contrasted (ἀλλὰ) with ἁμαρτάνειν is likewise the reason why the sinner is outside of fellowship with Christ who is life, gives life and takes away sin.

[Pearson (p. 539) says: "The law of God is the rule of the actions of men, and any aberration from that rule is sin: the law of God is pure and whatsoever is contrary to the law is impure. Whatsoever therefore is done by man, or is in man, having any contrariety or opposition to the law of God, is sin. Every action, every word, every thought, against the law, is a sin of omission, as it is terminated to an object dissonant from, and contrary to, the prohibition of the law, as a negative precept. Every omission of a duty required of us is a sin, as being contrary to the commanding part of the law, or an affirmative precept. Every evil habit contracted in the soul of man by the actions committed against the law of God, is a sin constituting a man truly a sinner, even then, when he actually sinneth not. Any corruption and inclination in the soul, to do that which God forbiddeth, and to omit that which God commandeth, howsoever such corruption and evil inclination came into the soul, whether by an act of his own will, or by the act of the will of another, is a sin, as being something dissonant from, and repugnant to the law of God. And this I conceive sufficient to declare the nature of sin."—M.]

2. *The nature of righteousness*, as the opposite of sin, is therefore a conduct consonant with the νόμος, a doing regulated by the divine ordinances of life, from the work of our hands to the act of thinking and the power of the will.

3. *The corruption* of sin is manifest in that it entangles men in a relation to Satan which at once defines his attitude and shows itself in it It comes from Satan and is the act of Satan, so that living in sin and the working of sin are evidences of the sinner's dependence on the devil, his appurtenance and similarity of nature to the devil. Although man's sin is the sin of the seduced, in virtue of such seduction he is yet as much doomed to the power of the kingdom of the Evil One as he is guilty before God; and he that ought and might have become a child of God, has become a child of the devil. As surely as fellowship with God and righteousness are gained in Christ, so surely does sin evidence fellowship with the devil.

4. *Satan* is a person, opposed to God, the opposite of God and not only of Christ, who came to take away sin and to destroy the works of the devil. Strauss (*Dogmatik* II. 15) justly observes: "The whole idea of Messiah and His kingdom is as impossible without its counterpart of a kingdom of demons with a personal head, as the north pole of a magnet without the south pole. If Christ came to destroy the works of the devil, there was no necessity for His coming if there was no devil; if there is a devil, but only as the personification of the principle of evil—well, then we ought also to be satisfied with a

Christ as an impersonal idea." Besides to deny the existence and personality of the devil is to give up the personality of God Himself. God would be *the Absolute* and not the absolute Personality, if in this Johannean complex of ideas we are permitted to understand Satan to be only a principle, though it be the cosmical.—But there are here no data whatsoever for a dualistic conception. *Two* things are certain; *First:* the devil's opposition to God cannot be so construed as to give the devil the character of the contestant counter-god from all eternity and to divest him of the attributes of the creature; the text contains no warranty for either; the purpose of Christ's manifestation and the circumstance that this purpose must be supposed to be fully accomplished and accomplishing in all essential points, warrant us rather to conclude that said true assumptions, as a perfectly *dualistic* opposition of the devil and God, are incompatible with the fundamental views of the Apostle. *Secondly:* it cannot be inferred from this passage that men are naturally and essentially devilish. For John plainly declares that not the devil's *nature* (to which he does not make the faintest allusion), but the devil's work shows itself in the sins of men and that Christ came not to destroy the nature of the devil but to destroy the works of the devil. Nor must it be overlooked that, as contrasted with the terms *γεγεννημένος ἐν τοῦ θεοῦ, σπέρμα θεοῦ ἐν αὐτῷ, ἐκ θεοῦ εἶναι, ἐκ αὐτῷ μένων, τέκνον θεοῦ*, the Apostle is very sparing in his reference to the devil and does not go beyond saying *ἐκ τοῦ διαβόλου εἶναι* and *τέκνον τοῦ διαβόλου*, opposing the latter term, as it were by constraint, to the phrase "child of God," so that *Augustine* justly refers to an *imitari diabolum*, observing: "*Omnes peccatores ex diabolo nati sunt, in quantum peccatores. Adam a deo factus est, sed quando consensit diabolo, ex diabolo natus est, et tales omnes genuit qualis erat.*" There is not the faintest intimation for the supposition that man does not sin of his own will, not *voluntaria* but *naturaliter*, and that the sin which he commits is not his fault, but solely the devil's fault; the contrary is evident from the exhortation in v. 7 and the paracletical tendency which lies at the bottom of the whole. Neither dualism nor determinism can be deduced from this passage. But concerning subjection and personal transactions reference is made to cosmical powers in God the Father with the Son and in the devil, as the ultimate and chief factors of all personal development.

5. The *work* of Satan is sin, and sin from the beginning, *i. e.* from the beginning of sin on the part of mankind, which is the only subject under notice here. Hence he is most truly *the* sinner, the original sinner. As he was actively engaged in the first sin, so he still is actively engaged in every sin. But beyond this fact nothing is said as to the nature of his activity, as to its concurrence with that of man which is not excluded, and as to the manner how sin comes to pass. But it is intimated that contrary to *Christ* who was *manifested* and did appear in order to destroy the works of the devil, the *devil* was not manifested but remained and continued to walk *in concealment*, and that the children of God and the children of the devil cannot be identified at once, even as the world (which knows neither God nor the children of God (v. 1), nor itself) does not discover the devil's work in its own sin; for the reference is to *πνευματικὰ τῆς πονηρίας* (Eph. vi. 12). It is just the man, who, as St. James says (ch. i. 14 sq.), is incited and enticed by *his own lust* (*ὑπὸ τῆς ἰδίας ἐπιθυμίας ἐξελκόμενος καὶ δελεαζόμενος*) and commits sin without an inward struggle, without offering any resistance, in a calm course of development (*ἡ ἐπιθυμία συλλαβοῦσα τίκτει τὴν ἁμαρτίαν*), has the devil as the father of sin and is himself a child of the devil. In sins it becomes manifest that the anti-divine on earth is intimately and vitally connected with the kingdom and influence of the devil and that ultimately the whole matter resolves itself into a world-combat between God and the devil, and a world-victory of God in Christ over the devil (compare Harless, *Ethics* § 28. ***: Nitzsch, *System*. p. 244. sqq.)

6. *Redemption from sin is the work of the Sinless One, the purpose of the manifestation* of the Sinless One, whose aim it is not to bring a *new* doctrine but to produce a new *life*. According to this the most important thing is, of course, not the *exposition* of the law marked by the utmost profoundness of apprehension and lucidity of statement, but the *exhibition* of the law to its full extent in a pure life, which not only evinces its strength in suffering and the assumption of human sin, but also satisfies and reconciles the Father, so that for the Son's sake He now once more turns to mankind as hallowed and mankind overcome and attracted by the Sinless One, parts company with sin and turns away from it. It is inconceivable to have known and understood the Sinless One and yet to continue in sin all the same; to abide in Christ and to abide in sin are incompatible opposites; the one excludes the other. John, to be sure, has respect only to the principle or the result, as the issue is a life that terminates not in a moment but has its historical course and internal development. This is predicated of the life in Christ (vv. 2, 3,) and by analogy we are constrained to assume it of the life in sin.

7. *Being* determines the *doing*, the doing does not determine the being, but we know the being from the doing. The being is the cause, the doing the effect. Hence he that does not commit sin but worketh righteousness (vv. 6, 7, 8, 9) must be born of God (ch. ii. 29; iii. 9, 10) and have seen and known Christ (ch. iii. 6), but he that is of the devil, commits sin and worketh no righteousness (v. 8). So Luther (*Erlangen ed.* 27, 191): "Good, pious works nevermore make a good, pious man, but a good pious man will do good, pious works. Evil works nevermore make an evil man, but an evil man will do evil works. Consequently the person must everyways be good and pious prior to all good works, and good works must follow and proceed from the good, pious person (Matth. vii. 18)." Hence a man must have become righteous by justification, before he can act righteously in sanctification. This is the truth and the right of the Lutheran and Reformed confessions in opposition to Rome; but on the subject of *becoming* righteous John confines himself to saying that it takes place (out) of God in Christ by regeneration and propitiation; hence it simply indicates the objective ground and not the subjective accomplishment. On this point no

other particulars can be inferred from our passage.

8. While the *not-sinning* and the *impossibility of sinning* on the part of a Christian born of God, must be held fast as a fact, we must be on our guard against hasty inferences therefrom, for which John gives us no warrant. In the first place this passage (v. 9) must be susceptible of a construction that does not contradict ch. i. 8 sqq., for John could not have made both statements, if they were incompatible with one another. Hence the Roman Catholics are as much in the wrong for holding, as de Lyra says, that it is the prerogative of the saints, *i. e.* only individuals in virtue of special grace in regeneration, not to sin and not being able to sin, as are the Lutherans for contending that *all* truly regenerated persons live without sin; for such an assertion is as arrogant as that contained in the sentence of Seneca, the Stoic (see Düsterdieck II. 148 from Wetstein): "*Vir bonus non potest non facere, quod facit; in omni actu par sibi, jam non consilio bonus, sed more eo perductus; ut non tantum recte facere possit, sed nisi recte facere non possit.*" 1 Jno. i. 8 sqq. forbids such a construction of ch. iii. 9. The Gichtelites, who in virtue of Matth. xxii, 30 used to call themselves the brethren of the angels and refusing to be considered a sect laid claim to being the invisible Church, and the Molinists who were Quietists, claimed with some Pietists such a state of perfection, and being called Perfectists by their adversaries, called them in turn *Conatists;* the Methodists who maintain that they stand daily and hourly in need of the atoning merits of Christ do not belong to this category although they hold the sinless perfection of the regenerate; but this certainly exposes them like the Roman Catholics to the danger of regarding or treating concupiscence as a matter of indifference. The Synod of Dort, moreover, cannot on the strength of this passage reject the following proposition (see Niemeyer, p. 719 sub III): "*Vere credentes et regenitos non tantum posse a fide justificante, item gratia et salute totaliter et finaliter excidere, sed etiam reipsa non raro ex iis excidere atque in æternum perire,*" nor is *Calvin* warranted to say: "*Johannes non solum docet, quam efficaciter agat semel deus in homine, sed clare affirmat, spiritum suam gratiam in nobis* AD EXTREMUM USQUE PERSEQUI, UT AD VITÆ NOVITATEM INFLEXIBILIS PERSEVERANTIA ACCEDAT," because the Apostle teaches here not a word on that subject. He neither says ch. i. 8 sqq. that the regenerate in reality does not seldom fall from grace and perish eternally (!), but only, that his sinning notwithstanding, his sins would be forgiven him, nor here at ch. iii. 9, that the gift of sonship and regeneration can never be lost again or impaired, or that the σπέρμα is and must be brought to perfection in every child of God, or that the *donum perseverantiæ* is added by God to the gift of His grace, so that the two are intimately united and inseparable. A view hitting the truth may be found already in *Jovinian* (at the end of the fourth century) as stated in the controversial writing of his opponent (Hieronymus *adv. Jovinianum* libri II), if we remember that he said besides what here follows, viz: "*eos, qui plena fide in baptismate renati sunt, a diabolo non posse subverti,*" or "*a diabolo non posse tentari: quicunque autem tentati fuerint, ostendi eos aqua tantum et non spiritu baptizatos*"—that the Christian is not called upon to fight and to labour "*ut majora præmia accipiat*" but only "*ne perda quod accepit,*" and that he did add "*qui suum baptisma servaverint.*" For John neither affirms nor excludes by an intimation that the work and act of God to man must be accepted and received by man, that man with the divinely-given strength must become self-acting so that he not only do not resist and thus not resisting, *obicem non ponens*, become sanctified after having been justified, but also that entering into the work and act of God he exercise himself by his own personal efforts and thus appropriate more and more and receive into his own nature that which is God's, by giving up and sacrificing his self without doing injury to his seity. All these things John does not touch upon because he is not concerned with subjective execution but solely with the objective ground and foundation. Hence he says: he that is born of God, as such (as God's child), without any reference to his former condition and its reaction, does not really sin in the literal acceptation of the term; sin may still take place in him, but *he* himself, as the child of God, in the power of regeneration, *does* not and *cannot* commit it (cf. Harless *Ethics* § 26. **).—Hence we cannot see at all why the regenerate, if he neglects, in conflicts and collisions which may arise, to be on his guard and to hold fast all that God has given to him, done for him and is offering to him, may not by degrees fall entirely from grace, and such an issue necessitates or justifies the assumption that God did not seriously intend, energetically will and efficiently accomplish his regeneration and that lastly the lapsed was right and God in the wrong, that it is God's fault that he, though already redeemed from the power of the devil, had again fallen a prey to the devil. Heb. vi. 4 sqq. which only declares that it is impossible to recover those who have fallen away from such true regeneration has no connection with this passage (in opposition to *Ebrard*), but we ought rather to take note of *μένων* in v. 6., which points to that unexpressed train of thought. Cf. Rom. vii. 15 sqq. where mention is made of the ἔσω ἄνθρωπος as the σπέρμα θεοῦ and the ἐγὼ of the regenerate warring against the old *ego*.—[Düsterdieck: "The difference between the older and more modern expositors[1] lies in this, that the former are more anxious to moderate the details of the Apostle's sentiment, and to tone down his assertion to the actual life of Christians, while the moderns recognize the full precision of the text as it stands, but then remind us that the ideal truth of the principle announced by St. John continually, so to speak, floats above the actual life of believers as their rule and aim, and that, in so far, the Apostle's saying finds in such actual life only a relative fulfilment. None however of all the expositors, who in any way has recognized the ideal character of St. John's view, has overlooked the fact, that even in the actual life of all that are born of God there is something which in full verity answers to the ideal words "they cannot sin." The children of God, in whom the Divine

1. Lücke, Rickli, de Wette and Neander.

seed of their eternal life abides, have, in reality, a holy privilege, as Steinhofer says,—they sin not and they cannot sin, just in proportion as the new Divine life, unconditionally opposed to all sin, and manifesting itself in godlike righteousness, is present and abides in them. Expositors of all these logical tendencies, in all times, *e. g.* Didymus, Oecum., Estius, Schlichting, Luther, Hunnius, Seb. Schmidt, Calov, Bengel, Joachim Lange, Rosenmüller, Lücke, Neander, etc. point to this, that the new life of believers, veritably begotten by regeneration from God, is simply incompatible with sin[1]; the life which essentially alienates the spirit from all sin,[2] fills it with an irreconcilable hate against every sin, and urges it to an increasing conflict against all unrighteousness. Luther excellently says, that a child of God in this conflict receives indeed wounds daily, but never throws away his arms or makes peace with his deadly foe. Sin is ever active, but no longer dominant; the normal direction of life's energies in the believer is against sin, is an absence of sin, a no-will-to-sin and a no-power-to-sin. He that is born of God has become, from being a servant of sin, a servant of righteousness; according to the Divine seed remaining in him, or, as St. Paul says, according to the inner man[3], he will and he can work only that which is like God,—righteousness, though the flesh not yet fully mortified, rebels and sins: so that even in and by the power of the new life sin must be ever confessed, forgiveness received[4], the temptation of the evil one avoided and overcome[5], and self-purification and sanctification carried on."—M.].

9. *John* speaks of being born in order to live, *Paul* of dying in order to live.

[Ezek. Hopkins: This place may, perhaps, be among the number of those, that had been more clear, if they had been less expounded. I shall only give you the genuine native sense of the words and then proceed to manage them to my present purpose. *Whosoever is born of God doth not commit sin.* Some from hence have concluded a possibility, at least, of a sinless state in this life: others, the infallible certainty of it; not only that a child of God might attain to such a perfection as is exclusive of all sin, but that whoever is a child of God cannot upon that very account be guilty of any sin; so like are errors to precipices, that, if a man lose his firm footing, usually he falls headlong; nor does he stop, till he dash himself against the bottom and foundation of all religion and piety: had these men but seriously pondered what the same Apostle saith in his first chapter, vv. 8, 10: "*If we say that we have no sin, we deceive ourselves, and the truth is not in us;*" and "*If we say that we have not sinned, we make God a liar,*" they would not have entertained such an over-weening conceit of a spotless perfection of life here; whereof the greatest part is no better than sin and the best of it, but too, too much defiled with it. Others interpret thus: So long as we are the children of God, we cannot sin; and so the Papists go; but these go upon an erroneous supposition, that every mortal sin, as they call them, makes an intercision of justifying grace; and doth, as it were, annihilate the new creature. Others interpret it thus: *in quantum sumus filii Dei:* we cannot sin under that respect and notion, as we are the children of God; but even so far as we are, the best of us in the most part, unrenewed; though this is a certain truth, yet it is but a dilute and waterish exposition of this place; and it amounts to no more than this, that a regenerate man sins not as he is regenerate, that the principle of grace in him is not that principle from whence sinful actions proceed; and certainly, no man, that considers the weight of this Scripture expression, will think that the Apostle, by such an instance and ingemination, would press so thin a meaning as this is. The interpretation, therefore, that I judge to be the most natural and unforced is this: He, that *is born of God, doth not commit sin;* that is, he doth not sin in that malignant manner, in which the children of the devil do: he doth not make a trade of sin, nor live in the constant and allowed practice of it. Neither can he thus sin, because *his seed remaineth in him;* that is either the energy of the word of God whereby he is begotten again to a spiritual life, or the complexion of the graces of the spirit that are as it were the seminary and the seed-plot of glory. Nor he cannot sin, *because his seed remaineth in him:* this seed remains, and keeps him, that he cannot sin; either as apostates do who totally forsake the ways of God, or as profane persons do, who never embraced them. There is a great difference betwixt regenerate and unregenerate persons, in the very sins that they commit: all, indeed, sin; but a child of God cannot sin; that is, though he doth sin, yet he cannot sin after such a manner as wicked and unregenerate men do: there is a vast difference betwixt them, even in that wherein they do most of all agree: see that place in Deut. xxxii. 5. *Their spot is not the spot of his children:* even deformities themselves are characteristic: and a true Christian may come to know by his sins, that he is not a sinner. And, as they differ in the committing of sin, so much more in the opposing of it."—M.].

HOMILETICAL AND PRACTICAL.

Thou art wont in other respects to attach importance to the right name and the right word. Well, sin is immorality; what thou callest a slip, an error, an infirmity or a foible, is essentially—immorality.—Be not concerned as much about earthly losses or disgrace before men as about outraging the Divine majesty, which marks the nature of sin even more graphically than the outrage done to thy own soul.—What does it avail thee to be praised of men, even in newspapers, if God regards thee as a transgressor?—Remember the case of Chrysostom, Bishop of Constantinople, who was hateful to the Emperor; the courtiers said: "Burn him, confiscate his property, put him in irons, and have him killed." But others replied, saying: "You will not gain anything by all this; for in exile he would find a home with his God; you deprive the poor, not him, of property; he kisses his chains, death

1. Didymus: ἀκόλουθον καὶ ἀνάρμοστον.
2. Oecumenius: ἀνεπίδεκτον ἁμαρτίας τὸν νοῦν ἡμῶν ποιεῖ.
3. Rom. viii. 15.
4. Ch. i. 8 sqq.
5. V. 18.

opens heaven to him. There is only one way to render him unhappy; force him to sin; *he fears nothing in the world but sin.*"—Dost thou honestly abide the law of the land, especially the fundamental law—then maintain also the law of God's kingdom, His fundamental law.—The sinner does the very thing which Christ desires to remove: he twines for Him a crown of thorns and crucifies Him anew.—Hold fast the sinlessness and death of Christ. Why was it necessary for the Sinless One to die if not for the sin of men? What is he that does not like the Sinless One and does every thing in his power to put Him out of the way? What is the public opinion which crowned that attempt with success? Of what consequence must sin be, if He had to die by and for it?—He did not come for the sake of the doctrine, which did not take away sin, that the prophet might be praised, but He came for the sake of sin, that the Lamb of God and the High priest might be praised together.—He came to acquire for Himself a people that it might live of and by Him; He came not to receive from it what were its possessions, but to take away from it, what is its grievance and to grant to it His glory.—A Christian, as a Christian, never *does* sin, he only *suffers* it.—In and with Christ we lose all pleasure in sin and loathe its service.—Sin dazzles men and prevents their seeing and knowing the glory of Christ.—To overlook the glory of Christ denotes not a low degree of immorality.—The illumination of our spirit is not without the purification of our heart, without the deliverance of our will from the chains of sin.—As sin is ever growing so that thin threads of lust become cords of vanity and cart-ropes of unrighteousness (Is. v. 18), the small rent of doubt grows into a shipwreck concerning faith (1 Tim. i. 19) and a little spark causes a great fire (Jas. iii. 5), so in like manner the forgiveness of sins in justification grows to the annihilation of sin in sanctification, and the regenerate grows into manhood, so that while Ahab, though wholly mail-clad, was mortally wounded in one place, Paul though bitten by a venomous viper, shook off the beast into the fire and remained unhurt.—Christ is the point where men must choose the way that leadeth to the kingdom of darkness, or that which conducts to the kingdom of light.—Man's way ends in the former kingdom with his belonging to Satan, but it *begins* in the latter with his regeneration.—Just those who are the devil's know least of him, deny his existence and personality; those who with God resist him, know his nature and power much better than his servants.—Be not deceived, 1. Concerning the nature of sin; 2. Concerning the glory of Christ; 3. Concerning the activity of Satan; 4. Concerning the power of regeneration.—Fear sin! 1. It breaks the ordinance of God; 2. It is the cause of Christ's sufferings; 3. It leads to the slavery of Satan; 4. It destroys thy adoption of God.—Child of God, rejoice! 1. God's law is a sure and straight path; 2. The merit of Christ affords thee a mighty help; 3. The gift of the Spirit will yield thee precious fruit.

AUGUSTINE:—The doing of righteousness does not precede but succeed justification.

STARKE:—Whatever is contrary to the law of God, whether done inwardly or outwardly, in thought, manner, words or works—is sin.—Let every one diligently study the law of God so that he may learn what is right and wrong and not do ignorantly what might have been avoided.—Sin must be a terrible and horrible thing, because for its sake Christ had to come, to suffer and to die. Every thing is in harmony: begone, sin! there is no room for thee with the redeemed! It is apostasy from the law, the opposite of the Image of Christ, the progeny of Satan, a mark of his slaves.—Thou sayest: I am a sinful man and not a sinful angel! True; but if thou art truly a believing Christian, sin must not reign in thee, but thou must reign over sin and not serve sin in any particular.—Not certain, believers are exposed to the danger of being seduced.—Appearance, propriety of conduct, and observance of the externals of worship are not paramount in Christianity, but the heart must be changed and that takes place in regeneration.—It is ill-befitting a Christian to appeal to and boast of his illustrious descent, the distinction of his family and connections; the grace of regeneration, which invests him with the prerogatives of the adoption, truly ennobles him before God and men.—The children of Satan are often unknown, but more to themselves and those like them than to the godly.—The godly also are often hidden, but more from the ungodly than from themselves, for they know very well in virtue of the spirit of adoption both what they have received and what is promised to them.—There is a difference between the children of God and the children of the devil; they may and ought to be identified, but the identification requires a spiritual discernment, otherwise it cannot take place.—Honest preachers must not give evangelical consolation to those who are openly ungodly, though they say that preachers cannot condemn. True; they cannot condemn but they can denounce the damnable condition.

BENGEL:—"*Iniquitas horribilius quiddam, apud eos præsertim, qui legem et dei voluntatem magni faciunt, sonat, quam peccatum. Ex lege agnitio peccati. Linea curva cernitur per se; sed magis, ad regulam collata.*"

STEINHOFER:—The children of God in whom the divine seed of their eternal life is truly abiding, have really the holy privilege of not being able to sin.

HEUBNER:—Not the hurtfulness of sin is its nature, for that is accidental, but its opposition to God.—The chief purpose of the manifestation of Christ was the cancelling of sin, the atonement for our sin, and sanctification by means of reconciliation. Hence continuing in sin frustrates the purpose of Christ and contradicts His holiness.—Christianity is not *gnosis*, but an honest mind and conversation.—Recollect that as long as sinning is thy element, thou art in the devil's sphere and exposed to his influence.—Take note: 1. That the destruction of the works of the devil is not something that has been done, finished and perfected once for all but is progressive in its nature, advancing to perfection to the end of time. 2. That Christ has laid the foundation by His suffering and death as well as by the establishment of His Church, that incessant warfare may be waged against the kingdom of the devil and that at the last it shall be entirely destroyed. 3. That Christ has enabled all who believe in Him and receive His power to overcome Satan. The power of Satan is broken in believers. The works of the devil are being destroyed in proportion as the Gospel spreads intensively and extensively. 4. That the absolute and total destruction of the kingdom of the devil will take place at the second coming of Christ. Then it will be fully consummated. At present believers are only called upon to make war against Satan.—As the seed does only push forth the fruit it contains, and cannot produce a fruit different in kind, and as it is peculiar to the nature, even to the germinating principle in the seed to produce the right fruit, so it is also with those in whom is laid the seed of God, the Spirit of God; its germinating principle prompts godliness of living. But this does not warrant the assertion of absolute sinlessness.—It is not a physically absolute impossibility, but a moral impossibility; it is impossible to the *sanctified* will.—The indwelling spirit effects so essential a difference among men, that it seems as if they were wholly different races. But because it is invisible, God causes it to become *manifest* in its *persevering* fruit.—How sharply does Holy Scripture distinguish between men; they are either the children of God or the children of the devil; it knows nothing of half-Christians, of an amphibious race; man can only be one or the other.—Be not deceived by this sharp dichotomy, as if it were unkind and uncharitable thus to judge, for it is not taught here that we should thus judge and classify *others* (for that is the prerogative of God), but that we should judge and range *ourselves*.

REINHARD:—Christ takes away

1. The *deception and fraud of sin*—by His *doctrine*.
2. The *punishment* of sin—by His *death*.
3. The *dominion* of sin—by His *Spirit* and *example*.

BESSER:—With God every transgression is a crime; the Judge above does not treat sin as a trifle, a peccadillo (*peccatilio*, a little sin). Every sin and all sin has the character of treason.—True Christians *know* that the Saviour was manifested as the enemy and atoner of sin, and they agree with Him in heart and mind in pronouncing the same sentence on sin which was passed upon it in His bitter sufferings and painful death. Every one that *abides in Christ*, to whom he belongs once for all, *does not commit sin*, but says *no* to sin, which belongs to the old man, and resists its foreign power. The Christian's will, his *ego* resting in and governed by Christ is not one with sin but one with Christ in whom there is no sin. Hatred of sin is the feeling which the children of God have in common, the love of sin the universal dowry of the children of the devil. Just as only those truly love *good* who know *the Good One*, so they only hate *evil* with perfect hatred who hate the *Evil One* as actively engaged in every evil and abhor sin as the work of the beginner of sin.—The will which worketh sin, is of the devil and not of God. Out of the new, divine life-ground laid in the children of God grows up the pure delight in the good and perfect will of God, and whatever is displeasing to the Father (and sin is unrighteousness and wrong) is equally displeasing to the child.

THOLUCK:—*Do not trifle with sin.* 1. Because our *hope is so glorious.* Here the blessed *rights* of children, there the splendour and joys of children; should not he shun sin that hath such a hope? Ingratitude is one of the meanest vices; he that does not experience the necessity of gratitude for benefits received is one of the poorest and most hopeless of men. Christ who burst the chains and shunned no indignity in order to help us, should we not be grateful to Him—by fighting against sin? 2. *Because sin is so culpable.* Sin, did it only hurt *us*, we might get over it, but as it hurts *God*, it becomes a more fearful thing. The true child of God ceases to *commit* sin and greatly grieves at the presence of any and every sin. [A stanza of a German hymn.—M.] Every, even the smallest sin always hits the nerve of the law, unlike the eye, where the skin only and not the ophthalmic nerve needs to be injured; and the sinful lust is followed by the culpable word and the culpable word by the culpable deed. Misfortune is seldom alone and sin even more seldom. To become free from sin is the *life-task* of the Christian. He knows of no care greater than that of getting rid of a *diseased conscience.* Repentance cuts the *nerve* away from the lust of sin.

GEROK:—(on ch. ii. 28—iii. 8). *Of the paradise of the divine sonship.* 1. of the noble state *of being a child;* 2. of the holy *duty of a child;* 3. of the blessed *children's right* of the children of God.

[V. 7. BURKITT:—The Scriptures speak of doing righteousness in two senses: 1. in a *legal* sense, which consists in an exact obedience and fulfilling of the law; and thus there is "*none righteous, no not one;*" 2. in an *evangelical* sense, which means walking uprightly according to the rules of the Gospel, conscientiously avoiding all known sin, and performing every commanded duty, observing a constant course of holy actions and making it our daily care to please God in all that we do. And it is the duty of every Christian, who would not be deceived as to his spiritual condition, to try himself by this infallible mark: "He that doeth righteousness is righteous;—whosoever doeth not righteousness is not of God."—M.].

[V. 8. BP. HALL:—He that gives himself over to the commission of sin, and makes it his willing practice, that man is not of God but of the devil: for it is and hath been, the trade of that wicked spirit, even from the beginning, ever since his fall [?], to sin against God, and to draw others into sin and condemnation with him.—M.].

[SECKER:—Herein is the plain trial of our condition. If we are destitute of "the fruits of the spirit," it is bad; if we find them in our hearts and lives, we have proof enough of its being good, and need never disquiet ourselves for want of any other. Being able to tell the very moment when we became pious and virtuous, is not material, provided we are so now; and happiest of all are they, who remember not themselves ever to have been otherwise. All feelings are imaginary and deceitful, unless they be accompanied with that one, which the Apostle experienced and mentioned: "For our rejoicing is this, the testimony of our conscience, that in simplicity and godly sincerity we have had our conversation in the world." 2 Cor. i. 12. Our Saviour's rule of "knowing every tree by its fruits" Luke vi. 44, is the only sure way to judge of ourselves as well as of others. And though we may perhaps be sometimes at a loss how to judge, or inclined, and even strongly, to fear the worst; yet if this arise not from presumptuous sins or habitual negligence, but merely from excessive humility or weakness of spirits, a modest diffidence will never hinder our future happiness, nor will a bold positiveness ever forward it. Good men may be cast down and bad men elevated without any reason. The former may see much in themselves to dislike; and yet God may see enough of what He approves to accept them: they may experience little joy in serving Him, and yet "walk" more completely "worthy of the Lord unto all pleasing," Col. i. 10, for doing it without the encouragement of a present reward. The latter, on the other hand, may build upon groundless fancies of their own, mistaking them for Divine communications: may be absolutely confident, wonderfully transported, yet find themselves at last fatally deceived. It is not, therefore, by their fears, or their hopes, or their raptures, that men are to judge of their spiritual condition. "Hereby," saith St. John, "do we know that we know God, if we keep His commandments," ch. ii. 3. "Little children, let no man deceive you: he that doeth righteousness is righteous; he that committeth sin is of the devil."—M.]

[TUCKER:—As therefore we are well assured, that repentance will re-instate us, and that obedience will continue us, in the Divine favour, according to the gracious terms of the Gospel, so let us likewise remember, that he who wilfully and habitually committeth sin, whatever evidence of his new birth or justification, his adoption or acceptance, he may fancy himself possessed of, is actually no other than the servant of sin and the slave of the devil. In short, virtue and vice, holiness and wickedness, Christ and Belial, can never, never unite together. If therefore we design ourselves to be the candidates for heaven, we must endeavour to acquire such qualifications as will render us fit for that holy place. Because unless we really acquire them during the present state, the alternative is dreadful indeed: for he who committeth sin is of the devil. How shocking even to repeat; yet much more shocking to feel! to feel not only for a time but forever! Whereas on the contrary, "he who doeth righteousness is righteous, even as He is righteous;" righteous he is, because he will have, not only his manifold failings and imperfections all forgiven, through the mercies of the Gospel-covenant, but even his deliberate sins and offences cancelled and blotted out on his sincere repentance: and what is still more than ever could have been thought of, much less petitioned for, he will find himself permitted to appear before God as "holy, unblameable and unreproveable in His sight," Col. i. 22.—M.].

[VER. 9. PYLE: *Whosoever is born of God*, etc. As if he had said: In fine, while a man preserves his Christian principle, and answers the character of a true member of God's Church, he can never be guilty of deliberate and habitual vice. Make it therefore a sure test to whom a man belongs, in whose service he is listed, and from whom he may expect his wages, whether of God or of the devil, by the good or wicked practices of his life, by his behaviour towards God and towards his brethren.—M.].

[HAMMOND:—The phrase "born of God" is not to be taken here, as to denote the single transient act of regeneration; but rather a continued course, a permanent state, so that a regenerate man and a child of God are of the same meaning, and signify him that lives a pious and godly life and continues to do so. For the phrase "a child" or "a son" of any kind of father, signifies a resemblance or similitude of inclinations and actions; as a child of the devil, Acts xiii. 10; sons of Belial, Judges xix. 22; children of Abraham, Gal. iii. 7. And so generally in this Epistle, he that is "born of God," signifies a man truly pious, an obedient servant of God: and such is the subject of this proposition when of such an one it is said, that "he cannot sin:" not affirming that he cannot cease to be what he is, cannot fall off from the performance of his duty, of the possibility of which the many warnings and exhortations that are given to pious men are evidences, see ch. ii. 1; 1 Cor. x. 12; Heb. iii. 12; 2 Pet. iii. 17; but that remaining thus, a pious follower, imitator, and so a "child of God," he cannot yield deliberately to any kind of sin.—M.].

[WHITBY:—*He cannot sin.* Now that doth not import a good man cannot be overtaken with a fault (Gal. vi. 1). No, even those "little children" whose "sins are forgiven," and who have "known the Father," may and will be obnoxious still to some infirmities and wanderings out of the way. (ch. ii. 1). They may "sin not unto death," and therefore may still have the spiritual life remaining in them (v. 16–18). But the true import of that phrase is this (Ita de Catone Minore Velleius Paterculus: *Homo virtuti simillimus, et per omnia ingenio diis quam hominibus proprior, qui nunquam recte fecit ut facere videretur, sed quia aliter, facere non poterat.* Hist. R. II. 34. *Omnibus humanis vitiis immunis.* Ibid.): That he hath such an inward frame of heart, such a disposition of spirit, as renders sin exceeding odious and hateful to him; so that he cannot entertain the thoughts of doing it, or a temptation to commit it, without the utmost detestation and the greatest horror, and so can very rarely, and only through surprise, or want of due deliberation, or through such violent temptations as prevent or hinder his consideration, be obnoxious to sin; and when he comes to consider of such an action, is presently condemning himself for it, bitterly repenting of it, and for the future watching most carefully against it. Cf. Matth. xii. 34; xvii. 18; Jno. vii. 7; viii. 43; xii. 39; xiv. 17; Rom. viii. 7, 8; 1 Cor. ii. 14; Rev. ii. 2.—M.].

He that committeth sin is of the devil. It is not he who committeth one or more sins of infirmity, for so did Christ's disciples while they were with Him; nor he who committeth one great sin through the power of a strong temptation, of which he bitterly repents, and from which he returns to his obedience; for thus did David and Peter, who yet were not then the children of the devil; *but they who comply with the lusts of Satan and who will do them.* Jno. viii. 44. The other interpretations which are given of these words seem either vain or impertinent, or false and dangerous, and

1. *Vain* is that sense which some put on these

words: "He that is born of God, *non debet peccare*, ought not to sin," or that it is absurd for him to sin; for the Apostle speaks not of what he ought not to do, but of what he doth not. Such is that also of those fathers, who interpret this of him who is perfectly born of God by a παλιγγενεσία, or "a resurrection from the dead," for the Apostle doth not speak of what he shall do hereafter, but of what he doth not do at present.

2. *False* seems to be the sense which Origen, Jerome, and Ambrose put upon the words, that "he that is born of God sinneth not, *quamdiu renatus est*, whilst he is born of God, because he ceaseth to be a child of God when he sins; for this is not only confuted by the examples of David and Peter, whose faith under that great miscarriage failed not (Luke xxii. 32), but by the words of the Apostle, 'Little children, if we sin we have an Advocate with the Father, Jesus Christ the Righteous, and He is the Propitiation for our sins'" (Jno. ii. 1), who yet is only the Advocate for the sons of God. For the same reason I cannot assent to that exposition which saith: "A child of God cannot be guilty of any great or deliberate crime," as Tertullian, *de pudicitiâ* c. 19.

3. *Dangerous* is the exposition of Bernard (*In Septuag.* Serm. 1), that "they who are born of God sin not, *quia etiamsi peccata illis neutiquam imputentur*, because their sins will never be imputed to them;" and of those who think it sufficient to say, "He sins not without great reluctancy, or not willingly, the evil that he doeth being that which he would not do;" for the will of that man, who, after some contest in his soul, yields to the commission of sin, is more strongly inclined to sin than to the avoiding of it, and so is not renewed. Nor doth the Apostle say, he that is born of God sins not willingly, or without reluctance; but absolutely, "He doth not commit sin."

[I conclude with Gataker: "He that is born of God sinneth not," that is: *Vitam a peccato immuneum quantum potest sibi proponit, nec peccato unquam sponte dat operam; si aliquando præter animi propositum deliquerit, non in eodem persistit, sed errore agnito, ad institutum vitæ pristinum quamprimum quantumque potest, festinus revertitur.*"—M.].

---

4. *Brotherly love is the sum-total of the Divine law.*

CHAPTER III. 10*b*–18.

10*b* Whosoever[1] doeth not righteousness is not of God, neither[2] he that loveth not his
11 brother. For[3] this is the message[4] that ye heard from the beginning, that we should
12 love one another. Not as Cain, *who* was of that wicked one,[5] and slew his brother.
And wherefore slew he him? Because his own[6] works were evil, and[7] his brother's
13 righteous. Marvel not, my brethren,[8] if the world hate[9] you. We know that we
14 have passed from[10] death unto life, because we love the brethren. He that loveth not
15 *his* brother[11] abideth in death. Whosoever[12] hateth his brother is a murderer:[13] and
16 ye know that no murderer[13] hath eternal life abiding in him. Hereby perceive[14] we
the love *of God*, because he laid down his life for us: and we ought to lay down[15]
17 *our* lives for the brethren. But whoso hath this world's good,[16] and seeth his brother
have need, and shutteth up his bowels *of compassion*[17] from him,[18] how dwelleth the[19]
18 love of God in him? My[20] little children, let us not love in word, neither in[21] tongue;
but in deed and in truth.

Verse 10*b*. [1 πᾶς ὁ="Every one that." So German. M.]
[2 καὶ="And." So German, and most foreign versions.—M.]

Verse 11. [3 ὅτι="Because." So German.—M.]
4 ἀγγελία A. B. G. K.; ἐπαγγελία C. Sin. and a few, unimportant Codd.—The context admits the sense "promise" only on the artificial interpretation that it is a gift and a happiness to love.

Verse 12. [5 οὐ καθὼς Κάϊν ἐκ τοῦ πονηροῦ ἦν. German: "Not as Cain was of the wicked one."—Lücke: "Some supply after οὐ: ἀγαπῶμεν, others ποιῶμεν and the like. But in the first case there arises an irony unsuitable in this connection; and in both cases a second supplement becomes necessary, to wit, of ὅς after Κάϊν, which, as the omission of the relative pronoun is in classic as well as in N. T. Greek without example, could hardly be justified. Much simpler is it with Grotius to complete the sentence thus: οὐκ ὦμεν ἐκ τοῦ πονηροῦ, καθὼς Κάϊν ἐκ τοῦ πονηροῦ ἦν." Winer: "Properly, there is nothing to be supplied (ὦμεν or ποιῶμεν would not suit οὐ), but, the comparison being negligently expressed, the reader easily adjusts the clauses for himself: *that we love one another, not as Cain was of the wicked one*, etc., shall it or may it be so with us." For further authorities see Lillie.—M.]
[6 German: "Because his works were *wicked*, but his brother's righteous." It is difficult to determine the right reading, whether it is αὐτοῦ, αὑτοῦ or ἑαυτοῦ (B.) Most probably αὐτοῦ.—The correspondence between Κάϊν ἐκ τοῦ πονηροῦ ἦν and τὰ ἔργα αὐτοῦ πονηρὰ ἦν should by all means be brought out.—M.]
[7 δὲ="but," not "and," as E. V.—M.]

Verse 13. [8 German: "Marvel not, brethren," agreeing with Sin. G. K. Rec. al. in omitting μου.—M.]
[9 μισεῖ. German, Wiclif. al. retain the Indicative mood.—M.]

Verse 14. [10 German: "We have passed out of death into life."—M.]
11 Ἀγαπῶν *without* τὸν ἀδελφὸν, A. B. Sin.; *with* it C. G. K., although less authentic, and rather inserted than omitted. [German: omits the words, and renders: "He that loveth not abideth in death."—M.]

Verse 15. [12 πᾶς ὁ=Every one.—M.]
[13 ἀνθρωποκτόνος; German: "man-murderer," but better to render, "*man-killer*" (Lillie following Rhemish vers. at Jno. viii. 44), which is free from the extenuating force suggested by the technical use of such words as "*homicide*" or "*man-slaughter*."—M.]

Verse 16. [14 German: "Hereby have we known."—M.]
15 θεῖναι A. B. C. Sin. al., decidedly preferable to τιθέναι G. K. al.

Verse 17. [16 German: "Life-sustenance." *Goods* might be used in that sense.—M.]
[17 German: "His inwards;" but "bowels" without the supplement "compassion" should by all means be retained.—M.]
18 ἀπ' αὐτοῦ A. B. C. Sin.; the words are omitted only by several unimportant Codd.
[19 German: "Abideth."—M.]
20 μου after τεκνία occurs in Rec. after G. K., but is wanting in the best Codd.—M.]
21 The Article τῇ before γλώσσῃ is wanting in Rec. Sin., but found in A. B. C. G. K. and most of the Codd. verss. and editions. [German: "with the tongue."—M.]; ἐν, omitted by K., is found in almost all the authoritative Codd., including Sin.

EXEGETICAL AND CRITICAL.

The transition. v. 10*b*.

VER. 10*b*. **Every one that doeth not righteousness, is not of God.**—Thus the Apostle compresses the one, positive, formally taken and described side of the preceding section and having thus fully, concisely and distinctly recapitulated, he now quickly adds the essential characteristic of that righteousness as the leading theme of what follows, viz:

And he that loveth not his brother.—Calvin: "*Hoc membrum vice expositonis additum est.*" It is interesting to compare the progress of thought in this part with that in the first part: this section ch. iii. 10–18 is related to ch. ii. 29 and iii. 1–10 like ch. ii. 6–11 to ch. i. 5 and i. 6—ii. 5; ii. 6, 7, 11: ἡ ἐντολή, ὁ λόγος, ἡ ἀγγελία brotherly love, and ch. iii. 11 the ἀγγελία, ch. ii. 7: ἣν εἴχετε—v. 11: ἣν ἠκούσατε ἀπ' ἀρχῆς as in ch. iii. 11; the ὀφείλειν ch. ii. 6 and iii. 16; and both times after the example of Christ; respectively disclosing our relation to death and life here (vv. 14, 15) and to light and darkness there (ch. ii. 9–11). But this section draws more on life (Cain and Abel v. 12, poverty and benevolence vv. 17, 18) and reaches more into life.

Πᾶς ὁ ποιῶν δικαιοσύνην refers back to ch. ii. 29; iii. 7, but the omission of the Article renders the idea more general and indicates the leading thought with the self-evident reference to God and Christ. Thus ἐκ τοῦ θεοῦ εἶναι denotes here both to be born of God and to be the child of God. Καὶ before ὁ μὴ ἀγαπῶν τὸν ἀδελφὸν αὐτοῦ is epexegetical, and explains δικαιοσύνη as ἀγάπη; hence it is neither=*proinde* (Episcopius) nor adds a new particular, something different (Rickli, Socinus, who defines ἀγάπη as Christian virtue excelling Jewish legality); nor is ἀγάπη a part or moment of δικαιοσύνη (Bengel, Spener, Neander, Gerlach), but its "substance and nature" (Huther,* also Düsterdieck). Cf. Rom. xiii. 8-10; Gal. v. 14; Col. iii. 14; 1 Tim. i. 5; Jno. xiii. 34 sq.; xiv. 15; xv. 12, 17. "Brotherly love is the sum-total of all right-doing" (Besser), love is the fulfilling of the law. Ἀλλήλους, in the Johannean passages like ἀδελφὸν αὐτοῦ here, denotes brotherly love, the love which Christians have for one another; so also in the corresponding sections ch. ii. 9–11 and iv. 20, 21. Ἀδελφὸς is consequently not=πλησίον Luke x. 36 (Ebrard, who sees here a contradiction to Matth. v. 44; 1 Cor. iv. 12, but without sufficient reason; Rickli and others).

[* Huther in a note [2d ed. p. 163] replies to the objection of Ebrard and Myrberg that this could only apply to our love of God and not to our love of the brethren, that in John's opinion Christian love of the brethren is identical with the love of God, because the Christian loves his brother as one born of God. He suggests also that ἀγάπη might be better defined as the "essential exhibition" of δικαιοσύνη—M.].

The commandment of Christ. v. 11.

VER. 11. **Because this is the message which ye have heard from the beginning, that we should love one another.**—He that loves the brother must be (out) of God, and brotherly love is the deed of righteousness, *because* the commandment is from Him. Ἀγγελία is here =ἐντολή ch. ii. 7. Bengel's remark is only half true: "*liberalissima appellatio, nunquam legem appellat;*" ἐντολή occurs often, but νόμος never. But the *message* implies the *commandment* as indicated by ἵνα. The reading ἐπαγγελία, promise, cannot be sustained without a forced interpretation: it is the goodness, power and grace of God that we should love one another. The commandment of brotherly love has been given from the beginning, since the Gospel has been preached, since you have been Christians; it is and remains indissolubly united with the Gospel and Christianity; ἠκούσατε ἀπ' ἀρχῆς applies to the *first* and to *all* Christians. Ἵνα denotes the *purpose*, the *work to be done* and not only the *substance* or *contents* of the ἀγγελία (Huther), for the reference is not only to the substance of a commandment, but to a commandment specified by means of the message, which lies in the *message given* as a *task*, a *work to be done*.

The opposite in Cain. vv. 12, 13.

VER. 12. **Not, as Cain was of the wicked one and slew his brother.**—The sentence is imperfect like Jno. vi. 58, and is a *breviloquentia*, of frequent and diversified occurrence in the classics; cf. Winer, p. 646, who cites in a note a parallel sentence from Demosthenes (Mid. p. 415). The comparison is left incomplete, as in animated conversation when there is no room for misunderstanding; there is nothing to be supplied; the reader or hearer knows from the context what is meant. In the present case: Not, as Cain was of the wicked one and slew his brother, (shall it or may it be so with us). [See note 5 in Apparat. Crit.—M.]. Hence it is neither an independent exclamation (Sander); nor need we supply ὦμεν ἐκ τοῦ πονηροῦ (Grotius, Lücke), nor ὅς (Beza, Socinus), nor *sitis* or the like.—Ἐκ τοῦ πονηροῦ refers back to v. 8 as contrasted with ἐκ

-οῦ θεοῦ v. 10*b*. Hence the reference is to the wicked *one.* The sentence specifies the reason of that action, even as v. 8. ποιεῖν τὴν ἁμαρτίαν and ὁ διάβολος ἁμαρτάνει are correlates. [The wild notion of the Rabbis concerning the diabolical nature of Cain may be interesting to the student (Zohar in Genes. iv. 1): "*Rabbi Eleazar dixit: Cum projecisset serpens ille immunditiem suam in Evam, eaque illam suscepisset, remque cum Adam habuisset, peperit duos filios, unum ex latere illo immundo et unum ex latere Adami; fuitque Cain similis imagine superiorum h. e. angelorum et Abel imagine inferiorum h. e. hominum, ac propterea diversæ fuerunt viæ istius ab illius viis. Equidem Cain fuit filius spiritus immundi, qui est serpens malus; Abel vero fuit filius Adami; et propterea quod venit de parte angeli mortis, ideo interfecit fratrem suum.*"—M.]. The verb σφάζειν denotes *cultro jugulum aperire ut sanguis effluat*, then to kill, in sacrifice, as the martyrs were slain by the ungodly. Rev. v. 6; vi. 4, 9; xviii. 24. Hence the word does not warrant the inference that the knife was the instrument of the murder (Piscator), but rather denotes that the death of Abel was martyrdom inflicted by an ungodly hand, or finely intimates that Cain, in his hatred, offered a sacrifice to his God, the devil. The next clause, at all events gives prominence to the diabolical character of Cain's deed, the eager question "**And wherefore slew he him?**" being promptly answered thus: "**Because his works were wicked, but his brother's righteous.** Τὰ ἔργα αὐτοῦ πονηρὰ ἦν answers to ἐκ τοῦ πονηροῦ ἦν, and denotes Cain's whole manner of life" (Spener), of which the murder of his brother was one form of expression, his whole manner of life as well as this specific exhibition of it being identical as to cause and origin—namely the devil. For if the wicked one had not influenced Cain's whole manner of life and if that had not been wholly wicked, he would not and could not have committed this specific act of fratricide. The term πονηρὸς, as distinguished from κακός is very significant. πονηρὸς, from πονεῖν or πόνος, denotes toil or hardship (and is opposed to χρηστός, good, honest, useful, friendly, serviceable) and then malignity, *malignus;* κακός, bad, *malus*, is the opposite of ἀγαθός, good and valuable. Rev. xvi. 2; Sir. xxxi. 4; Matth. vii. 11; xii. 35; v. 11; Luke xii. 35; 3 Jno. 10. The inwardly evil nature is κακόν, that which is inimical, hurtful and displeasing to others is πονηρόν. Ὁ πονηρὸς is the most suitable term to describe the nature of Satan, the enemy of God, His kingdom and His people, as well as the works of the devil's children. The additional clause τὰ δὲ τοῦ ἀδελφοῦ αὐτοῦ δίκαια the context requires us to refer to ἐκ τοῦ θεοῦ εἶναι, as pointing out that the piety and the walk of the children of God exactly answering to the law of God are loathsome to the anti-divine world. That devilishness continues still Jno. iii. 19; vii. 7; xvii. 14. Hence the monition:

VER. 13. **Marvel not, brethren, if the world hateth you.**—The same idea is already expressed in v. 1 (διὰ τοῦτο); Cain is the type of the κόσμος (ch. ii. 15–17). "*Magis esset mirabile, si diligerent eos.*" (Didymus). The address ἀδελφοὶ in this connection exerts a beneficial influence: John expresses his love of those whom the world hates and this expression contains a ground of their rejoicing and conveys to them the sweet consolation of the fellowship of love. The particle εἰ is and remains=*if;* if it had been the Apostle's object to describe the hatred of the world as actually present, he might have used ὅτι; but he signifies by εἰ that the readers collectively or individuals at the time being, will not in the end have to endure hatred; but the Indicative μισεῖ denotes that the case will doubtless arise. So Mark. xv. 44 (Vulgate falsely: *si jam odisset*); Acts. xxvi. 8; Winer, *Grammar* p. 307; Kühner, ii. 480 sq. Hence Sander, who makes εἰ=ὅτι, S. Schmidt who makes it=*etiamsi*, and Ebrard who explains=if ever the case occurs, are in the wrong, for the reference is to a necessary condition. ["Εἰ denotes neither a doubt nor only a possibility, for it is not only possible but from the nature of the case *necessary*, that the world hates the children of God; only the form of the sentence is hypothetical, not the thought it expresses. Cf. Jno. xv. 18." Huther. —M.].

Amplification of the Antitheses: Love and Life, Hatred and Death; vv. 14, 15.

VER. 14. **We Know.**—In ἡμεῖς John includes himself among those he had just called ἀδελφοὶ and expresses their confident assurance, the world and its hatred notwithstanding, which is and ought to be a source of strength and consolation. The object affirmed in the sequel shows that the reference is to the experience of believers, of the children of God, and not to the Apostles only, (Lyra) or that it is only the conclusion drawn on the ground of a good conscience, (Estius).

That we have passed over out of Death into Life.—The Prefect μεταβεβήκαμεν signifies an action of the past or the past of an action still continuing in the present, in the condition that has been effected: we *are* those *who have passed over*, Winer, *Grammar*, p. 288, 299. The Perfect must not be taken *per enallagen*, for the Future (Schlichting) or the Present (Didymus, Oecumenius), or the verb must not be construed =*jus* or *spem habere ad vitam* (Grotius, Carpzov). Cf. Jno. v. 24: ὁ πιστεύων—μετεβέβηκεν ἐκ τοῦ θανάτου εἰς τὴν ζωήν. Of course ἐκ τοῦ θανάτου εἰς τὴν ζωὴν cannot be taken physically but spiritually, but it must be taken as a real fact; it is=γεγεννῆσθαι ἐκ τοῦ θεοῦ, ch. ii. 29: for ἡ ζωὴ is the real life, divine, eternal life (ch. i. 1, 2; ii. 17, 25),=the φῶς and the ἀλήθεια (ch. i. 5; ii. 21, 22) of which the children of God are partakers; the θάνατος is the opposite of this life,=the σκοτία and the ψεῦδος, all of which belong to the ἐκ τοῦ διαβόλου. The Apostle, therefore, does not speak of a sentiment (Paulus) or *caligo, infelicitas moralis* (Semler), but of relations and conditions, of regeneration, of the new life of the reconciled child of God. This implies that those who have not yet passed over, are still or will be ἐν τῷ θανάτῳ before this transition into life in Christ; hence there is not the faintest colour for the assertion of Hilgenfeld, that the Apostle did share the gnostic view of the original metaphysical difference of men.

Because we love the brethren.—From this conduct we may know that relation, from these acts of brotherly love that state of adoption by God. Hence the former is the first and this the second and it is false to consider brotherly love as the cause of regeneration or even as a part of justification in order to complete it, and as *conditio gratiose a Deo requisita*, as do the R. Catholics (Estius, Lyra) and the Pelagians (Episcopius). Brotherly love is only the condition of the certainty of the knowledge that we are justified and the children of God, and not the condition of this new life itself. [ζωή and ἀγάπη are really one and the same thing with this difference that ζωή is the *state* and ἀγάπη the *activity* of the believer; from this blissful, eternal life groweth love, and love in its turn worketh happiness and eternal life; hence the Apostle adds—(Huther)—M].

He that loveth not, abideth in death.—As usual (ch. i. 8, sqq., ii. 22, sqq.), the negative is added in a concise, pregnant form. [See note 11 in Appar. Critic.—M]. The statement is quite general "*he that loveth not,*" without specifying the object, viz. the brother. The force of the Present μένει should be retained. To be in death is connected, as something permanent, with not loving. They are one in the other, yet not so that the not loving is the cause of the abiding in death, but, as is manifest from the context, so that we may know the abiding in death from the not loving. [The two are identical. Besser, "Where hatred is there is death, where love is there is life; yes, love is life itself."—M.].

VER. 15. **Every one that hateth his brother is a man-killer.**—Πᾶς denotes the universal application of this thought. Not loving is described as equal to hating one's brother. [Not to love=to hate.—M.]; "pure indifference is impossible to the *living* spirit of man" (Huther). Luther rightly observes: *Nova sententia coram mundo, quod non diligere sit occidere.*" Bengel: "*Omne odium est conatus contra vitam; at vita vitam non insectatur; qui odit fratrem, aut illum aut se ipsum vult occidere.*" Lyra (*odisse pejus quam non diligere.*"), Schlichting ("*Qui non amat, nec bene vult nec male; qui vero odit, male vult*"), and others are wrong. Not loving is only the state of quiescence exhibited in acts of hatred. According to our Lord's exposition of the fifth commandment (Matth. v. 21–26) he is an ἀνθρωποκτόνος that hateth his brother. "*Nam quem odimus, vellemus periisse*" (Calvin); hatred is not only a beginning or cause of murder, but a murder in heart, be it a wish, a thought or a purpose or only the passion which afflicts the brother's life without thinking of his death. "*Latro es, antequam inquines manum*" (Seneca). Here is evidently a reference to Cain, v. 12; the case of Cain shows plainly how hatred of one's brother and homicide go together. The word ἀνθρωποκτόνος, only here and Jno. viii. 44, in this place applies to Cain who slew Abel, his brother, in the Gospel to Satan who destroyed, murdered Adam. Notwithstanding this difference, the two passages are connected with each other, the one shedding light on the other. Cf. Lange on John viii. 44; Vol. IV. p. 244 sq.—The devil, having seduced Eve, and Adam through her to sin, to the transgression of the divine law of which death was the penalty fixed by God.—Sin causing mortality is itself a kind of dying, the fall or falling into death [German: The fall of sin, *i. e. the* fall, a fall of death.—M], and sin, born of lust, when it is finished, bringeth forth death (Jas. i. 15); the first sin was a falling from the life created (out) of God into death threatened as a punishment. Thus Satan became the murderer of Adam and Eve in the strictest sense of the word (Wisd. i. 11–13; ii. 23, 24). With the entrance of sin, moreover, there died in Eve the love of her husband whom she had seduced, and in Adam the love of his wife whom he accused to God and on whom he laid the guilt. There hatred and death are again together. In Cain also there was the hatred of his brother united with the murder of his brother, whereby he showed that he was ἐκ τοῦ διαβόλου. Cf. Stier, *Reden Jesu*, Vol. IV. 414 sqq.

And ye know that no man-killer hath eternal life abiding in him.—This concludes the thought: μὴ ἀγαπῶν τὸν ἀδελφὸν v. 10*b* led the Apostle to speak of μὴ ἀγαπῶν v. 14, then of μισῶν τὸν ἀδελφὸν v. 15 and in remembrance of Cain of ἀνθρωποκτόνος; he first said οὐκ ἔστιν ἐκ τοῦ θεοῦ v. 10*b* μένει ἐν θάνατῳ, but here οὐχ ἔχει ζωὴν αἰώνιον ἐν αὐτῷ μένουσαν. Before he said, he is in death, but now, in him is not eternal life, consequently death is in him. The Apostle denies that he "possesses permanently and fully" (Lücke) eternal life and thus denotes the "permanent state of death" (Düsterdieck) of him that hates and kills his brother. The Present ἔχει has respect to this present life; it is not *habebit* (a Lapide). Hence ζωὴ αἰώνιος not the future glory (a Lapide, Bede and others). Μένουσαν certainly intimates the existence of eternal life, of baptism, etc., out of or in the word of God by means of Christian instruction and the Christian family-discipline; for the Apostle speaks of and to Christians. But even such gifts of God are consumed by hatred abiding; hence he loses entirely the possession of eternal life, so that nothing thereof abideth in him; μένουσαν is therefore not an intensified *to be* (Huther), nor must the want of the Article be pressed as if the reference were only to powers of the future world (Ebrard). This the Apostle lays down as an undeniable fact of Christian experience and consciousness (οἴδατε); hence they know it not from the fifth commandment (S. Schmidt) or from the Old Testament with its death-penalty in the case of murderers, spiritually interpreted (Grotius, Lücke).

Description of brotherly love, vv. 16–18.

VER. 16. **Hereby have we known love that He laid down His life for us.**—S. Schmidt: "*Ne quis vel se ipsum decipiat, vel ab aliis decipiatur, exponendum etiam erit, quæ sit vera et Christiana caritas.*" First after the example of Christ. On ἐν τούτῳ cf. on ch. ii. 3; on ἐκεῖνος, vv. 3, 7; ii. 6; ἐγνώκαμεν = *cognitum habemus.* Τὴν ἀγάπην should be taken in a general sense without any further qualification: *love.*—Bengel: "*Amoris natura.*" In Christ may be known love, the being and nature of love. Hence we must not supply τοῦ Χριστοῦ (Carpzov and others), or τοῦ θεοῦ (Grotius, Calov, Spener, al.); the Vulgate (*amorem Dei*) constrains the Romanists to do so. Ebrard's explanation is rather forced: "we have known love as consisting in this," as if we had ἐν τούτῳ οὖσαν, and this were described in the following ὅτι as the predicate and as if ἐγνώκαμεν had only an introductory and secondary sense. Both the form (the position of the words) and the thought (to give His life=love) render that exposition untenable. The point is that *whereby* love is known: τὴν ψυχὴν τιθέναι (Jno. xv. 13; cf. x. 11, 15, 17, 18; xiii. 37, 38)=*vitam ponere* (Cicero *ad Fam.* ix. 24); this is the highest proof of love; for love imparts her very best, her most precious goods, παραδοῦναι the ψυχή or ἑαυτόν (Gal. ii. 20; Eph. v. 2); this makes Christ the object of the Father's love (Jno. x. 17). The context required here ὑπὲρ ἡμῶν, for our protection; literally over us, who had fallen, were wounded, in danger of perishing from our wounds or in the hands of enemies, fighting against the enemies, protecting us, becoming our substitute and assuming the fight for us: hence it is not exactly identical with ἀντί, and yet the two prepositions touch each other in thought "in indissoluble correlation" (Düsterdieck) cf. ch. ii. 2.

And we ought to lay down our lives for the brethren.—From the act of Christ's love for us springs a duty towards our brethren, incumbent on us (ὀφείλομεν); the thought is similar to ch. ii. 3, 6. The example of Christ must not be without corresponding works on our part (ch. iii. 3, 7). The essential union of believers to Christ must exhibit itself in the real moulding of their life after the pattern of Christ, in the use of the imparted gifts and the solution of the task assigned to us by the bestowal of that gift. Cf. Jno. xiii. 34; xv. 12, 13; xxi. 18, 19; Rom. xvi. 3, 4.

VER. 17. **But whoso has the world's goods** (*sustenance of life*).

By the adversative δὲ "John denotes the progress from the greater, which is justly insisted upon, to the less, the non-performance of which, therefore, appears as a correspondingly greater violation of the rule just laid down." (Düsterdieck), Ὃς δ' ἂν makes the sentence quite general. The proverb quoted by Grotius: "βίος βίου δεόμενος οὐκ ἔστι βίος" gives the double sense of life, and the necessaries of life, or the means of sustaining life.. Cf. Mark xii. 44 (Luke xxi. 4); Luke viii. 45; xv. 30. Col. v. 12. Beza: "*res mundanæ,*" "*des biens de ce monde.*" The Genitive τοῦ κόσμου simply points to the sphere to which the βίος belongs, and, according to ch. ii. 17, denotes the profane and worthless character of these goods, as contrasted with the eternal love and the eternal life in Christ. Βίος τοῦ κόσμου is the antithesis of ζωὴ αἰώνιος; the Christian shares the latter with Christ, the former with the world. The reference is not to uncommon wealth, but rather to any kind of property (ἔχῃ, emphatically in anteposition), though it be in limited circumstances, a mere mite, or bread and potatoes. He that hath the means to give and

Seeth his brother have need.—θεωρεῖ pictorially describes the attitude and activity of the spectator; it is not a hasty look, but permanent looking on and into it (Matth. xxvii. 35; Mark xv. 40, 47; xii. 41; Luke xxi. 6; xxiii. 35; Jno. ii. 23; vi. 19, 62; vii. 3; ix. 8; x. 12; xiv. 17; xvi. 10, 16); he has it before him like a picture which he contemplates with calmness and attention, τὸν ἀδελφὸν αὐτοῦ χρείαν ἔχοντα. On the expression and the thought cf. Eph. iv. 28; Mark ii. 25; Acts ii. 45; iv. 35; xx. 34; xxviii. 10; Phil. iv. 6. [He beholds the brother's need with unmoved eye—M.].

And shutteth up his bowels [inwards] **from Him.**—After the analogy of the Hebrew רַחֲמִים, σπλάγχνα is=καρδία, Prov. xii. 10 and very often in the New Testament. Bengel: "*Cum visceribus clauditur vel aperitur res familiaris. Aspectus miserorum corda spectatorum illico pulsat vel etiam aperit.*" The heart ought to open itself in compassion and sympathy and move and open the hand to communicate; but it is under the aggravating circumstances of his having the means and beholding his brother's need that he shutteth up his heart and turns away from him (ἀπ' αὐτοῦ). The same pregnancy of thought occurs at ch. ii. 28. A similar use of κρύπτειν ἀπὸ may be seen at Luke xix. 42; Jno. xii. 36 *b*. Hence we need neither supply ἀποστρεφόμενος (Carpzov), nor ἀπὸ=*coram* (Socinus). [This was the case of Dives. He *saw* Lazarus flung at his gate, Lazarus desiring to be fed with the crumbs which fell from the rich man's table, but he desired *in vain;* Dives *saw* him lie in misery; the dogs had pity and sympathized with the poor man, but Dives, who fared sumptuously *every day*, looked with unpitying eye on his brother's distress; he saw in him a *beggar*, not a *brother*. See Augustine, Serm. 178, c. 3, and Massillon's beautiful Lent Sermon on this subject.—M.]—The negative is emphatically expressed with an implied paracletical inference in the interrogative sentence:

How abideth the love of God in him?—A similar construction may be seen ch. iv. 20; Jno. iii. 12; v. 47. The substance of the question answers to v. 15: οὐκ ἔχει ζωὴν αἰώνιον ἐν αὐτῷ μένουσαν, where eternal life not abiding and even not being in him is inferred from the non-existence of brotherly love, while here the non-existence of the love of God is inferred from the same premises. Ἀγάπη τοῦ θεοῦ is our love to God and indicates the motion of eternal life to its fountain, as in ch. ii. 5. This love to God does not abide, where it does not become operative and preserve its vitality in the active exhibition of brotherly love. Hence it is neither *God's love to us* (Calov), nor *the love prescribed by God* (Socinus, Grotius), nor the love which answers to that of God and Christ (S. Schmidt).

Final exhortation. v. 18.

VER. 18. **Little children, let us not love** [German: *that we do not love*] **in word, nor with the tongue, but in deed and in truth.**—The affecting address, τέκνια, denotes at once the geniality and zeal of John; his earnestness is brought out in the rapid, hortatory, all-embracing expression: μὴ ἀγαπῶμεν. The four substantives occur in pairs and as correlates. First: λόγῳ and τῇ γλώσσῃ to describe false love; then: ἐν τῷ ἔργῳ and (ἐν) ἀληθείᾳ. It is important to note that the first pair in the *Dative* indicates only the means by which love is or becomes operative, while the preposition ἐν which by the copula καὶ belongs also to ἀληθείᾳ denotes the element wherein it moves (Jno. iv. 24). The first pair simply denotes the outwardness of a love which only makes use of words and the tongue, while the contrast indicates that it is destitute of *deed* and *truth*, that it is of real activity and inward heartiness which are the characteristics of true love. The Apostle accordingly annexes to λόγος, the word, which possibly might announce or accompany the deed, the emphatic μηδὲ τῇ γλώσσῃ, the Article serving the purpose "*of rendering the expression more conspicuous*" (Lücke); *the* tongue, "*as the member appointed to utter the word*" (Huther); so that love is not simply the word which might flow from the heart and be the instrument of its application, but stops with the tongue, the means and sole instrument of the word which does not proceed from the heart. Therefore λόγῳ is contrasted with ἐν ἔργῳ and τῇ γλώσσῃ with ἐν ἀληθείᾳ.—Ἔργον and λόγος frequently connected together, as in Luke xxiv. 19; Acts vii. 22; sometimes λόγος and δύναμις (1 Cor. iv. 19, 20), or λόγος and δύναμις καὶ πνεῦμα ἅγιον καὶ πληροφορία (1 Thess. i. 5) are placed in opposition. Bengel: "*Sermone otioso, lingua simulante.*" Lyra says excellently: "*Verbo, facto nihil; lingua fallaci; hic amor non solum, fictitius et vanus, sed etiam proditorius.*" Τῇ γλώσσῃ denotes "the hollow nothingness," "the purely outward babble which without inward truth produces only a hypocritical show" (Düsterdieck). Hence we need not supply μόνον to λόγῳ (Bede, Socinus, Sander and others); and Grotius is also wrong who chiastically [*i. e.* crosswise—M.] opposes: λόγῳ and ἀληθείᾳ, γλώσσῃ ἔργῳ, thus: "Verbo *amat qui prædicat a se diligi proximum, non autem* vere *diligit;* lingua *diligit qui egenti* dat *bona* verba." Nor is Huther right, who takes τῇ γλώσσῃ and ἀληθείᾳ as epexegetical additions without introducing a difference to λόγῳ and ἔργῳ respectively, as if the two words of each member expressed only *one* idea [He says, to express the idea mathematically, that λόγῳ: γλώσσῃ=ἐν ἔργῳ: (ἐν) ἀληθείᾳ. —M]. Compare ἀγαπᾶν ἐν ἀληθείᾳ 2 Jno. i.; 3 Jno. 1, and Jas. ii. 15, 16.

DOCTRINAL AND ETHICAL.

1. All the doings (ποιεῖν τὴν δικαιοσύνην v. 10*b*, ἔργα δίκαια and ἔργα πονηρὰ v. 12) and all the dispositions (ἀγαπῶν v. 10*b* and v. 14, ὁ μισῶν v. 15) of men points to a deeper ground, a fellowship with God or with Satan which is not discernible *per se*, neither to others nor to the respective persons themselves, but discernible by their disposition and doing.

2. The grossest transgression, e. g. the fratricide of Cain, is never alone, but exhibits itself as one of many, as one of a greater complex of manifold transgressions and plainly indicates, that matters must be had in other respects, because otherwise this would not have happened (v. 12).

3. Like attracts like, unlike repels unlike: love and antipathy are reciprocal. The Christian need not be surprised that the world from which he has separated himself, has turned away and remains alienated from him, dislikes and hates him; it is just so with himself, with this difference, that the world hates to persecute and destroy, whereas the Christian strives to improve and to overcome.

4. Before it can be said: μεταβεβήκαμεν ἐκ τοῦ θανάτου (v. 14), we are ἐν τῷ θανάτῳ, ἐκ τοῦ πονηροῦ. Consequently:

1. Before such a stepping forth has taken place and without it, no one is a child of God.

2. Such stepping forth is indispensable in the case of any and every one who desires to become a child of God.

3. It is possible to all who are called to become the children of God.

4. The children of God and the children of the world are perfectly alike in kind and nature before the difference connected with such transition sets in.

5. Consider that those who are not yet brethren, may and shall become brethren as well as thou.—Indeed, it is not said *here* how it comes to pass, but it is plainly stated and may be seen at Jno. v. 24, a passage to which the Apostle unmistakably refers here, and from which may be inferred what is said here and well expressed by *Scholiast* II.: τὸν λόγον αὐτοῦ δεξάμενοι, of course ἐν πίστει. But we must not by any means say with the *Roman Catholics* that although *faith* produces the *beginning* of our justification before God, yet *the love to God and to our neighbour increases the same.* This love is simply the sign and mark of recognition that our justification has taken place, that we are justified. Augustine accordingly says very correctly: "*Redeat unus quisque ad cor suum; si ibi invenerit caritatem fraternam, securus sit—jam in dextera est.*"

5. The principle affirmed at v. 16 as a duty (ὀφείλομεν) with reference to the example of Christ *that we also should lay down our lives*, is a general one. We must not regard it with the Roman Catholics as a counsel (*consilium*), but view and observe it with Evangelical Christians as a precept (*præceptum*). It applies not only to priests or saints, but to all Christians: "*Ministri verbi non debent fugere in periculo pestis*" (Luther); neither physicians in case of a pestilence, nor parents and brothers and sisters, nor the government in seasons of insurrection, nor soldiers in war, in the fight, before a battle, nor a mother when she has to nurse her child, nor a man when duty calls. This saying, moreover, must not be treated casuistically after the manner of Socinus, who thinks a Christian ought to die for a non-Christian if thereby his soul may be saved, or if the preservation of a brother is more necessary to the common weal than his own; or after that of Ammon (*Sittenlehre* 3, 24 sq.) be set aside, who thinks it right that in common danger of shipwreck, fire or self-defence, men are justified to kill others if they cannot save their own life in any other way. Düsterdieck rightly observes: "Concrete directions respecting the practical application of the principle can only be given in the connection of a complete system of Ethics in which especially the duties of Christian self-preservation and the virtues of Christian prudence and simplicity as well as those of Christian self-denial and Christian courage must be exhibited not as limitations, but as sacred ordinances of the fully valid evangelical principle as described by St. John." As St. Paul says 1 Cor. iii. 22: πάντα ὑμῶν ἐστιν—εἴτε ζωὴ εἴτε θάνατος and at Phil. i. 21 calls: τὸ ἀποθανεῖν κέρδος, so the giving up of one's own life in the calling and for the love of Christ is an ἀποθανεῖν τῷ κυρίῳ (Rom. xiv 8). Cf. Matth. x. 39; xvi. 25.—

6. The duty of beneficence is universal; it relates as much to the rich as to the poor; it is immaterial whether a man has much or little of the

βίος τοῦ κόσμου. The having much or little determines the giving with or without self-denial, with or without deprivation, consequently the giving with ease or with difficulty. But nothing is said here on that head or on the situation of the necessitous, his greater or lesser need, which may be very extraordinary; nor is any thing said of the worthiness or unworthiness of the necessitous. But the remark of Luther has a very important bearing on the care of our parochial poor; he says: "*Vult nos de nostro largiri; non de alieno aut communi, sicut stulti Anabaptistæ faciunt, qui tollunt proprietatem rerum, sine qua non possunt respublicæ consistere.*" *Private charity*, even *personal* charity, is here distinctly referred to. In this connection it must be supposed as ranged under the *fifth* commandment.—Its opposite is *Stoicism* which includes also compassion among the passions to be left off: σοὶ μὴ ὀργὴν εἶναι, μὴ μῆνιν, μὴ φθόνον, μὴ ἔλεον.

7. We must not think lightly of the *word* and its instrument, the *tongue*. But as the *mouth-work of hypocrisy* is hateful to the Lord (Matth. vi. 5), so the *mouth-work of brotherly love* is equally hateful to John, since neither the word nor the tongue is in the service of the love of the heart and speaks or is spoken *separate* from the heart and *contrary to* the life in the heart. The friendly utterance of the mouth must and ought to be in the case of Christians the friendly utterance of the heart. Otherwise it is only a μόρφωσις τῆς εὐσεβείας without the δύναμις (2 Tim. iii. 5). For the contrary see, Matth. xii. 34, 35; Rom. x. 8–10.

8. These concrete particulars of the laying-down of our lives, of communicating the sustenance of life and of the love to our brother in deed and in truth plainly and pathetically indicate that regeneration and adoption by God, (ch. ii. 29) if it is a reality, penetrates, as the central life-power the whole periphery of life, so that we read not only of a εὐσέβεια but of εὐσέβειαι, 2 Pet. iii. 11 and even of the θεοσέβεια δι' ἔργων ἀγαθῶν (1 Tim. ii. 10). For the diversity of good works induced by the faith of the heart makes it evident to others that the Christian sonship is not a show, but power and truth; his conduct towards the brethren *reveals* his relation to God the Father and this relation *produces* such conduct.

[The Apostle's declaration that every one that hateth his brother is a murderer or man-killer embodies the well known ethical principle that the moral quality of an action does not belong to the outward act, nor to the conception of it, nor to the resolution to carry it into effect, but to *the intention.* Hatred in St. John's view, is murder committed in intention, and he that cherishes hatred towards his brother stands convicted of murder before God and at the bar of his own conscience.—M.]

HOMILETICAL AND PRACTICAL.

The twofold piety of a child of God; 1. Obedience to the Father; 2. Love of the brethren.—Like the elder brother thou mightest stay with the Father and work in His field, be envious of and take offence at the friendly reception accorded to the younger son by the Father in the parable of the prodigal (Luke xvi). Cain was the elder brother. This applies primarily to the servants of the Church but it applies also to many others. Cain did not hate Abel because of his herds, for he had his fair fields; or because of his parent's love, for he was his mother's pride; or because of personal beauty or any outward, temporal good; but he hated him because of his piety, on account of the favour he found before God.—Cain [קַיִן a lance a spear, a weapon.—M.], called by Eve in feminine rashness her weapon, and in maternal vanity favoured and spoiled by her, made his offering of anything he found without any particular discrimination as to its quality, while Abel, disregarded and neglected, carefully selected the best of the best and presented it as an offering to his God.—Thou art able to take the life of thy brother's body but in doing so thou forfeitest thy own immortal life; thou becomest a man-killer in respect of thy brother's body, but in respect of thyself, a suicide, even a suicide of thy soul; depriving thy brother of his bodily, earthly life, thou deprivest thyself of thy spiritual, eternal life.—Three difficult questions: 1. Canst thou hate those whom God loves? 2. Darest thou shorten or waste the term of grace which God accords? 3. Wilt thou cast from thee the gift of God in thee, eternal life?—Threefold exhibition of brotherly love: 1. Laying down one's life for the brethren at duty's call. 2. Communication of one's possessions to the needy brethren. 3. Friendly and sincere readiness to oblige and aid the brethren.—Three things thou hast for the benefit of others: Body and life, goods and property, hand and heart.

EPISTLE TO DIOGNETUS [cap. vi]:—As the soul is in the body, so are Christians in the world The soul dwells in the body but is not of the body; so Christians also dwell *in* the world, but are not *of* the world. The invisible soul is, as it were, keeping guard in the visible body; this is the mark of Christians as long as they remain in the world: their piety is invisible. The flesh hates and wars against the soul, which (the soul) is, however, by no means wronged [ἀδικουμένη= *affecta injuria.*—M.] by it because it (the soul) forbids the indulgence of the lusts of the flesh; so the world hates the Christians, although they by no means wrong it but only resist the lusts of the world. The soul loves the flesh and the members which hate it; so also Christians love their enemies. [Cf. Matth. v. 44.—M.]

BASILIUS:—Because the devil's hatred cannot reach God, he seeks to hurt and destroy man, the image of God.

AUGUSTINE:—The Christian lives, but, as it were, in winter; the root is alive but the boughs look dry; the living pith and marrow is within, and within are hidden the leaves and the fruits—but they wait for summer.

AMBROSE:—"*Nemo dicat proprium, quod commune est; esurientium panis est, quem tu detines; nudorum indumentum est, quod tu recludis.*"

LUTHER:—The world is a den of murderers, subject to the devil. Would we live on earth we ought to be satisfied with being guests therein and putting up at an inn whose host is a roguish host, whose house bears the sign and title over the door: "*Murder and lie.*" For Christ Himself did affix such a sign and title to his house right over the door by saying that He is a murderer and a liar. A murderer to destroy the body; a liar to seduce the soul.

STARKE:—Because God is Love and loves those who are born of Him, therefore love of the brethren is also the mark of the regenerate.—Art thou tempted with the thought that thou art without the grace of God, without the adoption, without salvation: be of good courage! If thou really and heartily lovest the godly, yea even the wicked and thy foes, thou mayest be quite sure that all these blessings are thy own.—Good Christian, whenever thou readest and hearest some portion of Divine truth, consider well the purpose of God in announcing it and shape thy course accordingly.—Contrary dispositions are not uncommon among actual brothers; the one may be good, the other bad, the one may be saved, the other damned.—The power of Satan over those children is so great that he changes even natural love into hatred.—Mad features of the ungodly! they cannot bear that the works of others are good—why? What is it that envy will not do? They also do not like it because it puts them to shame and sometimes becomes the means of their punishment.—Happy state of believers as contrasted with that of unbelievers! The former truly live, the latter are dead though their body is alive. We mourn for the dead—how much more ought we to mourn for the ungodly, for they are spiritually dead, before they die, and if they die, they fall into eternal death.—God has not only connected the hand but also the mouth and the heart with the fifth commandment.—Hatred is not a trifling sin of infirmity compatible with a man's continuing in a state of grace, but so great a sin as to entail the loss of eternal life, which is irrecoverably lost while hatred lasts. He that hates is a double murderer, he wants to hurt others and deprives himself of eternal life.—To have had life does not render us blessed; but he is blessed with whom eternal life *abides*.—It is one thing to have this world's goods and another to covet them: the one is the blessing of God, the other covetousness.—Poverty is no disgrace: a man may be poor and yet be the child of God, the brother of Christ and of good Christians.—Doing good to the poor is not only incumbent upon the rich, possessed of great abundance, but to every one who has this world's goods and is able to communicate; even as every one has to work, also for this purpose, that he may have something to give to the poor.—Love is blind in not having respect to the person of the poor, whether it be known or unknown, strange or native; but it is not blind in taking cognizance of the need it is to relieve.—Do not always wait for a poor brother's application, begging, supplication and appeal to thy love; many are ashamed to disclose their need; but if thou knowest thy brother's case, show pity unasked and joyfully.—If unable to do anything else, thou canst love with the tongue by words of good counsel and consolation; but see that thy heart be with thy tongue.—The greatness of a benefaction does not determine its worth before God, nor does its smallness lessen it; a great benefaction without sincere love is small, even nothing before God; but a small benefaction prompted by sincere and hearty love is great in God's sight.

NEANDER! As Cain hated and slew Abel in consequence of the contrast between a godly and an ungodly disposition, so the world hates and slays the children of God in consequence of the same contrariety of disposition. Hence the world and the children of God are ever at war like love and selfishness. Hence Christians need not be surprised, if the world hates them. This is to them the stamp of the divine life, the possession of which renders them the opposite of the world.

HEUBNER. Being without love makes men like Cain, whose kind is not extinct. The mind of Cain is to destroy the hated children of God; literary murder also belongs to this head. As to its secret, inmost tendency, all hatred aims at murder.—The duplicity of mankind was prefigured in the case of Cain and Abel; this dichotomy runs through the whole Bible. Cain is the prototype of the evil and unloving, Abel the prototype of Christ.—A Christian *Nil admirari*, Ps. xxxvii. Hatred and enmity is that which disquiets, vexes, excites and disconcerts the natural man most. But the Christian is bidden not even to be surprised at it! He knows the world, is aware of what he has to expect of it, he is at peace with God, lives a life of introversion, is so well rooted and grounded in God, so abundantly satisfied with the grace of God, that the world's hatred does not disturb him. God is his fortress: but he must not leave that fortress.—Where the hatred of the world has not yet fully developed, there is most surely a want of decided Christianity.—Love displays its most glorious beauty under the world's hatred. The Christian loves while the world has no idea of the existence of his love.—Formerly this world was extra-Christian, but now there is a world on the soil of the Christian Church. Is it offensive, hostile, presumptuous to speak of this difference? then it is the fault of the Bible, of Jesus Christ. We ought to hold up a mirror to all: you are either this or that. But it would be presumption to refer individuals to the class to which they belong, for this is the prerogative of God.—*Death* is the state of insensibility and impotence with respect to whatever is good and godly, the conscience is blunted and without receptivity, the heart is dead without any emotion, or interest in religion. *Life* is activity, emotion, a sense for, an impulse to and ability for the holy, a work after the will of God, a state of holiness, of a walk well-pleasing to God. *Brotherly love* is mentioned as a criterion, as a test of life.—Think of hatred as the root and beginning of murder. Often a bitter grief is to others more deadly and vitally injurious than a gross bodily injury.—Distinguish between that which passes with men and that which passes with God.—Never make room for secret anger: or life, the Holy Ghost will depart from thee.—The unloving thinks more highly of lifeless, worthless metal than of the living man created in the image of God.—What can you accomplish with the metal? Refresh the weary, comfort their hearts and dry their tears! Then you transmute stones into bread, earthly treasures into heavenly.—The word is only the shadow of the deed and by no means an equivalent of love or gratitude. (Themistius).

BESSER:—Where hatred is, there is death

where love is, there is life; yea, love itself is the life.—Thus Luther showed that he was willing to lay down his life for the brethren when in the year 1527 he stayed at Wittenberg with those who were stricken with the plague. So the ancient historian Eusebius narrates how a pestilence at Alexandria brought out the difference between the Christians and the pagans. So *Hans Egede* laid down his life when for the sake of the poor Greenlanders he exchanged his comfortable parish for hunger and cold, for unspeakable toil and sufferings; and the coast of Africa, also, lined with grave-hills with the seed of the negroes proclaims the love which is stronger than death. Would that it might be said of the Christians of our time what Tacitus said of the Christians, viz.: that they are as inflexible concerning their faith, as they are ready in the exhibition of mercy.—How can he live on God's compassionating love in whom no compassionating love does live?

On the Epistle for the second Sunday after Trinity, 1 *Jno. iii.* 15–18.

HEUBNER, during the siege of Wittenberg, in 1813, preached on the hatred of the world to which Christians are exposed, and said, notwithstanding the presence of the French garrison, when he came to speak of deserved hatred: the hatred is deserved, which visits the tyrant who sacrifices thousands and the welfare of thousands to his lust of rule.

The Christian under the hatred of the world. 1. How dignified is his demeanour in bearing it a. with calmness, composure and patience (v. 13); b. with the consciousness of his innocence, his love, as known to God (v. 14); c. with the hope of being one day justified (v. 2); 2. how holily he uses it: a. as a warning against all the motions of hatred (v. 15); b. as a challenge to become more like Christ in love (v. 16); c. as an instrument to reconcile the world to himself by love (vv. 17, 18).

Motives of comfort for Christians under the world's hatred. 1. (v. 13). They are unknown and misunderstood; 2. (v. 14); they become conscious of their life; 3. (v. 15); they are encouraged to fight against all unlovingness; 4. (v. 16); they resemble Christ; 5. (v. 17); become more and more assured of the love of God; 6. (v. 18); they hope to gain their enemies over.

The mind of the Christian and of the world opposed to each other in love and hatred. 1. To hate is natural to the world, to love to the Christian (vv. 13, 14); 2. Hatred destroys, love sacrifices the life (vv. 15, 16); 3. The world shuts up, the Christian opens the heart (v. 18).

Whither do we come if the spirit of love leaves us? 1. Answer: we come from the fellowship of the saints to the fellowship of the world (v. 13), from the life of God to spiritual death (v. 14), to vice and shame (v. 15), to forfeiting our salvation and the fruits of the death of Christ (v. 16).—2. Application: learn the worth of true love (v. 16), fight against every motion of unlovingness (v. 17), practise love in deed and in truth (v. 18).

The strong warnings given to Christians against an unloving mind.—Love appears most beautiful under the world's hatred.—Love, a sign of life.—It is only by love that a Christian can know whether he is a child of God or regenerate. 1. The truth. 2. The laying to heart being reminded of this truth.

F. A. WOLF:—*The Apostolical refutation of the principal errors prevailing on the subject of Christian love:* 1. The *fate* of love, 2. The *reign* of love, 3. The *value* of love, 4. The *origin* of love.

CASPARI:—*Of the nature of true love:* 1. Its consolation, 2. Its powers, 3. Its purity.

KAPFF:—*How necessary true brotherly love is,* 1. As a test of our spiritual life; 2. As a condition (?) of eternal life.—*The Law and the Testimony: Of Brotherly Love.* I. Motives. 1. The contrast of Cain; 2. Marks of discipleship and regeneration; 3. The passing away and perdition of the hater. II. Marks. 1. Laying down one's life; 2. Communication of one's goods; 3. Love in deed.

The true life in love and certain death in hatred: 1. The ground, fruit and nature of the true life; 2. Certain death in hatred of the brethren, as to ground and nature.

Brotherly love. 1. Who are our brethren? 2. How do we love the brethren? 3. What moves us to such love?

How operative is the love which flows from the living knowledge of the sacrificing love of Christ! 1. It takes us from death to life; beloved of God in Christ, we love. 2. It alone is able to bear the hatred of the world without ceasing to love (Matth. v. 39–42). 3. It is not only love in words and with the tongue, but in deed and in truth.

We know that we are born of God, for, 1. The world hates us; 2. We love the brethren; 3. We hate hatred, but not the hater; 4. We lay down our life for the brethren.

A heart-test of what spirit we are (Luke ix. 55, 56; Jer. viii. 6). 1. For the satisfaction of the righteous who in their love grieve over the world's hatred; 2. For the terror of the ungodly who hate their neighbour without fear or anxiety; 3. for the awakening of the hypocrites who love their neighbour only in appearance.—*Questions of Confession.*

[IGNATIUS:—(*ad Smyrm,* 6.): "Observe those who are heterodox with regard to the grace of Christ, how contrary they are to the mind of God. They have no regard for love,—περὶ ἀγάπης οὐ μέλει αὐτοῖς—they do not care for the widow, or the orphan, or the hungry or the thirsty."—M.].

[WORDSWORTH: (on v. 16).—"*And we ought to lay down our lives for the brethren;*" a remarkable saying on the duty of Christian martyrdom. It was probably suggested by the seductive tenets of the false teachers (οἱ πλανῶντες mentioned 1 Jno. ii. 26; iii. 7), who courted popularity in times of persecution; by alleging that provided a man had *knowledge* of the doctrines of Christianity as delivered by them, and adopted their theories, it was not necessary for him to *expose* himself to any *danger* in the maintenance of the faith, much less to *endure martyrdom and to lay down his life for the brethren:* but that he might freely associate with *the heathen in their worship,* and eat things *offered to idols.* This was particularly the doctrine of the *Simonians* (Origen *c. Cels.* VI. p. 282; Euseb. II. 13), and of the *Nicolaitans* (Rev. ii. 15. Irenæus I. 23) and of the *Cerinthians* (Philastr. *hær.* c. 36).—Tertullian wrote his book called *Scorpiace* against these notions and he refers to this passage in proof of the *duty of martyrdom,* c. 12.—M.].

[MACKNIGHT: (vv. 14. 15):—According to the Apostle in this place, the surest mark, by which we can know our actual state, is to consider whether we possess that characteristic disposition towards our brethren, which the Christian religion enjoins. The high encomiums, passed in this and the following verse on love to mankind, are not to be so understood, as if no virtue but benevolence were necessary to complete the Christian character. The virtues have all such a connection with each other, that they cannot subsist separately. And therefore, if one really loves his brethren, he will not only be charitable to the poor, but he will be just in his dealings, true to his promises, faithful in all the trusts committed unto him. In short, he will carefully abstain from injuring his neighbour in any respect, and will perform every duty he owes to him, from a sincere principle of piety towards God, whereby his whole conduct will be rendered uniformly virtuous.—M.].

[SECKER:—If we do a person no harm, yet if we *wish* him harm, St. John has here determined the case, "Whosoever hateth his brother is a murderer." For indeed, hatred not only leads to murder, and too often, when indulged, produces it unexpectedly; but it is always, though perhaps for the most part in a lower degree, the very spirit of murder in the heart; and it is by our hearts that God will judge us.—M.].

[CLARKE: (on v. 15).—This text has been quoted to prove, that *no murderer can be saved.* This is not said in the text; and there have been many instances of persons who have been guilty of murder, having had deep and genuine repentance; and who, doubtless, found mercy from His hands who prayed for His murderers, *"Father, forgive them, for they know not what they do."* It is, however, an awful text for the consideration of those who shed human blood on frivolous pretences; or in those *wars* which have their origin in the worst passions of the human heart.

(On v. 17).—Here is a *test* of this love: if we do not *divide our bread* with the hungry, we certainly would not *lay down our life* for him. Whatever love we may pretend to mankind, if we are not charitable and benevolent, we give the lie to our profession. If we have not bowels of compassion, we have not the love of God in us: if we *shut up* our bowels against the poor, we shut Christ out of our hearts and ourselves out of heaven.

(On v. 18). There is a good saying in *Yalcut Rubeni*, p. 145, iv. on this point: "If love consisted in *word only*, then love ceaseth as soon as the word is pronounced. Such was the love between Balak and Balaam. But, if love consists not in *word*, it cannot be *dissolved;* such was the love of Abraham, Isaac, Jacob, and the rest of the patriarchs which were before them."—M.].

[TROWER: (on v. 17).—"What a picture is here brought before us, of a Christian possessed of this world's good, and seeing his brother have need; yet turning away his eyes, and hardening his heart against the claims of charity, shutting up his bowels of compassion from him! How unlike Him who, though He was rich, yet for our sake became poor, that we through His poverty might be rich. May we learn more and more that whatever share we enjoy of "this world's good," is intrusted to us as stewards for God; and that all pretence of possessing Christian love is vain, unless we minister freely to the necessities of our brethren what we have so freely received. Hereby alone can we know that we are of the truth, and can assure our hearts before Him."—M.].

[STANHOPE:—The good we would do, but cannot, shall be rewarded; and the evil, which we are disposed to do, though not actually done, shall be punished. Hence, if a man keep malice, though but in his heart, if he wish or rejoice at the misery or harm of his brother, this man is, in the eye of God, and of the Gospel dispensation, a murderer.—If some sudden change befalls my neighbour's fortunes, the diminution of his honour or estate, the blemishing his credit and reputation, and I feel a secret pleasure in such calamities, can it be charity that ties up my tongue from bitterness or slander, or my hands from invasion and cruelty? No, certainly.—He that triumphs in mischief and doth not act it himself; he that is fond of and cherisheth a scandal, but forbears to raise or spread it; it is not religion, but some other consideration, by which even this man is restrained. But alas! how few are there, in comparison, who think themselves bound to stop here! How few who, while they hold their hands from action, make no scruple to give their tongues a liberty of speaking "all words that may do hurt," and so contribute to the disgrace and grief of their injured and afflicted brother! and if they, with these sharp razors, wound and mangle a bleeding reputation, would not the same malice unsheath their sword and thrust it into his bowels, if their own safety, the fear of human laws, or some other prudential consideration, did not bind their hands, which leaves their tongues and thoughts at liberty? For, were religion, were the fear and love of God, their check, they would prevent the very beginnings of malice. This tells us that we must be compassionate and kind; that we must do to every man whatsoever we would that he should do unto us; that but to meditate or delight in evil is a sin, and that no instance of goodness should be wanting which the circumstances of any brother render seasonable for him to receive, and ours have put in our power to give; that a design of making him uneasy is not one whit less murderous and guilty, because not prosecuted in tenderness to one's self, and not to be effected with impunity. Thus God interprets it, and by this rule He will proceed with us; for He declares Himself a trier of the heart, and that in our last great reckoning, "every secret thing shall be brought into judgment."—M.].

5. *The glorious consequences of our adoption by God.*

CHAPTER III. 19–24.

19 And[1] hereby we know[2] that we are of the truth[3], and shall assure[4] our hearts before
20 him. For[5] if our heart condemn us[6], God[7] is greater than our heart, and knoweth
21 all things. Beloved, if our heart condemn us not[8], *then* have[9] we confidence toward
22 God. And whatsoever we ask[10], we receive of[11] him, because we keep[12] his command-
23 ments, and do those[13] things that are pleasing in his sight. And this is his com-
mandment, That we should[14] [15]believe in the name of his Son Jesus Christ, and love
24 one another, as he gave us commandment. And he that keepeth his command-
ments dwelleth[16] in him, and he in him. And hereby we know that he abideth in
us, by[17] the Spirit which he hath given us.

Verse 19. [1] Καὶ, though wanting in A. B., is found in C. G. K. *Sin.*, many cursives and versions.
[2] γνωσόμεθα with A. B. C. Sin; γιγνώσκομεν G. K.; another reading is γινώσκομεθα, *cognoscemur*. [German: We shall know.—M.]
[[3] German: "Out of the truth."—M.]
[[4] German: "And shall *persuade* our hearts before Him."—M.]
Verse 20. [5] ὅτι, is written by Lachmann ὅ τι, only after A, which reads ὅτι ἂν. [German: "because."—M.]
[6] καταγινώσκη in the reading of the best *Codd.* also of *Sinait;* elsewhere καταγινώσκει.
[7] ὅτι before μείζων, B. C. G. K. Sin. is well authenticated [and adopted in the German which reads: "Because God is greater etc."—M.]
Verse 21. [8] καταγινώσκη, elsewhere καταγινώσκει, Sin;—κω, is at all events an error of the pen like ἔκπροσθεν v. 19, ἔσσφαξὲν v. 12.—Besides A. omits the first, and B. C. the second ἡμῶν, but both occur in G. K. Sin; and B. C. testify for the former, A. for the second.
[9] ἔχομεν well supported instead of ἔχει B, ἔχωμεν, *habeamus.*
Verse 22. [[10] German: "And whatsoever we may ask."—M.]
[11] ἀπ' αὐτοῦ A. B. C. *Cod. Sin;*—παρ' αὐτοῦ G. K.
[12] τηρῶμεν A. K. *Sin.* is probably a slip of the pen for τηροῦμεν.
[[13] καὶ τὰ ἀρεστὰ κ.τ.λ. "And do *the things*, etc.;" the demonstrative pronoun is unnecessary and is not used in most of the versions, the German renders "and do the well-pleasing before Him."—M.]
Verse 23. [14] πιστεύσωμεν B. G. K.—A. C. Cod. Sin. πιστεύωμεν.
[15] ἡμῖν after ἐντολὴν in Cod. Sin. before or after ἔδωκεν in the best authentic *Codd.*
Verse 24. [[16] German: "abideth" to be retained to preserve the uniformity.—M.]
[[17] ἐκ τοῦ πνεύματος=of the Spirit; so German.—M.]

EXEGETICAL AND CRITICAL.

Transition and first consequence: the assurance of being of the truth.

VER. 19*a*.—**And hereby we shall know that we are of the truth.**—The connection is by the copula καὶ; the Future γνωσόμεθα is occasioned by the hortatory form of v. 18: μὴ ἀγαπῶμεν, the sense being: "If we love ἐν ἔργῳ καὶ ἀληθείᾳ, we shall know thereby that etc." (Huther); the object of our knowing, ὅτι ἐκ τῆς ἀληθείας ἐσμέν, is defined by what is said in v. 18. Thus close is the connection of the Apostle's argument with the preceding section in which he treated of obedience to the commandments of God and more particularly of brotherly love (v. 10—v. 18). Ἐν τούτῳ refers to what precedes, as in ch. ii. 5b., and not to what follows as in ch. ii. 3.—V. 19 is plainly connected with v. 18, not with v. 10 (Rickli, de Wette), or v. 14 (Lucke). The Future has here the same sense as in Jno. vii. 17; viii. 31, 32; xiii. 35, denoting the possibility of a case which may justly be expected to arise. Winer, *Grammar*, p. 294, sq.—Ἐκ ἀληθείας εἶναι requires to be interpreted like ἐκ θεοῦ εἶναι, τέκνον θεοῦ εἶναι both on account of the force of the preposition ἐκ which signifies *principium vel ortum*, and of the pregnant sense which John attaches to the word ἀλήθεια. It is the truth eternal, originating in and springing from God revealed in Christ, testified to by the Holy Spirit as the Spirit of truth, the real substance of the Gospel, and designed to be expressed in the life of believers; it comes nearest to the idea of φῶς, and we ought therefore to compare the term: υἱοὶ φωτός (Jno. xii. 36). Cf. Jno. xviii. 37.—It is not covered by ἐκ θεοῦ εἶναι, but should be combined with it. The truth (out) of God is the nature of those who love the brethren and a well of life in them.—Hence we must not explain with Bede: "*ex veritate quæ Deus est*" (so also Calvin, Rickli and others), or with Calov: "*ex verbo veritatis*" (so also Spener, Bengel, Lücke, de Wette), and still less understand with Jachmann "*the true religion*," or with Nösselt: "*doctrina divina*," or with Semler: "*perfectior vita.*" These definitions do not explain the idea ἀλήθεια. Nor must we weaken the force of the preposition ἐκ and explain with Oecumenius: "ἀληθεύειν," or with a Lapide: "*veracem esse, veraciter ambulare*," or with Socinus: "*vere talem esse, ut quis se esse se profitetur*," or with Grotius: "*congruere evangelio.*"

Second consequence: An assured heart before God, vv. 19*b*. 20.

VER. 19*b*. **And we shall persuade our hearts before Him.**—Πείθειν either to convince or to persuade; the object καρδίας ἡμῶν points to a difference within the personality, qualified by καταγινώσκῃ and hence perceptible. It is an ethico-religious difference: the accusation and condemnation of our heart against our own person. The Apostle designates by καρδία the inmost seat of the emotions (Jno. xiv. 1, 27; xvi. 6, 22), the source of our actions (ch. xiii. 2), and here also the judge within; συνείδησις in John, occurs only in the spurious passage ch. viii. 9, but is frequently used by Paul (Rom. ii. 15; ix. 1; xiii. 5; 1 Cor. viii. 7; 2 Cor. v. 11; Acts xxiv. 16) and also at 1 Pet. iii. 16, 21; Heb. xiii. 18. Origen cites v. 21, plainly either as: "ἐὰν μὴ ἡ συνείδησις καταγινώσκῃ ἡμῶν," or as "ἐὰν ἡ συνείδησις ἡμῶν μὴ καταγινώσκῃ." The Greeks take καρδία simply for συνείδησις. Although καρδία is more comprehensive than συνείδησις, yet the latter is contained in the former, viz., conscience is in the heart, which we must conceive to be disquieted and excited by and with the conscience. The connection requires us to construe πείθειν aimed at the point "*ut desistant condemnare*" (Bengel), as at Matth. xxviii. 14: πείσομεν αὐτὸν, *i. e.*, the ἡγεμόνα and ἀμερίμνους ποιήσομεν the soldiers on guard who had fled on the morning of the resurrection. According to the context and conformably to usage πείθειν denotes a pacifying persuasion. The antithesis v. 21: ἐὰν μὴ καταγινώσκῃ—παῤῥησίαν ἔχομεν likewise makes ἐὰν καταγινώσκῃ—πείσομεν denote to pacify, to quiet as the effect of persuasion. Hence Fritsche's explanation: "*flectemus animos—ad amorem ostendendum*," is false and wholly repugnant to the context. The reference however is not to the last judgment when the final decision and separation will take place, but rather to the inward transactions, which though prophetical of the last judgment, precede the same during this our earthly life. Accordingly, ἔμπροσθεν αὐτοῦ is not *coram illo* in the last judgment and πείσομεν relates not to eternity (as Socinus, Lücke, de Wette construe), but only *coram illo*, in His presence, in His light. As the accusing heart on the ground of the Divine word, and in virtue of the impulse of and the fellowship with the Holy Spirit is disquieted, and the voice of God is heard in the conscience, so the heart must be quieted before God, on the ground and in virtue of His word and promise and in the fellowship with Him, so that the following words: "μείζων ἐστὶν ὁ θεὸς καὶ γινώσκει πάντα" explain ἔμπροσθεν αὐτοῦ; imaginings of our own spirit and worldly diversions do not promote such quieting. Compare Düsterdieck. Hence we should construe the Future πείσομεν in coördination with γνωσόμεθα and so connected with καὶ that it is also governed by ἐν τούτῳ, although the latter connected zeugmatically with γνωσόμεθα denotes *thereat*, with πείσομεν, *thereby;* this is the more practicable, because ἐκ τῆς ἀληθείας εἶναι intervenes and completes ἐν ἀληθείᾳ ἀγαπᾶν and γνωσόμεθα introduces πείσομεν. It is therefore wrong to begin a new sentence with ἔμπροσθεν (Paulus, Fritzsche, Ebrard).

VER. 20. **Because, if the heart condemn us, because God is greater than our heart, and knoweth all things.**—The reading ὅτι ἐὰν—ὅτι μείζων is so well established that neither a conjecture like that of Stephanus, who proposes to read ἔτι μείζων, nor the cancelling of the second ὅτι, as done by Grotius, warrants us to lessen or remove the difficulties which are also rather contained in the thought. We have now the reason specified that we shall quiet our hearts before Him in case our heart should condemn us and find a verdict against us. Hence ἐὰν with the Subjunctive is perfectly right. Winer, *Grammar*, pp. 307, 308.—"Καταγινώσκειν stands midway between κατηγορεῖν, to accuse (Rom. ii. 15), which is still accompanied by an ἀπολογεῖν (Rom. ii. 15), and κατακρίνειν, to sentence [in a bad sense—M], condemn (Jno. viii. 10 sq.); the latter includes the judicial punishment (Jno. viii 10; Col. iv.), while καταγινώσκειν denotes only the verdict found against a person accused to be followed by the punishment corresponding thereto. Cf. Deut. xxv. 1, 2. The term is therefore very significant with respect to the verdict found by our own soul against ourself, which is more than the mere accusation, because the καταγινώσκειν implies also the guilt of the person accused, so that the condemnation to the punishment, the κατακρίνειν, may justly be expected" (Düsterdieck). In the heart there is not only a party, but also a judge; the conscience is a court of justice. Hence it denotes here not only *reprehendere* or accuse (*Vulgate*, Augustine, Lücke, al.). Why the heart finds a verdict against us the context indicates "in a relative play on the words" γνωσόμεθα—καταγινώσκῃ, exactly like Jno. xv. 2. (Düsterdieck). Consequently [it finds the verdict against us—M.] that we are not wholly of the truth, that we do not perfectly, gladly and uninterruptedly love the brethren; for these are correlates of extraordinary difference in degree up to perfection. The explanation of the Greek commentators, who think of v. 18, and that of Düsterdieck, who connects it with v. 19, should be combined against those of Luther and Nösselt, who think of every defect except that of brotherly love; but every other defect would also show itself with respect to brotherly love, and render it deficient. Of course, the reference cannot be to a complete relapse, to a knowingly and grossly repeated case of untruthfulness in love or of unlovingness, since the lying words of love would have no corresponding deed (Estius, Episcopius, Lücke, al.) though we may and should think not only of lesser but also of graver offences, seeing that the conscience of Christians is sufficiently tender and acute to find an adverse verdict also with respect to lesser defects of love. The repetition of ὅτι before ἐὰν and μείζων is not peculiar to this passage but occurs also at Eph. ii. 11, 12. Lücke cites an example from Xenophon, Anab. 7, 4, 5 and 5, 6, 19 remarking, however, that while ὅτι in both places signifies *that*, it denotes here "*because*." The reason of the epanalepsis is not the forgetfulness of the author, but the importance of the thought which allows and requires such a rhetorical emphasis. Lücke admits the epanalepsis without hesitation, Winer, (*Grammar* p. 604, note 3,) is undecided, Huther hesitates and decides against it, the older and many modern commentators (Calvin, Wolf, Sander, Düsterdieck) are for it. There is hence no reason to read with Bengel, Baumgarten-Crusius, Lachmann, *ed. maj.* and others ὅταν or ὅ τι ἐὰν=*quicquid* like ὃ ἐὰν in v. 22 instead of ὅτι. It cannot be maintained with Düsterdieck that this is not Greek, and from the circumstance that ὃς ἐὰν or even ὅστις ἐὰν never occcurs in the New Testament without the variant reading ἂν, while ὅστις ἂν frequently occurs without a variant reading, it cannot be inferred that ὅ τι ἐὰν cannot be read here. Cf. Winer, *Grammar*, p. 322, sq.—Matth. viii. 19 ὅπου ἐὰν occurs without the variant reading ἂν, and ὅστις ἐὰν is as well authenticated as ὃς ἐάν. But on that account it is only possible to read here ὅ τι ἐὰν which is occasioned by the reading ἂν in A; καταγινώσκειν, which may have its object in the Accusative, also allows that reading. But the context forbids it; for it is hardly true that we can quiet our heart at *every* accusation, and the reason of such quieting to be connected with πείσομεν is too much separated, while the putting and assumption of the case, as stated in v. 20, and required at v. 21, in which the heart stands in need of such quieting, is all but wiped out.—The main difficulty is, that in the circumstance of God being greater and knowing all things must be found, and that it really contains, a quieting of the heart under its accusations.—The word μείζων is of frequent occurrence in the writings of John; in a similar connection at ch. iv. 4; v. 9; in other connections, particularly at Jno. iv. 12; v. 36; viii. 53; x. 29; xiii. 16; xiv. 28; xv. 20. The context invariably supplies the sense in which it is used; here the sentence καὶ γινώσκει πάντα furnishes the necessary explanation; He γινώσκει, while the heart καταγινώσκει. "*Dulce parëgmenon in Græco*" (Bengel). God is here called greater in comparison with our heart; the heart accuses: it is not that He accuses more than our heart, but that He judges differently, more justly than our heart; for He knoweth *all* things which our heart does not perceive, know or observe in giving sentence. Πάντα of course points into the heart itself and to the immediate surroundings; what is that? The context answers that question: v. 2: οὔπω φανερώθη τί ἐσόμεθα, v. 9: σπέρμα αὐτοῦ ἐν αὐτῷ μένει, we do not altogether know ourselves, we have only the beginnings and germs of the life from Him; Christ, His life, His bearing and taking away sin (vv. 5, 6), His destroying the works of the devil (v. 8), objectively completed, but subjectively to be gradually completed from a life-principle of the regeneration (ch. ii. 29), and moreover passing through man's own weakness and sin (v. 3: ἁγνίζει ἑαυτὸν), and through the hatred of the world (v. 13: μισεῖ ὑμᾶς ὁ κόσμος). God knows the whole (πάντα) of the new life of man even to the ὅμοιοι αὐτῷ ἐσόμεθα (v. 2), while man knows only the particular, the particular error of which the heart accuses him; God knows the power of His gift to man and its preservation in penitence, its growth and development both in the hope and the faith in him. Therefore God is greater and knoweth all things; therefore, this greatness of the God who is our Father is a ground of quieting when the heart accuses us, and in its vitality and tenderness finds a verdict against us. So Besser: "Our heart knows some things and pronounces against us: God knows all things and pronounces not against us, but for us, because the seed of the truth out of which we are born, is not concealed to Him." He knows, as Sander says, even the smallest spark of faith in the glimmering wick, or even the hidden germs of true love (Rickli). "*Conscientia pusilla est et scit aliquid nostri duntaxat, at Deus magnus est, novit omnia nostra, præsentia, præterita, futura, et omnium, et habet jus voluntatemque condonandi*" (Bengel).—Hence this verse is, *sensu evangelico*, to be understood of the love which *forgives* and *destroys* sin (Luther, Spener, Bengel, Besser, Düsterdieck, Huther and others), and not *sensu legali*, of judging righteousness and omniscience (Calvin, Beza, Socinus, Grotius, Calov, Lücke, Neander, Ebrard and others). Ebrard begins a new sentence and explains thus: And before the face of God we shall *convince* our heart, mind, conscience, not the understanding, *that* if (already) our (easily deceived smaller) heart accuses us (that we do not practise love), God, the Omniscient, is greater than our heart (and that we so *much the less* can stand before Him, have παῤῥησία).—Nor must we construe: For, if the heart accuses us, because God is greater than our heart, He also knoweth all things; so de Wette *sensu legali*, Brückner *sensu evangelico*. Rather the importance of the thought justifies the epanalepsis of the ὅτι.

Third consequence. Filial confidence. vv. 21, 22.

VER. 21. **Beloved, if our heart condemn us not.**—Ἀγαπητοί as in ch. ii. 7; iii. 2; iv. 1, 7, 11 is here connected with the enjoyment of the forgiving love of God in order to bring out a new and other feature. The recurrence of the words ἡ καρδία καταγινώσκῃ ἡμῶν indicates the connection with the foregoing (although, as Bengel maintains, καρδία, v. 20, καταγινώσκῃ has the emphasis), in the same sense, in order to mark a particular case (ἐάν with *conjunct.*), which is sure to arise, and only the negative μή marks the antithesis; the word used is μή and not μηκέτι, which would make the supposed case the consequence of what goes before (as Huther supposes). A similar construction occurs at ch. i. 8, 9.

We have confidence towards God.—The words παῤῥησίαν πρὸς τὸν θεὸν ἔχομεν denote the state of the peace of the soul and of undisturbed confidence to God-ward which is opposed to that described before by πείθειν τὰς καρδίας ἡμῶν, like at Rom. viii. 15. The παῤῥησία ch. ii. 28; iv. 17 is indeed the child-like free confidence before the Father in the time of judgment; the reference here also is to a judgment, in the court of the conscience, in one's own heart, but not to the future and final judgment. Hence Estius explains falsely: *fiducia evadendæ damnationis in die judicii*. But the limitation of παῤῥησία to confident prayer and supplication is neither warranted by the word itself (2 Cor. vii. 4), the context, nor the construction with πρός, which simply indicates the direction and relation as in Rom. v. 1: εἰρήνην—πρὸς τὸν θεόν, nor by the parallel-passage at ch. v. 14. Here it denotes joyful confidence to God ward at every moment of life (Rickli, Düsterdieck and others), but not *fiducia in nostris necessitatibus recurrendi ad ipsum* (Lyra), or the girdle or mendicant's bag of all manner of necessaries (Luther), *fiducia in rogando* (Bengel). [Alford: "To God-ward, in our aspect as turned towards and looking to God.—It must be remembered that the words are said in the full light of the reality of the Christian State,—where the heart is awakened and enlightened, and the testimony of the Spirit is active: where the heart's own deceit does not come into consideration as a disturbing element."—M.]. But hereby it is not denied that the specific, yea the most significant feature of this filial confidence (Düsterdieck) is, what follows—

VER. 22. **And whatsoever we may** (perchance, German: *etwa*) **ask, we receive from Him.**—The conjunction καί connects a particular already contained in παῤῥησία like καί in v. 10*b* (Düsterdieck). Ὃ ἐὰν αἰτῶμεν is to be taken quite generally and to be limited only by the subject asking, namely *the child of God* and his wants (Düsterdieck, Huther). [The latter beautifully adds: "*The child of God* asks for nothing which is contrary to the will of his Father"—M.]. The same holds good of λαμβάνομεν ἀπ' αὐτοῦ (θεοῦ). The Present must not be taken for the Future (Grotius); it rather denotes the present, constant intercourse between the child of God with his God. Cf. Jno. xiv. 13; xvi. 24. Augustine: "*Caritas ipsa novit, caritas ipsa orat, contra hanc aures claudere non novit, qui illam dedit; securus esto, caritas roget, et ibi sunt aures dei; non fit, quod vis, sed fit, quod tibi expedit.*"

Because we keep His commandments and do the things which are pleasing in His sight.—Here is evidently a parallelism: ἐντολὰς—τηρεῖν and τὰ ἀρεστὰ ἐνώπιον αὐτοῦ ποιεῖν, so that the two together constitute one idea. At Jno. viii. 29, τὰ ἀρεστὰ αὐτῷ occurs in a connection similar to the present. Besides this also in Acts vi. 2; xii. 3.—The term εὐάρεστός of frequent occurrence in the Pauline writings (Rom. xii. 1; xiv. 18; 2 Cor. v. 9; Eph. v. 10; Phil. iv. 18), with the Dative τῷ θεῷ or τῷ κυρίῳ is used Col. iii. 20 of the fourth commandment, and the parallel passage Eph. vi. 1, has δίκαιον. Cf. 1. Tim. v. 4: ἀπόδεκτον ἐνώπιον τοῦ θεοῦ. Hence we must also connect τὰ ἀρεστὰ with the commandments. But while the first clause of the parallel sentence specifies the commandments, the second clause marks that which is pleasing in His sight and the kind of obedience, because God requires not a slavish service, but filial obedience, and that an active one (ποιοῦμεν). Hence we must not explain with the Roman Catholic expositors ἐντολαὶ of *præcepta* and ἀρεστὰ of *consilia evangelica*. The greater difficulty is the right construction of the connection with ὅτι, which indicates the reason why our prayers are heard. But the ground is not necessarily *causa meritoria* as the *Greek* writers think who assume an ἀντιδιδόναι on the part of God; and the *Roman Catholics* and the *Rationalists* of course agree with them. The context, especially with respect to ch. ii. 29; iii. 6, 9, 23, 24, shows that while prominence is given to their conduct the reference is to the relation in which they stand, or with the description of their activity to the ground on which they move. The relation between God and themselves which conditions and regulates their conduct is the cause why their prayers are heard, because their conduct conditioned by that relation also regulates their prayers according to the will of God (κατὰ τὸ θέλημα αὐτοῦ ch. v. 14); the prayers as they are made, so they are heard, because we are the children of God. The expression of Hunnius, that the particle ὅτι is not *causalis* but *rationativa*, is beside the mark, although the idea is correct. Cf. Düsterdieck. [Huther has *multum in parvo:* "ὅτι in close connection with the immediately preceding λαμβάνομεν indicates the ground of the Divine exhibition of love in hearing prayer; this ground, which must not be taken as *causa meritoria*, is the filial obedience of the person asking, whereby God identifies him as His child; the idea of obedience is expressed in two coördinated sentences (resembling the Hebrew parallelism); τὰς ἐντολὰς αὐτοῦ and τὰ ἀρεστὰ ἐνώπιον αὐτοῦ are synonymous; ποιεῖν marks the obedience as being *active;* the second sentence points to the circumstance that it does not consist in servile subjection to the *commandment*, but in the filial performance of that which is *well-pleasing* to God." Alford, adverting to the Romish misinterpretation, excellently expounds: "Out of Christ, there are no good works at all: entrance into Christ is not won or merited by them. In Christ, every work done of faith is good and is pleasing to God. The doing of such works is the working of the life of Christ in us: they are its sign, they are its fruits: they are not of us, but of it and of Him. They are the measure of our Christian life: according to their abundance, so is our access to God, so is our reward from God: for they are the steps of our likeness to God. Whatever is attributed to them as an efficient cause, is attributed not to us, but to Him whose fruits they are. *Because* Christ is thus manifested in us, God hears our prayers, which He only hears for Christ's sake: *because* His Spirit works thus abundantly in us, He listens to our prayer, which in that measure has become the voice of His Spirit. So that no degree of efficacy attributed to the good works of the child of God need surprise us: it is God recognizing, God vindicating, God multiplying, God glorifying His own work in us. So that when e. g. Corn. a Lap. says, "*Congruum est et congrua merces obedientiæ et amicitiæ, ut si homo faciat voluntatem Dei, Deus vicissim faciat voluntatem hominis,*" all we can reply is that such a duality, such a reciprocity, does not exist for Christians: we are *in God*, He in us; and this St. John continually insists on. We have no claim *ab extra:* He works in us to do of His good pleasure: and the works which He works, which we work, manifest before Him, and before all, that we are His children."—M.].

Fourth consequence: Fellowship of the Spirit with particular reference to the ground of these consequences, vv. 23, 24.

VER. 23. **And this is His commandment.**—Ch. i. 5: καὶ ἔστιν αὕτη. Καὶ is simply copulative and connecting with τὰς ἐντολὰς αὐτοῦ specifies the most essential contents of ἡ ἐντολή, which indeed embraces two commandments, faith and love, but which two commandments, being indissolubly united, contain the sum-total of the being determined by the Divine Will in Christ. Ἐντολή refers neither to the first commandment (J. Lange), nor must it be construed in a sense it does not bear (de Wette); it is and remains the expression of the Divine Will (Düsterdieck). Αὐτοῦ of course is=τοῦ θεοῦ. [Oecumenius: ἔχοντες ἐντολήν, ἵνα τῇ πίστει τῇ ἐν τῷ ὀνόματι τοῦ υἱοῦ αὐτοῦ Ἰησ. Χρ. ἀγαπῶμεν ἀλλήλους. Bede: *Singulari numero mandatum præmisit, et duo subsequentia adjungit mandata, fidem scilicet et dilectionem, quia nimirum hæc ab invicem separari nequeunt. Neque enim sine fide Christi recte nos alterutrum diligere, neque vere in nomine Jesu Christi sine dilectione possumus credere.*—M.].

That we should believe on the name of His Son Jesus Christ and love one another.—Here ἵνα indicates the *purpose* and not only the *contents* of the commandments, as Huther explains [But the strong *telic* sense of ἵνα can hardly be pressed here; see ch. iii. 1, 11.—M.]. The Aorist πιστεύσωμεν is not only the best authenticated and *difficilior lectio*, but also mor thoughtful than the πιστεύωμεν formed after the pattern of ἀγαπῶμεν, and denotes by the side of the Present ἀγαπῶμεν, that the former precedes the latter, πίστις as the pre-supposition, not as being done once for all (against Düsterdieck), but as a root of vital strength, and ἀγάπη as the stem, as in Gal. v. 6: πίστις ἐν ἀγάπῃ ἐνεργουμένη, or 1 Tim. i. 5: ἀγάπη—ἐκ πίστεως. Faith conceived as an ἔργον θεοῦ (Jno. vi. 29) and Jno. xvi. 9 (ἁμαρτία, ὅτι οὐ πιστεύουσιν εἰς ἐμέ) as the ground of a holy being, of the whole obedience, is yet man's *work* and hence may be required in the commandment, more especially since the construction πιστεύειν τινι (Jno. iv. 21; v. 24, 46, 47; viii. 45) denotes the *assensus* with which man's agency awakes, while πιστεύειν τινα describes the received *notitia*, and πιστεύειν εἰς τινα the God-wrought *fiducia*, which embraces the least, the *notitia*, and also the moment next to it, the *assensus*. The object of faith is τὸ ὄνομα τοῦ υἱοῦ αὐτοῦ Ἰησοῦ Χριστοῦ. This ὄνομα is the revelation of the being of the Son of God, and contains within itself and discloses to believers what is testified of Him and by Himself, and is to be testified; it includes both the *prædicatio* (Rom. x. 14) as Calvin and Beza explain, and the *meritum* and the *promissiones Christi et de Christo*, as pointed out by S. Schmidt and others. *Doctrina Christiana* (Episcopius), and *the dignity of the Messiah* (S. G. Lange), are consequently insufficient. [Alford: "To believe the Gospel-message concerning Him, and Him as living in it, in all His fulness."—M.]. Conformably to the close connection of faith and love (Jno. xvi. 4, 7 sqq.) the Apostle now annexes the Present ἀγαπῶμεν to the Aorist by the copulative καὶ.—The additional clause—

As He gave us commandment, being a further qualification of love (ch. ii. 7, 8; iii. 16; Jno. xiii. 34; xv. 12, 13), belongs to the latter part of the sentence (Myrberg: *non modo amandum est, sed etiam vere et recte amandum*), and not to the former (πιστεύσωμεν), as Estius, Bengel, Sander.—Hence Christ, and not God, is and remains the subject of this lateral idea. Christ, on whom, as the Son of God, we have to believe, is the origin and standard of brotherly love.

VER. 24. **And he that keepeth His commandments, abideth in Him and He in Him.**—Passing over the lateral idea and the ἐντολή, v. 23, and resuming the ἐντολὰς τηρεῖν, v. 22, the Apostle now makes prominent the fourth consequence, the fellowship of God with us and our fellowship with God, according to which He is in us and we are in Him. Hence αὐτοῦ, αὐτῷ, αὐτὸς—all three—describe God and not *Christ* (Neander, Besser, Sander).

And hereby we know that He abideth in us, from [out of] the Spirit that He gave us.—God's abiding in us is the object of knowledge; and it is important to notice that God's abiding in us is not specified here as *res minus verisimilis* (Socinus), but as the condition of our abiding in God; the two mutually include each other and must be taken in that sense. And this is known ἐν τούτῳ=ἐκ πνεύματος. Ἐν τούτῳ obviously refers to what follows, as ch. ii. 3, and not to what precedes, as ch. ii. 5. Surprising is the transition from the formula ἐν τούτῳ, placed at the beginning of this sentence and so current in John, to ἐκ πνεύματος, but the transition may be explained by the circumstance that after ὅτι μένει ἐν ἡμῖν the clearness and beauty of the structure required substantive proof, and that this substantive proof occasioned the fine and thoughtful description of the source and origin of that knowledge by the preposition ἐκ. Cf. ch. iv. 6: ἐκ τούτου γινώσκομεν. The πνεῦμα is the Holy Spirit who moves us, the living and powerful principle of our life from (out of) and in God. Here we should remember the χρίσμα, ch. ii. 20-26. Inadequate is de Wette's explanation, that πνεῦμα denotes the Divine appropriated in faith and life, but that the reference here is to the right knowledge and doctrine of the person of Jesus, and even more inadequate is the opinion of Socinus, that πνεῦμα is love.—In the annexed relative sentence οὗ must not be taken as a *genit. partitivus*, but as the result of attraction. Winer, Part III. § 24.

DOCTRINAL AND ETHICAL.

1. The Christian should *not be or remain in a state of uncertainty* whether he really is a child of God (out) of the truth; his redemption and the reconciliation of God to him and his reconciliation to God and his salvation need not be to him a doubtful or only probable state. But clear and firm knowledge on this subject he does not acquire at one stroke, over-night; he must learn it by living and exercising himself in love. The Christian in process of being [*i. e.*, in the development of this Christian life—M.] is in a state of fermentation, or engaged in single combat, without a survey of the whole field, the battle conducing to victory, although here and there defeats occur, and he is forced to retire even unto flight—without being able to imperil the ultimate victory. Hence he has misgivings which he can and ought to discard, fearless and full of confidence and reliance on the Lord of hosts and of the victory.

2. *The final cause* of such assurance of faith and blessed certainty of salvation, constantly exposed to the danger of being disturbed by the accusations and charges of the heart discerning and reproving the ever-recurring omissions and imperfections and transgressions in thought, word and deed, lies not in ourselves, neither in the mark, in brotherly love and, generally, in obedience to the commandments of God, nor in such acts of reproof of an anxious and contrite heart, but in God Himself, in that which He has promised and imparted to us, and that He abides by His word and work, also in our hearts, nursing and furthering the same even unto completion. Three things are clearly and distinctly asserted.

a. If the Christian looks at himself, anxiety and doubts concerning the state of grace are justified; Heb. vi. 4-6; x. 26-31, in which passages Luther found "a hard knot," and on which see R. Stier, point to the possibility of a relapse, as also Rom. viii. 13; Gal. vi. 7, 8. This is contrary to Calvin's assumption of the *donum perseverantiæ* given with regeneration, and which is not taught at Jno. x. 28, 29. But if the Christian looks up to the mercy of God, he acquires confidence and joyfulness and the Holy Spirit bears witness of his adoption and Divine life-fellowship (v. 24, Rom. viii. 16–27). This is contrary to the Roman Catholic doctrine except by that the Christian, special revelation, *cannot* have any certainty concerning his state of grace.

b. The point in question is not a mathematical *certitudo*, an *actus intellectus*, but only *fiducia* as well as confidence in the pureness of a man's disposition.

c. The certain assurance of standing in God's grace is not identical with nor to be confounded with the certainty of being predestinated. The *Council of Trent* was right, in opposition to the Reformed, to reject this certainty (vi. 15, 16) but wrong in rejecting the former assurance (vi. 9): "*Sicut nemo pius de Dei misericordia, de Christi merito deque Sacramentorum virtute et efficacia dubitare potest, sic quilibet, dum se ipsum suamque propriam infirmitatem et indispositionem respicit, de sua gratia formidare et timere potest, quam nullus scire valeat certitudine fidei, cui non potest subesse falsum, se gratiam Dei esse consecutum.*" Here, as we may readily perceive, truth and falsehood are suspiciously mixed up. Cf. Frank, *Theologie der K. F.* 2. 78, 141. Thiersch, *Vorlesungen über Protestantismus und Katholizismus*, 2, 149–159.

3. The two cases that conscience finds a verdict against us and not against us are opposed to each other, but nevertheless facts belonging to the Christian life and perfectly compatible with it, even as ch. i. 8, 9 and ch. iii. 9 do not cancel each other. These propositions cannot be classed among the paradoxes, which may not be without truth, as stated by Luther, e. g. "*Si in fide fieri posset adulterium peccatum non esset,*" and Proposition 32 in *Grund und Artikel*, which were unjustly condemned by the Romish bull (1520, Erlangen, 24, 138): A good work done in the very best manner, is still a daily sin, etc.—Nor dare we try to aid the establishment of a morality for the people, and another morality for the saints by drawing with the Roman Catholics a distinction between *præcepta* and *consilia evangelica*, between a selfish *amor concupiscentiæ* calculating on salvation and an *amor amicitiæ* surrendering itself in pure fidelity. We may neither separate by false distinctions the objectively given commandments with the will of God nor the subjectively imposed obligations, nor, worse still, men from one another. But we ought to contemplate both truths, that our natural disposition which is sinful before God ever and again mingles without, and contrary to the Christian's will with the works done by the motions of the Spirit from above and in faith, and that the Christian born of God has before his eyes and in his heart the one will of God, as revealed in the Law and in Christ, which aims not at a higher or a lower morality [but at one morality—M.], and that his obedience is well-pleasing to God, not because of his own doings or nature, but solely for the sake of Christ. Our life here on earth is made up of alternate joy and grief, of rising and falling, of forgiveness of sins and cancelling and the commission of sin. Sin, moreover, is more sinful in the children of God than in the servants of perdition, for they have a more profound and lively sense of the slightest stirrings of the wrath of God, because and though their falling is not yet a falling from grace, as at Gal. v. 4 (τῆς χάριτος ἐξεπέσατε). Not every falling involves the loss of grace. But obedience and patience in good works remain marks of the state of grace. Cf. C. A. 6, 20, f. C. 4, 5, 6, Frank 1, 1; 2, 177 sq.; 181 sq.; 139 sqq.; 369 sqq.

4. Filial confidence which does not begin with the entrance upon our inheritance [but here on earth—M.], has a παῤῥησία not only in the day of judgment, but already here on earth, and it evidences itself both by zealous efforts towards self-sanctification based on the assurance of the forgiveness of sins, and by confident prayer "Prayer is as essential to man as his conscience because the conscience, in proportion to its clearness and vitality, necessarily passes into prayer" (Löber, *Lehre vom Gebet* p. 1.). If the conscience is pacified, prayer will be sure of being heard. If man is so circumstanced that he lives and moves in God's word, his word in prayer to God will also prevail with God, in whose being (as we may learn from the case of the praying God-man), as well as in man's being prayer has its ultimate reason. Harless, therefore, has not very judiciously classed *prayer* among the *subjective means* of Christian virtue (*Ethik* §. 33).—A limitation of prayer that may be heard beyond the pattern-prayer of the Lord's Prayer is not permitted; you may in the state of grace pray for every thing assured of being heard, but equally assured that nothing is said of the time when and the manner how your prayers will be heard. God hears whatever we ask, but not exactly as we ask.

5. Faith in God, who is Love, and (in virtue of our belief in the love of God) love of the brethren are intimately connected, the reference being to "faith as the transition from darkness to light and love as the walk in the light" (Hofmann, *Schriftbeweis* XI., 2, 337, cf. v. 14).

6. It follows from the testimony of the Holy Spirit within thee (cf. No. 2 above), that thou art a *temple* of God (1 Cor. iii. 16), or a *tabernacle* of God among men (Rev. xxi. 3).

HOMILETICAL AND PRACTICAL.

Much depends on knowledge, more on knowledge of the truth, most on the knowledge whether we are ourselves of the truth.—He is to be pronounced happy in whom the difficult self-knowledge was acquired and carried out as the knowledge of sin, but more happy he in whom the knowledge of God forces itself through the knowledge of himself.—Four marks of our adoption or four evidences of our being of the truth: 1. Peace of the soul under the accusations of conscience (vv. 19, 20); 2. Filial trust under the wants and deprivations of life (vv. 21, 22); 3. Assurance and decision under the manifold and different requirements (x. 23); 4. Joy of fellowship in solitude or desertion.—How can you pacify your heart disquieted by the accusings of conscience? 1. Know what God has hitherto done for you not in vain: He desires to save you; 2. Feel how in such a judgment the holiness of

God is working in you: He desires to purify you; 3. Hope that He will gloriously accomplish it, as He has promised: He is the Master and your life will be a masterpiece *at the last.*—Prayer and commandment are essentially related to each other; thy word addressed to God in *prayer* will surely be heard, if God's word addressed to thee in the *commandment* is observed. God will not be *asked* in vain by those who suffer themselves to be *commanded* by Him. The hearing of prayer is not affected by the conduct of man fixed by his relation to God, but by this relation which produces in man childlikeness, childlike obedience, childlike trust, childlike disposition and childlike ways, even as it affords paternal fidelity and paternal aid. With faith in the name of His Son Jesus Christ thou hast the love of God above all things, or the fulfilment of the commandments of the first table; and from faith in the paternal love of God revealed in Christ flows Christian brotherly love, or the fulfilment of the commandments of the second table.—*He is in us,* this is ever the first and most important thing; His commandments are before our obedience to them; and He is with and in them. But if we do not value His commandments we do not value ourselves, we become ruins and a desert. In desert ruins He does not dwell; we must be builded up, if not into temples, at least into tabernacles. He builds—even the tabernacle into the temple, and instead of cares of the soul in indigence of the Good and the Eternal Good, jubilant hymns of praise for the inheritance of the saints swell in majestic fulness and strength.—Without Christ, the Son of God, God is not thy Father but without the Spirit of the Father and the Son, thou hast neither God the Father nor the Saviour.

Luther:—Although our conscience make us afraid and represent to us God as angry, yet God is greater than our heart. Conscience is but a single drop, but the reconciled God an ocean of consolation.—When a man is rebuked and condemned by his conscience, he grows terrified; but against this darkness of the heart we may say, God knoweth all things. Conscience is always fearful and shuts the eyes; but God is deeper and higher than thy heart and searches its inmost state most thoroughly.

Starke:—We believers do not indulge in idle imaginings and suppositions, but have sure, firm, irrefragable grounds and testimonies, wrought by the Holy Ghost Himself that we are of the truth and born of God.—A man may have a great temptation and yet be a child of God.—Away with forged letters and testimonials! if the inward witness of the conscience contradicts and condemns. Conscience is more than a thousand witnesses. How false is the charge that Christianity causes melancholy and gloominess! Sorrow may indeed be found among Christians but without any fault of Christianity or of God, and moreover with them true knowledge is followed by their sorrow being turned into joy.—A heart rejoicing before God is a great treasure; O, the happiness of being permitted to appear before God in His majesty with joyfulness; therefore let us pray: Lord, give us a cheerful heart!—The spirit of joyfulness is also a spirit of prayer. Believers will receive what they ask of God in the *manner* which He has promised and at the *time* He thinks proper.—Nothing can be required of a Christian beyond faith and love; believers will not be taken captive by statutes, but they stand in liberty.—Be ashamed to say or order anything *without* the commandment of God, and again be ashamed to do anything *in opposition* to the commandment of God.—To *live* a good life requires us to *abide* good; it is not enough to have *come* into God, one must also *abide* in Him.—The believer is a great miracle, seeing that the infinite and immeasurable God wholly dwells and walks in him.

Heubner:—Is here perchance taught work-confidence? No! faith remains the ground of justification but we may hope that the genuineness and purity of our faith will follow love.—The Christian's prayer is never unheard; for God gives us that which is good although not always that to which we gave utterance, not that which we intended; the Christian ever desires the Good and the Good only, and the better we grow, the more do all our desires coincide with the will of God. Only those are able to ask who are in a state of grace; a serious, pious, honest mind is the condition of prayer; a braggart cannot pray.—The presence and continued operation of the Spirit in keeping us in the right discipline, warning, moving, strengthening and comforting us, is the sign that we belong to Christ, if He leaves us we are separated from Christ.

Adapted from Ziel (*Gesetz and Zeugniss,* 4):—How happy they who are of the truth! 1. They may pacify their heart before Him. 2. They have a joyful confidence toward God; 3. They are they that will receive from Him whatsoever they ask.—Compare here hymns like Paul Gerhard's: "*Ist Gott für mich, so trete* (If God is for me, etc.).

Sein Geist spricht meinem Geiste *Manch süsses Trostwort zu;* *Wie Gott dem Hülfe leiste,* *Der bei Ihm suchet Ruh;* *Und wie Er hab' erbauet,* *Ein' edle neue Stadt* *Da Aug' und Herze schauet,* *Was es geglaubet hat.* *Da ist mein Theil und Erbe* *Mir prächtig zugericht't;* *Wenn ich gleich fall und sterbe,* *Fällt doch mein Himmel nicht.* (*v.* 9.)	His Spirit cheers my spirit With words of comfort sweet; That they God's help inherit Who rest with Him do seek. And that He has upbuilded A city fair and new, Where eyes and heart forever What they believed shall view. For there in glory lying My lot is held in store With all my falls, and dying, My heaven falls nevermore.

Also ERDMANN NEUMEISTER'S: *Jesus nimmt die Sünder an* (Jesus, sinners does receive); especially v. 7.

Mein Gewissen quält mich nicht,	My conscience now is purified,
Moses darf mich nicht verklagen;	All plea to Moses is denied,
Der mich frei und ledig spricht,	He acquitteth me to-day
Hat die Sünden abgetragen (1 Jno. iii. 5),	Who all sin did take away;
Dass mich Nichts verdammen kann;	Nothing can condemn or grieve
Jesus nimmt die Sünder an.	Jesus sinners does receive.

[PYLE: vv. 19-21.—This will show us to be Christians indeed; and while the impartial testimony and inward sense of our own consciences assure us of the sincere performance of our own duty, we may safely conclude that God, the Searcher of hearts and Standard of all truth, will approve of and reward us. And on the contrary, whoever by the clear conviction of his own mind knows and feels himself to be a hypocritical transgressor of his moral duty, must be assured that God, who knows him better than he does himself, cannot fail to be his more severe judge and avenger.—M.].

[BULL: v. 20.—If a man be conscious to himself of his own wickedness, yea, the very secret wickedness and hypocrisy of his heart, sure God Himself, who set up in every man this "*candle*" of conscience, as Solomon calls it, Prov. xx. 27, cannot be ignorant of it; He being the fountain of all knowledge, and all knowledge in the creature derivative from Him, and so knowing all things that are knowable by any creature, and infinitely more.—M.].

[MACKNIGHT: v. 22.—This general declaration must be limited by the conditions, which in other passages of Scripture are made necessary to our petitions being granted by God; such as, that we ask things agreeable to His Will, ch. v. 14, 15; and that we ask them in faith, Jas. i. 6; that is, in the full persuasion of the Divine wisdom and goodness, and with sincerity and resignation. Such prayers, they who keep the commandments of God, may hope will be heard, because they keep His commandments by habitually doing the things which are well-pleasing to Him.—M.].

[PYLE: vv. 23, 24.—These verses may be thus paraphrased: In short, true faith in the doctrine of Christ, and true charity to mankind, especially to our Christian brethren, is the sum-total of our duty. And you, that have already duly performed it, have a sufficient pledge and earnest of your acceptance with God, as true disciples of Christ, by the gifts and graces of His Holy Spirit conferred upon you.—M.].

[RIDLEY: v. 24.—The way of the Spirit is not to be traced; the working of God is not to be perceived. The Divine Author and His operation are hidden from us; but His work is manifest. And though we cannot see God at any time, or feel the motion of the Spirit in our hearts, yet is there certain evidence whether we are brought on by Him or not. St. John gives us an infallible rule, that we may know that God, by His Spirit, dwelleth in us, if we keep His commandments.—M.].

[EZEKIEL HOPKINS:—*A clear conscience gives us boldness of access unto God.* Guilt abashes the soul, and makes it both ashamed and afraid to appear in the presence of God: and therefore Adam, as soon as he had sinned against his Maker, presently hides himself from Him. We may observe in ourselves, what a slavish dejectedness seizeth us when we come to God in duty, after we have wronged Him by any known sin: we come to Him suspiciously; and with such a misgiving fear, as if we would not have God take notice that we are before Him; and are still in pain, till the duty be over. But, when our consciences are clear, oh, with what delight do we haste to God, and with what content do we stay with Him! How doth the soul dilate and spread itself under the smiles of God, beating full upon it! "So, O Lord, here is a heart that I labour to make and keep void of offence; do thou fill it with thy promised grace and Spirit. It is not, indeed, a mansion pure enough for the pure and holy God; yet it is such, as thou wilt accept, and in which thou wilt dwell. There are still many hidden corruptions in it, but do thou search them out; and thou, who hast kept thy servant from presumptuous sins, do thou also cleanse me from secret faults." Thus a clear conscience, with a holy and reverend boldness, addresseth itself to God; and sweetly closeth up every duty and every prayer, with full assurance of obtaining mercy from God. So the Apostle (Heb. ix. 22): "Let us draw near . . . . in full assurance of faith:" how may we gain this full assurance, when we draw near to God? By "having our hearts sprinkled from an evil conscience:" get but a pure and clear conscience, and that will enable you to draw near to God in full assurance of faith, and so here (1 Jno. iii. 21): "Beloved, if our heart condemn us not, then have we confidence towards God:" if conscience be not evil to accuse us, then have we confidence towards God: when the face of man's conscience looks cheerful, and hath not a frown or a wrinkle upon it, this makes us joyfully to apprehend that God's face towards us is serene also, and that we shall be welcome at all times into our Father's presence: this conscience suggests to us, and makes us come with a holy, yet with an awful boldness unto God.—M.].

[BARROW:—No man can otherwise found any assurance of God's special love to him, than upon a good conscience: testifying that he doth sincerely love God, and endeavour faithfully to obey His commandments.—If we desire to judge reasonably about ourselves, or to know our true state, the only way is to compare our hearts and lives with the law of God, judging ourselves by that rule according to which God will judge us. If we find in our hearts the love of God and goodness (sincere although imperfect); if we perceive ourselves disposed to keep God's commandments (to live piously, righteously and soberly in this world); then may we have a satisfactory hope concerning our state; then "*we may* (as St. John saith) *have confidence toward God, because we keep His commandments and do those things that are pleas-*

ing to Him:" but if we do not find that mind in us, and that practice, we, in conceiting well of ourselves upon any other grounds, do but flatter and impose upon ourselves; if all the world should account us good, and take us to be in a good case, we should not at all believe them, or mind them; for *let no man deceive us, he that doeth righteousness, he* (and he alone) *is righteous*, is the most faithful advice and unquestionable sentence of St. John. It is therefore (that by resting on such false bottoms we be not abused, and drawn thence to neglect the amendment of our hearts and ways, in order to our final account) a duty incumbent upon us thus to search our hearts and try our ways, and accordingly to judge ourselves: the doing which with care and conscience would dispose us to prepare for the judgment we speak of; for, *If* (saith St. Paul) *we would judge ourselves, we should not be judged*, or not condemned. —M.].

[NEANDER:—(Christ), when about to part from His disciples, no more to be with them in His personal bodily presence, promised that He would be invisibly near and present among them, no less truly than during His earthly manifestation. The proof of this, His actual presence among them, should be the communication to them of His Spirit. This should be the medium between believers and their Saviour, until vision takes the place of faith; till that immediate view of Christ, enjoyed by His disciples in the familiar intercourse of his earthly life, is restored in heightened glory to believers. It is to this inward experience that the Apostle makes his appeal with these Churches and to it the inward experience of believers in all ages bears witness. Here, then, are conjoined two characteristic marks of fellowship with Christ which cannot be discovered from each other; the one inward, perceptible to the immediate inner consciousness, the other belonging to the outward life, but presupposing the former, of which it is at once the outward expression and the condition of its continuance. The first is–Participation in the Spirit —promised by Christ; the second, Obedience to His commandments, which is the fruit of that Spirit's agency, and in which such participation makes itself apparent. This being the Spirit's work, is also, as the evidence of this work, the condition of its continuance; all Divine gifts being conditioned upon the faithful use of what "is bestowed, according to the words of Christ: Whoso hath, to him shall be given."—M.].

[On vv. 19, 20 see *De corde condemnante*, Critici Sacri Thes. Nov. 2, 991.

v. 20. A *Sermon* by ROBERT SOUTH, D.D.
SERMON THEMES: *God greater than our heart.*
Conscience an earnest of the last judgment.
Use to be made of the misgivings of conscience.

vv. 20, 21. CHARLES SIMEON, *A good and evil conscience*, Works 20, p. 454.

v. 21. R. SOUTH, *The nature and measures of conscience*, 2 Sermons.

v. 23. ANDREW GRAY, *The mystery of faith opened up*, 6 Sermons.
ISAAC WILLIAMS, *The Gospel a feast of Love*, Serm. 2, 67.

v. 24. JOHN FLAVEL, *The Spirit's indwelling*, Works, 2, 328.
J. BASNAGE, *L'union de l'âme avec Jésus-Christ*, Serm. 2, 501. —M.].

6. *Warning and Exhortation with reference to the false teachers.*

CHAPTER IV. 1-6.

Beloved, believe not every spirit, but try the spirits whether they are of[1] God: be-
2 cause many false prophets are gone out into the world. Hereby know ye[2] the Spirit of
God: Every spirit that confesseth that Jesus Christ is come[3] in the flesh is of God:
3 And every spirit that confesseth not that Jesus[4] Christ is come in the flesh is not of[1]
God: and this is that *spirit* of antichrist, whereof ye have heard that it should come;
4 and even now already is it in the world.[5] Ye are of[1] God, little children, and have
5 overcome them: because greater is he that is in you, than he that is in the world. They
6 are of[1] the world: therefore speak they of[1] the world, and the world heareth them. We
are of God: he that knoweth God heareth us; he that is not of[1] God heareth not us.[6]
Hereby[7] know we the spirit of truth, and the spirit of error.

Verse 1. [[1] ἐκ, German: "out of."—M.]
Verse 2. [2] γινώσκετε A. B. C. G. al. Cod. Sin. has in the text γινώσκομεν, but corrected γινώσκετε.
[3] ἐληλυθότα A. C. Sinait.—B. reads ἐληλυθέναι; Vulgate: *venisse* conforming to the usage of Latin [German: "Every spirit which confesseth Jesus Christ come in the flesh."—M.]
Verse 3. [4] Instead of the reading of A. B. τὸν Ἰησοῦν, G. K. and Sin. have Χριστὸν ἐν σαρκὶ ἐληλυθότα, but G. has also the Article and Sin. reads κύριον instead of Χριστὸν. Both readings, the shorter τὸν Ἰησοῦν, and the longer agreeing with v. 2, are well authenticated, and either may pass for the original reading, it being equally probable that the longer reading was abbreviated into the shorter, and that the shorter was changed into the longer; the testimony for both renders the decision very difficult; but the shorter form seems to be the *lectio difficilior*.—By the side of the reading ὃ μὴ ὁμολογεῖ

τὸν Ἰησοῦν, the Church Fathers have the variation ὃ λύει τὸν Ἰησοῦν, among the Latins Tertullian (*negantes—et solventes*, adv. Marc. 5, 16), Augustine *qui solvit Jesum et negat in carne venisse*, also the two conjoined. It is repeatedly asserted, that the heretics suppressed λύειν (Socrates *h. l.* 7, 32; Fulbert and Hincmar: *Eraserunt*, in Tischendorf 1859 *editio major*). Bengel well observes: *humanam potius artem, quam apostolicam redolet* (λύει) *sapientiam*. It is a dogmatical *terminus technicus* to denote the Nestorianism which dissolves the union of the Godhead and the humanity in Jesus, Christ.

[Socrates, *H. E.* VII. 32: γέγραπτο ἐν τοῖς παλαιοῖς ἀντιγράφοις ὅτι πᾶν πνεῦμα ὃ λύει τὸν Ἰησοῦν, ἀπὸ τοῦ θεοῦ οὐκ ἔστιν. Irenæus (III, 8, p. 511 ed. Stieren): *Igitur omnes extra dispositionem sunt, qui sub obtentu agnitionis alterum quidem Jesum intelligunt, alterum autem Christum, et alterum Unigenitum, et alterum Salvatorem . . . Sententia enim eorum homicidalis, Deos quidem plures confingens et Patres multos simulans. Comminuens autem et per multa* dividens *Filium Dei; quos et Dominus nobis cavere prædixit, et discipulus ejus Joannes in prædicta epistola fugere eos præcepit dicens: "Multi seductores exierunt in hunc mundum, qui non confitentur Jesum Christum in carne venisse. Hic est seductor et Antichristus. Videte eos, ne perdatis quod operati estis." Et rursus in Epistola ait: "Multi pseudo-prophetæ exierunt de sæculo. In hoc cognoscite Spiritum Dei. Omnis spiritus qui confitetur Jesum Christum in carne venisse, ex Deo est. Et omnis Spiritus qui* solvit *Jesum, non est ex Deo, sed de antichristo est." Hæc autem similia sunt illi quod in Evangelio dictum est, quoniam "Verbum caro factum est, et habitavit in nobis."*—Origen on Matth. xxv. 14 (Vol. IV. 359–361 ed. Lommat.): *Secundum hanc divinitatis suæ naturam non peregrinatur, sed peregrinatur secundum dispensationem corporis quod suscepit . .—Haec autem dicentes non* solvimus *suscepti corporis hominem, cum sit scriptum apud Joannem "Omnis spiritus qui* solvit *Jesum non est ex Deo:" sed unicuique substantiæ proprietatem servamus. Si enim omnis homo fidelis "qui conjungitur Domino unus spiritus est:" quanto magis homo ille quem secundum dispensationem carnis Christus suscepit non est* solvendus *ab eo, nec alter est dicendus ab eo? Et vide quomodo ait: "Sicut homo peregre futurus" quoniam non erat homo, sed sicut homo et quasi homo peregrinabitur, qui erat ubique secundum divinitatis naturam."* While thus Irenæus and Origen clearly had the reading ὃ λύει before them, Polycarp, on the other hand, seems to quote, though loosely, the received text (Ep. ad. Philipp. cap. 7): Πᾶς γὰρ ὃς ἂν μὴ ὁμολογῇ Ἰησοῦν Χριστὸν ἐν σαρκὶ ἐληλυθέναι, ἀντίχριρτός ἐστι. καὶ ὃς ἂν μὴ ὁμολογῇ τὸ μαρτύριον τοῦ σταυροῦ ἐκ τοῦ διαβόλου ἐστί. καὶ ὃς ἂν μεθοδεύῃ τὰ λόγια τοῦ κυρίου πρὸς τὰς ἰδίας ἐπιθυμίας καὶ λέγῃ μήτε ἀνάστασιν μήτε κρίσιν εἶναι, οὗτος πρωτότοκός ἐστι τοῦ Σατανᾶ. [Alford].—Huther: Very singular is the opinion of Semler that ὃ λύει originated *oculorum vitio;* the reading may probably be accounted for from the polemics against Gnosticism (Grotius, Lücke, de Wette, Huther), and this supposition is borne out by the scholion in Matthæi p. 225: προώδευσαν γὰρ αὐτοῦ (τοῦ ἀντιχριστοῦ) αἱ αἱρέσεις, ὧν χαρακτεριστικὸν τὸ διὰ ψευδοπροφητῶν καὶ πνευμάτων λύειν τον Ἰησοῦν ἐν τῷ μὴ ὁμολογεῖν αὐτὸν ἐν σαρκὶ ἐληλυθέναι.—M.].

[German: "*And every spirit which does not confess Jesus is not of God.*"—M.]

[5 German: "*And this is the* [spirit] *of antichrist, of which ye have heard that it cometh, and now it is in the world already.*" So Alford.—M.].

Verse 6. [6] ὃς οὐκ ἔστιν ἐκ τοῦ θεοῦ, οὐκ ἀκούει ἡμῶν is wanting in A. G. (perhaps by mistake?)

[7] ἐκ τούτου B. G. K. Sinait; important on account of ch. iii. 24; ἐκ τοῦ πνεύματος.

[German: "*From this.*"—M.]

EXEGETICAL AND CRITICAL.

The difference of the spirits renders the trial necessary, v. 1.

VER. 1. **Beloved**:—The Apostle begins with ἀγαπητοί as ch. iii. 21 [cf. v. 7. ch. iii. 2.—M], in the joyful consciousness of the common blessings of the Divine adoption, and earnestly solicitous of inciting and exhorting those to the exhibition of brotherly love who are loved of God.

Believe not every spirit.—Here, as in ch. ii. 18–28, the Apostle adverts to the false teachers. Those who are to believe on the name of the Son of God (ch. iii. 23) in the power of the Holy Ghost (ch. iii. 24) given to them and bearing witness to their spirit that they are the children of God (cf. Rom. viii. 16), must not believe every spirit. The reference is to a plurality, a multitude of spirits (πάντι πνεύματι), not to a Dual but to a Plural. Hence, we must understand the expression of *the spirits of men* to whom *the spirit* bears witness. Every human spirit has its peculiarity, its special gifts and views, its mode of expression, which the animating, moving SPIRIT does not change or render uniform. Many a spirit might secure our approbation, sympathy and attention, which is not influenced by the Spirit of God. Hence the warning, to which, because of its great importance, there is forthwith annexed the exhortation: —"*But try the spirits whether they are of God.*" [Huther: The idea πνεῦμα is closely connected with ψευδοπροφῆται. The true prophets spoke, as we read 1 Pet. i. 21, ὑπὸ πνεύματος ἁγίου φερόμενοι; the source of the revelations whose utterers (πρόφημι) they are, is the πνεῦμα ἅγιον or the πνεῦμα τοῦ θεοῦ, whereby is described, not an affection of their mind, but the DIVINE POWER, different from their own individuality, which animates and influences them (δύναμις ὑψίστου, the synonyme of πνεῦμα ἅγιον, Luke i. 35.). This πνεῦμα speaks by the prophet, entering into his πνεῦμα and communicating to him the truth to be revealed; and thus the πνεῦμα of the prophet becomes a πνεῦμα ἐκ τοῦ θεοῦ. But since every prophet has his own πνεῦμα, there is, although the πνεῦμα ἅγιον is *One*, a plurality of prophetical spirits. The same relation takes place in an opposite direction, in the case of the pseudo-prophets. They also are under the influence of one spiritual being, to wit, under that of the πνεῦμα, that ἐκ τοῦ θεοῦ οὐκ ἔστι, the πνεῦμα τῆς πλάνης; this spirit also is *one*, but since it penetrates with its lie the πνεύματα of the pseudo-prophets and makes them like itself, we may say of the πνεῦμα of each individual prophet that is not of God, that it is not a πνεῦμα τῆς ἀληθείας, but a πνεῦμα τῆς πλάνης."—The rationalistic interpretation of Socinus ("*sensus hominis aliquo modo inspiratus*") and Episcopius ("*doctrina*"), and the figurative construction of the word πνεῦμα= λαλοῦντες ἐν πνεύματι of Lücke, de Wette and Calvin ("*pro eo qui spiritus dono se præditum esse jactat ad obeundum prophetiæ munus*"), are equally irrelevant.—M.].

But try the spirits whether they are of God.—John evidently speaks of a plurality of spirits (τὰ πνεύματα). Instead of a receiving surrender to and of agreeing with them, of the *assensus* (πιστεύειν) John requires a δοκιμάζειν, a cautious criticism before the κατέχειν (1 Thess. v. 21), and he requires it of all like Paul, Rom. xii. 2; Phil. i. 20; Eph. v. 10; I Cor. x. 15; xi. 13, although some may have a special gift in discern ing the spirits (1 Cor. xii. 10: διακρίσεις πνευμάτων Calvin: "*alloquitur—singulos fideles,*" as opposed to Lorinus: "*Non omnium est probare; unum oportet in ecclesia summum judicem quæstionum de fide moribusque; id est sine dubio Pontifex Maximus.*" [This may be conclusive reasoning to Romanists, but will be utterly repudiated by Protestants, as an arbitrary dictum repugnant to Holy Writ.—M.]. The falsity of this exposition is evident both from the object of this text which every man ought to know; εἰ ἐκ τοῦ θεοῦ ἐστίν, whether they are of, originate in or proceed from God: the confession of Jesus Christ come in the flesh (v. 2), and from the danger, urging such a test, to which every one is exposed and which necessitates the decision [the Apostle proceeds to specify the reason why this trial is necessary.—M.].

Because many false prophets are gone out into the world.—These ψευδοπροφῆται answer to the ἀντιχρίστοις (ch. ii. 18). Cf. Matth. vii. 15; xxiv. 11, 24 (where also ψευδόχριστοι are specified), 2 Pet. ii. 1 (where ψευδοδιδάσκαλοι are paralleled with the ψευδοπροφῆται of the Old Testament). The idea of predicting something future is not any more the prominent point here than it constitutes in general the leading characteristic of the prophet; he derives his name from πρόφημι, because he has, as it were, behind him the Spirit that inspires him, whose thoughts he speaks out and makes known. The true prophet must be clearly distinguished from the hidden πνεῦμα influencing him, the true prophet is ὑπὸ πνευμάτος ἁγίου φερόμενος (2 Pet. i. 21); this πνεῦμα δύναμις ὑψίστου (Luke i. 35). The point at which He unites with the prophet, is the prophet's πνεῦμα, which as an organ to be influenced, must be clearly distinguished from the πνεῦμα ἅγιον who operates through it; for the πνεῦμα ἅγιον is the Source and Principle of the revelation, enters into the prophet's πνεῦμα, moves and imparts to the prophet, animates and prompts him, and thus the prophet's πνεῦμα becomes a πνεῦμα ἐκ τοῦ θεοῦ, yet so that thereby the characteristics of the prophet's spirit are neither obliterated nor annulled, neither as to his temperament, nor as to his mode of utterance, nor as to qualification for specific relations of the spiritual or material worlds. Hence there are as many πνεύματα as there are προφῆται, notwithstanding the unity of the efficient principle which influences them. But alongside this πνεῦμα ἅγιον, πνεῦμα τῆς ἀληθείας, there is a πνεῦμα τοῦ ἀντιχρίστου (v. 3), τῆς πλάνης (v. 6), that makes the ψευδοπροφήτας and whose spirit must not be believed. The πνεῦμα and πνεύματα designate not absolutely ψευδοπροφῆται (Calvin, Lücke, de Wette and others), nor the *sensus hominis aliquo modo inspiratus* (Socinus), nor *doctrina* (Episcopius), nor the superhuman principle animating man (Greek Comment., Augustine, Luther, Spener, Bengel (*spiritui, quo doctor aliquis agitur*), Neander, Düsterdieck and others). Cf. Huther [whose note I have translated above, under "Believe not every spirit."—M.].—With ἐξεληλύθασιν εἰς τὸν κόσμον Düsterdieck appropriately compares γεγόνασιν ch. ii. 18. After ἐκ τοῦ θεοῦ we ought to supply a reference to the sending forth, the missionary activity which in the case of the false prophets is an aping of the Apostles and the prophets; they come from, proceed, go out from him that makes them prophets. Cf. Jno. viii. 42; xiii. 3; xvi. 27, etc. cf. ch. xvii. 18; Matth. xiii. 49. It is therefore neither=*in publicum prodire*, as Matth. xiii. 3; xxvi. 55; Mark i. 35; viii. 11; Acts vii. 7 (Grotius, Calov, Lücke, al.), nor=*ex apostolis et eorum ecclesia*, as in ch. ii. 19 (S. Schmidt), nor=*ex sedibus suis* 2 Jno. 7. (Bengel).—On εἰς τὸν κόσμον cf. Jno. vi. 14; x. 36. They come into the world, which Christ was sent to redeem, which belongs to Him, in order to destroy it with their αἱρέσεις ἀπωλείας. (2 Pet. ii. 1).

The standard of the trial. vv. 2, 3.

VER. 2. **In this know ye the Spirit of God.**—Ἐν τούτῳ here evidently points to the following sentence and γινώσκετε is not Indicative, but like πιστεύετε, δοκιμάζετε v. 1, the Imperative [on the other hand Alford, on account of the very frequent ἐν τούτῳ γινώσκομεν, would let analogy prevail and take it as Indicative; but Huther, de Wette, Lücke and most commentators take it as Imperative.—M.].—That τὸ πνεῦμα τοῦ θεοῦ denotes the Holy Spirit is evident both from the expression itself and from the antithesis τὸ τοῦ ἀντιχρίστου v. 3; the reference therefore is not to a *loquens de spiritualibus ex inspiratione divina* (Lyra). But the sequel shows that we have to think of the Divine Spirit working in the spirit of the prophets, to wit:

Every spirit which confesseth Jesus Christ come in the flesh, is of God.—Ὁμολογεῖν is the oral confession of a doctrinal truth (cf. 2 Jno. 10.), like ch. ii. 23 (Düsterdieck, Huther and al.); confession with a walk agreeing with a Christian is not indicated here (Greek comm., Augustine, Bede), even though only a confession with the mouth emanating from the faith of the heart under the influence of the indwelling Spirit of God can be meant here, as in Rom. x. 9, 10; cf. ch. v. 11 sq.; ii. 22 sq.—The object of the confession: Ἰησοῦν Χριστὸν ἐν σαρκὶ ἐληλυθότα. The form is that of a substantival objective-sentence; hence the participial form should be retained, and the rendering avoided which would make it an Infinitive thus: that Jesus Christ *is or has come* in the flesh; it is not a predicative sentence, but ἐν σαρκὶ ἐληλυθότα is added attributively; that which is known is added in the Accusative. The names are taken in their literal sense at ch. ii. 22; here they stand, as in ch. i. 3, in juxtaposition and must not be separated according to ch. ii. 22, as if they imported: *Jesus the Christ* who is come in the flesh; so Luther renders wrongly in his Scholia, and Huther inclines in that direction. In like manner ἐν σαρκὶ must be held fast and not be made equivalent to εἰς σάρκα, as maintained by Augustine, Luther, Calvin, Piscator, Sander and al.; ἐν σαρκὶ denotes the mode of existence, in which He appeared and came; nor is there any ground here to assume here a pregnancy common among the Greeks who conjoin ἐν with verbs of motion in order to describe the result, the *rest* (cf. Winer, p. 449), to wit, that He had come *into* the flesh in order to remain and work *in* the flesh; so S. Schmidt and others.—Jesus Christ came *in the flesh* from the time of His birth after He σὰρξ ἐγένετο and ἐσκήνωσεν ἐν ἡμῖν (Jno. i. 14) cf. ch. i. 1. sqq.—The *conversatio in carne, inter homines, in vera natura humana*, nor the *incarnatio*, which is pre-supposed as the transition, is meant here; nor is here a limiting reference to *innumera mala* and *ipsa cruenta mors*, as maintained by Socinus, who erroneously refers to Heb. ii. 14; v. 7, and Grotius who adverts to a Hebraism.—Ἔρχεσθαι indeed is often used to designate the appearance of teachers, but then it either occurs with a qualifying ἐπὶ τῷ ὀνόματι, Matth. xxiv. 5, or ἐν τῷ ὀνόματι, Jno. v. 43, or εἰς μαρτυρίαν, Jno. i. 7, or with an indication of the subject as ἐμπαῖκται, 2 Pet. iii. 3, or an addition like καὶ ταύτην τὴν διδαχὴν οὐ φέρει, 2 Jno. 10, or as in Matth. xi. 18, of John, μήτε ἐσθίων μήτε πίνων or as in Matth. xvii. 11 of Elias καὶ ἀποκαταστήσει πάντα, so that the context invariably marks either the appearance of the teacher, or distinctly states that he is not exclusively referred to as a teacher, namely in his vocation of teacher. Here also the reference seems not to be exclusively to the office of a teacher or a prophet, which is by no means indicated by ἐν σαρκί. But it is important to notice here the tense: for while we have in this place the *part. perfecti* ἐληλυθότα, ch. v. 6 gives the *part. aor.* ὁ ἐλθὼν and 2 Jno. 7 the *part. præs.* ἐρχόμενον; the Present denotes the fact which is not a single act, in a moment, like birth, but has a longer duration which may be seen and represents this in a timeless form; the Aorist denotes an act as purely historical, the Perfect an act which, though historically completed, has present continuance (Winer, Part III. § 40). Thus this confession contains the fundamental truth of the Gospel; Χριστὸς and ἐν σαρκὶ ἐληλυθότα indicate the dignity and existence of the Son of God and emphatically assert His humanity as a reality and a historical fact for all time. Bengel excellently remarks: "*In carne, est ergo Ipse aliquid præter carnem; hæreses veritatem carnis Jesu Christi negantes præsupponunt et eo ipso confirmant* DEITATEM *ejus, quippe cum qua non poterant conciliare carnem, tanquam ea dignam.*"

VER. 3. **And every spirit which confesses not Jesus, is not of God.**—Τὸν Ἰησοῦν comprehends what was said in v. 2, viz.; Χριστὸν ἐν σαρκὶ ἐληλυθότα, it is just the historical Christ and none other.—Ὃ μὴ ὁμολογεῖ=*if he does not* confess, while ὃ οὐχ ὁμολογεῖ would be=*who does not* confess. From this it is evident that John contemplates not so much distinct persons, as only distinct doctrines. Winer, part III. § 55. [Huther observes that μή denotes the *contradiction* of the true confession, while οὐ would express only a simple denial.—M.].

And this is the (spirit) **of antichrist, of which ye have heard that it cometh, and now it is in the world already.**—Τοῦτο refers to πνεῦμα, not to ὁμολογεῖν, and τὸ τοῦ ἀντιχρίστου is the (πνεῦμα) of antichrist; for τὸ pre-supposes a substantive or constitutes a substantival idea; were it, as Valla, Episcopius, Huther and al. render, *proprium antichristi*, matter of antichrist, τοῦτο would not refer to πνεῦμα but to ὁμολογεῖν; this would be rather an artificial construction and τὸ before τοῦ ἀντίχριστου would be superfluous. The passages adduced, viz. Matth. xxi. 21; 1 Cor. x. 24; 2 Pet. ii. 22; Jas. iv. 14, are somewhat different, for they import one and all a substantival idea, τὸ τῆς συκῆς, τὸ ἑαυτοῦ, τὸ τῆς παροιμίας, τὸ τῆς αὔριον [that of the fig tree, that of himself, that of the proverb, the event of the morrow—M.], while here the Genitive alone would have been sufficient.—Ἀκηκόατε refers not to the written word ch. ii. 18 where we have already ἠκούσατε, but to the previous oral instruction they had received. The last clause καὶ νῦν ἐν τῷ κόσμῳ ἐστὶν ἤδη, which emphatically asserts that the spirit of antichrist is already now, at the present time, working in the antichrists, is not governed by ἀκηκόατε but coördinated with καὶ τοῦτό ἐστιν τὸ τοῦ ἀντιχρίστου. Cf. ch. ii. 18.

Comfortable strengthening and assurance against the false prophets. vv. 4–6.

VER. 4. **Ye are of God, little children.**—The Apostle moved, and affectionately confident (τεκνία) that they all stand in the fundamental truth and are the children of God (ch. iii. 1, 2, 13, 14), urgently represents to them (ὑμεῖς emphatically placed first as in ch. ii. 24, 27), what is given to them: ἐκ τοῦ θεοῦ ἐστέ, agreeing with the leading thought ch. ii. 29 and the context: the trial to be made is εἰ ἐκ τοῦ θεοῦ ἐστίν (v. 1) and he that confesseth Jesus is ἐκ τοῦ θεοῦ ἐστίν (v. 3) and he that confesseth not Jesus ἐκ τοῦ θεοῦ οὐκ ἔστιν.

And have overcome them.—Αὐτοὺς are the ψευδοπροφήτας (v. 1), in whom the πνεῦμα τοῦ ἀντιχρίστου is operative and connected with their πνεῦμα. Hence not: *antichristum et mundum* (Erasmus); the Vulgate renders falsely *eum*, which Lyra interprets: *mundum, devincendo concupiscentiam*, and other Roman Catholics: *antichristum* or *spiritum antichristi in antichristis*.—The Perfect νενικήσατε as at ch. ii. 13, 14, where τὸν πονηρόν is the person overcome. The victory referred to there is inward in their hearts, here it is a victory not only in their hearts but also outward, visible in the life, in the sphere of their church-life, the Church; in the former place the victory is over Satan himself, here over his false prophets. But it is a victory actually achieved, and moreover a victory of continuous duration notwithstanding a succession of conflicts; through these very struggles and conflicts runs the victory already achieved and decisive, ye *have* overcome! ye have it! by your fidelity they with their seductive arts and temptations have been confounded (Ebrard). Cf. Jno. xvi. 33. Νενικήκατε is the Perfect not *propter futuritionis certitudinem* (Episcopius),=*potestis superare* (Rosenmüller). Calvin renders not very accurately: "*In media pugna jam extra periculum sunt, quia futuri sunt superiores.*" The ground of their victory and overcoming lies indeed in them, yet nevertheless above them.

Because He (that is) **in you is greater than he** (that is) **in the world.**—Ὁ ἐν ὑμῖν is He of (out of) whom they are, who abideth in them (ch. iii. 24; iv. 1, 2), that is ὁ θεός (Greek Comm., Calvin, Bengel, de Wette, Sander, Düsterdieck, Huther); this is also clear from the antithesis; it is understood of Christ by Augustine, Grotius, etc.—Ὁ ἐν τῷ κόσμῳ=ὁ διάβολος, whose children (τέκνα) the antichrists are, ch. iii. 10*a*—God is not only greater than our heart (ch. iii 20), but also greater than Satan, than all things (Jno. x. 29; 2 Cor. ii. 14); all things belong to Him (1 Cor. xv. 57; iii. 23).—[Huther: "Instead of the more specific ἐν αὐτοῖς the Apostle uses ἐν τῷ κόσμῳ to intimate that the former, though having been for some time in the Church, belong to the κόσμος, which is expressly declared in the words following. Socinus: "*Quamvis Johannes, non de eo, qui sit in falsis prophetis, sed de eo, qui sit in mundo, verba faciat, tamen necesse est, ut mundi appellatione falsos istos Prophetas comprehendat, vel potius plane intelligat, quod satis aperte declarant sequentia verba.*"—M.].

VER. 5. *The antithesis as to essence, work and success:*

They are of the world.—Ἐκ τοῦ κόσμου, *quatenus Satanas est ejus princeps* (Calvin), hence not ἐξ ἡμῶν (ch. ii. 19). Cf. Jno. viii. 23, 44. The reference is not only to worldly lusts and carnal desires but to the ground and source of their life determining the exhibition of their life (διὰ τοῦτο).

Therefore they speak of the world and the world heareth them.—The substance of what they speak and their success with the world are conditioned by their being of [*out of, from*—as to origin—M.] the world. This λαλεῖν ἐκ τοῦ κόσμου also is deep-reaching: *ex mundi vita ac sensu sermones suos promere* (Bengel). Huther capitally distinguishes λαλεῖν ἐκ τοῦ κόσμου from ἐκ τῆς γῆς λαλεῖν (Jno. iii. 31) by the remark that ἡ γῆ is not an ethical notion like ὁ κόσμος. Although the separate points made by Oecumenius (κατὰ τὰς σαρκικὰς ἐπιθυμίας), the Scholiasts (ἐκ τῆς πονηρᾶς αὐτῶν γνώμης), Luther (*ea quæ mundus intelligit ac probat*), Grotius (*mundi affectibus congruentia*) and others, are correct, yet they shed light only on particular points and not on the whole. The approval and agreement of the world constitute a proof against them on the principle τῷ γὰρ ὁμοίῳ τὸ ὅμοιον προστρέχει. Cf. Jno. viii. 37, 43, 47; xviii. 37. [The false prophets left the Church and went out into the world to which they stood in inward affinity, and proclaimed to it a wisdom that originated in it; therefore the world *heard* them, *i. e.* approved and assented to their word; τῷ γὰρ ὁμοίῳ κ. τ. λ. (Oecumenius); whereas the believers were hated and persecuted by the world, Huther.—M.].—Αὐτῶν ἀκούει denotes hearing attentively with inward delight, while ἀκούειν τινα signifies hearing in general without determining the sympathy of the hearer.

Inference and conclusion. v. 6.

VER. 6. **We are of God.**—A quickly added contrast of the false prospects without δὲ. After what precedes there are here implied the two thoughts which are not expressed: διὰ τοῦτο ἐκ τοῦ θεοῦ λαλοῦμεν καὶ ὑμεῖς ἡμῶν ἀκούετε, although the latter is indicated by ὁ γινώσκων τὸν θεὸν ἀκούει ἡμῶν. Hence the Apostle understands by ἡμεῖς himself with the Apostles and the teachers in the Church (and not himself and the Church ὑμεῖς), as opposed to αὐτοὶ (v. 5) and the ψευδοπροφῆται (v. 1). This is the view of most commentators in opposition to Calvin, Spener, Lücke and al.

He that knoweth God, heareth us; he who is not of God doth not hear us.—The antithesis ὁ γινώσκων τὸν θεὸν and ὃς οὐκ ἔστιν ἐκ τοῦ θεοῦ requires, as is well known, that we should understand in the former clause ἐκ τοῦ θεοῦ εἶναι and supply in the second γινώσκειν τὸν θεὸν as the consequence. Hence ἐκ τοῦ θεοῦ εἶναι must not be taken here differently from vv. 1–4 and according to the contrast in v. 5. It is consequently not a general drawing and impulse towards God (as held by Lücke and Neander), but the state of grace of God's children, and their understanding of and conduct towards the word of God as preached to them. But nothing is said here concerning the manner how they did come into this state, nor is here any reference to predetermination (Hilgenfeld) or predestination (Calvin); we know also from ch. ii. 2, iv. 14; cf. Jno. iii. 16; i. 10 sqq. 29, that *all* are desired and may enter into the sonship. [Alford: Here we must remember carefully what the context is and what its purpose. The Apostle is giving a test to distinguish, not the children of God from those who are not children of God, but the spirit of truth from the spirit of error, as is clear from the words following. And this he does by saying that in the case of the teachers of the truth, they are heard and received by those who apprehend God, but refused by those who are not of God. It is evident then that these two terms here, ὁ γινώσκων τὸν θεόν, and ὃς οὐκ ἔστιν ἐκ τοῦ θεοῦ represent two patent matters of fact, two classes open and patent to all: one of them identical with the κόσμος above: the other consisting of those of whom it is said above, ἐγνώκατε τὸν πατέρα . . . . ἐγνώκατε τὸν ἀπ' ἀρχῆς, ch. ii. 13, 14. How these two classes are what they are, it is not the purpose of this passage to set forth, nor need we here inquire; we have elsewhere tests to distinguish them, ch. iii. 9, 10 . . . . ; we have a striking parallel, in fact the key to these words, in the saying of our Lord to Pilate, John xviii. 37.—M.].

From this we know the Spirit of truth and the spirit of error (deception).—Ἐκ τούτου refers to hearing, but since the matter in hand relates to the trial of the spirits that teach, the reference is to hearing the false prophets and to hearing the Apostles and the ministers of the Divine word [*i. e.* to the reception given to both classes.—M.]. Hence we must not think here of the criterion specified in vv. 2, 3, as maintained by the Roman Catholic Comm., Calvin, Hunnius, Calov and Neander.

In γινώσκομεν John includes the Apostles and the Church. On τὸ πνεῦμα τῆς ἀληθείας, cf. Jno. xiv. 17; xv. 26; xvi. 13; from which passages it is evident that the Genitive indicates that which the Spirit gives, testifies, whereto He helpeth and whither He guideth and leadeth; He is that Spirit that proceedeth from God and teacheth the truth to men. In like manner, τὸ πνεῦμα τῆς πλάνης is the spirit proceeding from the devil, deceiving and seducing men (ch. i. 8; ii. 26; 2 Jno. 8, 1 Tim. iv. 1, 1 Thess. ii. 3; 2 Thess. ii. 11.) The latter is certainly in him whom the world hears, the former in Him to whom the children of God give ear.

DOCTRINAL AND ETHICAL.

1. Δοκιμάζειν is used here as by St. Paul, (see notes on v. 1, in Exegetical and Critical) and as the Lord Himself bids His Church do, Matth. vii. 15, 16. The Roman Catholic proposition: "*Ecclesia in suis prælatis est judex controversiarum*" is not true; they limit to the *ecclesia repræsentans* and to the [visible] head of that, what the Lord of the Church and his Apostles say to all believers. However it is important to remember that the Apostle restricts this right and duty of trial

simply to the question whether the teachers are of God, and that he does not mean questions affecting the learning, wisdom or eloquence of teachers, or questions of secondary importance and on controversial points; he only refers to that which is necessary to the salvation of our souls. On this head every Christian ought and may, if necessary, apply the test.

2. The believing Confession of One Jesus Christ uniting in Himself the Godhead and the Manhood, even the confession of the historical Christ is necessary to salvation and essentially Christian. John, of course, understands *ὁμολογεῖν* as engaging the powers of the whole Christian and not only the oral confession without the heart; for he adverts to the *πνεύματα*, specifies the antithesis *μὴ ὁμολογεῖν* and proceeds throughout in a contemplative manner. If this were not so, the true disciples of Jesus would have the same confession as the demons as their distinguishing mark (Luke iv. 41; Matth. viii. 29); hence the *contents* of the confession are not decisive *per se.* Cf. Harless, *Ethik* § 39** p. 174.—But Estius has no warranty for limiting St. John's direction to the apostolical age and for considering the confession of the Lord's Supper as the criterion now; on the former confession depends also the latter, for the doctrine of the Lord's Supper reflects of course the Christology, since the fellowship with Christ is accomplished in the most pregnant manner in the Sacrament of the Lord's Supper. Nothing is truly Christian without the living Christ.

3. According to the Johannean mode of expression the contrast brought out here is to be conceived as an error wholly gnostic, spiritualizing and misinterpreting the historic and directed more against the corporealness, *i. e.* the manhood of Christ than against his Godhead, an error rather Docetical than Ebionite. For *σάρξ* does not denote merely the human body apart from the human *ψυχή*, the human *νοῦς*, the human will or self-consciousness, which could not be done by the preposition *ἐν*, but it signifies the human nature, the manhood; and this is conceived in the precise manner in which He appeared in the world. Cf. Hofmann, *Schriftbeweis* ii. 1. p. 76, sq.

4. John does not predicate of man independence, self-glory and perfect freedom in the sphere of his spiritual life; either the Spirit of God or the spirit of Satan determines the spirit of man and conditions his views, inclinations, knowledge, words and deeds. Behind the *πνεῦμα* of man stands the directing, determining, operating and fulfilling *πνεῦμα*, which through the former and united with it, works on the world and on men.

5. But any disposition of the human spirit for the Spirit of God or the spirit of Satan is no more taken for granted here than that the Spirit of God and the spirit of Satan are or might be supposed to be in a state of coördination. Rather, we should say, does this victory, of which the Apostle discourses in such lofty strains (v. 4, cf. ch. ii. 13, 14; v. 4, 5), assert the superiority of the Divine Spirit to Satan and denote both the monarchy of God and the enmity of Satan, at the same time intimating however, that, though men may suffer themselves to be controlled either by God or Satan, all men ought to be and might become God's.

6. The Apostle contemplates the reality and the possession of the Divine sonship (*εἶναι ἐκ τοῦ θεοῦ=γεγεννῆσθαι ἐκ τοῦ θεοῦ*), which is evident from his specification of the marks whereby the existence of this relation may be determined; the reference, therefore, is not to the origin, the beginning of one's being of God, to the manner how it is attained. The same remark applies to Jno. xviii. 36, 37 and also to ch. viii. 43-47, as is manifest from v. 30: *πολλοὶ ἐπίστευσαν εἰς αὐτὸν* and v. 31: *ἐὰν μείνητε ἐν τῷ λόγῳ τῷ ἐμῷ.* The sonship or state of grace of faith in Jno. viii. is however quite young and only begun, while the case before Pilate and in the passage under notice respects the believing people in His Kingdom and under His Rule. According to the Johannean conception we have to view the sonship or state of grace of believers as complete from the beginning although ever progressing towards perfection and consummation and to the inheritance itself. A young babe or a suckling is surely a perfect man, a rational creature, though only as to the germ, and not yet a man, not yet fully developed in all the powers and gifts wherewith it is endowed.

[7. As supplemental to the exegetical notes on v. 3, and No. 3, above, it may be profitable to put together some of the interpretations of this difficult passage.

1. The *Socinian.*—Socinus: "*Jesum Christum,* i. e. *Jesum qui dicitur Christus, non modo mortalem hominem fuisse, sed etiam innumeris malis et denique ipsi cruentæ morti obnoxium.*" Grotius: "*Non cum regia pompa et exercitibus, sed in statu humili, abjecto, multisque malis ac postremum cruci obnoxio.*" But it has been shown that *ἐν σαρκί* cannot be construed in this sense.
2. Those *assertive* and not only implicative of our Lord's Incarnation. The commentators, most of them orthodox, who give this interpretation, either confound *ἐν σαρκί* with *εἰς σάρκα* (Augustine, Luther, Calvin, Piscator, Sander and al.), or waver between *ἐν* and *εἰς*, *e. g.* Hunnius: "*Tunc venire in carne dicitur Jesus Christus quando λόγος ex sua velut arcana sede prodiens assumta visibili carne se in terris manifestat.* Here we must also name the exposition of Augustine, who introduces in the train of the Incarnation the death and redeeming love of Christ, and makes the confession denial depend on "*caritatem habere*" (Alford); saying: "*Deus erat et in carne venit: Deus enim mori non poterat, caro mori poterat: ideo ergo venit in carne ut moreretur pro nobis. Quemadmodum autem mortuus est pro nobis? Majorem hac caritatem nemo habet, quam ut animam suam ponat pro amicis suis. Caritas ergo illum adduxit ad crucem. Quisquis ergo non habet caritatem, negat Christum in carne venisse.*"—To put the question in his own words; "Arius and Eunomius, and Macedonius and Nestorius own that Jesus Christ came in the flesh, are not they therefore of God?" and then replies that those hierarchs did *not* in fact *confess* Christ to have come in the flesh, because whatever they might do by *words*, they in their *works* denied Him (Tit. i. 16). "They have not *charity,*" he

says "because they have not *unity*, and therefore all their other gifts are of no avail." (1 Cor. xiii. 1–3).—But the Apostle says here nothing of charity, or unity, or of the love of Christ, but he simply asserts the true Manhood of our Lord, and this brings us

3. To the true interpretation which takes ἐν in its proper meaning and applies the passage to the case of the *Docetæ* who maintained that our Lord had only an apparent and not a real body. See also the extracts from Irenæus and Origen above in *Appar. Crit.* note 4.—M.].

HOMILETICAL AND PRACTICAL.

The command: Try! 1. The occasion (v. 1: many false prophets); 2. The importance (v. 1: whether they are of God); 3. The difficulty (v. 1: the spirits); 4. The right (v. 4: ye are of God); 5. The standard (vv. 1, 3: the confession and the contradiction, cf. v. 6.).—Be not afraid of the majority of votes, but fear the majesty of the truth of (out of) God; take care that thou do not violate it; the former cannot and must not have any influence in matters of eternal truth and of eternal life. Not from the masses comes the truth, but from One, with whom you ought to vote and to whom you ought to assent; but though it comes only *from* One it is nevertheless designed *for* all and should be brought to and diffused among the masses by means of preaching, testimony and confession.—You ought to regard as a Christian and a brother whoever clings to Christ in faith, no matter how heretical the sect to which he may belong.—Communities and Christians grow more and more imperfect, the former into sects and the latter illiberal in proportion as they strive to give undue prominence to any one point of the truth except that of a believing and vital confession of Christ. You may not even push into the background the sphere of creation with its appointments before redemption and its glory, for Christ is also the Creator of the world.—The question is the pursuit of victory in order to secure and preserve unimpaired eternal peace for eternity.—The fundamental truth is simple and ever plain to the simplicity of the heart. That with which you are familiar you understand and love; what you cling to, cleaves to you; that in which you live, lives in you; that, for and of which you speak, speaks out of you.—Either a prophet of God or a false prophet, either of God or of the world, moved either by the Spirit of God or by the spirit of antichrist, by the Spirit of truth or the spirit of error; a middle way and a third course are not provided.—Neither you nor any of your acquaintance may be able clearly to perceive your point of gravity, but it is there, and One, now a Saviour, but hereafter the Judge, knows where and what it is and will make it manifest in preliminary judgments here, but in the final judgment there.

STARKE:—Trust, believe, whom? It concerns not riches and possessions, but your soul and salvation. It is amazing that most men are concerned about false wares, whereby they incur certain and eternal loss. The prudent will make inquiries and not join in with an inconsiderate credit.—Lying spirit, that sayest that the Christian religion is founded on credulity: Gross lies! it requires faith, but rejects credulity. —We ought to believe sincere, experienced and honest teachers, yet so that we look only and solely to God and rest in Him as the author of the wisdom which they proclaim. Teachers should willingly subject their teaching to the trial of others, even to the trial of their own hearers, and consequently not only not deter them from it but also to urge them to it, and direct them away from themselves to God and His Spirit; otherwise they will not make honest Christians but render themselves suspicious.—The government alone has not the power of appointing teachers at its option regardless of the views and wishes of the whole Church (or congregation), whose wishes should be duly consulted, for God has clothed it also with the power and ability to try the spirits. [Such a caution, however relevant on the Continent of Europe, is of course unnecessary in the U. S.—M.].—Whatever obscures and lessens in word or deed the person, office, doctrine and glory of Christ, is heretical.—Be of good courage! though the world and the devil rage, thou hast a strong support, for God, who is with, by and in thee, is greater than all.—Whenever we are victorious, we ought to ascribe the glory of our victory not to ourselves but to God; otherwise if we take the least credit to ourselves, we rouse a new enemy, spiritual pride, most dangerous in this that it enables Satan easily to overcome us.—Like seeks like; the world loves its own but hates those who have gone out from the world.

HEUBNER:—The Christian spirit of trial is intimately connected with faith. Faith is not credulity.—This trying is a duty which belongs to every age and especially in our age when so many teach against the Scripture and still set up the pretension that they have the Spirit, and consider themselves full of spirit and others spiritless. It is the duty of all Christians; consequently, also the duty of the laity.—The conditions of this trial are simplicity of heart, a firm faith, and prayer to the Lord for clearness of perception (to open our eyes). The deceived have indeed excuses to offer; but there would not be so many of the deceived, if they had a pure mind and would try. Try the more frequently and carefully, the more the spirit of deceivers flatters thee and thy vanity, and the greater the number of these spirits grow.—Everything which lays irreverent hands on the Person of Christ, from any side, is decidedly unchristian.—Should John have given us a false criterion? Maintaining this is already the sign of a bad cause. Whatever is anti-christian shows its true character by its contradicting the Apostles. The superiority of the Spirit of Christ to the error-spirit of the world gives to the Christian the preponderance; he need not fear any assaults of unbelief. John foretells certain victory. All the shouts of victory on the part of unbelievers are nothing but false alarm. All antichristianity panders to the spirit of the world; it flatters, if not the loose morality, yet the vanity and conceit of the world which finds it burdensome and confounding to believe in the Crucified One.—The false apostles prove the dignity of the true Apostles.

BESSER:—Any pupil in a catechism-class, in order to be on his guard against the false prophets, may determine whether the teaching of a prophet has the grape-taste of Christ's vine or the sloe-taste of the thorn of the flesh and reason.—It is not because of the parts of the truth they hold in common with the Church, but because of the error wherewith they contradict the confession of the Church, because of the broken branch on the tree of truth, because of the cancer in the body of truth, that the sects are congregated as separate communities.

KRUMMACHER:—*The frontier of Christianity.* 1. *In which way is it decided?* Are the cumbersome trinity, God, virtue and immortality, or birth within the pale of Christendom, individual interpretation, the opinion of the majority of one's contemporaries—to determine Christianness? 2. *The final infallible decision,* over against the skeptics, those who are at variance with the confessions, those who only seek for the word of God in the Scriptures but do not receive the Scriptures as the word of God, is given by the fundamental fact of the *supernatural revelation* in Christ, the necessity of *regeneration,* the *personal preëxistence of Christ* or of the *Godhead.*

FRONMÜLLER:—*Of the trial of the Spirits.* 1. *Why it is necessary?* Many false spirits have gone out into the world, the spirit of antichrist is already now in the world—in the Church, in the school, in the family, in private life, in the great and in the small. 2. *Which is its end and aim?* Whether they are of God or not. 3. *Which is its rule?* The confession.

[BURKITT: v. 1.—*Believe not every spirit,* etc. That is, every teacher who pretends to be inspired, and every doctrine that lays claim to the authority of Divine revelation: "but try the spirits," that is, examine their doctrine by the rule of the word of God, and try from whom they come, whether from the Spirit of God or from Satan.—M.].

[BP. HALL: v. 2.—Every one who confesseth Jesus Christ to have been God from all eternity, and in the fulness of time to have taken our nature upon Him, and to be come in the flesh, to accomplish the perfect work of man's redemption, is of God and speaks from God. And so by the contraries v. 3.—M.].

[BARROW:—He was not only (as the Gnostics and some other heretics have conceited) in shape and outward appearance (as a spectre, deluding men's sight and fancy), but in most real truth, a very perfect man; having a real body, figured and circumscribed like ours, compacted of flesh and blood, visible and tangible; which was nourished and did grow, which needed and received sustenance, which was tender and sensible, frail and passible, which was bruised with stripes, torn with scourges, pricked with thorns, pierced with nails, transfixed with a spear; which was mortal and underwent death by expiring its breath, and being disjoined from the soul that enlivened it. He had also a soul, endued with the same faculties as ours; with an understanding capable of learning and improvement (for He was a man, ignorant of some things which He might know: and *He grew in wisdom and in stature*), with a will, subject and submissive to the Divine Will (see Mark xiii. 32; Luke ii. 52; Matth. xxvi. 39; Luke xxii. 42; Jno. v. 30; Matth. xxi. 18; Jno. iv. 6, 7), with several appetites, of meat, of drink, of sleep and rest (for we read that He was hungry, that He thirsted, that He was weary), yea with various passions and affections (φυσικὰ καὶ ἀδιάβλητα πάθη, I mean, that is, natural and irreprehensible passions), and these of the most troublesome and afflictive sort, such as zeal, pity and sorrow; the which were sometimes declared by very pathetical significations and are expressed in high terms; as upon occasion of His friend Lazarus's death it is said, *He groaned in Spirit and was troubled;* He then and upon other occasions, out of pity and sorrow, did *weep;* and ye know what excesses of sorrow, what anxieties and agonies, what tribulations, disturbances and amazements, the Evangelists, using those very terms, describe Him to have undergone at His passion; so that, as the Apostle to the Hebrews speaketh, "*We have not an highpriest that could not compassionate* (or sympathize with) *our infirmities, but who was in all points tempted* (or exercised and proved) *as we are, yet without sin.*"—M.].

[NEANDER:—Here is no other test of true faith, no other law for Christian union, than steadfast adherence to that one fundamental fact of the appearing of the Divine-human Redeemer. In all which proceeds from this belief, the influences of the Divine Spirit should be acknowledged. Hence it follows, that provided faith in this one fundamental fact be the soul of the Christian life, no minor difference of creed should be allowed to disturb Christian unity; that mistakes and alloys of Christian truth, which trench not on this one fundamental fact, should not hinder us from recognizing the Divine Stamp in him whose faith and profession have their root therein,—that the bonds of Christian fellowship should not thereby be sundered or loosened. Steadfast adherence to this one foundation is the mark of being from God, of the Spirit derived from God.—

Truth and error have each their peculiar history of development. As in the continued development of Christian truth, the Holy Spirit is ever revealing Himself in the inward consciousness of believers, that Anointing spoken of by St. John; so does error, proceeding side by side with this revelation, mingle therewith its own disturbing and adulterating influence,—rending single truths from their connection with the whole system of truth and giving them the stamp of error. These are the two currents, proceeding from the ever operative Spirit of Christ and from the spirit of the world; the latter mingling with the revelations of the former its own disturbing element and imitating them with a deceptive outward seeming.—M.].

[*Sermons and Sermon-themes.*

v. 1. AUGUSTINE, *Believe not every Spirit.* Libr. of Fathers, 20. 954.

TILLOTSON, ABP. *Of the trial of the Spirits.* Sermons 2, 29.

WATERLAND, DANIEL, *The springs and motives of false pretences to the Holy Spirit; with the rules and marks of trying and detecting them.* Sermons. Works 9, 336.

EDWARDS, JONATHAN, *The distinguishing marks of a work of the Spirit of God, applied to that uncommon operation that has lately appeared in New England.* 120. 1742. Works. 2, 254.

ZOLLIKOFFER, C. J. *Fanaticism in general.*
Fanaticism with regard to religious conceptions in particular. Sermons on prevalent errors and vices I. 95. 111.

SMITH, JOHN PYE, *On the means of obtaining satisfaction with regard to the truth of religious sentiments.* A Sermon, London, 1822.

v. 2. AUGUSTINE, *Every Spirit that confesseth not,* etc. Libr. of the Fathers 20, 960.
De probatione Spiritum. Cr. Sac. Thes. Nov. 2. 999.

vv. 2, 3. WILBERFORCE, R. I., *The sacramental system.* Serm. on the New Birth, 222.
VAUGHAN, I. C., *John's test of truth.* Sermons (1851), 121.

v. 4. SAURIN, I., *The superior evidence and influence of Christianity.* Sermons; 2, 323. In French, 7, 129.
Extraordinary gifts of the Holy Ghost.

vv. 4, 5. TILLOTSON, ABP., *The advantages of truth in opposition to error.* 2 Sermons. Serm. XI. 389.—M.].

7. *Brotherly love and Divine love as related to each other on the ground of Christ's advent.*

CHAPTER IV. 7–21.

7 Beloved, let us love one another: for[1] love is of God; and every one that loveth[2] is
8 born of God, and knoweth God. He that loveth not, knoweth[3] not God;[4a] for God is
9 love. In this was manifested the love of God toward[4b] us, because[5] that God sent his
10 only begotten Son[6] into the world, that we might live through him. Herein[7] is[8] love,
not that we loved God, but that he[9] loved us, and sent[10] his Son *to be* the propitiation
11 for our sins.[11] Beloved, if God so loved us, we ought also to love one another.
12 No man hath seen God at any time.[12] If we love one another, God dwelleth[13] in us,
13 and his love is perfected in us.[14] Hereby[15] know we that we dwell[16] in him, and he in
14 us, because[16] he hath given us of his Spirit. And we have seen and do testify that
15 the Father sent the Son *to be* the Saviour of the world.[17] Whosoever[18] shall confess[19]
16 that Jesus[20] is the Son of God, God dwelleth[13] in him, and he in God. And we have
known and believed the love that God hath to[21] us. God is love; and he that dwell-
17 eth[13] in love dwelleth[13] in God, and God in him.[22] Herein[23] is our love[24] made per-
fect,[25] that we may have boldness in the day of judgment: because as he is, so[26] are we
18 in this world. There is no fear in love;[27] but perfect love casteth out fear: because
19 fear hath torment.[28] He that feareth is not made perfect in love.[29] We love him,[30]
20 because he first loved us. If a man say,[31] I love God, and hateth his brother, he is a
liar: for he that loveth not his brother whom he hath seen, how[32] can he love God
21 whom he hath not seen? And this commandment have we from him, That he who
loveth God love his brother also.[33]

Verse 7. [1 German: "The love."—M.]
2 πᾶς ὁ ἀγαπῶν without τὸν θεὸν, B. C. Sin. al.—A. adds τὸν θεὸν.

Verse 8. [3 German: "Knew not God;" Alford: "hath never known God;" Lücke "hath never learned to know Him at all." The force of the Aorist that he hath not once known God should be brought out.—M.]
4a ὁ μὴ ἀγαπῶν οὐκ ἔγνω τὸν θεὸν is wanting in Cod. Sin., but adds ἔγνωκὲν instead of γινώσκει (from v. 7). A.

Verse 9. [4b ἐν ἡμῖν=German: "*in* us" (*an uns*) "in regard to us." Alford.—M.]
[5 ὅτι, not "because" but "that;" so German, Alford, Lillie.—M.]
[6 German: "His Son, the only begotten."—M.]

Verse 10. [7 ἐν τούτῳ; render "In this" as in v. 9. instead of the unnecessary variation "herein" of E. V.—M.]
[8 German: "exists" Wordsworth "consists."—M.]
9 αὐτὸς, the most authentic reading; A has ἐκεῖνος.
10 Instead of ἀπεστείλεν, Cod. Sin. reads ἀπέσταλκεν as in vv. 9, 14.
[11 German: "And sent His Son as propitiation for our sins." More correctly: "And sent His Son a propitiation for our sins." No need for the supplement *to be* in E. V.—M.]

Verse 12 [12 German: "God hath no one ever seen." Alford: "God hath no one ever beheld." But render more idiomatically: "No one has ever beheld God."—M.]
[13 μένει, μένομεν, etc., had better be rendered uniformly "abide."—M.]

[14] There is a great variation in the readings of the final words: ἐν ἡμῖν before τετελειωμένη ἐστίν A. Vulg; ἐν ἡμῖν after τετελειωμένη ἐστίν G. K. and many versions; ἐν ἡμῖν between τετελ. and ἐστίν Cod. Sin. B. [Alford: The love of Him is perfected in us.—M.]

Verse 13. [[15] ἐν τούτῳ="In this." See note 7 above.—M.]

[[16] German: "that."—M.]

Verse 14. [[17] German: "*As* Saviour of the world." So Alford, Lillie. No need for the supplement *to be* in E. V.—M.]

Verse 15. [18] Instead of ὃς ἄν, B. reads ἐάν.

[[19] German: "confesseth;" so Alford who justly objects to all Futures "shall confess," and *Futuri exacti* "shall have confessed" and recommends the English Present with an exegesis,—viz., "that this Present betokens not a repeated act and habit, but a great act once for all introducing the man into a state of ὁμολογῆσαι."—M.]

[20] B. adds Χριστός after Ἰησοῦς.

Verse 16. [[21] ἐν ἡμῖν. German: "*an uns*" literally "*at* or *on* us" to which "concerning us" or "in regard to us" come nearest.—M.]

[22] B. G. K. Cod. Sin. add μένει, which owing to the same conclusion of the preceding verse was more likely to be omitted than added.

Verse 17. [[23] "In this." See note 7 above.—M.]

[24] Cod. Sin. adds ἐν ἡμῖν after μεθ' ἡμῶν, probably an error (with reference to v. 12) as ἐν ἀγάπῃ τῆς κρίσεως is plainly a slip of the pen.

[[25] German: "In this love with us is perfected;" Alford: "In this is love perfected with us." The rendering "our" of E. V. is almost solitary and should be changed. See below in *Exeget. and Critical.*—M.]

[[26] German: "Because as He is, we also are in this world." So Alford and Lillie, who transpose, however: "Are we also, etc."—M.]

Verse 18. [[27] German: "Fear is not in love." Alford: "Fear existeth not, etc."—M.]

[[28] German: "Punishment;" so Lillie, see note in *Exeget. and Critical.*—M.]

[[29] German: "Is not perfected in love." Alford: "Hath not been perfected in [His] love."—M.]

Verse 19. [30] Cod. Sin. reads τὸν θεὸν after ἀγαπῶμεν; G. K. αὐτὸν [A. B. omit either.—M.] A inserts οὖν after ἡμεῖς.

[German: "We love God."—M.]

Verse 20. [[31] German: "If one says . . . hateth . . ." Translate: "If any say . . . hate . . ."—M.]

[32] πῶς, A. [K. L. al. Tischend. Alford—M.]; οὐ, B. Cod. Sin. [Lach. Buttm. al.—M.] The true reading cannot be determined by the analogy with ch. iii. 17 (Düsterdieck), or by the consideration that the interrogative is more expressive than the negative (Huther).

[German: "How can he love God (or: cannot love God) whom he hath not seen?"—M.]

Verse 21. [[33] German: "Also love his brother." Doddridge—"Love also his brother" Alford, Lillie.—M.]

EXEGETICAL AND CRITICAL.

Connection. The whole section vv. 7–21 insists upon the exhibition of brotherly love, because love is the very Essence of God (vv. 8, 16), as is evident from the sending and revelation of His Son (vv. 8, 10, 11, 14, 15), from our past and present experience of the love of God (vv. 10, 11, 16), from the experience of our confidence towards Him without fear (vv. 17, 18), and because as the children of God, we ought in grateful obedience prove our enjoyment of such love by the love of our brethren, His children (vv. 19–21). Based on the γεννηθῆναι ἐκ τοῦ θεοῦ (v. 7), this exhortation belongs under the great leading thought ch. ii. 29, and connects with the warning against the false teachers, because faith in Jesus, in whom the love of the Father has been manifested and brought near to us, and the fellowship of the Holy Spirit (v. 13), the Spirit of truth and the Witness of God's love in us, must evidence and manifest their truth and vitality in brotherly love.

Exhortation to brotherly love founded on the Being of God. vv. 7, 8.

VER. 7. **Beloved, let us love one another.**—Ἀγαπητοί, ἀγαπῶμεν, a very emphatic expression; being loved we must love; being in the enjoyment of love we are and dare not be without love; the exhortation, as ἀλλήλους shows, must be restricted to brotherly [Christian—M.] love and not be extended to general love of man. [But the ground, on which this exortation is based, viz. that God is Love (v. 8) and that He sent His Son εἰς τὸν κόσμον (v. 9), shows that the love of man in general is not excluded here. Cf. ch. iii. 13; so Ebrard.—M.].

Because the love is of God, and every one, that loveth, is born of God and knoweth God.—Ὅτι indicates the ground on which the preceding exhortation is made to rest. The demonstration is conducted on a general axiom of truth: *Omnis amor ex Deo est* (Bengel), *originem habet a Deo* (Calov). This thought especially strengthened by ἐκ, must not be weakened into: *caritas res divina maxime laudabilis* (Socinus, Episcopius), *Deo maxime placet* (Grotius), love is Divine as to its nature (de Wette), *Deus caritatis auctor est, quatenus nobis mutuæ caritatis causas abunde suppeditat* (Schlichting). Neither must we add with A. τὸν θεόν, nor supply "the brother" with S. Schmidt, Lücke and al.—[Didymus singularly understood ἀγαπή here of Christ,—ἥτινα οὐκ ἄλλην εἶναι νομιστέον ἢ τὸν μονογενῆ, ὥσπερ θεὸν ἐκ θεοῦ, οὕτω καὶ ἀγάπην ἐξ ἀγάπης ὄντα:—and Augustine fitting together "*Dilectio est ex Deo,*" and "*Dilectio est Deus*" infers that "*Dilectio est Deus ex Deo,*" which comparing with Rom. v. 5, he infers that love is the Holy Spirit (Tract. vii. 6). Alford—M.].—Now since love and life are and spring from God, a man that is born of God proves that he is born of God by loving; for he must have part of that which is in God and comes from Him. The Perfect also alongside the Present shows that here again *being born of God* is regarded as the antecedent fact, as the cause of love, and love as a consequence warrants and necessitates the back-inference of the truth and reality of being born of God. Cf. ch. ii. 29. Every one that is born of God knows also in his belonging to God, in his fellowship with God, God as the Source of love, and love as the Essence of God, and hence he must insist upon love and practise love, so that thereby he may prove his knowledge of and familiarity with God; to love and to know God are correlates, because love is of God. Hence Grotius (*ostendit se Deum nosse sicut oportet*) errs less than Calvin (*vera Dei cognitio amorem Dei necessario in nobis generat*).

VER. 8. **He that loveth not hath never known God.**—Consequently: he that lacks love in general, has not known God, has never learnt to know Him at all (Lücke), has never made even the beginning of the knowledge of God (Düsterdieck); this rendering is required by the

Aorist ἔγνω joined to ὁ μὴ ἀγαπῶν. The reason of this is given in the following:

Because God is love.—A proposition which in the negative formula, according to the well-known manner of the Apostle, still further defines the former assertion that "love is of God." This relation of the two propositions and of their contents requires us to give to ὅτι a causal construction; hence it indicates the reason and not the contents of ἔγνω (Tirinus: *non novit, Deum esse caritatem*); in that case ὁ θεὸς also ought to be wanting and it would be: οὐκ ἔγνω τὸν θεόν, ὅτι ἀγάπη ἐστίν. Cf. Acts xiv. 13. Winer, p. 469. Ὁ θεὸς ἀγάπη ἐστίν=*Deus nihil* est *quam mera caritas* (Luther), *Dei natura nihil aliud est, quam caritas, quam bonitas, quam summum bonum, sui ipsius communicativum* (Hunnius). The Being of God is Love; therefore love springs from God. The word is to be taken *essentialiter* with most Catholic [Anglican—M.] and Lutheran Commentators, and not ἐνεργητικῶς with Calvin and Beza: *Dei natura est homines diligere;* for this construction makes God's Love-*Essence* give place to God's *manifestation* of love and adds the limitation of its application to men, whereas angels and even the Trinitarian God are objects of the love of God. Still farther removed from the depth of this saying, even to shallowness, are the expositions of Socinus (*caritas est Dei ipsiusque voluntas effectus et is quidem maxime proprius*), Grotius (*Deus est plenus caritate*), Rosenmüller (*benignissimus*). In this, that God is love as to His essential Being, lies the reason, why he that is born of God, must also have love and live in love and why the love of God must be allied with the love of the brethren who are also born of God. [Equally shallow are the explanations of Benson: "God is the most benevolent of all beings; full of love to all His creatures," Whitby: "The Apostle intends not to express what God is in His Essence . . but what He is *demonstrative*, ἐνεργητικῶς, showing great philanthropy to men," and Hammond "God is made up of love and kindness to mankind."—Alford reviewing these quotations says that in them the whole force of the axiom as it stands in the Apostle's argument is lost; "unless he is speaking of the Essential Being of God, *quorsum pertineat*, to say that he that loveth not never knew God, because "God is love?" Put for these last words, "God is loving," and we get at once a fallacy of an undistributed middle: He that loveth not never knew what love is: God is loving: but what would follow? that in as far as God is loving, he never knew Him: but he may have known Him as far as He is just or powerful. But take ὁ θεὸς ἀγάπη ἐστίν of God's essential Being,—as a strict definition of God, and the argumentation will be strict: He that loveth not never knew love. God is love [the terms are co-essential and co-extensive]: therefore he who loveth not never knew God."—M.].

Revelation of the love of God through Christ. vv. 9, 10.

Ver. 9. **In this was manifested the love of God in** (*on*) **us.**—"We hear the lovely, the living echo of Christ, Jno. iii. 16." (Heubner). Ἐν τούτῳ points to the sequel. Ἐφανερώθη as contrasted with the hidden Being of the invisible God, annexes the objective, actual appearing and manifestation of the ἀγάπη τοῦ θεοῦ, of the love which is God's, in God, as in ch. i. 2; iii. 5; 1 Tim. iii. 16; there is no reference whatever to subjective knowledge. [Huther: "The Apostle does not want to say that the love of God has been *known* by us through the sending of His Son; cf. v. 16, but that therein it stepped forth from its concealment, and did in reality manifest itself."—M.].—Ἐν ἡμῖν defines either the sphere in which, or the object *at* which [with regard to which—M.] the manifestation took place; it should be connected with the verb and rendered, either *among* us, *with* us, or *at* [in, with regard to] us. But the context does not introduce us merely as spectators but as receivers of the Divine love (ἵνα ζήσωμεν); and this love is not only to us an object of contemplation, which would be expressed by the Dative ἡμῖν without the preposition; but we ourselves are objects of this love, every one of us believers has experienced it; hence we ought not to leave the matter undecided (Lücke), but must decide for the rendering *at* [in, with regard to—M.] us (Düsterdieck), according to the manifest analogy of Jno. ix. 3, where ἐν must be thus construed and explained; hence we may not connect it with ἀγάπη τοῦ θεοῦ (Huther and al.); for it was not the love of God in believers which was manifested, as if the believers existed before the manifestation of God's love in Christ, but the love of God appeared in Christ and was manifested not *to*, but *at* [in] the believers. On this account Bengel's explanation: "*Amor Dei, qui nunc in nobis est,*" is equally untenable. Still less admissible is it to make ἐν ἡμῖν=εἰς ἡμᾶς, as is done by Luther, Spener and al. Cf. Winer, pp. 231, 436.—Ἐφανερώθη is explained by what follows:

That God hath sent His son, the only-begotten, into the world.

This is the fact of the manifestation. The designation τὸν μονογενῆ the *only* child (Luke vii. 12; viii. 42; ix. 38; Heb. xi. 17; Jno. i. 14, 18; iii. 18), *ad auxesin valet* (Calvin); what love, that He sent His only son (Huther)! It is therefore not=ἀγαπητός, *omnium creaturarum longe carissimus, sibi dilectissimus* (S. G. Lange, Socinus, Grotius). John thus marks the exaltation of the Son, just as the term ἀπέσταλκεν εἰς τὸν κόσμον denotes His pre-existence (Jno. iii. 17; x. 36): to be sent, to be sent into the world can only be true of one already born, not of one who is only born in the world, but one existing above and before the world, 1 Jno. i. 1.

That we might live through Him.—Thus ἐν ἡμῖν is explained. This indication of the purpose, ἵνα, points as much to the life-fulness in Christ as to our poverty. Cf. ch. iii. 16, 17. [Baumgarten-Crusius. Μονογενῆ and ζήσομεν are the two emphatic words: The most exalted One for our salvation!—M.].

Ver. 10. **In this exists love.**—[German like Greek "*the* love," *i. e.* love in the abstract.—M.]. Ἀγάπη is to be taken quite general, as at ch. iii. 16 (Neander, Düsterdieck, Huther), without the supplement of τοῦ θεοῦ (Spener, Lücke, Sander, de Wette, Brückner and al.), as at Rom. v. 5.

Not that we loved God, but that He loved us.—The simplest construction is to supply ἐν τούτῳ to οὐχ and ἀλλά. Thus preparation is made for the comprehensive term πρῶτος v. 19; the initiation of loving is with God; the beginning and origin of love is in God (ἐκ τοῦ θεοῦ); ἡμεῖς and αὐτὸς are here emphatically contrasted like τὸν θεόν; *amari dignissimum*, and ἡμᾶς, *indignissimos* (Bengel), the self-existence, independence, of the Divine love are intimated by the prevenience of that love absolutely unconditioned by any merit on the part of men; the former is what is really said here (Huther), the other, as we may justly infer from what follows, (ἱλασμὸν) and from what precedes (ἵνα ζήσωμεν), is implied (Düsterdieck). Hence there is no reason whatsoever for rendering ὅτι once "*because*" and then "*that*" (Baumgarten-Crusius), or for translating both times "*because*" but only as protases, thus: not because we loved Him but because He loved us, did He send His Son (Lachmann), or for a transposition of the words as if we did read: ὅτι οὐκ (Grotius), or for taking the first proposition as a dependent clause=ἡμῶν μὴ ἀγαπησάντων (Meyer: that although we have not loved God before, yet did He love us). a Lapide erroneously assigns to the implication the first place saying: "*Hic caritatem Dei ponderat et exaggerat ex eo, quod Deus nulla dilectione, nullo obsequio nostro provocatus, imo multis injuriis et sceleribus nostris offensus, prior dilexit nos.*"

And sent His Son (as) **a propitiation for our sins.**—This is the proof in fact of αὐτὸς ἠγάπησεν ἡμᾶς. The Aorist ἀπέστειλεν, like ἠγαπήσαμεν, ἠγάπησεν, simply narrates, while the Perfect ἀπέσταλκεν v. 9 absolutely presentiates Christ's having been sent (Lücke). Ἀπέστειλε stands emphatically in ante-position in order to set the act of God in relief; ἱλασμὸν περὶ τῶν ἁμαρτιῶν ἡμῶν has an explanatory and substantiating reference to ζήσωμεν δι' αὐτοῦ v. 9. Cf. ch. ii. 2; iii. 16. Insufficient: *testatum fecit, se velle condonare* (Rosenmüller).

Brotherly love inferred. v. 11. [from vv. 9, 10, *and substantiating the exhortation* v. 7.—M.]

VER. 11. **Beloved**—ἀγαπητοί has a peculiar emphasis and distinct meaning, *i. e.* it designates those who stand in the enjoyment of the experience of the love of God.

If God so loved us.—Because εἰ with the Indicative introduces the aforesaid fact, it is described as an indubitable ground for an inference to be built upon it. [Alford calls attention to the difficulty of rendering this εἰ with an Indicative in English, which is neither any expression of uncertainty, nor=*since*, or *seeing that;* he describes it as "a certainty put in the shape of a doubt, that the hearer's mind may grasp the certainty for itself, not take it from the speaker." If (it be true that) . .—is perhaps the nearest filling up of the sense."—M.]. Οὕτως denotes the preceding description of love; it is here=*hac ratione*, prevenient without any merit on our part, in the sending of His Son for the propitiation of our sins; but it is not=*tanta caritate*, as in Jno. iii. 16 (where οὕτως—ὥστε requires such a construction, as Düsterdieck rightly observes). There is no warrant for the interpretation: *nullo hominum discrimine* (Grotius).

We also ought to love one another.—In the first place we have to take notice of ἡμεῖς—ἀλλήλους: *we*, first the object of the glorious love of God (ἡμᾶς) must now also regard and treat every Christian as an object of Divine love and consequently become the subjects of such experienced Divine love; to this necessitates us the brother whom God loves, and to this compels us the love with which we ourselves are loved. Hence the Apostle uses the word ὀφείλομεν not only because there is extant for it an objectively given commandment and example, but also a subjective preparation for it; as God's children, born out of Him who is Love, born out of His Love Being, we must love one another.

There is no fellowship with God without brotherly love. vv. 12, 13.

VER. 12. **No one hath ever beheld God.**—Cf. Jno. i. 18: ἑώρακεν. The Perfects there, like τεθέαται here are on account of πώποτε to be emphatically referred to the past with respect to its separate course and periods, and must not be construed according to a Hebraism, as carrying present force (Estius), or as comprehending the past and the present (Lücke). The word τεθέαται denotes calm, continued looking at and contemplation of a thing, but it is real seeing [in the literal sense of the word as distinguished from spiritual beholding, inward vision—M.]; this is the view of the Greek Commentators, (Augustine, Spener, Lücke and al.), as in v. 14 and=ἑώρακεν also v. 20. The sense is: God is invisible (1 Tim. vi. 16). Passages like Exod. xxxiii. 20, and Gen. xii. 7; xvii. 1 etc., are not contradictory, since where God did appear, it was not His face, but some assumed form that became visible. Consequently the passage must not be interpreted in a spiritual sense, as if it imported spiritual seeing and that God cannot be known and apprehended by man's own, natural powers (Piscator), or immediately (Rickli), or as He is (Estius), that He is consequently inscrutable (Neander). The explanation of this axiom follows from,

If we love one another, God abideth in us and His love is perfected in us.—The proposition: θεὸν οὐδεὶς πώποτε τεθέαται, obviously refers not to the proposition ἀγαπᾶν ἀλλήλους which contains a presupposition and a condition, but to the leading thought: ὁ θεὸς ἐν ἡμῖν μένει. The Apostle is wholly concerned with the inward life-fellowship, with the inward relation between God and man which is to be carried on to perfection and which manifests itself in brotherly love; hence brotherly love is only the presupposition and condition of the assertion and assumption of such life-fellowship with God, but not of that relation itself (contrary to Frommann). So especially Düsterdieck, Huther. The invisibility of God surely does not exclude our love to God (v. 20. cf. 1 Pet. i. 8); nor is the invisibility of God used here to direct us to brotherly love, as if we should show to the brethren what we cannot show to Him (Lücke and al.); in that case θεὸν οὐκ θεᾶσθαι and not ἀγαπᾶν ἀλλήλους would have been introduced with ἐάν. Ἀγάπη θεοῦ denotes His love, the love of God, even the love peculiar to and inhering in Him, which is in us, if He ἐν ἡμῖν μένει. In this life-fellowship with Him we participate in His love, which is τετελειωμένη, has become perfected [*i. e.* has reached its full completion and maturity.—M.]. This love has its history of growth and completion in us and corresponds *pari passu* with brotherly love: where the one is, there is also the other; they mutually conditionate each other; it is loving with God, (out) of God, in God, which with Him is in us as His Being; dutiful loving (ὀφείλομεν v. 11) is *natural* in believers. Hence the reference is not to God's love to us (Hunnius, Calov, Spener, Beza, Sander and al.), for the predicate would not suit such a construction; nor to our love to God (Luther, Calvin, Grotius, Lücke, Neander, Düsterdieck and others), nor to *ea dilectio quam Deus præscripsit* (Socinus), nor to the mutual relation of love between God and us (Ebrard).

VER. 13. **In this we know that we abide in Him and He in us, that He hath given us of His Spirit.**—The mark of recognition of the life-fellowship of God with us, and among ourselves with God, agrees exactly with the description at ch. iii. 24, as does also the reference to the gift of the Spirit (ἐν τούτῳ): ὅτι ἐκ τοῦ πνεύματος αὐτοῦ δέδωκεν ἡμῖν. Neither οὐ ch. iii. 24, nor the preposition ἐκ here, has partitive force; it rather answers to ἀπὸ τοῦ πνεύματος, Acts ii. 17; Joel iii. 1 (LXX.), while the Vulgate in conformity to the original text renders *spiritum meum effundam*, and denotes the origin and source of the Spirit in us, although we, as distinguished from Jesus who has the Spirit οὐκ ἐκ μέτρου (Jno. iii. 34), have only part in Him; the coarse notion of a divisibility or dismemberment of the Spirit must be strenuously excluded. The Spirit Himself is given to us; nothing is said here of His gifts; there is no reference to the διαιρέσις τῶν χαρισμάτων, 1 Cor. xii. 4, 11—(in opposition to Estius). His Spirit (τὸ πνεῦμα αὐτοῦ, the Love-Spirit of God) answers to ἀγάπη αὐτοῦ and confirms the explanation of v. 12, as given above, and supplements the fact that His Spirit mediates in us His love and its perfections.

Evidence of this inward life-fellowship as a certain fact. vv. 14, 15, 16.

VER. 14. **And we have beheld and testify.**—Antithesis to v. 12: No one has ever beheld God, but we have seen the Son of the Father. Ἡμεῖς designates the Apostles and their associates, and this reference is confirmed by τεθεάμεθα καὶ μαρτυροῦμεν, which verbs point to an immediate, personal beholding as contrasted with the knowledge mediated by others (ch. i. 1, 2; Jno. i. 14), to their eye- and ear-witness (Jno. i. 34). What they have beheld, *that they* testify also; both verbs have the same object:

That the Father hath sent the Son as Saviour of the world.—In Jesus, the Sent One from God, they have beheld δόξαν αὐτοῦ, δόξαν ὡς μονογενοῦς παρὰ πατρὸς, πλήρης χάριτος καὶ ἀληθείας (Jno. i. 14), and therefore they beheld Him as the Sent One of God. Τοῦ κόσμου (cf. ch. ii. 2; Jno. iii. 16; iv. 42), implies that He is sent for every man, not only for the *electi in omnibus populis* (Piscator); the universality of salvation is also confirmed by the sequel:

VER. 15. **Whosoever confesseth that Jesus is the Son of God.**—This ὁμολογεῖν is the consequence of the reception of the μαρτυρεῖν of the Apostles. Cf. ch. ii. 2, 23. The reference here is neither to the confession in the fact of brotherly love (Bede), nor to the testimony of a holy life accompanying the confession with the mouth (Augustine, Grotius); but the faith of the heart, which receives the Apostolical μαρτυρία is taken for granted. Cf. v. 16.

God abideth in Him and He in God.—The confession, therefore, is to be taken as connected with the life-fellowship with God, and an ungodly conversation surely will not belie the confession; God in Christ Jesus will have appropriated salvation to the believer.

VER. 16. **And we have known and believed.**—The beginning καὶ ἡμεῖς exactly as in v. 14. But ἐγνώκαμεν and πεπιστεύκαμεν is matter of the disciples of Jesus without any exception whatsoever (Estius, Calov, Spener, Lücke, de Wette, Düsterdieck, Ebrard, Huther), not of the Apostles only, as in τεθεάμεθα καὶ μαρτυροῦμεν (in opposition to Episcopius, Rickli and al.). Cf. Jno. vi. 69: πεπιστεύκαμεν καὶ ἐγνώκαμεν; cf. Lange in this Commentary, Vol. IV., p. 166, German edition. "True faith is, according to John, a faith of knowledge and experience: true knowledge of faith" (Lücke); both are in one another; each conditions and promotes the other. Hence it is really immaterial which of the two is put first; the moral act of faith and the intellectual act of knowing are ultimately not without the working of God in His Spirit on our spirit. For the reception of the word of truth in faith is a receiving from the Lord of the word, just as the shining of this bright word into the heart and the luminous rise of the truth of the word in the heart, come also from Him. The two constitute the foundation of man's confession. Hence the Perfects which continue to operate in the present confession. The object follows, viz.:

The love which God hath in us.—Cf. Jno. xiii. 35: ἵνα ἀγάπην ἔχητε ἐν ἀλλήλοις. The Present is emphatically placed first after the preceding Perfects; ἐν is used here as in v. 9. It is, as in Jno. vi. 69 (ὅτι σὺ εἶ ὁ ἅγιος τοῦ θεοῦ), something objective, God's love *on* us, namely in Christ Jesus, wherefore Bede says: "*Quia videlicet cum haberet filium unicum, noluit illum esse unum, sed ut fratres haberet, adoptavit illi, qui cum illo possiderent vitam æternam.*" Hence neither the subjective love of God *erga nos* (Estius, Luther, Socinus, Grotius, Rickli and al.), nor the love of God indwelling in us (Wilke, *Hermeneutik des Neuen Testaments*, 11, 64,), nor our love, kindled in us by God's love (Ebrard).—Now follows the concluding summary,

God is love and he that abideth in love, abideth in God and God abideth in him.—A combination of vv. 8 and 15. Ἐν τῇ ἀγάπῃ denotes Love absolute, as the element of those who are born of God, and neither brotherly love (Lücke and al.), nor God's love to us (Ebrard); it occurs here without any qualifying addition. Μένων, however, denotes the love of man in which he abides and which dwells in him.

Perfecting of love in fearlessness. vv. 17, 18.

VER. 17. **In this, love is perfected with us.**—Ἀγάπη is again absolute as in vv. 16, 18, and must neither be construed as God's love εἰς ἡμᾶς, nor as our love εἰς ἀλλήλους (Socinus), nor to God (Lange), but simultaneously as the disposition and activity of love (Huther), as at ch. iii. 18; and μεθ' ἡμῶν must receive its full force of among, between, with us; see Winer, p. 336 sq.—Were it not parallel with ἐν ἡμῖν v. 12 we might think of fellowship, ecclesiastical fellowship, the Christian Church, within which love has been perfected; the context also points to the individual life and perfection of *Christians* and not to the life and perfection of the Christian

Church as such. Its most natural construction is with the verb τετελείωται (Lücke, de Wette, Düsterdieck and al.), not with ἀγάπη, of which it cannot be the object, since it is not=εἰς ἡμᾶς, as supposed by Luther, Calvin, Spener, Bengel, Sander, Besser and al. The position of the words is not more decisive for the connection with ἀγάπη here than at v. 9 (in opposition to Huther); μεθ' ἡμῶν denotes the place where love was perfected. Hence ἡμῶν must not be resolved into *God* and *we* (Rickli) and construed as the mutual love of God and Christians, which would be wholly inadmissible and repugnant to the spirit of the Gospel. Τετελείωται should be construed like τετελειωμένη ἐστίν, v. 12, and τελεία and τετελείωται in v. 18, this ἀγάπη in and on us is something to be perfected, and this perfection itself is not ready and accomplished at once; it has its stages and degrees. This is inconceivable and unpredicable of the love of God. But wherein is it primarily perfected? ἐν τούτῳ—ἵνα παῤῥησίαν ἔχωμεν:

That we have confidence in the day of judgment.—On παῤῥησία see Notes on ch. ii. 28 in *Exegetical and Critical.* Ἵνα, which follows αὕτη, ch. iii. 11, 23; Jno. xvii. 3 and also ἐν τούτῳ, Jno. xv. 8, gives the purpose of God in the perfecting of love with us; we *shall* have confidence. Ἐν τούτῳ therefore must neither be referred to what goes before v. 16 (Spener), nor, with the assumption of a *trajecta anticipatio*, connected with ὅτι (Grotius, Beza and al.), nor must ἵνα be construed in the sense of ὥστε (Episcopius, Bengel and al.). The ἡμέρα τῆς κρίσεως is ὅταν φανερωθῇ ch. ii. 28. Of course ἐν has its usual sense and must not be explained=εἰς; for the reference here is not to the confidence of expectation, the desire of its drawing near (Augustine, Calvin), where men are liable to deceive themselves. Of course, he that may and will have confidence *in* the judgment, will also have confidence *before* it takes place; however, it is to be borne in mind that even believers, notwithstanding their activity of love, will be surprised in the judgment (Matth. xxv. 31 sqq.); the reference is solely to confidence in the judgment, not to confidence beforehand. It is incorrect to combine the two with Rickli, Huther and al.; nor must τετελείωται be taken as a *futurum exactum.* [It is doubtful whether Braune's exegesis will carry conviction to the mind of the reader. It seems to be rather contradictory, for while he condemns the interpretation of Rickli and Huther, he seems to adopt it when he says that "of course he that may and will have confidence *in* the judgment, will also have confidence *before* it takes place." On the whole, Huther's explanation, which is substantially that of Alford, seems to be the most natural. He says: "The difficulty that something future (our attitude in the day of judgment), is to be valid as a mark of perfect love in the present, vanishes by the assumption that ἐν involves both the παῤῥησία of believers in the day of judgment, and their present παῤῥησία in anticipation of that day; this combination was natural to the Apostle who thought of the day of judgment not as very remote but as already dawning (ch. ii. 18). In his love this future παῤῥησία is to him already present."—M.].

Because as He is, we also are in this world.—Ὅτι annexes the reason of our confidence in the day of judgment. Ἐκεῖνος is Jesus and not God (Augustine, Calvin and al.). The Present ἐστί must not be construed=ἦν (a Lapide, Grotius, Rickli and al.), nor must the words ἐν τῷ κόσμῳ τούτῳ be referred to Christ. The comparison must be gathered from the context: it is very strict, καθὼς—καί. The point in hand is the μένειν ἐν τῇ ἀγάπῃ, which μένειν perfects love even unto filial confidence in the day of judgment (so Huther who cites Lorinus, "*reddit nos caritas Christo similes et conformes imagini filii Dei*"). Hence not likeness in suffering (Luther) or temptability (Rickli), not likeness in that, though we are in the world, we are not of the world (Sander); for nothing is said on these points; neither is here any reference to the adoption (Lücke), nor to δικαιοσύνη (Düsterdieck). Love is the eternal Being of Christ, cf. ch. iii. 7 (Huther). [The last named author lays stress on ἐστὶν and compares in the passage cited the words: καθὼς ἐκεῖνος δίκαιός ἐ σ τ ι ν.—Alford adopts the explanation of Düsterdieck, who thus develops his view: St. John does not say that Love is perfected in confidence in us, because we resemble Christ in Love; but he refers to the fundamental truth on which our Love itself rests and says: because we are absolutely like Christ, because we are in Christ Himself, because He lives in us, for without this there cannot be likeness to Him; in a word, because we are, in that communion with Christ which we are assured of by our likeness to Him in righteousness, children of God, therefore our love brings with it also full confidence. Essentially, the reason here rendered for our confidence in the day of judgment is the same as that given, ch. iii. 21 sq., for another kind of confidence, viz., that we keep His commandments. This also betokens the δικαιοσύνη, of which Christ is the essential exemplar and which is a necessary attribute of those who through Christ are children of God.—M.]. Ἐν τῷ κόσμῳ τούτῳ applied to ἐσμέν, denotes the place of abode, the earthly sphere of life, whereas Christ is in heaven, and is not an ethical idea, though we should supply with Bengel: *amoris experte judicium timente.*

VER. 18. **Fear is not in love.**—Antithesis of παῤῥησία ἐν τῇ ἡμέρᾳ τῆς κρίσεως. Quite general: In love is not fear; fear is not a part of love, it is something wholly foreign to it, which is only outside of it (Huther). According to the well known phrase: *oderint, dum metuant,* hatred and fear are congruous, but love and fear are wholly incongruous. There is nothing said of the fear of God which is the beginning of wisdom (Ps. cxi. 10), nor of love; hence neither our love to God, nor brotherly love (Lücke), and still less God's love to us (Calvin, Calov, Spener).

But perfect love casteth out fear.—Τελεία is more than *sincera, opposita simulationi* (Beza), and ἔξω is not out of itself (Lücke), as if it were in it, but out of the heart. "Love not only does not contain fear, but it also does not suffer it alongside of itself; the love which wholly drives away fear is not love in its first beginning, love as yet weak, but love in its perfection." (Huther). [Alford says of ἀλλά that it is not here the mere adversative after a negative clause, in which case it would refer to something in which fear *is, e g.* φόβος οὐκ ἔστιν ἐν τῇ ἀγάπῃ, ἀλλ' (ἐστιν) ἐν τῷ μισεῖ: but it is the stronger adversative, implying, "nay, far otherwise:" "*tantum abest ut . . . . ut;*" and renders: Fear *existeth* not in love, *nay*, perfect love casteth out fear, etc.—M.].—Where such love fills the heart, there is no room for fear,

Because fear hath punishment.—This is the reason why love does not suffer fear alongside itself. Κόλασις often used in the LXX., [Ez. xiv. 3, 4, 7; xviii. 30; xliv. 12, cf. Wisd. xi. 14; xvi. 2, 24; xix. 4.—M.], as in Matth. xxv. 46 in the sense of punishment, pain of punishment (Besser) under the menace of the κρίσις. Bengel: "*tormentum habet; nam diffidit, omnia inimica et adversa sibi fingit ac proponit, fugit, odit.*" Hence it is not consciousness of punishment (Lücke), for the punishment has not yet set in; nor condemnation pronounced in the final judgment on him who does not stand in the fellowship of love (Düsterdieck). 'Ο φόβος is neither *pro concreto:* he that fears (de Wette, Düsterdieck), nor is ἔχει=receives; and least of all: fear holds fast to, *tenet*, thinks of punishment, knows nothing of clemency and love (Baumgarten-Crusius).—["The pain felt in expectation of the punishment of Him who is feared" (Huther); "Fear by anticipating punishment has it even now" (Alford).—M.].

But he that feareth is not perfected in love.—Negative connected with the main proposition: ἡ τελεία ἀγάπη ἔξω βάλλει τὸν φόβον, and application to the beginning: φόβος οὐκ ἔστιν ἐν τῇ ἀγάπῃ. Hence δὲ is by all means to be retained, and neither to be cancelled, nor to be construed=οὖν or καὶ [δὲ is strictly adversative.—M.]. It is accordingly both owing to a want of perfection in the individual and to a want of perfection of love (τετελείωται ἐν τῇ ἀγάπῃ—ἡ τελεία ἀγάπη), if fear is present, fear, as in Rom. viii. 15: οὐκ ἐλάβετε πνεῦμα δουλείας πάλιν εἰς φόβον. Unnecessary [and diluting—M.] are the conjectures of Grotius, who proposes to read κόλουσιν (*mutilationem*) instead of κόλασιν (*metus amorem mutilat atque infringit, aut prohibet, ne se exserat*), and κολουόμενος instead of φοβούμενος (*qui mutilatur aut impeditur in dilectione*), and of Lamb. Bos who reads κώλυσιν instead of κόλασιν. [Oecumenius says that there are two kinds of godly fear, φόβος προκαταρκτικός, which afflicts men with a sense of their evil deeds and dread of God's anger, and which is not abiding; and φόβος τελειωτικός, of which it is said, "The fear of the Lord is clean and endureth forever," Ps. xix., and which δέους τοιούτου ἀπήλλακται.—M.].

The love of God is necessarily united with brotherly love. vv. 19, 20, 21.

VER. 19. **We love God.**—Φοβούμενος is contrasted with ἡμεῖς ἀγαπῶμεν θεόν, without an address, like ἀγαπητοί, v. 7. There is nothing here to indicate the Conjunctive or an exhortation. 'Ημεῖς,—emphatically placed first, who are born of God, His children,—rather notes the fact, the Indicative (Calvin, Beza, Aretius, Socinus, Spener, S. Schmidt, Bengel, Rickli, Neander, Ebrard, Erdmann, Huther, Hofmann, *Schriftbeweis* II. 2. 338); it corresponds, like the whole verse 19, with οὐχ ὅτι ἡμεῖς ἠγαπήσαμεν τὸν θεόν. Neither the comparison with v. 7, nor the ground and the further development in vv. 20, 21, can warrant the interpretation that we must assume here an imperative Conjunctive (as Düsterdieck does). For the majority of authorities favour the addition of the object, even the οὖν of A. implies as much. [Alford, who is on the same side, fixes the connection thus: "He that feareth is not perfect in love. Our love (abstract, not specified whether to God or our brother) is brought about by, conditioned by, depends upon His love to us first; it is only a sense of that which can bring about our love: and if so, then from the very nature of things it is void of terror, and full of confidence, as springing out of a sense of His love to us. Nor only so: our being new begotten in love is not only the effect of *a sense of* His past love, but is the effect of that love itself."—M.]. In the ground

Because He first loved us, πρῶτος is emphatic, and this seems to suggest a primary reference to our love to God, cf. vv. 9, 10. From our most natural love to God, grounded on our experience of the love of God, the Apostle now passes on to brotherly love.

VER. 20. **If any say, I love God, and hate his brother, he is a liar.**—'Εάν τις εἴπῃ, cf. ch. i. 6; ὅτι before ἀγαπῶ τὸν θεόν frequently introduces direct speech. This progress confirms the assumption of the Indicative in v. 19. Here the Apostle resolves the communicate form of speech into the singular form as a conclusion and proof. Μισῇ answers to the next following ὁ μὴ ἀγαπῶν. Cf. ch. iii. 14, 15. "To hate is the positive form of not to love." (Huther). Cf. Luke xiv. 26. *Col.* Matth. x. 37. Every defect of love makes room to hatred. Hence ψεύστης ἐστί, as in ch. i. 6. The reason:

For he that loveth not his brother whom he hath seen, how can he love God (or cannot love God) whom he hath not seen?—The main stress lies in the antithesis ὃν ἑώρακεν and ὃν οὐχ ἑώρακεν. The Perfect denotes sight continuing in its effect (de Wette, Düsterdieck, Huther); Lücke: ἑωρακέναι=to have before one's eyes; a Lapide: *vidit et assidue videt.* Socinus goes too far in emphasizing the Perfect so as to make it also intimate that it is enough to have seen and become acquainted with one, and that it is not necessary to have him still before one's eyes. The saying of Gregory: *oculi sunt in amore duces*, and the remark of Oecumenius: ἐφελκυστικὸν ὅρασις πρὸς ἀγάπην, supply what is understood in the inference. Love to God, the Invisible, is difficult; also 1 Pet. i. 8: ὃν οὐκ εἰδότες ἀγαπᾶτε express both joy and amazement. He therefore who performs the more difficult task of loving God whom he does not see, must also perform the easier work of loving his brother whom he does see. The Apostle's object, consequently, is not to lead us from the love to our brother to the love of God, but only to verify the latter by the former; love to God ever remains the first, the deepest and highest work, which must, however, evidence itself in brotherly love. The interrogative form is as strong and authentic as the simple negation; but the anteposition of the object τὸν θεὸν ὃν οὐχ ἑώρακεν greatly intensifies the thought. Πῶς or οὐ δύναται ἀγαπᾷν presupposes ἐάν τις εἴπῃ and denotes the supposition of the assertion of loving God [under the circumstances.—M.] to be impossible, and the assertion itself a lie. The Apostle's *argumentum ad hominem* applies only to the liar (Düsterdieck).

Bengel: *Sermo modalis; impossibile est, ut talis sit amans Dei, in præsenti.* Hence the reference to the *imago Dei*, which Augustine (*apostolus hic pro confesso sumit, Deus se nobis in hominibus offerre, qui inscriptam gerunt ejus imaginem; Johannes nil aliud voluit, quam fallacem esse jactantiam, si quis Deum se amare dicat, et ejus imaginem, quæ ante oculos est, negligat*), Sander, Ebrard (who suggests that it is not easier to love one who is visible before us, but has *hurt* us) and al., find here is by no means warranted, nor that of Grotius who calls man *opus Dei pulcherrimum.* De Wette also erroneously maintains that God, the ideal, invisible object could *only* be loved in reality in our brother, the visible, empirical object of love.

VER. 21. **And this commandment we have from Him.**—Καὶ simply adds a new reason: the reference is to a specific commandment. This is a *firmius argumentum* (Calvin): for *quomodo diligis eum, cujus odisti præceptum?* (Augustine). 'Απ' αὐτοῦ refers to God (Lücke, de Wette, Düsterdieck and al.), not to Christ (Calvin), Sander, Huther and al.). The fact that ϑεὸν is used afterwards does not militate against the application of αὐτοῦ to ϑεὸν, since Jesus in His intercessory prayer Jno. xvii, 3 mentions His own name instead of saying ἐμέ. The analogy of ch. i. 5; ii. 25 can not upset the context and ch. iii. 23. 24, and only indicate that αὐτὸς also may designate Christ, and that not ἐκεῖνος only does designate Him. The ἐντολή is and remains a commandment, and not=ἀγγελία, doctrine (Carpzov).

That he who loveth God, love his brother also.—But this commandment is nowhere found; not even at Matth xxii. 39. But the Apostle justly puts in the form of a definite Divine command the essential principle of Christian Ethics, which really and fundamentally carries everything which here (v. 7 sqq. iii. 10. 19. cf. Jno. xiii. 34, etc.) is told of the inviolable duty of brotherly love to those who are born of God and in filial love united to their Father (Düsterdieck); ἵνα denotes also here the end and aim and not only the substance of the command, as Huther supposes.

DOCTRINAL AND ETHICAL.

1. *God* is **Love**—a sentence, which "is the summary and most simple expression of what the Scripture, the whole Scripture teaches throughout" (Hofmann, *Schriftbeweis* I. p. 71), and has an important bearing retrospectively and prospectively. *Retrospectively* it bears even on the *Being of God* and on the *history of God's revelation* in Christ Jesus. If the Being of God is *Love* it must also be *personal* and cannot be substance only in the pantheistic sense. Yea, it points to the *Trinity* or God's vitality and fulness of life; Him that *loves*, who is yet not without Him that is LOVED, and *reciprocal Love*, as Augustine tried also this purely ethical construction of the Trinty alongside the psychological analogy (*memoria, intelligentia, voluntas*) in *De Trinitate* (VI. 5: and therefore there are not more than three: One who loves Him who is of Him, and One who loves Him of whom He is, and Love Itself. If this is nothing, how is God Love? If it is not Substance, how is God Substance? XI. 2: If I love something there are three,—I, what I love, and Love itself. For I do not love Love, if I do not love Him that loveth, for love is not where nothing is loved); hence he could, according to Rom. v. 5, understand in our passage (v. 7) by ἀγάπη the Holy Ghost, while Didymus explained ἀγάπη of Christ. In the middle ages Augustine was particularly followed by Richard of St. Victor, the mystic scholastic, or the scholastic mystic (cf. Liebner, *Hugo von St. Victor* p. 82 sqq.), in his work *De Trinitate*, especially III. 14—and in modern times, first of all, by Sartorius: *Die heilige Liebe*, Part. I. p. 1 sqq., and Liebner: *Christologie* I (in many places). See also Nitzsch on the Essential Trinity of God in the *Studien und Kritiken*, 1841, pp. 295—345, especially p. 337 sqq.

2. *Retrospectively*, traces of this truth may be found in the *History of the Revelation of God* in Ex. xxxiv. 6; Ps. ciii. 8–13; lxxxvi. 5, 15; Deut. xxxii. 6; Is. lxiii. 16: Jer. xxxi. 9. But John treats in the most comprehensive manner, with perfect ease and certainty this most profound thought which would never have occurred to any thinker out of his own strength and reason! The heavens declare the glory and majesty of God only, (Ps. xix.) His word alone declares His grace. In nature we meet His handiwork, His Power and Wisdom, in His word alone do we encounter His Love and Mercy. The axioms "God is a Spirit" (Jno. iv. 24), and "God is Love" set forth the most vital truths concerning the Nature and Being of God:—"Spirit is His Nature, Love His Life" (Schöberlein), or Spirit is the Substance and Nature, Love the character of God and not only in His attitude.

3. *Prospectively* this Johannean saying points to the life of knowledge and of demeanour. Sartorius in his "*Heilige Liebe*" has based on this saying the whole of his Ethics. Cf. also Köhler, "*Gott der allein Gute*" (God the Only Good One) in *Studien und Kritiken* 1856, p, 426 sqq. "*Practicam definitionem Dei proponit* 1 Joh. iv. 8: *Deus caritas est. Ex caritate omnia Dei opera procedunt, et Spiritus Sanctus a Patre et Filio ab æterno procedens est substantialis amor Patris et Filii. In tempore Deus ex caritate omnia creavit, ex caritate misit Filium ad opus redemtionis: præstandum, ex caritate dat Spiritum Sanctum, qui similes motus in cordibus credentium accendit, ex caritate in vita æterna a facie ad faciem beatis sese intuendum præstabit.—Omnia in caritate et ex caritate agit* (Joh. Gerhard *Exeg.* ii. p. 71). But we must guard against straightway identifying Love, which is the Nature of God, with the Personality of God which is the logical presupposition of the former (against Liebner, i. 1, 111), and to take care not to combine Love with Truth and Righteousness (as does Nitzsch, *System* § 63. 1), for communication of self is implied in the nature of Love, but not in the nature of truth and holiness, and what becomes of the difference between παιδεία and κόλασις, of the anti-scriptural conception of ἀποκατάστασις τῶν πάντων and the wrathless God in Origen and Schleiermacher? Cf. Thomasius, *Christi Werk und Person*, i. p. 127 sqq.; Philippi, *Glaubenslehre*, ii. p. 79 sqq.

4. The love of God was *revealed in the sending of His only begotten Son.* vv. 2, 9, 10, 12, 14. Hence He is called μονογενής=μόνος γεννώμενος (Jno. i. 14, 18; iii. 16, 18), and not πρωτότοκος (Rom. viii. 29; Col. i. 15, 18; Hebr. i. 6; Rev

i. 5). The greatness of the Sent One and the object of His Mission are designed to mark the love of Him that sent Him. The reference to the first-born would mark the success of the Mission and the work of the Sent One. There is no other proof of the love of the Father, equal to this: Christ, the Son of God by His appearing and message compensates us for the want of seeing the Invisible God (v. 12. Jno. xiv. 9). Hofmann, *Schriftbeweis*, i. 71.

5. To see, know, believe on, confess and testify of Jesus the Son of God on the part of the Apostles, to hear, know, believe and confess on the part of the Church, is indispensable to the life-fellowship of God with us, and of us with God, since, through and through ethical, it can only be acquired and preserved by an ethical process. With the new birth out of God, spiritual regeneration, begins the life-process of sanctification. To remain untouched, unmoved in the presence of Jesus, or only to be turned to Him outwardly, or even to turn away from Him, to deny Him in doubt or decided unbelief, is immorality.

6. The nature of this life-fellowship, begun with our regeneration, is mutuality in continuous reciprocity of action; He to and in us, we in Him, believingly knowing and confessing Him, living and loving, we full of confidence, He in His ever prevenient grace and work of grace to and in us.

7. The degrees of development are given by Bengel thus: "*Sine timore et amore, cum timore sine amore, cum timore et amore, sine timore cum amore.*" And Augustine: "*Timor quasi locum præparat caritati. Si autem nullus timor, non est, qua intret caritas. Timor Dei sic vulnerat, quo medici ferramentum. Timor medicamentum, caritas sanitas. Timor servus est caritatis. Timor est custos et pædagogus legis, donec veniat caritas.*" Though man in his sin begin with servile fear before God, in the presence of God's Nature of Love and attitude of Love he will progress in filial fear even unto fearlessness and confidence in all humility.

8. Brotherly love is and remains the measure of our life from God, from whom comes all love; he that abideo in God, oannot be without love, and he that is without love cannot be in God, nor can God abide in him. He, who is Love, has thus ordained it Himself; it is His Will, His explicit commandment, even as it is in conformity with His Nature.

9. [Wordsworth on v. 10: "A statement of the doctrine of the *Atonement*, and a statement the more remarkable, because it *anticipates* the *objections* that have been made to it in later times.—These objections have taken the following form. *God*, it is said, *is Love* (1 Jno. iv. 8). He loves us, and He loves His *only-begotten* Son. We are sinners; and as long as we are sinners, and without pardon from God, we have no hope of heaven. As sinners we owe an *infinite debt* to God, which we can never pay. But God is *infinite in Love*; He willeth *not that any should perish* (2 Pet. iii. 9), but *that all should be saved* (1 Tim. ii. 4). He can forgive us the debt. He can do this freely. To suppose that He cannot do so, is to set limits to His Omnipotence. To imagine that He will not do so, is to disparage His Love. To allege, that He will require an *equivalent* for the debt, is to represent the God of mercy as a rigorous exactor, and to believe that He required *such a price* for our pardon, as the *blood of His own beloved Son*, and that He exposed Him who is *perfectly innocent*, to the death of the cross for *our sakes*, at the hands of wicked men, is to charge God with cruelty, injustice and weakness; and to suppose Him to be *angry* with us, at the same time that we say that "He *loved* us," and gave His only Son to die for us (1 Jno. iii. 16; iv. 10), is, it is alleged, to involve ourselves in inconsistency, and to misrepresent God, as if He were affected by human passions. And lastly, to say that Christ shed His blood as a ransom to deliver us *from the captivity* of Satan, is, it is argued, to make the Son of God tributary to the Evil One. Such are the objections made by Socinians and others, to the doctrine of the Atonement.—These objections rest on fallacious grounds. They proceed on the supposition that as sinners we are only *debtors* to God. But in His relation to us, God is not only a *Creditor*, but He is our *Lawgiver* and *Judge*, our *King* and *Lord;* and He is perfectly *just* and *holy*.

Besides, as St. John teaches (ch. iii. 4), the essence of *sin* is, that it is a violation of God's *Law*, and *all* are sinners (ch. i. 10). And God represents Himself in Scripture as a Moral Governor, infinite in justice, and when we contemplate *Him* as He is represented by Himself in His own Word, and when we regard *sin* as it is in His sight, and as it is described in the Holy Scriptures, we must conclude that He is grievously offended by sin; and He has declared in His word that He *is* angry with it and will punish it. The *wrath* of God is *revealed* against *all ungodliness* (Rom. i. 18). The wages of sin is death (Rom. vi. 23).—But this proposition is not at variance, as has been alleged, with St. John's declaration, that God *loved us*, and sent His *own Son*, the only *begotten*, that we *might live through Him;* and that herein consists *Love*, not *that we loved God, but that He loved us, and sent His Son a propitiation for our sins*.

That which God loved in us was *not* our *sin*, but our *nature*. It was *that* nature which God Himself had made in His own likeness, and which we had marred, and which He desired to repair. And because He hates sin, and knows its consequences, even death eternal, and because He loved our nature which was exposed by it to everlasting perdition; and because being infinitely just, He must punish sin, which He, who is infinitely pure, must hate, and which He who is infinitely true, has declared that He will punish; and because the sins of the whole world are so heinous, and because they demand a satisfaction infinite in value, and because *without shedding of blood there is no remission* (Heb. ix. 22); therefore, in His immense love for our nature, which He had made and which we had marred by sin, He sent His own Son, God of God, to *take that Nature*, the Nature of *us all*, in order to be the substitute of *all*, and Saviour of *all*, and to become our *Emmanuel, God with us* (Matth. i. 23), *God manifest in the flesh* (1 Tim. iii. 16), partaking of our flesh and blood and to be the *Lord our Righteousness* (Jer. xxiii. 6; xxxiii. 16), and to suffer death, the wages of sin, in our nature, as our Proxy and Representative, and to *appease God's wrath* by an adequate *propitiation*, and to take away our guilt, and to *redeem* us from bondage and death by the priceless *ransom* of His own blood, and to deliver us by His death from him who had the power of it, even the devil, and to reconcile us to God, and to restore us to His favour, and to effect our *atonement* with Him, and to purchase for us the heavenly inheritance of everlasting life. See Heb. ii. 14, 17.—As Origen says (in Matth. xvi.): "Homo *quidem non potest dare aliquam commutationem pro animâ suâ* (Ps. xlix. 9; Matth. xvi. 26); Deus *autem pro* animabus omnium dedit *commutationem, pretiosum sanguinem Filii sui* (1 Pet. i. 18)." "*Si non fuisset peccatum, non necesse fuerat Filium Dei Agnum fieri; nec opus fuerat Eum in carne positum jugulari; sed mansisset hoc, quod in principio erat, Deus Verbum. Verum, quoniam introiit peccatum in hunc mundum, peccati autem necessitas* propitiationem *requirit, et propitiatio non fit nisi per* hostiam, *necessarium fuit provideri hostiam pro peccato.*" (ibid. hom. 4 in Num.) If it be said that according to this statement the *just suffer for the unjust*, and that the beloved Son of God was delivered to death for the offences of those who did not love Him, but were at enmity with Him, this is perfectly true; it is the assertion of God Himself in Holy Scripture, see 1 Pet. iii. 18; 2 Cor. v. 21; 1 Pet. i. 19.—The Just suffered for the unjust. Yes, suffered for a *time.* But this is not at variance with daily experience. Parents suffer for children; brethren for brethren; friends for friends; subjects for sovereigns, and sovereigns for subjects. And if we are to reject the doctrine of the Atonement on the plea that *vicarious* sufferings are not reconcilable with justice, we cannot stop short of Deism or even of Atheism. Cf. Bp. Butler's *Analogy of Religion*. Part II. ch. v.

If any victim was to take away sin, that victim must be innocent. In order to take away infinite guilt, it must be infinitely innocent. The price paid for Infinite Justice must be infinite in value. In order to suffer for men the victim must be human; and in order to satisfy God, it must be Divine. Be it remembered also that the Son of God suffered *willingly*. He *gave* Himself a ransom for all (1 Tim. ii. 6). The Good Shepherd *giveth* His life for the sheep (John x. 11). Cf. Matth. xx. 28; Gal. i. 4; ii. 20; Eph. v. 2; Tit. ii. 14; Heb. ix. 14.—They also for whom He gave Himself are His own flesh and blood. He is their Head, they His members. They are one with Him.—Still further.—By His meritorious sufferings in that human nature, which He has taken, and joined forever in His own Person to the Nature of God, He has delivered that nature from sin and death, and has exalted it to the right hand of God. Therefore He suffered *joyfully*. To *do* evil is indeed evil; and to *suffer* evil in *eternity*, is dreadful; but to *suffer* evil *in time*, in order that others by our means may be happy in eternity, is not evil, but glorious. Earthly conquerors die with joy in the hour of victory. Much more Christ. He knew that suffering was His path to glory. He knew that *because he was obedient to death, even to the death of the cross, therefore God would highly exalt Him, and give Him a Name above every name* (Phil. ii. 8, 9). He saw of the travail of His soul and *was satisfied* (Is. liii. 11). Doubtless, in His human flesh He shrank from the cup of agony and from the anguish of the cross. But even in the glorious hour of His transfiguration He had talked with Moses and Elias of His *death* (Luke ix. 31). His Divine eye pierced through the clouds of suffering, and saw the visions of glory to which it would lead, a victory over Satan, a world rescued from his grasp, God's justice satisfied, His wrath appeased, His love glorified; and so the cross became a triumphal chariot, in which the Conqueror rode in victory (Col. ii. 14), and mounted to heaven, and bore mankind with Him through the gates of the heavenly palace of the everlasting capital and was greeted by the song of the angels, "Lift up your heads," etc. Ps. xxiv. 7.

It has been alleged that if by sin we were prisoners to *Satan*, therefore the price of Christ's blood which He paid upon the cross for our liberation from Satan was *paid to Satan*. But this we deny. See Greg. Nazianzen, Orat. 45, p. 862, ed. Paris, 1778. It might as well be said that the ransom paid for the delivery of prisoners from a king's prison, is paid to the gaoler in whose custody they are. We, by our sins, had made ourselves slaves of Satan; and as a just punishment for our sins, we were made prisoners of Satan. Satan was God's executioner against us. He was our gaoler. *Tophet is ordained of old* (Is. xxx. 33), *as one of God's instruments of death* (Ps. vii. 14). But Christ, by dying for us, delivered us from death. He rescued us from the hands of Satan, and paid the price of our ransom, not to Satan, but *to God.* He delivered us from Satan by offering Himself to God. (Cf. Rom. iii. 23–26).

They who contravene the doctrine of the Atonement often claim the credit of exercising their *Reason*, and deny that unbelief of the doctrine of the Atonement rests on the foundation of reason. But a *right use* of reason leads to a firm belief in the doctrine of the Atonement; and a denial of it proceeds from an *abuse* of reason.—

The doctrine of the Atonement cannot be *discovered* by reason. No; but we can prove by reason that the Holy Scriptures are from God, and that the doctrine of the Atonement is clearly revealed in the Holy Scriptures. And thus this doctrine rests on the foundation of reason. Being a portion of *supernatural* truth revealed by God in Scripture to the world, it is not to be *discovered* by reason, or fully *comprehended* by reason, but it is to be heartily embraced and surely held fast by *faith*, which *implies a right use of reason.* And reason teaches us, that it would be very unreasonable to expect, that what is contained in a revelation from such a Being as God to so frail a creature as man, in his present state on earth, should be fully comprehended by reason; and that, if reason could understand everything, there would be no use in revelation, and no place for faith. Right reason itself teaches us that to *deny the Lord who bought us* (2 Pet. ii. 1), because we cannot *understand*, why God allowed sin to prevail, which required the sacrifice of the death of His own ever-blessed Son, would be to renew the indignities of the crucifixion, and to smite our Redeemer with a reed, the reed of our unregenerate reason, when we ought to fall down and worship in faith. Reason itself teaches us that it is very reasonable to expect mysteries in revelation; and that they are our *moral discipline*, and exercise our humility, patience, faith and hope, and teach us to look forward to that blessed time, when we, who now see through *a glass darkly* (1 Cor. xiii. 12), shall behold the clouds removed, etc. Thus reason leads us to the door of the Holy of Holies; and then we pass within the veil by faith; and there we stand, and with the eye of faith, we behold God enthroned upon the Mercy Seat, *sprinkled by the blood of Christ*. Further, as reasonable men, looking at the cross of Christ, we see there the most cogent reasons for *presenting* ourselves, our souls and bodies *a living Sacrifice, holy and acceptable to God, which is our reasonable service* (Rom. xii. 1).

This *doctrine* of the Atonement is the root of Christian *practice*, and they, who impugn that doctrine, are not only undermining the foundations of Christian *faith*, but also of Christian *morality*. This was clearly evinced even in the Apostolic age, by the licentiousness and profligacy, engendered by heretical doctrines, against which St. John contends in his Epistles, concerning the Incarnation and Death of Christ.

We cannot adequately estimate the moral heinousness of sin, without considering the sacrifice which it cost to redeem us from its power and guilt. We cannot duly understand the obligations of love and obedience, under which we lie to Christ, and the motives which constrain us to holiness, without remembering that we are *not our own*, but *have been bought with a price*—the blood of Christ—and are therefore bound to glorify Him in our bodies which are His. See 1 Cor. vi. 20.

Accordingly, St. John, having stated the doctrine of the Atonement, proceeds and continues to the end of the Epistle, to enforce the *moral duties* consequent on this *doctrine*. "Beloved, if God so *loved us*, *we* also ought to *love one another*." He teaches us to contend earnestly for the doctrine of the Atonement, as the groundwork of Christian duty to God and man. Cf. Pearson on the Creed, art. x. pp. 670–688.—M.].

HOMILETICAL AND PRACTICAL.

In love, even in God's glorious Love thou livest—well, let love live also in thee!—the primal fount of the Love in God streams round thee, and onward to thee, also through thy heart; wilt thou enjoy it without having part thereof?—*Out of thee* must shine forth that which has been manifested *to thee*, even the love and kindness of God thy Saviour, which seeks that which is lost. *Brotherly love* must grow warm in *filial love* which has been kindled at the Father's heart.—In thy child people recognize a member of thy family, thy race; and ought not our heavenly Father to be recognized in thee? Therefore exercise thyself in love of the brethren!—Dost thou boast of thy knowledge of God, of understanding the Holy Scripture? prove it in thy brotherly love!—In nature thou seest His handiwork, the traces of His Omnipotence, in Christ the love-purpose of His heart, His peace-thoughts respecting thee (cf. *Doctrinal and Ethical* No. 2). He takes care that thy sins be atoned for, that thou become not estranged from Him, or keep remote from His life; do not build anew at the wall of partition between Him and thee; such building destroys thy life and thy salvation.—The anticipating offices of friendship are gratifying and humiliating; realize and receive the prevenient grace of God.—As He took the initiative in creation, so He had to take it also in redemption, which is also a creation; and how has He done it! Though without thee He could create thee, yet He neither can nor will save thee without thee.—Above thee rules thy Father, for thee the Son is sent, in thee works His Spirit; do not hinder the work of God for and in thee; do not in unkindness to thyself and thy brethren arrest the perfecting of His work of love.—Do not reject the testimony of eye- and ear-witnesses; surrender to it, receive it in faith, hold it fast in confession; exercise thyself in the love which thou believest and knowest. For to be unloving is to be ungodly, and to be ungodly is to be unloving. If thou art disposed to disparage confession, recollect that like love it radiates from faith; confession is the love of the mouth, love is the confession of the deed, and both come from the heart.—Behind the judgments in the world's history and in the history of thy life, there is a judgment, to stand in which is salvation and bliss.—The unloving must be undone in the judgment of Him who is Love, before the Judge who desired to become the Saviour.—That cannot be our desire in life which does not give us confidence in the last judgment.—Fear, which does not strengthen but expels love, is worthless; so is also that love, which is unable to overcome fear (cf. *Doctrinal and Ethical*, No. 7).—Brotherly love, in comparison with the love of God, is as inferior as is rendering unto Cæsar the things that are Cæsar's, in comparison with rendering unto God, the things that are God's; but on that account both must not be undervalued, for both are enjoined upon us. Still it is certain that when the less is wanting, the greater has no room and cannot find the ability to practise it.—Behold of brotherly love: 1. The origin. 2. The measure. 3. The power. 4. The growth. 5. The prize and victory.—Only in obedience to the will of God thou growest in the nature of God and art changing from a creature into a child, from a servant into an heir of God.—The glory of love: 1. Whence is it? 2. Where was it manifested? 3. What does it effect? 4. Whither does it lead?—The power of love 1. on earth with reference to the brethren, even to hostile ones; 2. in heaven, in the judgment, before God and Jesus Christ, the Holy One.—The perfecting of love to the brethren is 1. difficult, 2. appointed, 3. sure, 4. glorious.

BERNARD:—God is Love: what then is more precious than love? And he that abides in love, abides in God; what then is more sure than love?

AUGUSTINE:—Thou beholdest the Trinity, when thou beholdest Love, for there are three, he that loveth, he that is loved, and reciprocal love.

LUTHER:—For what shall one say much of it? If one says in a lengthy way, that it is a lofty, noble *qualitas* in the soul and the most precious and perfect of virtues, as the philosophers and work-teachers discourse of it; all this is nothing in comparison with this word which he pours forth in overflowing eloquence that "*God is Love*," and that His Being and Nature is wholly Love. If any one would paint and produce a likeness of God, he must produce a picture which is wholly love; as if the Divine Nature were nothing else than an oven and fire of love, filling heaven and earth. And again, if Love could be painted and portrayed, it ought to be a picture that is neither real and human, nor angelic and heavenly, but God Himself. See thus the Apostle understands to paint here, that he represents God and Love as identical, in order that by such a noble, precious and lovely picture He may draw and attract us more to Himself and to make us strive to have love among ourselves and to beware of envy, hatred and discord. For as Love is a picture of God, neither a dead picture nor painted on paper, but a living Being of Divine Nature, burning and overflowing with whatever is good, so hatred and envy are a veritable picture of the devil, not human or devilish only, but the devil himself, who is nothing in his nature but an eternal burning of hatred and envy of God and all His works, both man and all creatures; so that that would be the best picture of the devil which would represent all hatred and envy.—As there are also among us still many who hear and teach the Gospel with us, use the same sacraments and affect the manners of genuine Christians: but they are among us like chaff among the wheat; if the battle approaches it becomes manifest whose they are and whither they belong. For there is nothing but pride, vanity, envy, contempt and the devil himself.—It is not a great art to begin a Christian life and love; but it is an art and a task to abide therein and perseveringly to continue therein especially in the presence of temptation and opposition. Although there still are many rough, coarse people that fall off spontaneously like rotten worm-eaten apples or pears, and proceed drowned in their avarice, pride, envy, etc., they are spoiled, useless fruit, wholly unprofitable, that shall and can not remain. But we refer to those who are blown off or struck down by wind and weather, that is, those who suffer themselves to be changed by temptations and thoughts like these: Why should I abide by the doctrine? I well perceive, that it yields no other returns than those of being burdened with the disfavour, contempt, enmity, rage and fury of all the world, that I must risk my body and life, and must ever take the lead against the devil, the world and the flesh, etc. Who can come up to this and persevere, if that is all he is to get?—But it is not to be so; the true course is rather to tear through all opposition, to proceed without heeding obstacles, whether we meet with the sour or the sweet, however it fare with us, be it friend or enemy, or the devil himself and ever to think: I have not entered upon this work in order that the people should give, love or reward me; and therefore no desisting from it though I receive the reward of ingratitude, envy and hatred. It (the world) shall not be so ill to me, as to overcome me with its ill: I will the rather, in opposition to it, continue to do good, regardless of thee or any one else, but for the sake of my Lord Christ, even as He did and still doeth.

STARKE:—Have we become partakers of the Divine Nature, if we are heavenly-minded and lead a heavenly life? It is infallible. As much true love, so much resemblance to God. He is a wise teacher who grounds his exhortations more on the Gospel than on the Law. The power and efficacy of encouragements are in proportion to their friendliness and lovingness.—You say much concerning God, but lack the best thing. You know Him in words, but deny Him in works. You do not know Him at all and will not be known of Him.—In order that one, provoked to anger, may not be overcome by the temptation and succumb, he should forthwith remember that "God is Love." That will be a good medicine to him and preserve him.—None can attain the life of glory without having first experienced here on earth the life of grace in Christ.—Holy Scripture does not expatiate in multiplied phrases which mean the same thing; but what it does repeat, is peculiarly emphatic, and intended to be carefully remembered.—Nothing can be more sweet, agreeable and delightful to us poor men in the vale of misery of this world, than to hear and to receive the assurance that God loves us. The love of God is the cause and rule of our love.—Love is not the cause of our union with God, but it assures, cements, confirms, and preserves it.—Beloved, though sometimes you do not feel any thing of the grace of the union of God and your heart, if you love cordially and abide in love, you have sufficient evidence that you are nevertheless united with God.—None is able to commend love to others with a good conscience, joyfulness and success, who does not himself walk in love. Preachers, more especially, ought to remember that when they exhort others to love, they themselves should copy the example of Christ and practise love.—God is willing, if we do not hinder Him, to make His love more full and to increase its efficacy; and then all the powers of the inner man do also grow in us, and among their number, the love of our neighbour.—Of what avail are the best testimonials if conscience contradicts them? A heart, full of love, is the best witness of friendship with God that endures also in the fire of temptation.—Thou art pleased when a loved friend comes to see thee, and is thy guest for a few days. Rejoice! God, thy best friend, dwells in thee, abides with thee, and possesses thee altogether, but thou art His property and possession. With God thou hast all things.—The love of God manifested in Jesus Christ, is the most excellent object of our faith and knowledge. The more we study it, the greater is our taste of its sweetness.—A glorious mark of the Christian religion as the only Divine religion, viz.: it effects so great a union between man and God, that God is in man and man in God.—O, wicked man, how canst thou be joyful in anticipation of the judgment-day? Beware that thou do deceive thyself with a false security instead of joyfulness!—Good Christian, whenever thou art about to do or to omit a thing, ask thyself: did my Saviour also do or omit this? It will be of great benefit to thee and happily further thee in thy Christian course.—Be not afraid if thou art summoned before an earthly court of justice; if thou lookest joyfully forward to the great judgment of the world, why shouldest thou not be equally joyful in respect of a little human judgment day? Wherever a Christian may be, he should always suffer himself to be seen without fear or dismay. [Verse of old German hymn.—M.].

A. H. FRANCKE:—One droplet of faith is more glorious than a whole ocean of science, even though it be the historical science of the Divine word.

HEUBNER:—Love has illuminating power, while hatred darkens the soul. The more you love, the greater the brightness of your knowledge; the more you love, the less it is possible for you to be deceived.—Want of love is a token of want of real knowledge of God. All knowledge, all theology must be rooted in love. Theology without the love of God is deception and show. What dry metaphysics have often been called religion and philosophy of religion, without containing a breath of love!—God who is Love can only be known *e praxi, ex usu;* as long as I have not made *personal* experience of the infinite Love of God, I can at the most only repeat what others say of God. Lauding the love of God from what is seen of Him in nature, is not the shadow of the love of God in Christ.—Proud philosophy could assert virtue and morality without the love of God and even go as far as to maintain that virtue without religion is even stronger and purer [than virtue with religion—M.].—Want of love to God is the most telling proof of the fall. For in the *statu integro* our first sign of life ought to be love to God, even as a babe is naturally drawn to its mother's breast. It is true that our love to God proceeds from a sense of shame, from conviction [of sin and ingratitude—M.]; but that cannot now be altered: and he that would deny it ought first to turn the whole world round. And who will most readily own it? They who have *begun* to love God: they are painfully aware how little they love God!—If there had been no apostasy, no breach, what necessity would there be for reconciliation? If reconciliation could have been effected without the Son, by our own efforts, by our own improvement and amending, what purpose would have been served by the sending of the Son?—This is the miracle of love in God, that He kept immovable in His Love and continued to love His creature now as ever, sought the creature although the creature had rebelled in enmity against Him. The love of God, therefore is eternal, unchangeable and having its cause in Himself, without having ever been greater or less than it is. This miracle of love no man can know before he has become aware of his misery, has had his eyes opened and seen with tearful eyes how loving the Lord is.—God has loved *us;* He has also deemed my neighbour worthy of His love: if *God* loves him, am I to refuse loving him? A knowledge of the love of God that has remained unfruitful, is not yet perfected.—There is sympathy or antipathy between the plants of God's planting and of those of his enemy's planting. The children of God are sensible of the spirit of affinity or antipathy in others. So it is said of Coccejus, who beyond all other things strove after a pure heart, that he frequently knew men at the first encounter.—He that underrates historical evidence, overthrows the whole foundation of Christianity and opens the gate and the door to all deception and delusion. Historical knowledge and personal spiritual life-experience *together* constitute true Christianity. God is through and through Love, His whole Essence, His real Nature is Love, *i. e.* is essentially His property to communicate Himself, to impart Himself, to cause His glory and felicity to stream forth on others [*i. e.* His creatures—M.], as it is the essential property of the sun to shine. It is true that the love of God, like the heat of the sun, manifests itself to men only by way of gradation. God is Love to all who stand in love and turn to His Love, but He is a consuming fire to those who stand outside of love. Love spurned brings torment: evil men, because of their own guilt, experience a sense of wrath. Every thing depends upon the attitude of men towards God.—The *Bible* is, as it were, the trumpet of the love of God, not *nature*, by a long way; it is only to *believing* Christians that nature becomes the trumpet of the love of God. The first tones of the love of God may be heard in Gen. i. and iii.; but they sound loudest in the New Testament.—Man is not lost as long as he believes in love; but he is lost, when he loses that belief. Chrysostom says that the devil would be saved if he could believe in the love of God.—Love changes God the Judge into God the Father.—He that cannot confide in love, is unable to endure the look of the Most Loving. Who but those who have pure and indefatigable love are in this world like God and representatives of God?—Where we experience fear, a secret dread, aversion to and distrust of God, love is not yet perfected; fear is the first discipline of boys.—v. 19. The whole wonderful structure of the Christian system; the one half is morality: to love God with every thing implied therein; the other half the doctrine of faith, the conditioning ground: the love of God to us sinners in Christ. The ground must be before the superstructure.—Love is most touching where it prevents the unworthy.—We can only exhibit our love to God the Unseen in His children that are seen.—Christianity indissolubly unites the love of God and the love of the brethren; its characteristic is that in it religion and virtue commingle in the Spirit of love.

GEROK (1 Jno. iv. 7–12). *Love the fundamental law of the world:* 1. As written *in heaven:* for God is Love. 2. As written *on the cross:* for Christ is Love. 3. As written in *our hearts:* for Christianity is Love.

LEONHARDI (1 Jno. iv. 9): *The manifestation of the love of God to us in holy Christmas.* It shines forth: 1. *from the Divine Christmas-gift*, and 2. *from its blessed destination for us.* It was manifested 1. in God sending *His only-begotten Son* into the world, 2. *in that we should live through Him.*

CLAUSS:—*The sending of Christ is the greatest proof of Divine Love.* 1. Christ is the *Only Begotten.* 2. He brings *life to the world.*

The same (on 1 Jno. iv. 12-16):—*The mystery of the Divine Essence.* 1. In which sense does It always remain concealed? 2. In what form has It been revealed? 3. With what eye only are we able to recognize It?

WILHELM:—*The Church of the Lord.* 1. The *good* it has; 2. The *confession* it makes: the *signs* whereby it is known.

LEONHARDI:—*Whereon is based our Trinity-rejoicing?* 1. We know that the Father sent the Son to be the Saviour of the world (vv. 14, 15); we have learned in the Son the love which the Father has in regard to us (vv. 15, 16); we know from our love to one another, that He has given us of His Spirit.

LUTHARDT (1 Jno. iv. 9, Advent-Sermon):—*The love of God in Christ is our life.* I. The love of God; 2. The sending of his Son; 3. Our life.

SPURGEON (1 Jno. iv. 19):—*Real love* viewed 1. as to its origin, 2. as to its maintenance, 3. as to its progress.

AHLFELD (Marriage address on 1 Jno. iv. 19, and Sermon on 1 Jno. iv. 9–16):—*With threefold bonds are we tied to the Triune God.* 1. In *the love among one another* God abides in us; 2. In *the Holy Ghost* we abide in God and God in us; 3. In the *confession of the Son of God*, God abides in us and we in God.

On the Epistle for the first Sunday after Trinity, 1 Jno. iv. 16–21.

HEUBNER:—*The belief, that God is Love, our only consolation in evil times.* 1. Why is it thus? 2. How do we become capable of this consolation? *The Divine nature of love.* 1. Proof (vv. 16–18); 2. Inferences (vv. 19–21).—*God is Love.*—1. Explanation. 2. Proof (also Defence); 3. Duties, arising therefrom, incumbent upon us.—*Belief in the love of God.* 1. Description of what it is, and whereon it is founded; 2. The power of this belief; 3. Inferences (resistance to attacks on that belief; its animation by the imitation of Christ).

C. J. NITZSCH (1813 during the siege of Wittenberg, inaugural Sermon on the Epistle for 1st Sunday after Trinity, 1 Jno. iv. 16–21):—*The value of true love under the fear of exciting prospects of the future.* Love exalts us above the whole of our earthly future. Her pains are deep, her complainings sincere; yes, she looks so much the more sadly out into the future, because she can never suffer for herself alone, but true love can nevermore cease to confide or despair of deliverance. To all true love is accorded the privilege of overcoming the world and to soar beyond time in the strength of true faith. She casts the brightest looks into the shadow of the future. She is not blind through fear, and knows that every time will have its own salvation, its own footprints of Divine Love, from the ruins of the old there will spring up the new and the better, in the school of distress there will mature and prosper a nobler liberty and wisdom of the nations, our children and the grandchildren of our race in a rejuvenated world will think with emotion and edification of their fathers, and we ourselves shall never fall short of the assistance and comfort which we need in our weakness. And bright-eyed love has also an indefatigable arm; it makes the best provision for whatever may be in store.

SCHLEIERMACHER:—*Perfection of love.* 1. The token, indicated by the Apostle, of the perfection of love. 2. That that, whereof he treats, can only be achieved by the perfection of love.

KAPFF:—*God is Love, and love only makes us one with God.*

GEROK:—*Another love sermon.* 1. The eternal fountain of love. 2. The holy duty of love. 3. The true test of love. 4. The blissful happiness of love.

RANKE:—*Life in love is the noblest life!* let that be our *conviction; we will abide in this love!* let that be our resolve; *then God will abide with us*, let that be our blessing.

J. MÜLLER:—*Love, the Essence of the Christian life.* 1. The Christian life *begins* with love to God through Christ; 2. it *develops* into love to our neighbour; 3. it *perfects* itself in the perfection of this twofold love.

HARLESS:—*Who knows and loves the living God who is Love?* 1. He who instead of deifying his own love, knows and loves God in His love-manifestation in Christ; 2. he who, instead of loving God without fear, in his love fears God without torment; 3. he who, instead of calling in such love all the world his brethren, loves every one, but after the manner of God in Christ.

SPITTA:—*The word of the Holy Apostle John concerning love.* 1. A word of doctrine, wherein he teaches us love; 2. A word of exhortation, wherein he exhorts us to practice love.

CLAUS HARMS:—*Let us love God!* Consider 1. The *ground* of the love of God, 2. its power and manifestation *inwardly*, 3. its power and manifestation *outwardly*.

BOBE:—God is love! 1. A confession of gratitude (v. 8); 2. a voice of comfort (vv. 17, 18); 3. a rule of life (vv. 19, 20).

FLOREY:—*The hallowing power of love on the heart of man.* 1. It *unites* the heart of man separated from God (v. 16); 2. it *calms*—the anxious heart (vv. 17, 18); 3. it *warms*—the cold heart (v. 19); 4. it *purifies*—the impure and sinful heart (v. 20); it *animates* and *fructifies*—the dead heart (v. 21).

GENZKEN (Confession-address):—*What do I yet lack of true Christianity?* 1. Its *beginning* is that we know *the love which God has to us.* 2. Its *progress*, that we *abide in this love;* 3. Its *full measure*, that *the experience of its hallowing power* expels *the fear of death and the judgment;* 4. The *test* of all this is *brotherly love.*

[PEARSON:—v. 9. Our belief in Christ, as the eternal Son of God, is necessary to raise us unto a thankful acknowledgment of the infinite love of God, appearing in the sending of His only-begotten Son into the world to die for sinners. This love of God is frequently extolled and admired by the Apostles. See Jno. iii. 16; Rom. viii. 5; viii. 32. If we look upon all this as nothing else but that God should cause a man to be born after another manner than other men, and when he was so born after a peculiar manner, yet a mortal man, should deliver him to die for the sins of the world; I see no such great expression of His love in this way of redemption more than would have appeared, if He had redeemed us in any other way. It is true indeed, that the reparation of lapsed man is no act of absolute necessity in respect of God, but that he hath as freely designed our redemption as our creation: considering the misery from which we are redeemed, and the happiness to which we are invited, we cannot but acknowledge the singular love of God, even in the act of redemption itself, but yet the Apostles have raised that consideration higher, and placed the choicest mark of the love of God in choosing such means, and performing in that manner our reparation, by sending His Only-begotten into the world; by not sparing His own Son, by giving and delivering Him up to be scourged and crucified for us, and the estimation of this act of God's love must necessarily increase proportionably to the dignity of the Son thus sent into the world; because the more worthy the Person of Christ before He suffered, the greater His condescension unto such a suffering condition; and the nearer His relation to the Father, the greater His love to us, for whose sakes He sent Him to suffer. Wherefore to derogate any way from the Person and Nature of our Saviour before He suffered, is so far to undervalue the love of God, and consequently to come short of that acknowledgment and thanksgiving which is due unto Him for it. If then the sending of Christ into the world were the highest act of the love of God which could be expressed; if we be obliged to a return of thankfulness some way correspondent to such infinite love; if such a return can never be made without a true sense of that infinity, and a sense of that infinity of love cannot consist without an apprehension of an infinite dignity of nature in the Person sent; then it is absolutely necessary to believe, that Christ is so the Only-begotten Son of the Father, as to be of the same substance with Him, of glory equal, of majesty coëternal.—M.].

[BARROW: (on v. 9).—How indeed possibly could God have demonstrated a greater excess of kindness to us, than by thus, for our sake and good, sending His dearest Son out of His bosom into this sordid and servile state, subjecting Him to all the infirmities of our frail nature, exposing Him to the worst inconveniences of our low condition? What expressions can signify, what comparisons can set out, the stupendous vastness of this kindness? If we should imagine that a great prince should put his only son (a son most lovely, and worthily most beloved) into rags, should dismiss him from his court, should yield him up to the hardest slavery, merely to the intent that he hereby might redeem from captivity the meanest and basest of his subjects, how faint a resemblance would this be of that immense goodness, of that incomparable mercy, which in this instance the King of all the world hath declared toward us His poor vassals, His indeed unworthy rebels?—And what greater reason of joy can there be, than such an assurance of His love, on whose love all our good dependeth, in whose love all our felicity consisteth? What can be more delightful than to view the face of our Almighty Lord so graciously smiling upon us?—M.].

[BERNARD, de Nativ. Serm. 1. *Apparuerat ante potentia in rerum creatione, apparebat Sapientia in earum gubernatione; sed benignitas misericordiæ nunc maxime apparuit in humanitate.*

P. LEO M., de Nativ. Serm. 1. *Semper quidem diversis modis, multisque mensuris humano generi bonitas divina consuluit, et plurima providentiæ suæ munera omnibus retro seculis clementer impertiit; sed in novissimis temporibus omnem abundantiam solitæ benignitatis excessit; quando in Christo ipsa ad peccatores misericordia, ipsa ad errantes veritas, ipsa ad mortuos vita descendit, etc.*—M.].

[SECKER: (on v. 18).—For want of cultivating the love of God, the thoughts of Him are dreadful to the generality of men. Too many are tempted to wish in their hearts, if they durst, that He were not, or had no regard to human conduct; and if any of them can but persuade themselves for a while on the strength of some poor cavil, to hope what they wish, they triumph in the imagined discovery, that sets them so much at ease. From the same default, humbler and righter minds consider Him very often in no better light, than as a rigid lawgiver arbitrarily exacting a number of almost impracticable duties, and enforcing them with the dread of insupportable punishments: whence they are ready to sink under the terrors of religion, even while they are conscientiously fulfilling its precepts. Looking on God as the object of love would rectify these mistaken conceptions entirely. We should all see and feel, that a Being of infinite goodness, directed by infinite wisdom, is the highest blessing: and the want of such an one would be the greatest calamity that is possible: we should be satisfied that the strictest of His laws, and the severest of their sanctions, are means which He knows to be needful for our good; that His mercy will forgive on repentance our past transgressions of them; that His grace will strengthen us to keep them better; and that He will never reject a soul affectionately devoted to Him. In proportion then as we are so, all terrifying apprehensions will vanish from us. "There is no fear in love" saith the Apostle; "but perfect love casteth out fear: because fear hath torment."—M.].

[JORTIN:—The love of God differs so much from the love of sensible objects, and from our other passions, that it can hardly be called a passion in the same sense in which they are so called. It differs in this, that it is at first raised, and afterwards kept up, by reason. It is therefore a religious habit and virtue, which no other passion is, unless it hath God and morality and religion for its objects. In this also it differs from them, that being both produced and preserved by reason, it is a sober and moderate affection, accompanied with no blind impetuosity, no restless uneasiness, no violent commotion of mind, like other passions; and as it riseth not to the same height with them, so neither does it sink as low at other times, but shews itself in an uniform and sedate love of righteousness, of every thing that God approves. Some persons, not duly considering this, sincerely desire to please God, and carefully endeavour to lead a good life; and yet sometimes are afraid that they have no love for God, because they experience not in themselves that warmth of affection, to which others pretend, and which is expressed and required in some books of devotion. They may learn from the Scriptures, that where there is obedience there is always love; and that whoever delights in holiness, and justice, and goodness, and mercy, and truth, may reasonably conclude that his heart is right towards God. Others looking upon the love of God as upon a mere passion, a disposition of mind producing devotion and ending there, have excited in themselves a high zeal and affection for God, and a firm persuasion, that they were His favourites: and, having done this, have thought themselves arrived at Christian perfection; whilst at the same time they have perhaps been under the dominion of evil habits, and addicted to wrath, malice, covetousness, censoriousness, injustice, pride, ambition, sensuality. This strange mixture of hypocrisy, vice and enthusiasm, hath been common in all ages, and ever will be so. There are always those, whose religion and devotion is, to use the words of St. Paul, "sounding brass," or clamour and confidence; whilst true goodness is modest and unaffected, and teaches men to make less noise, to live more honestly. To preserve us from such delusions, Christ hath told us, that we should either keep His commandments, or not pretend to love Him; and that it signifies nothing to say to Him, "Lord, Lord," and not to do what He requires.—Other love towards God than this the Scriptures know not: they never recommend that spiritual fever, those warm transports, and that bold familiarity, which some zealots affect; nor that cold, refined, mysterious, and disinterested devotion, which another sort of fanatics require: for, first, the love of God is sober reason, and not blind passion; reverence, and not presumption: secondly, it is gratitude; and we "love Him, because He first loved us."—M.].

[HORNE: (on v. 21).—Observe the firm basis on which is forever fixed the morality of the Gospel. How clear in its principles! how powerful in its motives! "We love God, because He first loved us;" "and sent His Son to be the propitiation for our sins. If God so loved us, we ought also to love one another." For "he who loveth Him that begat, loveth Him also that is begotten of Him." The head of the most unlearned cannot but comprehend the meaning of these few words: and the heart of the most learned must feel the force of them. Such is the ground of that charity, which performeth every duty of social life, and fulfilleth the law. To inculcate and produce in us this heavenly disposition, is the end of the Gospel and all its doctrines. It is deduced in Scripture even from those that may seem to be of the most mysterious and speculative nature: the unity of the Divine Persons; the Divinity and the satisfaction of Christ; doctrines, which cannot therefore be denied or degraded, without removing or proportionably lessening the most endearing and affecting incitements to the Christian life. Indeed the happy temper of a Christian is the natural and kindly effect of the great evangelical truths, when treasured up in the mind, and made the subjects of frequent meditation. The ideas of a reconciled God; a Saviour and Intercessor on high; a gracious Spirit, informing our ignorance, purifying our hearts, relieving our necessities, alleviating our cares, and comforting our sorrows: such ideas as these enable us to bridle the appetites of the body, and to calm the emotions of the mind; to bear with patience and cheerfulness the calamities of life: they sweeten the tempers, and harmonize the affections, resolving them all into one, diversified according to the different situation of its proper object; of which grief laments the absence, and fear apprehends the loss; desire pursues it; hope has it in view; anger rises against obstruction, and joy triumphs in possession. Thus religion fixes the heart on its treasure, in faith without wavering, and resignation without reserve: it draws the affections upwards towards heaven, as the sun does the exhalations of the earth, to return in fruitful showers, and bless the world. M.].

[*Sermons and Sermon Themes.*

v. 8. LELAND, JOHN, The goodness of God. 4. Serm. Disc. I. p. 225.

DWIGHT, T., Benevolence of God is proved by the works of creation and providence.—Benevolence of God, as exhibited by revelation.—Theology I. pp. 119, 139.

SCOTT, T., God is Love. Works, 4, 69.

v. 9. TILLOTSON, ABP., The love of God to men in the incarnation of Christ. Serm. 6, 3.

vv. 9, 10. SIMEON, C., The love of God in giving His Son for us. Works 20, 479.

v. 10. HENRY, PHIL., Christ is our Propitiation. M. Henry's Works. Appendix, 40.

vv. 10, 11. The unpurchased love of God in the redemption of the world by Jesus Christ, a great argument for Christian benevolence.

v. 11. HORNE, BP., Charity recommended on its true motive. Disc. 5, 441.

v. 18. SAURIN, La tranquillité qui nait de la parfaite charité. Serm. 6. 483.

vv. 18–21. M'CHEYNE, R. M., The perfect love of God to us. Remains, 368.

v. 19. ERSKINE, R., Preventing love; or God's love the cause of our love to Him. Works, 2, 1.

WARDLAW, R., On the question how far disinterestedness is an essential quality in legitimate love to God. Christian Ethics, 278.

CHALMERS, T., Gratitude, not a sordid affection. Works, 8, 222.

v. 20. HOWE, JOHN, The love of God and our brother, considered in Seventeen Sermons. Works, 6, 1.

WILLIAMS, ISAAC, Love the mark of God's children. Serm. 2, 51.

v. 21. SMALRIDGE, BP., The necessary connection between the love of God and our brother. Sermons 310.

WILBERFORCE, S., The love of the brethren. Sermons on several occasions. 78.—M.]

8. *The power of faith* (vv. 1-5), *its testimony* (vv. 6-10), *and substance* (vv. 11. 12)

Chapter V. 1-12.

Whosoever[1] believeth that Jesus is the Christ[2] is born of God: and every one that
2 loveth him that begat loveth him also[3] that is begotten of him. By this[4] we know
that we love the children of God, when we love God, and keep his commandments.[5]
3 For this is the love of God, that we keep his commandments: and his commandments
4 are not grievous. For[6] whatsoever[7] is born of God overcometh the world: and this is the
5 victory that overcometh[8] the world, *even* our[9] faith. Who is he[10] that overcometh the
6 world, but[11] he that believeth that Jesus is the Son of God? This is he that came by
water and blood,[12] *even* Jesus Christ[13]; not by water only, but[14] by water and blood.[15]
7 And it is the Spirit[16] that beareth witness, because the Spirit[17] is truth. For there are
three that bear record[18] in heaven, the Father, the Word, and the Holy Ghost: and these
8 three are one. And there are three that bear witness in earth, the spirit, and the water,
9 and the blood: and these three agree in one.* If we receive the witness of men, the
witness of God is greater: for[19] this is the witness of God which[20] he *hath* testified of
10 his Son. He that believeth on the Son of God hath the witness[21] in himself: he that
believeth not God[22] hath made him a liar; because he believeth not the record that
11 God gave of his Son.[23] And this is the record, that God hath given to us eternal
12 life, and this[24] life is in his Son.[25] He that hath the Son[26] hath life; *and* he that
hath not the Son of God hath not life.[27]

Verse 1. [[1] German: "Every one that believeth," and so E. V. in second clause.—M.]
[[2] German: "That Jesus is Christ."—M.]
[3] Καὶ before γεγεννημένον is the reading of A. Sin. (which has τὸ instead of τὸν) and several minusc.
[German: "loveth also Him that is begotten of Him."—M.]

Verse 2. [[4] Ἐν τούτῳ, in this, hereby.—M.]
[5] τηρῶμεν, cannot be considered to be supported by A. which omits the following words αὕτη γάρ ἐστιν ἡ ἀγάπη τοῦ θεοῦ, ἵνα τὰς ἐντολὰς αὐτοῦ, so that τηρῶμεν there might come from v. 3, although the omission of said words is more easily accounted for, even if we read τηρῶμεν and not ποιῶμεν (B. and al.) v. 2; but Sin. G. K. al. abundantly sustain the reading in question.

Verse 4. [[6] German: "because" so Alford.—M.]
[[7] πᾶν τὸ; German: "all that;" so Alford.—M.]
[[8] ἡ νίκη ἡ νικήσασα τὸν κόσμον; German: "the victory which *hath* overcome the world;" Alford: "has conquered."—M.]
[9] ἡμῶν; so A. B. G. K. Sin.; ὑμῶν, only in unimportant Codd.

Verse 5. [10] Sin. reads δὲ after τίς, B. K. have δὲ after τίς ἐστιν; others read γὰρ; *e. g.* Syriac; others prefix καὶ, while A. and al. [G. Vulg., Lachm., Tischend., Alf.—M.] have no conjunction at all. [German: "But who is it, that etc."—M.]
[[11] German: "If not he;" Alf. "except he."—M.]

Verse 6. [12] καὶ πνεύματος after αἵματος, though found in A. Sin., several minuscules and versions, is evidently an interpretation, like the still less authentic καὶ ἐν τῷ πνεύματι after ἐν τῷ αἵματι.
[13] The Article ὁ before χριστός found in B., is omitted by A. G. Sin. al.
[[14] German: "not *in* the water only" so Alford.—M.]
[[15] German: "but in the water and in the blood."—M.]
[[16] German: "And the Spirit is it that testifieth."—M.]
[17] The reading χριστὸς, instead of τὸ πνεῦμα before ἡ ἀλήθεια is only very feebly supported. Equally devoid of all firm foundation are several readings in this verse which do not even touch the sense, *e. g.* μόνῳ, ἀλλὰ καὶ, ἀλήθεια without the Article.

Verse 7. [[18] German: "For they are three that bear witness;" Alford "For those who bear witness are three." German: "And the three are one." Alford: "And the three concur in one."—M.]

Verse 9. [[19] German: "because."—M.]
[20] ὅτι is the reading of A. B. Sin. al. instead of ἥν, Rec. [K. L. al. German: "because that is the testimony of God, that He hath testified of His Son." Alford: "The testimony of God is this, that He hath borne testimony concerning His Son."—M.]

Verse 10. [21] The addition of τοῦ θεοῦ after μαρτυρίαν in A, is wanting in B. Sin. al.
[22] τῷ θεῷ in B. G. Sin. is more authentic than τῷ υἱῷ of A. and in better agreement with the context.
[[23] German: "He that believeth in the Son of God, hath the testimony in himself; he that believeth not God, hath made Him a liar, because He hath not believed in the testimony, which God hath given concerning His Son." The last clause is more correctly rendered thus: "which God hath testified concerning His Son." The variation "record" in this verse in E. V. should by all means be avoided.—M.]

Verse 11. [24] ἐστιν, generally at the end of the verse; in A. between αὕτη and ἡ ζωὴ.
[[25] German: "And this is the life in His Son."—M.]

Verse 12. [26] τοῦ θεοῦ after the first τὸν υἱὸν, as Luther reads, is too feebly supported; it is wanting in the best Codd., also in Sin.
[[27] German: "hath not the life."—M.]

* For particulars concerning this passage see *Critical Note* on vv. 7, 8.—M.

CRITICAL NOTE ON VERSES 7 AND 8.

After ὅτι τρεῖς εἰσὶν οἱ μαρτυροῦντες in v. 7, follows: ἐν τῷ οὐρανῷ, ὁ πατήρ, ὁ λόγος καὶ τὸ ἅγιον πνεῦμα. καὶ οὗτοι οἱ τρεῖς ἕν εἰσιν v. 8, καὶ τρεῖς εἰσὶν οἱ μαρτυροῦντες ἐν τῇ γῇ·—Thus Cod. 173, not however in the original Cod. of the 11th century, but only in a copy of it made in the 16th century; Codd. 34 and 162, belonging to the same period, viz. the 15th and 16th centuries, omit the words καὶ οἱ τρεῖς τὸ ἕν εἰσιν, and the Articles before πατήρ, λόγος and ἅγιον πνεῦμα, which shows the mechanical translation from the Vulgate. Said words are wanting in ALL THE GREEK CODICES, also in the CODEX SINAITICUS, in ALMOST ALL THE ANCIENT VERSIONS, INCLUDING THE LATIN, as late as the 8th century, and since that time they are found in three variations. Notwithstanding the trinitarian controversies, they are not referred to by a SINGLE GREEK FATHER, OR BY ANY OF THE OLDER LATIN CHURCH FATHERS. For the allusions of Tertullian (adv. Prax. 25. *connexus Patris in filio et filii in Paracleto, tres efficit cohærentes alterum ex altero;* QUI TRES UNUM SUNT), and of Cyprian (ep. ad Jubaianum: *cum* TRES UNUM sunt) are to Jno. x. 30; xvi. 5; and if the latter says in De Unitate Ecclesiæ p. 79. "*Dicit Dominus: ego et Pater unum sumus;* ET ITERUM *de Patre et Filio et Spiritu Sancto Scriptum est:* ET HI TRES UNUM SUNT, the reference in *iterum* is clearly to this place, but to v. 8, to wit, according to the symbolical interpretation [of the words τὸ πνεῦμα, τὸ ὕδωρ and τὸ αἷμα of the Trinity, as given in the Schol. by Matthæi: οἱ τρεῖς δὲ εἶπεν ἀρσενικῶς, ὅτι σύμβολα ταῦτα τῆς τριάδος, and in the Schol.: τουτέστι τὸ πνεῦμα τὸ ἅγιον καὶ ὁ πατὴρ καὶ αὐτὸς ἑαυτοῦ, and on ἕν εἰσιν: τουτέστι μία θεότης, εἷς θεός], as Facundus of Hermiane in the 6th century understood Cyprian, in *Pro defens. trium capitum* 1, 3 [*tres sunt qui testimonium dant* (*in terra?*). *Spiritus, aqua et sanguis, hi tres unum sunt .... quod Joannis apostoli testimonium Cyprianus .... de Patre, Filio et Spiritu Sancto intelligit.*—M.], who was not unacquainted with and free from mystical interpretations (the seamless coat, a type of Church unity, etc.). The aforecited Greek scholia contain unmistakable traces of the allegorical interpretation. The reading may gradually have originated in them and the passages from Cyprian, whose interpretation of the Persons of the Trinity was placed in *juxtaposition* with the text on which it was based. These words were mentioned first in a work which is to be ascribed to Vigilius of Thapsus, at the close of the 5th century; they occur more frequently afterwards and are found in most *Latin translations* [also in several German translations made from the Vulgate—M.]. After a Greek translation of the transactions of the Lateran Council of 1215 they were first inserted in Greek in the Complutensian edition (of 1502 to 1514). Erasmus, who did not insert them in his editions of the Greek New Testament of 1516 and 1518, received them in the version of 1521, and the third edition of 1522, yielding to the pressure of the Church (*pium. est, nostrum sensum semper ecclesiæ judicio submittere*), and with reference to the Codex Britannicus (=codex 34), in order to justify himself before the learned. [Erasmus had committed himself to their insertion if they were found in any Greek Manuscript. Learning that they were found in said Codex Britannicus, he inserted them in the 3rd edition of 1522 and added the note: "*Ex hoc igitur Codice Britannico reposuimus, quod in nostris dicebatur deesse: ne cui sit ansa calumniandi. Tametsi suspicor codicem illum ad nostros esse correctum.*"—M.]. Then Robert Stephanus received them 1546–1569, Beza 1565–1576 and the Text. Recept. sanctioned the citizenship of this reading. Luther never translated these words, but commented upon them in his second commentary on this Epistle, although he had pronounced them spurious in his first commentary. They are omitted in all German *Wittenberg* Bibles from 1522–1545; they are first inserted in Lehmann's Quarto Wittenberg edition of 1596, although they are still wanting in later editions and in the Quarto edition of 1620. They appear first in the *Zürich* edition of 1529; the next edition of 1531 has this passage in smaller type, the later editions insert it in brackets, which were not abandoned until 1597. The *Basle* edition of 1552 gives it already without brackets. Of the *Frankfort* editions, the Quarto of 1582 was the first in which this passage is inserted, although it is omitted in the Octavo edition of the same year. It was of no avail that Luther considered these words as a clumsy addition directed against the Arians which was wanting in the Greek Bibles, and that Bugenhagen, on the appearance in 1549, of a lectionary, containing these words, at Wittenberg, gave this warning: "*Obsecro chalcographos et eruditos viros, ut illam additionem omittant et restituant græca suæ priori integritati et puritati propter veritatem.*"—The genuineness of this passage was still attempted to be defended in the 17th century. Lastly Bengel still upheld it [but with the arbitrary assumption, that the text read originally thus: "ὅτι τρεῖς εἰσιν οἱ μαρτυροῦντες ἐν τῇ γῇ. Τὸ πνεῦμα κ. τ. λ. εἰς τὸ ἕν εἰσιν. v. 8. Καὶ τρεῖς εἰσιν οἱ μαρτυροῦντες ἐν τῷ οὐρανῷ, ὁ πατήρ, ὁ λόγος καὶ τὸ ἅγιον πνεῦμα· καὶ οὗτοι οἱ τρεῖς ἕν εἰσιν. Apparat. Crit.—M.], who was followed by v. Meyer, Sander, Besser and Mayer.—Compare Griesbach's *diatribe ad h. l. in ed. a.* 1806; Rickli on this passage; Tischendorf *editio major* 1859, *tom.* 2. p. 225–228.—This critical, external evidence is fully sustained by internal evidence, viz. the exegetical reasons against these words. The idea of a witness ἐν τῷ οὐρανῷ cannot be carried out. Hence certain commentators, *e. g.* a Lapide, change the *testari in cœlo* into a *testari de cœlo*, or find in it a description of the nature of the testimony (S. Schmidt, Spener), or of the witnesses (Bengel). *Moreover* the collocation of the words ὁ πατήρ and ὁ λόγος is altogether contrary to John's diction, which gives only ὁ θεός and ὁ λόγος or ὁ πατήρ and ὁ υἱός in juxtaposition (Jno. i. 1 sqq.; v. 21 sqq.; xiv. 9 sqq.) *Again* τὸ ἕν can only be interpreted of unity of essence and the context affords no ground for such an interpretation. The advocates of the passage have *also* recourse to arbitrary expedients, *e. g.* Bengel who places v. 8 before v. 7 [see above—M.]. *Lastly* we cannot consider them to have been inserted by orthodox Christians against the Arians (as Luther thinks), the reference being to a testimony *on earth*. The fact is that they cannot be used without arbitrariness grammatically, dialectically or logically. Cf. Huther 2d edition, p. 228 sq.—[Huther: Luther remarks on this passage: "It seems that this verse was inserted by the orthodox with reference to the Arians, *which insertion however was not congruous*, because he does not discourse of the witnesses in heaven, but of the witnesses on earth, here and there." This is the opinion of most modern expositors, excepting Besser and Sander. If we look at the contents of the *whole* Epistle, it is indeed not difficult to harmonize the thought of the three witnesses in heaven with scattered sayings in this Epistle; but it does not follow from this that it is appropriate or even necessary at the place where it occurs. On the contrary this is manifestly not the case, since neither the verses immediately following or preceding, with which v. 7 is intimately connected by ὅτι, contain any reference whatsoever to such a trinitarian testimony in heaven. The specification of the three witnesses: πνεῦμα, ὕδωρ, αἷμα, is clearly and plainly substantiated by what precedes, but this is not the case with respect to that of the three witnesses: ὁ πατήρ, ὁ λόγος, τὸ πνεῦμα ἅγιον; this trinity is introduced abruptly, without any preparation; but the sequel also militates against it, especially since it is altogether uncertain which testimony is meant by the μαρτυρία του θεοῦ, v. 9, that of the three in heaven, or that of the three on earth.—To this must be added that these two different testimonies are placed in juxtaposition without being connected together; it is said, indeed, that the two three witnesses agree together, but nothing is said of the relation of the two threes to one another.—The thought *per se*, moreover, lacks clearness; for what are we to understand by a testimony in heaven? Bengel (with whom Sander agrees) says indeed: "*Non fertur testimonium in cœlo, sed in terra: qui autem testantur, sunt in terra, sunt in cœlo; i. e. illi sunt naturæ terrestris et humanæ, hi autem naturæ divinæ et gloriosæ.*" But the untenableness of this proposition is evident, on the one hand, from the circumstance that ἐν τῷ οὐρανῷ does not belong to εἰσιν, but to μαρτυροῦντες, that consequently the text absolutely says nothing of a being in heaven, but asserts *a testifying in heaven*, and on the other, from the consideration that the πνεῦμα which is afterwards connected with ὕδωρ and αἷμα is to be conceived as something earthly and human.—Add to this the non-johannean character of the diction, for though in John we meet the collocations ὁ θεός and ὁ λόγος, and ὁ πατήρ and ὁ υἱός, we never encounter that of ὁ πατήρ and ὁ λόγος; Sander, to be sure, has recourse to the rather easy expedient of assuming here an ἅπαξ λεγόμενον, but that assumption cannot be admitted here, because those words are of constant occurrence in John—and the collocation is not accidental, but founded on the nature of the case. The interpolator evidently wrote λόγος because he thought that term to be purely Johannean, not reflecting however that its connection with πατήρ was un-johannean. Lastly, καὶ οὗτοι οἱ τρεῖς ἕν εἰσι, is also surprising. Bengel explains: *Unum sunt essentia, notitia, voluntate, atque adeo consensu testimonii;* and properly begins with the *unity of essence*, for that is indicated by said words—but this unity of essence is irrelevant here, where the reference is rather to the *unity of the testimony*.—I subjoin here also Sir Isaac Newton's PARAPHRASTIC EXPOSITION: "*Who is he that overcometh the world, but he that believeth that* JESUS *is the Son of God*, that Son spoken of in the Psalms, where He saith, 'Thou art my Son, this day have I begotten thee.' *This is He that*, after the Jews had long expected Him, *came*, first in a mortal body, *by* baptism of *water*, *and* then in an immortal one by shedding His *blood* upon the cross, and rising again from the dead; *not by water only, but by water and blood*, being the Son of God, as well as by His supernatural birth of the Virgin (Luke i. 35). *And it is the Spirit* also, *that* together with the water and the blood, *beareth witness* of the truth of His coming; *because the Spirit is truth*, and so a fit and unexceptionable witness. *For there are three that bear record* of His coming; *the Spirit*, which He promised to send, and which was since sent forth upon us in the form of cloven tongues, and of various gifts; *the* baptism of *water*, wherein God testified, 'this is my beloved Son;' *and* the shedding of His *blood*, accompanied with the resurrection, whereby He became the most faithful martyr or witness of the truth. *And these three*, the Spirit, the baptism, and passion of Christ, *agree* in witnessing *one* and the same thing (namely, that the Son of God is come); and therefore their evidence is strong: for the Law requires but two consenting witnesses, and here we have three, *and if we receive the witness of men, the* threefold *witness of God*, which He bare of His Son, by declaring at His baptism 'This is my beloved Son,' by raising Him from the dead, and by pouring out His Spirit upon us, *is greater;* and therefore ought to be more readily received."—"This," Sir Isaac Newton observes, "is the sense plain and natural, and the argument full and strong; but if you insert the testimony of the three in heaven, you interrupt and spoil it; for the whole design of the Apostle being here to prove to men by witness the truth of Christ's coming, I would ask how the testimony of the 'three in heaven' makes to this purpose? If their testimony be not given to men, how does it prove to them the truth of Christ's coming? If it be (given), how is the testimony in heaven distinguished from that on earth? It is the same Spirit which witnesses in heaven and in earth. If in both cases it witnesses to us men, wherein lies the difference between its witnessing in heaven and its witnessing in earth? If in the first case it does not witness to them to whom does it witness? And to what purpose? And how does its witnessing make to the design of St. John's discourse? Let them make good sense of it who are able. For my part, I can make none. If it be said, that we are not to determine what is Scripture, and what not, by our private judgments, I confess it in places not controverted, but in disputable places, I love to take what I can best understand."—M.]

EXEGETICAL AND CRITICAL.

Connection. That which in the *preceding* verses had been repeatedly noticed as a proof of the love of God, the appearing of Jesus Christ (vv. 9, 10, 14, 19), and as the immediate consequence of it, had been indicated as the exhibition of our life-fellowship with God,—faith, knowledge and confession—(vv. 15, 16), the Apostle places with emphatic prominence at the end of this section with a primary reference to brotherly love (v. 1), then with respect to the love of God and obedience to His commandment (vv. 2, 3), with reference to the victory over the world (v. 4), viz. faith in Jesus the Christ (v. 1*a*), the Son of God (v. 5), who is confirmed as such by God Himself (vv. 6–9), and in His work or gift, eternal life (vv. 10–12). Bengel: "*Concinne Apostolus in hac tractationis parte mentionem amoris ita collocat ut fides tanquam prora et puppis totius tractationis, in extremo spectetur.*"

Efficacy of faith in Christ. vv. 1–5.

VER. 1. **Every one that believeth that Jesus is Christ, is born of God.**—The only limitation of the universality (πᾶς) is believing (πιστεύων) and the object of faith (ὅτι Ἰησοῦς ἐστιν ὁ χριστός); the faith may be weak and imperfect, provided that it be sincere (subjective) and right (objective), and consequently true. This believing involves knowledge, inclination, yielding and trust and genders susceptibility for receiving. It is clear from v. 5 that ὁ χριστὸς refers to the inward nature of Him that has been manifested,=ὁ υἱὸς τοῦ θεοῦ, although these ideas are not identical and may occur in juxtaposition (iii. 23): the Divine Sonship makes the Man Jesus the Christ=Saviour. Cf. ch. iv. 15 and ii. 22. The tenses, the Present πιστεύων and the Perfect γεγέννηται denote the regeneration, the birth out of God as the ground, and faith, which is a Divine work (Eph. ii. 8), as the consequence; only a child of God believes in Jesus the Son of God.

And every one that loveth Him that begot him, loveth also him that is begotten of Him.—Πᾶς ὁ ἀγαπῶν is a parallel of πᾶς ὁ πιστεύων, and gives prominence to what was given along with and received in faith. Hence there is no need of an ellipsis to be filled up, like that specified by Huther: "he that is born of God loveth God." The object (γεννήσαντα) is evidently God, and hence ἐξ αὐτοῦ=θεοῦ, and τὸν γεγεννημένον ἐξ αὐτοῦ denotes the believer (v. 2: τὰ τέκνα τοῦ θεοῦ). *Argumentum ex communi naturæ ordine sumtum* (Calvin), or *a propensione naturali, quæ cernitur in hominibus* (Estius). Cf. Eph. v. 28–30. The reference therefore is not to Christ as maintained by Augustine, Hilary and others. The Present ἀγαπᾷ by the side of ὁ ἀγαπῶν denotes the interconnection of brotherly love and the love of God [i. e. *our* love of our brother and of God—M.], the simultaneousness and duration of the relation of both. The Apostle lays it down as a fact, not as something which he requires; he shall love.

VER. 2. **In this we know, that we love the children of God, when we love God and keep His commandments.**—It is clear that the reference here is to something which every one may and must know from his own experience and not from that of others. Again it is clear that this something is brotherly love, even the love to our brethren, who are τέκνα θεοῦ. Lastly it is clear that the token and sign of it is our love to God and our keeping His commandments. For ὅταν followed by the Indicative ἀγαπῶμεν (Winer, p. 325), is a conditional particle, although it is qualified by the idea of time, =whensoever; there may be fluctuations, disturbances, pauses, or ebbs in our love to God; but when it is in us, brotherly love surely is also in us. Hence John annexes to ἀγαπῶμεν τὸν θεόν, τὰς ἐντολὰς αὐτοῦ τηρῶμεν in order to designate the living love to God by an obedience rooted in the love of God, so that brotherly love should be considered as one of the commandments of God, and, at the same time, as the necessary consequence of our love to God, as of the necessary ground. [Huther: He that loves God, has in this his love a testimony that he also loves his brethren, even as τέκνα τοῦ θεοῦ—because brotherly love is the *necessary consequence* of the love of God; but the converse is also true, that he who loves the brethren, has in this his love a testimony that he also loves God, because his love to God is the *necessary ground* of his love to the brethren. Alford: And indeed so inseparable are the two, that as before iv. 20, our love to our brethren was made a sign and necessary condition of our love to God, so conversely, our love to God, ascertained by our keeping His commandments, is itself the measure of our love to the children of God. Either of the two being found to be present, the presence of the other follows.—M.]. While John elsewhere (ch. ii. 3; iv. 20, 21) makes the knowledge of God and love to God to be ascertained from our keeping His commandments and loving our brethren, *i. e.* the ground from the consequence, so he conversely makes us ascertain the consequence from the ground, which, considering the unity of the Divine life, is the less surprising, since the former references point to the truth and purity of our disposition, while here the concluding reference is to the consolation which we need in the discharge of an important and difficult duty. Hence it is wrong and unnecessary, to assume here, with Grotius following Oecumenius, a trajection, or to construe, with de Wette, the sentence τὸν θεὸν ἀγαπῶμεν as simply accompanying the sentence immediately following, so that obedience is to be considered only as emanating from the love to God, or still worse, to alter the text, as some of the ancient versions (the Ethiopic and Arabic), and several unimportant expositors, have dared to do. [Calvin also gives a wrong turn to the thought in the remark: "*Nunc docet, recte et ordine amari homines, quum Deus priores obtinet; vult sic mutuam coli inter nos caritatem, ut Deus, praeferatur.*"—M.].

VER. 3. **For this is the love of God, that we keep His commandments.**—The connection of our love to God with our keeping His commandments doubtless occasioned this saying, in order to take in its unity that which had been treated as simply coördinate [viz. the ideas expressed in the two preceding clauses.—M.]. Huther.—Αὕτη—ἵνα, as in ch. i. 9; iv. 17, denotes the requirement and tendency of love; ἐστιν describes its nature, not=it implies, it includes the effort (de Wette). The context (v. 2) shows that the love of God here is our love to God.

And His commandments are not grievous; this clause is added by John "encouragingly in the full and joyous consciousness of his Divine sonship," (Düsterdieck). Cf. Matth. xi. 30: φορτίον ἐλαφρόν; Luke xi. 46; φορτία δυσβάσταται. The connection requires us to apply this only to regenerate Christians, to whom is given the ability to keep the commandments of God. So most Commentators. Cf. *Doctrinal and Ethical* on this section below. [Oxford Catena: *εἴ τις προσελθὼν αὐταῖς μὴ ὃν δεῖ τρόπον λέγει αὐτὰς βαρείας, τὴν ἑαυτοῦ ἀσθένειαν ᾐτιάσατο· Φίλον γὰρ τοῖς ἄγαν ἀποβάλλουσιν ἰσχὺν βαρέα νομίζεσθαι καὶ τὰ πανύ ἐλαφρὰ καὶ κοῦφα.*—Spener: "The reference is to the difficulty of a burden so oppressive as to be insupportable and painful."—Calov: "*Dicit ea non esse gravia, quia non aggravant, aut instar molis onerosæ premunt renatum.*"—Huther: "The commandments of God as the requirements of man created after His Image, cannot be difficult to man; but if they are, the reason is, that man has left his original relation to God; they are not difficult to the believer, because, as the child of God, he has returned to the original relation of love to God."—Alford: "This declaration, that His commandments are not grievous, has, as did ch. iii. 9, furnished some of the Roman Catholic Commentators with an opportunity of characterizing very severely the Protestant position that none can keep God's commandments. But here as there the reply is obvious and easy. The course of the Apostle's argument here, as introduced in the next verse by ὅτι, substantiates this *βαρεῖαι οὐκ εἰσίν* by showing that all who are born of God are standing in and upon the victory which their faith has obtained over the world. In this victorious state, and in as far as they have advanced into it, in other words in proportion as the Divine life is developed and dominant in them, do they find those commandments not grievous. If this state, in its ideality, were realized in them, there would be no difficulty for them in God's commandments; it is because, and in so far as sin is still reigning in their mortal bodies and their wills are unsubdued to God's will, that any *βάρος* remains in keeping those commandments." The reader is also reminded of Augustine's saying, "*Da quod jubes et jube quod vis*" (Confess. 10, 29), and referred to Ausonius (ad. Theodos. 13), "*Juvat qui Jubet,*" and Bp. Sanderson, Serm 3. p. 316.—M.].

VER. 4. **Because all that is born of God overcometh the world.**—Now follows (ὅτι) the reason why the commandments of God are not grievous. Hence *πᾶν τὸ γεγεννημένον* as in Jno. iii. 6, 37, 39; xvii. 2 (*πᾶν—αὐτοῖς*, like here *πᾶν—ἡμῶν*), denotes universality. See notes on ch. i. 1, Winer, p. 191, 5=*πάντες οἱ γεγεννημένοι.* The reference is to *persons*, not to disposition, *virtutes* and *charismata* (Oecumenius, Paulus), or to the dignity of the Divine sonship (Baumgarten-Crusius).—*Κόσμος* is here taken collectively, as the opposite of the kingdom of God, as whatever opposes its progress, estranged from and hostile to God and the Divine, within and without men (Calvin [*quicquid adversum est Dei spiritui. Ita naturæ nostræ pravitas pars mundi est, omnes concupiscentiæ, omnes Satanæ actus, quicquid denique nos a Deo abstrahit.*—M.], Beza, Spener, Lücke, Düsterdieck, Huther, and al.); hence not merely inwardly the love of the world and of self (de Wette), or outwardly *homines virtute et pietate adversantes*, their *machinationes*, even to the *persecutiones* (Grotius), nor merely *ecclesia judaica et judaismus* (Schöttgen). [Alford: "The argument then is this: The commandments of God are not grievous: for, although in keeping them there is ever a conflict, yet that conflict issues in universal victory: the whole mass of the born of God conquer the world: therefore none of us need contemplate failure, or faint under his struggle as a hard one."—M.].—The Present *νικᾷ* denotes the constant victory in the conflict to be endured; "the children of God fight with the world only as conquerors" (Düsterdieck), cf. ch. ii. 13, 14; iv. 4. But *νικᾶν* must not be diluted into "keeping oneself, unseduced" (Baumgarten-Crusius).

And this is the victory which hath overcome the world: our faith.—*Αὕτη νίκη* refers to *πίστις, ἡμῶν* is not explained here but in the next verse. *Νίκη*, being further qualified by *νικήσασα*, does not denote the action which conquers the world (Ebrard), but *victoria parta*, the fact of the victory, the faith, not the cause of, but the participation in the victory and the reception of the power of continuing, maintaining and consummating the victory. Lorinus: "*Victoria proprie non vincit, sed comparatur vincendo, sed energiam continet ea formula, denotans in quo sita sit vincendi ratio, unde victoria parta.*" Huther: "Faith is here intended to be extolled not as the result of a conflict, but as the combatant who has gained the victory." Hence faith itself is not yet the victory (Baumgarten-Crusius, Neander), nor must the Aorist be explained to former, departed Christians (Socinus). Cf. ch. ii. 13, 14, 23; iv. 4; v. 12.

VER. 5. **But who is it that overcometh the world, if not he that believeth, that Jesus is the Son of God.**—While v. 4 brought in *ἡμῶν πίστις*, this verse gives emphatic prominence to the *contents* of the faith qualified by *ἡμῶν* in a triumphant question well suited to this section of the victory over the world. Bengel: *Credens omnis et solus vincit.* Episcopius: *Lustrate universum mundum et ostendite mihi vel unum, de quo vere affirmari possit, quod mundum vincat, qui christianus et fide hac præditus non sit.* The Apostle, in this question, appeals to the experience of his Church. The Present *ὁ νικῶν*, which, with respect to the fact: *ἡ νίκη νικήσασα* (v. 4), denotes the person conquering in the conflict, indicates the existing and present attitude and relation of the believer. But by the variation: *ὅτι—ὁ υἱὸς τοῦ θεοῦ* instead of *ὁ χριστός* v. 1, the Apostle refers to the essential glory of Jesus, and also to the fact that believers, as partakers of His glory and as the children of God, of course conquer with Him and participate in His victory. The believer, who is Christ's and whose is Christ the Son of God, is a conqueror in his character of being a child of God. If only faith is true, and the believer born again, born of God, which may be ascertained from love to the brethren and love to God and a hearty obedience to the commandments of God,—the victory over the world also is indubitable. And with this the Apostle is here particularly concerned.

Jesus is really confirmed as the Son of God. vv. 6–9.

VER. 6. **This is He that came by water and blood, Jesus Christ.**—*Οὗτος* refers to the Person Jesus, whose dignity is proved and confirmed. Ὁ *ἐλθών* must be taken substantively as at ch. i.

5; Jno. i. 15, 33; iii. 13, 31; the Article requires this and forbids the connection of the Participle with the preceding ἐστιν, as if it were=this one came; for we read not ἐστιν ἐλθών, but ἐστὶν ὁ ἐλθών. But we must here hold fast the usual form of the *Partic. Aoristi*, which simply narrates that which has happened, and does not denote present events or past events continuing in the present; this would require ἐρχόμενος or ἐληλυθώς (ch. iv. 2). How He came is stated in the words δι' ὕδατος καὶ αἵματος, viz. by means of, by water and blood; διά denotes the medium; immediately afterwards we have ἐν ὕδατι, which indicates surrounding or accompaniment. There must therefore be facts, and facts at once historical and external, by which He came, and which are important and efficacious to demonstrate Him, who He is. Moreover the connection of the two requires us to understand acts equal in kind and relation. Hence we must explain δι' ὕδατος καὶ αἵματος of the baptism, which He received of John in Jordan and which by its immersion pointed to death, while the voice of the Father uttered over Him pointed out His filial dignity, and of His death upon the cross with its atoning sacrificial virtue; in both facts He proved His obedience to the will of the Father, while His obedience proved Him to be the Son of God, the Holy and Innocent One.—Now the apposition Ἰησοῦς=οὗτος, χριστὸς=ὁ ελθών δι' ὕδατος καὶ αἵματος, comprises what is here said into one whole as the result. A similar turn may be seen in Rom. i. 3, 4. Consequently we must not, contrary to the grammar and the dialectics of the text, refer οὗτος to the Predicate ὁ υἱὸς τοῦ θεοῦ v. 5 (with Knapp, Huther 1st ed.), but to the Subject (Lücke), or to the Subject qualified by the Predicate (Huther 2d ed.); we must and cannot explain contrary to grammatical usage (Matth. xi. 3; Luke vii. 19 sq.; Jno. xi. 27), ὁ ἐλθών of the Messiah, like ὁ ἐρχόμενος, and connect ἐστιν with δι' ὕδατος καὶ αἵματος (Hofmann, *Schriftbeweis* ii. 1, p. 469), or take ἐστιν ἐλθὼν as a circumlocution of the *verbum finitum* the Article notwithstanding, and thus overlooking the force of the Aorist, explain it as a Present: He comes (Luther and al.), or as a Perfect: He has come and comes (de Wette, Sander and al.). There is no reference here to the water and blood which flowed from His side pierced on the cross (Jno. xix. 34, Augustine and al.), because the passage in John has αἷμα before ὕδωρ, and because that does not constitute a phase of His life, but is something which, after death had set in, took place in His body, so that concerning it we cannot predicate ὁ ἐλθὼν διά. The symbolical reference of this passage to the two Sacraments, Baptism and the Lord's Supper, is inadmissible (Luther I, S. Schmid, Bengel, Sander, Besser and al.), since the term ἐληλυθὼς is not used here, and αἷμα is not used to describe the Lord's Supper; but since the two ideas are parallel, ὕδὼρ cannot be referred to the Sacrament of Baptism (ὕδωρ moreover cannot be made to designate Baptism Jno. i. 26, 33), as instituted by Christ, nor αἷμα to the death He suffered (de Wette, Rickli, Düsterdieck, Ebrard and al.), nor both together to Baptism only (Luther I), since Baptism was administered into the death of Christ; the *double* reference is, by all means, to be held fast. It is either historically or grammatically unwarranted to explain ὕδωρ of *vita purissima* (Grotius), *doctrina pura* (Socinus), *regeneratio et fides* (Clemens Alex.), of tears, and αἷμα of the blood shed at the circumcision, *expiatio* (Cameron), *redemptio* (Bullinger), *cognitio* (Clemens Alex.). Compare particularly Huther on this passage. [Huther, who has changed his view expressed in the first ed. of his commentary, says in the 2d ed. p. 221. "There are two points in the life of Jesus which answer to the terms ὕδωρ and αἷμα, to wit, *His Baptism* at the *beginning* of His Messianic career, and *His bloody death* at the *end* of the same; by *Baptism* Jesus entered upon His office, which is the office of reconciliation; it constitutes the *initiatio* (Erdmann, Myrberg) of it; this initiation, however, did not take place only by that which occurred during His Baptism, but by the act of the Baptism itself, since thereby Christ consecrated Himself to death, which was symbolized by the act of immersion; by His *death* He effected reconciliation in cancelling with His Blood the debt of the world of sinners, for χωρὶς αἱματεκχυσίας οὐ γίνεται ἄφεσις (Heb. ix. 22). The Apostle therefore rightly designates Christ as the Reconciler, as Him that came δι' ὕδατος καὶ αἵματος. The view that ὕδωρ and αἷμα are to be explained of the Sacraments instituted by Christ is confuted not only by the circumstance that they are only *the means of appropriating* the reconciliation effected by Him, whereas we are here concerned with *the accomplishment of the reconciliation itself*, but also by the use of the Aorist ἐλθών, instead of which in the former case we ought to have the Present, and by the fact that the term αἷμα, used alone, is in the New Testament *not once* applied to the Lord's Supper; in 1 Cor. xii. 13 also ἐποτίσθησαν does not allude to the Lord's Supper, but to the communication of the Spirit in Baptism.—The opinion that though αἷμα denotes the death which Christ suffered, ὕδωρ does not signify the Baptism He received is opposed by the following considerations: 1. The close connection of the two words (διά not being repeated before αἵματος) is only fitting if the ideas correspond the one to the other, which they do not if δι' ὕδατος is referred to an institution of Christ, and αἵματος to the blood shed by Christ. 2. The simple term ὕδωρ is ill-suited to designate Christian baptism (for Christian Baptism is distinguished from John's Baptism in that the former is *essentially* not ὕδωρ like the latter; even as John the Baptist distinguishing himself from Christ said: ἐγὼ βαπτίζω ἐν ὕδατι Jno. i. 26, while Jesus had been indicated to him as ὁ βαπτίζων ἐν πνεύματι ἁγίῳ, Jno. i. 33. 3. Since the institution of Baptism took place *after* the death of Christ and necessarily presupposed that death, John, had he understood by ὕδωρ Christian Baptism, would surely have put ὕδατος not *before* but *after* αἵματος. Hilgenfeld and Neander have justly maintained that if ἔρχεσθαι δι' αἵματος denotes something relating to the Messiah personally, ἔρχεσθαι δι' ὕδατος must do so likewise. The relation must be the same in both terms. If αἷμα signifies the death to which Christ submitted, ὕδωρ also can only signify the Baptism to which He in like manner submitted."—Passing to that class of commentators who substantially admit the views expressed by Huther, but superadd a secondary or implied sacramental reference, we give the language of Alford who says that "ὕδωρ represents the Baptism of water which the Lord Himself underwent and instituted for His followers, αἷμα, the Baptism of blood which He Himself underwent and instituted for His followers. It is equally impossible to sever . . . . from these words the historical accompaniments and associations which arise on their mention. The Lord's Baptism, of itself, was indeed rather a result than a proof of His Messiahship: but in it, taking St. John's account only, a testimony to His Divine Sonship is given, by which the Baptist knew Him to be the Son of God: ἐγὼ ἑώρακα κ. μεμαρτύρηκα ὅτι οὗτος ἐστιν ὁ υἱὸς τοῦ θεοῦ, are his words, Jno. i. 34; and when that blood was poured from His "riven side," he that saw it again uses the same formula ὁ ἑωρακὼς μεμαρτύρηκε. It cannot be that the word μαρτυρία being thus referred to two definite points of our Lord's life, should not apply to these two, connected as they are with ὕδωρ and αἷμα here mentioned, and associated by St. John Himself with the remarkable preterite μεμαρτύρηκεν, of an abiding μαρτυρία in both cases. But these past facts in the Lord's life are this abiding testimony to us, by virtue of the permanent application to us of their cleansing and atoning power."—Wordsworth, as usual, adopts the Patristic and symbolical interpretation, and as the views of other classes of commentators have been given at considerable length, we add as a *curiosum* his exposition of this passage in a condensed form. "Jesus Christ *came*, as the Messiah and Son of God, in various ways.

1. 'He *came* in all the purifications that were made by *water* and *blood* under the Old Law, which was dedicated with blood and water. Heb. ix. 22; because all those purifications were typical of, and preparatory to, His sacrifice on the Cross, and derived all their efficacy from it. . . . . . .

2. 'He *came* by *water* in His Baptism; and by *blood* in His circumcision, and especially in His agony and bloody sweat in Gethsemane, and by the blood shed in His scourging before His passion, and in the crown of thorns, and the piercing of His hands at the crucifixion. . . . .

3. 'He *came* both by *water and blood* at once, in a special manner, on Calvary after His death. . . .

'Thus St. John in his Gospel prepares us to understand the words of this Epistle; and in his Epistle also he elucidates what had been recorded in his Gospel. His words therefore may be thus paraphrased: 'This is He who *came*—that is, proved Himself to be what He was pre-announced to be by the types and prophecies of the Old Testament, and what He proclaimed Himself to be in the New—the "*Coming One*," "*The Comer*" (ὁ ἐρχόμενος); the *Messiah*, the true *Paschal Lamb*, and *Very Man*, a true *Sacrifice for Sin;* and yet *Very God*, the *Everlasting Jehovah*, of whom the prophet Zechariah spoke (Zech. xii. 10), when he prophesied of His being pierced at His death.

'He came by *blood* and *water*. He proved thereby the reality of His *humanity* and of His *death;* and thus He has given a practical refutation—which St. John saw with his own eyes—to the heretical notions of those in the Apostolical age, such as Simon Magus and the Docetae, who alleged that Christ had *not a real human body*, but was merely a spectral phantasm, crucified in show; and therefore Irenæus in the next age after St. John, infers this fact of the piercing of the side and the flowing out of the blood and water, recorded by St. John, as conclusive against their heresy. . . .

'In the words, "*not* by *water* only," there seems also to be a reference to another heresy of the Apostolic age, that of Cerinthus, who said that Christ came in the *water of baptism*, and descended into the Man Jesus; and afterwards departed from Him, when He shed His *blood* on the cross. In opposition to this notion St. John says, "This is He who came by water and blood; *not by water only*, but by water and *blood*."

4. 'Further it is to be observed that in this passage of his Epistle St. John is speaking of Christ's *generation*, and of our *regeneration*.—Every one who believeth that Jesus is the Christ, *hath been born*, and *is born*, of *God; i. e.*, is *regenerate;* and every one who loveth Him that *begat*, loveth Him also that is *begotten of Him; i. e.*, whosoever loveth God the *Father*, loveth Him who by *generation* is the only-begotten *Son of God;* and every thing that is born of God (*i. e.*, is *regenerate*) overcometh the world; and who is he that overcometh the world, but he that believeth that *Jesus*—the *Very Man* Jesus—is also the *Son of God?*

'St. John then proceeds to describe the *means* by which *our regeneration*, or *New Birth*, is communicated to us from God, through His Son Christ Jesus, Very Man and Very God, and how the *new life*, so communicated, is sustained *in us*. He does this by saying, This is *He who came*—came to us—by water and blood, Jesus Christ; not by water only, but by water and blood.

'The *natural* life which was imparted to Eve—the Mother of all living, the type of the Church, the Spouse of the Second Adam, Jesus Christ—was derived from the first Adam's side, opened when he was *asleep* in Paradise. In like manner, the *spiritual life* is given to the spiritual *Eve*, the Church, and to all her faithful members, from the side of the second Adam, Jesus Christ, *sleeping in death* on the cross; and it is communicated through His *death* by means of the *water* and *blood* of the *two sacraments*, which derive their quickening, cleansing and invigorating virtue from the Divinity, Incarnation and Death of our crucified Lord and Saviour, and by which the benefit of that death is applied to our regeneration and revivification; and which were visibly exhibited in the *water* and *blood* flowing from His precious side, pierced on the cross. . . . [See Augustine, Serm. V.—M.].

'He came by water, which is our λουτρὸν, and by blood, which is our λύτρον. His Baptism of blood is our λύτρον, or *ransom* from death; and His Baptism by water is our λουτρὸν, or *laver* of birth. And the *water* of the λουτρὸν derives its efficacy from the *blood* of the λυτρόν, shed on the cross, which works in and by the water of baptism. He has washed us from our sins in His own *blood* (Rev. i. 15). His *blood cleanseth* us from all sin (1 Jno. i. 7). In baptism we pass through the Red Sea of His blood, and are delivered from our enemies thereby."—For further particulars connected with the symbolical interpretation, the reader is referred to Wordsworth himself, and for a good account of all the interpretations, to Huther's Commentary, 2d edition, pp. 217-219.—M.].

Not in the water only, but in the water and in the blood.—The preposition ἐν should be connected with ἐλθὼν, and, as compared with διὰ, signifying the medium through which, introduces a new shade of thought, viz., the surrounding, accompaniment and sphere [or "element in which"—M.]; a similar change occurs at Heb. ix. 12, 25 (Delitzsch, pp. 390, 434). *Articulus habet vim relativam* (Bengel) to what has just been specified, which must be taken in the same sense as before. Μόνον after ὕδατι renders the latter very emphatic, and is not followed by ἀλλὰ καὶ because it is not connected with οὐ. Consequently not only in the Baptism received at the hands of John the Baptist has Jesus been proved to be the Christ, the Son of God, but in both. This refutes the opinion of those heretics who alleged that the Son of God was with Jesus at His Baptism, but not at His death upon the cross, that He left Him before His death (Huther [*i. e.*, the heresy of Cerinthus.—M.]). The distinction of Jesus from the Baptist, who baptized with water only, is out of the question, the reference being not to Jesus' baptizing, but to His being baptized (against Lücke, Düsterdieck, Ebrard and others).

And it is the Spirit that testifieth.—Καὶ superadds a further and third particular, an additional witness (ἐστιν τὸ μαρτυροῦν cf. ὁ ἐλθὼν). The Article before the Participle compels us to understand τὸ πνεῦμα as the absolute, objective Spirit, as the Holy Spirit, and the Present denotes the continuance of the office of witnessing (Jno. xv. 26) wherein He leads into all truth, mediates fellowship with Christ, and secures eternal life. Τὸ πνεῦμα must not be explained of the spirit of believers, of the spiritual life wrought in believers by the Holy Spirit (Episcopius, Sander and others); this is forbidden by the context, and the grammatical usage of the New Testament disallows such a construction without any further qualification Nor is it=ὁ πνευματικός, *i. e.*, the Apostle John himself (Ziegler, Stroth), nor a third sacrament of *absolution* (Augustine), nor the word, the ministry of the word (Luther, Piscator, al.). [In order to complete the catalogue of curious and fantastic views begun in the text, we mention those of Oecumenius and Knapp, who regard τὸ πνευμᾶ=ὁ θεός—διὰ δὲ τοῦ πνεύματος, ὅτε ὡς θεὸς ἀνέστη ἐκ νεκρῶν· θεοῦ γὰρ τοῦτο μόνον λοιπόν, τὸ ἀνιστᾶν ἑαυτόν. τῇ δὲ τοῦ πνεύματος φωνῇ σημαίνεται ὁ θεος: thus making the threefold witness to the υἱοθεσία of Jesus, τὸ βάπτισμα, ὁ σταυρός, ἡ ἀνάστασις; of Socinus, Schlichting, Grotius, Whitby and al. who understand the Divine power by which Christ wrought His miracles: '*id est*,' says Grotius, '*per μετωνυμίαν, admiranda ejus opera, a virtute divina manifeste procedentia*,' of Bede, who understands the Spirit which descended on the Lord at His Baptism, and of Wetstein, who considers τὸ πνεῦμα to signify the *psychical* element which, along with ὕδωρ and αἷμα the *physical* elements, constituted the human nature of Christ.—The interpretation given by Braune is that of Scholiast I., Estius, Corn. a-Lapide, Tirinus, Calvin, Calov, Lücke, Rickli, de Wette, Huther, Neander, Düsterdieck, Alford and Wordsworth. It is the *Holy Spirit*, whom Christ in fulfilment of His promise, sent to His Church on the Day of Pentecost, and who is a permanent witness of the Divine Sonship of Jesus.—M.].

Because the Spirit is the truth.—This clause does not contain the substance of the testimony, which is determined by the context (viz., that Jesus, the Son of God, is the Christ), but the reason of the testimony, as being a reliable one; ὅτι is=*because*, not=*that* (Luther, Besser, al.). Ἡ ἀλήθεια designates the Truth revealed in the word of God, and received in faith, in its perfect fulness, which Truth is the nature of the Spirit who is the Spirit of the Truth into which He leadeth (Jno. xiv. 17; xv. 26; xvi. 13). Christ, who has the Spirit without measure (Jno. iii. 34 sq.), and who with the Father sends Him (Jno. xv. 26; xvi. 7), is of course in the same sense the Truth according to His nature (Jno. iv. 6). We must not construe ἡ ἀλήθεια=ἀληθές, as Grotius does. [Estius: "*Testimonium ejus haudquaquam rejici potest, quoniam Spiritus est veritas, quam sit Deus, ideoque nec falli potest, nec fallere.*"—M.].

Vv. 7, 8. **For three are the witnesses, Spirit, water and blood.**—[Grotius: "*Johannes hic causam reddit, cur locutus fuerit non de Spiritu tantum, cujus præcipua in hoc negotio est auctoritas, verum etiam de aqua et sanguine, quia in illis etiam non exigua est testimonii fides, et ternarius numerus in testibus est perfectissimus.*"—M.]. This formula is precisely like that of the preceding verse (v. 6). Οἱ μαρτυροῦντες of course must be construed substantively and in the same sense as v. 6, nor must be supplied another object of the testimony; in like manner τὸ πνεῦμα καὶ τὸ ὕδωρ καὶ τὸ αἷμα bear exactly the same meaning here as in v. 6. The historical facts, previously specified merely as evidencing the Divine Sonship of Jesus, are now introduced in the Masculine Gender, in order to designate them as concrete witnesses, like persons (Lücke and al.); but of course so, that they are subordinated to the Spirit, who is the principal, and alone absolute Witness, employing and making use of the facts in the life of Jesus. The verb denotes the activity of the testifying, with reference to the condition of being μάρτυρ, and the Present signifies the permanent character of that activity, wherefore it is not necessary to think here of objects at present existing, *e. g.*, the sacraments, but we have only to hold fast that these facts in the history of the life of Jesus, like that history itself, are fixed in the Gospels, and that these facts, even without such written fixedness, continue to be permanently operative during the years of salvation [*i. e.*, the dispensation of grace.—M.] with world-historical import [*i. e.*, exerting a permanent influence on the world's history during the dispensation of grace. —M.].—Τρεῖς, with reference to Deut. xvii. 6; xix. 15; Matth. xviii. 16; 2 Cor. xiii. 1; Heb. x. 28, 29, denotes the assurance of the perfectness of the testimony. This sentence is annexed with ὅτι=for, in order to represent now in a compressed form the testimony, particularized in v. 6, as a weighty confirmation and substantiation of the truth, that Jesus, the Son of God, is the Christ.

And the three are one.—The Article οἱ τρεῖς denotes here, as also previously, the witnesses already designated and well known, and likewise in εἰς τὸ ἕν the one Truth in question, the object of the testimony (ch. v. 1, 5). Εἰς, like εἰς ἕν in Jno. xi. 52; xvii. 23, denotes *in unum consentire.*—Hence we need neither assume with de Wette, an ellipsis between vv. 6 and 7, 8, nor take ὅτι in the sense of *jam vero* (Grotius), *consequently, therefore* (Baumgarten-Crusius, Meyer), nor understand τρεῖς οἱ μαρτυροῦντες, with Bengel, of three different classes of men (*prophetas, baptistas, apostolos*), or of symbols of the Trinity. Lastly we must not interpret the being one, with Luther, as a being together, a being joined together. [Alford renders "and the three concur in one" and explains, that they contribute to one and the same result: viz., the truth that Jesus is the Christ, and that we have life in Him. Wordsworth explains the passage of the Trinity and the sacraments and paraphrases: *these three* (Persons) who are bearing witness *are joined into one* (ἕν one *substance*, neuter). He collects, as usual, many Patristic and Anglican notices and gives in his exegesis the following:—'The *Spirit*, who begins the work of regeneration by applying all quickening grace to man.—The *Water:* the symbol and instrument of the new birth derived from God the Father, who is the original *Well-spring* and *Fountain* of all life and grace to man. The natural heavens and the earth were formed out of the *Water*. There was their origin (2 Pet. iii. 5). So it is with the spiritual life; it is formed from out of water. Water therefore is a proper symbol of the Paternity of God.—The *Blood*, symbolizing the *Incarnation* and *Passion* of *God, the Son through* whom all grace descends *from* the *Father, by* the *Holy Spirit.* 2 Cor. xiii. 13.—These three Persons are joined consubstantially *into one Godhead;* and their *Witness* is *the witness of God.* (Andrews: "*Water* notes *Creation; Blood* notes *Redemption* by Christ; the *Spirit* notes *Unction*, to complete all").—There is an image of the Trinity in the Christian sacraments. There is *baptismus* FLUMINIS, the baptism of *water*, the work of *Creation* by the *Father;* there is *baptismus* SANGUINIS, the baptism of *blood*, the work of Redemption by the *Son;* but these are not enough, unless there be also the *baptismus* FLAMINIS, the Baptism of the *Spirit.* Thus the work of the Ever-Blessed Trinity is done in the soul.' In addition to the notes on the spurious passage given above, the reader is referred to a sketch on this subject in Horne's Introduction, vol. IV. pp. 355–388.—M].

VER. 9. **If we receive the testimony of men.**—Εἰ denotes an undoubted fact; hence the Indicative, but the fact is put down as the premise of a conclusion. [It is an *argumentum a minori ad majus.*—M.]. Winer p. 307 sq. [also *ibid*, p. 642.—M.]. In τὴν μαρτυρίαν τῶν ἀνθρώπων. the Article opposes the human testimony to the Divine, without in any way specifying one qualified by its substance (Brückner). The reference therefore is neither to the prophecy of Christ (Bede), nor to John the Baptist, to eye- and ear-witnesses (Wetstein, Stier), nor to prophets, baptists and Apostles (Bengel). Grotius takes λαμβάνειν=*judicio approbare*, and Düsterdieck understands any human testimony, provided that it possess the necessary requirements.

The testimony of God is greater.—Here ἡ μαρτυρία τοῦ θεοῦ is not particular, but quite general [The particular is specified in the sequel. Supply in the argument: much more must we receive the testimony of God (Winer).—M.]. As the testimony of God it is greater than that of men and requires so much the more its reception and validity.

Because this is the testimony of God. Now follows the definite testimony of God, which must be received as the testimony of God. Here is evidently an ellipsis, viz.: but a Divine testimony is really extant, namely this . . . . (Düsterdieck).

That He hath testified of His Son.—The clause beginning with ὅτι depends on αὕτη, and notes the testimony as a historical fact, μεμαρτύρηκε, which has been given, but must be understood to be continuous and permanent in its operation, namely the threefold testimony specified in vv. 7, 8. Hence ὅτι cannot be rendered "because," which would especially designate the author of the testimony, in which case αὐτὸς could hardly be wanting before μεμαρτύρηκε; nor is here any reference to internal testimony (Düsterdieck) introduced afterwards, and still less to the testimony vouchsafed to John the Baptist (Jno. i. 33), as maintained by Ebrard.

The possession of eternal life in the faith on Jesus the Son of God, is the inward confirmation of the Divine testimony vv. 10–12.

VER. 10. **He that believeth in the Son of God, hath the testimony in himself.**—The result as well as the purport of the Divine testimony is faith in Jesus as the Son of God; hence we now have ὁ πιστεύων εἰς τὸν υἱὸν τοῦ θεοῦ. Such an one ἔχει τὴν μαρτυρίαν ἐν ἑαυτῷ. The addition τοῦ θεοῦ is unnecessary; the context precludes any other testimony than that of God; the Article designates that which has been specified and is known. "The outward has become to him something inward" (Huther). ["The object of the Divine testimony being, to produce faith in Christ, the Apostle takes him in whom it has wrought this its effect, one who habitually believes in the Son of God, and says of such an one, that he possesses the testimony in himself. What it is, he does not plainly say till below, v. 11. But easily enough here we can synthetically put together and conjecture of what testimony it is that he is speaking: the Spirit by whom we are born again to eternal Life, the water of baptism by which the new birth is brought to pass in us by the power of the Holy Ghost (Jno. iii. 5; Tit. iii. 5), the Blood of Jesus, by which we have reconciliation with God, and purification from our sins (ch. i. 7; ii. 2), and eternal life (Jno. vi. 53 sqq.),—these three all contribute to and make up our faith in Christ, and so compose that testimony, which the Apostle designates in v. 11 by the shorter term which comprehends them all." Alford following Düsterdieck.—M.].—Ἔχειν bears the same sense here as in. v. 12; ch. iii. 3; ii. 23. Ἐν ἑαυτῷ might be wanting, but John specifies besides the having, the possession of the sphere, the believer's own inward testimony for it. It is wrong to render, *to have with him* (Luther), more wrong, *recipit in se* (Grotius), nor is it=τηρεῖ (Baumgarten-Crusius), nor=he *not only receives it, but is also firmly convinced of it* (Lücke), nor=*he has* *received it in and with himself* (de Wette).—As usual, the Apostle continues in the negative.

He that believeth not God, hath made Him a liar.—The Dative refers not to the object of faith, but to the witness; hence the reading τῷ υἱῷ is not in agreement with the text, as is τῷ θεῷ τῷ μεμαρτυρηκότι (Huther); this is confirmed by αὐτὸν, which must be referred to God, but would have to be connected with υἱῷ, if that were the reading. The Perfect πεποίηκεν indicates the still continuing and operating animus of the disbeliever: he has told and ever tells God to the face: thou liest (Luther). The reason follows:

Because he hath not believed in the testimony, which God hath given concerning His Son.—Οὐ πεπίστευκεν and not μὴ, because John refers to him, whom he had supposed not to believe (ὁ μὴ πιστεύων), as a definite individual, who in point of fact, objectively, has not become believing. Jno. iii. 18: ὁ δὲ μὴ πιστεύων ἤδη κέκριται, ὅτι μὴ πεπίστευκεν, because there the reference is to the judgment of the judge, and not simply to a fact *per se*. See Winer, p. 495 sq. The Perfects denote continuing and permanent facts.

VER. 11. **And the testimony is this, that God hath given us** [better *gave us*—M.] **eternal life.**—John now annexes by καὶ what follows, and this is the substance, the testimony consists in this (αὕτη ἐστὶν ἡ μαρτυρία); the reference is not to *intentio, finis* of the same (Lyra), nor to its use, fruit and blessing (Calov, Spener), nor to its exhibition, test, experience (Lücke, Neander, Huther). The testimony of God is in himself eternal life, which at the Baptism of Jesus, at His death, in the Holy Spirit, makes itself felt and perceptible, and testifies for the Son of God. Hence ὅτι=that, and ἔδωκεν, like μεμαρτύρηκεν points to a giving, with a present continuing of that past giving; it cannot be *dare decrevit, promisit* (Socinus, Carpzov), any more than ζωὴ αἰώνιος is *vita æterna in spe* (Bede), to be given only in heaven *in re*. Ἡμῖν designates the οἱ πεπιστευκότες. To the principal idea, ζωὴ αἰώνιος, placed first, the Apostle now adds

And that is the life in His Son, (or: *and this life is in His Son*).—This clause is co-ordinate with the one preceding and not dependent on ὅτι. Αὕτη ἡ ζωὴ is ἡ αἰώνιος, and this is in Jesus the Son of God; ἐν is not *per* (Grotius), or in communion with Him, nor ἐστιν=*contingit*. The eternal life is οὐσιωδῶς (Jno. i. 4; xi. 25; xiv. 6), σωματικῶς (Col. ii. 9), ἐνεργητικῶς (2 Tim. i. 10) in Christ. It became manifest in Him, because it really was in Him, and the believer participates in the eternal life, because he has part in the Son of God. Hence the conclusion.

VER. 12. **He that hath the Son hath the life; he that hath not the Son of God, hath not the life** (or: *the life he hath not*).—Very fine and pointed is Bengel's note: "Habet versus duo cola; in priore non additur *Dei*, nam fideles norunt *Filium;* in altero additur, ut demum sciant infideles, quanti sit, non habere. Priore hemistichio cum emphasi pronunciandum est *habet;* in altero *vitam*." This is also indicated by the arrangement of the words (Düsterdieck). Ἔχει τὴν ζωὴν is not=*habet jus certum ad vitam æternam* (Grotius). Cf. i. 3; ii. 23; Jno. xvii. 3. [Alford: "*The having the Son* is the possession of Christ by faith testified by the Spirit, the water and the blood: and the *having the life* is the actually possessing it, not indeed in its most glorious development, but in all its reality and vitality."—M.]. Ὁ μὴ ἔχων points to a supposition: if one has not; which implies that he might have, but only through faith vv. 10, 11. [Düsterdieck has remarked that the use of ὁ μὴ ἔχων, not ὁ οὐκ ἔχων (cf. οἱ οὐκ ἠλεημένοι, 1 Pet. ii. 10) shows that the Apostle is contemplating, at all events primarily, rather a possible contingency than an actual fact: and thus is, primarily again, confirming his saying to those to whom the Divine testimony has come. To them, according as they receive or do not receive it, according as they are οἱ ἔχοντες or οἱ μὴ ἔχοντες τὸν υἱὸν τοῦ θεοῦ, it is a savour of life unto life, or of death unto death."—M.].

DOCTRINAL AND ETHICAL.

I. CONCERNING THE PERSON OF CHRIST.

1. In Christ, as the Son of God is the life eternal, so that it is as well said: God has given us the eternal life (v. 11), as: He gave His only begotten Son (Jno. iii. 16); and he that hath the Son, hath the life, the eternal (v. 11). Beside Him there is no salvation (Acts iv. 12).

2. The essential nature of the Son was unmistakably exhibited in His obedience to the will of the Father, both at the commencement of His ministry by the baptism in Jordan, and at the close of it in His death upon the cross (v. 6).

3. The testimony of the Holy Spirit for the Divine Sonship of Christ must not be separated from the historical facts of His life, even as these cannot become witnesses without the Holy Spirit, who has the office of testifying (vv. 6–8); the history on earth must not be severed from the Spirit of God. One might almost find here the principle of the Lutheran Church that the *finitum* may become *infiniti capax*, in opposition to the [German] Reformed principle: *finitum infiniti non capax*.

4. The Father hath so definitely appointed all things, that He who does not believe in the Divine Sonship of Jesus, refuses to believe God (v. 10), as in Jno. xiv. 1.

II. CONCERNING THE ACQUISITION OF SALVATION.

1. *The origin of faith*: *Regeneratio præcedit fidem* (v. 1).

2. *The nature of faith:* it is essentially an ethical act laying hold of the merit of Christ, of the love of the Father in the Son, so that it has (ἔχει) that on which it believes (vv. 12, 10, 11): it includes therefore love, and is not to be joined only to it, as set forth in the Roman Catholic representation of the *fides formata*. Nor does John allow faith to be described as the second condition, nor even as the first condition by the side of love and morality (v. 1), as de Wette holds and expresses it.

3. *The virtues of faith: a.* with reference to *men*—it makes all believers brethren, because it makes them the children of God (v. 2); *b.* with reference to the *commandments of God*—it makes us strong and cheerful in obedience (v. 3), so that Bengel rightly observes: *in se sunt suavia; sed τὸ non gravia contradicit et occurrit iis, qui gravia esse putant; c.* with reference to the *world*—

it imparts courage for the conflict and power for the victory (vv. 4, 5). This it works with reference to men, at the same time changing them, transforming children of men into children of God, and causing such change to be perceived and received; with reference to the law of God and the world, it only changes believers by first giving to them the powers of the eternal life, and afterwards clear perception and a deeper understanding of the justice and blessing of the law and the transitoriness of the world.

4. *The necessity of faith:* without it one has neither Christ, nor God the Father, nor the Holy Spirit, nor the eternal life; consequently, without it and beside it there is no justification, no forgiveness of sins, no sanctification, no salvation (v. 12).

5. *The liberty of faith:* all men are to believe according to the will of God, but coërcion of faith is not ordained; every man has the power of resistance (*ὁ μὴ ἔχων τὸν υἱὸν τοῦ θεοῦ=ὁ μὴ πιστεύων*, vv. 10, 12).

6. *The immorality of unbelief* follows from v. 1, and especially v. 10: not to believe God, to consider Him a liar, is like misbelief and despair, a shameful thing, and, as Luther says in the Catechism, a vice.

III. Concerning the Law.

1. It should be considered as a fact of the revelation of love, of paternal discipline.

2. It answers to the originally God-ordained human nature, which sin has corrupted and grace has healed; the burden and grievousness of it to men proves their state of sin, joy in it and obedience to it, their state of grace.

3. Of his own strength man cannot fulfil a single commandment; in this the Evangelical Church is right.

HOMILETICAL AND PRACTICAL.

Do not separate faith and love! This is forbidden, 1. by the *origin* of faith in the regeneration from God who is Love, and 2. by its *object*, Jesus the Christ, in whom the love of God was manifested, and 3. by its *task*, to conquer the world through love.—Do not fail to distinguish between faith and love in the work of regeneration which is secured by the former, not by the latter, but do not sever them in the sphere of sanctification, where faith is the root of love, and love the many-branched crown of faith.—You may ascertain whether you have faith and are born again from 1. your love to God the Father, 2. from your love of the brethren, 3. from your obedience to the Divine commandments, 4. from your fight with the world in and around you.—Dr. Christian Friedrich Richter, physician at the Orphan House of Halle, in Franke's time, was the author of the Christian song: *Es kostet viel ein Christ zu sein*, etc. 'It costeth much to be a Christian and to live conformably to the mind of the pure Spirit, for nature finds it very hard, ever to be reconciled to the death of Christ,' and the companion verse: 'It is not difficult to be a Christian and to live conformably to the mind of the pure Spirit, for though nature finds it very hard, etc.' Both are true and good. For the law is only a burden to man enfeebled by sin, but not to the Christian strengthened by grace, the one, indeed, is only *enjoined* to be good, but the other is enabled to be good.—Obedience to the Divine commandments notes the recovery of the Spirit, disobedience notes its decay. Nothing is more natural, nothing more adapted to human nature created by God after His own Image, than the Will of God, consistent with His Nature and expressed in the lovingly ordained Law for the benefit of His Kingdom, which was given, not against man, but for man, not against man, but against sin.—Learn from John how to contend with error! With all his resoluteness and decision, he is so objective and calm, and reasons so joyfully on the foundation of truth, that we are not even induced to make a personal application of his reasoning to others, but rather influenced to make it the test of our own standing.

Augustine:—*Qui habet in memoria et servat in vita, qui habet in sermonibus et servat in moribus, qui habet audiendo et servat faciendo, aut qui habet faciendo, et servat perseverando, ipse est, qui diligit Deum. Opere est demonstranda dilectio ne sit infructuosa nominis appellatio.*—You adore the Head, and offend the members. He loves His Body. Just as if somebody would desire to kiss your head, and at the same time trample with nailed shoes on your feet. Would you not decline the proffered demonstration of honour and exclaim: What are you about? You tread on my feet? The head would cry more for the trodden members than make account of being honoured.

Spener:—The meaning is not, that the keeping of the Divine commandments does not require considerable pains, labour and diligence, for that would contradict Luke xiii. 24; 2 Tim. iv. 7.—The difficulty applies to a burden so oppressive and painful as to be unbearable.—Spiritual life is, as to its nature, an eternal life, and consists as well in the grace of God which forgives sin and imparts new Divine strength, as also in the enjoyment of eternal felicity and glory.

Starke:—Christianity is not a sham, but a true and honest thing which has its foundation, its coat of arms and tokens, its works and fruits, its profit and happiness.—If thou hast a sense of shame and honour, thou wilt surely not hurt the saintly children of a saintly father; look, believers are the children of thy heavenly Father; if instead of loving, thou hate them, thou art truly an enemy of God, their Father, and He, in His turn, thy enemy.—If thoughtful preachers stop long at one matter, and perhaps repeat it several times, and with changed phraseology make it more clear, be not impatient of it, but take note of their zeal and of the importance and necessity of the matter treated of.—O, how much pain, burden, difficulty and anxiety attend the children of the world in their sins and iniquities, of which the children of God are free and delivered! Thus many a child of Satan has more trouble to find hell, than a child of God to find heaven.—O man, do not persuade thyself and do not suffer thyself to be persuaded, that the world cannot be overcome. This is the infallible sign of true and false faith: viz., whether thou conquerest the world, or sufferest the world to conquer thee.—The children of God are soldiers and knights. The crown must be fought for; faith is victorious. Wretched man, if conquest and the crowning do not attend thy course! World begone beneath my feet. We will trample under foot lions and vipers. Come hither, sword of the Lord! The blessed state of a righteous man in Christ, his Head! He does not fortify the walls of houses and cities, but the empire of Satan and the walls of Jericho in his heart.—The stronger thy faith, the greater thy victory over sin, the world, death, the devil and hell.—The Bible surpasses, and should be preferred to, all books; all other good books are conducted like rivulets from this river.—Christ is not only the foundation, but also the true centre and chief work of our faith, at which alone the believer under the practice of self-denial, is ever aiming, and into which he does, as it were, ground himself.—As there is nothing more excellent than faith, so is nothing more dishonourable than unbelief. Faith honours God, and is the mother of all virtues; unbelief dishonours God, and is the mother of all vices.—Man must not seek the true life any where except in Christ; nor cherish any hope of life beside Him. As long as he is without Christ, he has no life; whereas the degree to which he is in Christ and partaker of His Being, is also the measure of his life.—A true Christian is a veritable Christophorus, who carries Christ in his heart, and leads his life in Him.—

BESSER:—If thou art a conqueror, thou must have thy spoils to show.—The lust of the flesh, the lust of the eyes and the pride of life are the chief trophies, of which the soldiers of Christ divest the conquered world, and which they suspend from the victorious banner of the cross.—

HEUBNER:—Without prejudice to the general love of man, a Christian must be especially attracted to those who are of one mind with him; he must value the true children of God infinitely more than the unconverted.—The genuineness and holiness of human love betokened by its religious character.—All love is worthless without religion, a mere natural impulse, or masked selfishness.—True love is allied to strict conscientiousness; love must not render us languid or indulgent in respect of duty.—If the love to God requires obedience, the true love of man also must consist in obedience, fidelity and conscientiousness.—Struggle for this strength (v. 3); to be ever complaining is a bad sign.—1. The light of faith conquers the errors, illusions and delusions of false wisdom, it sees through them, perceives their nothingness and masters them; the word of Christ is the eternal, unchangeable truth; faith the pole-star, that we do not swerve from the truth. 2. Faith conquers the allurings and fascinations of the world which we encounter in its lusts, its riches and honours; it conquers them by the love of Christ, by the heavenly riches and the eternal glory, which it discloses. 3. It conquers the threatenings of the world, the obstacles which it raises, its persecutions; the call of Christ to us is too mighty, and the crown of honour offered to us causes us to despise the contempt of the world.—This (viz. the conquest of the world) is an idea peculiar to Christianity, because it only teaches the contrast of the kingdom of God and the world.—A lofty thought, to face the whole world and to conquer it! This is a greater task than that of the world-conquerors; they are servants of the world.—Unbelief is an offence against the Majesty of God, a denial of the holy miracles in the moral world, which God has wrought.—

V. 1. L. in Gesetz und Zeugniss, 1859:—*When does the feast of the Nativity become to us the birth-day of a new life?* When its glad tidings excite in us anew 1. *the undoubting faith* that Jesus is the Christ; but also 2. *grateful love* to God, and to all those who are our brethren in Christ.

On v. 4. SPURGEON:—*A great victory, a great birth, a great grace.*

DANNEIL:—*The Christian's warfare.* 1. The *warrior* (born of God); 2. The *enemy* (the world); 3. The *victory* (faith).

GENTHE, on the tercentenary Anniversary, 1860, Baptismal Address. *How Melanchthon conquered the world in the strength of faith;* 1. The *temptation* of the world; 2. The *opposition* of the world; 3. The *fear* of the world.

V. 5. SCHLEIERMACHER:—*Our Christmas-joy is closely connected with the fact that the faith, that Jesus is the Son of God, is the victory which conquers the world.* 1. The object of the festal joy, that in Jesus is born the Son of God, surpasses all similar events in our family and social life, for through Him we are made well-pleasing to God. 2. The world is destined to be conquered, judged, and destroyed as to its transitory and corruptible side, but to become more and more blessed as to its Divine side, and this has been done in Christ and through Christ in believers, so that it is one and the same thing to say: the the Son of God conquers the world through our faith, and our faith conquers the world through Him.

Vv. 9–12. F. A. WOLF:—*Christ the Author and Giver of a living religion.* 1. Explain and prove that this is true of Christ as a *Witness*, an *Ensample*, and a *Surety*. 2. The inferences: *a.* Christianity has nothing to fear from all-changing time, from false love of novelty, and from true zeal for improvement; *b.* test the genuineness of your own Christianity by the vitality of the faith that is in you.

Vv. 1–13. PETRI:—*The Easter-faith, that Jesus is the Christ.* 1. That we become anew conscious of the wholesome virtues of this faith; 2. and edify ourselves on this our most holy faith.

On the Epistle for *Dom. Quasimodogeniti* [First Sunday after Easter—M.] vv. 4–10.

HEUBNER:—*The great value of faith in Jesus Christ.* 1. How it manifests itself: *a.* in its *power*: it makes us the children of God and conquers the world (vv. 4, 5); *b.* in its *certainty:* it is supported by the testimony of God (vv. 6–8); 2. The duties it enjoins upon us: *a.* it warns us against contempt of faith (v. 9), and *b.* it lays us under the obligation to receive the testimony of God (v. 10).

Faith in Christ the good part of younger Christians (Candidates for Confirmation). 1. Proof: this faith makes them the children of God; preserves them from the world. 2. How do they acquire this faith? By diligent consideration of the testimonies for Jesus, and by ready obedience.

Continued provision for grown-up children, 1. In what it consists; 2. What makes it our bounden duty.—

R. STIER:—*What John means by conquering the world?* Our faith must conquer 1. The *unbelief* of the world; 2. The *sin and seduction* of the world; 3. The *enmity* of the world.—

What sort of faith does conquer the world? 1. Faith in Him, who also was not of the world, but the eternal brightness of the glory of the Father, and the express image of His Person; 2. Faith in Jesus, the Conqueror of the world.—

KAPFF:—*The Confirmation of regeneration.* 1. How the regeneration of mankind is confirmed in Christ; 2. How it is confirmed in individual hearts; 3. What influence in that direction outward confirmation has.

GENZKEN:—Build yourselves up on faith by the Holy Ghost. 1. *This is needful* for the regenerate, as feeble newly-born persons (v. 4); 2. *But the foundation, which is laid, stands firm like a rock* (v. 5); and the Prince of life evermore joins us in the Holy Communion (v. 6); 3. The *Holy Spirit* bears testimony concerning *the truth of His word*, and the *power of His life* (vv. 6, 8–11).

F. W. KRUMMACHER:—The threefold testimony for Jesus the Messiah and Saviour of the world 1. in the water; 2. in the blood; 3. in the Holy Spirit.

BEYER (in Gesetz und Zeugniss for 1862):—*A test of Faith!* 1. Dost thou know the *victory*, whereby faith verifies itself? 2. The *fountain*, whence it daily draws fresh nourishment? 3. The *testimony* which gives it assurance?—

The testimony of God concerning His Son, 1. to us; 2. in us; 3. by us.

The victorious power of faith, 1. against the sin of the world, 2. against the lie of the world.

Our faith is the victory which conquers the world. 1. What sort of faith is it? 2. How is it obtained? 3. How does it conquer the world?—

[VER. 2. MACKNIGHT:—The intention of the Apostle was to show, how we may know when we love the children of God in a right manner. Now this was necessary to be shown, since men may love the children of God because they are their relations, or because they are engaged in the same pursuits with themselves, or because they are mutually united by some common bond of friendship. But love proceeding from these considerations is not the love of the children of God which He requires. By what mark then can we know, that our love to the children of God is of the right sort? "By this," saith the Apostle, "we may know that we love the children of God" in a right manner, "when we love God and" from that excellent principle, "keep His commandments," especially His commandment to love His children, because they bear His Image. True Christian love therefore is that which proceeds from love to God, from a regard to His will, and which leadeth us to obey all His commandments.—M.]

[VER. 3. PUSEY:—"For nothing is grievous or burdensome to him who loves. They are not grievous, because love makes them light; they are not grievous, because Christ gives strength to bear them. Wings are no weight to the bird, which they lift up in the air until it is lost in the sky above us, and we see it no more, and hear only its note of thanks. God's commands are no weight to the soul, which, through His Spirit, He upbears to Himself; nay, rather, the soul, through them, the more soars aloft and loses itself in the love of God."

VER. 4. "'They are not grievous, because every thing which is born of God overcometh the world.' He saith not only whosoever, but 'every thing which,' showing the largeness of the gifts. 'Every thing,' of every sex or age time or clime, 'which is born of God, overcometh the world,' and that not of themselves, but of the gift of God; not they, but the power, through their new birth, in-born in them, faith, love, grace, from God, unto God, and they, as wielding in them a power not their own, overcome the world.—'The commandments of God are not grievous,' because we have a power implanted in us mightier than all which would dispute the sway of God's commandments and God's love, a power which would lift us above all hindrances, carry us over all temptations, impel our listlessness, sweep with it whatever opposes it, sweep with it even the dulness or sluggishness of our own wills, the Almighty power of the grace of God."

"This is the victory, by which the martyrs overcame, by which the weak became strong, and, in Divine strength, mastered the strong; the strength of endurance wearied out the brutal might of affliction; children overcame their oppressor; the ignorant took captive the learning of the world; fishermen and the tent-maker subdued the world; the dying conquered the living; the blood of martyrs became the harvest-seed of the church. By faith, St. Paul says, 'they subdued kingdoms;' by faith St. Peter bids us resist the evil one. For faith knits us to Christ; faith obtains for us the power of Christ; faith prevails with Him who is Almighty, and overcomes the world, for it has power with Him who has power over the world."

"Faith binds us to Him, who is Almighty; but faith, too, opens our own eyes to things invisible. It imparts to us of the power of the All-Powerful, of the wisdom of the All-Wise. It gives us to see the nothingness of all things which are but for a time. It opens our eyes to the majesty and beauty of things eternal. What to us are things which perish in the grasp? What to us are things of time and sense, save as they speak of that which lives when time shall cease to be, or as they shall themselves live on, purified but indestructible? One only is above us, He who made us. All we see is below us. His friends we may be, His we have been made, who is Lord of the world. The world itself, and all which is in the world, is for our use, subject to us, as we to God. All things beautiful to sight, sweet to taste, transporting in sound, pleasant to smell, and thrilling to touch, all things are ours and for us, if used in obedience to their and our Maker. But we are above them. They were made for us, not we for them; they are made to serve us, not we to be slaves to them. Faith shows us Him who is above all things, but in all things; immortal, invisible, incomprehensible, in light unapproachable, yet who willeth to come unto us, and make His abode in us. God made us, because He willed to impart Himself to us. He made us, not that He needed us, but to show us His love. He has made us for Himself, He willed not to make us apart from Himself. He willed to join us to Himself. He who hath and is all things, of which we have the shadow here below, 'the true riches of wisdom, and spiritual delight, royal glory, eternal peace, a kingdom incorruptible, eternal joy, overflowing peace, true bliss, certain knowledge' (Laurentius), pleasure for evermore, He willeth to give thee all which is His, and much more, He willeth to give thee Himself. Why shall we not trust Him with the things of time, or with ourselves, who must trust Him with our eternity? Why not trust that, for these few days and years, He will provide for us, whom He has made for His love, if He will not have it, in those countless ages which time measures not?"—M.].

[SECKER:—Presumption in our strength is destructive to our virtue; confidence of our own merit is injurious to our Maker; but a deep sense of human unworthiness and of Divine grace will inspire us with that lowliness of heart, which God will accept, and that vigilance of conduct, which He will bless. "This," therefore, "is the victory that overcometh the world, even our faith."—M.].

[VER. 6. PYLE:—"Nor are the effects and influences of this great truth more excellent and noble than is the ground and foundation of it strong and certain. The testimonies given Him at His baptism, when God by a voice from heaven declared Him to be His beloved Son, the Saviour of mankind: the miracles at His crucifixion, when at the shedding of His innocent blood, we saw both water and blood come out of His side; the sun was darkened; the earth trembled, and the vail of the temple was rent; the signs and wonders done by Him, and by others in His name; these three, respectively denoted by 'the water,' 'the blood,' and 'the Spirit,' are all testimonies of the authority of His Person and mission, most unexceptionable, as being evidences of that Holy Spirit that cannot deceive us."—M.].

[VER. 12. SHERLOCK:—"If we reflect upon the holiness of God, and His hatred of sin and iniquity, and begin to fear that He can never be reconciled to sinners; let us take courage; the work is difficult, but the Son of God has undertaken it; and how great soever the distance between God and us is, yet through the Son we have access to Him. If we still fear for ourselves, that all may again be lost through our own weakness and inability to do good; even here help is at hand, the Spirit of God is our support, He is the pledge and earnest of our redemption. These being the necessary means of salvation it was necessary to reveal to the world the doctrines concerning the Son and the Holy Spirit: and the belief of these doctrines is necessary to every Christian, as far as the right use of the means depends on the right faith and belief of the doctrines. 'He that hath the Son,' saith St. John, 'hath life: and he that hath not the Son of God hath not life;' and again: 'whosoever denieth the Son, the same hath not the Father.' For since we can only come to the Father through the Son, to deny the Son is to cut off all communication between us and the Father. The same may be said of the blessed Spirit, through whom we are in Christ: 'If any man,' says St. Paul, 'have not the Spirit of Christ, he is none of His.' Our blessed Lord has Himself told us, that 'this is life eternal, that we may know the only true God, and Jesus Christ whom He hath sent.'"—M.].

[*Sermons*, etc.

v. 1. HOWE, JOHN, On Regeneration. Works, 8, 484.

v. 3. TILLOTSON, Abp., The Precepts of Christianity not grievous. Serm. i. 152.
OSTERWALD, J. F., Qu'il est nécessaire et facile de garder les commandements de Dieu. Sermons, 79.
WARDLAW, R., On the identity of morality and religion. Christian Ethics, 240.
SHERLOCK, W., Obedience the best evidence of our love to God. Sermons, ii. 44.

v. 4. ALLEINE, R., The world conqueror. 8vo. 1676.
HARE, J C., The victory of faith.
Faith the victory that overcometh the world.—Faith a practical principle.—Office and province of faith.—Power of faith in man's natural life.—Power of faith among the heathen and among the Jews.
PYLE, P., The Christian's victory over the world. Sermons, iv. 503.

vv. 7, 8. Among the controversial writers on these verses the following have supported their *genuineness*: Dr. MILL, T. SMITH, KETTNER, DAVID MARTIN, CALAMY, CALMET, SLOSS, TRAVIS, HEY, BUTLER, MIDDLETON, NOLAN, HALES, ALBER, BP. BURGESS, JOHN JONES, CARD. WISEMAN; the following assert their *spuriousness*: SIMON, EMLYN, SIR ISAAC NEWTON, BENSON, PORSON, MARSH, GRIESBACH, A. CLARKE, JOWETT, TURTON, ORME, SCHOLZ, HORNE and the authors named above in *Exegetical and Critical*. Our limits do not allow us to give the titles of the books in this controversy, which is a library in itself.

v. 10. BAXTER, W., Christ's witness within us, the believer's special advantage against temptations to infidelity. Works, xx. 129.
WATTS, I., The inward witness to Christianity. 3 Serm. Works, i. 1.
MELVILL, HENRY, The witness in oneself. Lecture 58.

vv. 11, 12. STEDMAN, ROWLAND, The mystical union of believers with Christ; or a treatise wherein that great mystery and privilege of the saints' union with the Son of God is opened. 8vo. London 1668.—M.].

IV. THE CONCLUSION.

CHAPTER V. 13-21.

13 These things have I written[1] unto you that believe on the name of the Son of God;
that ye may know that ye have eternal life, and that ye may believe[2] on the name of
14 the Son of God. And this is the confidence that we have in him[3], that, if we ask any
15 thing[4] according to his will, he heareth us: And if we know that he hear[5] us, what-
16 soever we ask[6], we know that we have the petitions that we desired of[7] him. If any
man see his brother sin a sin[8] *which is* not unto death, he shall ask, and he shall give
him life for them that sin not unto death. There is a sin unto death: I do not say
17 that he shall pray for it[9]. All unrighteousness is sin: and there is a sin not[10] unto
18 death. We know that whosoever is born of God sinneth not; but he that is begot-
19 ten[11] of God keepeth himself, and that[12] wicked one toucheth him not. *And* we know
20 that we are of God, and the whole world lieth in wickedness[13]. And[14] we know that
the Son of God is come, and hath given us an understanding[15], that we may know[16] him
that is true[17]; and we are in him that is true[17], *even* in his Son Jesus Christ. This is
21 the true God, and eternal life[18]. Little children, keep yourselves[19] from idols. Amen[20].

Verse 13. [1 German: "These things wrote I."—M.]
2 τοῖς πιστεύουσιν B. Cod. Sin.; οἱ πιστεύοντες A.; this reading is preferable on account of the witnesses and because it is *difficilior*.—Text. Rec. inserts after ὑμῖν, "τοις πιστεύουσιν εἰς τὸ ὄνομα τοῦ υἱοῦ τοῦ θεοῦ," and continues after αἰώνιον, "ἵνα πιστεύητε εἰς τὸ ὄνομα κ. τ. λ;" but this reading is not sufficiently authenticated, and probably not without dependence on Jno. xx. 31. [The Codd. A. B. Sin. al. Vulgate, Syriac, Coptic, Aethiopic, Armenian, Cassiod., Bede, al. are all against the reading of Rec.—But the reading οἱ πιστεύοντες, though found in A. and many Versions, is not clearly established; it seems to have been the basis of the reading of Text. Rec.—Αἰώνιον before ἔχετε Sin. G. K. al. Theoph., Oecum.; after ἔχετε A. B. al. Vulg. Syr. Rec. Cassiod., Bede.—The most probable reading is: ὑμῖν, ἵνα εἰδῆτε ὅτι ζωὴν ἔχετε αἰώνιον, τοῖς πιστεύουσιν εἰς τὸ ὄνομα τοῦ υἱοῦ τοῦ θεοῦ. Huther, Alford.—M.]
[German: "These things wrote I unto you, that ye may know, that ye have eternal life, ye that believe in the name of the Son of God."—M.]

Verse 14. [3 German: "towards Him."—M.]
4 ὅτι ἐάν τι B. Sin.; ὅ τι ἄν A. [German: "If we ask something."—M.]

Verse 15. 5 καὶ ἐὰν οἴδαμεν, ὅτι ἀκούει ἡμῶν, omitted in A. and Sin., but added by a later hand. [German: "And if we know, that He heareth us."—M.]
6 ὃ ἐὰν Sin. B. G. al.; ὃ ἂν A. K. al. The Codd. are undecided here, and in the beginning after καὶ, between ἐὰν and ἄν. [German: "whatsoever we may ask."—M.]
7 ἀπ' αὐτοῦ B. Sin.; παρ' αὐτοῦ A. G. K. [German: "which we have asked from Him;" Lillie, Alford.—M.]

Verse 16. [8 German: "If any man see his brother commit a sin not unto death;" Alford, Lillie: "sinning a sin."—M.]
[9 German: "Concerning that I do not say, that he shall pray." Similarly Alford, Lillie, al.—M.]

Verse 17. 10 οὐ πρὸς θάνατον is well authenticated; Vulg: Aeth. omit οὐ; μὴ is too feebly sustained.
[11 German: "Born of God" as in the beginning of the verse; the variation is unnecessary.—M.]
[12 German: "And the wicked one."—M.]

Verse 19. [13 German: "And the whole world lieth in the wicked one." So Alford, Lillie, following Syriac, Vulg. and many others.—M.]

Verse 20. 14 οἴδαμεν δὲ B. K. Sin.—A. al. καὶ οἴδαμεν.—G. al. omit δὲ and καὶ, as in the beginning of v. 18. [German: "But we know," so Lillie; Alford "Moreover, etc."—M.]
[15 German: "a sense."—M.]
16 γινώσκομεν A. B.* G. Sin; γινώσκωμεν, B.** K. al.
17 After τὸν ἀληθινόν A., several minusc., versions, al. insert θεόν; Sin. had originally τὸ, but corrected into τὸν. [German: "The true One," so Lillie, Alford, following many translators.—M.]
18 ζωὴ αἰώνιος, without the Article, is well authenticated; some minusc., add it. John nowhere makes use of ἡ ζωὴ αἰώνιος, but ζωὴ αἰώνιος, or ἡ αἰώνιος ζωὴ, or ἡ ζωὴ ἡ αἰώνιος.

Verse 21. 19 ἑαυτοὺς is better authenticated than ἑαυτά.
20 ἀμὴν G. K. al.; [it is omitted in A. B. Sin. al.—M.]—The subscription: ΙΩΑΝΝΟΥ A., Sin. and al.

EXEGETICAL AND CRITICAL.

The Conclusion. v. 13. **These things wrote I.**—Ταῦτα ἔγραψα, like ταῦτα ἔγραψα ch. ii. 26, might be referred to the verses immediately preceding, if the words annexed permitted such a construction:

That ye may know, that ye have eternal life, ye that believe in the name of the Son of God.—Quite similar to the closing verse of the Gospel, ch. xx. 31. The purpose of the writing ἵνα εἰδῆτε ὅτι ζωὴν ἔχετε αἰώνιον corresponds with the χαρά at the beginning of the Epistle, which χαρά was to be filled by the testimony of the eye- and ear-witnesses of the λόγος τῆς ζωῆς; hence ταυτα ἐγραψα answers to ταυτα γράφομεν ch. i. 4 (Bengel), the certainty of the possession of eternal life being the ground and strength of the joy, which John has, and to which he adverts. The words τοῖς πιστεύουσιν εἰς τὸ ὄνομα τοῦ υἱοῦ τοῦ θεοῦ, annexed to ὑμῖν, primarily refer back to ch. iii. 23, but find their last resting-place in the κοινωνία ἡ ἡμετέρα μετὰ τοῦ πατρὸς καὶ μετὰ τοῦ υἱοῦ αὐτοῦ, ch. i. 3. Hence ταῦτα must be referred neither to vv. 6-12 (Huther), nor to vv. 1-12 (S. Schmid), but to the whole Epistle (Luther, Bengel, Lücke, Düsterdieck and al.), though the inducement to the choice of this expression lies in verses immediately preceding, and preparing the concluding portion of the Epistle, and there still follow several verses which constitute that concluding portion. Noteworthy is the difference between the closing verse of the Gospel, ch. xx. 31, which adverts to the future believing and obtaining eternal life of the readers, while our passage asserts their present belief and possession of eternal life. [Alford sees here with Düsterdieck something like an anticipatory close of the Epistle. Huther maintains, that this verse still belongs to the second main part of the Epistle beginning with ch. iii. 23, on the ground that ζωὴν αἰώνιον goes back to the verses immediately preceding, and that πιστεύειν εἰς τὸ ὄνομα τοῦ υἱοῦ τοῦ θεοῦ, refers back to ch. iii. 23.—M.].

The confidence that prayer is heard. vv. 14, 15.

VER. 14. **And this is the confidence which we have towards Him.**—Καὶ connects with what goes before, *i. e.*, it connects παῤῥησία ἣν ἔχομεν with ζωὴν ἔχετε αἰώνιον. This confidence consists in this:—

That if we ask any thing according to His will, He heareth us.—It is consequently the confidence in God, which has the intercourse of prayer with Him; this confidence rests on the ζωὴ αἰώνιος, springs from it, points back to it, and reacts also on it, strengthening and confirming it. Cf. ch. iii. 21, 22.—Πρὸς αὐτὸν and τὸ θέλημα αὐτοῦ must be referred to God the Father, because the idea of possessing the ζωὴ αἰώνιος involves the idea of the Divine Sonship, and the παῤῥησία is connected with both. While ἐάν τι leaves the object of the prayer quite general and indefinite, κατὰ τὸ θέλημα limits it, so that it is a *conditio æquissima, latissime patens* (Bengel), as we may see from the fourth and seventh petitions of the Lord's Prayer, in connection with the others. (Cf. *Doctrinal and Ethical* No. 1.).—Ἀκούει ἡμῶν denotes an attentive, sympathetic hearing, while ἡμᾶς would signify a mere hearing.—This is an undoubted fact:

VER. 15. **And if we know that He heareth us whatsoever we may ask.**—Hence ἐὰν with the Indicative οἴδαμεν. Winer, p. 310, sq.—Ὃ ἐὰν αἰτώμεθα denotes the general character of the object of prayer. It follows that:

We know that we have the petitions which we have asked from Him.—Ἔχομεν, emphatic, placed first. By the side of ἀκούει ἡμῶν, we must distinguish ἔχομεν τὰ αἰτήματα (Lorinus: *res petitæ*), although the two belong together; God hearing our prayers and our having go hand-in-hand. The additional clause: ἃ ᾐτήκαμεν ἀπ' αὐτοῦ indicates that the having is the consequence of prayer preceding it, so that the having in point of time does not coincide with the prayer, as does the believer's prayer with God's hearing; but our having is secured; ἔχομεν is not=λαμβάνομεν (Lachmann and al.), nor must it be construed like a Future (Grotius: *statim exaudit, at non statim dat*).—Ἀπ' αὐτοῦ, as in Matth. xx. 20, belongs to ᾐτήκαμεν, not to ἔχομεν; παρ' αὐτοῦ, as in Acts iii. 2, (see Appar. Crit., No. 7,), could not, at any rate, denote prayers as deposits made with God, as Ebrard maintains.

Intercession for a brother sinning not unto death. vv. 16, 17.

VER. 16. **If any one see his brother commit a sin, not unto death.**—Here is supposed a specific case, in which the confident petition becomes an intercession for the purpose of keeping an erring brother,—after the example of Christ (ch. ii. 1; cf. Luke xxii. 31, 32; Jno. xvii 9; Heb. vii. 25),—with his Saviour and salvation, in fellowship with the Redeemer and in the participation of eternal life. *Additur casus omnium maximus; ut possis orare etiam pro altero in re gravissima* (Bengel). Ἐάν τις ἴδῃ supposes an objective possibility; it is not said that some one does see, but it may be, the event will show it; consequently: If any one *should see* it. Winer, p. 306, sq. The reference is to an event which may be seen, to a fact susceptible of observation, as in ch. iii. 17.—Τὸν ἀδελφὸν αὐτοῦ, denotes a member of the Christian Church, and τις requires to be taken in the same sense. The reference is consequently to intimate converse, and to what happens and becomes manifest there. This the Apostle brings out emphatically in the participial form: ἁμαρτάνοντα ἁμαρτίαν: the sinning brother stands, as it were, before our eyes. Here we have μὴ πρὸς θάνατον, not as in v. 17: οὐ πρὸς θάνατον, because the reference is to the subjective judgment of the observer, not to an objectively valid principle, not to the establishment of a dogmatically real idea. Winer, p. 496.—Ἀδελφὸς is therefore not=*proximus quicunque* (Calov); non-christians are excluded (against Ebrard), although the reference may not be exactly to "a regenerate person" (Düsterdieck).

He shall ask and give him life.—The Future αἰτήσει denotes that the intercession may be confidently expected, since καὶ δώσει neither warrants us to construe the Future, in the decisive language of the legislation of the Old and New Testament (Matth. v. 21, 27, etc.,) as an Imperative, nor gives an occasion to assume a purely ethical possibility, as Luke xxii. 49: κύριε, εἰ πατάξομεν; Rom. x. 14: πῶς οὖν ἐπικαλέσονται; shall we smite? how shall they, how can they call? See Winer, pp. 294, 295, 331. Hence it is not=*licebit petere* (S. Schmidt). The subject is the intercession, τις, not the Church (Neander), or the *saints* (Meyer). The same subject, αἰτῶν, belongs also to δώσει; it is neither=*dabitur* (variation of the Vulgate, approved by Bede and others), nor to be derived from the idea of prayer, αἰτούμενος, *rogatus Deus* (Beza, Bengel, Lücke, Winer, p. 553, and al.). [The Æthiopic version brings out the right meaning: *rogans vivificabit; i. e.* the asker shall be instrumental in bestowing life on the erring brother for whom he intercedes.—M.]. The grammatical requirements of our passage are fully borne out by the cycle of thoughts current in the New Testament (Acts iii. 6; Jas. v. 15, 20). John here simply contemplates the result as a fact, without adverting to the instrumentality, its ways and stages within the brother's heart, which was the object of intercession; repentance and faith, moreover, are not excluded, and the interceding brother is not viewed as the Saviour, or the representative of the Redeemer. Neither may we think of an *admonitio et correptio fraterna* (Matth. xviii. 15; S. Schmid), nor of the proper demeanour of the asker towards his erring brother, as the result of his intercessory prayer (Rickli). The final effect of intercession is ζωὴ (αἰώνιος), which is weakened and disturbed by every sin [Alford; This bestowal of life by intercessory prayer, is not to be minutely inquired into, whether it is to be accompanied with "*correptio fraterna*,"—whether it consists in the giving to the sinner a repentant heart (Grotius, al.), but taken, as put by the Apostle, in all its simplicity and breadth. *Life*, viz.: the restoration of that Divine life from which by any act of sin he was indeed in peril, and indeed in process of falling, but this sin was not an actual fall.—M.].

To them that sin not unto death.—The Plural τοῖς ἁμαρτάνουσι belongs to αὐτῷ, which *generaliter positum est* (Erasmus); the Plural takes the supposed case from the sphere of singularity; τις has collective force. See Winer, p. 553. It is forced and ungrammatical to refer αὐτῷ to him that asks, understanding θεός as the subject, and taking τοῖς ἁμαρτάνουσι as *Dativ. commodi*: "God will give him life for the persons sinning," as Bornemann (*Biblische Studien der Sächs. Geistlichen* I. p. 71,) does.—Μὴ πρὸς θάνατον qualifies ἁμαρτάνειν ἁμαρτίαν, or ἁμαρτάνειν, and has consequently adverbial force. θάνατος, only, if taken in the sense of spiritual death, corresponds with the context, viz., with the παῤῥησία of prayer being heard on the ground of our possession of the ζωὴ αἰώνιος, for ζωή in the intercession on behalf of the erring brother, and the preposition πρός, as denoting the aim towards which something is directed (Winer, p. 423), require us to think of a sinning, which in the conviction of the person interceding, must not terminate in θάνατος, the emptying of all ζωὴ αἰώνιος, and accordingly must not absolutely annul fellowship with Christ, faith in Him. This is brought out more clearly in the next clause.

There is a sin unto death.—Thus the Apostle circumscribes the domain of sinning not unto death: it is not infinite. This is directed against any possible laxity in the judgment of the Church on the sins of believers. Πρὸς θάνατον has the same meaning here, as in the preceding clause. The reference is accordingly to a specific sin, to a simple act perceptible (ἴδῃ) in the brother, within the limits of Christian fellowship (τὸν ἀδελφὸν αὐτοῦ), not to a particular, outwardly marked category of sins, but to a sinning, and committing of sin, which renders it clear to the careful observer, that the fellowship of faith with Christ, the fountain of eternal life, has been cut off, that consequently the ethical life-form appears to be inwardly decayed and dying, that the moral status of that brother shows itself to be in a state of hopeless dissolution, so that it is of no avail to pray for such an one, and that therefore intercession is not proper. Hence it is wrong to transfer to this passage the Old Testament idea of חֵטְא לָמוּת, ἁμαρτία θανατηφόρος (Numb. xviii. 22), and to refer to capital crimes, *e. g.* idolatry, adultery, murder, incest, which are punishable with death under the secular or Mosaic law (Morus, al.), or to the sins ecclesiastically punishable with excommunication, as if intercession had to conform to the secular code of punishment; nor is the reference to sinning unto the end of man's earthly existence (Bede and al.), in which connection de Lyra rightly observes: "*Qui sit peccator non ad mortem, sciri non potest nisi per divinam revelationem*;" πρὸς θάνατον cannot be rendered "*usque ad mortem*." Nor is the reference to the physically sick, Jas. v. 14 (Steinhofer); nor to definite, gross crimes, *peccatum gravissimum, quod vix remittitur* (Ambrose), *moechia port baptismum commissa* (Tertullian), *peccatum invidentiæ* (Bede). Nor is here any description of a condition, "*Talis animæ status, in quo fides et amor et spes, in summa, vita nova exstincta est; si quis sciens volensque mortem amplectitur, non ex illecebris carnis, sed ex amore peccati, sub ratione peccati; repudium gratiæ proæreticum.*" (Bengel). Augustine thought first of *invidentiæ faces post agnitionem Dei*, and added afterwards: *si in hac perversitate finierit vitam*, and then: *fidem deserere usque ad mortem.* Lastly the reference is neither to a purely inward act, like obduracy (Ebrard), apostasy (de Wette, Lücke), nor to sin, perceptible in the walk of men, like the antichristian denial expressed in words (Düsterdieck), nor to the sin against the Holy Ghost (Calvin, Sander and al.). The reference is simply to sinning, from which it may be perceived either, that no inward absolute severance from the faith and denial of Christ may or can be assumed, or that the latter is either recognizable or highly probable. To the latter case apply the words:

Concerning that I do not say that he shall pray.—The simple negation is, that the the Apostle says (οὐ—λέγω), that prayer should be made for him who sins unto death. He only makes prominent the circumstance that he confines himself to saying that intercession should be made for the person not sinning unto death. Hence those commentators are right, who do not see here a prohibition (Socinus, Grotius, Neander, Lücke, Huther and al.). But it is certainly not said that we ought, or only are permitted, to pray for him (Neander). It is important to note the difference of the words employed by the Apostle, for whereas before he made use of the word αἰτήσει, he now uses ἐρωτήσῃ: ἐρωτᾶν is= *rogare*, and implies equality on the part of the asker with him from whom the favour is sought; Jesus designates His praying by that term (Jno. xiv. 16; xvi. 26; xvii. 9, 15, 20); on the other hand αἰτεῖν is—*petere*, and implies inferiority (Düsterdieck), while Bengel regards αἰτεῖν as *species humilior* under the *genus* ἐρωτᾶν. This word ἐρωτᾶν denotes the confident petition of the child, praying inquiringly and expecting the gift. Hence, due regard being had to the force of the term employed, we may discover here the sanction of intercession for a brother sinning unto death, yet without any assurance of success or that the intercession will prevail. But since the Apostle advocates this very παῤῥησία and *Deus non vult, ut pii frustra orent* (Bengel), it is probably *locutio morata et attica* for a prohibition. Deut. iii. 26. This is also suggested by ἵνα; in the present instance he does not wish to excite and promote the purpose of praying. (Cf. *Doctrinal and Ethical* No. 4).

VER. 17. **All unrighteousness is sin.**—The subject πᾶσα ἀδικία reminds us of the predicate ἡ ἀνομία ch. iii. 4. Ἀνομία is in contradiction with the objectively given law of God, ἀδικία is the contradiction and negation of the δικαιοσύνη and is concerned with the subjective disposition, though it be wrought from above and subject to the law. And this harmonizes with the fact that we are concerned with the moral status of the sinner in this sinning unto death, and sinning not unto death. John manifestly desires to guard against any ἀδικία being too lightly dealt with, being not considered as ἁμαρτία, though it be μὴ πρὸς τὸν θάνατον. The Roman Catholics, therefore, have no warrant for determining from the sin itself, whether it is *peccatum mortale* or *veniale*.

And there is a sin not unto death.—Καὶ simply connects the sequel; it is not=*et quidem*, and the sense: *quodlibet nefas est peccatum non ad mortem* (Bengel); Bengel's clause: '*sed ne quisquam id levius interpretetur, præmittit: est peccatum*' is only a moral reaction against the perversion of the Johannean thought: all unrighteousness is sin. The sequel, because of the intercession recommended, is added by way of emphasis. Οὐ πρὸς θάνατον implies the objectively real fact, the actual occurrence of such sin; it defines ἁμαρτία, not ἐστιν, as Luther supposes.

[There are one or two questions, in connection with this section, which require to be treated somewhat more fully. First, v. 17, involves a prohibition, or what is equivalent to it. But this has been denied by many commentators. "*Ora si velis, sed sub dubio impetrandi*". (Corn. a Lapide); Neander supposes that the offering of prayer is permitted, though the obtaining of it will be difficult, and arbitrarily imagines the prayer in question to be the collective prayer of the Church, and that one who sins πρὸς θάνατον should not be included in the common prayer of the Church, lest he might be confirmed in his sin; Huther finds in οὐ λέγω not more than a denial of the Apostle that the case of one sinning unto death came within the purview of his command. Lyra qualifies the prohibition, though "*non est orandum pro damnatis*," yet we may pray, "*ut minus peccaret, et per consequens minus damnaretur in inferno*."—Calvin recognizes the prohibition, but limits it to extreme cases, adding: "*Sed quia rarissime hoc accidit, et Deus, immensas gratiæ suæ divitias commendans, nos suo exemplo misericordes esse jubet: non temere in quemquam ferendum est mortis æternæ judicium, potius nos caritas ad bene sperandum flectat. Quod si desperata quorundam impietas non secus nobis apparet, ac sic Dominus eam digito monstraret, non est quod certemus cum justo Dei judicio, vel clementiores eo esse appetamus*."—Alford sums up: "Certainly this seems, reserving the question as to the nature of the sin, the right view of the οὐ λέγω. By an express command in the other case, and then as express an exclusion of this case from that command, nothing short of an implied prohibition can be conveyed."—

Secondly, the question: *What is the sin unto death?*—The canons of interpretation for its solution, and some of the principal divergences, chiefly from Düsterdieck, collected by Alford, are here produced.

"The FIRST canon of interpretation of the ἁμαρτία πρὸς θάνατον and οὐ πρὸς θάνατον is this: that *the θάνατος and ζωή of the passage must correspond*. The former cannot be bodily death, while the latter is eternal and spiritual life. This clears away at once all those commentators who understand the sin unto death to be one for which bodily death is the punishment, either by human law generally, as Morus and G. Lange, or by the Mosaic law (Schöttgen),—or by sickness inflicted by God, as Whitby and Benson; or of which there will be no end till the death of the sinner (thought possible by Bede, and adopted by Lyra). This last is evidently absurd, for how is a man to know, whether this will be so or not?

"The SECOND canon will be, that this sin unto death being thus a sin leading to eternal death, being no further explained to the readers here, must be presumed as *meant to be understood by what the Evangelist has elsewhere laid down*, concerning the possession of life and death. Now we have from him a definition immediately preceding this, in v. 12, ὁ ἔχων τὸν υἱὸν ἔχει τὴν ζωήν· ὁ μὴ ἔχων τὸν υἱὸν τοῦ θεοῦ τὴν ζωὴν οὐκ ἔχει. And we may safely say that the words πρὸς θάνατον here are to be understood as meaning, "involving the loss of *this life* which men have only by the union with the Son of God." And this meaning they must have, not by implication only, which would be the case, if any obstinate and determined sin were meant, which would be a *sign* of the fact of severance from the life which is in Christ (see ch. iii. 14, 15, where the inference is of this kind), but directly and essentially, *i. e.* in respect of that very sin which is pointed at by them. Now against this canon are all those interpretations, far too numerous to mention, which make *any* atrocious and obstinate sin to be that intended. It is obvious that our limits are thus confined to *abnegation of Christ*, not as inferred by its fruits otherwise shown, but as the act of sin itself. And so, with various shades of difference, as to the putting forth in detail, most of the best commentators, both ancient and modern: *e. g.*, Aretius, Luther, Calvin, Beza, Piscator, Corn. a Lapide, Tirinus, Baumgarten-Crusius, Lücke, Huther, Düsterdieck.

"The THIRD canon will help us to decide, within the above limits, what especial sin is intended. And it is, that by the very analogy of the context, it must be *not a state of sin, but an appreciable* ACT *of sin*, seeing that which is opposed to it *in the same kind*, as being not unto death, is described by ἐάν τις ἴδῃ ἁμαρτάνοντα. So that all interpretations which make it to be a *state* of apostacy, all such as, *e. g.*, Bengel's (see above), do not reach the matter of detail which is before the Apostle's mind.

"In enquiring what this is, we must be guided by the analogy of what St. John says elsewhere. *Our* state being that of life in Jesus Christ, there are those who have gone out from us, not being of us, ch. ii. 19, who are called ἀντίχριστοι, who not only "have not" Christ, but are Christ's enemies, denying the Father and the Son (ch. ii. 22), whom we are not even to receive into our houses nor to greet (2 John 10, 11). These seem to be the persons pointed at here, and this is the sin: viz. the denial that Jesus is the Christ, the incarnate Son of God. This alone of all sins bears upon it the stamp of severance from Him who is the Life itself. As the confession of Christ, with the mouth and in the heart, is salvation unto life (Rom. x. 9), so the denial of Christ, with the mouth and in the heart, is sin unto death. This alone of all the proposed solutions seems to satisfy all the canons above laid down. For in it the life cast away and the death incurred strictly correspond: it strictly corresponds to what St. John has elsewhere said concerning life and death, and derives its explanation from those other passages, especially from the foregoing v. 12: and it is an appreciable act of sin, one against which the readers have been before repeatedly cautioned (ch. ii. 18 sqq.; iv. i. sqq.; v. 5, 11, 12). And further, it is in exact accordance with other passages of Scripture which seem to point at a sin similarly distinguished above others: Matth. xii. 31 sqq., and so far as the circumstances there dealt with allow common ground, with the more ethical passages, Heb. vi. 4 sqq., x. 25 sqq. In the former case, the Scribes and Pharisees were resisting the Holy Ghost (Acts vii. 51), who was manifesting God in the flesh in the person and work of Christ. For them the Lord Himself does not pray (Luke xxiii. 34): they knew what they did: they went out from God's people and were not of them: receiving and repudiating the testimony of the Holy Ghost to the Messiahship of Jesus."—M.].

Assurance of redemption. vv. 18, 20.

VER. 18. **We know that every one who is born** (out) **of God, sinneth not.**—Each of these three concluding verses begins with οἴδαμεν; Bengel: *anaphora.* The Evangelist refers to εἰδῆτε v. 13, and thus describes the proper consciousness of the Christian in his attitude to sin (v. 18), the world (v. 19), and the Redeemer (v. 20). Πᾶς γεγεννημένος ἐκ τοῦ θεοῦ signifies every one who is, and abides, born of God; the power of regeneration, of the life given and received in regeneration, operates from the past into the present; as such οὐχ ἁμαρτάνει, as such sin is foreign to him, Rom. vii. 20; cf. ch. iii. 9. —It is unnecessary to supply πρὸς θάνατον (Bede, Beza and al.), and arbitrary to understand an abiding in sin, or a falling from grace (Calvin), or the not frequent occurrence of the sin unto death and sin in general (de Wette).

But he that hath been born of God, keepeth himself, and the wicked one doth not touch him.—The opposite (ἀλλά), refers not only to the predicate, but, since the subject is particularly specified, to the whole clause, and the two clauses (οἴδαμεν ὅτι—and ὁ γεννηθεὶς κ. τ. λ.) are independently coördinated. The Aorist indicates the historical fact; that *hath been* born again (in opposition to Sander who discovers this in the Perfect, and Bengel, "*præteritum grandius quiddam sonat, quam aoristus; non modo qui magnum in regeneratione gradum assecutus, sed quilibet, qui regenitus est, servat se.*") Τηρεῖ αὐτὸν indicates moral effort and self-exertion; οὐ φύσει εἰς ἀναμαρτησίαν προβαίνει (Oecumenius); sin occurs, approaches, but he sustains the conflict, guarding himself in his peculiar nature and the Divine gift of eternal life, which hinders, spoils and drives away sin. Thus sin destroys man himself; it is in virtue of his self-guarding that the σπέρμα τοῦ θεοῦ abides in him (ch. iii. 9); we must neither supply ἁγνόν (1 Tim. v. 22), nor ἄσπιλον (Jas. i. 27. Carpzov, Lücke, al.), nor take τηρεῖσθαι in the sense of being on one's guard (Ebrard). Cf. ch. iii. 3. [Alford justly objects to this and similar expositions, and retaining the reading αὐτόν A. B. Vulg. Jer., renders "*it* keepeth him," viz. the Divine birth, adding, "it is this, and not the fact of his own watchfulness, which preserves him from the touch of the wicked one, as in ch. iii. 9, where the same is imported by ὅτι τὸ σπέρμα αὐτοῦ ἐν αὐτῷ μένει, καὶ οὐ δύναται ἁμαρτάνειν, ὅτι ἐκ τοῦ θεοῦ γεγέννηται. The rationalistic commentators insist on τηρεῖ ἑαυτόν, as showing, as Socinus, "*aliquid præstare eum atque efficere, qui per Christum regeneratus fuerit;*" and the orthodox commentators have but a lame apology to offer. Düsterdieck compares ἁγνίζει ἑαυτόν, ch. iii. 3. But the reference there is wholly different—viz. to a gradual and earnest striving after an ideal model; whereas here the τηρεῖσθαι must be, by the very nature of the case, so far complete that the wicked one cannot approach: and whose self-guarding can ensure this even for a day? Cf. Jno. xvii. 15, ἵνα τηρήσῃς αὐτοὺς ἐκ τοῦ πονηροῦ, which is decisive."—M.]. The clause annexed by καὶ notes the difficult but successful conflict. The enemy, ὁ πονηρός, ch. iii. 12, is Satan, οὐχ ἅπτεται αὐτοῦ, though he would fain do it, hostile attacks, Satanic assaults, temptations are not wanting (1 Pet. v. 8); but the point of complication between Satan and the regenerate is not reached, the wrestling is wanting; the regenerate keeps Satan at a distance, wards him off; Bengel: *malignus appropinquat, ut musca ad lychnum, sed non nocet, ne tangit quidem.* "In the πανοπλία τοῦ θεοῦ he is guarded against all the μεθοδεῖαι τοῦ διαβόλου Eph. vi. 11 sqq." (Huther). Luther and Calvin also refer to the armour of God, so that, as in John xvii. 11, 12, 15; Rev. iii. 10, God is the Preserver [Calvin: "*Utut malignus renatum ad peccatum solicitet, tela tamen illius irrita cadunt, quoniam renatus scuto fidei munitus ea repellit et diabolo per fidem resistit.*"—M.]. But here the Apostle contemplates only the result, and not the way to it. Additions such as *letaliter* (Calvin), *finaliter* (E. Schmid), are unnecessary. But ὁ πονηρὸς οὐχ ἅπτεται αὐτοῦ depends of course on the careful τηρεῖν ἑαυτὸν (Düsterdieck, Huther). [Alford: "As the Prince of this world had nothing in our blessed Lord, even so on His faithful ones who live by His life, the Tempter has no *point d'appui*, by virtue of that their γέννησις by which they are as He is."—M.].

VER. 19. **We know that we are** (out) **of God.**—The second οἴδαμεν repeats by way of introduction and in pregnant abbreviation (ἐκ τοῦ θεοῦ ἐσμέν), and with application to himself and his church, the believer's consciousness of his Divine sonship. There is no occasion whatever to understand here the peculiar revelation vouchsafed to the Apostles, or to explain εἶναι ἐκ τοῦ θεοῦ=*a Deo pendere illique adhærere* (Socinus). The principal sentence is the independent clause, annexed like vv. 18, 20, by καί, viz.:

And the whole world lieth in the wicked one.—For the world is the territory and domain of Satan, on which account, and because ὁ πονηρός occurs in v. 18, and we have here an antithesis to ὁ θεός, τῷ πονηρῷ is masculine, and not neuter (Lyra, Socinus, Grotius, who however allows an allusion to Satan, Spener, Rickli and al.). Ἐν τῷ πονηρῷ κεῖται denotes like ἐν τῇ συγκλήτῳ κεῖται (Polyb. VI. 14, 6), both the competency of Satan and dependence on him as the controlling power; in (ἐν) him lies the world, [it is circumscribed by him and in his power—M.]; κεῖται denotes the passiveness of the state, of the situation; he ἅπτεται τοῦ κόσμου continually in the most powerful and destructive manner

The ethical medium of sin is not expressed here, only the result is indicated. Referring here, with Spener and Steinhofer, to Is. xlvi. 3, and explaining it in analogy with regeneration, as if the world were lying in the wicked one like a child in its mother's womb, is false *per se* and not warranted by that passage wrongly rendered by Luther.—Ὁ κόσμος ὅλος refers to all the unregenerate; God's children do not belong to the world, though ἐν τῷ κόσμῳ, yet are they not ἐκ τοῦ κόσμου (Jno. xvii. 11, 16), not ἐκ τοῦ διαβόλου (ch. iii. 8). Bengel well observes: "*Totus mundus, isque universus, eruditos, honestos, aliosve complectens omnes, exceptis duntaxat, qui Deo se et Christo vindicarunt, non modo non tangitur, sed plane jacet* (remains lying), *per idololatriam, cæcitatem, fraudem, vim, lasciviam, impietatem, malitiam omnem, in malo, expers et vitæ ex Deo et* διανοίας (1 Cor. v. 10; xi. 32). *Brevi hac summa vividissime denotatur horribilis status mundi. Commentarii loco est ipse mundus et mundanorum hominum actiones, sermones, contractus, lites, sodalitia.*" Hence our passage does not contradict ch. ii. 2; iv. 14. God aims at the redemption of the whole world through Christ and He is enough for the whole world; but Satan also, as the antagonist of God, aims at the whole world. The world is to be taken as the territory which embraces all, not as the sum-total produced by the adding together of all individuals. [Alford: "Had not Christ become a propitiation for the sins of the whole world, were He not the Saviour of the whole world, none could ever come out of the world and believe on Him; but as it is, they who believe on Him, come out and are separated from the world; so that our proposition here remains strictly true: the κόσμος is the negation of faith in Him, and as such lies in the wicked one, His adversary."—M.].

VER. 20. **But we know, that the Son of God is come.**—The third οἴδαμεν whose object: ὅτι ὁ υἱὸς τοῦ θεοῦ ἥκει, *i. e.*, has come; he conditions the εἶναι ἐκ τοῦ θεοῦ which continues in εἶναι ἐν τῷ θεῷ; had He not come, we should still lie like ὁ κόσμος ἐν τῷ πονηρῷ. Hence it is=ἐφανερώθη ch. iii. 8 and not *adest* (Bengel referring to Mark viii. 3).—["δὲ closes off and sums up all: cf. 1 Thess. v. 23; 2 Thess. iii. 16; Hebr. xiii. 22 al. This not being seen, it has been altered to καί, as there appeared to be no contrast with the preceding." Alford.—M.].

And hath given us a sense that we know the true One.—The subject of δέδωκεν is ὁ υἱὸς τοῦ θεοῦ, not as Bengel *Deus*, as the Sender, ordaining the coming of Jesus. For Jesus is also the Mediator of the truth and of knowledge [*i. e.*, He bestows to us the truth and this knowledge—M.], (Düsterdieck). Διάνοια is the faculty or sense of knowing, not insight or knowledge (Lücke, de Wette), nor the activity of thinking out all the points in contrast with a faith void of thought (Paulus), 2 Pet. iii. 1; Eph. iv. 18; i. 18 (ὀφθαλμοὶ τῆς καρδίας or τῆς διανοίας), or mind (Matth. xxii. 37; Luke i. 51; Eph. ii. 3; Col. i. 21; 1 Pet. i. 13; Hebr. viii. 10; x. 16), *sensus cognoscendi* (Lyra), *sensus et gustus rerum divinarum* (a Lapide), the spiritual sense (1 Cor. ii. 12, 14), whose aim (ἵνα), but not whose substance is γινώσκειν τὸν ἀληθινόν. Cf. ch. ii. 3, 4; Jno. xvii. 3. The object of this cognition is evidently God, *qui re vera Deus est, ut eum ab idolis omnibus discernat* (Calvin), in contrast with every *Deus fictitius*. Bengel refers to the Son without any warrant for doing so.

And we are in the true One, in His Son Jesus Christ.—Another independent proposition annexed by καὶ, as in v. 19. Ἐσμὲν ἐν τῷ ἀληθινῷ, designates, as before, God, which is also evident from the pronoun in ἐν τῷ υἱῷ αὐτοῦ. This is the extreme antithesis of κεῖται ἐν τῷ πονηρῷ, the climax of εἶναι ἐκ τοῦ θεοῦ. The words ἐν τῷ υἱῷ αὐτοῦ Ἰησοῦ Χριστῷ fully denotes the Mediator, the ground and stay both of the knowledge and of the position of the believing child of God, and it denotes this by ἐν, not by διά, *in*, not *per*, in order to mark the permanent character of this life-fellowship; *inserimur in Christum et unum efficimur cum Deo.* Cf. ch. ii. 3–6; iii. 2. It is therefore no opposition, as seems to be assumed by the Vulgate (which connects by *et simus* with the clause beginning with ἵνα), Lyra, Erasmus and al.

This is the true God and eternal life.—Οὗτος like ἐκεῖνος, does not refer, as it were, in a merely mechanical manner, to the literally or locally nearest or more remote noun, but also to the noun, psychologically nearer or more remote. Winer, p. 175. Thus in v. 16, ἐκείνη did not refer to the grammatically and locally distant ἁμαρτία μὴ πρὸς θάνατον, but to the immediately preceding ἁμαρτία πρὸς τὸν θάνατον. So here the mediating Son is not in point of sense the nearest, but ὁ ἀληθινός. Under the influence of the christological conflicts it may have been natural, with reference to the Arian heresy which was joined by the more modern antitrinitarians, to refer οὗτος to the Son; but the discipline of grammar and language requires us to refer it to the Father (this has been done by most commentators, also by Hofmann, Schriftbeweis I. 146, down to Sander, Ebrard, Besser, Stier [*ad* Jno. xvii. 3. Vol. 5, p. 392] of our time), though the arrangement, the reference taken locally, might induce us to think of Christ, yet this is not the case, if the internal structure of the thought,—in which God the Father is the chief, and the Son simply the Mediator,—is attentively considered. But what does οὗτος refer to? To ἐν τῷ ἀληθινῷ. That would make: οὗτος (ὁ ἀληθινός)= ὁ ἀληθινὸς θεός, but that would be weak and shallow. But if we take οὗτος, δεικτικῶς, of Christ, it is a terse and strong conclusion of the Epistle, and a powerful motive for the concluding exhortation.—The words: καὶ ζωὴ αἰώνιος belong to οὗτος. Grammatically it is not singular (Winer, p. 144), still less in point of thought: for God is essentially ζωή, and so is Christ (Jno. xiv. 6), even ζωὴ αἰώνιος. In like manner He is called φῶς (ch. i. 5), ἀγάπη (ch. iv. 8, 16), πνεῦμα (Jno. iv. 24). Bengel, on *vita æterna*, has the subtle note: "*initium epistolæ et fines conveniunt.*" It is therefore wrong to contend, that οὗτος ἐστιν ὁ ἀληθινὸς θεὸς καὶ ζωὴ αἰώνιος ought to be referred to the Son, as if His Divinity rested on this passage, and at the same time to overlook, that ἐν τῷ ἀληθινῷ denotes primarily God the Father, nor is it right to overlook here the tautology (this One, the true One, is the true God), and to apprehend an identification of the Father and the Son, which would be un-johannean, if the clause were referred to the Son. Now John distinguishes between the Father and the Son, but not between God and not-God. In the Son from the Father we have the Father, eternal life, and all that which is the Father's, and only in Him; hence this turn to the Son and the warning against all idols; the Son is the living Image, the Christian is in no point idolatrous! [Alford: "The grounds on which the application to *Christ* is rested are mainly the following: 1. that οὗτος, most naturally refers to the last mentioned substantive: 2. that ζωὴ αἰώνιος, as a predicate, more naturally belongs to the Son than to the Father: 3. that the sentence, if understood of God the Father, would be aimless, and tautological. But to these it has been well and decisively answered by Lücke and Düsterdieck: 1. that οὗτος more than once in St. John belongs not to the nearest substantive, but to the principal one in the foregoing sentence, *e. g.*, in ch. ii. 22 and in 2 Jno. 7: and that the subject of the whole here has been the Father, who is the ὁ ἀληθινός of the last verse, and the Son is referred back to Him as ὁ υἱὸς αὐτοῦ, thereby keeping *Him*, as the primary subject, before the mind; 2. that as little can ζωὴ αἰώνιος be an actual predicate of Christ, as of the Father. He is indeed ἡ ζωή ch. i. 2, but not ἡ ζωὴ αἰώνιος. Such an expression, used predicatively, leads us to look for some expression of our Lord's, or for some meaning which does not appear on the surface to guide us. And such an expression leading to such a meaning we have in Jno. xvii. 3, αὕτη δέ ἐστιν ἡ αἰώνιος ζωή, ἵνα γινώσκωσιν σὲ τὸν μόνον ἀληθινὸν θεόν, καὶ ὃν ἀπέστειλας Ἰησοῦν Χριστόν. He is eternal life in Himself, as being the fount and origin of it: He is it to us, seeing that to know Him is to possess it. I own I cannot see, after this saying of our Lord with σὲ τὸν μόνον ἀληθινὸν θεόν, how any one can imagine that the same Apostle can have had in these words any other reference than that which is given in those; 3. this charge is altogether inaccurate. As referred to the Father, there is in it no tautology and no aimlessness. It seems to identify the ὁ ἀληθινός mentioned before, in a solemn manner, and leads on to the concluding warning against false gods. As in another place the Apostle intensifies the non-possession of the Son by including in it the alienation from the Father also, so here at the close of all, the ἀληθινὸς θεός, the fount of ζωὴ αἰώνιος, is put before us as the ultimate aim and end, to be approached ἐν τῷ υἱῷ αὐτοῦ, but Himself the One Father both of Him and of us who live through Him."—M.].

Final request. v. 21: **Little children, keep yourselves from idols.**—Τεκνία indicates the affectionate warmth and depth of the Apostle. The exhortation φυλάξετε ἑαυτούς reminds them of great danger, against which they must be courageously on the alert; they themselves are exposed to great corruption. Bengel: "*Elegantia activi verbi cum pronomine reciproco plus dicit, quam: custodimini. Custodite vos ipsos, me absente,—neque solum ab eorum cultu, sed etiam ab omni eorum communione et communionis specie.*" Ἀπὸ τῶν εἰδώλων denotes, that believers must withdraw from the idols, surrounding and in immediate proximity to them, in order to be guarded against them. The εἴδωλα are figures of imaginary deities, and as contrasted with the true God, who is Eternal Life, denote the manufacture of the creature; the decisive point, or the thing decided here is not whether they are made with hands for the grossest forms of heathenism, or in imagination and thought for its more subtle forms; the real point is that they are self-made, untrue, unliving, and strictly speaking, nothing. 1 Thess. i. 9; 1 Cor. x. 19; xii. 2. Düsterdieck, therefore, is wrong in following here an *Etymologicum ineditum* in Biel, *sub voce* (τὸ μὲν εἴδωλον οὐδεμίαν ὑπόστασιν ἔχει, τὸ δὲ ὁμοίωμα τινῶν ἐστιν ἴνδαλμα), and making εἴδωλον tritons or centaurs, and ὁμοίωμα, constellations, men and beasts; the Diana of the Ephesians, forsooth, was also an εἴδωλον. Cf. Rom. i. 23, 25.—We are fully warranted to refer here, with Tertullian, Oecumenius, Düsterdieck and others, to idols proper, but equally warranted to refer also (with Bede, Rickli, Sander and others) to the self-made representations and ideas of the false teachers and their dupes, which, like the truth, they require to be received and submitted to. We may even see, with Ebrard, a reference to images of God or gods or saints in reality, or in imagination, for whom heathenish worship is required. The εἴδωλα are so dangerous because they are the objects of εἰδωλολατρεία. As this applied then to the church-frontier in contact with heathenism, so it applies at this time to the Mariolatry in the Church of Christ, and to the worship of genius, to Schiller-worship, etc., in His Church. [The literal and *figurative* reference in this closing charge, seems to be required by the context, and, in fact, by the whole tenor of the Epistle; the reference being both to literal idols, and to spiritual idolatry.—M.].

DOCTRINAL AND ETHICAL.

1. The assurance that our prayers will be heard rests upon the life-fellowship with God the Father through faith in Christ, and forbids its being circumscribed, as to the substance of our prayers, within limits narrower than those given by the Lord Himself (Matth. vi. 9-13), but neither pursues any other course than that indicated in Matth. vi. 33, sq., viz., it expresses in the way of ethical effort what life really stands in need of. So St. Paul in Rom. viii. 14-17. Absolutely exaudible*, is the prayer for the Holy Spirit and spiritual gifts (Luke xi. 13), relatively exaudible are our prayers for temporal gifts *quantum non est impedimento ad salutem* (Matth. xxvi. 39).

2. Intercession is very potent (v. 16); it is a work of love, an act of kindness.

3. Every sin is, properly speaking, unto death, which is the wages of sin; there is no sin, which is not *per se* unto death, unto condemnation. In this respect, the maxim of the Stoics and Jovianus holds good, that *omnia peccata paria*, no matter how different they may be; and there is only one way towards the forgiveness and cancelling of sin, viz., Christ and His high-priestly work, and the fellowship of faith with the Sinless One. Consequently it is not the species or greatness of sin, *per se*, which constitutes it a sin unto death, but rather the effect of sin on the sinner's relation to the Redeemer, or the nature of the disturbance of this relation, as evidenced by sin

* [I coin this word, which signifies "that which may be heard or granted," for want of a better term.—M.].

The sin which indicates a permanent falling away from Christ, is sin unto death. The Romish distinction of *peccatum mortale* and *peccatum veniale* and the restriction of the former to seven, is wrong; for there is always the danger that the sin assumed to be *peccatum veniale*, and received in excuse of it, may turn into *peccatum mortale*, and that that which from a lower standpoint appears as *peccatum veniale*, is afterwards in its further progress *peccatum mortale*.

4. Intercession for those who sin unto death is improper, because such intercession is inexaudible, because such sin cannot be forgiven. Cf. Riehm, *Lehrbegriff des Hebräerbriefs*, II., pp. 763–775. The words *ἀδύνατον—πάλιν ἀνακαινίζειν εἰς μετάνοι—αν* (Heb. vi. 4–6), as well as *οὐκ ἀφεθήσεται αὐτῷ οὔτε ἐν τούτῳ τῷ αἰῶνι οὔτε ἐν τῷ μέλλοντι* (Matth. xii. 32) distinctly indicate the reason why the Apostle neither requires, nor advises us to make intercession for those sinning unto death. Cf. Hofmann, Schriftbeweis, II., p. 340, sqq. Intercession for suicides must, at all events, be judged from this stand-point.—[Jeremy Taylor: "Every Christian is in some degree in the state of grace, so long as he is invited to repentance, and so long as he is capable of the prayers of the Church. This we learn from those words of St. John: 'All unrighteousness is sin, and there is a sin not unto death,' that is, some sorts of sin are so incident to the condition of men, and their state of imperfection, that the man who hath committed them is still within the method of pardon, and hath not forfeited his title to the promises and covenant of repentance; but 'there is a sin unto death;' that is, some men proceed beyond the measures and economy of the Gospel, and the usual methods and probabilities of repentance, by obstinacy, and preserving a sin, by a wilful, spiteful resisting, or despising the offers of grace and the means of pardon; for such a man St. John does not encourage us to pray; if he be such a person as St. John described, our prayers will do him no good; but because no man can tell the last minute or period of pardon, nor just when a man is gone beyond the limit, and because the limit itself can be enlarged, and God's mercies stay for some longer than for others, therefore St. John left us under the indefinite restraint and caution; which was derogatory enough to represent that sad state of things in which the refractory and impenitent have immerged themselves, and yet so indefinite and cautious, that we may not be too forward in applying it to particulars, nor in prescribing measures to the Divine mercy, nor in passing final sentences upon our brother, before we have heard our Judge Himself speak. 'Sinning a sin not unto death,' is an expression fully signifying that there are some sins which though they be committed and displeased God, and must be repented of, and need many and mighty prayers for their pardon, yet the man is in the state of grace and pardon, that is, he is within the covenant of mercy; he may be admitted, if he will return to his duty: so that being in a state of grace is having a title to God's loving-kindness, a not being rejected of God, but a being beloved of Him to certain purposes of mercy, and that hath these measures and degrees."—M.].

5. The regenerate, as such, according to the spirit, does not sin, though the flesh ever and anon causes him to fall.

6. The sins of the regenerate are not unto death, because forgiveness and atonement are sought and found in Christ.

7. None but believing Christians, born of God, are not subject to the world-power of Satan; those who are subject to it, are least sensible of it; the Christian, who has become free, perceives and feels it in its hostility to him and his resistance to it.

8. Vital piety finds rest only in God, from whom it comes.

9. Although the absolute and immoveably fixed assurance (*certitudo*) of salvation, such as the Methodists and Baptists suppose to possess, is neither possible nor biblically established, yet we may attain unto a sure confidence (*fiducia*), and maintain it in opposition to the Romish decrees, which not only reject the impossibility of final apostasy, but also deny this confidence of the Christian (*Conc. Trid. Sess.* vi. 9, 15, sq.).

10. The Reformed are fully justified in their rejection of altars, images and similar *instrumenta superstitionum* with respect to the abuses of the Roman Catholics, and even down to the present time with their extreme Mariolatry, but they err in confounding the abuse of the several objects with the objects themselves and in changing the one into the other, in lodging complaints against the natural sphere of art instead of pressing it into the higher service [of religion—.]. The liberty of the Lutheran Church cannot be over-estimated.—Images of God will always remain hazardous, not only in the Zwinglian or Puritan sense.—

HOMILETICAL AND PRACTICAL.

Care for thy friends, that they may be and remain assured of the possession of eternal life, despite the temptations and troubles on earth.—Thou hast confidence in the purity of mind of some loved man, how much more shouldest thou confide in the true God?—If distrust is disgraceful and fraught with much unhappiness in our intercourse with men, how much more disgraceful and productive of unhappiness is distrust of the glorious God?—Seeing the light of the world in regeneration is no warrant that this Sun will always smile in His brightest light, unclouded and without stormy days, on the firmament of the soul; but we know, without the gift of prophecy, as the children of God, as Christians, that it is day.—Pray for everything, but be urgent unto intercession for thy erring brother. Prefer to speak of an erring brother to God than to other men.—Dismal is the high-mindedness which fancies that it can never fail with God, but equally dismal is the pusillanimity, which afraid that all is to no purpose, conducts to despair.—As a Christian be not a minor, but volunteer also to act as guardian.—Sin violates not only the Divine command before us, and the Majesty of God above us, but also the Image of God in us!—Every sin may become a sin unto death, as long as it remains unforgiven.—Every sin checks and disturbs the eternal life in thee; the greatest danger, however, is not the commission of, but consenting unto sin, and this is the more dangerous, as your sensibility has become more acute and your will more resolute under the growth of sanctification.—Beware of genius-worship!—

LUTHER:—Thou must learn to cry and not sit down by thyself, or lie on a bench, with drooping head, or shaking it, and lacerate or consume thyself with thy anxious thoughts, caring and fretting how to get free, and regarding nothing except thy own misery and ill-fortune, and wretchedness. But come, idler that thou art, fall down on thy knees, lift up thy hands and eyes to heaven, sing a psalm or say the Lord's prayer, and lay thy trouble before God, and with streaming eyes pour forth thy supplications and make known thy wants.—Prayer, the opening of our grief, the lifting up of our hands, are the sacrifices which are most acceptable to God.—He Himself desires thee to acquaint Him with thy distress, instead of burdening and oppressing, of torturing and lacerating thyself with it, and thus multiplying one calamity into ten or a hundred. He wants thee to be too weak to carry and overcome such a load, that thou mayest learn to grow strong in Him, and that He may be glorified in thee through His strength. Behold the opposite course makes people who are *called* Christians, but nothing else than vain babblers and praters, who see much of faith and the Spirit, but know not what it is, or what they see.

STARKE:—Holy Scripture is our Epistle of God to us, in which He reveals to us His gracious will, as it were, in His own handwriting, and His purpose to give us eternal life.—Faith is never too strong; it may and must grow stronger. Where is confidence of faith, there is joyfulness. The more faith gets filled with the riches of God, the more jubilant is its rejoicing in the abundance of its satisfaction: it is heaven on earth!—The prayer of the lip must be joined to the desire of the heart.—Wouldest thou pray so that thy prayers shall be heard, thou must be full of faith, holy, and a child of God, otherwise thou art abominable.—Prayer is not only a Christian duty, but a glorious benefit. Simplicity is not ignorance. The former befits the Christian, but not the latter. Christians must know. Ignorant Christians are unchristian.—Learned but ungodly men are unlearned; the regenerate are truly learned, as those who through the knowledge of Christ have been made apt for the kingdom of heaven and eternal salvation.—Subtle idolatry is not better than gross idolatry.

BENGEL:—The lamentable state of the world is most aptly described in the brief summary: "*The whole world lieth in the wicked one*," and the world itself, the doings and workings of the children of the world, their sayings, their dealings, their society, etc., are the best exposition of this passage. It is not so much matter of surprise that they are so wicked, as that they are not more wicked.—

HEUBNER:—A sin is not excusable, because it is not yet a sin unto death. A pardonable sin may become a sin unto death; therefore we should abhor every sin.—The wicked one will not touch him: 1. The power of Satan is not irresistible; 2. The Christian, while he continues in a state of regeneration, is proof against all the assaults of Satan.—Fine threads are often more dangerous than coarse chains.—*Faith in the Son of God.* I. A holy, blissful, assured faith:—*a.* as to its substance: in the Image of God, in the Saviour of love; *b.* as to its ground: in the testimony of God; *c.* as to its effects: eternal life. II. It is a faith possible unto all: *a.* provided they diligently read and lay to heart what is written, in order to attain unto faith; *b.* provided they pray God with child-like trust, to give unto them the true faith.—

BESSER:—A singular saying! They believe, and he writes that they may believe. What need is there of an exhortation to believe, if we believe already? (Luther). It is not possible to have to-day's life through yesterday's faith. Here no stand-still is allowed; he that believes, let him go on believing.—After every prayer of a child of God, the Father hears the expressed or unexpressed petition: Thy will be done.—I have read of a pious Christian who was in the habit of keeping a record of his daily prayers and intercessions that he invariably concluded his daily record with the passage 1 Jno. v. 15.—Sin is to the children of God like a robber, against whom they defend themselves all their life long. As a sentry stands before a king's palace, so there stands a sentry with shield and sword before the habitation of God in the heart of His children.—The Epistle of St. John itself is such a preservative.

[EZEKIEL HOPKINS:—God's will, in bestowing a desired mercy upon us, is best known by the promises that He hath made to us. Which promises are of two kinds: some refer to temporal blessings, and others refer to grace and glory.

1. Grace and glory are promised *absolutely* It is that, which we are commanded, all of us, to seek after: and, therefore, here we cannot mistake, while we beg these; for there is no doubt while we pray for grace and glory, but that we do it according to the will of God. Here, we may be earnest and importunate, that God would sanctify and save our souls: and, while we ask this, and make this the matter of our requests, we are under an impossibility of asking amiss; yea, and the more violent we are, and the more resolute to take no denial at the hands of God, the more pleasing is this holy force, since it shows a perfect conformity and concurrence in our wills to His will, who hath told us, It is His will, "*even*," our "*sanctification*:" 1 Thess. iv. 3. This was one part of that violence which our Saviour saith the kingdom of heaven suffered in the days of John the Baptist. It is an invasion that is acceptable to God, when we storm heaven by prayers and supplications, with strong cries and tears: when we plant against it unutterable sighs and groans, this is such a battery, that those eternal ramparts cannot hold out long against it.

2. Though we may pray thus absolutely and with a holy boldness, for grace and glory, saying to God as Jacob to the angel that wrestled with him, I will not let thee go, until thou hast blessed me with spiritual blessings, in heavenly things, in Jesus Christ: yet, secondly, for the degrees of grace and for the comforts of the Holy Ghost, we must pray *conditionally*: if the Lord will. For

these things are not absolutely necessary, neither are they absolutely promised to us by God. Neither any degree of grace, nor any consolation of the Spirit is absolutely promised to us. But, however, our prayers ought to be so much the more fervent and importunate for these things, than for outward, temporal things; by how much more these are of far greater concern than the other.

3. To pray for outward and worldly blessings is *not contrary* to the will of God, for He hath promised to bestow them.—But then, as His promise is conditional, if it is consistent with our good: so, truly, must our prayers be conditional, that God would give them to us, if it is consistent with His will and with our good. Whatsoever we thus ask, we do it according to the will of God; and we are sure of speeding in our request, either by obtaining our desires, or by being blessed with a denial. For, alas, we are blind and ignorant creatures, and cannot look into the designs and drift of Providence, and see how God hath laid in order good and evil in His own purpose: oftentimes, we mistake evil for good, because of the present appearance of good that it hath; yea, so short-sighted are we, that we can look no farther than outward and present appearance. But God, who sees the whole series and connection of his own counsels, knows, many times, that those things, which we account and desire as good, are really evil: and therefore it is our wisdom, to resign all our desires to His disposal, and to say, "Lord, though such temporal enjoyments may seem good and desirable to me at present, yet Thou art infinitely wise, and Thou knowest what the consequence and issue of them will be: I beg them, if they may stand with Thy will; and if Thou seest they will be as really good to me, as I suppose them now to be. If they be not so, I beg the favour of a denial." This is the right frame, in which a Christian's heart should be when he comes to beg temporal mercies of God; and, whilst he thus asks any worldly comforts, he cannot ask amiss. It was an excellent saying of the Satirist, "We ask those things of God which please our present humors and desires: but God gives those things which are best and fittest for us: for we are dearer to Him," saith the heathen, "than we are to ourselves." "And," says another, very well, "It is mercy in God, not to hear us, when we ask things that are evil:" and when He refuseth us in such requests, it is that He might not circumvent us in our own prayers; for, indeed, whilst we ask rashly and intemperately, whatever we foolishly set our hearts upon, God need take no other course to plague and punish us, than by hearing and answering us."—M.].

[Bp. Hall: v. 16:—"If any man see his brother fall into and continue in such a sin as may be capable of forgiveness, let him earnestly sue unto God for pardon of that offender: and God, who is great and infinite in mercy, shall graciously incline His ear unto his prayers, and give remission and life to such an one. There is indeed a sin unto death, for which there is no forgiveness with God, because there is no capacity of repentance for it in the committer of it; I mean the Sin against the Holy Ghost; when a man having received the knowledge of the Gospel by the illumination of the Holy Spirit, and professed the belief thereof, shall in a devilish malice wilfully blaspheme and persecute that known truth."—M.].

[Jortin:—"What makes sin exceedingly sinful and most provoking, is a determined insolence and an obstinate impenitency, a guilt without remorse, and without relenting, without shame and without fear. This is what appears most odious and offensive in the sight of God, as also in the sight of man; and to this incorrigible temper, and abandoned behaviour, indignation and wrath are denounced by Him, who will by no means acquit those that are guilty in this way. "There is a sin unto death," saith St. John, "and there is a sin not unto death." The sin unto death, of which the Apostle speaks, was in some manner peculiar to those times. It was an apostasy from Christianity, and these apostates were persons who had seen the miraculous proofs of its truth, and had themselves been partakers of some extraordinary gifts. When such persons renounced Christ, and fell away from the Church, it was plain that nothing more could be done to amend and reclaim them. And even now it is possible, that sinners may offend so long and so heinously as at last to provoke God, either to take them out of the world by a secret judgment, and so it is a sin unto temporal death; or to give them up to their own hard hearts, and so it becomes a sin unto spiritual death. But let an observation be added, which may be necessary to quiet melancholy and desponding minds; and it is this: If any one be afraid that he is in such a condition, this very fear shows that in all probability he is not in such a condition; because it is usual for such sinners to have no consideration, no shame, no remorse, and no fear at all."—M.].

[Ezekiel Hopkins:—"Beware therefore, then, that you do not entertain any slight thought of sin: nor think, with the Papists, that there are some sorts of sins, that do not deserve death; which they call *venial* sins, in opposition to other more gross and heinous sins, which they allow to be *mortal*. Believe it, the least prick at the heart is deadly; and so is the least sin to the soul. And, indeed, it is a contradiction, to call any sin venial in their sense, who hold it is not worthy of damnation, for *the wages of sin is death;* if it be not, how is it venial?"—M.].

[Rieger: on v. 21:—"Those who were called to the light of God, readily knew that an *idol* is nothing in the world, and that idolatry and idol-worship are abominable. But there were at that time temptations which did not render superfluous this concluding admonition. They might be invited to idol-sacrifices and thus be drawn into a sort of communion with idols, Rev. ii. 20; 2 Cor. vi. 16. Sometimes, in order to escape bitter persecution, Christians might venture to go too far. Yes, notwithstanding idols have at this present time sunk into still greater contempt, there yet arises always something which injuriously affects the knowledge of God in Christ Jesus, or the worship of God in spirit and in truth, which tries to find out some other way to God than by Christ, and to seek acceptance with God in another service than in His Son. It becomes therefore every one who is of the truth to sigh, O God, keep me in the mind, which Thou hast given me of Thy Son, and in which thou hast strengthened me by this testimony of St. John! Amen."—M].

[*Sermons and Sermon Themes.*

Ver. 13. If we must aim at assurance, what should they do who are not able to discern their own spiritual condition? THOMAS DOOLITTLE. Morn. Exerc. I. 252.

Ver. 16. LIGHTFOOT, JOHN. A sin unto death Sermons; Works, 6, 331.

CHALMERS, T. The nature of the sin unto death. Sermon: Works, 9, 225.

Ver. 16, 17. BENSON, G. Concerning a sin unto death, and a sin not unto death. A Paraphrase, etc. 2, 647.—M.].

THE

SECOND AND THIRD EPISTLES GENERAL OF JOHN

INTRODUCTION.

§ 1. CONTENTS OF THE EPISTLES.

1. The Second Epistle, after the Address and Salutation (vv. 1–3), expresses the Apostle's joy on finding the children of the *κυρία* walk in the truth of the Gospel (v. 4), a monition of the commandment of brotherly love (vv. 5, 6), not without a solemn warning against the doctrine of the false teachers, who confess not the coming of Jesus Christ in the flesh (vv. 7–9), and against fellowship with them (vv. 10, 11). Disinclined to write, and in the hope of early oral intercourse, the Epistle concludes with greetings of the sister's children (vv. 12, 13).

2. The Third Epistle, addressed to Caius (v. 1), after a salutation, importing his wish for the prosperity of Caius, expresses the Apostle's joy over his walking in the truth (vv. 2–4), commends his hospitality to missionary brethren (vv. 5–8), deplores the opposition they have to encounter at the hands of the ambitious Diotrephes, notwithstanding his Epistle of commendation, and the readiness of the Church to comply therewith, with an intimation of his intention to take a personal stand against him (vv. 9, 10), warns against his example and commends Demetrius, the probable bearer of the Epistle (vv. 11, 12). Disinclined to write, and in the hope of a speedy meeting, the Epistle concludes with greetings from the Apostle and friends to friends (vv. 13–15).

§ 2. CHARACTER OF THE EPISTLES.

1. These two brief Epistles, besides which reference is made to a similar Epistle, which has been lost (3 Jno. 9), are two instructive monuments of the Apostle's mode of dealing with individuals. Ewald justly observes that these Epistles lack the rich flow and fusion of language found in a similar Epistle addressed by Paul to Philemon, but unmistakeably evince a loftier assurance, and with all their gentleness and affability, a brevity and earnestness which point to an Apostle little disposed to write much, and greatly preferring oral dealings and instruction.

2. While the Second Epistle exhibits in forcible energy the most lively joy in his converts' walking in the truth coupled with the most tender solicitude for them with respect to the false teachers, and warns them in the most decided terms against intimate intercourse with them, the Third Epistle exhibits the same joy, coupled with a reference to the aiding sympathy with missionary brethren as the inviolable duty of individuals and the Church, and censures, threatens and entreats with great power.

3. The two Epistles exhibit a remarkable similarity. The beginning of 2 Jno. 1 is precisely like that of 3 Jno. 1 (*ὁ πρεσβύτερος—ἀγαπῶ ἐν ἀληθείᾳ*); 2 Jno. 4 and 3 John 3 (*ἐχάρην λίαν*); particularly the conclusion 2 Jno. 12 (*πολλὰ ἔχων—οὐκ ἐβουλήθην διὰ χάρτου καὶ μέλανος —ἀλλὰ ἐλπίζω —στόμα πρὸς στόμα λαλῆσαι*), and 3 Jno. 13, 14 (*πολλὰ εἶχον—οὐ θέλω διὰ μέλανος καὶ καλάμου—ἐλπίζω δὲ—στόμα πρὸς στόμα λαλήσομεν*).—These Epistles, which resemble each other like twin sisters

(Düsterdieck after Hieronymus, *Ep.* 85), must have been written by one and the same author. This is the opinion of those who ascribe their authorship to the Apostle St. John, of Ebrard, who ascribes them to the Presbyter John, and of Baur, who regards them as writings of Montanistic origin.

§ 3. OCCASION AND SCOPE OF THE EPISTLES.

1. Although similar in plan and form, they are different as to their objects and tendency.—From his acquaintance with some of the children of the κυρία, who were stanch Christians, the author of the Second Epistle took occasion to express his joy to their mother, who, as Düsterdieck, and probably correctly, supposes, had been known and endeared to him for some time, and to make known to her his paternal sympathy and encouragement, coupled, in particular, with a warning against false teachers and fellowship with them, who might prove especially dangerous to a Christian lady, for the purpose that her joy might be full (v. 12) and remain undisturbed; the announcement of his visit does not seem to belong to the real scope of the Epistle, (Düsterdieck).—The Author of the Third Epistle has been informed by missionary brethren that owing to the ambitious and domineering attitude of Diotrephes, who had also maligned the author of the Epistle for his interest on behalf of said missionaries, these had not been permanently received in the Church, with which Caius was connected, and had been compelled to move on, notwithstanding the hospitality of Caius and several other church-members similarly disposed. On this account the author of the Epistle gives notice of his coming in a short time, with a view to removing such disunion and disorder and to encouraging Caius to fearless care of the brethren.

2. In view of these simple, unequivocal relations, Baur, the head of the Tübingen School, describes the situation in a truly marvellous manner, with shocking arbitrariness. On the ground of the passage from Clement of Alexandria, cited below in § 5, Baur maintains that ἐκλεκτή is the Church, which is holy, and that the Montanists portray the *ecclesia* or *Sponsa Christi vera, pudica, sancta;* that the allegorical term *Babylonia* refers to Rome, as in 1 Peter v. 13; that opinions were divided in respect of Montanism; that one party led by Diotrephes, had denied church-fellowship to the Church with which the author of the Epistle was connected, but that the other party was on terms of amity and union with said Church, that this second Epistle was addressed to the *Montanistic* party of the Church at *Rome;* that *Diotrephes* is not a real name, but a symbolical designation of the Roman bishop, yet not of Victor (193-202), as assumed by Schwegler (*Montanism* p. 284), because Irenæus and Clement of Alexandria were already acquainted with these Epistles, but perhaps of Anicetus (157–168), Soter or Eleutheros (to 193); that due consideration should be given to the *partisan spirit* of the author of the Epistle, which made him designate the followers of Diotrephes as heathens (3 Jno. 7); that the Second Epistle was addressed to the Church to which Caius belonged, and that the Epistle, alluded to at 3 Jno. 9, was written to Caius.—Baur bases all this on the notice of Clement of Alexandria that the Second Epistle was written by the Apostle St. John, and Diotrephes (Διοτρεφής), one nourished and brought up by Jews, is said to be the symbolical designation of an orthodox bishop at Rome. A Montanist is named as the author of these Epistles, which contain no Montanistic views and are not even referred to by Tertullian, the Montanist!—Hilgenfeld regards the Second Epistle as an excommunicatory writing, designed to be the official expression of an Apostolical sentence of repudiation directed against fellowship with the Gnostic false teachers, and the Third Epistle as an ἐπιστολὴ συστατική emanating from the Church of John, for the purpose of vindicating the right of that Church to issue such Epistles of commendation, which the Jewish Christians considered to be the prerogative of their venerated James, the author of the Epistle having recognized the utility of such an ordered passport-system during the Gnostic storms and commotions; cf. Huther, p. 253, sqq.

§ 4. READERS OF THE EPISTLES.

On the κυρία see notes on 2 Jno. 1, and on Caius, notes on 3 Jno. 1 in Exegetical and Critical.—Very curious is the view of Ewald, who supposes that the two Epistles were sent to one Church, namely, the Second Epistle addressed to the *elect glorious one,* to the Church; but because it might be feared that Diotrephes the elder, through whose hands the Epistle had to pass, would prevent its being publicly read at Church, the Third Epistle was on that account addressed to another well-disposed elder, viz., Caius, of the same Church. The poor support which this view derives from 3 Jno. 9 is evident and shown in the Exegesis on that passage. He further alleges that the great stress of the times induced John to omit the name of the Church, which must have been one of considerable importance, because three of its elders, viz., Diotrephes, Caius, Demetrius, are mentioned. Pure conjectures!

§ 5. THE AUTHOR OF THE EPISTLES.

1. *History* answers the question, 'Who is the author of these Epistles?' in the following particulars: The oldest testimony for these Epistles is that of the Muratorian Canon of the New Testament which was composed until about A. D. 170 (as stated in the Introduction to the first Epistle § 3, 1. p. 4.), and makes mention of the First and Second Epistles. From the excellent essay of Wieseler, referred to there, we have still to supply an observation on the Pauline Epistles to Philemon, Titus and Timothy. In said Canon we read (p. 828): *Verum ad Philemonem una, et ad Timotheum duæ pro affectu et dilectione, in honorem tamen ecclesiæ catholicæ, in ordinatione ecclesiasticæ disciplinæ sanctificatæ sunt.*—"The Epistle to Philemon probably followed immediately after the Epistles addressed to Churches, because it was addressed not only to Philemon, but also to Apphia and Archippus and to the Church in Philemon's house (v. 2), and because the Apostolical salutation and benediction had also reference to them (vv. 3, 25). It constituted, therefore, a sort of transition to the Epistles addressed to individuals only, viz., to those to Titus and Timothy. Yet the circumstance, that such a distinction was really drawn in the Christian Church between Epistles addressed to individuals, and Epistles addressed to whole Churches, and that our author deemed it necessary, in the words beginning with *pro affectu et dilectione*, to justify the grounds on which the Epistles to Titus and Timothy were notwithstanding received into the Ecclesiastical Canon,—has a most important bearing on the history of the Canon." (Wieseler, l. c. p. 839). Hence it can neither be thought singular, nor subject to doubt, that, while the Second Epistle, because of its more instructive character and because the term κυρία was supposed to refer to a Church and not to an individual person, was received along with the First Epistle into the Canon, the Third Epistle, addressed to an unknown personage and without the intrinsic weight of the Pauline Pastoral Epistles, was not received into the Canon; but this of course does not deny its Johannean origin, still this is the way how it came to be reckoned among the Antilegomena. The additional clause: *"ut sapientia ab amicis Salomonis in honorem ipsius scripta,"* does not belong to the words preceding them which refer to the Epistle of John, but to those following: *"apocalypsis etiam Johannis."* The latter, therefore, is said to have been composed by the friend of John, not by himself, but this is not asserted concerning the Epistles, as many, because of the false connection with the words preceding said clause, would like to maintain (Wieseler, l. c. p. 846 sq.). Hence Düsterdieck's use of the Muratorian Canon (II. p. 464 sq.), and also Huther's (p. 248 sq.), require to be rectified in this respect.—Clement of Alexandria, the successor of Pantænus A. D. 190–220: *"Secunda Johannis epistola, quæ ad virgines scripta est, simplicissima est; scripta vero est ad quandam Babyloniam Electam nomine, significat autem electionem ecclesiæ sanctæ."* (Opp. ed. Potter p. 1011). Origen, who says in his eighth homily on Joshua: *"addit et Joannes tuba canere per* EPISTOLAS *suas,"* knew several Epistles; but he says according to Euseb. *Hist. Eccl.*, VI. 25: οὐ πάντες φασὶ γνησίους εἶναι ταύτας.—Dionysius of Alexander, the disciple and successor of Origen A. D. 233, from A. D. 248 bishop, for the purpose of illustrating the Johannean diction makes use also of the Second and Third Epistles, takes accordingly no offence in the appellation: ὁ πρεσβύτερος, and calling the Second and Third Epistles φερομένη Ἰωάννου, designated them as generally received as Johannean, by tradition.—Irenæus, the disciple of Polycarp and Papias, † A. D. 202, cites 2 Jno. 7 mistakenly, as Guericke says (p. 478), owing to an error of memory, as forming part of the First Epistle (*adv. Hær.* III. 16. 8), but still as from the Epistles of John; he cites, however, correctly 2 Jno. 11 (adv. Hær. I. 103), as from the Epistle of John (Ἰωάννης δὲ, ὁ τοῦ Κυρίου μαθητής.)—It is of course natural, that these two private Epistles were not translated in the earliest age of the Church, and consequently not inserted in the Peschito,

which contains only three Catholic Epistles (James, 1 Peter, 1 John), although Ephrem the Syrian knew both Epistles,—and that citations from them are more rare occurrences, so that Tertullian and Cyprian do not make mention of them. Although Cyprian did not cite them in his own writings, he still says in relating (*De Hær. bapt.*) the opinions of the various bishops in the council of Carthage: "*Aurelius a Chullabi dixit: Joannes Apostolus in epistola sua posuit dicens, si quis ad vos venit,*" etc. 2 Jno. 10; [thus clearly showing that this Epistle was received as Apostolical and Canonical in the North African Church.—M.]. On that account Eusebius (*Hist. Eccles.* III. 25) reckons the two Epistles among the antilegomena of the first class [still Eusebius's own opinion may be gathered from his *Demonstratio Evangelica,* III. 5, where he says of St. John ἐν μὲν ταῖς ἐπιστολαῖς αὐτοῦ οὐδὲ μνήμην τῆς οἰκείας προσηγορίας ποιεῖται, ἢ πρεσβύτερον ἑαυτὸν ὀνομάζει, οὐδαμοῦ δὲ ἀπόστολον οὐδὲ εὐαγγελιστήν, whence it would appear that he received the two smaller Epistles as genuine." Alford.—M.]. Jerome (*de vir. illustr.* c. 9): "*Scripsit autem Johannes et unam epistolam—quæ ab universis ecclesiasticis et eruditis Viris probatur: reliquæ autem duæ quarum principium* SENIOR *Johannis Presbyteri asseruntur.*" But he calls (cap. 18) this view "*opinio, quam a plerisque retulimus traditam,*" and Oecumenius and Bede decidedly reject this view.—The Epistles, after having been regarded without any doubt as Johannean in the Middle Ages, were first referred to the authorship of John the Presbyter by Erasmus, who was followed by Grotius, J. D. Beck (*observ. crit. exeget. specim.* I.), Fritzsche (*Observations on the Epistles of John* in Henke's *Museum,* vol. 3, 1), Ammon (*Life of Jesus* I. p. 45 sq.), and especially Ebrard. Almost all the modern commentators (Lücke, de Wette, Brückner, Düsterdieck, Huther) receive them as Johannean Epistles. The Tübingen school disputes their Apostolical origin and considers them, according to the opinion of its leader, as writings of *Montanistic* origin; but Hilgenfeld, at least, makes them originate in the *subapostolic age* (cf. § 3).

2. The result of the examination of the most ancient documents respecting the author of these two Epistles, which requires us to regard them as the writings of the Apostle St. John, is confirmed by the writings themselves.—The *first* point to be considered here is the term ὁ πρεσβύτερος. Here the author observes an incognito to all persons except those to whom he wrote, and who knew, of course, who this presbyter was. It surely was not his intention to write anonymously, because he addresses private individuals in clear and definite terms, and apprizes them of his coming to see them. The expression in question describes a superior position in general terms and in language reflecting a friendly and affectionate disposition. This is precisely St. John's manner both in the First Epistle and in the Gospel; he thus describes himself, that only those whom it concerns, may recognize him. Bede and Oecumenius leave it undecided whether the Apostle called himself ὁ πρεσβύτερος on account of his age or on account of his office; had he used said appellation on account of his advanced years, he ought to have put either ὁ πρεσβύτης, or ὁ γέρων. Hence Piscator, Er., Schmidt, Wolf, Carpzov, Sander and al., [who take this view—M.], are mistaken. The official sense of that appellation is advocated by N. de Lyra, Bartholomæus Petrus (=*Episcopus, totius Asiæ primus*), a Lapide, Beza, Lücke, Huther, Düsterdieck and others. Cf. 1 Pet. v. 1: συμπρεσβύτερος, and Eusebius, *Hist. Eccl.,* III., 39, where the Apostles are called πρεσβύτεροι. John might have called himself ὁ ἀπόστολος, ὁ ἐπίσκοπος; but he prefers thus to moderate his privileged position. Ewald assumes that it was also on account of the stress of the times that he omitted to give his own name, as well as that of the Church to which he sent the second Epistle (see above in § 4). Düsterdieck combines the official reference of this appellation with a reference to age, the then advanced years of the Apostle presupposing the years during which he had held converse with the Lord Himself; so also Aretius, Guericke, (*Gesammtgeschichte des Neuen Testaments,* 1854, p. 485, sq.), Benson and others. But seeing that there did exist, according to the testimony of Papias in Eusebius, *Hist. Eccl.,* III., 39, a person different from the Apostle, called John the Presbyter, who was called ὁ μαθητὴς τοῦ κυρίου, it has been thought, especially on the above-cited testimony of Irenæus, that this latter was the author of these Epistles. This opinion is strenuously advocated by Ebrard. But in that case the name ought not to be wanting, as Lücke, Düsterdieck and Huther, rightly and emphatically contend; for it cannot be proved that said personage bore that name κατ' ἐξοχήν, especially since

the diction of the Epistles clearly points to the Apostle.—The *second* point relates to the impress of Johannean diction and thought left on our Epistles. Compare only the following expressions: 2 Jno. 1: ἐγνωκότες τὴν ἀλήθειαν, v. 2: μένειν ἐν, v. 3: ἐν ἀληθείᾳ καὶ ἀγάπῃ, v. 4: περιπατεῖν ἐν, v. 5: ἐντολὴν—καινή, ἣν εἴχομεν ἀπ' ἀρχῆς (1 Jno. ii. 7), v. 6: αὕτη—ἵνα (1 Jno. iii. 11, 23; v. 3), καθὼς ἠκούσατε ἀπ' ἀρχῆς, v. 7: πλάνοι ἐξῆλθον (1 Jno. ii. 18, sq.), οἱ μὴ ὁμολογοῦντες Ἰησοῦν χριστὸν ἐρχόμενον ἐν σαρκί (1 Jno. iv. 1, 2), ὁ ἀντίχριστος, v. 9: μένων ἐν τῇ διδαχῇ, θεὸν οὐκ ἔχει (1 Jno. ii. 23), καὶ τὸν υἱὸν καὶ τὸν πατέρα ἔχει, v. 12: ἵνα ἡ χαρὰ ἡμῶν ᾖ πεπληρωμένη (1 Jno. i. 4), 3 Jno. 1: ἐν ἀληθείᾳ, vv. 3, 4, ἐν ἀληθείᾳ περιπατεῖς, v. 11: ἐκ τοῦ θεοῦ ἐστίν, οὐχ ἑώρακεν τὸν θεὸν (1 Jno. iii. 6, 10; iv. 8). The connection of thesis and antithesis, without simple antithesis, leading to a progression in the thought, occurs at 2 Jno. 9; 3 Jno. 11. How freely is carried out the theme of 2 Jno. 3: ἐν ἀληθείᾳ καὶ ἀγάπῃ, and then vv. 4–11. Do we not identify the independent position of the author by the ἐρχόμενον ἐν σαρκί (2 Jno. 7), as compared with the Perfect (1 Jno. iv. 2), and the Aorist (1 Jno. v. 6), and his free, easy handling of his subject. This independence is recognizable in the salutation, perfectly analogous to that in the pastoral Epistles of Paul, by the ἔσται μεθ' ὑμῶν being placed first, and then by the παρά following, instead of which Paul uses ἀπό (see note on the passage), and the omission of ἡμῶν, supplied by Paul. On this, as well as on the severity, alleged to be bordering on lovelessness in 2 Jno. 10, compare the notes below, in Exegetical and Critical.—After what has been said, we can neither refer, with de Wette, to εἴ τις (2 Jno. 10) instead of ἐάν τις, διδαχὴν φέρειν (*ibid.*), περιπατεῖν κατά (v. 6), κοινωνεῖν (v. 11), μειζότερος (3 Jno. 4), τὸ κακόν, τὸ ἀγαθόν, as proofs against the Johannean origin of the Epistle, nor characterize, with the same intent, with Fritzsche, as Pauline the following expressions: ὑγιαίνειν, εὐοδοῦσθαι (3 Jno. 2), προπέμπειν ἀξίως τοῦ θεοῦ (v. 6), φιλοπρωτεύειν (v. 9), φλυαρεῖν (v. 10), especially since the expressions used in 3 Jno. 6, 9, 10, are not found either in the writings of Paul. It is moreover rather hazardous to prove such things from single and isolated words, especially here, since the matters introduced in the Third Epistle are altogether specific, and do not bear the faintest resemblance to the circumstances, relations and subjects discussed in the First Epistle; such a disparity, of course, involves the use of different expressions. Ebrard's attempt also, to prove that the Third Epistle, as being most unlike the First, and the Second Epistle nearly related to the Third, were not written by the Apostle St. John, but by John the Presbyter, is a failure. He discovers in the passages used, allusions, intentional reminiscences, and actually citations, and acknowledges the Author's independence neither in the passages given above, nor "in the striking circumstance" that he uses at 2 Jno. 10, εἴ τις instead of ἐάν τις, and that "at 3 Jno. 11 he reproduces Johannean *forms of thought*, in wholly unjohannean *language*." Even Ebrard is compelled to admit the similarity of the Second Epistle to the First, both as to the identity of the doctrine taught, and the form of its expression.—Under these circumstances it seems impossible to deny the Apostolic and Johannean origin of these Epistles. They were both written by one and the same author, by an independent man, and the Second Epistle necessitates us to go back to the author of the First, while there is at least nothing in the Third to prevent such a mode of procedure.

§ 6. DATE OF THE EPISTLES.

One thing is clear: the two Epistles were written at about the same time. It cannot be inferred from the affinity of the Second Epistle with the First, that the former was composed after the latter, as Ebrard alleges, since only the identity of the Authors is established, but not the use of the First in the Second. Nor can any inferences be drawn from the First Epistle not being mentioned (S. G. Lange), from the more vigorous spirit of the Second Epistle (Eichhorn), from the youthful fire in the *rigoristic* saying at 2 Jno. 10, 11. (Knauer).—But they were probably written about the same time as the First, since the circumstances of the times are probably identical in all three Epistles.

§ 7. PLACE WHERE THEY WERE WRITTEN.

Probability points to Ephesus, as the place where they were written, before a tour of visitation (Eusebius, Hist. Eccl., III., 23; Lücke, Huther, Düsterdieck).

§ 8. LITERATURE.

See Introduction to the first Epistle. § 10. Also the following:

J. SOMMELIUS, *Isagoge in 2 et 3 Joh. Ep.* Land. 1798.

J. RAMBONNET, *De sec. ep. Johannea,* Traj. 1818.

C. A. HEUMANN, *Commentar über den dritten Brief des Johannes,* Helmstädt. 1778.

[AUGUSTINE MARLORATE, 4to. 1588.

WILLIAM JONES, on the Second and Third Epistles of John, in the *Commentary on Philemon, etc.* Folio. London, 1635.

SAMUEL SMITH, *Exposition of the Second Epistle of St. John.* 1663.

F. D. MAURICE, on the 2d and 3d Epistles of St. John. Truth in the woman and the man Epistles of St. John, 316.

J. B. CARPZOVIUS, *Commentatio in Epistolam, 2 Joannis de charitate et veritate; in Joannis Epistolam tertiam brevis enarratio.* T. Rapolti Opera. 4to. Lips. 1693.—M.].

COMMENTARY.

THE SECOND EPISTLE GENERAL OF JOHN THE APOSTLE

(*Ἰωάννου β*. B. Cod. Sin. Several codices add *ἐπιστολή*, and others *ἐπιστολή καθολική*. Several have after *Ἰωάννου*: *τοῦ ἐπὶ στηθοῦς*, G: *τοῦ ἁγίου ἀποστόλου—τοῦ θεολόγου*).

I. THE ADDRESS (vv. 1–3).

The elder unto the elect lady and her children, whom I love in the truth;[1] and not I only, but also all they that have known the truth; for the truth's sake, which dwelleth in us,[3] and shall be with us for ever. Grace be[4] with you,[5] mercy, and *peace* from God the Father, and from[6] the Lord Jesus Christ, the Son of the Father, in truth and love.

Verse 1. [1 German: "Whom I love in truth." So Alford, Lillie.—M.].
2 B. Cod. Sin.: *καὶ οὐκ ἐγὼ*; A.; *οὐκ ἐγὼ δὲ*; G: *καὶ οὐκ ἐγὼ δὲ*. [The reading of A. may have arisen from a desire to mark the antithesis more strongly.—M.]
Verse 2. 3 *μένουσαν* is the reading of B. Sin. and most and the best codd. A. reads *ἐνοικοῦσαν*, but is evidently an interpretation. [German: "which abideth in us."—M.]
Verse 3. [4 German: "There shall be with you."—M.]
5 A. omits *ἔσται μεθ' ὑμῶν*—evidently by a mistake, occasioned by the conclusion of v. 2. B. G. Sin. read *ἡμῶν* which is also occasioned by v. 2.
6 G. K. Sin insert before *Ἰησοῦ* the word *κυρίου*; this addition, as well as the exchange of the preposition *παρὰ* for *ἀπὸ* are probably transcribed from the beginnings of the Pauline Epistles.

EXEGETICAL AND CRITICAL.

The address proper. V. 1. **The elder,** *ὁ πρεσβύτερος*; the definite Article notes a person, the word without the Article would give prominence to his official position. That John the Apostle is meant we have endeavoured to prove in the Introduction § 5. Thus Peter also calls himself, in an exhortation addressed to presbyters, *συμπρεσβύτερος*. (1 Pet. v. 1).

To the elect lady, *ἐκλεκτῃ κυρίᾳ*; these words have been very differently explained. Grammatically they present a perfect analogy to 1 Pet. i. 1: *ἐκλεκτοῖς παρεπιδήμοις*, to elect strangers; *κυρίᾳ* therefore cannot well be taken as a proper name, which would require as at v. 13, and 3 Jno. 1: *Γαΐῳ τῷ ἀγαπητῷ,—κυρίᾳ τῇ ἐκλεκτῇ* Cf. Phil. i. 2. Rom. xvi. 5, 8, 9, 10, 12, 13 etc. To what purpose is it that *κυρία* was a female proper name, as may be seen in *Gruteri inscript.* p. 1127. N. xi., and that this was maintained by Athanasius, and later by Benson, Heumann, Bengel, Krigele (*de κυρία Joannis*, Lips. 1758). S. G. Lange, Carpzovius, Paulus, de Wette, Brückner, Lücke, Düsterdieck and others? Düsterdieck and Lücke notice a certain irregularity and inconsequence, which is not explained by but consists in the adjective preceding the noun, as long as *κυρία* is treated as a *nomen proprium*. But the difficulty is even greater in treating *ἐκλεκτή* as a proper name, as is done by de Lyra, Cappellus, Wetstein, Grotius and al. For the sister, v. 13, is also called *ἐκλεκτή*.—But how are we to take the *elect lady*? The context requires us to think of an individual: the *ἐγὼ* of the writer answers to the *σύ* of the person addressed (vv. 1, 4 sq.); she as a mother with her children is mentioned (vv. 3, 6, 8, 10, 12); her sister and her sister's children salute her (v. 13). Epictetus (cap. 62) observes that: *αἱ γυναῖκες εὐθὺς ἀπὸ τεσσαρεσκαίδεκα ἐτῶν ὑπὸ τῶν ἀνδρῶν κυρίαι καλοῦνται*. Huther is wrong in saying that the term *κυρία* does not answer to the German *Frau* [=the English *Mistress*, the word used to address married ladies—M.], but to the German *Herrin* [=the English Mistress or lady of the house—M.]; for *Frau* is the feminine of *fro*, the Master, (*Frohndienst, Frohnveste, Fronleichnam*), and *Frau* =*Herrin* (see Jütting, *Biblisches Wörterbuch* 1864, s. v. *Frauenzimmer* p. 61 and s. v. *Frohnvogt* p. 65); nor need that author designate *κυρία* only as *a polite form of address*, nor Düsterdieck pronounce it a *title* only suited to *worldly politeness*. It may just as well be taken as the standing designation of an esteemed woman, and it is neither unworthy of a Christian, nor of an Apostle to call a church-member, according to a prevailing usage, "*Frau*" (lady or mistress)=*κυρία*, so

Luther, Piscator, Beza, Heidegger, Rittmeier, *de electa domina*, Helmst. 1706), Wolf, Baumgarten-Crusius, Sander and al.; a Lapide reports her to have been called Drusia or Drusiana. Carpzovius supposes that Martha, the sister of Lazarus, is the person addressed; Knauer (*Studien und Kritiken*, 1833, pp. 452–458), suggests Mary, the mother of the Lord—but all these views are wholly untenable. It is true, that unfortunately the name of the person addressed is not given in the address, so that one might almost feel inclined to take κυρία as a proper name. But the name of the person addressed might be wanting just as well as that of the writer; the messenger may and probably did make up for such omission.—But the circumstance that this "note" (*Handbillet*-Augusti) found its way among the Catholic Epistles, should not occasion any difficulty. Just as well as the third Epistle to Caius; it is no more unworthy of the Canon than St. Paul's Epistle to Philemon; the individual, also a woman, is worthy of due regard and consideration, I confine myself to making mention of Priscilla (Acts xviii. 2, sq.; 26, sq.; Rom. xvi. 3, sq.).—It is far more hazardous to understand κυρία to signify the Christian Church in general, or some particular congregation; the former is recommended by Jerome, the latter by the Scholiast I.; they are followed by Calov, Hofmann (*Weissagung und Erfüllung* II., p. 321; *Schriftbeweis*, I., p. 226, sq.), Hilgenfeld, Huther and al. Serrarius guessed Corinth, Whiston argued for Philadelphia, Whitby for Jerusalem, the mother of all Churches, and Augusti for Jerusalem, because founded by the Lord Himself, though such a "*note*" would certainly be less suited to a Church than to an individual church-member. Hammond has the curious notion that κυρία is=*curia, ecclesia*, and Michaelis, that it designates the Church assembled on the Lord's day. But wholly unfounded, and devoid of all possibility of proof is the hypothesis of Besser and al., that κυρία is the ἐκκλησία to which 3 Jno. 9, was written, and that the 2d Epistle of John is the one there referred to. Hofmann adverts to the Church being called νύμφη and γυνή in the Apocalypse, to שׁוּלַמִּית and שְׁלֹמֹה, and to ἡ ἐν Βαβυλῶνι συνεκλεκτή (1 Pet. v. 13). Huther also rightly observes in opposition to Ebrard, that the Church, which in respect of Christ is an obedient handmaid, may be considered both in her subordinate relation to Christ and in her superior relation to individual members, and as such be described as κυρία by the side of κύριος; but that v. 12 requires us to understand a single congregation and not "*all orthodox Christendom*" (Hilgenfeld), and that our Epistle is not an Encyclical. But in that case the address ought to have given the name of that congregation. Nor would ἐκλεκτή exactly suit κυρία=ἐκκλησία; for ἡ ἐν Βαβυλῶνι συνεκλεκτή is somewhat different, and, in juxtaposition with and as distinguished from ὁ Μάρκος, can hardly designate the Church in that place (see Fronmüller on 1 Pet. v. 13, in this Commentary). The relation indicated at Gal. iv. 26: ἥτις ἐστὶν μήτηρ ἡμῶν, can hardly have been applied here to a single congregation, so that it might be called κυρία. After all that has been said, the choice lies between κυρία as a *nomen proprium*, or κυρία=lady. [Among recent English commentators, Alford takes the former view, while Wordsworth elaborates the interpretation, according to which κυρία is a Church.—M.].

And her children (τοῖς τέκνοις) should be taken literally; a family is always an important circle of men! But if κυρία is construed as a Church, the children designate Church-members.

Further particulars. vv. 1, 2.

Whom I love in truth.—Οὕς after τέκνα imports sons, but does not exclude daughters, the κυρία had sons and daughters, but more sons than daughters; hence it would have been improper to say τοῖς υἱοῖς, as Huther maintains, who, if κυρία designates a Church, refers to Gal. iv. 9 (τεκνία μου—οὕς), Matth. xxviii. 19 (τὰ ἔθνη—αὐτούς), passages which fully justify the given explanation, and prove that τέκνα need not be sons only (de Wette and al.); nor does οὕς refer to κυρία and her children (Beza, Bengel, Sander [al.]). Ἐγώ emphatically asserts the Apostle's personal relations to that family-congregation; that which makes that family-congregation the object of the Apostle's love and of that of all believers, implies the reason of this Epistle and its importance. Though ἐν ἀληθείᾳ along with ἀγαπῶ should be construed adverbially, yet it signifies more than: "in sincerity," for it denotes also Christian love. Bengel: "*Amor non modo verus amor, sed veritate evangelica nititur.*" Lücke: "It designates genuine Christian love." Ebrard: "I love thee with that love which is love in truth," cf. i. Jno. iii. 18, 19. The additional clause has respect to objective truth (Düsterdieck, Huther 2d ed.).

And not I only, but also all who have known the truth.—Bengel pointedly observes: "*communio sanctorum.*" He assumes in his own case, as well as in the ἀγαπᾶν ἐν ἀληθείᾳ, the ἐγνωκέναι τὴν ἀλήθειαν. The term πάντες must not be restricted to Ephesus and its environs, the supposed place of writing (Grotius, de Wette and al.), but only to those who were acquainted with the κυρία and her children (Lücke), yet so that those, who afterwards might get acquainted with her, are included. The restriction lies not in the word itself, but in the *situation* (Ebrard). It is not necessary to think here of only one Church (Huther).—The reason of this love is stated in

Ver. 2. **For the truth's sake, which abideth in us.**—Ἡμῖν designates the persons loving and beloved, (Huther); it must not be altogether construed in a general sense or applied, as if by implication, to the persons specified in v. 1 (Bede, Düsterdieck and al.). This is also the ground of the definition of ἀγαπᾶν ἐν ἀληθείᾳ and of believers as οἱ ἐγνωκότες τὴν ἀλήθειαν (v. 1), not as Huther maintains, in πλάνοι (v. 7). The common life-sphere is just ἡ ἀλήθεια, and moreover not only that which is objectively sure, but also that which subjectively is securely kept. In order to note the former point, the Apostle adds:

And shall be with us forever.—The reason why the Participle, instead of being followed by a further participial sentence, is here followed by the *Verb. finit.*, is the writer's intention to give greater prominence to this thought. Winer, p. 600. The Future is not the expression of a *wish*, as Grotius, Lücke, Ebrard and others suppose, but the confident assertion of certain duration. Hence εἰς τὸν αἰῶνα must not be restricted to the duration of the life of the persons interested (Benson and others). Μεθ' ἡμῶν denotes the objectivity of Divine truth as well as our subjectively developed activity. Cf. Jno xiv. 16; 1 Jno. ii. 20, 27; especially Matth. xxviii. 20. Hence ἐν and μετὰ must not be taken as substantially equivalent (Winer, p. 430), since ἐν notes the subjective side, and μετὰ also the objective side.

The *greeting.* v. 3. **There shall be with you.**—Singular, and proof that we have not to deal here with the imitation of a forger; who would have adhered to usual and current forms of expression, like the addition ἐν ἀληθείᾳ καὶ ἀγάπῃ, here Future; it is qualified by the preceding words with which it is connected. It is not=ἔστω, but *votum cum affirmatione* (Bengel); the certainty of the expectation excels the wish of the greeting.

Grace, mercy, peace.—1. Tim. i. 2; 2 Tim. i. 21 have also χάρις, ἔλεος, εἰρήνη.—Χάρις is free grace, which, without any merit on the part of man, lovingly condescends to men and denotes the thoughts of peace in the paternal heart of God, the *mind* of Him who is Love (Rom. iii. 24; Eph. ii. 4–10); ἔλεος describes the mercy which energetically lays hold of, and enters into the *misery* of man (Luke x. 30–37), and denotes the *act* of love; εἰρήνη is the *gift* of love, the effect of χάρις and ἔλεος. [Trench, *Synonyms of the New Testament*, p. 225: "Χάρις has reference to the sins of men, ἔλεος to their misery. God's χάρις, His free grace and gift, is extended to men, as they are guilty, His ἔλεος is extended to them, as they are miserable. The lower creation may be, and is, the object of God's ἔλεος, inasmuch as the burden of man's curse has redounded also upon it (Job. xxxviii. 41; Ps. cxlvii. 9; Jonah iv. 11), but of His χάρις man alone; he only needs, he only is capable of receiving it. In the Divine mind, and in the order of our salvation as conceived therein, the ἔλεος precedes the χάρις. God so *loved* the world with a pitying love (herein was the ἔλεος) that He *gave* His only-begotten Son (herein the χάρις) that the world through Him might be saved: cf. Eph. ii. 14; Luke i. 78, 79. But in the order of the manifestation of God's purposes of salvation the grace must go before the mercy, the χάρις must make way for the ἔλεος. It is true, that the same persons are the subjects of both, being at once the guilty and the miserable, yet the righteousness of God, which it is just as necessary should be maintained as His Love, demands that the guilt should be done away, before the misery can be assuaged; only the forgiven can, or indeed may, be made happy; whom He has pardoned, He heals; men are justified before they are sanctified. Thus in each of the Apostolic salutations it is first χάρις and then ἔλεος, which the Apostle desires for the faithful (Rom. i. 7; 1 Cor. i. 3; 2 Cor. i. 2; Gal. i. 3; Eph. i. 2; Phil. i. 2, etc.); nor could the order of the words be reversed."—M.]—This might be wanting soonest, since the χάρις of the Almighty, of course, cannot remain idle; see Tit. i. 4; Rom. i. 7; 1 Cor. i. 3; 2 Cor. i. 2; Gal. i 3; Eph. i. 2; Phil. i. 2; Col. i. 2; 1 Thess. i. 1; 2 Thess. i. 2. But it is just χάρις which is omitted in Jude 2 (ἔλεος ὑμῖν καὶ εἰρήνη καὶ ἀγάπη πληθυνθείη), since these two, with respect to εἰρήνη, belong together. But the order is established. Bengel observes very well: "GRATIA *tollit culpam*, MISERICORDIA *miseriam*, PAX *dicit permansionem in gratia est misericordia*." [Alford: "Εἰρήνη is the whole sum and substance of the possession and enjoyment of God's grace and mercy; cf. Luke ii. 14; Rom. v. 1; x. 15; Jno. xiv. 27; xvi. 33."—M.].

From God the Father, and from Jesus Christ the Son of the Father.—The employment of παρὰ instead of the ἀπὸ commonly used in the Pauline writings, points to the independence of our author; and so does the circumstance that the pronoun ἡμῶν is omitted after πατρός. Thus, in this connection, God is to be taken primarily as the Father of Jesus Christ, especially since the words τοῦ υἱοῦ τοῦ πατρός are annexed, and the Sonship is rendered peculiarly prominent, also since the preposition παρὰ is repeated, as denoting the Divine nature and character of the object desired by the Apostle, whereas ἀπὸ denotes only their procession from God; παρὰ designates them as the gifts *of God*, ἀπὸ as Divine *gifts*. Cf. Winer, 382 sq. Note should also be taken here of the independence of the Son by the side of the Father, as importing their equality.

In truth and love.—Also a peculiar addition; it belongs to ἔσται μεθ' ὑμῶν, the preposition ἐν denoting the two life-elements (Huther) of believers, in which the Divine exhibitions of grace, mercy and peace have to be received and enjoyed (Düsterdieck); these words contain also a reference to the contents of the Epistle (Bengel, Ebrard). Hence it is wrong to join ἐν ἀληθείᾳ καὶ ἀγάπῃ with τοῦ υἱοῦ τοῦ πατρὸς, as if it were=*filio verissimo et dilectissimo* (Barth. Petrus), or to explain *ut perseveretis vel ut crescatis* (a Lapide), or like Grotius: *per cognitionem veri et dilectionem mutuam, nam per haec in nos Dei beneficia provocamus, conservamus, augemus;* for ἐν is not = *per*, and *our* conduct is not the reason of the χάρις etc. (Huther).

DOCTRINAL AND ETHICAL.

1. God is primarily the Father of Jesus Christ and Christ the Son of God, and it is not until we are in Christ, that he is our Father, and we are His children.

2. By the side of the Personality of the Father the Personality of the Son is a fundamental view.

3. The grace of God is the ground of our peace.

4. Our peace is the end and aim of the Divine grace and mercy.

5. All true love rests upon the truth of revelation.

6. Love with its all-embracing power is coextensive with truth.

HOMILETICAL AND PRACTICAL.

Love is truth, and truth is love!—Truth and love are the fundamental elements of the Chris tian life. Peace is really nothing but the health of the soul.

STARKE: In Christ there is neither male nor female.—Caution is needed, not to call any man elect, of whose true and firm faith we are not sufficiently convinced.—The abuse of titles should be abolished; but their right use should be preserved; honour to whom honour is due!—What! each and every person are not to be allowed to read the Holy Scriptures? and yet the Holy Spirit caused a special Epistle to be written to a pious matron and her children!—Preachers ought to pasture sheep and lambs, to teach great and small, in various ways, the ways of the Lord.—It is a rare example to meet a whole family of pious people.—A hireling loves the sheep for the sake of their fleece; but a true shepherd only for the truth's sake, because of God and with self-denial.—Truth is beautiful as such; but it is unprofitable, if it is not, and does not remain, in us.—Truth holds out longest.—Truth is founded on God, it has consequently an eternal root and will never perish. The greeting of Christians is a part of prayer.—None does truly receive peace, unless he have received the grace of God, hence that peace, which is not the daughter of grace, is the offspring of corrupt nature, and a carnal security.—God deems none worthy of peace or grace, who do not deem themselves unworthy of either or both, well knowing, that in virtue of his greatest misery he does not merit any thing, but that he stands in need of mercy.—The grace of God is not with us, unless it be also in us, and be worthily received by us.

HEUBNER: Love towards a Christian presupposes the knowledge of the truth, and the love of it. But Christ is the truth. For the truth's sake the shepherd should love his flock.—All greetings ought to have a Christian foundation.

BESSER: Every pastor is a successor to the office of the Apostles, and according to the Divine right, there is no difference between bishops, and pastors, and parsons. [On this point I beg leave to differ with the Author, although this is not the place to discuss so important a question.—M.]. *Grace*, which removes our guilt, *mercy*, which delivers us from misery, *peace*, into which grace and mercy translate us.

---

2. *Exhortation to walk in truth and love.*

vv. 4–11.

4 I rejoiced greatly that I found[1] of thy children walking in truth, as we have re-
5 ceived a commandment from the Father.[2] And now I beseech thee, lady, not as
though I wrote[3] a new commandment unto thee, but that which[4] we had from the
6 beginning, that we love one another. And this is love, that we walk after his com-
mandments. This is the commandment,[5] That, as ye have heard from the beginning,
7 ye should walk in it.[6] For many deceivers are entered[7] into the world, who confess
not that Jesus Christ is come in the flesh.[8] This is a deceiver and an antichrist.[9]
8 Look to yourselves, that we lose[10] not those things which we have wrought,[10] but that
9 we receive a full reward.[10] Whosoever transgresseth,[11] and abideth not in the doc-
trine of Christ, hath not God. He that abideth in the doctrine[12] of Christ, he hath
10 both the Father and the Son.[13] If there come any unto you, and bring not this doc-
11 trine, receive him not into *your* house, neither bid him God speed:[14] For[15] he that
biddeth him[16] God speed is partaker of his evil deeds.[17]

Verse 4. [1 German: "That I have found." So Alford, Lillie.—M.]
2 Instead of ἐλάβομεν Cod. Sin. reads, ἔλαβον, evidently a writing error; A. and others have ἀπὸ, instead of παρὰ; B. omits τοῦ.

Verse 5. 3 A. B. G. K. Sin. γράφων; elsewhere γράφω. The arrangement of A. Sin. is: ἐντολὴν καινὴν γράφων; that of B., al.: ἐντολὴν γράφων σοι καινήν. Might the former have been corrected from 1 Jno. ii. 7? [German: "Not as if I write," better "not as writing," Alford, Lillie.—M.]
4 Cod. Sin. inserts ἐντολὴν before ἣν.

Verse 6. 5 G. Cod. Sin.: αὕτη ἐστὶν ἡ ἐντολή; B. D. K. αὕτη ἡ ἐντολή ἐστιν.
[6 German: "As ye heard from the beginning, that ye should walk in it." So Lillie and Alford, who supplies however "even" before "as ye heard, etc."—M.]

Verse 7. 7 B. Sin. ἐξῆλθον; A. ἐξῆλθαν; G. K. εἰσῆλθον. [German: "went out," Alford: "went forth." —M.]
[8 German: "who did not confess Jesus Christ, who cometh in the flesh;" "who confess not Jesus Christ coming in (the) flesh" (Alford), so Lillie, who omits the definite Article before flesh.—M.]
[9 German: "This is the deceiver and the antichrist." So Alford, Lillie.—M.]

Verse 8. 10 G. K.: ἀπολέσωμεν—εἰργασάμεθα—ἀπολάβωμεν;. Cod. Sin.: ἀπολῆσθε (with the correction: ἀπολέσητε)—εἰργάσασθαι (ε)—ἀπολάβητε; thus also A.; but B.: ἀπολέσητε—εἰργασάμεθα—ἀπολάβητε; this is decidedly preferable as the *lectio difficilior* and *mater lectionum*. Bengel, on very slender grounds, recommends: ἀπολέσητε, εἰργάσασθε—ἀπολάβωμεν.
[German: "Look to yourselves, that ye do not lose, what things we have wrought, but that ye receive full reward."—Alford: " . . that ye lose not the things which we wrought but receive reward in full."—Lillie: " . . but receive a full reward."—M.]

Verse 9. 11 A. B. Cod. Sin.: προάγων; G. K.: παραβαίνων. The former reading is supported by the versions with the variations: *præcedit, procedit.*
[German: "Every one that progresseth;" Alford: "goeth before you." . . .—M.]
12 A. B. Cod. Sin. omit τοῦ Χριστοῦ, which are perhaps repeated from the former half of the verse [German: "He that abideth in the doctrine;" so Alford.—M.].
13 B. Cod. Sin.: καὶ τὸν πατέρα καὶ τὸν υἱὸν; A.; καὶ τὸν υἱὸν καὶ τὸν πατέρα.
Verse 10. [14 German: "And do not bid him welcome;" Alford: "Do not bid him good speed:" Lillie: "neither bid him hail." The introduction of the Divine name both in this verse and the next, is avoided by almost all the versions.—M.]
Verse 11. 15 A. B. Cod. Sin.: ὁ λέγων γάρ; G. K. ὁ γὰρ λέγων. The former reading is preferable because of the weight of authority by which it is supported, and also because of its singularity.
16 A. B. G. Cod. Sin.: αὐτῷ; αὐτὸν is probably an error; there is not sufficient reason for its omission.
17 The Vulgate (*ed. Sixtin.*) concludes thus: *Ecce, prædixi vobis, ne in diem domini condemnemini (ut in diem—non confundamini).* The words are found in Greek in the Lectiones Veleſian. (Tischendorf). They are interpolated.

EXEGETICAL AND CRITICAL.

Ver. 4. *Joy in* [*the lady's children*—M.] *walking in the truth.* **I rejoiced greatly.**—The Aorist ἐχάρην answers to the Perfect εὕρηκα and notes the time, when he did make the discovery, hence it is not=I rejoice (Luther). The Pauline Epistles begin with similar expressions of joy in the Christian standing of Churches; we have here, however, not an imitation but only the expression of the same Christian mode of viewing things. Cf. Rom. i. 8 sqq.; 1 Cor. i. 4 sqq.; 2 Cor. i. 3 sqq.; Eph. i. 3 sqq.; Phil. i. 3 sqq.; Col. i. 3 sqq.—

That I have found of thy children walking in truth.—The first reference here is to ἐν ἀληθείᾳ v. 3. [Alford: "not only in honesty and uprightness, but in that truth which is derived from and is part of the truth of God in Christ."—M.].—Ἐκ τῶν τεκνῶν σου is not=τὰ τέκνα σου, but should be taken in a partitive sense, though there is no need of supplying τίνας (Beza), as in 1 Jno. iv. 13; Jno. xvi. 17; Matth. xxiii. 34. The omission of the Article before περιπατοῦντας does not import that her other children did not walk ἐν ἀληθείᾳ. Ebrard's remark—"It is a *delicate* way, how the presbyter conceals the *censure* he has to express in a mere limitation of praise"—is overfine, for it cannot be maintained that the same praise of walking in truth could not be accorded to all. Εὕρηκα simply states that the Apostle had found them, but there is here no intimation how he found them, whether accidentally, or in consequence of inquiries to that effect. But περιπατοῦντας denotes sons, whom the Apostle was more likely to encounter on his missionary journeys than daughters; hence the reference seems to be rather to an accidental meeting. Lücke, not without some ground (v. 12), thinks that he met the children without their mother, elsewhere than in the family. Bengel: *Hos liberos in domo materteræ eorum invenerat Johannes*, v. 13. But this uncertainty does not favour, as Huther thinks, the hypothesis of a Church, but [rather]. that of a lady.—On περιπατεῖν ἐν ἀληθείᾳ, denoting not only the Christian state, but true, vital Christianity, see 1 Jno. i. 6, 7; ii. 6; cf. 3 Jno. 3, 4; Jno. viii. 12.—

According as we received commandment from the Father.—The clause introduced by καθώς expressly refers to objective Divine truth, as the ground of Christian walking. Ebrard falsely understands καθώς in the sense of "even as we," and turns the thought "even as we have (indeed) a command from the Father (that we should walk in the truth)." But the clause in question should not be taken argumentatively, but as an apposition and explanation. Ἐντολὴν does not refer to the commandment of brotherly love (Lücke), but denotes the περιπατεῖν ἐν ἀληθείᾳ taken as ἐντολή (de Wette, Huther, Düsterdieck).—On παρὰ τοῦ πατρός see v. 3. The interpretation of Oecumenius that Christ is here referred to as the Father of believers cannot be upheld by Is. viii. 18; Hebr. ii. 13. But the mediation of Christ is to be supplied. [Huther—M.].

Reference to ἐν ἀγάπῃ (v. 3). vv. 5, 6.

Ver. 5. **And now I beseech thee, lady.**—Καὶ νῦν as in 1 Jno. ii. 28. The connection is not temporal but logical, and moreover with the whole of v. 4, not with the subordinate clause beginning with καθὼς only (as Düsterdieck thinks); nor does it belong to ἐρωτῶ in order to mark the point of time. On ἐρωτῶ Schlichting says: "*blandior quædam admonendi ratio;*" Düsterdieck calls it an entreaty with a reference to the inviolable authority of the Divine law of love. Hence the Apostle adds:

Not as writing to thee a new commandment, but that which we had from the beginning.—Cf. 1 Jno. ii. 7: **that we should love one another.**—Ἵνα ἀγαπῶμεν ἀλλήλους, as the object of ἐρωτῶ, indicates its end and aim. Hence it does not describe or specify the substance of ἐντολή (Baumgarten-Crusius).

Ver. 6. **And this is love, that we should walk according to His commandments.**—Ἀγάπη is left undefined and nothing is said beyond its being exhibited in our walking according to the commandments of God; so that the reference is neither to love to the brethren (Benson), nor to love to God (Grotius, Carpzov., and al.), but to love in general, as in 1 Jno. iv. 7, 16 sqq.—This is the view of most and the best commentators. The end of all the commandments of God regulating the conduct of men, is love; hence ἵνα, as at 1 Jno. v. 3. Hence also κατὰ τὰς ἐντολὰς αὐτοῦ, is here followed by ἐντολή in the Singular, as denoting their unity.

The commandment is this,—cf. 1 Jno. iii 22, 23; it is further described as to its contents

As ye heard from the beginning, as in v 5. It is not a secondary aim of the commandment, as such (de Wette, Lücke).

That ye should walk in it.—Ἵνα denotes the aim and scope; ἐν αὐτῇ refers to ἀγάπῃ which should be supplied; for ἐν ἐντολῇ περιπατεῖν does not occur, and would be an intolerable tautology (against Sander). Thus the Apostle describes the identity of love, especially of brotherly love, and of obedience to God; both stand and fall together.

Description of the false teachers: v. 7.

For many deceivers.—Ὅτι grounds the reason of this exhortation to brotherly love on the Apostle's fear of its being marred by the influence of false teachers (Huther). But ὅτι is not governed by ἐρωτῶ σε (Lücke, Ewald), nor should there be mentally repeated ἐρωτῶ σε (de Wette), nor should any thought be supplied, *e. g.* "seeing that ye have the true Christianity, I have to warn you, for" (Heumann), or "*hoc non temere dixi, nam*" (Beza); nor does ὅτι introduce a protasis, followed by v. 8 as apodosis (Grotius, Carpzov), wholly unlike the Johannean diction. Bengel's remark also is wrong: "*ratio cur jubeat retinere audita a principio.*" The love required (vv. 5, 6) rests on the truth (v. 7), and the ἐντολή (v. 6) embraces also the truth (v. 7, Düsterdieck). Cf. vv. 1–3, and 1 Jno. iii. 23, 16. The false teachers are called πλάνοι on account of their influence and effect on believers. 1 Jno. ii. 26; 1 Tim. iv. 1.

Went out into the world.—1 Jno. ii. 19; iv. 1; **Who do not confess Jesus Christ coming in flesh.**—Οἱ μὴ ὁμολογοῦντες denotes that whereby, or how these are πλάνοι. Winer, p. 146. But Winer (p. 405) errs in assuming a genus on account of μή: all those who do not confess, *quicunque non profitentur.* If we had οὐχ it would be equal to: οἱ ἀρνούμενοι. But the reference here is not to simple, open denial, but to a contradicting, which by various turnings and twistings, evades and endangers the definite confession. Cf. 1 Jno. iv. 2, 3. Ἐρχόμενον ἐν σαρκί is different both from ἐληλυθότα (1 Jno. iv. 2), and from ὁ ἐλθών (1 Jno. v. 6). The Present denotes the thought *per se* "without any reference to time" 1 Cor. xv. 35 (Düsterdieck), "separate from all consideration of time" (Huther); so also Lücke, de Wette, Sander and al.—This may intimate that the false teachers denied the *possibility* of the Incarnation (Lücke). Bengel (*qui veniebat*) is beside the mark, for 3 Jno. 3, where the Participle Imperfect is clearly indicated by ἐχάρην, is not apposite here; and so is Oecumenius, who *per enallagen temporis* suggests the second advent of Christ.

This is the deceiver and the antichrist.—Οὗτος refers to οἱ μὴ ὁμολογοῦντες, and expresses plurality (πολλοὶ πλάνοι) in unity: ἐστιν ὁ πλάνος; it is a transition from the Plural to the distributive Singular; Winer, pp. 186, 654. The words καὶ ὁ ἀντίχριστος give prominence to a further characteristic of πλάνος (Huther); we must not say, however, that the πλάνος is in reality only in the many that have the πνεῦμα πλάνης (Lücke, Huther); but he is personally behind the many, who are his forerunners. Cf. 1 Jno. ii. 18, 22.

Warning against the false teachers. vv. 8, 9.

VER. 8. **Look to yourselves**, βλέπετε ἑαυτούς. They are to consider what would be the loss entailed upon themselves by being deceived, viz., the loss of fellowship with the Father and the Son, the loss of truth and love. Bengel's explanatory clauses "*me absente*" would be in point, if we had here: βλέπετε ὑμεῖς ἑαυτούς, as in Mark xiii. 9. Moreover they themselves had to look to themselves, even though the Apostles were present.

That ye do not lose.—Ἵνα μή denotes the end and aim of their precaution. Matth. xii. 16; xxvi. 5; Luke xviii. 5; John vii. 23; 1 Cor. xvi. 10. The object is to avoid a loss, even a loss on the part of the readers. But of what?

What things we have wrought.—The Apostles of Jesus Christ had done, wrought and accomplished something by their labours and preaching, even a possession of truth and love with their fruits (ἃ εἰργασάμεθα), which possession will be lost, if they give ear to false teachers (Düsterdieck, Huther). This a bold self-testimony (1 Jno. i. 3; iv. 6). It is unnecessary to add ἐν ὑμῖν, as Lücke thinks, for the context supplies it. The first person does not require us to understand that the Apostle must have converted the children of the κυρία; he only includes himself in the number of the Apostles and genuine witnesses of Christ, whom he opposes to the recipients of their preaching, without determining through whose instrumentality the children of the κυρία were converted; but the teachers and their hearers are not taken together.

But that ye receive full reward.—Μισθός denotes the blessing of truth and love in one's own heart, in life with its joys and sorrows, and in eternity; μισθὸν πλήρη is the full reward, uncurtailed, as it falls to the lot of perfect fidelity (Huther, Düsterdieck); it is not=πολύν (Carpzov), nor is it said that they had only received it in part, and that they were to receive it fully in eternity (Grotius, Ebrard), for this fulness is relative; there is even here on earth a full reward, a full peace, a full παῤῥησία, etc., in conformity to the relations of this present time. But Bengel rightly observes: "*nulla merces dimidia est, aut tota amittitur, aut plena accipitur,*" but his next remark is irrelevant, viz., "*consideranda diversitas graduum in gloria;*" for the blessed have their full reward on the lowest grade. But ἀπολάβητε designates the receiving as a gift, a present (Col. iii. 24; Gal. iv. 2; Luke xvi. 25). Taking all the verbs in the first person, weakens the thought as much as taking them all in the second person (see Apparatus Crit. Note 10); in the former case the teachers and hearers are taken together, in the latter the teachers are wholly excluded, and the delicate touches, the Apostle's right of warning them, and the weight of the Apostolical warning are all lost.

VER. 9. **Every one that progresseth and abideth not in the doctrine of Christ.**—This describes him who does not receive the full reward, of whom they are warned, whereby they lose the reward. Ὁ προάγων and μὴ μένων designate the same persons, positively and negatively. Προάγειν denotes a progression, a going before, which in the opinion of the προάγων is the reaching of a higher degree of knowledge, a decided progress, but in reality is a departure from the truth, ἐν διδαχῇ τοῦ χριστοῦ, a going beyond the limits of Christian doctrine. Huther errs in seeing here an ironical allusion (Düsterdieck); it is a bitter truth of the actual fact. On προάγειν cf. Matth. xxi. 9; 1 Tim. i. 18; v. 24. On the characteristics of those who know and learn without knowledge, see 2 Tim. iii. 7. The *lectio rec.* παραβαίνων, passing by, τὴν διδαχήν (according to Matth. xv. 3), or ἐκ τῆς διδαχῆς (Acts i. 25), and the exposition: "ἀπάγων ἑαυτόν" (Oecumenius), are clearly untenable; and in the variation of the Vulgate *recedit* instead of *praecedit*, it is more probable that the former arose from the latter, than that the latter arose from the former. St. Paul also insists upon the μένειν, 2 Tim. iii. 14; i. 13; Tit. i. 9.—Ἡ διδαχὴ τοῦ χριστοῦ signifies that Paul calls the ὑγιαίνοντες λόγοι (2 Tim. i. 13); the Genitive is subjective (Düsterdieck, Huther al.). Agreeably to constant usage (Matth. vii. 28; xvi. 12; xxii. 33; Mark i. 22; iv. 2; xii. 38; Acts ii. 42; v. 28), it cannot be the Genitive of the object (Bengel, Lücke, Sander, al.). Cf. Jno. viii. 31: μείνητε ἐν τῷ λόγῳ τῷ ἐμῷ. It is the doctrine which Christ Himself brought and taught and caused to be propagated by His Apostles. But, of course, the principal part of its contents, is Christology.

Hath not God.—cf. 1 Jno. ii. 23; v. 12.—Truth, life and God are inseparable.

He that abideth in the doctrine hath both the Father and the Son.—The same thought, not only repeated positively, but completed by the addition of καὶ τὸν υἱὸν, as in 1 Jno. ii. 23. [Alford: "The order in the text is the theological one, the Father being mentioned first, then the Son. That in A. etc. is the logical and contextual one, seeing that the test is, abiding in the doctrine of Christ. Thus he has Christ, and through Him, the Father: which of the two is original, it is impossible to decide."—M.].

Warning against fellowship with the false teachers. vv. 10, 11.

VER. 10. **If any cometh to you.**—Εἴ τις ἔρχεται shows that the case supposed actually existed. Winer, p. 307. Ἐὰν with the subjunctive denotes a possibility. There is hence no occasion for surprise, as if this were unjohannean (de Wette, Ebrard), since it cannot be unjohannean to suppose a case as actually existing. Πρὸς ὑμᾶς, as in 2 Tim. iii. 6, refers to the forwardness of the false teachers and their calculating on the greater receptivity and mouldableness of women.

And bringeth not this doctrine.—Καὶ adds the capacity and character in which such persons come, not as soliciting aid, as necessitous persons, but as false teachers (Bengel: *quasi doctor aut frater*). The use of οὐ φέρει, instead of μή, also shows that the case mentioned is actually true, and imports the simple denial of φέρειν. Similar is φέρειν κατηγορίαν, Jno. xviii. 29 (Acts xxv. 7). It is unnecessary to supply here that the contrary doctrine is brought (de Lyra), and that the true doctrine is disputed (Tirinus); this is self-evident from 1 John iv. 2, 3. Ταύτην τὴν διδαχὴν is τὴν διδαχὴν τοῦ χριστοῦ. *Non de iis, qui alieni semper fuerunt ab ecclesia* (1 Cor. v. 10), *sed de iis qui volunt fratres haberi et doctrinam evertunt* (Grotius).

Receive him not into (your) **house.**—On the above supposition the point in question is not an act of φιλοξενία (Heb. xiii. 2; Rom. xii. 13); for the reference is not to the necessitous. The injunction simply bears upon the false teachers not being received into the house (αὐτὸν εἰς οἰκίαν λαμβάνειν), on account of the danger *per se*.

And do not bid him welcome, which was unavoidable if they were received into the house; the two circumstances should be taken together; for while the former would be dangerous, the latter would be untrue; χαίρειν, joy, good speed, prosperity, cannot be said to the false teacher; only to ὁμοτρόποις and ὁμοπίστοις is due the Christian, fraternal greeting, in its deeper import (Oecumenius, Calov, Bengel, Lücke, de Wette, Huther, Düsterdieck and al). This χαίρειν μὴ λέγετε must therefore not be limited to the *salutatio* as a conventional form of politeness (Clemens Alex.), or as an expression of friendship (Grotius), or be taken quite generally: *velut hic Joannes omne colloquium, omne consortium, omne commercium cum hæreticis* (a Lapide), or applied to excommunication (Vitringa, *de syn. vet.* p. 759); nor must it be referred to the κρίσις which was necessary only at that time (Lücke), nor must it be construed, according to the now prevailing loftier view that man, all his errors notwithstanding, remains man and an object of esteem and love, as an act of intolerance which may have been justifiable at that time (de Wette), or be charged to the fiery temperament of the Apostle, according to the notices contained in Luke ix. 54 and Euseb. Hist. Eccl. III. 28; IV. 14. The reference is simply to the cultivation of personal acquaintance and fraternal intercourse with the false teachers; this is, and continues to be, forbidden; brotherly love in its depth, truth and blessedness has its limits. Hofmann, *Schriftbeweis* II. 2, p. 339.

VER. 11. **For he that biddeth him welcome, partaketh in his deeds, the evil ones.**—Γὰρ gives the reason of the injunction: in the words ὁ λέγων αὐτῷ χαίρειν the Apostle gives prominence to the one point which is closely connected with the other: αὐτὸν εἰς οἰκίαν λαμβάνειν. The clause κοινωνεῖ τοῖς ἔργοις αὐτοῦ shows that we have here not simply an outward conventional form of politeness, but an "inward relation of communion" (Huther), which is fostered. The ἔργα τὰ πονηρά are primarily acts of communicating false doctrine, but secondarily also the whole ethical conduct connected with it, which injures God, Christ, the Church, the truth, individual communities, believers and their souls.

DOCTRINAL AND ETHICAL.

1. The knowledge of the truth from God is acquired in the way of obedience to the will of God (v. 4).

2. The law of God should only be viewed as the revelation of His love, and as it originates in love, so it impels to love (vv. 5, 6).

3. The acme and ground of all error is the denial of the Incarnation of Christ (v. 7). He that breaks with Christ come in the flesh and as the Son of man ever the Coming One, breaks brotherhood with believers and forces them to break brotherhood with him. Besser truly says: "The doctrine *of Christ* is through and through *from Christ*. 'It is I,' is the fundamental theme of the Gospel, preached by Himself and the holy Apostles, from beginning to end." Believing Catholics, Lutherans, Reformed, United, are brethren and remain brethren, because they are living Christians, the children of God and coheirs with Christ. But he ought hardly to have used this passage for the purpose of warning against the union nor to have said: "Yes, people reverse the meaning of John and are perchance afraid to hold private intercourse with manifest blasphemers and revilers of the Divine truth, perhaps to take coffee with them, but—

alas! *our* table has become more holy to us than *God's* table." For these things occur, inside the same communion, every where and at all times, if instead of putting blasphemers, he had said: hypocrites or adulterers.

4. False teachers corrupt not only the christological truth, but also the work of the Church and the salvation of individual church-members (vv. 7, 8).

5. The promised reward is not a merit of good works, but a consequence of Divine appointment, and a communicated gift (v. 8).

6. True progress is only possible in the maintenance and on the foundation of Christian truth (v. 9). For men come short not so much in the desire to be furthered, as in the judgment as to what constitutes true progress, and what is the true mode of progressing. A striving forward with a good conscience will always be a diligent and faithful road-maker bridging over the chasm between himself and signal successes, by the most faithful and scrupulous discharge of duty.

7. In the converse among Christians love must not be practised at the expense of truth and truthfulness (vv. 10, 11), nor must the truth be spoken at the expense of love!

HOMILETICAL AND PRACTICAL.

Compare Doctrinal and Ethical.

STARKE:—Preachers should rejoice most when they see that young children are well trained, grow in grace and make the beginning of their wisdom in the fear of the Lord.—Christians have also their joy in the world, though not of the world.—Godly children are their parents' joy, the ornament of the Church and the joy of all godly people. Young plants of righteousness look more beautiful in the garden of the Lord, than old trees on the point of decaying.—Truth is not only to be investigated and meditated upon, but it must be practised, and men should walk in it.—A preacher should not always use severity and earnestness, but also lenity and gentleness, not command but entreat his people to become godly.—Whenever thou lackest the mind to follow, thou art wont to cry: it is a novelty! Thou utterest a falsehood! Hear what St. John says: To love, which contains all the commandments, has been from the beginning.—Christianity needs no new commandments, but it requires the constantly renewed inculcation of the old commandments.—It is not enough that the truth be preached, falsehood must also be denounced. The heresies, persecutions and abuses in the Church of God must not cause us to waver, and doubt the truth of the Christian religion, but rather strengthen and confirm us while we are exposed to their danger.—Alas, by nature we all have an antichristian mind and antichrist in our hearts; he who does not know and expel him, will nevermore know or avoid the outward antichrist.—Ye that are wise overmuch and are anxious about unnecessary things, ye that judge and censure every thing, hear what St. John says: "Look to yourselves."—Delightful reward of faithful ministers, if they see in their hearers the fruit of their labour arranged according to the mind of Christ.—The less regard a minister pays to the temporal reward in his office, the more is he faithful, and the greater will be the reward which he shall receive from Christ, the Great Shepherd.—What can a man lack who has God, and what can a man possess who has not God? If none may receive into their houses wicked and false teachers, how much the more ought they not to be introduced into the sheepfold of Christ, which would be like taking wolves among sheep! It is injurious to have fellowship with false people, but still more injurious to open to them the door of our heart; where the first is done, the latter is wont not to be wanting.—Who enters into a pest-house? Do we not flee a bedfellow affected with a venomous disease? Why not likewise a deceiver, a servant of Satan? The opposite takes place in the world: be friendly to everybody except to Christ in His members!—The greetings of Christians should not be merely conventional, but spring from the ground of truth and love.—A Christian should be on his guard not only against his own sins, but also against those of others, of which he may easily and in various ways become partaker.

HEUBNER:—The children of the same family are not always of one mind; a godly mother may have unbelieving children.—Christian mothers, Christian families are a blessing to the world.—Those also who run already in the Christian course need stirring up.—A Christian's treasure is liable to be lost as long as he continues to live among deceivers and enemies; hence the necessity of foresight, courage and fidelity of vigilance over himself and in respect of temptation: the more precious the treasure, the more carefully should it be guarded. It is slowly acquired, but may be lost at once. The number of those who once had grace and then lost it, will one day appear very great.—John teaches us what we should ask of every one that comes to us, to wit: do you bring Christ with you or not? Reception was denied to a false teacher, because it would have been a token of brotherly acknowledgment; but this was so much the more to be denied, because such reception took place in the name of the Church, and hence would have been a declaration that the whole Church did receive him as a brother. But on that account we need not in a case of emergency deny to such an one our bounden private love.—Love should never be prejudicial to the confession of our faith. Love at the expense of faith, to its injury or with its denial is no love. This commandment was falsely applied in the case of John a Lasco, who having been expelled from England in the reign of Mary, A. D., 1553, was denied reception in Denmark, both he and his congregation (Salig, *Hist. Conf. Aug.* II., 1090).

BESSER:—It is an idle speech that Christians and antichristians have one and the same God. "We are believers in one God" is sung in truth by those only who continue: "We also believe in Jesus Christ, His Son and our Lord."

THE CONCLUSION.

vv. 12, 13.

12 Having many things to write unto you, I would not *write*[1] with paper and ink; but[2] I
13 trust to come[3] unto you, and speak face to face,[4] that our[5] joy may be full. The chil-
dren of thy elect sister greet thee.[6] Amen.[7]

Verse 12. [[1] German omits "*write*" supplied in E. V.—M.]
[2] ἀλλα ἐλπίζω is the reading of the best and of most Codices, also of Cod. Sin. A. al. read ἐλπίζω γάρ.
[3] πρὸς ὑμᾶς γενέσθαι is the most authentic reading; ἐλθεῖν *lect. rec.* supported by G. K.; Coptic version has ἰδεῖν ὑμᾶς according to 3 Jno. 14.
[[4] German: "mouth to mouth;" Alford, Lillie.—M.]
[5] Cod. Sin. G. K.: Χαρὰ ἡμῶν; A. B. ὑμῶν. The former, on account of 1 Jno. i. 4 is *lectio difficilior*.
Verse 13. [[6] German: "There greet thee the children of thy sister, the elect one." Alford: "There greet thee the children of thine elect sister."—M.]
[7] Ἀμὴν, at the conclusion, is wanting. Cod. Sin. A. B.; Ἰωάννου β'· Others add ἐπιστολὴ, others τοῦ θεολόγου, and still others καθολική.

EXEGETICAL AND CRITICAL.

Breaking off, v. 12.

Ver. 12. **Having many things to write to you.**—His heart is full; he had only written very little of what he had in his heart. Hence it is unwarrantable to see, with Ebrard, in most of these verses, simply citations from the First Epistle.

I would not [write them] **with paper and ink.**—The Infinitive from the preceding clause: πολλὰ ἔχων ὑμῖν γράφειν should, of course, be supplied here. Διὰ χάρτου καὶ μέλανος denotes the written character of his communication; the more common phrase is: διὰ μέλανος—καὶ καλάμου, 3 Jno. 13.—Ὁ χάρτης is the Egyptian papyrus, probably the so-called Augustan or Claudian, for letters; τὸ μέλαν, also 2 Cor. iii. 3, ink made of soot, water and gum; ὁ κάλαμος, the writing reed, probably split (μεσοσχιδής, μεσότομος). Cf. Lücke on this passage. The Aorist οὐκ ἐβουλήθην, from the standpoint of the readers on receiving the Epistle, because he wished to communicate it personally, orally.

But I hope to come to you and to speak [say it] **mouth to mouth.**—The antithesis of γράφειν διὰ χάρτου καὶ μέλανος is πρὸς ὑμᾶς γενέσθαι καὶ στόμα πρὸς στόμα λαλῆσαι; because he hopes for the latter, he has broken off the former; but this does not import that he did reserve part of the doctrine necessary to salvation for oral tradition (Barth. Petrus); for he surely spoke only what he had written in the first Epistle. On γένεσθαι πρὸς ὑμᾶς see Jno. vi. 21, 25; Acts xx. 16; xxi. 17; xxv. 15; 1 Cor. xvi. 10; Jno. x. 35; Acts x. 13=to turn towards a person or place. On στόμα πρὸς στόμα λαλῆσαι, cf. 1 Cor. xiii. 12; Xenoph. *Mem.* II., 6, 32; and פֶּה אֶל־פֶּה, Numb. xii. 8.

That our joy may be fulfilled [filled full].—The aim (ἵνα) is to fill up his own and the readers' joy, and then that of the hearers. Cf. notes on 1 Jno. i. 4. The object of joy is not the personal presence of the Apostle (Bengel), but the full communication of the truth in oral intercourse.

The greetings, v. 13.

Ver. 13. **There greet thee the children of thy sister, the elect one.**—To explain τῆς ἀδελφῆς of a Church, and τέκνα of church-members is not warranted by any thing found here; the reason why the sister herself does not send greetings, may be death, or absence, but "can neither be ascertained, nor is it a proper question" (Düsterdieck *versus* Huther). Bengel: "*Suavissima communitas! Comitas apostoli, minorum verbis salutem nunciantis.*"

HOMILETICAL AND PRACTICAL.

Starke:—Both what the Apostles wrote and what they spoke is the word of God, and we do well to bear this in mind.—A true reader is he, who not satisfied with the written Epistle or the printer's work on paper, suffers the Holy Spirit to write in his heart and thus becomes himself an Epistle of the living God.—It is a blessing of God if we have the opportunity given to us of conferring with friends on matters of importance and of enjoying the benefit of their counsel.—The children of the world imagine that the life of the godly consists in nothing but dejected looks and constant sorrowing; but here applies that saying: as sorrowful, yet always rejoicing.—He is the servant of his belly, but not the servant of Christ, who seeks in his office other joy than the salvation of his hearers.—It is and ever will be a beautiful custom to interchange cordial greetings with friends in Epistles and in other ways, and thus to desire for them all temporal and spiritual prosperity.—Happy are those sisters and brothers who besides being united by the ties of nature, are also firmly united by the tie of Divine grace. For it is eternal grace only, which works alliances of eternal friendship.

Heubner:—With us it is often the opposite; we have much to write and little to speak, when we do meet.—When those who are one in faith, meet and converse together of the grace of God, of which they have made experience, they have a foretaste of heavenly joy.

THE

THIRD EPISTLE GENERAL OF JOHN THE APOSTLE.

(Ἰωάννου γ in B. and Cod. Sinait. C. adds ἐπιστολή, G. τοῦ ἁγίου ἀποστόλου.)

I. *The Address.*

v. 1.

The elder unto the well beloved Gaius, whom I love in the truth[1].

Verse 1. [[1] German: The presbyter to the beloved Gaius, whom I love in truth.—M.]

EXEGETICAL AND CRITICAL.

VER. 1. On ὁ πρεσβύτερος see Introduction § 1. It can hardly be determined whether this Gaius is one of the two or three persons of that name, who are mentioned as friends and companions of Paul in Acts xix. 29; xx. 4; Rom. xvi. 23; 1 Cor. i. 14. Lücke thinks that our Gaius is identical with Gaius of Derbe mentioned Acts xx. 4, Wolf, in his *Curis ad. h. l.*, that the Gaius mentioned 1 Cor. i. 14 is meant here. Others suppose that the Gaius, mentioned Constit. Ap. 7, 46, and appointed by John Bishop of Pergamus, is the one referred to here (Whiston); but this is also purely hypothetical. Nor can it be inferred from v. 8 of this Epistle that Gaius was a presbyter. As John adds to the address the term τῷ ἀγαπητῷ, so he also addresses him as ἀγαπητέ in vv. 3, 5, 11, and superadds as in 2 John 1, the words: ὃν ἐγὼ ἀγαπῶ ἐν ἀληθείᾳ (Oecumenius: ὁ κατὰ κύριον ἀγαπῶν ἐνδιαθέτῳ ἀγάπῃ).

HOMILETICAL AND PRACTICAL.

STARKE: Those who wish to be loved of men, must be lovable and worthy of love; this is done, if they give up the love of the world, and love God only.—Truth and love are precious jewels of Christians, which must be linked together and are more ornamental than golden chains. The one cannot exist without the other; truth without love is dead, and love without truth is blind.

The Apostle's joys and sorrows.

vv. 2–11.

2 Beloved, I wish above all things[1] that thou mayest prosper and be in health, even
3 as thy soul prospereth. For[2] I rejoiced greatly when the[3] brethren came and testified
4 of the truth that is in thee,[4] even as thou[5] walkest in the truth.[6] I have no greater
5 joy than[7] to hear that my children walk in truth.[8] Beloved, thou doest faithfully[9]
6 whatsoever thou doest[10] to the brethren, and[11] to strangers; Which have borne witness of thy charity before the church[12]: whom if thou bring forward on their journey
7 after a godly sort, thou shalt do well:[13] Because that for his name's sake[14] they
8 went forth, taking nothing of the Gentiles.[15] We therefore ought to receive[16] such,
9 that we might be fellow helpers to the truth[17]. I wrote unto the church[18]: but Dio

10 trephes, who loveth to have the preeminence among them,[19] receiveth us not. Wherefore, if I come, I will remember[20] his deeds which he doeth, prating against us with
malicious words[21]: and not content therewith, neither doth he himself receive the
brethren, and[22] forbiddeth them that would, and casteth *them* out of the church.
11 Beloved, follow[23] not that which is evil, but that which is good. He that doeth good
12 is of God: but[24] he that doeth evil hath not seen God. Demetrius hath good report
of all *men*, and of the truth itself[25]: yea, and we *also* bear record; and ye know[26] that
our record[27] is true.

Verse 2. [[1] German: "In all things." So Lillie. "Concerning all things." Alford.—M.]

Verse 3. [2] Cod. Sin. and several minusc. omit γὰρ after ἐχάρην.
[[3] German: "When brethren came." Lillie.—M.]
[[4] German: "And testified to thy truth;" so Alford, Lillie.—M.]
[5] σὺ is emphatic, omitted in A., but inserted in B. C. G. K. Cod. Sin.
[[6] German: "In truth," without the Article; so Alford, Lillie.—M.].

Verse 4. [7] The best authorities read τούτων; ταύτης found only in minusc. and versions, is doubtless a correction.—Some read χάριν instead of χαρὰν. [German: "Greater than this I have no joy, that;" Lillie: "Greater joy than this I have none, to hear;" Alford: "I have no greater joy than this, that."—M.]
[8] A. B. ἐν τῇ ἀλησείᾳ; C. Cod. Sin. al. omit the Article.

Verse 5. [[9] German: "Beloved, thou actest faithfully." So Lillie.—M.]
[10] B C. G. K. Cod. Sin. al. read ἐργάσῃ, so that the ἐργάζῃ of A cannot stand.
[11] A. B. C. Cod. Sin. al. have καὶ τοῦτο, instead of καὶ εἰς τοὺς, of G. K. [German: "And that strangers." So Alford.—M.]

Verse 6. [[12] German: "Who have testified to thy love before the Church;" so Lillie and Alford, who renders however: "in the presence of the Church."—M.]
[[13] German: "Whom thou shalt do well to conduct (forward) worthily of God." Alford: "Whom thou wilt do well if thou forward on their way, worthily of God;" Lillie: "Whom thou shalt do well to forward their way, in a manner worthy of God."—M.]

Verse 7. [[14] German: "For they went out on behalf of the name;" Lillie: "For in behalf of the name they went forth." Alford: "On behalf of."—M.]
[15] A. B. C. Cod. Sin. al. read ἐθνικῶν, instead of ἐθνῶν, the reading of G. K. [German: "Receiving nothing from the heathens."—M.]

Verse 8. [16] A. B. C. Cod. Sin. al.: ὑπολαμβάνειν; G.K.: ἀπολαμβάνειν.
[17] Τῇ ἀληθείᾳ; Cod. Sin.: τῇ ἐκκλησίᾳ, with the emendation τῇ ἀληθείᾳ. [The latter reading, without the emendation, occurs also in A.—M.]

Verse 9. [18] A. B. C. Cod. Sin. read τι; a hand has added ἄν in Cod. Sin. [German: "I wrote somewhat to the Church;" so Alford.—M.]
[[19] German: "But he who loveth to be the first of them, Diotrephes, does not receive us;" Lillie: "But he who loveth to be foremost among them, Diotrephes, doth not admit us;" Alford: "Howbeit, Diotrephes, who loveth preëminence over them, receiveth us not."—M.]

Verse 10. [[20] German: "Therefore, if I come, I will bring to remembrance;" so Lillie; Alford: "Bring to mind."—M.]
[[21] German: "Wicked words."—M.]
[[22] German: "And not contented with this, neither does he himself receive the brethren, but also, those who would do it, he hindereth, and casteth out of the Church."—M.]

Verse 11. [[23] German: "Imitate not evil, but good;" so Alford.—M.]
[24] ὁ κακοποιῶν is best authenticated [A. B. C. K.—M.]; ὁ δὲ κακοπ., *text. rec.*, is only feebly supported. [German: "He that doeth evil," omits the "but" of E. V., so Alford.—M.]

Verse 12. [25] C. inserts τῆς ἐκκλησίας καὶ before τῆς ἀληθείας. Instead of ἀληθείας A. probably reads ἐκκλησίας. [A. corrected, B. G. K. read ἀληθείας. German: "Unto Demetrius testimony hath been borne by all, and by the truth itself."—M.]
[[26] German: "And thou knowest; A. B. C. al. Vulg.: οἶδας; οἴδατε l. r. according to the G. K. al. several versions, etc.—M.]
[[27] German: "That our testimony is true."—M.]

EXEGETICAL AND CRITICAL.

Wish for the prosperity of Gaius. vv. 2–4.

VER. 2. **Beloved**:—Joy in and care for Gaius account for the accumulation of terms of endearment.

In all things I wish that thou mayest prosper.—Περὶ πάντων is simply idiomatic: with respect to all things: περὶ, with the idea of including, encircling, shutting in, both in connection with substantives and absolutely, is found at the head of whole sentences in the sense of *adtinet ad*; 1 Cor. xvi. 1. Cf. Winer, p. 390, sq. Connected with εὔχομαι, which signifies "to wish," but carries here also the force of intercession (cf. Jas. v. 15), the most natural sense is "praying for, concerning all things," without any necessity for recurring to the Homeric usage of the preposition, viz. *prae*=above all things, as alleged by Schott, Düsterdieck and others. Rather than giving it that construction, we may connect περὶ πάντων with εὐοδοῦσθαι (Bengel, Huther, al.), which connection is affected neither by the rhetorical emphasis of the position of περί πάντων (Lücke), nor by the circumstance that it cannot belong to ὑγιαίνειν.—The prosperity referred to (εὐοδοῦσθαι) is general, *in re familiari* (Bengel), in all outward relations of life. Εὐοδοῦν, to make, lead a good way (εὐοδία) is transitive, while εὐοδεῖν to have a good way, is intransitive; hence the Passive, which carries the same force as the intransitive verb. Cf. Rom. i. 10; 1 Cor. xvi. 2; Lücke, Düsterdieck and al.—Καὶ ὑγιαίνειν singles out a particular point. Possibly Gaius had been sick (Düsterdieck), or was in delicate health; but this cannot be inferred with certainty as a fact, for health *per se* is important enough, if outward prosperity is the matter referred to.

Even as thy soul prospereth.—Oecumenius: ἐν τῇ κατὰ τὸ εὐαγγέλιον πολιτείᾳ, consequently in that it has the truth, and that he walks in it (v. 3); the words καθὼς εὐοδοῦταί σου ἡ ψυχή contain a high encomium on Gaius and the object of the Apostle's particular rejoicing.

VER. 3. **For I rejoiced greatly.**—On ἐχάρην γὰρ λίαν see 2 Jno. 4. These words give the reason of the encomium, as of a well authenticated fact.

When brethren came and testified to thy truth.—The connection with the Aorist ἐχάρην requires us to continue the Participles ἐρχομένων καὶ μαρτυρούντων as Imperfects, as in Luke xvii. 12 (Lücke, Huther, Düsterdieck al.); the Dative σου τῇ ἀληθείᾳ governed by μαρτυρεῖν (as in vv. 6, 12; Jno. v. 33; xviii. 37; iii. 26) denotes the truth become subjective in Gaius; hence not=*sinceritas* (a Lapide, Beza and al.), but inward, Christian life, born of the truth, and itself truth (Lücke, Huther, Düsterdieck and al.); the restriction to *liberalitas* (Lorinus), is inadmissible.

As thou walkest in truth.—This clause contains the testimony of the brethren, hence it is an indirect clause recording the Christianity of Gaius as evidenced by his walk; on that account we have also ἀκούω in v. 4, so that it is not the testimony of the Apostle added to that of the brethren (Besser). So Brückner, Huther, Düsterdieck, and al. The express and emphatic σὺ denotes that the testimony of the brethren had been different with reference to others, for instance in the case of Diotrephes vv. 9, 10.

VER. 4. **I have no greater joy than this.**—Here the Apostle expresses his mind in general. On μειζοτέραν, a double comparative, like Eph. iii. 8, see Winer, p. 81. Grotius: "*Est ad intendendam significationem comparativus e comparativo factus.*" The Genitive τούτων is not=ταύτης, the neuter Plural, carrying a general reference, is restricted by the following ἵνα to one idea. Winer, p. 175 compares ἐφ' οἷς and ἀνθ' ὧν, also μετὰ ταῦτα and καὶ ταῦτα *idque*, Heb. xi. 12, and cites Jno. i. 51.

That I hear my children are walking in the truth.—On ἵνα see Jno. xv. 13. It signifies the Apostle's desire to hear this; this is his whole aim. Τὰ ἐμὰ τέκνα are the Christians committed to John; the members of the Churches confided to his care and placed under his paternal direction (Huther).

Praise and necessity of hospitality. vv. 5–8.

VER. 5. **Beloved,** as in v. 2.

Thou actest faithfully.—πιστὸν ποιεῖς; Oecumenius: ἄξιον πιστοῦ ἀνδρός. Bengel: "*Facis quiddam quod facile a te pollicebar mihi et fidelibus;*" this explanation is too narrow, the reference to the πίστις which lays hold of the ἀλήθεια and carries out in love being too definite. But it is not on that account=πίστιν ποιεῖσθαι (Ebrard).

Whatsoever thou doest for the brethren.—Ὃ ἐὰν (ἂν)=*quodcunque* denotes that this activity had various modes of expression and made itself felt in different directions. On ἐργάζεσθαι εἰς, cf. Matth. xxvi. 10.

And that strangers.—Καὶ τοῦτο, as in 1 Cor. vi. 6; Eph. ii. 8; Phil. i. 28, is not different in point of sense from καὶ εἰς τοὺς ξένους: *and that=this too for* (*towards*), *strangers.* This additional particular shows that the brethren were unknown and strangers, and acknowledges and praises the hospitality of Gaius as more liberal and not confined merely to brethren personally known to him. On the importance of φιλοξενία, cf. Heb. xiii. 2; Rom. xii. 13; 1 Tim. iii. 2; Tit. i. 8; 1 Pet. iv. 9.

VER. 6. **Who have testified to thy love before the Church.**—Οἳ ἐμαρτύρησαν are the strange brethren; not only some of their number singled out (de Wette). Ἐνώπιον τῆς ἐκκλησίας denotes the Church where the Apostle was at the time of writing (Grotius, Huther, Düsterdieck al.), before which they gave an account of their experience [on their missionary journey—M.], like in Acts xiv. 27, and made mention of the love of Gaius. Bengel's "*publice commemorabantur exempla ad hortandum*" goes too far.

Whom thou shalt do well to conduct (forward) worthily of God.—The reading: οὓς καλῶς ποιήσεις προπέμψας is established; the Future with the *part. aor.* is difficult. The Future is simple and clear; Gaius will do well; we must not construe it, with Huther, as *Futur. exactum.* For at Mark xiii. 13, the being saved (σωθήσεται) does not take place until after the enduring is accomplished (ὁ ὑπομείνας εἰς τέλος). Cf. Winer, p. 306, where only the *part. aor.* carries the force of the *futur. exact.* But the action of Gaius is not finished until he has accomplished the providing and speeding forward of the brethren; this is the sense of the *part. aor.* In such a connection the Future indicates a certain expectation, not without the direction softened by the Future, even as the ὀφείλομεν, v. 8, is *morata formula hortandi* (Bengel). It is more allowable to see here with Luther, a vagueness of expression than to venture with Ebrard on the correction ἐποίησας. As καλῶς qualifies ποιεῖν (Acts x. 33; Phil. iv. 14), so ἀξίως τοῦ θεοῦ qualifies προπέμπειν, to fit out for a journey (Tit. iii. 13; 1 Cor. xvi. 11); in a manner worthy of God [whose messengers they are—M.], with all care and love (Lücke); the *viaticum* (Grotius), *commeatus* (Bengel), will not be wanting; but this is not all. Cf. 1 Thess. ii. 12; Col. i. 10.

VER. 7. **For they went forth on behalf of the name.**—Ἐξῆλθαν; the reason why they went forth is intimated by ὑπὲρ τοῦ ὀνόματος, as in Acts v. 41, on behalf of the name of Christ, cf. Jas. ii. 7, even for the purpose of preaching it, as in Rom. i. 5, so that they went forth as missionaries, as in Acts xv. 40 (Lücke, Huther, Düsterdieck and others). Hence the reference is neither to the name of God, which would require αὐτοῦ, and then to be referred back to τοῦ θεοῦ, v. 6, nor only to the Christian religion, and least of all to the name of the brethren who were called missionaries (Paulus). The connection of ἐξῆλθαν with ἀπὸ τῶν ἐθνικῶν is untenable (Beza, Bengel, al.), which belongs to λαμβάνοντες.

Receiving nothing from the heathens.—The *Part. Præs.* with μηδὲν denotes the maxim of the missionaries not to receive any support from the heathens (Huther, Düsterdieck), agreeably to Matth. x. 8. The Mathematical astrologers and thaumaturgs did, on the contrary, make a business of religious affairs. But compare also the practice of St. Paul (1 Cor. ix. 18; 2 Cor. xi. 7, sqq.; xii. 16, sqq., 1 Thess. ii. 9, sqq.), although he might not take any thing from the younger Churches. On the construction of λαμβάνειν ἀπό, cf. Matth. xvii. 25, and Winer, p. 388, note 1.

VER. 8. **We therefore ought to receive such persons.**—In contrast to τῶν ἐθνικῶν the Apostle begins with: ἡμεῖς οὖν [οὖν because they receive nothing from the heathens, *therefore* we, etc.—M.]. The communicative Plural denotes the general Christian duty to take part in missions; hence ὀφείλομεν. There is a fine play on the word ὑπολαμβάνειν after μηδὲν λαμβάνοντες; *elegans antanaclasis* (Carpzov). According to Strabo's definition: οἱ εὔποροι τοὺς ἐνδεεῖς ὑπολαμβάνουσι, this word implies both the προπέμπειν (v. 6), and the λαμβάνειν εἰς οἰκίαν (2 Jno. 10).

That we may become fellow-workers (for) the truth.—The purpose (ἵνα) is a noble one, viz. to serve the truth and work for it. The Dative τῇ ἀληθείᾳ denotes the object to which the work of the missionaries is devoted; we should become the assistants and fellow-workers of the missionaries; συν also refers back to τοιούτους, not to τῇ ἀληθείᾳ as Luther, Bengel and Besser allege. Our view is also held by Brückner, Huther, Düsterdieck. Cf. Col. iv. 11: συνεργοὶ εἰς τὴν βασιλείαν τοῦ θεοῦ; 1 Thess. iii. 2; συνεργὸν ἐν τῷ εὐαγγελίῳ; 2 Cor. viii. 23: εἰς ὑμᾶς.

Complaint of a hostile person. vv. 9, 10.

VER. 9. **I wrote somewhat to the Church.**—Ἔγραψα designates a lost Epistle; τι does not imply that the writing was specially important, but brief, he wrote somewhat (Lücke, Huther, Düsterdieck), the writing was not particularly valuable [nothing is said one way or another, τι leaves the matter quite indefinite and merely imports that he had written somewhat—M.]. The reference here cannot be to the *first* Epistle (Wolf, Stier al.), or to the *second*, for they contain not the remotest allusion to the relations here specified. Diotrephes might have withheld it from the Church (Huther).—The Church to which he had written (τῇ ἐκκλησίᾳ), is that of which Gaius was a member, who was to correct and repair the injuries done by Diotrephes (vv. 5–8, 11). Hence it is wrong to hold with Bengel ("*illius loci, ex quo exierunt. Occupatio: ne Cajus dicat, cur itur ad nos?*"), with whom Besser agrees, that the reference here is to the Church from which the missionaries went forth.

But he who loveth to be foremost among them, Diotrephes, doth not receive us.—We have no particulars concerning Diotrephes; it neither may be affirmed nor denied that he was a presbyter or deacon of the Church. But φιλοπρωτεύων renders it more improbable than probable. It is a pure conjecture to describe him as an opponent of the Jewish Christians (Grotius), or as a gnostic or judaistic false teacher; he was *ambitiosus;* this is known. Schol. I. defines φιλοπρωτεύων thus: ὁ ὑφαρπάζων τὰ πρωτεῖα.—Αὐτῶν is taken from ἐκκλησία, [the collective noun—M.], and designates the members of the Church who, as Huther supposes, were wont to meet at his house. Ἐπιδέχεσθαι ἡμᾶς signifies to receive us; hence not: to acknowledge our Epistles and exhortations (de Lyra, Grotius, Lücke, de Wette and al.).—Huther 1st ed. [corrected in the 2d—M.]. In not complying with the directions given in the Apostle's Epistle, Diotrephes virtually delined to receive the Apostle himself (v. 10).

VER. 10. **Therefore, if I come, I will bring to remembrance the works which he doeth.**—With διὰ τοῦτο the Apostle bases his coming and censure on the refractory conduct of Diotrephes. On ἐὰν ἔλθω see 1 Jno. ii. 28. That it would take place soon is indicated by εὐθέως, v. 14. It is not necessary to supply αὐτὸν (Huther), or ἐκκλησίαν (Paulus) after ὑπομνήσω; the Accusative of the person which is added in Jno. xiv. 26; Tit. iii. 1 is also wanting in 2 Tim. ii 14.—It was the Apostle's intention to censure not only Diotrephes, who was not singular in his reprehensible conduct, but had a friendly party backing him. Bede: "*In omnium notitiam manifestius arguendo producam.*" Although the connection requires us to understand the feature of censure (de Lyra: *puniam*, Bengel: *notabo, ut sentiat, animadvertam*), the idea of an instructive calling to mind is by all means to be retained; the censure lies in the matter being mentioned and that publicly. Αὐτοῦ τὰ ἔργα, ἃ ποιεῖ are the object of ὑπομιμνήσκειν, and these consist in the sequel, viz.:

Prating against us with wicked words —On λόγοις πονηροῖς see 2 Jno. 11; 1 Jno. iii. 12. They were slanderous words calculated to lower and detract from the Apostle's influence, but idle, worthless tattle, untenable falsehoods; hence φλυαρῶν, "*apposite calumnias Diotrephis vocat garritum*" (á Lapide); the intransitive verb has a transitive reference to ἡμᾶς taken from the λόγοις πονηροῖς; a similar construction may be seen in μαθητεύω, Matth. xxviii. 19; θριαμβεύω, Col. ii. 15 (properly *nugari*, cf. i. Tim. v. 13.)

And not contented with this.—Ἀρκεῖσθαι with the Dative only, occurs at Luke iii. 14; Heb. xiii. 5 instead of ἐπὶ τούτοις; μὴ ἀρκούμενος with φλυαρεῖν against the Apostles, he wrongs the missionary brethren in two ways, viz.:

Neither doth he himself receive the brethren.—Οὔτε followed by καὶ is of frequent occurence, see Winer p. 516, 7. Αὐτὸς answers to βουλομένους. Ἐπιδέχεσθαι signifies literally to receive, to entertain hospitably, 2 Jno. 10. The reference is to the ἀδελφοί mentioned v. 7.

But also, those who would do it, he hindereth.—There was consequently no lack of well-disposed Church-members; but he κωλύει by force, imperiousness, cunning tricks and speeches.

And casteth out of the Church.—Ἐκβάλλειν ἐκ τῆς ἐκκλησίας may signify: to excommunicate, but according to the context also to turn out of the local congregation. In the latter case κωλύει and ἐκβάλλει would have the same object; but in the former ἀδελφοί would be the object with αὐτούς understood. The former, adopted by Düsterdieck on account of the meaning of the word and the construction, seems to be improbable, because excommunication in a case which had no reference to false doctrine or immorality of life, would be immoderate and unheard of, and hardly conceivable at that time. But it might be possible that Diotrephes was wont to hold, or caused to be held, the meetings of the Church in his own house, and refused admittance to those who were opposed to him; but that would not be an excommunication. Huther, who maintains the other view, seems to enter more fully into the circumstances hinted at, and to avoid untenable conjectures.

Exhortation and Commendation. vv. 11, 12.

Ver. 11. **Beloved**; peculiarly emphatic as following what goes before. 1 Jno. iv. 1, 7, 11.

Imitate not evil but good.—On *μὴ μιμοῦ* see Hebr. xiii. 7; 2 Thess. iii. 7, 9; Eph. v. 1. Τὸ *κακόν in Diotrephe*, Τὸ *ἀγαθόν in Demetrio* (Bengel). De Wette erroneously asserts that the diction here is "*unjohannean*," for we have *τὰ ἔργα πονηρὰ* and *δίκαια* in 1 Jno. iii. 12; *τὸ κακόν* in Jno. xviii. 23; *τὰ ἀγαθά* and *τὰ φαῦλα* in Jno. v. 29: the diction is generally biblical, 1 Pet. iii. 10, 11.

He that doeth good, is (out) **of God.**—Cf. 1 Jno. iii. 10. Ὁ *ἀγαθοποιῶν* is general, as before (1 Pet. ii. 14; xv. 20; iii. 6, 17); a Lapide, Grotius, Paulus and al. erroneously apply and restrict this expression to benevolence and hospitality.

He that doeth evil, hath not seen God.—It is inconceivable how Lücke and de Wette can call this expression "*unjohannean*," considering that *ἐκ θεοῦ ἐστίν* with the constantly recurring *ἐκ θεοῦ εἶναι* (1 Jno. iv. 2, 3, 4, 6; iii. 10; v. 19) is manifestly "*johannean*," and that we read at 1 Jno. iii. 6: *οὐχ ἑώρακεν αὐτὸν* notwithstanding the addition there of *οὐδὲ ἔγνωκεν αὐτὸν*, and at 1 Jno. iv. 8: *οὐκ ἔγνω τὸν θεόν*, 1 Jno. ii. 3: *ἐγνώκαμεν αὐτὸν*.

Ver. 12. **Unto Demetrius testimony hath been borne by all, and by the truth itself.**—Demetrius was probably the bearer of this Epistle (Lücke, Düsterdieck, Huther), and John commends him to Gaius. Hence he cannot be one of the *βουλόμενοι*, whom Diotrephes is said to have hindered and excommunicated (Ebrard); in that case he would have been a member of the congregation to which Gaius belonged, and known to him. The Perfect *μεμαρτύρηται* denotes a testimony which has been given and continues to be valid; used absolutely, without any further qualification, it always denotes a good testimony (Acts vi. 3; x. 22; xvi. 2, etc.). In *ὑπὸ πάντων* the reference is to Christians; for the matter in question bears on the Christian excellence of Demetrius (Lücke); the restriction to those who know him, is self evident, and hence otherwise than in 2 Jno. 1. Limiting it to the brethren vv. 5, 7, 10 (Ebrard), or extending it to Jews and Gentiles (Oecumenius), cannot be done; there is nothing to warrant either construction; the former would require a further qualification, the latter is limited to his congregation by the context.—*Καὶ ὑπ' αὐτῆς τῆς ἀληθείας* imports a personified and independent testimony running parallel with that of the *πάντες*, equal to it, real, and the truth itself giving that testimony. Hence we cannot agree with the explanation of Huther who thinks that the Apostle wanted to give prominence to the circumstance that the good testimony of all was not founded on their human judgment, in the testimony of the *ἀλήθεια* dwelling in them, and refers to Jno. xv. 26, 27. There the truth does not bear testimony concurrent with, and outside of the *πάντες*, but in them and out of themselves. We ought rather to think with Düsterdieck of the walk and conversation of Demetrius, in which the *ἀλήθεια* dwelling in him, shows itself as vital and bearing testimony to him; he is an image of the truth, which is personified in him, in his walk and nature. It is not sufficient to think here only of the *res ipsa*, or *res ipsæ*, the reality (a Lapide, Grotius, Beausobre); the Divine Truth is the witness here. [Alford reproducing, and, as so often, improving on Düsterdieck: "The objective Truth of God, which is the Divine rule of the walk of all believers, gives a good testimony to him, who really walks in the truth. This witness lies in the accordance of his walk with the requirement of God's Truth. It was the mirror in which the walk of Demetrius was reflected; and his form, thus seen in the mirror of God's Truth, in which the perfect form of Christ is held up to us (1 Jno. ii. 6; iii. 3, 16), appeared in the likeness of Christ: so that the mirror itself seemed to place in a clear light his Christian virtue and uprightness, and thus to bear witness to him."—M.].

But we also bear testimony.—John adds now his own testimony, as a third [and independent testimony—M.]; *καὶ ἡμεῖς δὲ* makes this testimony of the Apostle very emphatic. Cf. notes on 1 Jno. i. 8.

And thou knowest that our testimony is true.—The reference is only to the personal testimony of the Apostle; Grotius explains erroneously: "*alii, qui Ephesi sunt.*" Cf. Jno. xix. 35; xxi. 24. Gaius knows and values it as a true and reliable testimony; not however because of the episcopal, apostolical and canonical dignity of John (a Lapide), but because of his personal truthfulness.

ETHICAL.

1. Outward prosperity, and more especially physical health, are of sufficient value to become the objects of a Christian wish in the form of intercession, but must always be subordinated to the health, or rather by Divine grace to the recovery of the soul walking in the truth of God. A parallel passage is 2 Cor. xii. 7 (*σκόλοψ τῇ σαρκί*) cf. v. 9—(*ἀρκεῖ σοι ἡ χάρις μου, ἡ γὰρ δύναμις ἐν ἀσθενείᾳ τελεῖται*).

2. The greatest joy of the servants of Christ is, not to labour in vain in their congregations, though they labour for nothing (v. 4).

3. Participation in the work of missions is the sacred duty of individuals (vv. 5—8) as well as of Churches (v. 10), and a life-token of the truth in them (vv. 8, 11). Missionaries are objects of Christian love.

4. Ambition destroys the efficiency and position of men, so that they not only work evil themselves, but also hinder good.

5. Church-visitation is an official work, derived from the Apostolical Church.

6. We should look to and imitate in our walk and conversation those who have a good testimony in truth, not those who err and commit sin.

HOMILETICAL AND PRACTICAL.

Compare Ethical.—Health is the foundation of all human activity. A sickly man cannot even think healthily. Men would be surprised, if they were able to take such a survey, to find how many of the things which have filled the world with feuds and laden with errors, may be traced back to a disordered stomach. Who would go to sea in a leaky vessel?

STARKE:—Christians should bless and greet one another, wish one another good, pray for one another, so that all of us may be benefited.—There is none so weak but that he may be of use to others; though it be done only by wishing and praying, yet it is a great service.—A faithful teacher may be known by this token, that he rejoices over the spiritual growth of his hearers and others, and thanks God for it.—The evangelical truth is not still, it walks and causes those to walk who have it.—The natural life is not concluded with one step; sure, the spiritual life is a constant progression unto death.—Preachers have anxiety and toil in their ministry, they meet with hatred and envy, opposition and persecution, mockery and derision, but their joy in the fruits of their labour overcomes all the rest.—Would that all evangelical ministers might become zealous and imitators of the holy men of God, who have faithfully performed the work of the Lord. Let every one be of good cheer and courage in the discharge of his duty and he will be exalted to their society in heaven.—He who seeks only temporal and transitory things in the ministry is an antichrist and brings shame on the name of Christ.—It is very injurious to the course of the Gospel, if its servants seek only their own advantage; this makes more atheists than Christians.—Those who while exhorting others to the practice of godliness, include themselves, not only set a higher value on their exhortation, but also render it more telling and efficacious.—Those who receive the servants of Christ, receive Himself. Should we then not eagerly long to receive Him in His members? He will richly pay for His entertainment.—He that is of the truth and loves the truth must seek to further it in every possible way; this is the mark of a true one.—Be not surprised if thou findest no room with the clear truth among false teachers and prophets; for Christ Himself and His Apostles did not find it.—When loose talkers have exhausted words and proofs, they forthwith have recourse to detraction, slander and abuse.—Devilish malice—not to do good yourself and actually to hinder others who would do good.—False teachers are opposed to the children of God and avoid their company; but this very course shows plainly that they are not the children of God.—Heretics and false teachers foster not only errors of the understanding, but these are also allied to perversity and a malicious will.—The knowledge of the letter [of the Scriptures], is vastly remote from illumination.—He who does not see God by faith here, will not see Him in glory hereafter.—Benefits which have been shown to us, should be publicly acknowledged.

HEUBNER:—Here we are reminded of the double health. How rarely do we ask after the health of the soul: it is thought unbecoming, and yet it is the most important matter.—Let the sick in body be specially anxious for the health of the soul (2 Cor. iv. 16).—Spiritual paternal joys may compensate us for the want of bodily ones (2 Cor. i. 14; 1 Thess. ii. 19).—Where do we now find a congregation interested in the spiritual condition of another congregation?—The exhibition of love to the messengers of the Gospel, is a duty we owe to the Gospel itself. Such love exalts the praise of Christianity and of the Church.—Diotrephes probably turned them away as vagabonds. There were of course those who went begging in the name of the Gospel, idle begging brothers [*Grussbrüder*], like the *μητραγύρται* among the heathen went begging in the name of Mother Cybele.—The hatred of strange, calling and visiting Christians which is also found among clergymen, proceeds from a secret, wicked malice; they do not want strangers to become acquainted with the condition of their congregation, or to bring the Gospel which they themselves do lack; they are afraid of being eclipsed and of having their credit impaired (1 Thess. ii. 16).—Demetrius is so faithful and simple that the truth itself commends him in speaking forth from him. This is the best commendation, which we can have through ourselves and through faith (2 Cor. i. 12).—You cannot give a testimonial to others, unless you have out of themselves [*i. e.*, from their life and conversation.—M.] a testimony of the truth.

BESSER:—Hospitality was a conspicuous virtue of the first Christians, and St. Paul enumerates it among the qualities of an unblamable bishop (1 Tim. iii. 8; Tit. i. 8). Every parsonage, yea, every Christian house was a home to travellers, where expelled brethren, or brethren travelling as evangelists met with hospitable welcome.—Instead of causing his name (*Diotrephes*, one nursed by Jupiter, the great mythological god of the heathen) to be mistaken and of becoming a *Theotrephes*, one nursed by God, he continued in the captivity of the love of the world.—The elder would not have admonished a confirmed obdurate man.—When a Diotrephes desired to be highly esteemed, a John had to be little esteemed. Where it is impossible to obey the law of God, there we ought not to be possible.

THE CONCLUSION.

VV. 13, 14.

13 I had many things to write,[1] but I will[2] not with ink and pen write[3] unto thee:[4]
14 But I trust I shall shortly see thee, and we shall speak face to face.[5] Peace *be* to
thee. *Our* friends[6] salute thee. Greet the friends[7] by name.[8]

Verse 13. [1] A. B. C. Cod. Sin. read: γράψαι σοι.
[2] B. C. Cod. Sin.: οὐ θέλω. The reading οὐκ ἐβουλήθην in A. originated from 2 Jno. 12, and like οὐκ ἤθελον formed after it.

[3] B. C. Cod. Sin.: σοι γράφειν; A: γράφειν σοι.

[[4] German: "I should have much to write unto thee, but I will not write unto thee with ink and pen."—M.]

Verse 14. [[5] German: "But I hope soon to see thee, and we shall speak mouth to mouth."—M.]

[6] B. C. G. K. Cod. Sin. read: φίλοι; A. ἀδελφοί. [German: "The friends salute thee."—M.]

[7] Several unimportant Codd. read ἀδελφούς instead of φίλους.

[8] G. inserts ἀμήν.—A. B. Cod. Sin. have the subscription: Ἰωάννου γ. The usual additions occur here and there, but are not sufficiently authenticated.

EXEGETICAL AND CRITICAL.

Close of the Epistle. vv. 13, 14.

VER. 13. **I should have much to write to thee.**—Πολλά, emphatic, placed first. The Imperfect εἶχον without ἄν, is idiomatic Greek and must be rendered in the Subjunctive in German. See Winer p. 283 sqq.; [The objection to the rendering of E. V. "I had many things to write" is that the Apostle does not advert to the past but to the present. So Luther 2d ed. "I should have much to write" brings out this shade of thought in English.—M.].

But I will not write unto thee with ink and pen.—Cf. 2 Jno. 12.

VER. 14. **But I hope, soon to see thee.**—The contrast to writing, for which the Apostle has no further inclination (Düsterdieck), is oral intercourse which he hopes soon to realize.

And we shall speak mouth to mouth.—The Future λαλήσομεν denotes the assurance of hope. The object is πολλά v. 13, and the particulars indicated in the Epistle.

Greetings v. 14.

VER. 14. **Peace be to thee.**—The greeting of the Apostle to the beloved Gaius. As at the beginning of the Epistle the simple χαίρειν is not sufficient for the fulness of the Christian greeting, so at the close the common ἔρρωσο (Acts xxiii. 30; xv. 29) is displaced by richer and deeper forms. There the wish of peace is most appropriate (Gal. vi. 16; Eph. vi. 23; 1 Pet. v. 14; 2 Thess. iii. 16; Rom. xv. 33 and al.), because peace may be regarded as the sum-total of the Divine gifts of grace in Christ (Luke. ii. 4; Jno. xiv. 27) as N. de Lyra correctly explains it: "*Pax interna conscientiæ, pax fraterna amicitiæ, pax superna gloriæ*" (Düsterdieck). [Alford: "Remember our Lord's legacy, Jno. xiv. 27; and His greeting after the resurrection, εἰρήνη ὑμῖν, Jno. xx. 19, 26."].—Joy moreover is health of the soul.

The friends salute thee.—Bengel: "*Rara in N. T. appellatio, absorpta majori fraternitatis. Errant philosophi, qui putant amicitiam non instrui a fide.*" Jno. xv. 15. The expression suits a purely private Epistle, written on purely personal relations (Lücke). Bede: "*Amicis gratiam pacis mandat et salutis et per hæc Diotrephen ceterosque veritatis inimicos a salute et pace vestra monstrat extraneos.*" Among the ἀδελφοί, which are generally saluted (Phil. iv. 21; 1 Cor. xvi. 20; Eph. vi. 23), John, according to 2 Jno. 9–11, probably included Diotrephes, because he acted only as an *ambitiosus*, but does not seem to have been wrong and erred in the doctrine of Christ's incarnation; but he and his party were not φίλοι to the Apostle, like Gaius and Demetrius. Cf. Jno. xi. 11; Acts xxvii. 3.

Greet the friends by name.—Κατ' ὄνομα = ὀνομαστί (Jno. x. 3); Bengel: "*Non secus ac si nomina eorum præscripta essent.*" The greetings, and especially those by name, have so deep an import and so great a value, that Paul fills a whole chapter of his Epistle to the Romans (ch. xvi. 1–24) with them, and often adds a series.

HOMILETICAL AND PRACTICAL.

STARKE:—It is not advisable to confide every thing to the pen; many things may be better and more effectively stated orally than in writing.—It is not a small benefit, if the children of God may visit each other and delight in friendly conversation.—We are in the company of the holy men of God whenever we hear or read their writings.

HEUBNER:—We see, how even letters of friendship are hallowed by faith. Everything should have the impress of our evangelical frame of mind. A mind wholly penetrated by the spirit of Christianity will not deny itself even in unimportant letters of friendship. Examples may be seen in Sailer's Christian letters of every century, in the letters of Luther, Tersteegen and John Newton.—The children of peace receive peace (Luke x. 5, 6).

BESSER: John greets the friends by *name*; he carries them all in his heart, and every one in particular. This is presbyter-fidelity.—

[WORDSWORTH: The good pastor imitates that Good Shepherd, who "calleth His sheep by *name*." Jno. x. 3.—M.].